CRITICAL SURVEY
OF
POETRY

CRITICAL SURVEY
OF
POETRY

Foreign Language Series

Authors

A-D

1

Edited by
FRANK N. MAGILL

Academic Director
WALTON BEACHAM

SALEM PRESS
Englewood Cliffs, N. J.

LIBRARY OF CONGRESS CATALOG CARD NUMBER: 84-5365
Complete Set: ISBN 0-89356-350-1
Volume 1:   ISBN 0-89356-351-X

PRINTED IN THE UNITED STATES OF AMERICA

PREFACE

MAGILL'S *Critical Survey of Poetry*, Foreign Language Series, is a continuation of the eight-volume English Language Series on poetry published in 1982. The Drama Series, now in preparation, and the Foreign Language Series on Long Fiction, scheduled for release in 1985, will complete this forty-one-volume project.

The format of this Series follows that of the earlier works in the project. The first four volumes provide critical studies of 197 poets whose works have had an important influence on the literature of their native language.

The individual articles include seven sections: Principal poems and collections; Other literary forms; Achievements; Biography; Analysis (by far the most extensive section); Major publications other than poetry; and Bibliography. Volume Five comprises a collection of twenty-seven comprehensive essays centering on special areas of poetry, useful background material often demanded in an extensive study of the genre. This volume also includes the index for the set, adequately cross-referenced to provide prompt access to the pertinent information included on any poet represented in the volumes.

One of the most striking—and obvious—differences to be noted in this continuing study of the world's great poets is the fact that we can now introduce the "grandfathers" of our poetic heritage—missing in the earlier set but here much in evidence. Separated earlier by design—time and language—many great poetic forebears can at last be brought into focus in this work to open the doors on our distant past, a legacy whose influence has been enormous and continuing. Perhaps the most obvious new name is that of Homer, followed by Hesiod, Theocritus, Ovid, Vergil, and Dante, to mention only a few. Such majestic figures could not, by definition, be dealt with in the first eight volumes but are here made available for study in comprehensive critical assessments.

For the same reasons, a number of superior Far Eastern poets may now be presented for study. Among them are Tu Fu, considered by many scholars to be China's greatest poet; Li Po, perhaps China's most popular poet; and Li Ch'ing-Chao, called China's greatest woman poet—her lyrics especially admired for their vision and sensibility. Those readers seriously interested in Chinese poetry will find worthy of careful study an extended essay on the subject entitled "Chinese Poetry"; it appears in the essay volume on page 1776. The two essays on Japanese poetry are also most instructive, as is the individual article on Matsuo Bashō, called the "Father of haiku poetry."

For an extended study of medieval German poetry, the reader may wish to examine the earlier part of the essay "German Poetry to 1800." The essay provides a fairly detailed early history of the people, leading gradually into the literary beginnings. The early stirrings of chivalry (sparked in part by tales of gallantry from the Crusades) were augmented by recountings of the exploits of Christian knights. Feudalism also helped to nurture the ideas. Out of these elevated exploits grew a highly imaginative saga, *The Nibelungenlied*. The ground was thus prepared for the great medieval poet Hartmann von Aue to introduce the Arthurian legend into Germany, perhaps borrowed from France's Chrétien de Troyes.

One of the great achievements of German medieval poetry was Wolfram von Eschenbach's *Parzival*, which evoked much admiration among the contemporary audience and from other poets as well. The work is considered by some scholars to be an early forerunner of the *Bildungsroman*. Another Middle High German poet who lived at the same time as Wolfram was Walther von der Vogelweide, perhaps the most famous Minnesinger and love poet of medieval Germany. Walther was very prolific and greatly praised in his day not only for his lyrics but also for the quality of his singing voice.

As the centuries passed, German lyric poetry developed to near perfection. Perhaps the preeminent poet of the Romantic period was Joseph von Eichendorff, who often found religious themes ideal for his creative impulses. His reputation as the Romantic lyricist nonpareil was acknowledged by contemporaries and successors alike, figures such as Heinrich Heine, Friedrich Hölderlin, Hugo von Hofmannsthal, Rainer Maria Rilke, and even the twentieth century novelist Thomas Mann.

The two essays on French poetry, "French Poetry to 1700" and "French Poetry Since 1700," provide excellent coverage historically as well as literarily. They are admirably complete and together offer a point of departure for a rewarding review of French poetry from the Middle Ages forward. These articles may profitably be augmented by the individual essay on the eloquent medieval stylist Alain Chartier.

The consistently imaginative French thread runs down to the present time. Among those well remembered for their contributions are Alfred de Vigny, the "Father of French Romanticism"; Théophile Gautier, whose theory of "art for art's sake" was very influential for a time; the great Victor Hugo; and Arthur Rimbaud, whose dual personality sought communion with God but expressed itself most freely in *A Season in Hell* (1873). Also well remembered are Paul Valéry, famous for his notebooks; André Breton, the "Father of Surrealism"; Paul Éluard, one of the founders of Surrealism and also involved in the Dada movement; and the contemporary René Char. These few citations are but a sample of the extensive French coverage available here.

Besides those names already mentioned, the contributions of Italy loom large indeed in this discussion of non-English-language poetry. Of these figures, none looms larger than Petrarch, whose great reputation and high honors were well deserved. The work of this greatest of Latin/Roman poets has been revered and studied for centuries. In his day, he left the medieval period behind and looked ahead to the Renaissance, a philosophy more in keeping with his humanistic values. Other early contributors to the period include Poliziano, Pietro Bembo, and Ludovico Ariosto, whose *Orlando furioso* became one of the most influential works of the Italian Renaissance.

In 1554, Gaspara Stampa, a woman of Padua, produced some very good love lyrics, her work modeled after that of Petrarch, whose style was emulated by innumerable followers. Torquato Tasso's *Jerusalem Delivered*, an epic poem dealing with the First Crusade, found enthusiastic audiences throughout much of Europe during the Renaissance. Important and influential poets of a later period include Ugo Foscolo, Giacomo Leopardi, and Alessandro Manzoni, the latter greatly admired by Johann Wolfgang von Goethe not only for his innovative style but also for the balanced treatment exhibited in his religious poetry. Others include Nobel Prize winner Giosuè Carducci; Giovanni Pascoli, whose influence on many twentieth century Italian poets has been substantial; Gabriele D'Annunzio, a prominent figure in Italian affairs during much of his lifetime and a leader of the literati of his day; and Eugenio Montale, whose Nobel Prize was not awarded until 1975, when Montale was nearly eighty.

As stated, the mission of this five-volume set is to survey briefly the creative works of significant poets whose means of verbal expression is non-English. In addition to those poets already discussed, limited space demands subjective selectivity. Few, however, would question the suggestion for study of Luís de Camões' *The Lusiads*, the work of Portugal's greatest poet, a sensitive artist who wrote out of his own tragic experience. Neighboring Spain, prior to her Golden Age, produced her greatest poet, Garcilaso de la Vega, whose classically inspired style became the model for those who followed. During Spain's literary Golden Age, Lope de Vega Carpio appeared and became another great poet and playwright, a consummate artist who yet seemed at times to live with the flamboyance of one of his characters.

During Spain's Golden Age, the influence and language were set for much of an entire Hemisphere. One might begin with Mexico's seventeenth century poet Sor Juana Inés de la Cruz, and refer also to Enrique González Martínez, Alfonso Reyes, and Octavio Paz. Others of the Western Hemisphere include Nicaragua's Rubén Darío, Peru's César Vallejo, and Chile's Pablo Neruda. These are only a few of the worldwide outstanding poets whose mother language is Spanish.

Another continent, Africa, has recently begun to impress the world with its new poets. Léopold Senghor, a native of Senegal born in 1906, spent much of his early career in France, and became president of his own country in 1961. Well educated, he became a leader among the expatriate blacks in Paris prior to World War II. His poetry, while strictly original and grounded in the land of his birth, is nevertheless influenced at times by French Symbolism. One of his strongest political positions is the elimination of illiteracy in his own country.

Kofi Awoonor is another poet of African background whose early poems revere the land and acknowledge a debt to his native ancestors. Although his works have gained sophistication with maturity, the poet has never entirely divorced himself from the artistic innocence of his apprenticeship, when communion with nature and the eternal presence of death in life were always in the background. Awoonor has seen the world—China, Russia, Indonesia— and has conducted poetry readings in many universities in the United States and Europe. Still young, he will undoubtedly yet share with the world much more of his cultural wisdom in the years ahead.

This preface is not meant to be a detailed survey of world poetry, but it should not close without mentioning a few other countries whose authors' poetry has contributred much to the value of this reference work.

Represented here from Russia, among many others, are Boris Pasternak, Vladimir Mayakovsky, Mikhail Lermontov, and Alexander Pushkin, often called the "Father of modern Russian literature," whose splendid talent was foolishly squandered in a duel while he was still in his thirties. Included from Poland are Adam Mickiewicz, Zbigniew Herbert, Juliusz Slowacki, and Tadeusz Różewicz; from Lithuania, Czeslaw Milosz, winner of the Nobel Prize in 1980.

Romania is represented by Paul Celan and Itzik Manger; Czechoslovakia by Karl Kraus; Hungary by Endre Ady, Mihály Babits, and Miklós Radnóti; Austria by Ingeborg Bachmann and Stefan Zweig; Yugoslavia by Miodrag Pavlović, Jovan Dučić, and Vasko Popa; Sweden by Tomas Tranströmer and Gunnar Ekelöf; and Belgium by Guido Gezelle and Émile Verhaeren.

Among the many Greek poets represented, in addition to the Ancients mentioned earlier, are George Seferis, the first Greek to win the Nobel Prize; Odysseus Elýtis, who won the Nobel Prize in 1979; Nikos Kazantzakis, a poet with a keen philosophical mind at work; and Constantine P. Cavafy, his poetry more admired after his death than before.

Ancient Persia is represented by Omar Khayyám and Sa'di, both of whom flourished in the eleventh or twelfth century. India's Rabindranath Tagore, a prolific poet and a painter, is here; he won the Nobel Prize for Literature in 1913.

This five-volume work completes our current studies on world poetry. I wish to express my appreciation to all those who have contributed to the development of the Series.

FRANK N. MAGILL

CONTRIBUTORS

Writing Staff for Essays

Stanislaw Barańczak

Richard P. Benton

Patricia J. Boehne

András Boros-Kazai

Mitzi M. Brunsdale

Robert Colucci

Lillian Doherty

Paul A. Draghi

Ken Goodwin

Donald D. Hook

Irma M. Kashuba

Richard Keenan

John Richard Law

Robert W. Leutner

Dieter P. Lotze

Richard Peter Martin

Vasa D. Mihailovich

Makarand Paranjape

Peter Petro

J. Thomas Rimer

Sven H. Rossel

Patrizio Rossi

Joachim Scholz

Jack Shreve

Thomas J. Sienkewicz

Richard Spuler

James Stone

Writing Staff for Author Articles

Claude Abraham

Paul Acker

Robert Acker

Sidney Alexander

Lowell A. Bangerter

James John Baran

Stanislaw Barańczak

Theodore Baroody

Jean-Pierre Barricelli

Enikő Balnár Basa

Fiora A. Bassanese

Todd K. Bender

Robert Bensen

Peter Bien

M. D. Birnbaum

Franz G. Blaha

András Boros-Kazai

Harold Branam

Anne Kelsch Breznau

Joseph Bruchac

Glauco Cambon

H. W. Carle

John Carpenter

Leonard R. Casper

Francisco J. Cevallos

Luisetta Elia Chomel

Peter Cocozzella

Steven E. Colburn

Robert Colucci

Julian W. Connolly

Victor Contoski

Carrie Cowherd

J. Madison Davis

Andonis Decavalles

Lillian Doherty

Lee Hunt Dowling

Cliff Edwards

Clara Estow

Welch D. Everman

Christoph Eykman

Rodney Farnsworth

William L. Felker

Margot K. Frank

Daniel H. Garrison

Katherine Gyékényesi Gatto

Keiko Matsui Gibson

Morgan Gibson

Donald P. Haase

Shelley P. Haley

Todd C. Hanlin

Robert Hauptman

Ann R. Hill

Elizabeth A. Holtze

Kenneth A. Howe

Karen Jaehne

Alfred W. Jensen

Juan Fernández Jiménez

Judith L. Johnston

Irma M. Kashuba

Theodore L. Kassier

Jürgen Koppensteiner

Philip Krummrich

Katherine C. Kurk

Norris J. Lacy

Jeanne Larsen

Carolina D. Lawson

John M. Lee

Raymond LePage

Marie-Noëlle D. Little

John D. Lyons

Dennis McCormick

Cherie R. Maiden

David Maisel

John Marney

Richard Peter Martin

Richard A. Mazzara

Laurence W. Mazzeno

Vasa D. Mihailovich

Leslie B. Mittleman

C. L. Mossberg

Adriano Moz

Monique Nagem

Károly Nagy

Moses M. Nagy

David Nerkle

Evelyn S. Newlyn

Hermine J. van Nuis

David J. Parent

John P. Pauls

La Verne Pauls

Margaret T. Peischl

Susan G. Polansky

Rado Pribic

James R. Reece

Sylvie L. F. Richards

Helene M. Kastinger Riley

J. Thomas Rimer

Sven H. Rossel

Norman Roth

Victor Anthony Rudowski

Stephanie Sandler

Minas Savvas

Paul J. Schwartz

Roberto Severino

Jack Shreve

Thomas J. Sienkewicz

Janet L. Solberg

Madison U. Sowell

Richard Spuler

Kenneth A. Stackhouse

CONTRIBUTORS

Laura M. Stone

George Thaniel

Rogelio A. de la Torre

Janet G. Tucker

Thomas A. Van

David Allen White

Pauline Yu

Harry Zohn

LIST OF AUTHORS IN VOLUME 1

ENDRE ADY

Born: Érdmindszent, Hungary; November 22, 1877
Died: Budapest, Hungary; January 27, 1919

Principal collections

Versek, 1899; *Még egyszer*, 1903; *Új versek*, 1906 (*New Verses*); *Vér és arany*, 1908 (*Blood and Gold*); *Az Illés szekerén*, 1909 (*On Elijah's Chariot*); *A minden titkok verseiből*, 1910 (*Of All Mysteries*); *Szeretném, ha szeretnének*, 1910 (*Longing for Love*); *A menekülő élet*, 1912 (*This Fugitive Life*); *A magunk szerelme*, 1913 (*Love of Ourselves*); *Ki látott engem?*, 1914 (*Who Sees Me?*); *A halottak élén*, 1918 (*Leading the Dead*); *Margita élni akar*, 1921; *Az utolsó hajók*, 1923 (*The Last Ships*); *Rövid dalok egről és másról*, 1923; *Poems of Endre Ady*, 1969 (includes *New Verses*, *Blood and Gold*, *On Elijah's Chariot*, *Longing for Love*, *Of All Mysteries*, *This Fugitive Life*, *Love of Ourselves*, *Who Sees Me?*, *Leading the Dead*, *The Last Ships*).

Other literary forms

Endre Ady was a journalist who wrote numerous articles, reports, reviews, criticisms, essays, and short stories for the press. These were collected after his death under the titles *Az új Hellász* (1920; new Hellas), *Levelek Párizsból* (1924; letters from Paris), *Párizsi noteszkönyve* (1924; Paris notebook), and *Ha hív az aczélhegyű ördög* (1927; if the steel-tipped devil calls). In his lifetime, Ady published *Vallomások és tanúlmányok* (1911; confessions and studies), containing his important prose writings, both political and literary. Some of these writings are available in English translation in *The Explosive Country: A Selection of Articles and Studies, 1898-1916* (1977). His collections of short stories combine subjective, personal confession, with a depiction of early twentieth century Hungary. They are: *Sṕadt emberek és történetek* (1907; pale men and stories), *Így is történhetik* (1910; it can happen thus also), *A tízmilliós Kleopátra és egyébb történetek* (1910; Cleopatra of the ten millions and other stories), *Új csapáson* (1913; on a new track), and *Muskétás tanár úr* (1913; Professor Muskétás). His letters have been published in *Ady Endre válogatott levelei* (1956; selected letters of Endre Ady), with an introduction by Béla György.

Achievements

Ady is one of Hungary's greatest lyric poets. Inspired by Western European models, primarily French, he created a new lyrical style that both shocked and inspired his contemporaries. At the same time, he revitalized indigenous Hungarian literary traditions, looking back to the seventeenth and eighteenth centuries rather than to the example of his immediate predecessors. His topics, too, were considered revolutionary: physical passion and erotic love, political and social reform. He remained, however, within the tradition of the great nineteenth century Hungarian poets who expressed the spirit of the nation in their works. Ady came from the deep center of the nation, and he sought to raise the nation to a new consciousness, just as János Arany and others had done before him. Ady was an innovator because the literary and political establishment had failed to grasp the need for change. Ady's "Hungarianness" is a central part of his work; he was intensely aware of his struggle "with Europe for Europe."

Ady never abandoned his native traditions. He built instead on folklore, the *kuruc* poetry of the eighteenth century, the folk-song-inspired lyrics of Mihály Csokonai Vitéz, and the revolutionary verse of the great national poet of nineteenth century Hungary, Sándor Petőfi. Ady also drew heavily on Hungarian Calvinism and the rich vernacular tradition of Protestant writings to create a highly personal modern style, animated by the tension between Hungarian and Western European influences. His great love poems to Leda and Csinszka, his poems on materialism and on national traditions—all incorporated European philosophies, preoccupations, and styles, reflecting the influence of Friedrich Nietzsche and Henri Bergson as well as of Charles Baudelaire and Paul Verlaine. Today, Ady is recognized as one of the most important of the generation of writers and thinkers who transformed the intellectual life of Hungary in the first decades of the twentieth century.

Biography

Endre Ady's heritage and birthplace had a profound influence on his poetry. His ancestry was the relatively poor nobility, or gentry, which on his mother's side also boasted a tradition of Calvinist ministers. In the small village of Érdmindszent, he came to know the peasantry intimately, for his own family's life differed little from theirs. His father wished him to enter the civil service, so he was educated with a view to obtaining a legal degree. The area in which Ady grew up (today Sălaj, Romania) is situated in the Partium, a region of eastern Hungary that had stormy ties to Transylvania during the sixteenth and seventeenth centuries, when that principality had been a bulwark of Hungarian autonomy and traditions while the rest of the country was under Turkish or Habsburg rule. The Partium was thus doubly a frontier area in whose Calvinist and *kuruc* (anti-Habsburg) traditions Ady saw justification for his own rebellious, individualistic nature. He was always proud of his ancestry and considered himself much more Magyar than many of his contemporaries with more mixed ethnic backgrounds.

After completing five elementary grades in his village, Ady was sent first to the Piarist school in Nagykároly, then to the Calvinist gymnasium at Zilah, which he regarded as his alma mater; he always fondly remembered his teachers there. Several of his classmates were later to become prominent among the more radical thinkers and politicians of the early years of the twentieth century. He also read voraciously, both earlier Hungarian literature and European Naturalistic writers, and became acquainted with the works of Arthur Schopenhauer. After a brief period in law school in Debrecen and time spent as a legal clerk in Temesvár (Timisoara, Romania) and Zilah (Zălău), he realized that his true vocation was in journalism. He followed this career until his death.

Ady first worked in Debrecen, and in this period not only did his horizons widen, but his critical theses began to crystallize as well. "Life" and "truth" became important bywords for him, and he continued his readings: Auguste Comte, Herbert Spencer, Nietzsche, Henrik Ibsen, Fyodor Dostoevski, and especially the late eighteenth century poet Mihály Csokonai Vitéz, a native of Debrecen. It was in Nagyvárad (today Oradea, Romania) that Ady became familiar with the life of a large city and the more cosmopolitan society it represented. He wrote for liberal papers, and for a while his political views agreed with the pro-government stance of such journals. In time, however, he became disillusioned with their reluctance to press for universal suffrage and other reforms affecting the poor and the national minorities. It was at this time that he became acquainted with *Huszadik szazad*, a progressive journal begun in 1900.

The years in Nagyvárad were also important in Ady's personal life and poetic development, for it was during this period that he met Adél Brüll, whom he was to immortalize as the Leda of his poems. This older, married woman (her married name was Diósi)—more experienced, more worldly, more cultured than he—was an important influence on his life. Their passionate and at times tempestuous love affair, which finally ended in 1912, is recorded in poems that were to revolutionize Hungarian love poetry. When Ady went to Paris as the foreign correspondent of his paper, Adél Brüll was there, and his impressions of the French city were acquired under her tutelage. When he returned from the 1904 trip, he burst on the world with a new poetic style.

By 1905, Ady was working in Budapest for the liberal *Budapesti napló*. In numerous articles, he wrote of the need for radical reforms; independence from Austria was also debated. At this time, Ady turned his attention to the social problems that were destroying the country; in both his poetry and his prose writings, he championed the disenfranchised. The important journal *Nyugat* was started in 1908, and Ady soon became associated with it—all the more so as his increasingly radical views did not agree with the middle-of-the-road liberalism of the *Budapesti napló*.

When war broke out in 1914, Ady opposed Hungarian participation in the conflict, increasing his isolation from official political life. His antiwar poems were inspired by humanism and patriotism. The poor and the politically powerless suffered most heavily, Ady argued, and he believed that the war was being fought against Hungarian interests, purely for Austrian goals. During this time, Ady lived mostly in Érdmindszent and at Csucsa, the estate of Berta Boncza, whom he had met in 1914 and married the following year. Berta, the daughter of a well-to-do nobleman and prominent politician, was considerably younger than Ady; she had been attracted to him some time earlier, when she read his *Blood and Gold* while still in school in Switzerland. The poems written to her reflect a different mood from that of the Leda poems: The love is deeper and less intensely erotic. They project the hope that Csinszka (as Berta is called in the poems addressed to her) will preserve the thoughts and ideals of the poet. By this time, Ady was gravely ill with the syphilis that had been progressively destroying him since his Nagyvárad days.

The revolution that Ady had awaited came to Hungary in October of 1918. Ady went to Budapest, where the revolutionary government celebrated him, even though he had reservations about the Socialist system. He also doubted whether the Karolyi government's courting of the Entente powers would bring any positive results. As it turned out, his instincts were right, and the Entente did little for Hungary. Ady died in January of 1919, spared the knowlege that Hungary's territory would be drastically reduced and that his own birthplace and home region would be awarded to Romania.

Analysis

Endre Ady's first two volumes of verse, *Versek* (poems) and *Még egyszer* (once more), did not attract great interest; they were relatively insignificant collections in the traditional vein. In 1906, however, Ady's own style emerged in *New Verses*. Here, he presented new subjects and new themes, new images and a fresh, new style. The emphasis in *New Verses*—an emphasis continued in Ady's next three collections—was on brevity and impact: short, concise lines; short poems packed with meaning; condensed language with multiple levels of reference. Many of the early poems develop a single metaphor. A very conscious innovator, Ady prefaced *New Verses* with a manifesto that identifies the tension which persists throughout his oeuvre: Hungary is a nation caught at the crossroads between East and West. While proudly claiming his descent from the conquering Hungarians of the ninth century, who came through the Eastern gate, he asks if *he* can break in from the *West* with "new songs of new times." Answering in a defiant affirmative, he states that, in spite of opposition by conservatives, these poems "are still victorious, still new and Hungarian."

After the burst of energy that characterized his style in the period from 1906 to 1909, Ady paused in mid-career to adopt a quieter style and grayer moods. His themes and concerns remained much the same, but there was a deepening of thought, and a more pessimistic note entered his poems. His concern for the fate of the country, particularly its ordinary citizens, grew as he saw policies that could only bring ruin being blindly followed by the political elite. His relationship with Adél Brüll also cooled. After 1914, during the war years, Ady's style underwent another transformation. His sentences became more complex as his verse became increasingly reflective, and he turned from softer, French-inspired tones to the somber and sublime style of the Bible and of sixteenth century Calvinist poetry. In this late poetry, Ady retained two themes from his earlier collection: patriotism, which broadened into humanitarianism, and love—no longer the unfulfilled and unsatisfying erotic encounters of earlier years, but the deeper, more fulfilling passion of the Csinszka poems.

Ady's poems can be organized thematically into four large groups, though there is considerable overlapping; also, some important minor themes are eventually subsumed into one or another of the major ones reflecting Ady's intellectual development. One of Ady's most enduring themes was romantic love. The Leda cycles, with their portrayal of destructive yet irresistible passion, reveal the influence of Baudelaire. These poems represented a break with Hungarian tradition in their emphasis on the physical aspects of love. Ady's poems to his wife, on the other hand, are more in the tradition of Petőfi, in which the emotional-spiritual content is on a par with the physical. It would be misleading, however, to dismiss the Leda poems as purely physical: Adél Brüll offered Ady much more than physical excitement, and these poems reflect a world of shared ideas. They are more significant and generally more successful than the poems on fleeting alliances with insignificant partners.

"Félig csókolt csók" ("Half-Kissed Kiss") from *New Verses*, and "Léda a kertben" ("Leda in the Garden"), from *Blood and Gold*, emphasize the intense desire that cannot be satisfied even in physical union. The "half-kissed kiss" is a metaphor for an erotic relationship that leaves the lovers still restless for fulfillment: "tomorrow, then perhaps tomorrow." Nature sympathizes with them in their eternal hunger, as an image from "Leda in the Garden" suggests: "even the poppy/ pities us, [itself] satisified." Consummation, Ady suggests in "Héja nász az avaron" ("Kite-Wedding on the Loamy Earth"), can come only in death. In "A mi násznagyunk" ("Our Best Man"), Ady returns to this theme. There are also love poems of great tenderness in the Leda cycles, as "Add nekem a szemeidet" ("Give Me Your Eyes"), illustrates. The beloved's eyes "always see him grand . . . always build, have mercy . . . see him in a better light," yet "they kill, burn, and desire." The poem, comprising four stanzas of three lines each, repeats the title line as the first line of each stanza and follows it with two rhymed lines. This *abb* tercet in anapestic meter echoes the lyrical mood and the melody of the words as well as the expansive ideas.

The 1910 volume *Of All Mysteries*, chronicles the waning of Ady's love for Adél Brüll. This collection offers a virtual outline of Ady's characteristic themes, as is indeed suggested in the poem's motto: "youthful All vanquished, with the spear of Secrecy, Death in my heart: but my heart lives, and God lives." Here, Ady seems determined to hope in spite of disappointments. The pose of earlier poems as decadent is shed as the poet develops a real faith in man that culminates in the humanism of the war poems. Each of the six cycles in *Of All Mysteries* is devoted to a "secret": of God, of love, of sorrow, of glory, of life, and of death. In the "Love" cycle, dedicated to Leda, the poem "A türelem bilincse" ("The Fetters of Patience") significantly refers to the "fetters" of their love in the past tense. Their whole life was fetters, yet the "kisses, exhaustions, flames, oaths" were all good fetters. The farewell becomes explicit in "Elbocsátó, szép üzenet" ("Dismissing, Beautiful Message"), where pity wins over the regretful remembrance of love. The poems of 1912 to 1914 show a man in search of love. In the final volumes, this love is found. "A Kalota partján" ("On the Banks of the Kalota") records the "security, summer, beauty and peace" brought to his life by Berta Boncza. The poem's two long free-verse stanzas depict a summer Sunday in which the peace and joy of the service and of the feast (Pentecost) mingle to overwhelm the poet, and the eyes of his beloved draw him into a magic circle.

Ady saw life and death not as opposing forces but as two components of the same force. "Párizsban járt az ősz" ("Autumn Passed Through Paris") is a beautiful evocation, through the breath of autumn on a summer day, of the presence of death. Although death comes for all men, it need not be accepted passively, as Ady suggests in the melodic "A halál lovai" ("Death's Horsemen"). The riderless horse with the unclaimed saddle is always in the troop of death's horses, but "He before whom they stop/ Turns pale and sits into the saddle." The act is presented as voluntary. In "Hulla a búza-földön" ("Corpse on the Wheat-Field"), a corpse, forgotten on the snowy plain, will not have carnations, artemisia, and basil blooming on its grave, but "the victorious wheat-kernel" will win through; life will triumph.

To some extent, Ady's God-fearing poems continue the life-death theme. They chronicle the same doubts and seek answers to the same questions. In time, Ady found the answers and the refuge, but as with John Donne, the struggle was a fierce one; indeed, Ady's love poems, much as in Donne's case, have a close and direct relationship to his religious verse. While many of Ady's religious poems describe his struggle to achieve union with God, others reflect the peace of childlike faith. Ady seeks rest and forgiveness and creates powerful symbols to concretize these feelings. In "A Sion-hegy alatt" ("Under Mount Sion"), he creates an image of God as a man in a huge bell coat inscribed with red letters, ringing for the dawn Mass. The figure is kindly yet sad; he cannot answer the poet's plea for simple, unquestioning faith. The poem is a poignant expression of the dilemma of modern man. In "Hiszek hitetlenül Istenben" ("I Believe, Unbelieving, in God"), Ady longs for belief in the great mystery of God, convinced that such faith will bring peace to his tormented soul. The poems from the cycle "Esaias könyvének margójára" ("To the Margins of the Book of Isaiah"), often prefaced by biblical quotations that emphasize their prophetic intentions, transcend the personal religious quest to become pleas for the nation and for humanity. "Volt egy Jézus" ("There Was a Jesus") not only testifies to a personal acceptance of Christ but also proclaims the need for all mankind to heed His teachings on peace and brotherhood. "A szétszóródás elött" ("Before the Diaspora"), another poem with a biblical inspiration, scourges the nation for its sins, concluding with the powerful line: "And we were lost, for we lost ourselves."

Many of Ady's poems can be classified as patriotic. This group, however, unites several different themes that were significant at different points in his career. Two important early threads are the "I" poems and the "money" poems. The I poems are more than personal lyrics; they present the speaker (the poet) as a representative of the nation. As such, they evolve into the patriotic poems in a fairly direct line. The money poems startled readers with their "nonpoetic" theme: Ady went beyond complaints against poverty to question the role of money in society at large.

An important thread in Ady's patriotic-revolutionary poetry is the use of the *kuruc* theme. *Kuruc* was the name applied to the supporters of Ferenc Rákóczi II, who had led a popular uprising against the Habsburgs in the eighteenth century. In Ady's vocabulary, the *kuruc* is the true but disenfranchised Hungarian, a fighter for national goals betrayed by his self-serving masters to Austrian interests. In the war years, Ady identified the *kuruc* with the common man everywhere, oppressed by political power plays.

Ady's last poem, "Ember az embertelenségben" ("Man in Inhumanity"), was an appeal to humanity addressed to the victors of the war. He appealed, fruitlessly, to the Allies "not to tread too harshly" on Hungarian hearts. The nation sought reform, but suffered instead "War, the Horror." Defeated in a war fought against Hungarian sentiments and Hungarian interests, Hungary paid for its all-too-recent union with Austria with the loss of much of its territory and millions of its citizens. Foreseeing this tragedy even before the war, Ady offered a poignant comment on its aftermath.

While Ady was a very subjective poet, one of the first purely personal lyric voices in Hungarian poetry, he did not break with the national tradition of committed literature. Deeply influenced by Western European models, he transformed what he took by the force of his genius, exploiting the rich resources of the Hungarian tradition in the service of a powerfully modern vision. Thus, it is not surprising that Ady continues to inspire poets in Hungary today.

Major publications other than poetry

SHORT FICTION: *Sápadt emberek és történetek*, 1907; *A tízmilliós Kleopátra és egyébb történetek*, 1910; *Így is történhetik*, 1910; *Muskétás tanár úr*, 1913; *Új csapáson*, 1913.

NONFICTION: *Vallomások és tanúlmányok*, 1911; *Az új Hellász*, 1920; *Levelek Párizsból*, 1924; *Párizsi noteszkönyve*, 1924; *Ha hív az aczélhegyü ördög*,

1927; *Ady Endre válogatott levelei*, 1956; *The Explosive Country: A Selection of Articles and Studies, 1898-1916*, 1977.

Bibliography
Bóka, Lazlo. "Endre Ady the Poet," in *The New Hungarian Quarterly*. III, no. 5 (January-March, 1962), pp. 83-108.
Cushing, G. F. "Introduction," in *The Explosive Country: A Selection of Articles and Studies, 1898-1916*, 1977.
Hatvany, Lajos. *Ady: Cikkek, emlékezesek, levelek*, 1974.
Nyerges, Anton N. "Introduction," in *Poems of Endre Ady*, 1969.
Reményi, Joseph. *Hungarian Writers and Literature*, 1964.
Szerb, Antal. *A magyar irodalomtörténet*, 1959.

Enikő Molnár Basa

ANNA AKHMATOVA
Anna Andreyevna Gorenko

Born: Near Odessa, Russia; June 11, 1889
Died: Moscow, U.S.S.R.; March 5, 1966

Principal poems and collections

Vecher, 1912; *Chetki*, 1914; *Belaia staia*, 1917; *Podorozhnik*, 1921; *Anno Domini MCMXXI*, 1922, 1923; *Iz shesti knig*, 1940; *Izbrannye stikhotvoreniia*, 1943; *Stikhotvoreniia*, 1958, 1961; *Poema bez geroa*, 1960 (*A Poem Without a Hero*, 1973); *Rekviem*, 1963 (*Requiem*, 1964); *Beg vremeni*, 1965; *Sochineniia*, 1965; *Poems of A.*, 1973; *Selected Poems*, 1976; *Requiem, and Poem Without a Hero*, 1976.

Other literary forms

In addition to poetry, Anna Akhmatova wrote an unfinished play and many essays on Russian writers. Her spirited book *O Pushkine: Stat'i i zametki* (1977), published in its complete version posthumously, is one of the most discerning tributes to the greatest Russian poet by a fellow poet. Akhmatova also translated poems from the Old Egyptian, Hindu, Armenian, Chinese, French, Italian, and many other languages, most of these in collaboration with native speakers.

Achievements

Akhmatova enriched Russian literature immeasurably, not only with the quality of her poetry but also with the freshness and originality of her strong talent. Through Acmeism, a literary movement of which she was one of the founders and leading members, she effected a significant change of direction in Russian poetry in the second decade of the twentieth century. The Acmeists' insistence on clarity and precision of expression—much in the spirit of the Imagists, although the two movements developed independently of each other—represented a reaction against the intricate symbols and otherworldly preoccupations of the Symbolists. Akhmatova's youthful love poems brought her early fame, and her reputation was further enhanced during the long reign of terror in her country, through which she was able to preserve her dignity, both as a human being and as a poet. With Boris Pasternak, Osip Mandelstam, and Marina Tsvetayeva, Akhmatova is universally regarded as one of the four great poets of postrevolutionary Russia. Having been generously translated into English, Akhmatova's works are constantly gaining stature in world literature as well.

Biography

Anna Akhmatova—the pen name of Anna Andreyevna Gorenko—was

born in a suburb of Odessa in 1889, into the family of a naval officer. Akhmatova began to write poetry when she was eleven, and her first poem was published in 1907. She achieved great popularity with her first books *Vecher* and *Chetki*. After joining the literary movement called Acmeism, she played an important part in it together with Osip Mandelstam and with her husband, Nikolay Gumilyov, from whom she was later divorced. During World War I and the Russian Revolution, Akhmatova stood by her people, even though she did not agree with the ideas and methods of the revolutionaries. Never politically inclined, she saw in the war and the Revolution an evil that might eventually destroy the private world in which she had been able to address herself exclusively to her own problems. When the end of that world came, she refused to accept it, believing that she would be able to continue her sequestered life. She also refused to emigrate, saying that it took greater courage to stay behind and accept what came. The effect of the Revolution on her life and creativity was not immediately evident, for she subsequently published two more collections of poetry. When her former husband and fellow Acmeist Gumilyov was shot, however, Akhmatova realized that the new way of life was inimical to her own. Compelled to silence, she ceased to exist publicly, instead remaining an inner émigré for eighteen years and occupying herself mostly with writing essays and translating. This silence may have saved her life during the purges of the 1930's, although she was not spared agony while trying to ascertain the fate of her only son, a promising scholar of Asian history, who had been sent to a labor camp three times. Only World War II brought a change to Akhmatova's dreary and dangerous life. Like many Soviet writers and intellectuals, she once again sided with her people, suppressing her reservations and complaints. She spent the first several months of the war in besieged Leningrad and then was evacuated to Tashkent, where she stayed almost to the end of the war. In Tashkent, she was brought closer to the other part of her ancestry, for her grandmother, from whom she took her pen name, was a Tartar.

When the war was over and the authorities again resorted to repression, Akhmatova was among the first to be victimized. In a vitriolic speech by Andrei Zhdanov, the cultural dictator at that time, she and the satirist Mikhail Zoshchenko were singled out as examples of anti-Soviet attitudes among intellectuals and charged with harmful influence on the young. They were expelled from the Writers' Union, and their works ceased to be published. Thus, Akhmatova vanished from public view once again in 1946, this time involuntarily, and did not reappear until ten years later. In 1958, a slender collection of her poems was published as a sign of rehabilitation. A few more of her books were subsequently published, both at home and abroad, thus reinstating the poet as an active member of society. During the last decade of her life, she wrote some of the best poetry of her career. Shortly before her death, she received two richly deserved accolades for her work. Ironically, the recognition came from abroad: she was awarded the prestigious Italian Etna Taormina Prize in 1964, and an honorary doctorate from Oxford University in 1965. Ravaged by long illness, she died in 1966, having preserved her dignity and independence by asking for and receiving a church funeral according to the Russian Orthodox rites. After her death, Akhmatova was almost unanimously eulogized as the finest woman poet in all of Russian literature.

Analysis

Anna Akhmatova's poetry can conveniently be divided into three distinct periods: 1912 to 1923, 1940 to 1946, and 1956 to 1966 (with a few poems published in 1950). The interim periods were those of enforced silence. The first silence, from 1923 to 1940, came as a result of tacit admission on her part that the changed way of life in Russia was not fully acceptable to her. The second, from 1946 to 1956, was a direct result of the authorities' intervention. Needless to say, Akhmatova kept busy by further refining her poetry, by writing essays, and by translating.

Akhmatova's development as a poet can be traced from book to book. Her first books, *Vecher* and *Chetki*, impressed readers with the freshness of a young woman's concern about her feelings of love. In almost all the poems having love as a focal point, Akhmatova presents love from a woman's point of view, in a form resembling a diary. It is difficult to say whether the female voice in these poems belongs to the poet herself; probably it does, but in the last analysis it is immaterial. The beloved is almost always silent, never fully revealed or described, and at times he seems to be almost secondary—only a catalyst for the woman's feelings. She is so entranced by his mere presence that, in her anguish, she draws her "left-hand glove upon [her] right." The poet expresses the whole spectrum of love—from the playfulness of a young woman trying to dismay her partner in order to prove that she, too, can wield some power over him, to moments of flaming passion. To be sure, passion is presented implicitly, in the time-honored tradition of Russian literature, yet it is also vividly indicated in unique ways. As she says, "In human intimacy there is a secret boundary,/ Neither the experience of being in love nor passion can cross it/ Though the lips be joined together in awful silence/ And the heart break asunder with love." Her fervent passion is coupled with fidelity to her partner, but as her loyalty is professed time and again, a note of frustration and a fear of incompatibility and rejection become noticeable. The prospect of unrequited love is confirmed by betrayal and parting. The ensuing feeling of loneliness leads to despair and withdrawal. The woman's reaction shows a mixture of anger, defiance, even resignation: "Be accursed . . ./ But I swear by the garden of angels/ By the holy icon I swear,/ By the passionate frenzy of our nights,/ I will never go back to you!" (These lines, incidentally, prompted Zhdanov, in his merciless attack many years later, to call Akhmatova "a nun and a harlot.") Thus, celebration, parting, and suffering receive equal play in Akhmatova's approach to love, although the ultimate outcome is a markedly unhappy one. Her love poetry is a vivid testimony both to the glories and to the miseries of her sex.

The feminine "I" of the poems seeks refuge, release, and salvation in religion, nature, and poetry. The refuge in religion is especially evident in *Chetki*. The work has a peculiar religious tone, pervaded, like Akhmatova's sentiments of love, with a mood of melancholy and inexplicable sadness. The persona seems to have found consolation for unhappiness in love when she says: "The King of Heaven has healed my/ Soul with the icy calm of love's/ Absence." Her prayers are mostly in the form of confession or intercession. It is easy to see, however, that they are used primarily to compensate for her feeling of loneliness and weariness of life. Thus, privations and misfortunes are closely tied to her religious feelings; sin and atonement are inseparable, and her passions of the flesh are tempered by spiritual fervor. Akhmatova's poems with religious overtones have little in common with customary religious experience. They are also much more complex and psychologically laden than any of her other poetry.

In Akhmatova's third collection, *Belaia staia*, a new theme joins those of love and religion: a presentiment of doom. Nourished by the horrors of war and revolution, this presentiment grows into a wake for a world on the verge of annihilation. As the Revolution dragged on, Akhmatova's mood turned bleaker and more hopeless. She sought rapport with the events by writing poetry with political motifs, but to no avail. The poems in *Anno Domini MCMXXI* clearly reveal Akhmatova's state of mind and emotions at this difficult time, as well as her awareness that an era had come to an end. "All is sold, all is lost, all is plundered,/ Death's wing has flashed black on our sight,/ All's gnawed bare with sore, want, and sick longing," she laments in one poem. She refused to emigrate, however, knowing instinctively, as did Boris Pasternak many years later when he was threatened with expulsion from the Soviet Union, that for a poet to leave his or her native land is tantamount to a death worse than physical death. She did not hesitate to criticize those who had left their country in its worst hour: "Poor exile, you are like a prisoner/ To me, or one upon the bed/ Of sickness. Dark your road, O wanderer,/ Of wormwood smacks your alien bread." These lines have been quoted often by Soviet critics for propaganda purposes, although Akhmatova wrote them sincerely, as a poet who could not tear herself away from her own land.

In the poems in which Akhmatova grappled with the problems of present-day reality, a gradual shift away from intimate love poetry toward more worldly themes can be seen. This shift can be considered as an overture to another kind of Akhmatova's poetry. Tormented by the turbulent years of war and revolution, in which she made many personal sacrifices and witnessed many tragedies (the loss of friends, for example, including her former husband Nikolay Gumilyov), she was forced to face reality and to express her feelings and opinions about it. The silence imposed on her in 1923 only postponed further development in that direction. When she was allowed to reappear shortly before World War II, she wrote little in her old idiom. In many poems written during the war, she extols the beauty of her land and the magnitude of the martyrdom of her people under attack by a ruthless enemy. Leningrad, the city of her life and of her dreams, is especially the object of her affection. Tsarskoe Selo—a settlement near Leningrad that was the residence of the czars, the town of young Alexander Pushkin, and the town of Akhmatova's favorite poetry teacher Innokenty Annensky, as well as of her own youth—remained vividly and forever etched in her memory, even when she saw it almost totally destroyed in the war.

Leningrad and Tsarskoe Selo were not the only places to which Akhmatova paid homage; indeed, all of Russia was her home. Her attitude toward her country is typical of many Russian intellectuals, who, despite a thick veneer of cosmopolitanism, still harbor a childlike, sentimental, and irrational love for their country. From her earliest poems to her last, Akhmatova expressed the same feeling for Russia, a strange mixture of abstract love for her country, on the one hand, and down-to-earth concern for its people, on the other. In the poem "Prayer," for example, she prays to the Lord to take even her child and to destroy "the sweet power of song" that she possesses if it would help to change "the storm cloud over Russia . . . into a nimbus ablaze." This willingness to sacrifice what is dearest to her if it would benefit her country is no mere affectation—it is expressed with utmost sincerity and conviction. In a poem written almost thirty years later, "From an Airplane," she again expresses her love for her country in no less sincere terms: "It is all mine— and nothing can divide us,/ It is my soul, it is my body, too." Perhaps the most profound and meaningful testimony to her patriotism can be found in the poem "Native Land," written in the last years of her life. For her, her country was "the mud on our gumboots, the grit in our teeth . . . And we mill, and we mix, and we crumble/ This innocent earth at our feet,/ But we rest in this earth at the roots of the flowers,/ Which is why we so readily say: It is ours!"

Akhmatova did not limit her gaze to European Russia, where she was reared and where she spent most of her life. Through her experiences in Tashkent, the city in which her ancestors had resided, she acquired a great admiration for, and understanding of, the Asian mind and soul. A mystical bond with Asia inspired her to write some of her most beautiful descriptive poems, such as "From the Oriental Notebook."

Nevertheless, Akhmatova could not close her eyes to the Soviet reality, in which she was personally caught in a most tragic way. In a unified cycle of poems, *Requiem*, a masterpiece still unpublished in the Soviet Union, she expresses her deep sorrow not only about her personal loss but also about the suffering to which the Russian people were being subjected. *Requiem* was her closest approach to public castigation of the regime in her country. The tone for the entire work is set by the motto, which sadly admits that the circumstances are not those of a foreign country but, more personally, those of the poet's own country and people. In a short foreword in prose, Akhmatova tells how during the horrible years of the purges she spent seventeen months waiting in line in front of a prison in order to discover the fate of her son. Another woman recognized her and whispered, "Can you describe this?" "Yes, I can," Akhmatova replied. She kept her promise by writing *Requiem*. Although much of it reflects the universal sorrow and despair of a mother on the verge of losing her son, it is the *injustice* of her suffering that most pains the poet. Using her personal sorrow to speak for all human beings who suffer unjustly, the poet created in *Requiem* a work of lasting value. Moreover, there is much encouragement to be gained from *Requiem*. The persona does not lose hope and courage. She perseveres, knowing that the victims are unjustly persecuted and that she is not alone in suffering. In the epilogue, she recalls the trying hours and the faces she has seen in those seventeen months; in her final words, she begs that her monument be erected in front of the prison where she has stood for "three hundred hours," so that the thawing snow from the face of her monument will glide like tears. Even if overt references to the political terror are overlooked, *Requiem* is still one of the twentieth century's most eloquent poetic testimonies to human tragedy.

Akhmatova's poetry from the last decade of her life shows the greater maturity and wisdom of old age. Her approach to poetic themes is more epic and historical, with a deeper perspective. This mature poetry is also more philosophical and psychological. The best example is the autobiographical *A Poem Without a Hero*, a panoramic view of the previous century as it pertains to the present. It is a subtle and at times complex poem, difficult to fathom without a proper key. In her last poems, she speaks as if she has realized that her active role is over and that nothing else can hurt her. Her work at this time shows a mixture of sadness, resignation, relief, and even slight bewilderment as to what life really is after more than seven decades of coping with it: "The grim epoch diverted me/ As if I were a river./ I have been given a different life. In a new bed/ The river now flows, past the old one,/ And I cannot find my shores. . . ." She finds solace in her increasing loneliness, contemplating the past, trying to reevaluate it and to find the correct perspective on it. In one of her last poems, written slightly more than a year before her death, she speaks of the "Supreme Mystery." It has been on her mind from the beginning, changing its face from period to period. In her early poetry, it was the mystery of the man-woman relationship. Later, it became the mystery of the man-to-man relationship, with the emphasis on the cruelty of man to man. In her last years, it became the mystery of the relationship of man to eternity, indeed the mystery of the meaning of existence. Through such organic development, Akhmatova reached the pinnacle of her poetic power, the power found in Pasternak's late poetry and in the work of other great poets of the century.

The stylistic aspect of Akhmatova's poetry is just as important as the thematic one, if not more so. She shows several peculiarly Akhmatovian features. Above all, there is the narrative tone that points to a definite affinity with prose. Zhirmunski calls her entire oeuvre "a novel in verse." It is this affinity that enables her to switch easily from emotion to description. Connected with this skill is a dramatic quality, expressed either through inner monologue or dialogue. The second striking feature is the brief lyric form, usually consisting of three to four stanzas, rarely five to seven, and never more than seven. (Later in her career, Akhmatova wrote many poems in free verse.) Parallel to the brevity of form is a pronounced laconism: a few carefully selected details suffice to convey an entire picture. Akhmatova's economy of words, spare almost to the point of frugality, led her to the epigrammatic form and to fragmentation, understatement, and improvisation. As a result, her sentences are sometimes verbless and even without a subject (that being quite possible in Russian). Another peculiarity is the concreteness of her images, especially with reference to space and time. She tells the reader exactly where and when, almost to the minute, the events in her poem take place. The colors are vividly and exactly given. She avoids metaphors, instead using pointed, explanatory epithets. Finally, her intonation, never scrupulously measured or regulated, is that of a syncopated rhythm, approaching the rhythm of some forms of folk poetry. Many of these stylistic features result from her adherence to the tenets of Acmeism, but many others are uniquely her own and are easily recognizable as such.

Of the poets who influenced her, Akhmatova herself admits indebtedness to Gavrila Derzhavin, Pushkin, and Annensky. The latter two can be said to have exerted the greatest influence on her, although traces of other poets' influences—Nikolai Nekrasov, Aleksandr Blok, Mikhail Kuzmin—can be found. Even Fyodor Dostoevski, who never wrote poetry, is sometimes mentioned as a possible source of influence. As for her impact on other poets, Akhmatova's influence—like that of her great contemporaries, Mandelstam, Pasternak, and Marina Tsvetayeva—is pervasive, elusive, impossible to measure. In her old age, she recognized the talent of Joseph Brodsky—then only twenty-two years old—and passed on her mantle, as Nadezhda Mandelstam has said, in a kind of poetic succession. Anna Akhmatova, "Tragic Queen Anna," as Alexander Werth calls her, is a poet without whom modern Russian literature is unthinkable and by whom world literature has been significantly enriched.

Major publication other than poetry
NONFICTION: *O Pushkine: Stat'i i zametki*, 1977.

Bibliography
Dobin, E. *Poeziia Anny Akhmatovoi*, 1968.
Driver, Sam N. *Anna Akhmatova*, 1972.
Eikhenbaum, Boris. *Anna Akhmatova: Opyt analiza*, 1923.
Haight, Amanda. *Anna Akhmatova: A Poetic Pilgrimage*, 1976.
Pavlovskii, A. I. *Anna Akhmatova*, 1966.
Verheul, Kees. *The Theme of Time in the Poetry of Anna Akhmatova*, 1971.
Vinogradov, Viktor. *O poezii Anny Akhmatovoi: Stilisticheskie nabroski*, 1925.
Zhirmunskii, V. M. *Tvorchestvo Anny Akhmatovoi*, 1973.

Vasa D. Mihailovich

RAFAEL ALBERTI

Born: Puerto de Santa María, Spain; December 16, 1902

Principal collections

Marinero en tierra, 1925; *La amante*, 1925; *El alba del alhelí*, 1927; *Cal y canto*, 1929; *Sobre los ángeles*, 1929 (*Concerning the Angels*, 1967); *Consignas*, 1933; *Verte y no verte*, 1935 (*To See You and Not to See You*, 1946); *Poesia, 1924-1938*, 1940; *Entre el clavel y la espada*, 1941; *Pleamar*, 1944; *A la pintura*, 1945; *Retornos de lo vivo lejano*, 1952; *Baladas y canciones del Paraná*, 1954; *Poesías completas*, 1961; *Rafael Alberti: Selected Poems*, 1966 (Ben Belitt, translator); *The Owl's Insomnia*, 1973; *Alberti tal cual*, 1978.

Other literary forms

Although Rafael Alberti established his reputation almost entirely on the basis of his poetry, he became involved in drama after emigrating to Argentina, writing plays of his own and adapting Miguel de Cervantes' *El cerco de Numancia* (c. 1585, discovered in 1784; *Numantia: A Tragedy*, 1870) for the modern stage in 1944.

Alberti's most notable achievement in prose, a work of considerable interest for the student of his poetry, was his autobiography, *La arboleda perdida* (1942; *The Lost Grove*, 1976). In addition, he was a talented painter and supplied illustrations for some of his later volumes.

Achievements

Alberti had at once the ill luck and the singular good fortune to flourish during Spain's second great literary boom. Despite his acknowledged worth, he was overshadowed by several of his contemporaries—in particular, by Federico García Lorca. Although Alberti's name is likely to come up in any discussion of the famous *generación del 27*, he generally languishes near the end of the list. On the other hand, the extraordinary atmosphere of the times did much to foster his talents; even among the giants, he earned acceptance and respect. He may occasionally have been lost in the crowd, but it was a worthy crowd.

Commentators on Alberti agree in their praise of his astonishing technical mastery. Despite his relative lack of formal education, he proved able to compose flawlessly in many forms and styles. His first volume, *Marinero en tierra*, won Spain's National Prize for Literature, and throughout his long career, his virtuosity never faltered. Always a difficult poet, he never gave the impression that his obscurity stemmed from incompetence.

Alberti's technical skill did not allow him to stagnate. He might continue in the same vein for three volumes, but he would invariably break new ground in the fourth. His massive corpus of poetry comprises a remarkable array of styles, themes, and moods. His political ideology—Alberti was the first of his circle to embrace Communism openly—led him to covet the role of "poet of the streets," but Alberti will be remembered more for his poems of exile, which capture better than any others the poignant aftermath of the Spanish Civil War.

Ultimately, Alberti stands out as a survivor. Many of his great contemporaries died in the civil war, or simply lapsed into a prolonged silence. Despite his wholehearted involvement in the conflict, Alberti managed to persevere after his side lost and to renew his career. He continued to publish at an imposing rate, took up new activities, and became a force in the burgeoning literary life of Latin America. Consistent in his adherence to Communism, he received the Lenin Prize for his political verse in 1965. Oddly enough, then, Alberti emerges as a constant—an enduring figure in a world of flux, a practicing poet of consistent excellence during six decades.

Biography

Rafael Alberti was born December 16, 1902, near Cádiz in Andalusia, and his nostalgia for that region pervades much of his work. His genteel family had fallen on hard times, and Alberti's schoolmates made him painfully aware of his inferior status. In 1917, the family moved to Madrid, where Alberti devoted himself to painting in the Cubist manner, attaining some recognition. Illness forced him to retire to a sanatorium in the mountains—a stroke of luck, as it happened, for there he subsequently met such luminaries as García Lorca, Salvador Dali, and Luis Buñuel and began seriously to write poetry. He won the National Prize for *Marinero en tierra*, his first volume, and thereby gained acceptance into the elite artistic circles of the day. Personal difficulties and an increasing awareness of the plight of his country moved Alberti to embrace Communism. In 1930, he married María Teresa León, also a writer, and together they founded the revolutionary journal, *Octubre*, in 1934.

Alberti's new political credo enabled him to travel extensively and to encounter writers and artists from all parts of Europe and the Americas. After participating actively in the civil war, he emigrated to Argentina in 1940. There, he began to write for the theater, gave numerous readings, and resumed painting. Hard work and fatherhood—his daughter Aniana was born in 1941—preserved Alberti from embittered paralysis, and his production of poetry never slackened. Indeed, many of his readers believe that he reached his peak in the late 1940's.

In 1964, Alberti moved to Rome, where he lived until 1977, when he was finally able to return to Spain, after almost thirty-eight years in exile. He proceeded to run for the Cortes, giving poetry readings instead of speeches, and won. Alberti resigned his seat after three months in order to devote himself to his art. The lost Andalusian had returned home at last.

Analysis

Throughout his long career, Rafael Alberti proved to be a remarkably versatile poet. His facility of composition enabled him to shift smoothly from fixed forms to free verse, even within the confines of a single poem. Whether composing neomedieval lyrics, Baroque sonnets, or Surreal free verse, he always managed to be authentic. His deep emotions, sometimes obscured by his sheer virtuosity, found expression in all modes.

Although he was a natural poet with little formal training, Alberti always kept abreast of current developments in his art—indeed, he kept himself in the vanguard. He associated with the best and brightest of his time and participated in their movements. When the luminaries of Spain reevaluated Luis de Góngora, Alberti wrote accomplished neo-Baroque poetry; when Dali and Buñuel were introducing Surrealism in Spanish art and film, Alberti adapted its principles to Spanish poetry; when most of the intellectuals of Spain were resisting General Franciso Franco and embracing Communism, Alberti was the "poet of the streets." He remained, withal, a genuine and unique lyric voice. Even his political verses are not without poetic merit—an exception, to be sure. Alberti changed by adding and growing, never by discarding and replacing; thus, he became a richer talent with each new phase of his creative development.

Alberti's poetry is suffused with nostalgia. The circumstances of his life decreed that he should continually find himself longing for another time, a distant place, or a lost friend, and in his finest poems, he achieves an elegiac purity free of the obscurity and self-pity that mar his lesser works. From first to last, the sadness for things lost remains Alberti's great theme, one he explored more fully than any other poet of his generation.

The doyens of Spanish letters received *Marinero en tierra* with immediate enthusiasm, and the young Alberti found himself a *de facto* member of the *generación del 27*, eligible to rub elbows with all the significant writers of the day. Although Alberti seems to have been happy in the mid-1920's, his early volumes glow with poignant nostalgia for the sea and the coasts of his native Andalusia. He expresses his longing in exquisite lyrics in the medieval tradition. Ben Belitt, introducing his translations collected in *Rafael Alberti: Selected Poems*, confesses that he could find no way to render these lyrics in English. They depend entirely on a native tradition, the vast trove of popular verses from Spain's turbulent Middle Ages. Alberti's genius is such that the poems have no savor of pedantry or preciosity. Luis Monguió, in his introduction to Belitt's translations, suggests that "it is far from unlikely that they are being sung in the provinces today by many in complete ignorance of their debt to Rafael Alberti." The notion is a tribute both to the poet and to the tradition he understood so well.

The verses themselves may seem enigmatic, but only because the modern reader is accustomed to probe so far beneath the surface. One of the best of them, "Gimiendo" ("Groaning"), presents the plaint of a sailor who remembers that his shirt used to puff up in the wind whenever he saw the shore. The entire poem consists of only six brief lines; there is only one image, and only one point. That single image conveys a feeling close to the hearts of those born within smell of the sea—a need unfulfilled for Alberti. He speaks for all seamen who are marooned inland, the sailors on land.

"Pradoluengo," an aubade in the same style, is only seven lines long and conveys an equally simple message. The beloved to whom the poem is addressed is told that the cocks are crowing, that "we need cross only river waters, not the sea," and is urged to get up and come along. With all the richness of the genre, Alberti hints at a wealth of erotic possibilities and natural splendors. Only William Butler Yeats, in modern English poetry, matches this exquisite simplicity and feeling for tradition.

As noted above, Alberti took a leading role in the Góngora tricentennial of 1927, and many of the poems in *Cal y canto* owe much to the Baroque model. Here, Alberti reveals a new facet of his technical mastery, particularly in his handling of the sonnet, perhaps the most difficult of forms. "Amaranta," a sonnet that frequently appears in anthologies, shows how completely Alberti was able to assimilate the poetics of Góngora and to adapt them to the twentieth century. The octave describes, in ornate and lavish terms, the beauty of Amaranta; as with Góngora, the very exuberance of the description disquiets the reader. Her breasts, for example, are polished "as with the tongue of a greyhound." The sestet conceals the scorpion sting so often found in Góngora's conclusions: Solitude, personified, settles like a glowing coal between Amaranta and her lover. In this poem, Alberti displays his affinity with Góngora in two respects: an absolute control of his idiom and an obscurity that has deprived both poets of numerous readers. As Alberti himself remarked in his autobiography, "this was painterly poetry—plastic, linear, profiled, confined."

Concerning the Angels differs sharply from Alberti's previous work. Bouts of depression and a loss of faith in his former ideals drove him to abandon nostalgia and to confront despair. Suddenly, all the joy and tender sorrow of his early work is gone, replaced by anguish and self-pity. The revolution in content corresponds to a rebellion in form: free verse prevails as more appropriate to the poet's state of mind than any traditional order. Alberti does not despair utterly, as Monguió indicates, but the overall tone of the collection is negative.

"Tres recuerdos del cielo" ("Three Memories of Heaven"), a tribute to the great Romantic poet Gustavo Adolfo Bécquer, constitutes a noteworthy exception to the depressing tone of the volume. Here, Alberti displays the subtlety and tenderness that characterize his work at its most appealing. Evoking a condition of being before time existed, Alberti recaptures the tenuous delicacy of Bécquer, the sense of the ineffable. The meeting between the lovers, for example, takes place in a world of clouds and moonlight: "When you, seeing me in nothingness/ Invented the first word." Alberti imitates Bécquer masterfully, at the same time finding a new way to express his own nostalgia.

"Three Memories of Heaven," however, is atypical of the collection. Virtually all the other poems treat of "angels" and ultimately of a world turned to wormwood and gall. "El ángel desengañado" ("The Angel Undeceived") debunks the ideals of the younger Alberti, particularly in its desolate conclusion: "I'm going to sleep./ No one is waiting for me." "El ángel de carbón" ("Angel of Coals") ends no less grimly: "And that octopus, love, in the shadow:/ evil, so evil." Several of the poems offer a kind of hope, but it is a wan hope, scarcely better than despair. Like the T. S. Eliot of "The Hollow Men," however, Alberti maintains his poetic control, even with the world withering away around him.

Two pivotal events in Alberti's life helped him out of this quagmire: meeting his future wife and becoming a Communist. The political commitment, while it did little to benefit his poetry, provided him with a set of beliefs to fill the void within. Of his proletarian verse, one can say only that it is no worse than most political poetry. Like his friend and contemporary Pablo Neruda, Alberti mistook a sincere political commitment for an artistic imperative; like Neruda, he eventually returned to more personal themes, although he never wholly abandoned doctrinaire verse.

Even at the height of his political activism, however, Alberti was capable of devoting his gifts to the elegy; the death of Ignacio Sánchez Mejías in the bullring moved him to write the sonnet series that makes up *To See You and Not to See You* in 1935. The same tragedy also inspired Federico García Lorca to compose one of the most famous poems in the Spanish language, "Llanto por Ignacio Sánchez Mejías" ("Lament for Ignacio Sánchez Mejías"). A comparison of the two poems reveals the radical differences between these two superficially similar poets. García Lorca chants compellingly, "At five in the afternoon," evoking the drama of the moment and the awful immediacy of the bull. Alberti reflects on the bull's calfhood, its callow charges as it grew into the engine of destruction that destroyed Sánchez Mejías. García Lorca goes on to convey, in muted tones, his sense of loss. Alberti expresses that sense of loss in terms of distance: as his friend dies in the bullring, Alberti is sailing toward Romania on the Black Sea. The memory of the journey becomes permanently associated with the loss of the friend and thus a redoubled source of nostalgia.

As usual, García Lorca enjoys the fame, and Alberti is lost in his shadow. No doubt García Lorca's elegy speaks more clearly and more movingly; it probably *is* better than its counterpart. Alberti himself admired the "Lament for Ignacio Sánchez Mejías" without reservation. The pattern, however, is only too familiar: Alberti, so like García Lorca in some ways, found himself outmatched at every turn while his friend and rival was still alive. Alberti wrote exquisite medieval lyrics, but García Lorca outdid him with the *Romancero gitano* (1928; *The Gypsy Ballads*, 1953). Alberti captured the essence of Andalusia, but the public identified Andalusia with García Lorca. Alberti wrote a noble and moving elegy for Ignacio Sánchez Mejías, but his rival composed such a marvelous lament that Alberti's has been neglected.

All this is not to imply conscious enmity between the two poets. Alberti had cause to envy his contemporary's fame, and his bitterness at playing a secondary role may have been reflected in *Concerning the Angels*. Indeed, although Alberti gave many indications, in verse and prose, of his profound regard for García Lorca, his relationship with the poet of Granada represents an analogue to the dilemma of his literary life. The competition must have stimulated him, but, because his poetry was less accessible and less dramatic in its impact, he tended to be eclipsed. After the Spanish Civil War, Alberti emigrated to Argentina, mourning his slain and dispersed comrades, including García Lorca, who was senselessly gunned down at the outset of the hostilities. The war poems in the Alberti canon compare favorably with any on that subject, not least because his lively imagination enabled him to look beyond the slaughter.

For all his faith, the poet soon found himself across the Atlantic, listening to reports of World War II, picking up the pieces. Somehow he managed to recover and to emerge greater than ever. A poem from his first collection published outside Spain, *Entre el clavel y la espada*, (between sword and carnation), sounds the keynote of his renewed art:

> After this willful derangement, this harassed
> and necessitous grammar by whose haste I must live,
> let the virginal word come back to me whole and meticulous,
> and the virginal verb, justly placed with its rigorous adjective.

The poem, written in Spain, anticipates the purity of Alberti's poetry in exile. The poet forgot neither the horrors he had seen nor his love for his homeland.

Another elegy deserves mention in this context. Written after news of the death of the great poet Antonio Machado, "De los álamos y los sauces" (from poplar and willow) captures the plight of Alberti and his fellow exiles in but a few lines. The man in the poem is caught up "in the life of his distant dead and hears them in the air." Thus, Alberti returns grimly to his leitmotif, nostalgia.

With his return to this leitmotif, Alberti reached his full potential as a poet during the 1940's and 1950's. He poured forth volume after volume of consistently high quality. *Retornos de lo vivo lejano* (returns of the far and the living), a book wholly devoted to his most serviceable theme, may well be the finest volume of his career. The poems are at once accessible and mysterious, full of meaning on the surface and suggestive of unfathomed depths.

"Retornos del amor en una noche de verano" ("Returns: A Summer Night's Love") recalls in wondrous imagery the breathlessness of a time long past. For example, two pairs of lips, as they press together, become a silent carnation. "Retornos de Chopin a través de unas manos ya idas" ("Returns: Chopin by Way of Hands Now Gone") evokes some of the poet's earliest memories of his family. After many years, the poet is reunited with his brothers by an act of imagination, supported by the memory of Frédéric Chopin's music as played by the poet's mother. This is the quintessential Alberti, the master craftsman and the longing man in one.

Amid the melancholy splendor of his poems of exile, Alberti distilled a curious volume entitled *A la pintura* (to painting). In contrast to all that Alberti lost in exile, painting stands as a rediscovered treasure, and the Alberti of the early 1920's comes face to face with the middle-aged émigré. The collection includes sonnets on the tools of painting, both human and inanimate; free-verse meditations on the primary colors; and poems on various painters, each in a style reminiscent of the artist's own. Beyond its intrinsic value, the volume reveals much about the mutual attraction of the two arts.

One more poem, from *Baladas y canciones de Paraná*, deserves special mention here. "Balada del Andaluz perdido" ("Ballad of the Lost Andalusian"), as much as any single poem, reflects Alberti's self-image as a poet in exile. Written in terse, unrhymed couplets, it tells of a wandering Andalusian who watches the olives grow "by the banks of a different river." Sitting alone, he provokes curious questions from the Argentine onlookers on the opposite bank of the river, but he remains a mystery to them. Not so to the reader, who understands the pathos of the riderless horses, the memory of hatred, the loneliness. The final question admits of no answer and in fact needs none: "What will he do there, what is left to be done/ on the opposite side of the river, alone?"

Alberti was a poet who could grow without discarding his past. The youthful poet who composed marvelous lyrics persisted in the nostalgia of exile; the angry poet of the streets reasserted himself in diatribes against Yankee imperialism in Latin America. At ease in all forms and idioms, forever the Andalusian in exile, always growing in his art and his thought, Alberti wrote a staggering number of excellent poems. In the vast treasure trove of twentieth century Spanish poetry, he left a hoard of pearls and sapphires—hidden at times by the rubies and the emeralds, but worthy nevertheless.

Major publications other than poetry

PLAYS: *El hombre deshabitado*, 1930; *El trébol floride*, 1940; *El adefesio*, 1944; *El cerco de Numancia*, 1944 (adaptation).

NONFICTION: *La arboleda perdida*, 1942 (*The Lost Grove*, 1976).

Bibliography

Malahat Review, The. XLVII (July, 1978). Special Alberti issue.
Monguió, Luis. *The Poetry of Raphael Alberti: An Introduction*, 1966.
Morris, C. B. *Rafael Alberti's "Sobre los ángeles,"* 1966.
Salinas de Marichal, S. *El mundo poético de Rafael Alberti*, 1968.

Philip Krummrich

VICENTE ALEIXANDRE

Born: Seville, Spain; April 26, 1898

Principal collections

Ambito, 1928; *Espadas como labios*, 1932; *La destrucción o el amor*, 1935 (*Destruction or Love*, 1976); *Pasión de la tierra*, 1935; *Sombra del paraíso*, 1944; *Mundo a solas*, 1950; *Nacimiento último*, 1953; *Historia del corazón* 1954; *Mis poemas mejores*, 1956; *Poesías completas*, 1960; *En un vasto dominio*, 1962; *Retratos con nombre*, 1965; *Poemas de la consumación*, 1968; *Poems*, 1969; *Diálogos del conocimiento*, 1974; *Twenty Poems*, 1977 (Lewis Hyde and Robert Bly, translators); *A Longing for the Light: Selected Poems*, 1979; *A Bird of Paper: Poems of Vicente Aleixandre*, 1982.

Other literary forms

Vicente Aleixandre has published a great number of prologues, critical letters, memoirs, and evocations of friends and literary figures, many of them later included or rewritten for his major prose work, *Los encuentros* (1947; the encounters). Aleixandre has also made several speeches on poetry and poets, later published in pamphlet or book form.

Achievements

After receiving the Nobel Prize for Literature in 1977, Aleixandre stated that the prize was "a response symbolic of the relation of a poet with all other men." In Aleixandre's own estimation, winning the Nobel is his only worthy achievement. All other influences that he may have had on the development of poetry are insignificant compared to the poet's call to speak for his fellowman.

The extent of Aleixandre's influence is considerable, however, even if he denies its importance. He is a member of the Royal Spanish Academy (1949), the Hispanic Society of America, the Academy of the Latin World, Paris, the Royal Academy of Fine Arts of San Telmo, Málaga, the Spanish American Academy of Bogotá, the Academy of Arts and Sciences of Puerto Rico, and, as of 1972, an Honorary Fellow of the American Association of Spanish and Portuguese.

All of these honors recognize Aleixandre's lifelong devotion to the production of a unified body of poetry. A member of the celebrated *generación del 27*, including Jorge Guillén, Pedro Salinas, Federico García Lorca, Rafael Alberti, and Gerardo Diego, Aleixandre is one of the central figures of Spanish Surrealism. Although influenced by André Breton and his circle, the Spanish Surrealists developed to a great extent independently of their French counterparts. While French Surrealism is significant for its worldwide impact on the arts, it produced a surprisingly small amount of lasting poetry. In

contrast, Spanish Surrealism—both in Spain and, with notable local variations, in Latin America—constitutes one of the richest poetic traditions of
the twentieth century, a tradition in which Aleixandre has played a vital role.

Biography

Vicente Aleixandre Merlo was born on April 26, 1898, in Seville, Spain,
the son of Cirilo Aleixandre Ballester, a railway engineer, and Elvira Merlo
García de Pruneda, daughter of an upper-middle-class Andalusian family.
Married in Madrid, Aleixandre's parents moved to Seville, the base for his
father's travels with the Andalusian railway network. Four years after Aleixandre's birth, the family moved to Málaga, remaining there for seven years,
spending their summers in a cottage on the beach at Pedregalejo a few miles
from the city.

Aleixandre seems to have been very happy as a boy in Málaga, where he
attended school, frequented the movie theater across the street from his house
(he particularly liked the films of Max Linder), and read the Brothers Grimm
and Hans Christian Andersen. Happy memories of Málaga and the nearby
sea appear frequently in Aleixandre's poetry: He calls them "ciudad del paraíso" (city of paradise) and "mar del paraíso" (sea of paradise), respectively.

In 1911, the family moved to Madrid, where Aleixandre continued his
studies at Teresiano School, but he found the strict requirements for the
bachelor's degree tedious and preferred reading the books in his grandfather's
library: classical and Romantic works and detective novels, especially those
by Sir Arthur Conan Doyle. Aleixandre frequently visited the National Library,
where he read novels and drama from Spain's Golden Age to the *generación
del 98*. During the summer of 1917, his friend Dámaso Alonso lent him a
volume by Rubén Darío, a book which, Aleixandre says, revealed to him the
passion of his life—poetry. The next year, he discovered the works of Antonio
Machado and Juan Ramón Jiménez, as well as the Romantic world of Gustavo
Adolfo Bécquer, and his interest in poetry was firmly established.

At the age of fifteen, Aleixandre began to study law and business admini-
stration, finishing the two programs in 1920. He became an assistant professor
at the School of Commerce of Madrid and worked at night editing a journal
of economics in which he published several articles on railroads. In 1921, he
left his teaching post to work for the railway company, but when in 1925 he
suffered an attack of renal tuberculosis, he dropped all professional and social
activities, dedicating himself to his poetry, reading, and traveling with his
family through Portugal, France, England, and diverse regions of Spain.

Aleixandre's first poems appeared in *Revista de occidente* (journal of the
West) in 1926, and two years later his first collection, *Ambito* (ambit) was
published. In 1929, he discovered Sigmund Freud, James Joyce, and Arthur
Rimbaud, and, although he suffered a relapse into his tubercular condition
in 1932, this period of his life was very productive, resulting in three collections

published between 1932 and 1935.

After the removal of his diseased kidney in 1932, Aleixandre retired to Miraflores de la Sierra to convalesce, but in 1933 he returned to Madrid. Carlos Bousoño reports that during this year, Aleixandre read French translations of the German Romantic writers Ludwig Tieck and Novalis, as well as *Les Romantiques allemands* (1933; a translation of Ricarda Huch's *Blüthezeit der Romantik*, 1899; the German Romantics). He completed this new spiritual phase with the lyric poetry of William Shakespeare, John Keats, Percy Bysshe Shelley, and William Wordsworth. In 1934, Aleixandre's mother died, and there were more travels through England, France, and Switzerland. During the years of the Spanish Civil War (1936-1939), Aleixandre was isolated from political turmoil, spending much of the time in convalescence after renewed bouts of illness. The death of his father in 1939 brought him even closer to his sister Concepción.

Aleixandre's work reflects his psychological and physiological state as a vitally passionate man and a chronically sick man, as a calm, patient man and a creative man. His poetic production has been sustained over a lifetime, although a great many years have often passed between his published collections. In his own words, "The poet dies only when the man dies. And then, his poetry lives forever."

Analysis

In the work of Vicente Aleixandre's first period, the poet is interested primarily in terrible mythic elements of nature without people; he is chaotic, delirious, and grotesque. His is a kind of rebellion against the middle class that hems him in, but he is not yet aware that to save himself from its oppression he must transform his blind, ineffective rebellion into a conscious, efficient one. In his middle period, although Aleixandre continues to take refuge in myth to escape the horrible realities of the day, he faces them as he recalls his family and past, realizing that he cannot remain aloof from history, politics, and other realities when people believe in him. Finally, in his later work, the poet becomes academic, literary, cultured, and decorative; gradually, finding historical and telluric man and his own dialectical reality, Aleixandre identifies with the public, and the amorous solidarity of the man and poet with all creation is complete.

The idea that love equals death is the leitmotif of almost all Aleixandre's poetry; it appears most clearly in his recurring images of the sea. In addition to repressed sexuality, a neurotic and somewhat limited group of fantasies recur throughout his oeuvre, many of them associated with the sea. His early years in Málaga impressed the sea on his consciousness, so that it became for him a symbol of youth, equated in turn with innocence, happiness, and his mother (in psychoanalytic dream interpretation, the sea often symbolizes the mother). His desire to return and merge with that happiness and all it represents implies his death as an individual, as he is absorbed by a larger unit. Intrauterine life, being premortal (except to the Church), is easily equated with postmortal life—life before birth equals life after death.

The sea occupies a high place in Aleixandre's poetic scale of values. Among the 336 poems of his *Poesías completas*, the sea appears 182 times; moreover, it is used as a central theme in sixteen poems. The sea, a recurring symbol or archetype which integrates all Aleixandre's characteristic themes, represents primitive, instinctive life, true values lost by modern civilized man and maintained by simple sea creatures, a constant interplay between Thanatos and Eros, and a variety of sensual, erotic states involving repressed sexuality. Often Aleixandre juxtaposes the sea with images of forest, beach, teeth, tongue, birds, sun, moon, and breast. The sea in Aleixandre's poetry is pathognomonic in its psychological connotations, rooted in the painful dynamic of Aleixandre's own life, although at times it evokes a happy, innocent childhood, much as the gypsy symbolized the childhood of García Lorca. Aleixandre disguises the relationship between the symbol and its meaning at unconscious levels; he distorts and represses it so that the symbols may lend themselves to many interpretations, which only psychoanalysis can fully reveal.

Indeed, a catharsis comparable to psychological analysis is accomplished by Aleixandre's poetry, except that here the patient ministers to himself; for example, unconscious forces account for the breast motif associated with the sea, one of Aleixandre's most constant neurotic projections. Throughout his poems, Aleixandre uses the sea as a surface on which to project his images, according to which it takes on various hues, colors, and attributes. It can be an "unstable sea," an "imperious sea," or a "contained sea," and it serves as the principal, though not the exclusive, vehicle for the projection of neurotic fantasies in which the poet employs symbols to convey meaning he might consciously wish to suppress. Aleixandre's sea imagery irrationally yet imaginatively challenges the reader's preconceptions, as the poet attempts deliberately or otherwise to recapture an unconscious knowledge and create a unity of perception.

Aleixandre's interest in Freudian analysis made him particularly receptive to Surrealism, yet he never accepted the "pure" Surrealism of André Breton. Breton defined Surrealism as a psychic automatism through which he proposed to express the real functioning of thought without control by reason and beyond all aesthetic or moral norms, revealing the relationship between the real and the imaginary. For Breton, perception and representation are products of the dissociation of a single original faculty which the eidetic image recognizes and which is to be found in the primitive and the child. The distinction between the subjective and the objective lost its value as the poet sought to engage in a kind of automatic writing. Aleixandre rejected the notion of automatic writing, but in his preoccupation with the subconscious and his powerful, irrational imagery, he introduced Surrealism to Spanish poetry, where it found extremely fertile soil.

Ambito (ambit), Aleixandre's first collection, is related to the much later volume, *Sombra del paraíso* (shadow of paradise). *Ambito*, composed of seven sections and eight "Nights" (including an initial and final "Night" and one "Sea"), contains classical and Gongoristic forms—not unexpected at the time, since the collection was composed partly during the tercentenary of Luis de Góngora y Argote, when Baroque formalism ruled the day. Nature is everywhere; although there is a faint reflection of the cosmic force, the poet is largely descriptive and objective in a somewhat traditional way. Here, he contemplates nature, while in later works he will seek to possess it and be one with it. Written during his first serious illness, the book sensually examines the fleeting aspects of time. Within his own boundary—the limits of his sickroom, where he lived a solitary existence—he waxed both tender and uncontrollably passionate. Yet *Ambito's* formal beauty, pleasure in the contemplation of nature, desire for perfection, and joy in life reflect both Juan Ramón Jiménez and Jorge Guillén more than the later Aleixandre. The poetry deals with the world of the senses, classic and cold at times but also warm and romantic. The elusive imagery resembles the reverberations of a musical instrument. The poet employs traditional ballad form instead of the free verse that he has since come to use almost exclusively, and his ten- and six-syllable lines reveal his great sense of rhythm. In this volume of youthful love, Aleixandre delicately renders his love affair with nature, a love whose equations frequently resist logical interpretation.

Begun in the summer of 1929, Aleixandre's second collection, *Espadas como labios* (swords like lips), concerns the central themes of life, death, and love—themes which the poet, in his moment of inspiration and suffering, views from a new perspective. An epigraph from Lord Byron, to the effect that the poet is "a babbler," serves notice that the volume eschews conventional "meaning." The work as originally presented was filled with poetic transpositions and capriciously arranged punctuation to help Aleixandre release what he considered his "interior fire." His intention was not to induce a surrealistic trance but to create a voluntary pattern of unusual images. Aleixandre, in his somewhat illogically and incoherently developed poetic structures, does not know exactly what theme he will develop. The diffuse emotion he creates in this confused and disturbed work gives rise to apparent indecision for the poet, which transfers to the reader. His liberty of form allows Aleixandre to cover a variety of subjects in a dream atmosphere that hovers between sensation and thought. *Espadas como labios*, in its examination of reality, petrifies it—or, as one critic phrases it, indulges in the immobilization of the moment. Aleixandre's bittersweet imagery of dead roses, coals of silence (because they lack life-giving flame), and other signs of loss and decay suggests a desire to embrace the reality of death.

If *Espadas como labios*, despite its striking images, lacks imaginative coherence, Aleixandre's third collection, *Destruction or Love*, is an undisputed masterpiece. Here, in fifty-four poems divided into six parts, the poet offers a visionary transfiguration of the world in flux, a world of mystery and darkness whose basic fabric is erotic love. Aleixandre's universe is a place of cosmic and human passion, of frustrated and desperate clamor, and of unchained telluric forces which often prove fatal to man, absorbing him and destroying him. In Aleixandre's vision, men can obtain love only by destroying themselves and fusing with the cosmos, for human love is fleeting, and a final fusion with the earth will prove to be the most enduring love of all. Aleixandre excludes the life beyond and salvation; absorbed in the living unity of nature, he acclaims a love without religious connotations. Aleixandre stresses the idea that the unity of the world includes man's works and his civilization, but they remain peripheral to the primary, instinctive life. Perhaps love can save him from society's mask—for love fuses all things, animal, vegetable, and mineral, into one substance—but to achieve fusion, one must give up his limiting structures. Thus, the title of the volume is intended to signify not a choice between mutually exclusive alternatives (*either* destruction *or* love) but rather an identification (as when the subtitle of a book is introduced by the word "or").

In *Destruction or Love*, the animal and the vegetable worlds constantly interact with the thoughts and feelings of the poet. In virgin forests, ferocious beasts surround man, who seeks fruitlessly to find himself, half glimpsing his salvation in an identification with nature in all of its forms and thus affirming rather than denying love for all creation. Animals, the forest, and the sea live in intimate union with elementary forces of nature, and tender, small animals exist with large, destructive ones: the beetle and the scorpion with the cobra, the eagle, lions, and tigers. Thus, the tiger is an elastic fire of the forest, and the eagles resemble the ocean. Like other aspects of nature, such as the ocean, the moon, or the heavens, these animals may be virginal and innocent or terrible and destructive. In this vision of nature as a physical whole in which violence and love are complementary forces, everything attacks, destroys, and loves everything and, in so doing, loves, attacks, and destroys itself. Life is death. The limits between flora and fauna dissolve into a new unity; the sea's fish appear to be birds; foam is hair; a body becomes an ocean; a heart becomes a mountain; man may be metal or a lion. Like the mystic poets of old—who had to die in order to find eternal life—Aleixandre offers a mystic fusion or death with the sea and the maternal earth.

Sombra del paraíso (shadow of paradise), begun in 1939 and finished in November, 1943, created a sensation among young poets even before its publication in book form; when it finally appeared in 1944, it won a wide and enthusiastic readership among the literary youth of the day. Here, Aleixandre returns to the innocent world of infancy, to a paradise beyond Original Sin and knowledge, to be one with the heavens and the creatures of the dawn.

He evokes a Garden of Eden where he may find lost happiness in order to escape the evil world of man, its folly and malignity. The poet narcissistically reinvents his own reality, remembers it, or perhaps imaginatively re-creates the world of childhood before the horrifying and inevitable loss of innocence. In his universe of serenity, order, and beauty, however, Aleixandre implies an awareness of the historical world, in which man must play his role. The tension between paradise and history is always just beneath the surface.

Sombra del paraíso is divided into six parts. Of its fifty-two poems, only a dozen have a definite metric form, but through them all there are patterns of association among rhythms of different kinds. The verse lines are of varying length, including hendecasyllables, pentasyllables, hexameters, exciting combinations of anapestic lines, and irregular meters. Avoiding monotony in his rhythmical movements by means of this prodigality of expression, Aleixandre uses exclamations, interrogatives, and an almost musical progression of scales to form a polyphonic richness. His fetish for rhythmic simplicity extends to his use of adjectives, which he occasionally employs adverbially and, rarely, in double or triple combination. Often his naked nouns convey his precise tone or mood; on other occasions, for special effect, he ends his poetic lines with a verb; infrequently, he employs gerundives experimentally.

Of Aleixandre's later collections, the most important is *Historia del corazón* (history of the heart). Many underlying crosscurrents of thought and emotion can be found in this volume, but its central theme is the need for human solidarity and compassion for the victims of injustice. *Historia del corazón* reveals a dramatic change in Aleixandre's conception of man. Here, no longer the creature of telluric forces, man is defined by the dolorous round of daily experience. Likewise, Aleixandre's conception of poetry has changed: The poet, a man, becomes all men, destined to live and die, without the assurance of paradise or eternal life, in a world where death is always present. Nevertheless, the poet proclaims, it is not necessary to live desperate, solitary lives; he sings for all mankind of fleeting time, social love, and human solidarity. The poet recognizes that he is aging, but without despair, and empathizes with his neighbor, who must also stoically face the end.

Aleixandre's poetry is a spiritual voyage, at times verging on the commonplace but for the most part permeated with the beauty of the profound. He speaks of love, of life and death, of nature, humanity, and fleeting time. Vigorous or gentle, as the occasion demands, he has not invented a new poetic language, but his ardent and opaque imagery added a new dimension to the poetry of his day.

Major publications other than poetry

NONFICTION: *Los encuentros*, 1947.

MISCELLANEOUS: *Obras completas*, 1977 (includes all Aleixandre's poetry and prose).

Bibliography

Bourne, L. M. "The Spiritualization of Matter in the Poetry of Vicente Aleixandre," in *Revista de Letras*. XXII (1974), pp. 190-199.
Durán, M. "Vicente Aleixandre, Last of the Romantics: The 1977 Nobel Prize for Literature," in *World Literature Today*. LII (1978), pp. 203-208.
Ilie, P. *The Surrealist Mode in Spanish Literature*, 1968.
Schwartz, Kessel. *Vicente Aleixandre*, 1970.

Richard A. Mazzara

ANACREON

Born: Teos, Greece; c. 571 B.C.
Died: Athens, Greece; c. 490 B.C.

Principal collections
Using the Ionic dialect of Greek, Anacreon wrote in most of the lyric meters and forms of his day. His melic songs, of mixed meters, were mostly monodic and included hymns, love songs, and convivial poems. Anacreon followed the Greek custom of writing commemorative poems, dedications, and epitaphs in the elegiac meter, and invective poetry in iambics. He may have also written *partheneia*, or choral songs sung by young girls; the evidence, however, is uncertain. Anacreon composed primarily for oral performance, but his poetry was certainly written down in his lifetime. The first known edition of Anacreon's works was made by the Alexandrian scholar Aristarchus, who arranged Anacreon's poetry into several books (at least three, possibly five or six) according to metrical principles. This edition does not survive. A few poems have survived under Anacreon's name in the *Palatine Anthology*, but not all of them are authentic. Most of Anacreon's extant corpus has been collected from papyri and from ancient citations. Consequently, only a very few of these extant fragments can be considered complete poems. The most complete modern edition of Anacreon can be found in Denys Page, *Poetae Melici Graeci* (1962), whose numerical references to Anacreon's fragments are used below.

Other literary forms
Anacreon is remembered only for his poetry.

Achievements
Included in the Alexandrine canon of nine Greek lyric poets, Anacreon has influenced generations of poets since classical times, although it is difficult to measure his influence precisely with such fragmentary texts. The surviving fragments show that Anacreon set a high standard for sophisticated, polished, short poems written in a variety of meters. While he appears to favor a combination of Glyconics and Pherecrateans in his extant verse, he is best known for the Anacreontic meter, an anaclastic Ionic dimeter to which he has given his name. He was probably most admired in antiquity for his love poems, his banquet poems, and his imagery and tropes, especially those dealing with Eros, which became standardized in later poetry.

Anacreon's style was copied by unknown Greek poets writing under his name; these spurious poems, usually called the Anacreonteia, survive in the *Palatine Anthology* and range in date from the Alexandrine period through late Byzantine times. The poetry of Horace and of other Roman lyric poets also shows conscious imitation of Anacreon, whose authentic works could still be read in Augustan Rome. Anacreon is better known in the modern world through the Anacreonteia than through his own works. The Anacreonteia, first printed in 1554, had a great influence upon several European literary schools: upon the French Renaissance poets Pierre de Ronsard and Rémy Belleau; upon such Italian lyric poets of the seventeenth and eighteenth centuries as Gabriello Chiabrera and Jacopo Vittorelli; upon such eighteenth century German poets as Friedrich von Hagedorn, Johann Gleim, and Johann Götz; and upon the British and Irish poets Robert Herrick, William Oldys, and Thomas Moore. These poets, often called Anacreontics, either made free translations of the Greek Anacreonteia into their own languages or wrote original poetry in the meter and style known as Anacreontic.

Biography

Anacreon's poetry reflects the aristocratic Greek society of the sixth century B.C. in which he lived. His was a society endangered by Persian encroachments on Ionic Greece, as well as by internal political upheavals marked by the rise and fall of antiaristocratic tyrannies. Although little is known for certain about Anacreon's life, much can be conjectured from ancient citations and, to a lesser degree, from the remains of his own poetry.

Anacreon, son of Scythinus, was born in the Ionian city of Teos (modern Sighalik, Turkey) about 571 B.C. Teos was seized by the Persian Harpagus soon after the fall of Sardis about 541 B.C. Many Teans, including Anacreon, escaped Persian rule by fleeing to Abdera on the coast of Thrace; fragments 391 P. and 419 P. may refer to this traumatic period in Anacreon's life. Anacreon's Thracian period is obscure; only a few fragments, including 417 P., reflect his experiences there. Anacreon's poetic reputation, however, certainly grew from that time, for he was at some point invited to the court of the Samian tyrant, Polycrates (ruled 540 to c. 522 B.C.), to tutor Polycrates' son in music and poetry.

Polycrates' political policy on Samos included a patronage of the arts which brought to the island not only Anacreon but also the West Greek poet, Ibycus of Rhegium, known for his choral song. Although Anacreon remained in Samos until the death of Polycrates, and is said by ancient sources to have made frequent reference to the tyrant in his poetry, only a few allusions to events in Samos (348 P., 353 P., and 426 P.) can be found in Anacreon's extant fragments. The surviving poetry suggests that Anacreon had little enthusiasm for political themes; he preferred to write about love and wine. Although Anacreon's love poetry was addressed primarily to young boys, this provides meager evidence for the poet's biography, since homoeroticism was a conventional poetic theme in his society (see, for example, Sappho).

With the fall of Polycrates about 522 B.C., Anacreon was brought to Athens by the Pisistratid Hipparchus, who, like Polycrates, practiced a policy of art patronage under the tyranny of his brother Hippias. Anacreon remained in Athens for the rest of his life, except for a brief interlude in Thessaly about 512 B.C., caused by the fall of the Pisistratids.

As he grew older, Anacreon introduced the theme of old age into his poetry, often combining it with his favorite themes of love and wine. It was for this type of poetry that he was best known in the aristocratic Athenian society for which he wrote. Anacreon's personality came to be so closely associated with love and wine that long after his death he was remembered as a drunken, amorous old man. Indeed, this may account for the ancient tradition that Anacreon died as a result of choking on a grape pip. Whatever the actual cause, Anacreon died probably about 490 B.C., since the ancients say that he lived to the age of eighty-five and that he lived long enough to experience the poetry of Aeschylus.

Analysis

The Greek poetic tradition in which Anacreon wrote was a particularly rich one, tracing its origins to the oral songs of the Homeric period. It was in many ways a conservative tradition; it restricted certain genres to specific meters, such as epic to hexameter and invective to iambic, and depended to a great extent on stock epithets, formulas, and vocabulary from Homeric epic. Yet, at the same time, it was a tradition which encouraged experimentation and novelty of expression. Thus, beginning in the late eighth century B.C., lyric poetry, distinguished by the use of the first person, blossomed, epecially in the Greek cities of Ionia and Aeolia, and produced Archilochus, Sappho, and Alcaeus in the seventh century B.C. All of these early lyric poets experimented with a poetic analysis of personal experience and emotion to which the late sixth century Anacreon was heir. While accepting the traditional metrical types and while continuing the lyric proclivity toward self-expression and introspection, Anacreon brought to this poetry not so much new emotions and feelings as the skill of a meticulous craftsman who chose his words carefully and knew when to inject exaggeration and humor for the proper effect. Anacreon enriched Greek lyric with the novelties of a poetic experimenter who constantly sought new imagery and approaches for old themes. Certainly the themes of love and wine which dominate Anacreon's extant poetry are, for the most part, traditional. What is significant about Anacreon is that he strove to express these themes in new contexts and succeeded so well that the novel imagery and contexts he introduced, especially in the realm of love poetry, have generally become the clichés of later generations of poets.

Anacreon's goal of novelty in a traditional context is demonstrated in 357 P., a prayer to Dionysus. The prayer form had early been recognized to be well suited to lyric expression; these prayers are meant not for public ceremony but for private performance. Sappho's "Ode to Aphrodite" had already used the prayer poem in a love context with great success, and Anacreon may here be following Sappho. Anacreon's prayer is divided into two parts: the invocation, in which the deity is addressed and described; and the entreaty, or the request made to the god. Anacreon's invocation, striking in that it does not mention the god's name, identifies Dionysus only by his habitual companions and haunts. Dionysus is described as playing on the lofty mountaintops with Eros, nymphs, and Aphrodite. Novelty of expression is achieved by the use of new rather than stock epithets for Dionysus' companions. While the epithet "subduer," which Anacreon invents for Eros, is never used again in Greek literature, the concept of Eros as a tamer of men, which Anacreon implies through this epithet, is one which becomes commonplace in later lyric. Anacreon's descriptions of the nymphs as "blue-eyed" and Aphrodite as "rosy" are noteworthy both because these adjectives had never been applied to these deities before, and because they reflect another characteristic of Anacreon's style: a fondness for color contrasts. In a very few words, Anacreon is thus able to achieve a vivid, colorful, original description of Dionysus' world.

This formal invocation is followed by an equally formal entreaty. Anacreon maintains the solemnity of the prayer form here by employing standard expressions of entreaty: "I beseech you," "come kindly to us," and "hear our prayer." The climax to which the poem is leading is the specific request that the poet wants to make; the formality of structure and vocabulary suggests that the request is a serious one. Yet the next phrase, "be a good counselor to Cleobulus," shows that Anacreon is not serious. Anacreon's word for "good counselor," *sumbulus*, creates a pun on Cleobulus' name which is difficult to miss, since both Cleobulus and *sumbulus* are placed at the beginning of their respective lines. The humor of this phrase shatters the solemn tone of the prayer and prepares for the surprise of the last two lines, where Anacreon finally reveals that he is actually praying to Dionysus not for some lofty request, but for aid in a homosexual love affair. The manipulation of the prayer form to suit a love theme is already found in Sappho, but without the change in tone developed here. Sappho maintains in her poem an intensity of emotion which is not found in Anacreon. By adding a pun at the point when he is introducing the love theme, Anacreon emphasizes not his intense emotions but his artistic skill, his ability to control his poem through the careful selection of words.

Cleobulus is featured in several other poems, including 359 P., which again shows Anacreon's interest in form rather than emotions. This love poem is a sequence of three parallel statements about Anacreon's relationship with Cleobulus. Each line begins with Cleobulus' name used in a different case ending and concludes with a different verb in the first person singular: "I love," "I am mad," and "I gaze." The grammatical trope is probably borrowed from Archilochus, who uses it in a political context. Anacreon's application of Archilochus' technique to love poetry reflects a de-emphasis of emotional intensity which is suggested by the verbal sequence as well, where Anacreon moves from mad love for Cleobulus to mere gazing at the beloved. "I gaze at Cleobulus" suggests a distance between lover and beloved which is not evident in "I love Cleobulus." Such distance is critical to Anacreon's poetic stance, which is based on careful word study.

Another of his poems, 358 P., demonstrates not only Anacreon's use of special descriptive words, but also his experimentation with new imagery. In this piece Anacreon describes Eros' invitation to play ball with a girl from Lesbos. Anacreon may here be inventing the image of Eros as the "ball-player," a commonplace in later poets such as Apollonius and Meleager. The ball-playing, possibly derived from the *Odyssey* (c. 800 B.C.), where Nausicaa plays ball with her servant girls, is a successful variation on the traditional Greek theme of apple-tossing (as in the story of Atalanta). The play here is a double entendre. Anacreon's fondness for color contrasts, noted above, is evident in this poem as well, and with even more effect. Eros' ball is "purple," a rich and expensive color in the ancient world, while Anacreon transfers an epithet of Dionysus, "golden-haired," to Eros. The girl, too, is described with colors; she is the girl "with the motley slippers." The final, and perhaps most important, color reference is to Anacreon's white hair, implying that the girl rejects Anacreon because he is too old. This incompatibility of love with old age a theme which is repeated in Anacreon's extant corpus, is emphasized by the contrast of colors developed in the poem.

Old age, however, is not the only motive for the girl's rejection of Anacreon. She is from Lesbos and gapes after some "other" (female). To the modern reader this situation suggests an association of the island of Lesbos with female homosexuality which may not have been standard in Anacreon's day. Further, there is some ambiguity here, probably intentional, in the text. First, "female" is only grammatically understood and other nouns have been supplied, for example, "hair" (feminine in Greek), making the homosexuality theme more uncertain and, at the same time, enhancing the sexual double entendre. The epithet for Lesbos, "good to dwell in," is also ambiguous. While derived from a standard Homeric epithet for the island, this word is employed here with a meaning which is difficult to establish. The solemn Homeric word may simply be used, as David A. Campbell suggests, to contrast with the more playful tone of the poem as a whole. C. M. Bowra argues in *Greek Lyric Poetry from Alcman to Simonides* (1961) that the epithet, transposed to the girl, may suggest that she comes from a prosperous family and can pick and choose her mates. Bowra has also suggested that this epithet is a subtle dig at Lesbos, "well-established" in its sexual habits. Any and all of these interpretations may be correct, for in this poem, where Eros is depicted as a tease, perhaps the poet, too, is a tease through his use of ambiguity. Once again Anacreon is more interested in his poetic expression than in his emotions. Such a poetic distance from his emotions permits him to deal with sexual passion and with the frustrations of old age in a distinctively humorous way.

Anacreon also demonstrates a concern with novelty and effect. The fragment 376 P. combines two of the poet's favorite topics, love and wine, in the context of a traditional love theme: the spurned lover's desperate leap from the Leucadian Cliff. Anacreon uses this theme in a new way. The poet states that the climb onto the rock is being made "again," indicating that this particular leap is not a suicide, but rather a repeated occurrence. The emphasis is not on the despair of unrequited love, but on the loss of self-control caused by love. This helplessness is further stressed by the dive which the poet takes in the second line. Finally, the poet mentions that he makes the plunge "drunk with love." Inebriety may already have been associated with the traditional leap from the Leucadian Cliff, but Anacreon appears to have transposed the theme into a significant metaphor which was not there before and which has not left love poetry since. "To be drunk with love" is certainly a comical exaggeration which suits Anacreon's theme of loss of self-control and which underscores his evident mastery over his poetry.

Wine and love are also combined in 396 P., where the poet addresses the cupbearer, who played a role of honor at Greek drinking parties, and asks for water and wine, which the Greeks mixed before drinking, as well as a garland of flowers, another common trapping of a Greek drinking song. Anacreon, however, adds something new to the drinking song by introducing a love theme. "Bring me these things," he says, "that I may box with Eros." The boxing metaphor is apparently an invention of Anacreon, who may have used it at least once more (in 346 P.). Eros, who was represented as a youth in the sixth century and was not transformed into an infant until the Hellenistic period, is thus fitted by Anacreon with another apt metaphor, that of boxing, an image appropriate to Eros' pain-inflicting capabilities.

A final selection, 417 P., shows Anacreon not creating new imagery but rather using an old image in a strikingly new fashion. For the first time, perhaps, a lyric poet may be creating an entire poem out of a single metaphor, a comparison of women with mares, which had appeared earlier in the choral poetry of Alcman. Ibycus, Anacreon's poetic associate on Samos, also used the race-horse image for the lover controlled by Eros. In 417 P., however, Anacreon reverses Ibycus' imagery by making the girl the wild mare and himself the potential rider. The vocabulary of the poem is a remarkable combination of words with amatory undertones, such as "reins" and "mounter," and of elevated epic phraseology, such as "stubbornly" and "think me in no way wise" and "around the limits of the course."

These few examples of the surviving fragments of Anacreon's poetry suggest what a great loss the disappearance of his corpus has been. They demonstrate his consummate skill as a lyric poet who could manipulate poetic themes, imagery, vocabulary, and even his emotions for poetic effect. The reader of Anacreon, tantalized by the few extant fragments, must appreciate the poet's ironic position within literary tradition. A playfully original and prolific innovator, Anacreon became an authoritative model for many later poets, and, despite the ravages of time, he remains a major figure in literature through imitation by others rather than by the weight of his own writings.

Bibliography
Bowra, Cecil Maurice. *Greek Lyric Poetry from Alcman to Simonides*, 1961.
Campbell, David A. *Greek Lyric Poetry*, 1967.
Lobel, Edgar, and Denys Page. *Poetarum Lesbiorum Fragmenta*, 1955.
Page, Denys. *Poetae Melici Graeci*, 1962.
West, M. L. *Iambi et Elegi Graeci*, 1971-1972.

Thomas J. Sienkewicz

INNOKENTY ANNENSKY

Born: Omsk, Siberia; August 20, 1856
Died: St. Petersburg, Russia; November 30, 1909

Principal collections
Tikhie pesni, 1904; *Kiparisovy larets*, 1910 (*The Cypress Chest*, 1982).

Other literary forms
In addition to his two collections of poetry, for which he is best remembered today, Innokenty Annensky wrote four tragedies and was a critic and pedagogue of note. His tragedies include *Melanippa-Filosof* (1901), *Tsar Iksion* (1902), *Laodamiia* (1906), and *Famira Kifared* (1913). Annensky's major critical effort consists of the essays constituting the two collections entitled *Kniga otrazhenii* (1906) and *Vtoraia kniga otrazhenii* (1909). They were reissued in a single volume in 1969. The remainder of Annensky's critical and pedagogical essays have never been collected in book form; they remain scattered throughout the Russian journals in which they first appeared.

Achievements
Annensky has always been considered a "poet's poet" because of the subtlety of his poetic imagery and the intricacy of his thought. In contrast to such contemporary poets as Aleksandr Blok and Konstantin Balmont, who were enormously popular in their own time, Annensky's main impact was rather on the aesthetic theory of Acmeism, one of the great Russian poetic schools of the twentieth century. Two gifted and famous Acmeists, Anna Akhmatova and Osip Mandelstam, were especially drawn to Annensky both as a poet and as a formulator of poetic doctrine.

Although he has often been regarded as a member of the older, "first generation" of Russian Symbolists (in contrast to the younger or "second generation"), Annensky does not truly fit into a particular category. His style can be designated as Symbolist insofar as his use of literary allusions is concerned, yet his worldview and aesthetic ideals, as well as his treatment of non-Symbolist stylistic elements, set him apart from this movement. Annensky differs from his contemporaries in his aesthetic independence. He is considered unique among twentieth century Russian poets in that he combined aspects of Symbolism with experimental stylistic devices to produce verse that cannot easily be labeled. He is regarded today as one of the more interesting and significant modern Russian poets, and he has a reputation far exceeding that which he enjoyed during his own lifetime.

Biography
Innokenty Fyodorovich Annensky was born in Omsk, Siberia, on August

20, 1856, but the family returned to St. Petersburg in 1858. Both parents having died when Annensky was quite young, he was reared by his brother, Nikolay Fyodorovich Annensky, publisher of the important journal *Russkoe bogatstvo*. Nikolay and his wife, Alexandra Nikitichna Annenskaya, held liberal political and social views typical of the positivistic thinkers of their generation.

Educated at home, possibly because his health was poor, Annensky mastered several foreign languages, including Latin and Greek. He completed a degree in philology at the University of St. Petersburg in 1879; in the same year, he married a widow named Dina Khmara-Barshchevskaya. The marriage was apparently a happy one; he was close to his two stepsons, and his own son Valentin was born in 1880.

Annensky embarked on his pedagogical career following graduation. After teaching Greek and Russian in several private institutions in St. Petersburg, he went to Kiev between 1890 and 1893, where he became director of the Pavel Galagan College. He returned to St. Petersburg in 1893, assuming the directorship of a high school there, and in 1896, he was appointed head of the famous lyceum at Tsarskoe Selo. It was during his tenure at Tsarskoe Selo that he issued his first volume of original verse and translations, *Tikhie pesni*; the book was virtually unnoticed by the critics.

Annensky's last post was as inspector of the St. Petersburg School District; he also lectured on classical literature at a private university for women. During this period, his friendship with the Acmeist poet and theoretician Nikolay Gumilyov gave him entrée into the literary world of St. Petersburg and brought him belated fame. Annensky died of a heart attack on November 30, 1909, the very day his retirement had been granted.

Analysis

Innokenty Annensky's lyrics reflect an intimate knowledge of French poetry, particularly the verse of the Parnassians and the French Symbolists. Like many of these French poets, Annensky heeded Stéphane Mallarmé's dictum that to name was to destroy, while to suggest was to create. Like the French, Annensky concentrated a lyrical theme in one symbolically treated subject or in a complex of interconnected subjects. While he made use of symbol and suggestion, the fact that the lyrical theme was related to a single subject or a complex of related subjects lent greater impact to his poems.

Annensky's link with the French Symbolists was paralleled by his close ties with the Parnassians. The latter, particularly their principal poet, Théophile Gautier, advocated "art for art's sake" and the composition of a carefully constructed poetry equally removed from subjective emotions and contemporary events. The Parnassians also expressed a renewed interest in the classical world; indeed, the Parnassians had a greater impact on Annensky than did the Symbolists, for he shared with the former a cult of poetic form and a love of the word as such, as well as subscribing to their notion that there was no affinity between aesthetics and ethics.

Annensky's relationship with the Russian Symbolists is somewhat ambiguous, for there was an absence of any kind of organizational tie or even any close relationship between him and representatives of the "new poetry." Unlike his contemporaries, he considered Symbolism to be an aesthetic system rather than a literary school. He neither rebelled against civic poetry, for example, as the Symbolists generally did, nor rejected his poetic heritage. Unlike the later Symbolists, he did not regard art as a means of mystical escape, maintaining that Symbolism was intended to be literature rather than a new form of universal religion.

The approximately five hundred lyrics that Annensky wrote are the center of his creative work and can be divided into six major themes: death, life, dream, nature, artistic creation, and time. The themes of death, life, dream, and nature are actually subordinate to that of time, which binds all of them together. In this very emphasis on temporality, Annensky transcended Symbolism and anticipated later poetic movements. His exemption of artistic creation from the strictures of time illustrates the enormous emphasis he placed on aesthetics.

Death played an important role in Annensky's verse, for he considered it as an ever-intruding end to a life without hope. He devoted a number of lyrics to this theme, one of the most important of which was "Siren' na kamne" ("Lilac on the Gravestone"). Here Annensky touches on the transitory nature of man's life, on the contrast between life and death, and on the awareness that the seemingly infinite possibilities of the intellect are thwarted by the intrusion of an awareness of physical death. Annensky's realization that death is a physical, inescapable end demonstrates his acceptance of the limitations of the material world and stresses thereby one of the most significant differences between him and the Symbolists.

One of Annensky's major themes is life. This category is dominated by lyrics about *toska* (depression, melancholy, or yearning), as exemplified by the poem "Toska" ("Depression"). The persona in "Depression" is an invalid, suspended, as it were, between life and death. The setting for the poem is a sickroom decorated with flowered wallpaper, around which flies hover. The unnaturalness of the surroundings, coupled with Annensky's frequent use of participles rather than finite verbs, separates both persona and reader from the normal, lively world of action and imprisons them in a static, banal realm. Like his poems on death, Annensky's lyrics about life are characterized by pessimism derived from his constant awareness of the limitations and frustrations of life.

In *The Influence of French Symbolism on Russian Poetry*, Georgette Donchin suggests that, because the dream symbolizes an escape from reality, it was a common poetic theme for Russian Symbolists. The dream also occupies a special place in Annensky's poetry. Simon Karlinsky, in his 1966 essay "The Materiality of Annensky," argues that the dream represents a world divorced from the strictures of time, an alternative existence for the poet. Annensky's dream verses can be subdivided into three categories according to theme: disorientation, oblivion, and nightmare. In "Dvoinik" ("The Double"), the persona experiences a loss of orientation, with the primary differentiation of identity, that between the I and the non-I, blurred. Annensky's deliberate grammatical confusion of the first, second, and third persons destroys the normal distinctions between conversation and narration, even of existence. When the distinct separateness of the individual consciousness is eradicated, nothing is certain. Annensky has, in fact, placed the rest of the poem outside reality by erasing the conceptions of definite time and space, with all existence transformed into a dream.

In "Kogda b ne smert', a zabyt'e" ("If There Were Not Death, but Oblivion"), oblivion represents the cessation of time. It is a state divorced from temporality, which is seen in the poem as the creator and destroyer of beauty. The poet's awareness of the ephemerality of artistic as well as natural beauty is a source of torment for him; he is trapped by time and is doomed to solitude.

Unlike disorientation and oblivion, the nightmare threatens the sufferer with annihilation. In "Utro" ("Morning"), Annensky has erased the distinction between dream and reality, making the nightmare vividly real. When day comes at the end of the poem, it is not merely a unit of time but a symbol of the force of light against the power of darkness, good against evil, life against death.

Nature is the backdrop against which thoughts and emotions can be projected, the external mirror of human existence. As such, it constitutes a significant theme in Annensky's verse. The winter poem "Sneg" ("Snow") is characterized by a sharpness of line and by the specificity resulting from the repeated use of the definite demonstrative adjective *eto* (this). In addition to crispness of outline and color contrast, Annensky's employment of oxymoron makes his images clearer still. The clarity of nature has become a foil for the clarity of the thought of the persona.

In contrast to the later Symbolists, Annensky considered the poet a creator of clear, linear art. His divergence from the Symbolists is especially marked in the lyric "Poetu" ("To a Poet"), a lesson in how to write poetry. Annensky focuses on the importance of clarity and concreteness, opposing them to abstraction and indefiniteness. He asserts that poetry is a "science" governed by certain laws and is, within limits, exact, as the measuring triad of dimensions in the poem suggests. The figure with the triad is the Muse, who in turn symbolizes the art of classical Greece with its emphasis on clarity and beauty of form. The link with Greece is reinforced by the reference to Orpheus and the significance of form. The Muse is juxtaposed to veiled Isis, emblematic of the mystery and distortion of the later Symbolists. She perhaps stands for the figure of Eternal Wisdom that informed much of the philosophy of the Symbolist philosopher-poet Vladimir Soloviev. The poet is not an intermediary between the earth and a higher realm; he is not a seer or transmitter, but a writer.

Like "To a Poet," "Poeziia" ("Poetry") is a metapoem, in which art transcends the everyday world and allows the poet limited access to a realm of absolute beauty. The poem is set in the Sinai desert, a region of intense light and heat; the word "flaming" in the first line not only describes the concentrated heat of the desert, but in addition carries the religious connotation of the fire that can purge sin and memory (as in Alexander Pushkin's famous poem "Prorok," "The Prophet"). Annensky personifies poetry in the last stanza, where he speaks of the "traces of Her sandals." The narrator never sees Poetry directly; he entreats Her, although not "knowing Her."

The desert can be seen here as a haven from society and from the decay of the established religion (in this case, Symbolism) from which the poet seeks to escape. Poetry is contrasted to the vision of Sophia (Eternal Wisdom) that Soloviev saw in Egypt, and the poem as a whole may well represent Annensky's escape from a burdensome, "official" school of poetry in his quest for pure art.

Time is centrally important in Annensky's verse, for it is the regulator of the days and seasons, the ruler of life. Time connects and dominates all of Annensky's other themes, providing a focal point for understanding his conception of the material world and his emphasis on art. "Stalnaia cikada" ("The Steel Cicada") portrays time as an invention of the mind. In this lyric, Annensky has equated the timepiece with a cicada and has thus transformed it into something alive, thereby implying process and change. When the lid of the watch has been slammed shut in the last stanza, time has stopped. The intrusion of *Toska* (depression personified), having cut the poet off from external events (by shutting the watch lid), has stopped time.

Time, the medium of change, causes the alteration of moods and conditions that is the antithesis of depression. Annensky speeds up time through his poetic lexicon, employing short phrases without enjambment to achieve a staccato effect. Near the end of the poem, the persona has become reconciled to the return of Depression; his companionship with the cicada is called a "miracle" that will last only for a minute. With the removal of the cicada comes the realization that the passing moment is beyond recall. The poet's attempt to escape from constancy into a realm of change that he has invented himself (symbolized throughout the poem by the watch, a mechanical object) has failed. In the end, he is the victim of his own immutability.

For Annensky, time symbolizes process and the final disintegration that characterizes life, nature, and death, while life represents the temporary immersion in process. It is the poet's realization of the relentless flow of time that produces the psychological state of depression, an awareness that the extreme limitations of existence are nevertheless the highest human achievement. Annensky's cognizance of depression amounts to a rejection of mysticism, separating him irrevocably from the later Symbolists. Time represents reality and is inescapable except through the momentary conquest by the mind and spirit of the artist.

Although he did not experiment in metrics and rhyme, Annensky was more adventurous stylistically in his employment of personification. He frequently capitalizes the first letter of a word denoting an object or abstract term to identify it with a human being, utilizing the simile and metaphor for the same purpose. Annensky's reliance on personification causes the reader to view nature, at least within the scope of these poems, as an extension of the conscious mind. His poetic universe centers on the mind, extends to artifacts, includes surrounding nature (especially the garden), and is limited only by the clouds. Beyond the clouds lies infinity, which cannot be understood and hence cannot be encompassed within the realm dominated by the mind. Because his universe can be considered as having a rational basis, Annensky should be regarded as a precursor of the rationalism of the Acmeists.

Although classified as a Symbolist by a number of critics, Annensky should rather be regarded as a transitional figure between Symbolism and later poetic developments in Russia. Annensky differs from the Symbolists in his use of conversational elements and in his preference for concrete, distinct objects as poetic images. Like his thematic emphasis on time, his predilection for the concrete and real as opposed to the abstract and mystical denotes an acceptance of the actual world. His literary orientation was toward new poets rather than toward those who were already established. His later poetry contains stylistic elements more compatible with Acmeism, even with Futurism, than with Symbolism.

Annensky's ambiguous position in relation to the Symbolists is underscored by his avoidance of the polemics characterizing the Symbolist school. This may have been partially a result of the fact that he was not a professional poet but instead was an educator who lacked sufficient time or opportunity to develop extensive personal contacts with the Symbolists. His abstention from the literary quarrels that were to climax in 1910, the year after his death, indicates an unwillingness to involve himself in the intricacies of literary battles. In addition, Annensky's avoidance of Symbolist polemics parallels his emphasis on poetry as an artistic phenomenon rather than a literary school. He believed that the intrinsic aesthetic value of poetry precluded its use as a vehicle. His abstention from mysticism and literary polemics resulted from a desire to preserve the integrity of the art and thus to prevent its prostitution to other ends.

Annensky stood out from the poets of his time in devising a poetic world that was concrete rather than abstract, worldly rather than mystical. He employed personification and focused on images and objects that made his language concrete. Although he was interested in the musical elements of poetry, he emphasized its pictorial and visual aspects. He thus created a definitive background for the philosophical or aesthetic argument of a particular lyric. These factors, coupled with a respect for the intrinsic worth of art, relate him more closely to writers following him, particularly to such poets as the Acmeists, than to his contemporaries. In tracing the development of Russian poetry and, indeed, of Russian literature as a whole in the twentieth century, the pivotal position of Annensky and the great scope of his contribution must be taken into account.

Major publications other than poetry
PLAYS: *Melanippa-Filosof*, 1901; *Tsar Iksion*, 1902; *Laodamiia*, 1906; *Famira Kifared*, 1913.
NONFICTION: *Kniga otrazhenii*, 1906; *Vtoraia kniga otrazhenii*, 1909.

Bibliography
Balakian, Anna. *The Symbolist Movement: A Critical Appraisal*, 1967.
Bowra, C. M. *The Heritage of Symbolism*, 1943.
Donchin, Georgette. *The Influence of French Symbolism on Russian Poetry*, 1958.
Erlich, Victor. *The Double Image: Concepts of the Poet in Slavic Literatures*, 1964.
Poggioli, Renato. *The Poets of Russia, 1890-1930*, 1960.
Setchkarev, Vsevolod. *Studies in the Life and Work of Innokentij Annenskij*, 1963.

Janet G. Tucker

GUILLAUME APOLLINAIRE
Wilhelm Apollinaris de Kostrowitzky

Born: Rome, Italy; August 26, 1880
Died: Paris, France; November 9, 1918

Principal collections

Le Bestiaire, 1911 (*Bestiary*, 1978); *Alcools*, 1913 (English translation, 1964, 1965); *Calligrammes*, 1918 (English translation, 1980); *Il y a*, 1925; *Le Guetteur mélancolique*, 1952; *Tendre comme le souvenir*, 1952; *Poèmes à Lou*, 1955; *Oeuvres complètes*, 1966 (8 volumes).

Other literary forms

Besides poetry, Guillaume Apollinaire wrote a number of prose works. Among the most significant of his short stories and novellas are *L'Enchanteur pourrissant* (1909; the putrescent enchanter), published by Henry Kahnweiler and illustrated with woodcuts by André Derain; *L'Hérésiarque et Cie.* (1910; *The Heresiarch and Co.*, 1965), a contender for the Prix Goncourt; and *Le Poète assassiné* (1916; *The Poet Assassinated*, 1923). They are contained in the Pléiade edition, *Oeuvres en prose* (1977), edited by Michel Décaudin.

Apollinaire collaborated on numerous plays and cinema scripts. His best-known individual works in these genres are two proto-Surrealist plays in verse: *Les Mamelles de Tirésias* (*The Breasts of Tiresias*, 1961), first published in the magazine *SIC* in 1918, and *Couleur du temps* (the color of time), which first appeared in the *Nouvelle Revue française* in 1920. They are available in the Pléiade edition of *Oeuvres poétiques*. Apollinaire also published a great deal of art criticism and literary criticism in journals, newspapers, and other periodicals. In 1913, the articles published before that year were collected in *Peintres cubistes: Méditations esthétiques* (*The Cubist Painters: Esthetic Meditations*, 1944). In 1918, *Mercure de France* published his famous manifesto "L'Esprit nouveau et les poètes" ("The New Spirit and the Poets"), which later appeared, along with many other articles, in *Chroniques d'art, (1902-1918)* (1960), edited by L. C. Breunig. The same collection has been translated into English as *Apollinaire on Art: Essays and Reviews, 1902-1918* (1972).

Achievements

After Apollinaire, French poetry was never the same again. Writing at the end of the long Symbolist tradition, a tradition very apparent in his early works, Apollinaire moved into a new perception of the world and of poetry. In the world of his mature verse, spatial and temporal relations are radically altered. Apollinaire's was one of the first voices in French poetry to attempt to articulate the profound discontinuity and disorientation in modern society.

At the same time, however, his works reflect hope, frequently ecstatic, in the promise of the future.

Apollinaire's sense of radical discontinuity was reflected in his formal innovations, analyzed in considerable depth by Jean-Claude Chevalier in *Alcools d'Apollinaire*. Immediately before the publication of *Alcools*, Apollinaire went through the volume and removed all punctuation, a device which he continued to use in most of his later works. His most notable poems, such as "Zone," "Liens" ("Chains"), and "Les Fenêtres" ("Windows"), use free verse with irregular rhyme and rhythm; his most startling works are the picture poems of *Calligrammes*, a form which he falsely claimed to have invented. They consist of verses arranged to give both a visual and an auditory effect in an effort to create "simultaneity."

Like the Cubists and other modern painters who sought to go beyond the traditional boundaries of space and time, Apollinaire desired to create the effect of simultaneity. This ambition is evident in "Zone," with its biographical, geographical, and historical discontinuity. In this single poem, the poet leaps from his pious childhood at the Collège Saint-Charles in Monaco to the wonders of modern aviation and back to the "herds" of buses "mooing" on the streets of Paris. Perhaps his most obvious achievement in simultaneity, though less profound, is in "Lundi rue Christine" ("Monday in Christine Street"), which records overheard bits of conversation in a "sinistre brasserie," a low-class café-restaurant that Apollinaire had frequented as early as 1903.

The friend and collaborator of many important painters during the exciting years in Paris just before World War I, Apollinaire began associating with artists when he met Pablo Picasso in 1904, after which he frequented the famous Bateau-Lavoir on the rue Ravignan with Max Jacob, André Derain, Maurice Vlaminck, Georges Braque, and others. After 1912, he moved into the world of art criticism, not always appreciated by the artists themselves, as Francis Steegmuller has noted. Not unrelated to this interest was Apollinaire's tumultuous liaison with Marie Laurencin from 1907 to 1912. He frequently inspired works and portraits by artists, including Laurencin, Henri Rousseau, and Picasso. Apollinaire's own works further testify to his links with painters: *Bestiary* was illustrated by Raoul Dufy, and "Windows" was the introductory poem to the catalog of the Robert Delaunay exhibit in 1912. His poems often parallel the work of the painters in their spirit of simultaneity; in their subjects, such as the *saltimbanques* of Picasso; and in their moods, such as those of Marc Chagall's dreamworld and inverted figures.

After 1916, Apollinaire became the "chef d'école," the leader of a new generation of poets and painters. Among them were Pierre Reverdy, Philippe Soupault, Jean Cocteau, André Breton, and Tristan Tzara. His own works appeared in the most avant-garde journals: Reverdy's *Nord-Sud*, Picabia's *391*, and Albert Birot's *SIC*. His lecture "The New Spirit and the Poets" called poets to a new prophetic vision, imploring them to create prodigies with their imagination like modern Merlins. Like Paul Claudel, Apollinaire regarded the poet as a creator. The modern poet, he believed, must use everything for his creation: new discoveries in science, in the subconscious and the dreamworld, and in the cinema and visual arts.

The Surrealists, in their desire to revolutionize art and literature, saw in Apollinaire their precursor. It was he who coined the word "surréaliste," in the preface to his drama in verse *The Breasts of Tiresias*. In it, he explains that an equivalent is not always an imitation, even as the wheel, though intended to facilitate transportation, is not a reproduction of the leg. Apollinaire conveys his message with a lighthearted tone, employing incongruous rhythms, parody, and sexual imagery. This is essentially the technique he employs in his most avant-garde poetry, and *The Breasts of Tiresias* echoes poems from "Ondes" ("Waves," the first part of *Calligrammes*) such as "Zone," "Le Brasier" ("The Brazier"), "Les Fiançailles" ("The Betrothal"), and "Le Larron" ("The Thief"). Thus, Apollinaire indicated the path to follow in revolutionizing poetry, although much of his work was in some respects traditional. Like Victor Hugo, he served subsequent poets chiefly as a guide rather than as a model, but it was his "esprit nouveau" that gave considerable impetus to a new form of modern poetry.

Biography

Born in Rome on August 26, 1880, Wilhelm Apollinairis de Kostrowitzky was an illegitimate child; in "The Thief," he says that his "father was a sphinx and his mother a night." In reality, his mother was a Polish adventureress of noble ancestry, Angelique Kostrowicka, known in Paris mostly as Olga. His father's identity has never been definitively ascertained. The most plausible supposition points to Francesco Flugi d'Aspermont, a man from a noble Italian family which included many prelates. This theory is based on the careful investigation of biographer Marcel Adéma. Apollinaire's mysterious and involved parentage haunted the poet throughout his life, leaving unmistakable marks on his character and works.

Apollinaire received his only formal education at the Collège of Saint-Charles in Monaco and the Collège Stanislas at Cannes, from 1890 to 1897, where he acquired a solid grounding in religious and secular knowledge. Although his Catholic training was to remain firmly implanted in his memory and is evident in his poetry, he moved away from any outward adherence to religious beliefs after 1897. In 1899, he arrived in Paris, his home for most of the next nineteen years of his life and the center and inspiration of his literary activity. First, however, he made a significant trip to Germany's Rhineland in 1901, as tutor to Gabrielle, the daughter of the Viscountess of Milhau. There, he met and fell in love with Annie Playden, Gabrielle's English governess. This ill-fated romance and the beauty of the Rhineland inspired many of Apollinaire's early poems, which were later published in *Alcools*.

Apollinaire's return to Paris coincided with the beginning of friendships with artists and writers such as André Salmon, Alfred Jarry, Max Jacob, and especially Picasso. In 1903, he began his collaboration on many periodicals, which he continued throughout his lifetime. Most of his prose and poetry were first published in such journals, many of which—such as *Le Festin d'Esope* and *La Revue immoraliste*—were of very short duration. His works appeared under several pseudonyms, of which "Apollinaire" was the most significant. Others included "Louise Lalame," "Lul," "Montade," and "Tyl." In 1907, he met Marie Laurencin, an artist, whose talent Apollinaire tended to exaggerate. Their liaison continued until 1912 and was an inspiration and a torment to both of them. During this period, Apollinaire was deeply marked by the false accusation that he was responsible for the theft of the *Mona Lisa* from the Louvre. A series of six poems in *Alcools*, "À la Santé" ("At the Santé") describes his brief stay in the prison of La Santé in Verlainian imagery.

The year 1912 marked Apollinaire's break with Laurencin and his definite espousal of modern art, of which he became a staunch proponent. During the two years preceding World War I, he gave lectures and wrote articles on modern art and prepared *Alcools* for publication. The beginning of the war, in 1914, was to Apollinaire a call to a mission. Although not a French citizen until the year 1916, he embraced with great enthusiasm his *métier de soldat* as an artilleryman and then as an infantryman, according an almost mystical dimension to his military service. His poetry of these first two years reveals the exaltation of war and the idealization of two women, "Lou" (Louise de Coligny-Châtillon) and Madeleine Pagès, to whom he was briefly engaged.

Wounded in the head in 1916, Apollinaire required surgery and was then discharged from the service. He returned to the world of literature and art with numerous articles, lectures, two plays, and a volume of poetry, *Calligrammes*. In May of 1918, he married Jacqueline Kolb ("Ruby"), the "jolie rousse" (pretty redhead) of the last poem in *Calligrammes*. The marriage was of short duration, however, as Apollinaire died of Spanish influenza on November 9 of the same year.

Analysis

In his poetic style, Guillaume Apollinaire might be characterized as the last of the Symbolists and the first of the moderns. He is considered a revolutionary and a destroyer, yet the bulk of his work shows a deep influence of traditional symbolism, especially biblical, legendary, and mythical. Very knowledgeable in Roman Catholic doctrine from his years with the Marianists at Monaco and Cannes, he uses extensive biblical imagery: Christ, the Virgin Mary, and the Holy Spirit in the form of a dove. Robert Couffignal has analyzed Apollinaire's religious imagery in detail and considers his comprehension of the Bible to be "a cascade of superficial weavings." Scott Bates sees the Last Judgment, with its apocalyptic implications, as central to Apollinaire's works. The concept of Messianism and the advent of a new millennium is evident in both the early works and the war poems, which predict a new universe. In the Symbolist tradition, the poet is the seer of the new kingdom.

Many of Apollinaire's symbols are from the realm of legend and myth. Rosemonde, the idealized woman of the Middle Ages, is present in several poems, though she appears also as a prostitute. In "Merlin et la vielle femme" ("Merlin and the Old Woman"), the medieval seer foreshadows Apollinaire's vision of the future. Ancient mythology is the source for Orpheus, under whose sign *Bestiary* is written. Orpheus is also the symbol of Christ and the poet, as is Hermès Trismégiste. Ancient Egypt appears in frequent references to the Nile, the Israelites in bondage, and Pharaoh, the image of the poet himself. The fantastic abounds in Apollinaire's works: ghosts, diabolic characters, and phantoms, as found, for example, in "La Maison des Morts" ("The House of the Dead") and especially in the short stories.

Much of Apollinaire's early symbolism is directed toward the quest for self-knowledge; his choice of the name "Apollinaire" is a clue to his search. Though it was the name of his maternal grandfather and one of the names given to him at baptism, he seems to have chosen it for its reference to Apollo, the god of the sun. Indeed, solar imagery is central to his poetry, and the introductory poem of *Alcools*, "Zone," ends with the words "Soleil cou coupé" ("Sun cut throat"). Bates argues that the violent love-death relationship between the sun and night, with its corresponding symbolism, is as crucial to the interpretation of Apollinaire as it is to a reading of Gérard de Nerval or Stéphane Mallarmé. Along with love and death is death and resurrection. Apollinaire chooses the phoenix as a sign of rebirth and describes his own psychological and poetic resurrection in "The Brazier" and "The Betrothal," poems that he regarded as among his best. Fire seems to be his basic image, with its multiple meanings of passion, destruction, and purification.

Passion as a flame dominated Apollinaire's life and poetry. Of the many women whom he loved, five in particular incarnated his violent passion and appear in his work: Playden and Laurencin in *Alcools*; Lou, Madeleine, and Jacqueline in *Calligrammes* and in several series of poems published after his death. Apollinaire is capable of expressing tender, idealistic love, as in the "Aubade chantée à Lætare un an passé" ("Aubade Sung to Lætare a Year Ago") section of the "La Chanson du mal-aimé" ("The Song of the Poorly Loved") and in "La Jolie Rousse" ("The Pretty Redhead"), which closes *Calligrammes*. In most cases, Apollinaire is the *mal-aimé*, and as he himself says, he is much less the poorly beloved than the one who loves poorly. His first three loves ended violently; his last was concluded by his death. Thus, the death of love is as important as its first manifestation, which for him resembles the shells bursting in the war.

Autumn is the season of the death of love, wistfully expressed in such nostalgic works as "L'Adieu" ("The Farewell") and "Automne" ("Autumn"). Because the end of love usually involved deep suffering for him, the image of mutilation is not uncommon. The beloved in "The Song of the Poorly Loved" has a scar on her neck, and the mannequins in "L'Émigrant de Landor Road" ("The Emigrant from Landor Road") are decapitated, much like the sun in "Zone." Apollinaire perceives love in its erotic sense, and in many cases he resorts to arcane symbolism, as in the seven swords in "The Song of the Poorly Loved." "Lul de Faltenin" ("Lul of Faltenin") is also typical, with its subtle erotic allusions. Such themes are more overt in Apollinaire's prose; indeed, Bates has compiled a glossary of erotic symbolism in the works of Apollinaire.

Apollinaire was both a lyric poet and a storyteller. In the lyric tradition, he writes of his emotions in images drawn from nature. His work is particularly rich in flora and fauna. *Bestiary* shows his familiarity with and affection for animals and his ability, like the fabulists, to see them as caricatures of people. *Alcools*, as the title indicates, often evokes grapes and wine; it also speaks of fir trees (in "Les Sapins") and falling leaves. "Zone" contains a catalog of birds, real and legendary. The Seine comes alive in Apollinaire's ever-popular "Le Pont Mirabeau" ("Mirabeau Bridge"). In *Calligrammes*, the poet often compares the explosion of shells to bursting buds.

Apollinaire was the author of many short stories, and he maintains a narrative flavor in his poetry. "The House of the Dead" was originally a short story, "L'Obituaire," and it reads like one. Many of the picture poems in *Calligrammes* tell a story; "Paysage" ("Landscape"), for example, portrays by means of typography a house, a tree, and two lovers, one of whom smokes a cigar that the reader can almost smell. Apollinaire's technique often involved improvisation, as in "Le Musicien de Saint-Merry" ("The Musician of Saint-Merry"). Although he claims almost total spontaneity, there are revised versions of many of his poems, and he frequently borrowed from himself, rearranging both lines and poems. In particular, Apollinaire tells stories of the modern city, imitating its new structures as Arthur Rimbaud did in his innovative patterns, and, like Charles Baudelaire, Apollinaire peoples his verse with the forgotten and the poor, the prostitutes and the clowns.

Apollinaire had a remarkable sense of humor, displayed in frequent wordplays, burlesques, and parodies. The briefest example of his use of puns is the one-line poem "Chantre" ("Singer"): "Et l'unique cordeau des trompettes marines" ("And the single string of marine trumpets"). *Cordeau*, when read aloud, might be *cor d'eau* or "horn of water"—another version of a marine trumpet—as well as *corps d'eau* (body of water) or even *coeur d'eau* (heart of water). The burlesque found in his short stories appears in poetry as dissonance, erotic puns, and irreverent parodies, such as in "Les Sept Epées" ("The Seven Swords") as well as in "The Thief," a poem that Bates interprets as parodying Christ. Apollinaire's lighthearted rhythm and obscure symbolism tend to prevent his verse from becoming offensive and convey a sense of freedom, discovery, and surprise.

Bestiary is one of the most charming and accessible of Apollinaire's works. The idea for the poem probably came from Picasso in 1906, who was then doing woodcuts of animals. In 1908, Apollinaire published in a journal eighteen poems under the title "La Marchande des quatre saisons ou le bestiaire moderne" (the costermonger or the modern bestiary). When he prepared the final edition in 1911, with woodcuts by Raoul Dufy, he added twelve poems and replaced the merchant with Orpheus. According to mythology, Orpheus attracted wild beasts by playing on the lyre he had received from Mercury. He is the symbol of Gnosis and Neoplatonic Humanism, and is also identified with Christ and poetry, in a mixture of mystical and sensual imagery.

Apollinaire himself wrote the notes to the volume and uses as its sign a Δ (the Greek letter delta) pierced by a unicorn. He interprets it to mean the delta of the Nile and all the legendary and biblical symbols of ancient Egypt, also suggesting a D for Deplanche, the publisher, in addition to the obvious sexual symbolism. He added the motto "J'émerveille" (I marvel), thus giving a fantastic aura to the work. Roger Little sees in the volume a "delicious and malicious" wit, with metamorphoses, syncretism, pride in poetry, carnal love, and mysticism. Like all Apollinaire's early works, it is full of self-analysis. In "La Souris" ("The Mouse"), the poet speaks of his twenty-eight years as "mal-vécus" ("poorly spent").

The animals represent human foibles; the peacock, for example, displays both his best and, unbeknownst to him, his worst. They also speak of love: the serpent, the Sirens, the dove, and Orpheus himself. They point to God and things divine: the dove, the bull, or, again, Orpheus. They speak of poetry: the horse, the tortoise, the elephant, and the caterpillar. For Apollinaire, poetry is a divine gift. He concludes his notes by observing that poets seek nothing but perfection, which is God Himself. Poets, he says, have the right to expect after death the full knowledge of God, which is sublime beauty.

The most analyzed and the best known of Apollinaire's works is *Alcools*, a slender volume published in 1913 with the subtitle *Poèmes, 1898-1913*. A portrait of Apollinaire, an etching by Picasso, serves as the frontispiece. Apollinaire chose fifty-five of the many poems he had written from his eighteenth to his thirty-third year and assembled them in an order that has continued to fascinate and baffle critics. Michel Décaudin says that the order in *Alcools* is based entirely on the aesthetic and sentimental affinities felt by the author, or their discrete dissonances. Very few poems have dates, other than "Rhénanes" (September, 1901, to May, 1902) and "At the Santé" (September, 1911); nevertheless, critics have succeeded in dating many, though not all, of the poems.

The poems have several centers, though not all of those from one group appear together. More than twenty were inspired by Apollinaire's trip to the

Rhineland in 1901, including the nine in the cycle "Rhénanes." Several of these poems and some others, such as "The Song of the Poorly Loved," "Annie," and "The Emigrant from Landor Road," refer to his unhappy love affair with Playden. These poems and an interview with her as Mrs. Postings in 1951 by Robert Goffin and LeRoy Breunig are the only sources of information about this significant period in Apollinaire's life. Three poems, "Mirabeau Bridge," "Marie," and "Cors de chasse" ("Hunting Horns"), scattered throughout the volume, refer to Laurencin.

The poems exhibit great variety in form, tone, and subject matter. They range from the one-line "Chantre" to the seven-part "The Song of the Poorly Loved," the longest in the collection. Most of them have regular rhyme and rhythm, but "Zone" and "Vendémiaire," the first and the last, give evidence of technical experimentation. The poems range from witty ("The Synagogue") to nostalgic ("Autumn," "Hunting Horns"), from enigmatic ("The Brazier") to irreverent ("The Thief"). Critics have arranged them in various ways. Bates, for example, sees the volume as a "Dionysian-Apollonian dance of life in three major symbols: fire, shadow, alcools."

Apollinaire chose the beginning and concluding poems of the collection, "Zone" and "Vendémiaire," with great care. "Zone" is overtly autobiographical in a "Romantic-Symbolist ambience, yet its instant leaps in space and time make it very modern. Also modern is the image of the city, where Apollinaire can see beauty in a poster, a traffic jam, and a group of frightened Jewish immigrants. The city is also the central focus in the concluding poem, "Vendémiaire" (the name given the month of vintage, September 22-October 21, in the Revolutionary calendar), a hymn to the glory of Paris. The poet exuberantly proclaims his immortality and omnipresence: "I am drunk from having swallowed all the universe." Bates sees the end of the poem as a hymn to joy reminiscent of Walt Whitman and Friedrich Nietzsche.

The bizarre juxtapositions, the inner borrowings of lines from one poem to the next, and the absence of punctuation provoked various responses from critics. Cubists hailed Apollinaire as a great poet. Georges Duhamel, writing in the June 15, 1913, issue of *Mercure de France*, called the volume a junk shop. Recent critics such as Adéma, Décaudin, and Marie-Jeanne Durry analyze *Alcools* with depth and scholarship. They discover many platitudes and much mediocrity but find it redeemed by what Steegmuller identifies as a spirit of freedom.

Intended as a sequel to *Alcools*, *Calligrammes* is much more unified than *Alcools*, yet its importance was seen only much later. It consists of six parts. The first part, "Waves," is the most innovative and was written before World War I in the frenzied stimulation of artistic activity in Paris. The other five contain poems inspired by the war and by the poet's love for Lou, Madeleine, and—in the final poem—his future wife, Jacqueline.

Philippe Renaud sees the difference between *Alcools* and "Waves" as one of nature rather than degree. Even the most enigmatic poems of *Alcools* follow a familiar plan, he maintains, whereas in "Waves" the reader is in unfamiliar territory, disoriented in space and time. In "Waves" one feels both the insecurity and the indefiniteness that can only be called "modern art." The introductory poem, "Chains," uses the elements recommended by Apollinaire in "The New Spirit and the Poets" yet remains anchored in the past. It leaps from the Tower of Babel to telegraph wires in disconcerting juxtapositions, speaking of man's eternal, frustrating quest for unity. In "The Windows," the window opens like an orange on Paris or in the tropics and flies on a rainbow across space and time.

Beginning with "Waves," and throughout *Calligrammes*, Apollinaire uses what he calls "ideograms," or picture poems. They are the most attractive pieces in the book, though not necessarily the most original. They became excellent vehicles for the war poems, where brevity and wit are essential. The theme of war dominates the majority of poems in *Calligrammes*. The war excited Apollinaire, promising a new universe. He experienced exhilaration as he saw shells exploding, comparing them in the poem "Merveilles de la guerre" ("Wonders of War"), to constellations and to women's hair, to dancers and to women in childbirth. He saw himself as the poet-hero, the omnipresent seer, the animator of the universe. In "La Tête étoilée" ("The Starry Head"), his wound was a crown of stars on his head.

Apollinaire was as dependent on love as he was on air, and he suffered greatly in the solitary trenches of France. His brief romance with Lou was intense and violent, as his pun on her name in "C'est Lou qu'on la nommait" ("They Called Her Lou") indicates; instead of "Lou," the word *loup* (which sounds the same in French but means "wolf") is used throughout the poem. In his poems to Madeleine, he devours images like a starving man. The anthology ends serenely as he addresses Jacqueline, "la jolie rousse," the woman destined to be his wife as poetry was destined to be his life. This final poem is also his poetic testament, in which he bequeaths "vast and unknown kingdoms, new fires and the mystery of flowers to anyone willing to pick them."

Major publications other than poetry

NOVELS: *L'Enchanteur pourrissant*, 1909; *Le Poète assassiné*, 1916 (*The Poet Assassinated*, 1923).

SHORT FICTION: *L'Hérésiarque et Cie.*, 1910 (*The Heresiarch and Co.*, 1965).

PLAYS: *Les Mamelles de Tirésias*, 1918 (*The Breasts of Tiresias*, 1961); *Couleur du temps*, 1920.

NONFICTION: *Peintres cubistes: Méditations esthétiques*, 1913 (*The Cubist Painters: Esthetic Meditations*, 1944); *Chroniques d'art, 1902-1918*, 1960 (*Apollinaire on Art: Essays and Reviews, 1902-1918*, 1972).

MISCELLANEOUS: *Oeuvres en prose*, 1977 (Michel Décaudin, editor).

Bibliography

Adéma, Pierre-Marcel. *Apollinaire*, 1965.

Bates, Scott. *Guillaume Apollinaire*, 1967.

Breunig, L. C. *Guillaume Apollinaire*, 1969.

Chevalier, Jean-Claude. *Alcools d'Apollinaire*, 1970.

Couffignal, Robert. *L'Inspiration biblique dans l'oeuvre de Guillaume Apollinaire*, 1966.

Davies, Margaret. *Apollinaire*, 1964.

Décaudin, Michel. *Guillaume Apollinaire*, 1964.

Durry, Marie-Jeanne. *Guillaume Apollinaire: Alcools*, 1956-1964, 1965.

Little, Roger. *Guillaume Apollinaire*, 1976.

Renaud, Philippe. *Lecture d'Apollinaire*, 1969.

Steegmuller, Francis. *Apollinaire: Poet Among the Painters*, 1963.

Irma M. Kashuba

APOLLONIUS RHODIUS

Born: Alexandria, Egypt; c. 295 B.C.
Died: Alexandria, Egypt; c. 215 B.C.

Principal poem
Argonautica (third century B.C.).

Other literary forms
Apollonius is credited with several works besides the *Argonautica*. A collection of epigrams passed under his name, but only one has survived. Besides these, he seems to have written a poem or group of poems called *Ctisis* (third century B.C.), dealing with the founding of the cities of Alexandria, Naucratis, Cnidos, Rhodes, and Caunus; in this work, Apollonius might well have been poaching on Callimachus' preserve, since he wrote something similar. Apollonius also wrote philological works in prose, including *Against Zenodotos* (third century B.C.). A variety of other works are attributed to Apollonius, but it was not necessarily this Apollonius who wrote them, since the name was a common one.

Achievements
Apollonius' principal work, the *Argonautica*, which has survived in revised form, is a deliberate challenge to Callimachus' fundamental literary principle that poems should be short, for it fills four lengthy books with its 5,834 hexameter lines. It is a book of excellent stories told in good verse rather than a regular and unified epic poem, and its merit lies in its episodes, notably in the admirable recounting of the loves of Jason and Medea, which fills the third book and part of the fourth.

Biography
The birth of Apollonius Rhodius is placed by scholars at various times between 296 and 260 B.C., and the year of his death is equally uncertain. In fact, there is very little information about his life available today. There are two "lives" of Apollonius, both derived from an earlier biography which is lost. From these one learns that Apollonius was the son of one Silleus (or Illeus) and was born either at Alexandria or Naucratis. Possibly, as has been suggested, he was born at Naucratis and reared in Alexandria.

Apollonius lived during the reign of the Ptolemies and apparently was a pupil of Callimachus, the literary dictator of the time, an author of frigid, learned poems and a few highly polished epigrams, and the originator of the terse and generally true dictum that a big book is a big nuisance. Apollonius' opinions on the subject of lengthy poems were diametrically opposed to those of Callimachus and, hence, heretical. At a youthful age, the student-poet produced a long poem on the Argonautic expedition. It was a complete failure, and in his shame and distress, Apollonius left Alexandria and settled in Rhodes. There he revised and polished, and perhaps completed, his work. The Rhodians gave his book a far more favorable reception. He was given Rhodian citizenship, hence the surname Rhodius, and was held in high esteem. Years later, after the death of Callimachus, Apollonius returned to Alexandria to a better reception; indeed, one biographer reports that he followed Callimachus as head librarian there. He died probably about 215 B.C. and was buried near his old foe.

This traditional account of the life of Apollonius has been questioned by modern scholarship. Callimachus may never have been head librarian at Alexandria or even the teacher of Apollonius. Indeed, Apollonius and Callimachus may have been near contemporaries and thus more likely to be literary opponents. Some scholars, for chronological reasons, deny the librarianship of Apollonius, but it is clearly asserted by his biographer, Suidas, and the arguments against it are not conclusive.

In spite of these uncertainties, it seems clear that Apollonius' quarrel with Callimachus was a crucial event in his life. This quarrel apparently arose from differences of literary aims and taste but degenerated into the bitterest sort of personal strife. There are references to the quarrel in the writings of both. Callimachus attacks Apollonius in a passage at the end of his *Hymn to Apollo* (third century B.C.), but he attacks Apollonius most vociferously in the *Ibis* (third century B.C.), which Ovid imitated or perhaps translated in his poem of the same name. On the part of Apollonius, there is a passage in the third book of the *Argonautica* which is of a polemical nature and which stands out from the context, as well as a savage epigram attacking Callimachus. There is not enough data to determine the chronological order of the attacks and counterattacks. The *Ibis* has been thought to mark the termination of the feud on the curious ground that it was impossible for the abuse to go further.

Analysis

The chief characteristics of Alexandrianism, of which Callimachus was the leading proponent, were refinement in diction, precision of form and meter, erudition which often degenerated into pedantry and obscurity, and avoidance of the commonplace in subject, sentiment, and allusion. Apollonius shares some of these traits, and he seems to have written the *Argonautica* out of bravado, to show that he could indeed write an epic poem. The influence of the age, however, was too strong. Instead of a unified epic, there is merely a series of episodes. In the four books of his *Argonautica*, Apollonius tells of the quest for the Golden Fleece, and especially of Jason and Medea. The same story was known to Homer and certainly belonged in the repertory of old epic. It provided a splendid source of thrilling adventures and opportunities for excursions into the unknown, a literary device that varied the more straightforward episodes of epic. It demanded, however, a heroic sense of human worth and of perilous action, and this was precisely what Apollonius lacked. His Jason is the faintest of phantoms; he could hardly be otherwise, inasmuch as Apollonius lived in the metropolitan society of Alexandria and had little idea of how to depict a hero. There were other defects as well. Apollonius never forgot that he was an antiquarian and therefore he liberally garnished his poem with tidbits of erudite information. This is deadly, not only to the flow of the narrative, but also to the actual poetry. The delight in learning for its own sake was an especially Alexandrian characteristic. Literary allusions seeped into Alexandrian poetry without poets quite noticing how cumbersome and distracting they were. Apollonius must have thought such allusions gave richness and dignity to his story, but ultimately, they make it tedious and pedantic.

Not until the Hellenistic age and Apollonius' *Argonautica* was there a complete epic presentation of the Thessalian or Argonautic cycle of legends, among the oldest in Greek mythology. Poetry in all its forms had time and again turned to the legend of the Argonauts and the local history of the many places connected with it. Thus, Apollonius was faced with a rich tradition with many partly contradictory variants.

Apollonius' composition exhibits a systematic arrangement of the subject matter. The first two books describe the voyage to the land of Colchis, the third relates the adventures leading to the winning of the Golden Fleece, while the fourth tells of the dangers of the flight and the return home. The stress on details, however, is variously distributed; there are rapid transitions, but there are also passages over which Apollonius had lingered lovingly, typical of the rejection of symmetry and the tendency to variety found elsewhere in Alexandrian poetry.

While a proem with prayer formula is merely indicated at the beginning of book 1 and much of the preceding history is saved for later, the introductory passage offers an elaborate catalog of the Argonauts, geographically arranged in the manner of a circumnavigation and leading from the north of Greece, to the east and west, and then back to the north. The catalog tradition of ancient epic served as its model. The scenes of departure in Iolcus and on the beach at Pagasae are spun out in detail. Then follows the long series of stopping places and adventures on the way out, along the usual route to Colchis. For the voyage up to the treacherous passage through the Symplegades, which are thought to be at the entrance to the Pontus, the tradition had a number of effective, ready-made episodes upon which Apollonius elaborated successfully. First is the landing in Lemnos, where the women, under a curse of Aphrodite, have killed their husbands. Now, however, they are glad to entertain the Argonauts. The result is a delectable sojourn from which Heracles has to call his companions to action. That is followed by the initiation into the mysteries at Samothrace and the adventures in Cyzicus. Here the

Argonauts give the Doliones effective help against evil giants, only to become involved, through a misunderstanding, in a bitterly regretted nocturnal battle with their friends.

The next stop on the coast of Propontis provides the setting for the Hylas episode. When Apollonius tells how the beautiful youth Hylas is dragged down into a pool by a nymph who has fallen in love with him, he does it very well, since his dramatic economy avoids any kind of false pathos, and the reader witnesses the nymph's ruthless determination as she puts her arms around the boy who is stooping to get water. Heracles seeks Hylas in the woods and the Argonauts continue their voyage without him, since the sea-god Glaucus announces that the hero is destined to perform other deeds. This device eliminates from the narrative the greatest of the champions, beside whom the heroic Jason would pale by comparison.

The story continues without a stop from book 1 to book 2, which begins with Pollux's boxing match with Amycus, a barbarian king. In Bithynia, the Argonauts come upon the blind king Phineus, who, in deep misery, is doing penance for some ancient offense. The winged sons of Boreas liberate him from the Harpies, the predatory storm spirits who rob him of every meal, or defile it. As a reward, Phineus gives the Argonauts good advice for the rest of their voyage. The compositional significance of this preview is that it sums up the various minor episodes of the second half of the voyage. The passage through the Symplegades after a pigeon's test flight is depicted with dramatic power. Thereafter, the only sojourn worthy of mention is that on the island of Ares. There the Argonauts drive out the Stymphalian birds, and there they meet the sons of Phrixus. Their mother is Chalciope, Aeetes' daughter and the sister of Medea. Medea will play a significant role in the events in Colchis, thus the meeting in the island of Ares provides a dramatic link between the description of the voyage and the winning of the Golden Fleece.

Book 3 starts with a new proem and portrays the events in Colchis by means of a technique which often resolves the action into parallel strands. Medea's decisive intervention is first motivated in a scene in which the goddesses Hera and Athena enjoin Aphrodite to have Eros do his work. Independent from this motivation, however, Medea's awakening love, her hard struggle between loyalty to her father's house and passion for the handsome stranger, is presented as a drama full of tension with the girl's soul as the stage. Apollonius is at his best when he writes of love. What engages all his powers is not Jason's love for Medea (on which he leaves the reader uninstructed) but Medea's love for Jason, and it is this which makes book 3 of the *Argonautica* shine more brightly than the other three. Medea is still a girl, and she falls passionately in love at first sight. When she first sees Jason, he seems to her like Sirius rising from the ocean, and Apollonius, not without echoes of Sappho, describes how a mist covers Medea's eyes, her cheeks burn like fire, her knees are too weak to move, and she feels rooted to the earth. When, a little later,

Medea helps him in his ordeals to win the Fleece, the light playing on his yellow hair makes her willing to tear the life out of her breast for him, and her heart melts like dew on roses in the morning. When their love is fulfilled, Medea is entirely absorbed in him, but when he plans to return to Greece and in his callous indifference is ready to leave her behind, the fierce side of her nature emerges, and she bursts into bitter remonstrances, chiding him for his ingratitude. If he really intends to desert her, she invokes disaster and vengeance on him and prays that the Furies will make him homeless. In this part of his poem, Apollonius tells one of the first surviving love stories in the world.

Alongside this love story runs a subplot concerning Chalciope, which leads to her intervention and to the decisive talk between the two sisters, Chalciope and Medea. The composition of book 3 is particularly careful. Developing in several stages, it progresses to the meeting of Medea and Jason, when he receives the magic ointment.

Book 4, which begins with a brief invocation to the Muse, presents Apollonius with his most exciting challenge, to which he rises admirably. After receiving the magic ointment from Medea, Jason must yoke fire-breathing bulls, sow dragon's teeth, and destroy the armed men who spring out of them. Jason falls on the men like a shooting star, and the furrows are as filled with blood as runnels are with water. Apollonius presents the weird scene very vividly, capturing even the brilliant light shining from the armor and weapons. This struggle bears no resemblance to a Homeric battle, but, in its unearthly strangeness, it is convincing and complete. Apollonius glories in strangeness for its own sake, and it is this quality that makes him a pioneer of that kind of poetry which deals with remote and unfamiliar themes. The rest of book 4 describes the homeward voyage, two high points being the murder of Absyrtus, who has gone in pursuit of his sister Medea, and the marriage of Jason and Medea in the land of the Phaeacians. One of the most enchanting aspects of mythic geography is the way the return of the Argonauts was modified as the knowledge of foreign countries and seas increased, newly discovered facts and ancient mythic elements forming various and often grotesque combinations. After a series of less-than-dangerous adventures, the Argonauts return to Colchis.

Apollonius' epic has numerous qualities which depend largely on the literary and historical background of the work. Some readers find it pedantic, unpoetic, or dry, while others—and especially in recent times—are able to appreciate the truly poetical qualities of the *Argonautica*. In the first place, it should be clearly understood that the intellectual world in which this epic originated was separated from that of Homer by an immeasurable distance. When older poets molded the history of the heroic past for their people, they claimed that their verses imbued true events with splendor and permanence. In these events the gods were active everywhere; they were great spirits, inspiring faith and helpfully allying themselves with man or wrathfully striking out at him. By Apollonius' time, the living belief had become mythology or was proceeding toward this condition. Hardly anything can be said about Apollonius' personal religious feelings, but his attitude to tradition cannot have been very different from that of Callimachus. Apollonius' *stylos* was guided both by an erudite interest in mythical tradition and by a delight in the unfading beauty of its creations. Both can be discerned in his verse.

The tremendous distance from Homer's world is in exciting contrast with the fact that numerous and essential elements of ancient epic remain preserved. In Apollonius, the gods also act, but the very nature of the great Olympian scene at the opening of book 3 reveals the ornamental character of such passages. With Hera, Athena, and Eros a complete divine apparatus is developed, but Medea's love and its consequences are completely imaginable without it. Also, in the portrayal of the girl's emotional struggles, the poet can be recognized much more directly than in the conversations of the Olympians. While in Homer, man's actions are determined simultaneously by his own impulses and by the influence of the gods, in Apollonius this duality of motivation has resulted in separate spheres of action. The divine plot takes place on an upper stage; its connection with earthly happenings is neither indissoluble nor irrevocably necessary.

Apollonius retains important formal elements of Homeric epic. While he is sparing with metaphors, he uses similes with great frequency. Their free, Homeric spontaneity has been restricted in Apollonius in favor of a more direct bearing on the action, although the subject matter has been expanded in many directions. Illustrations of emotions by means of similes, found in the verse of Homer in rudimentary form, have been developed by Apollonius with great skill. Thus Medea's agitation and irresolution are elucidated by the image of the sun's ray which is reflected onto a wall by the ruffled surface of water. Apollonius also uses stock scenes, but he keeps recurrent formulas to a minimum. This is connected with another, fundamentally important observation. Apollonius' language is largely based on that of Homer. This does not mean that Apollonius accepted the tradition without due reflection or that he imitated it naïvely. Rather, the linguistic resources he borrowed are given new effectiveness through constant, well-planned variation, sometimes even by means of a shifting of the meaning.

The Homeric legacy, which functions as a sort of framework for the *Argonautica* with regard to themes and style, contrasts with the poem's Alexandrian element. Apollonius is a realist, although the term is to be taken in its broadest sense. In the final analysis, this realism is connected with the altered attitude toward myths, with the awareness of their illusory nature. Apollonius may be granted poetic ability, and there may be much that is praiseworthy in his work, but he was not truly a poet filled with the Muse; time and again, the reader is struck by the cool objectivity with which he describes legendary events. This also explains the great care he takes with motivation and establishment of cohesion.

The poet frequently accounts for contemporary customs by seeking explanations in early history, and in this way he links his own time with the mythical past. A true Hellenist, Apollonius devoted much of his poem to etiological matters, interspersing the narrative of the voyage with a wealth of such stories.

As a portrayer of emotions, especially of those which Eros brings to the human soul, Apollonius belongs entirely within the sphere of Hellenistic poetry. It has already been pointed out that his highest achievement was his description of Medea's pangs and doubts. After the long-winded description of the outward voyage, which at times sinks to the level of a learned guidebook, the realm of true poetry is entered. This is confirmed by the tremendous subsequent influence of book 3 in ancient literature. The characterization of Medea recalls Apollonius' predecessor Euripides in that the effective portrayal of individual emotion is more important than a finished portrait of a character. Medea the love-sick girl and Medea the great sorceress could not be readily combined in one description.

There is also an Alexandrian element in the many descriptions of nature which, in the traditional epic, would be unthinkable. Successful color effects are achieved in descriptions of seascapes, as in the sailing of the Argo when the dark flood foams under the beat of the oars, the men's armor flashes like fire in the morning light, and the long wake seems like a bright path in a green meadow. Apollonius also shares with the rest of Hellenistic art the discovery of children. The Eros of the celestial scenes of book 3, who in his day was a formidable god, has here been reduced to an ill-mannered boy. He is the epitome of the spoiled rascal who cheats his comrades at play and can be persuaded by his mother Aphrodite to perform a service only by means of an expensive present.

Apollonius cannot be characterized concisely. He proved himself to be a poet of considerable importance in several passages, but he was not completely successful in blending the rich epic tradition with his own creation. His fire was too weak to fuse all the heterogeneous elements into one whole.

Major publication other than poetry
NONFICTION: *Against Zenodotos*, third century B.C.

Bibliography
Bowra, C. M. *Landmarks in Greek Literature*, 1966.
Hadas, M. *A History of Greek Literature*, 1950.
Lesky, A. *A History of Greek Literature*, 1966.
Mooney, G. W. *Apollonius Rhodius: Argonautica*, 1912.
Rose, H. J. *A Handbook of Greek Literature*, 1951.

Shelley P. Haley

LOUIS ARAGON

Born: Paris, France; October 3, 1897
Died: Paris, France; December 24, 1982

Principal poems and collections

Feu de joie, 1920; *Le Mouvement perpétuel*, 1925; *La Grande Gaîté*, 1929; *Persécuté persécuteur*, 1931; *Hourra l'Oural*, 1934; *Le Crève-coeur*, 1941; *Brocéliande*, 1942; *Les Yeux d'Elsa*, 1942; *En Français dans le texte*, 1943; *Le Musée grévin*, 1943; *La Diane française*, 1945; *Le Nouveau Crève-coeur*, 1948; *Les Yeux et la mémoire*, 1954; *Le Roman inachevé*, 1956; *Elsa*, 1959; *Les Poètes*, 1960; *Le Fou d'Elsa*, 1963; *Les Chambres*, 1969; *Aux abords de Rome*, 1981; *Les Adieux*, 1982.

Other literary forms

Louis Aragon was one of the most prolific French authors of the twentieth century, and although lyric poetry was his first medium, to which he always returned as to a first love, he also produced many novels and volumes of essays. As a young man, he participated in the Surrealist movement, and his works of this period defy classification. In addition to the exercises known as "automatic writing," which had a considerable impact on his mature style in both prose and poetry, he wrote a number of Surrealist narratives combining elements of the novel (such as description and dialogue) and the essay. The most important of these, *Le Paysan de Paris* (1926; *Nightwalker*, 1970), is a long meditation on the author's ramblings in his native city and on the "modern sense of the mythic" inspired by its streets, shops, and parks. In the 1930's, after his espousal of the Communist cause, Aragon began a series of novels under the general title of *Le Monde réel* (The Real World), which follow the tenets of Socialist Realism. These are historical novels dealing with the corruption of bourgeois society and the rise of Communism. His later novels, however, beginning with *La Semaine sainte* (1958; *Holy Week*, 1961), show greater freedom of form and lack the explicit "message" characteristic of Socialist Realism; these later works incorporate an ongoing meditation on the novel as a literary form and on its relation to history and biography.

An important characteristic of Aragon's style that cuts across all of his works of fiction and poetry is the use of spoken language as a model: his sentences reproduce the rhythms of speech, full of parentheses, syntactic breaks, and interjections, and his diction, especially in prose, is heavily interlarded with slang. This trait is true to some extent even of his essays, although the latter tend to be more formal to both diction and rhetorical strategy. His nonfiction works are voluminous, for he was an active journalist for much of his life, producing reviews and essays on politics, literature, and the visual arts for a variety of Surrealist and then Communist publications.

Achievements

Like most writers who have taken strong political stands, Aragon was, during the course of his lifetime, the object of much praise and blame that had little to do with the literary value of his work. This was especially true of his series of novels, *Le Monde réel*, which was hailed by his fellow Communists as a masterpiece and criticized by most non-Communist reviewers as contrived and doctrinaire. It is probably too early to assess Aragon's importance in the history of literature. He was, with André Breton, one of the leaders of the Surrealist movement; his poetry after the mid-1940's combined elements of Romanticism and modernism, but his style evolved in a direction of its own and cannot be identified with that of any one school.

After his Surrealist period, during which he wrote for an intellectual elite, Aragon sought to make his work accessible to a wider public and often succeeded. The height of his popularity was achieved in the 1940's, when his poems played an important role in the French Resistance: written in traditional meters and using rhyme, so that they might more easily be sung, they became rallying cries for French patriots abroad and in occupied France. (Many of Aragon's poems have, in fact, been set to music by writers of popular songs, including Léo Ferré and George Brassens.) Beginning in the late 1950's, Aragon's work became much less overtly political, which contributed to its acceptance by non-Communist critics. At the time of his death in 1982, Aragon was considered even by his political opponents as a leading man of letters. Writers of lesser stature have been elected to the Académie Française, but Aragon never applied for membership, and it is hard to imagine such an ardent advocate of the common man, who used slang liberally in his own work, sitting in judgment on the purity of the French language.

For Aragon, who wrote his first "novel" at age six (and dictated a play to his aunt before he could write), writing was like breathing, a vital activity coextensive with living. He was a novelist whose eye (and ear) for telling detail never dulled, a poet whose lyric gifts did not diminish with age.

Biography

Until late in life, Louis Aragon was reticent about his childhood, and many biographical notices erroneously describe it as idyllic; in fact, his family (which consisted of his grandmother, mother, and two aunts) was obsessed with a concern for appearances that caused the boy considerable pain. The illegitimate son of a prominent political figure, Louis Andrieux, who chose the name Aragon for his son and acted as his legal guardian, Aragon was reared as his mother's younger brother, and although as a boy he guessed much of the truth, it was not until his twentieth year that he heard it from his mother (at the insistence of his father, who had previously insisted on her silence). Since his maternal grandfather had also deserted the family, his mother, Marguérite Toucas-Masillon, supported them all as best she could by painting china and running a boardinghouse. According to his biographer, Pierre Daix, the circumstances of Aragon's childhood left him with an instinctive sympathy for outsiders, especially women, and a great longing to be accepted as a full member of a group. This longing was first satisfied by his friendship with André Breton and later by Aragon's adherence to the Communist Party. (Indeed, his deep need to "belong" may help to account for his unswerving loyalty to the Party throughout the Stalinist era.)

Breton, whom he met in 1917, introduced Aragon to the circle of poets and artists that was to form the nucleus of the Dadaist and Surrealist movements. Horrified by the carnage of World War I (which Aragon had observed firsthand as a medic), these young people at first embraced the negative impulse of Dada, an absurdist movement founded in Zurich by Tristan Tzara. Their aim was to unmask the moral bankruptcy of the society that had tolerated such a war. Realizing that a philosophy of simple negation was ultimately sterile, Breton and Aragon broke away from the Dadaists and began to pursue the interest in the subconscious, which led them to Surrealism. Through the technique of automatic writing, they tried to suppress the rational faculty, or "censor," which inhibited free expression of subconscious impulses.

Politically, the Surrealists were anarchists, but as they became increasingly convinced that profound social changes were necessary to free the imagination, a number of them, including Aragon, joined the French Communist Party. At about the same time (1928), Aragon met the Russian poet Vladimir Mayakovsky and his sister-in-law, the novelist Elsa Triolet, at the Coupole, a Paris café. As Aragon put it, describing his meeting with Elsa many years later, "We have been together ever since" (literally, "We have not left each other's side"). In Elsa, Aragon found the "woman of the future," who could be her husband's intellectual and social equal while sharing with him a love in which all the couple's aspirations were anchored. Aragon celebrated this love in countless poems spanning forty years; some of the most ecstatic were written when the two were in their sixties. Elsa introduced Aragon to Soviet Russia, which they visited together in the early 1930's; she also took part with him in the French Resistance during World War II, publishing clandestine newspapers and maintaining a network of anti-Fascist intellectuals. Although he followed the "party line" and tried to rationalize the Soviet pact with the Nazis, Aragon was an ardent French patriot; he was decorated for bravery in both world wars and wrote hymns of praise to the French "man (and woman) in the street," who became the heroes of the Resistance.

After the war, Aragon redoubled his activities on behalf of the Party, serving as editor of the Communist newspaper *Ce Soir* and completing his six-volume novel *Les Communistes* (1949-1951). In 1954, he became a permanent member of the Central Committee of the French Communist Party, and in 1957, the Soviet Union awarded him its highest decoration, the Lenin Peace Prize. He was vilified by many of his fellow intellectuals in France for failing to criticize

Stalin; not until 1966, during the much-publicized trial of two Soviet writers, Andrei Sinyavsky and Yuli Daniel, did he venture to speak out against the notion that there could be a "criminality of opinion." In 1968, he joined with the French Communist Party as a whole in condemning the Russian invasion of Czechoslovakia. Throughout his life, Aragon continued to produce a steady stream of poetry, fiction, and essays. His wife's death in 1970 was a terrible blow, but he survived it and went on to write six more books in the twelve years that were left to him.

Analysis

Despite the length of Louis Aragon's poetic career and the perceptible evolution of his style in the course of six decades, there is a remarkable unity in the corpus of his poetry. This unity results from stylistic as well as thematic continuities, for even when he turned from free verse to more traditional metric forms, he managed to preserve the fluency of spoken language. In fact, his most highly structured verse has some of the qualities of stream-of-consciousness narrative. There are a variety of reasons for this. Aragon began to write as a very young boy and continued writing, steadily and copiously, throughout his life. As Hubert Juin has observed, Aragon never needed to keep a journal or diary because "his work itself was his journal," into which he poured his eager questions and reflections on what most closely concerned him.

This confessional impulse was reinforced and given direction in Aragon's Surrealist period by experiments with automatic writing, a technique adapted for literary use primarily by Breton and Philippe Soupault. By writing quickly without revising, and by resisting the impulse to edit or censor the flow of words, the Surrealists hoped to tap their subconscious minds and so to "save literature from rhetoric" (as Juin puts it). Literature was not all they hoped to save, moreover, for "rhetoric" had poisoned the social and political spheres as well; in liberating the subconscious, Aragon and his friends sought to break old and unjust patterns of thought and life. They also expected this powerful and hitherto untapped source to fuel the human imagination for the work of social renewal. Although Aragon repudiated the Surrealist attitude (which was basically anarchistic) when he embraced Communism as the pattern of the future, he never lost the stylistic freedom that automatic writing had fostered, nor did he become complacent about the "solution" he had found. Like his relationship with his wife, in which his hopes for the future were anchored, Aragon's Communism was a source of pain as well as of fulfillment: the deeper his love and commitment, the greater his vulnerability. Thus, poetry remained for him, as it had been in his youth, a form of questioning in which he explored the world and his relation to it.

There were, nevertheless, perceptible changes in Aragon's style during the course of his career. After the Dadaist and Surrealist periods, when he wrote mainly free verse (although there are metrically regular poems even in his early collections), Aragon turned to more traditional prosody—including rhyme—in the desire to make his verses singable. At the same time, he sought to renew and broaden the range of available rhymes by adopting new definitions of masculine and feminine rhyme based on pronunciation rather than on spelling. He also applied the notion of enjambment to rhyme, allowing not only the last syllable of a line but also the first letter or letters of the following line to count as constituent elements of a rhyme. Partly as a result of the conditions under which they were composed, Aragon's Resistance poems are for the most part short and self-contained, although *Le Musée grévin* (the wax museum) is a single long poem, and the pieces in *Brocéliande* are linked by allusions to the knights of the Arthurian cycle, whom Aragon saw as the symbolic counterparts of the Resistance fighters.

Aragon's postwar collections are more unified, and beginning with *Les Yeux et la mémoire* (eyes and memory), they might almost be described as book-length poems broken into short "chapters" of varying meters. Many of these "chapters," however, can stand alone as finished pieces; good examples are the love lyrics in *Le Fou d'Elsa* (some of which have been set to music, like the war poems) and the vignette from *Le Roman inachevé* (the unfinished romance) beginning "Marguerite, Madeleine et Marie," which describes Aragon's mother and aunts—whom he thought of as his sisters—dressing for a dance. Within his longer sequences, Aragon skillfully uses shifts of meter to signal changes of mood and does not hesitate to lapse into prose when occasion warrants—for examaple, when, in *Le Roman inachevé*, he is suddenly overwhelmed by the weariness and pain of old age: "The verse breaks in my hands, my old hands, swollen and knotted with veins. . . ." Such disclaimers to the contrary, Aragon was never in greater control of his medium than in these poems of his old age, culminating in *Elsa*, *Le Fou d'Elsa* (Elsa's madman), and *Les Chambres* (the rooms). *Le Fou d'Elsa* is perhaps his greatest tour de force, a kind of epic (depicting the end of Moslem rule in Spain, with the fall of Granada in 1492) made up of hundreds of lyric pieces, along with some dialogue and prose commentary. As Juin has remarked, Aragon tends to alternate between two tones, the epic and the elegiac, and *Le Fou d'Elsa* is a perfect vehicle for both. The grand scale of the book gives full sweep to Aragon's epic vision of past and future regimes, while the inserted lyrics preserve the reduced scale proper to elegy.

In order to appreciate the texture of Aragon's poetry—his characteristic interweaving of image and theme, diction and syntax—it is necessary to examine a few of his poems in detail. Choosing one poem from each of the three distinct phases of his career (the Surrealist, Resistance, and postwar periods), all dealing with his central theme, the love of a woman, makes it possible to demonstrate both the continuities and the changes in his poetry during the greater part of his career. All three poems are in his elegiac vein, the mode easiest to examine at close range and the most fertile for Aragon. The occasional false notes in his verse tend to be struck when he assumes the triumphalist pose of the committed Marxist. When he speaks of his wife, his very excesses suggest a shattering sincerity, especially when the subject is separation, age, or death.

"Poème à crier dans les ruines" ("Poem to Shout in the Ruins"), although addressed to a woman, is not addressed to Elsa, whom Aragon had yet to meet when it was written. The poem records the bitterness of an affair that has recently ended and from which the poet seems to have expected more than his lover did. Like most of Aragon's work, the poem is heavily auto-biographical; the woman involved was American heiress Nancy Cunard, with whom Aragon had lived for about a year, and the allusions to travel throughout the poem recall trips the couple had taken together. Although the poem opens with a passage that might be described as expository, and although it moves from particular details to a general observation and closes with a sort of reprise, it strikes the reader as more loosely organized than it actually is. This impression results from its rhythm being that of association—the train of thought created when a person dwells on a single topic for a sustained period of time. Because the topic is unhappy love and the bitterness of rejection, the process of association takes on an obsessive quality, and although the resulting monologue is ostensibly addressed to the lover, the title suggests that neither she nor anyone else is expected to respond. The overall effect, then, is that of an *interior* monologue, and its power stems not from any cogency of argument (the "rhetoric" rejected by the Surrealists) but from the cumulative effects of obsessive repetition. Thus, the speaker's memories are evoked in a kind of litany ("I remember your shoulder/ I remember your elbow/ I remember your linen. . . ."); later, struck by the realization that memory implies the past tense, he piles up verbs in the *passé simple* (as in "Loved Was Came Caressed"), the tense used for completed action.

The lack of a rhetorical framework in the poem is paralleled by the absence of any central image or images. Although many arresting images appear, they are not linked in any design but remain isolated, reinforcing the sense of meaninglessness that has overwhelmed the speaker. The "little rented cars" and mirrors left unclaimed in a baggage room evoke the traveling the couple did together, which the speaker now sees as aimless. Some of the details given remain opaque because they have a private meaning that is not revealed ("Certain names are charged with a distant thunder"); others seem to be literary allusions, such as Mazeppa's ride (described in a poem by Lord Byron) and the bleeding trees, which to a reader who knows the works of Dante suggest that poet's "wood of the suicides." (Not until many years later did Aragon reveal that he had attempted suicide after the breakup with Cunard.)

The use of such arcane personal and literary allusions was a legacy of the Symbolist movement; as a young man, Aragon admired both Arthur Rimbaud and Stéphane Mallarmé, two of the most gifted Symbolists. The Surrealist approach to imagery evolved directly out of Symbolism in its more extreme forms, such as "Le Bateau ivre" ("The Drunken Boat") of Rimbaud and the *Chants de Maldoror* (1869) of Comte de Lautréamont. Despite its hopelessness, "Poem to Shout in the Ruins" conveys the almost hallucinatory power the Surrealists saw in imagery: its ability to charge ordinary things with mystery by appealing to the buried layers of the subconscious. "Familiar objects one by one were taking on . . . the ghostly look of escaped prisoners. . . ." The poem also suggests, however, that Aragon is not content merely to explore his subconscious; he hungers for a real connection to a real woman. In his desperate desire to prolong the liaison, he tries fitfully to make a "waltz" of the poem and asks the woman to join him, "since *something* must still connect us," in spitting on "what we have loved together." Despite its prevailing tone of negation and despair, the poem anticipates two central themes of Aragon's mature works: the belief that love between man and woman should be infinitely more than a source of casual gratification, and the awareness of mortality (which the finality of parting suggests). This awareness is not morbid but tragic—the painful apprehension of death in a man whose loves and hopes were lavished on mortal existence.

"Les Yeux d'Elsa" ("Elsa's Eyes"), the opening poem in the collection of that name, is a good example of the metrically regular pieces Aragon produced in the 1940's (and continued to produce, together with free verse, until the end of his life). It is particularly characteristic in that, while each stanza has internal unity, the stanzas do not follow one another in a strictly necessary order; like those of a folk song or lyrical ballad, they offer a series of related insights or observations without logical or narrative progression. Many of Aragon's mature poems *do* exhibit such a progression (notably "Toi qui es la rose"—"You Who Are the Rose"), but in most cases it is subordinated to the kind of associative rhythm observed in "Poem to Shout in the Ruins."

The imagery of "Elsa's Eyes" is more unified than that of the earlier poem. Taking his wife's eyes as the point of departure, the poet offers a whole array of metaphors for their blueness (sky, ocean, wildflowers), brilliance (lightning, shooting stars), and depth (a well, far countries, and constellations). The last four stanzas are more closely linked than the preceding ones and culminate in an apocalyptic vision of Elsa's eyes surviving the end of the world. The poem as a whole, however, cannot be said to *build* to this climax; its power stems from the accumulation of images rather than from their arrangement. It should be noted that Aragon's Surrealist formation is still very much in evidence here, not only in the hallucinatory quality of his images but in their obvious connection with subconscious desires and fears. The occasional obscurities are no longer the result of a deliberate use of private or literary allusions; Aragon was already writing with a wider public in mind. Nevertheless, he continued to evoke his own deepest desires and fears in language whose occasional ambiguity reflects the ambiguity of subconscious impulses.

A relatively new departure for Aragon in this period, the serious use of religious imagery, is reflected in the references to the Three Kings and the Mother of the Seven Sorrows in "Elsa's Eyes." Although reared a Catholic, Aragon became an atheist in his early youth and never professed any religious faith thereafter. During World War II, however, he was impressed by the courage of Christian resisters and acquired a certain respect for the faith that sustained them in the struggle against Fascism. For his own part, Aragon began to use the vocabulary of traditional religion to extol his wife. Thus, for example, in "Elsa's Eyes," Elsa is described as the Mother of the Seven Sorrows, an epithet of the Virgin Mary; at the same time, Elsa is assimilated by natural forces and survives the cataclysm of the last stanza like a mysterious deity. This is partly attributable to Aragon's rediscovery, at about this time, of the courtly love tradition in French poetry, in which the lady becomes the immediate object of the knight's worship, whether as a mediatrix (who shows the way to God) or as a substitute for God Himself. Repeatedly in Aragon's postwar poetry, Elsa is endowed with godlike qualities, until, in *Le Fou d'Elsa*, a virtual apotheosis takes place: the "holy fool" for whom the book is named (a Moslem, not a Christian) is convicted of heresy for worshiping a woman— Elsa—who will not be born for four centuries.

Whenever he was questioned on the subject, Aragon insisted that his aim was not a deification of Elsa but the replacement of the transcendent God of traditional religions with a "real" object, a woman of flesh and blood who could serve as his partner in building the future. Thus, Elsa's madman tells his judge, "I can say of her what I cannot say of God: she exists, because she *will be*. . . ." At the same time, the imagery of "Elsa's Eyes" clearly indicates that on some level there is an impulse of genuine worship, compounded of love, fear, and awe, in the poet's relation to his wife; he turned to the courtly tradition because it struck a deep chord in him. From the very first stanza, Elsa is identified with forces of nature, not all of which are benevolent: "Your eyes are so deep that in stooping to drink/ I saw all suns reflected there/ All desperate men throw themselves there to die. . . ." In most of the early stanzas, emphasis is laid on her grief (presumably over the effects of war), which only enhances her beauty, but the insistence on her eyes also suggests that, like God, she is all-seeing. Aragon himself often referred to his wife as his conscience, and Bernard Lecherbonnier has suggested in *Le Cycle d'Elsa* that the circumstances of Aragon's upbringing created in him, first in regard to his mother and later in regard to his wife, "an obsession with self-justification that permitted the myth of god-as-love to crystallize around the person, and in particular the eyes, of Elsa." Such an attitude is especially suggested by the final images of the poem, that of "Paradise regained and relost a hundred times" and that of Elsa's eyes shining over the sea after the final "shipwreck" of the universe.

An attitude of worship can also be seen in "You Who Are the Rose" (from the collection entitled *Elsa*), but it is tempered considerably by the vulnerability of the rose, the central image around which the poem is built. Its tight construction makes this a somewhat uncharacteristic poem for Aragon, yet his technique is still that of association and accumulation rather than logical or rhetorical development. As in "Poem to Shout in the Ruins," short syntactic units give the impression of spoken (indeed, in this poem, almost breathless) language. With an obsessiveness reminiscent of the earlier poem, the speaker worries over the flowering of the rose, which he fears will not bloom "this year" because of frost, drought, or "some subterranean sickness." The poem has a clear dramatic structure: the tension of waiting builds steadily, with periodic breaks or breathing spaces marked by the one-line refrain "*(de) la rose*," until the miraculous flowering takes place and is welcomed with a sort of prayer. The images that accumulate along the way, evoked by the poet in a kind of incantation designed to call forth the rose, are all subordinated to this central image of flowering, yet by their startling juxtaposition and suggestiveness, they clearly reflect Aragon's Surrealist background. Thus, the dormant plant is compared to "a cross contradicting the tomb," while two lines later its roots are "like an insinuating hand beneath the sheets caressing the sleeping thighs of winter." The use of alliteration is excessive—as when six words beginning with *gr-* appear in the space of three lines—and although this serves to emphasize the incantatory quality of the verse, to hostile critics it may look like simple bad taste. Hubert Juin, a friendly critic, freely acknowledges that a certain kind of bad taste is evident in Aragon; he ascribes it to the poet's "epic" orientation, his desire to include as much of the world as possible in his design, which precludes attention to every detail. It seems more to the point to recall that for the Surrealists, editing was a kind of dishonesty; by writing rapidly and not revising, they sought to lay bare what was most deeply buried in their psyches. What often saves Aragon from *préciosité* or literary affectation is the realism of this stream-of-consciousness technique. Caught up in the speaker's own anxiety or fantasy, the reader does not stop to criticize the occasional banalities and lapses of taste; he follows in the poet's wake, eager to see where the train of thought will lead.

The poignancy of "You Who Are the Rose," as of so many of Aragon's late poems, stems from the contrast between his exaggerated hopes—still virtually those of a young man—and the fact of old age, which threatens to deprive him of his wife and of his poetic voice. There is also, in some of his later work, a hint of sadness (although never of disillusionment) at the failure of Communism to fulfill its promise within his own lifetime. It is worth noting that in France the rose has long been associated with Socialist ideals; the poet's fear for his wife in "You Who Are the Rose" may be doubled by a tacit fear that the promise of Marxism will not be fulfilled. The two fears are related, moreover, because Aragon saw the harmony between husband and wife as the hope of the future, the cornerstone of a just and happy (Communist) society. His anguish is that of the idealist who rejects the possibility of transcendence: his "divinity" is mortal, like him. This helps to account for the fact that he continued to write with undiminished passion until the very end of his life, for poetry held out the only prospect of immortality in which he believed. The rose is mortal, but she has a name, and the poet can conjure with it (as his conclusion emphasizes: "O rose who are your being and your name"). What is more, Elsa Triolet was herself a writer, and in the preface to an edition combining her own and her husband's fiction, she described their mutually inspired work as the best possible memorial to their love. Aragon will probably be remembered primarily as the poet of Elsa—"Elsa's Madman," perhaps, in his anguished self-disclosure—but above all as Elsa's troubadour, an ecstatic love poet who insists on the possibility of earthly happiness because he has tasted it himself.

Major publications other than poetry

NOVELS: *Anicet ou le panorama, roman*, 1921; *Les Aventures de Télémaque*, 1922; *Le Paysan de Paris*, 1926 (*Nightwalker*, 1970); *Le Monde réel* (The Real World) series, 1934-1944 (*Les Cloches de Bâle*, 1934, *The Bells of Basel*, 1936; *Les Beaux Quartiers*, 1936, *Residential Quarter*, 1938; *Les Voyageurs de l'impériale*, 1942, *The Century Was Young*, 1941; *Aurélien*, 1944, English translation, 1947); *Les Communistes*, 1949-1951; *La Semaine sainte*, 1958 (*Holy Week*, 1961); *La Mise à mort*, 1965; *Blanche, ou l'oubli*, 1967; *Théâtre/roman*, 1974.

SHORT FICTION: *Servitude et grandeur de français*, 1945; *Le Mentir-vrai*, 1981.

NONFICTION: *Le Traité du style*, 1928; *Pour une réalisme socialiste*, 1935; *L'Homme communiste*, 1946, 1953; *Introduction aux littératures soviétiques*, 1956; *J'abats mon jeu*, 1959; *Les Deux Géants: Histoire parallèle des États-Unis et de l'U.R.S.S.*, 1962 (with André Maurois; *A History of the U.S.S.R. from Lenin to Khrushchev*, 1963, 1964); *Entretiens avec Francis Crémieux*, 1964; *Écrits sur l'art moderne*, 1982.

Bibliography
Becker, Lucille F. *Louis Aragon*, 1971.
Daix, Pierre. *Aragon: Une Vie à changer*, 1975.
Garaudy, Roger. *L'Itinéraire d'Aragon: Du surréalisme au monde réel*, 1961.
Josephson, Hannah, and Malcolm Cowley. *Aragon, Poet of the French Resistance*, 1945.
Juin, Hubert. *Aragon*, 1960.
Lecherbonnier, Bernard. *Le Cycle d'Elsa*, 1974.

Lillian Doherty

JÁNOS ARANY

Born: March 2, 1817; Nagyszalonta, Hungary
Died: October 22, 1882; Budapest, Hungary

Principal poems and collections
Toldi, 1847; *Murány ostroma*, 1848; *Katalin*, 1850; *Nagyidai cigányok*, 1852; *Toldi estéje*, 1854; *Kisebb költeményei*, 1856; *Buda halála*, 1864 (*The Death of King Buda*, 1936); *Arany János összes költeményei*, 1867; *Toldi szerelme*, 1879; *Összes mvei*, 1851-1868; *Arany János összes munkái*, 1884-1885.

Other literary forms
János Arany's criticism and studies in Hungarian literature are in the best tradition of scholarship and remain useful. His translations of several of Shakespeare's plays and of Aristophanes' comedies are outstanding in the history of Hungarian translations.

Achievements
Arany contributed to Hungarian literature a poetic style and language—in fact, a poetic tradition—that united the best elements of native Hungarian verse, based to a large degree on folk song and folk poetry, with the learned traditions of Western Europe, particularly the traditions of the Enlightenment and of Romanticism. The result was a poetry that, while retaining its distinctively Hungarian character, joined the larger conversation of European literature.

Arany was not the only writer engaged in this literary development, nor was he the first. He built on medieval, Renaissance, and Baroque traditions, and his goals were shared by many of his contemporaries. His individual contribution rested above all on his knowledgeable and sensitive use of folk elements, his ability to recognize and reject undue foreign influence while using foreign models to enrich his own work, and his unerring sense for the forms and rhythms best suited to the Hungarian language. His affinity with the folkloric tradition, as well as his recognition of its role in preserving Hungarian cultural traditions, enabled him to put into practice the theories and plans of the reform movement. As a teacher and critic, he was further able to explain and elucidate reformist goals. He not only used native words but also explained their appropriateness and traced their history. He used meters based on folk song and wrote a thesis on Hungarian versification. Arguing that native themes and forms could equal the best in classical literature, he demonstrated this in his critical essays. Ever sensitive to literary developments abroad, he emphasized the need for literature to be realistic yet to avoid the excesses of Naturalism; in his view, the poet should show not so much what is, but rather its "heavenly counterpart."

Biography

János Arany was born the last child of György Arany and the former Sára Megyeri in Nagyszalonta, Hungary (now known as Salonta, Romania). Taught to read by his father, Arany began his studies in 1828 at Nagyszalonta. In 1831, he became a tutor at the school there, and in 1833, he transferred to the gymnasium (high school) at Debrecen on a scholarship. He took a leave of absence to serve as tutor in Kisujszállas for about a year, and in 1836 left Debrecen without taking a degree. He settled in Nagyszalonta and became a teacher, later taking a post as notary. In 1840, he married Julianna Ercsey, the orphaned child of a lawyer. A daughter, Juliska, was born in 1841, and a son, László, in 1844.

Although originally Arany had intended to give up his literary aspirations and devote his energies to building a secure future for his family, the friendship of István Szilágyi, who became rector at Nagyszalonta in 1842, drew him into the literary world. Arany had read widely in popular Hungarian literature since his childhood and had been introduced to earlier as well as contemporary Hungarian literature at Debrecen, but Szilágyi encouraged him to continue his studies of English and other foreign authors. Arany learned English to be able to read the works in the original, and he later translated from this language as well as from German, Greek, Italian, and other languages. In 1845, Arany's poem "Az elveszett alkótmany" (the lost constitution) won a literary prize. In 1847, his *Toldi* won even greater acclaim, and he became increasingly involved in the literary life of the country, as well as in the events leading up to the Revolution of 1848. He ran for a seat in Parliament but was defeated; he also served as a soldier during the siege of Arad.

After the defeat of the Hungarians by the combined forces of the Austrian and Russian empires, Arany, like most of his contemporaries, spent several months in hiding and naturally lost his teaching position. For a while, Count Lajos Tisza employed him as a tutor, and in 1851 he accepted a position as teacher in the gymnasium at Nagykörös. Arany never felt comfortable as a teacher, and in time the routine and the atmosphere of the small town depressed him. At first, however, there were brilliant colleagues who were similarly in hiding or exile during the years of terror, and he wrote a series of ballads, completed *Toldi estéje* (Toldi's eve) as well as several other narrative poems, and began the third poem of the Toldi trilogy, *Toldi szerelme* (Toldi's love). The notes for his lectures on Hungarian literature prepared at this time (never collected by him and published only after his death) show his sensitivity and the thorough critical and historical grasp he had of his subject.

In spite of his distance from the center of activity, Arany remained in close contact with literary developments. Recognition also came his way. On December 15, 1858, the Hungarian Academy of Sciences was allowed to resume its activity after a ten-year suspension, and Arany was elected a member. In his acceptance speech, he compared the epics of Miklós Zrinyi, a poet of the seventeenth century, with the work of Torquato Tasso. After repeated invitations by his friends to move to Budapest, Arany finally accepted the position of director of the Kisfaludy Társaság. In addition to administrative duties, he was active as an adviser and critic. He wrote a study on the Hungarian drama by József Katona, *Bánk bán* (1821, performed in 1833), and helped prepare Imre Madách's *Az ember tragédiája* (1861; the tragedy of man) for publication. Increasingly accepted as the unofficial laureate of Hungarian literature, he became Secretary of the Academy of Sciences in 1865. He continued writing, although he was unable to complete many projects. The major poem he worked on in this period was what he hoped would be a national epic, *The Death of King Buda*. It was, moreover, a period during which Arany was active as a translator, rendering William Shakespeare, Aristophanes, and selections from many writers in other languages into Hungarian. He had the obligation to oversee the translation and publication of the complete works of Shakespeare and of Jean-Baptiste Molière, as well as a comprehensive edition of Hungarian folk literature.

In 1879, Arany's third request for retirement was finally accepted by the Academy. In his last years, he enjoyed a resurgence of lyric power and, despite his ill health, was able to finish some earlier projects, notably *Toldi szerelme*. He published his *Prózai dolgozatai* (1879; prose essays) and was increasingly involved in linguistic studies.

Arany died on October 22, 1882, several days before the unveiling of the statue of his friend, the poet Sandor Petőfi, that still stands by the Danube in one of the city's old squares. Arany was laid out in state in the main chamber of the Academy and was eulogized by the important critics and poets of his day. His role as one of the major figures in Hungarian poetry and literary criticism, as well as a sensitive and learned molder of the language, continues to be recognized to this day.

Analysis

In 1845, János Arany won the prize of the Kisfaludy Társaság with his mock-heroic epic, "Az elveszett alkótmany." He had begun writing it spontaneously and with no thought of publication, learning of the competition only when the poem was well under way. Although he was later to regret the unevenness and coarseness of the work, it deserves attention, for it shows Arany's use of supernatural machinery, which is rooted in Hungarian folklore and popular mythology—a device he borrowed from Mihály Vörösmarty and others but which Arany was to use effectively in later poems. His portrayal of the petty bickering between progressive and liberal political parties, no less than the high-handed and illegal actions of the party in power, indicates his political concerns. He suggests in the conclusion that only with a widening of the franchise, with the inclusion of all segments of the population in the political process can Hungarian institutions fulfill their proper role.

It was *Toldi*, however, that established Arany's literary reputation. As the enthusiastic Petőfi wrote: "Others receive the laurel leaf by leaf,/ For you an entire wreath must be given immediately." What Arany did was to create a folk-epic style that conveyed the life of the Hungarian Plain and the sense of history shared by the nation. Arany, who felt strongly that folk poetry should be the basis of the new national literary style, ennobled the genre by blending with it the qualities of the epic. Indebted to Petőfi's *János Vitéz* (1845; *János the Hero*, 1920), also a folk epic, which had appeared a year earlier, Arany nevertheless was responsible for innovations of his own. *Toldi* was written in the old narrative meter, the Hungarian Alexandrine or twelve-syllable hexameter line rather than in the simpler quatrain of the folk song. Arany's hero was an actual historical personage, while the poem's setting was based on the realistic verse chronicle by Péter Selymes Ilosvay; in contrast, Petőfi's *János the Hero* had a fairy-tale setting. In the handling of his sources and the characterization of his hero, Arany established the method he was to use in later poems.

Arany turns Ilosvay's sketchy tale about Miklós Toldi, a man of prodigious strength who won fame at the court of Lajos the Great (1342-1382), into a tightly organized poem in twelve cantos. Arany is careful to motivate each action and to fit each episode into his framework. Arany also concentrates on the hero's emergence as the King's champion rather than attempting to cover all of his life. He deliberately refrains from beginning his poem *in medias res* and filling in background through digressions and backtracking, a method he believed would have been incompatible with the spirit of folk poetry.

The action of the poem covers nine days and falls into two sections: cantos 1 through 6 relate the crime of Toldi and give the reason for his leaving home to seek the favor of the King, while cantos 7 through 12 show how this is accomplished. Several episodes are intertwined, but all serve to illustrate the development of the hero's character.

In the course of a few days, Toldi emerges as a loyal, brave, generous, faithful, and compassionate man who uses his great strength for good—whether working in the fields or fighting in the lists. Arany, through an examination of Toldi's actions as well as of his underlying motivations, makes his hero representative of that which is best in the Hungarian character. Arany also makes him a representative of the entire nation, not restricting his ties to any one class; noble by birth, yet close to the peasants and servants on the farm, he embodies Arany's political views as well. In contrast to the affected, treacherous György, who seems to be both a parasite and a tyrant on his own land, Toldi is equally at home with the servants and at the court of the King.

Idealized and simplified in some respects, the hero retains many very human qualities. He is despondent and brooding when disappointed, gives way to anger quickly, and almost gives up while hiding in the swamp. On the other hand, he can rejoice with abandon as he celebrates the arrival of a gift from his mother and the opportunity to earn respect and recognition.

Arany's portrayal of Hungarian qualities, of the soul of the nation, as it were, is not, however, restricted to Toldi. Arany captures the essence of Hungarian life in his description of the activities of the people, whether in the fields or in the city, working or enjoying a festival. By projecting familiar details of the nineteenth century onto his fourteenth century setting, Arany was able, moreover, to give the epic a realism and intimacy it would otherwise have lacked. Far from being false to the medieval setting or an oversimplification of life in Buda and the court, this projection carries Arany's message that in the past, Hungarian society was more unified: Distinctions of rank were not chasms.

Like the overall concept and style of the poem, its language and form are based on folk literature. Arany, well aware of the power of native words, used these deliberately. He wished to make his poetry easily understood and enjoyed by all, but he also sought to introduce the *language* of the people, no less than their poetry and song, into Hungarian literature. An active language reformer, he felt that the written Hungarian language could be revitalized only by absorbing the pure speech of the common man, still rich in archaic words, local dialect, and variety. The form of *Toldi* is also rooted in folk poetry, for the Hungarian Alexandrine was the traditional verse of earlier narrative poems. It echoes the patterns of Hungarian speech and, as Arany showed, is capable of a wide range. In this first epic, Arany used the traditional accented line, divided by a caesura. Later, he was to use both accented and quantitative feet to fit the form to the theme.

Arany was deeply affected by the failure of the War of Independence, yet the early 1850's was one of his richer periods, even though many of the poems of this time are expressions of despair and disappointment. He not only criticized the newly evolving political and social life, but also questioned his own poetic style and creativity. In the two "Voitina levelei öccséhez" ("Voitina's Letters to His Brother"), he condemned the distortion of the folk style as well as the mere aping of foreign fashions, even as he himself sought the true possibilities of a popular national style. "Leteszem a lantot" ("I Lay Down the Lute"), an elegy for Petőfi, also expresses Arany's feeling that "he is no longer what he was,/ The better part has left him." No longer can he sing the hope of the future, nor can he even hope for the reward of immortality. The specter of the nation's death also haunted him in "Rachel" and "Rachel siralma" ("Rachael's Lament"). In "A nagyidai cigányok" ("The Gypsies of Nagyida"), he sought release from the disappointment and bitterness he felt at the failure of the Revolution.

In his ballads and narrative poems, Arany continued to develop the folk style and to set his stories in a real time and place. He excelled in capturing the many moods of the life of the people, in painting intimate village scenes and establishing characterizations with a deft touch. A relatively short descriptive poem, "Családi kör" ("Family Circle"), illustrates this method in the compass of thirteen stanzas, but it was used no less effectively in the epics and the ballads. Arany describes a village evening, giving each element its due place while creating a domestic scene. As the village retires for the evening, the trees "nod," the bugs make a final sortie before becoming still, the frogs move "as if clods of earth had grown legs," and the bat and the owl take over their domain. He then moves closer to the farm to describe participants in the evening's activities: the cow, just milked, now feeding its calf; the playful cat; the inviting hearth guarded by the faithful dog; as well as the human inhabitants. A young girl is ironing her Sunday clothes; children listen to tales as they play or do their chores. A father returns from work and, putting his tools away, prepares for supper. Arany's attention to detail adds movement and drama to this still life; the father brings home from the fields a rabbit which the children immediately make their pet. As they sit down to the evening meal, a disabled veteran comes by, is welcomed as a member of the family, and yet is made to feel like an honored guest. After supper, he tells them stories of the war, and again it is through a comment here and there that the scenes are given dramatic tension. The father gently chides the young boy: The stranger's story is not fiction. The marriageable daughter asks about "her brother," yet the comment that she will wait another year before marrying gives a clue that her relationship to the lost youth is something different: It would be unseemly to question a stranger about a lover. The final lines return the scene to the calm mood of the opening ones. Night has now completely fallen; the frame is complete. The family drama portrayed here is universal, while rooted nevertheless in the Hungarian village.

Within this seemingly simple poem, one that rivals Petőfi's "Szeptember végén" ("At the End of September") as a literary masterpiece, Arany creates a little gem of realistic description in which each detail has its place and in which each seems uncontrived and follows from the preceding one as if without artifice. Arany also comments obliquely on Hungarian life in the 1850's: The veteran tells tales of the War of Independence, and the daughter's lost "brother" is a casualty of the war, dead or in hiding from the Austrians. It is interesting that this quintessentially Hungarian poem was inspired by Robert Burns's "The Cotter's Saturday Night." Thus, it provides a good example of Arany's successful assimilation of Western European influences.

The ballad, a form that in Arany's hands was to reach a height unsurpassed by anyone in world literature, interested him throughout his life. He believed that the ballad, while remaining within the lyric sphere, achieved objectivity; such a blending of lyric emotion and objective setting was not possible in any other form. In range, the ballad allowed him to explore both historical incidents and psychological tragedies and even to blend the two. He was familiar with German and Scottish ballads and borrowed judiciously from these as well as from the Hungarian ballads of Transylvania. In vocabulary and form, he explored the possibilities of the language and metrical variations. In theme, he gave his readers a feeling for their history. By portraying Hungarian history through words and actions with which his audience could easily identify, he reinforced the unity and continuity of the nation.

Arany's earlier ballads, whether on historical themes or dealing with private tragedy, are less elaborate than the later ones. "Rákocziné" ("Rákoczi's Wife") is still in the direct folk-narrative style. "Rozgonyiné" ("Rozgonyi's Wife") also turns to a historical incident, the rescue of King Sigismund from battle by Cicelle Rozgonyi, but the emphasis is on the beauty and bravery of the lady who joins her husband in battle.

The Turkish wars provided Arany with much material. In "Török Bálint," he recounts the treachery of the Turks, who lure the champion of the widowed queen of Lajos II and her infant son into Turkish territory, then imprison the Queen's protector in Constantinople. The ballad focuses on the complicated political maneuverings of Bálint Török and the treachery of the monk György. The story is told through innuendo and dialogue: how the Queen was beset by both the Habsburgs and the Turks; Török's plan seemingly to unite with the Turks to gain victory; the suggestion that the monk betrayed him when he was invited to the Turkish camp after the victory; and how—while Török was ostensibly a guest of the Turks—the Turks took the city and drove out the Queen and her infant son. Others are given honors by the Sultan—Brother György is appointed governor—but the hero is imprisoned. Through this tale, Arany not only depicts the fall of Buda, but also suggests the fateful division of the country, beset by both the Turks and the Habsburgs and forced to choose one or the other, or, as Bálint Török did, to try to play off one against the other.

"Szondi két apródja" ("Szondi's Two Pages") records the faithfulness of the pages who sing the deeds of their fallen master and refuse to leave his grave in spite of the promises and threats of the Turkish Ali. Interwoven with this song are the words of the Turkish messenger, who gradually loses his patience: All saw the battle, all recognize Szondi's heroism—but Ali will be angry if his offer is refused.

In 1857, when Emperor Francis Joseph made a visit to Hungary and let it be known that he wished the poets to celebrate this event, Arany wrote "A walesi bardok" ("The Welsh Bards"). This ballad, based on a tradition that King Edward I of England had executed five hundred bards after his conquest of Wales, was a condemnation of the Habsburg ruler. Naturally, it was not published until later (1863), when the allusion was less obvious.

The ballad shows the influence of Scottish and medieval English models, which Arany had been studying for some time. The four-line stanza is in alternating iambic tetrameter and trimeter with an *abcb* rhyme scheme. Repetition and skillful variation are used both to move the narrative along and to paint the psychological mood. The scene is set with great economy, and the action is presented through dialogue. The opening lines, describing the triumphant march of the King, are repeated with significant variations at the beginning of each new section: "Edward the King, the English king/ Strides on his fallow horse/ Let's see, he says, just what the worth/ of the Welsh domains." He inquires about rivers and land and meadows ("Did the spilt patriot blood do it good?") and the people ("Are they happy . . . like the beast driven to the yoke?"). The courtiers assure him that all is well in words that echo the King's but with an ironic twist: "The people, the God-given people/ Are so happy here, Sire/ Its huts are silent, all silent/ Like so many barren graves."

The scene thus set in the first five stanzas is developed in the next section, which begins with the same two lines but intensifies the contrast between conqueror and conquered in the last two: "Edward the King, the English king/ Strides on his fallow horse/ Around him silence where'er he goes/ And a mute domain." The silence of the land puts its stamp on the banquet Edward holds that night, for the nobles sit in silence, and when Edward calls for song and toasts to celebrate his victory, "Words are choked, sound is suspended,/ Breath is caught" as an ancient bard rises. Arany presents three songs, or rather fragments of songs, for as each bard blesses the dead or curses Edward, he is sent to the stake. In the three songs, three different ages, three different styles are presented, symbolizing the united opposition of all. Edward flees the land, however, and in this final section, Arany gives the psychological retribution for the King's crime, which is not so much his conquest of the Welsh, but his presumption that the conquered should sing his praises: "Edward the King, the English king/ Gallops on his fallow steed,/ Around him burns earth and sky/ The entire Welsh domain." He is now fleeing a land that seems to be burning, yet it is only the fires of his own executioners. Nor does he find peace at home: All noise disturbs him, and drum, fife, and music will not drown out the curses of the Welsh banquet and the martyr-song of the five hundred.

Crime or sin upsets the balance of nature: It is this idea that lies at the heart of these ballads and dominates the series Arany wrote in 1877. In the late ballads, however, the scene is transferred to private life, and the crime itself becomes the focal point; the punishment often is more severe, and the role of the supernatural as a manifestation of spiritual disorder is more important. In "Éjfeli párbaj" ("Midnight Duel"), the Knight Bende's bride has been won in an unfair fight, and he has to duel with the ghost of his slain rival on three successive nights of the wedding festivities. Arany develops the mood gradually, from carefree joy to the bride's fear and the puzzling behavior of the host that forces the guests to leave. On the third night, Bende's guards watch as he hews and slashes the air, even killing some of them, thus fulfilling the ghostly foe's prediction that he will slay in the spirit, himself being a spirit. The interplay of the real and the imagined is at the core of the drama, as indeed it is in most of these ballads. Only the guilty see the supernatural forces, for these are projections of their own guilt and thus drive them mad. In "Az ünneprontók" ("The Defilers of the Sabbath") and "Hídavatas" ("Bridge Dedication"), supernatural punishment is meted out to groups rather than to sinful individuals: Sunday revelers are forced by a demoniac bagpiper to perform a dance of death, and a procession of suicides jumps again from a newly built bridge. It is interesting to contrast the concentration and technical skill achieved here with the style of certain earlier ballads of sin and retribution: "A Hamis tanú" ("The False Witness"), "Ágnes Asszony" ("The Woman Agnes"), and "Bor Vitéz." In these earlier ballads, Arany tends to exploit the supernatural for its own sake, although in "The Woman Agnes," the protagonist's punishment takes place in her own unbalanced mind.

"Tengeri hántás" ("Corn Husking") and "Vörös Rébék" ("Red Barbara") rely on folklore and superstition to create an eerie world where human actions seem to be ruled by supernatural powers. In the first poem, the Halloween atmosphere of cornhusking and storytelling in the fields at night provides the background for a tale of illicit and tragic love. In the second, a snatch of a folk song serves as the leitmotif for a tale of infidelity and murder. "Tetemre hívas" ("Ordeal of the Bier") also has ancient beliefs at its core: A murdered youth begins to bleed in the presence of his lover, who, in a teasing mood, had given him the fatal dagger. While the narrative is relatively straightforward, the mood of intrigue and the grand medieval setting give the poem a mysterious quality. The climax, in which the girl suddenly goes mad with horror, achieves the surprising psychological realism of which the ballad form is capable.

Throughout his life, Arany sought to create a popular national epic. The Toldi trilogy had not fulfilled these expectations fully, for it lacked the necessary historical component in the person of the central figure. The theme of the original settlement of Hungary would have been appropriate, but Arany found the historical and legendary material too limited. He projected events into an earlier period, that of the Hun conquest under the leadership of Attila. Originally, he planned a trilogy that would trace the fall of Attila and the fate of his son Csaba, who, according to legend, had led the remnant of Attila's forces back to their homeland, leaving a token force of Székelys in Transylvania. Their descendants later regained this patrimony and established the modern Hungarian state. Only the first poem, *The Death of King Buda*, was completed, but Arany did leave fragments of the other parts as well as several detailed outlines.

In *The Death of King Buda*, Arany united the archaic and the modern, the naïve and the sophisticated. He used a variety of sources and elements: Greek and Western history and legend, Eastern motifs in the tales and customs of the Huns, folklore, epic dreams and prophecies, even borrowings from *The Nibelungenlied* (c. 1200). All of these elements contributed to the realism of the poem, which was reinforced by Arany's attention to psychological conflicts.

Formally and stylistically, Arany broke new poetic ground in *The Death of King Buda*. In its form, the poem presents yet another variation of the Hungarian Alexandrine: The twelve-syllable line is an accented one with a definite caesura, and while Arany maintains the hexameter, two of the accented feet in each half are significantly stronger than the third, so that the line seems shorter and closer to ballad and other meters of folk poetry. The occasional alliteration enhances the archaic quality of the verse, although the couplet rhyme is maintained. In diction, Arany again turned to popular speech and to the Hungarian literary heritage. The numerous footnotes show how consciously he used both popular expressions and archaic forms and how carefully he researched chronicle and legend for each detail—but also the sound reasons he had for departing from these sources in any respect.

Arany's late lyrics, written mostly in 1877, are characterized by introspection and a peaceful acceptance of life, particularly of his old age and its infirmities. Originally intended only for himself, they are intensely personal yet reveal the same values that inform his more public poems. Whatever their point of departure, these late poems are about his love for his homeland (particularly the scenes of his youth on the Alföld) and the changes he has experienced over the years. They capture the mood of quiet meditation in forms that are as rich as any he had used.

"A tölgyek alatt" ("Under the Oaks") is a meditative lyric in which Arany recalls happy hours spent under oak trees in his childhood as he rests under the oaks at his retreat on St. Margit Island. The poem's dominant mood is quiet and resigned, yet it gathers a variety of colors and scenes ranging from childhood games to the sunsets of old age. "Vásárban" ("At the Market") also serves as a release for the poet's homesickness for the Hungarian Plain: A wagon from this region with its load of wheat reminds him of the activities, the sights, and the sounds of the harvest, in which he, too, once participated. He also expresses the hope that after many sorrowful years, the region—and the country—will see better times. Personal comment and a concern for his country, both the "smaller one" and the larger nation, mingle naturally in these poems, as do the poet's childhood memories and the concerns of his old age.

Drawn almost reluctantly into a literary career, Arany left a legacy rich in both creative and critical works. It has been said that if Hungary were suddenly to disappear, its history and life (at least through the nineteenth century) could be reconstructed from Arany's works. In many ways, he is a *national* poet. One reason that he is not better known abroad is that, aside from the difficulty of translating his rich language, it is difficult to convey the Hungarian scenes, ideas, moods, and emotions of his verse without an overabundance of notes and commentary. Nevertheless, Arany was a poet who dealt with universal themes and general human problems. While the setting of his poetry reflects what he knew best, the ideas come from his wide reading and perceptive studies of the Western tradition. His critical works and his own practice showed how native Hungarian themes and concerns could be integrated into the body of Western literature. When he is approached from this comparative perspective, Arany can offer his wealth to the non-Hungarian reader as readily as he has been inspiring Hungarian readers for generations.

Major publications other than poetry

PLAYS: *A Szent-Iván éji alóm*, 1864 (translation); *Hamlet, dán királyfi*, 1867 (translation); *János király*, 1867 (translation); *Aristophanes vígjátékai*, 1880 (translation).

NONFICTION: *Prózai dolgozatai*, 1879; *Zrinyi és Tasso*, 1885.

MISCELLANEOUS: *Arany János hátrahagyott iratai és levelezése*, 1887-1889.

Bibliography

Jones, David Marvyn. *Five Hungarian Writers*, 1966.

Keresztúry, Dezső. *Arany János*, 1971.

Reményi Jóseph. *Hungarian Writers and Literature*, 1964.

Riedl, Frigyes. *Arany János*, 1920.

Sőtér, István. *Nemzet és haladás: Irodalmunk Világos után*, 1963.

Enikő Molnár Basa

ARCHILOCHUS

Born: Paros, Greece; c. 680 B.C.
Died: Paros (?), Greece; c. 640 B.C.

Principal collections

Archilochus composed the earliest surviving first-person poetry in Western literature, especially hortatory and *iambus*, or blame, poetry. Probably intended for oral performance among a circle of friends or, sometimes, for cultic and official occasions, the bulk of his poetry is hortatory or invective. He is also known to have produced hymns, including a "Hymn to Heracles," partially preserved, which is said to have been sung to victors at the Olympic Games. It is doubtful that Archilochus produced an edition of his poetry in the modern sense, but his work was written down either by the poet himself or by an unknown contemporary and was thus preserved. The first known text (which includes a commentary as well) was compiled by the Alexandrian scholar Aristarchus of Samothrace (c. 217-145 B.C.), who, in his canon of three Greek iambic writers, included Archilochus. Aristarchus' edition, which is lost, probably divided Archilochus' poems along traditional metrical lines, into iambic, elegiac, and lyric groupings. Archilochus' work survives in extensive fragments, mostly quotations from ancient writers, although several major papyrus and inscriptional finds in the twentieth century have greatly increased knowledge of the poet and his poetry. The most complete modern edition of Archilochus is that of Max Treu (*Archilochos*, 1959). The numerical references to Archilochus' corpus used by Treu and in this article are those of Ernst Diehl (*Anthologia Lyrica Graeca*, 3rd ed., 1940).

Other literary forms

Archilochus is remembered only for his poetry.

Achievements

Archilochus was well-known in antiquity as an innovator, especially in metrics. His metrical forms include iambic trimeter, elegiac couplets, trochaic tetrameter, epodes (poems in which a longer metrical unit is followed by a shorter one), and asynartete (verses consisting of two units having different rhythms). While he is traditionally said to have been the inventor of iambic and epodic poetry, it is possible that earlier poems in these meters failed to survive. Archilochus' technical innovations, rather, may be seen in the skilled combination of established meters in his epodes and asynartete. Archilochus writes mostly in an Ionic Greek, imbued with the language and especially the vocabulary of the epic tradition. In fact, he was frequently admired by the ancients for his successful imitation of Homer, and Homeric influence, on both theme and vocabulary, can be seen in Archilochus' surviving fragments.

The view that Archilochus is an anti-Homeric poet, at least in his rejection of epic standards and values, is increasingly questioned today. Archilochus' elegiac poems generally reflect the martial or hortatory themes found in other archaic Greek elegists, including Tyrtaeus and Theognis; elegy was not specifically associated with lament until the fifth century B.C. In general, Archilochus' poems are unbound by any rigid restriction of particular themes to particular meters. Not all his elegiacs are about war, and not all his iambics possess the invective or satirical mood to which that meter was restricted later in the Hellenistic period. Nearly all of Archilochus' poetry is written in the first person, and he has often been called the first European lyric poet. Modern scholars, however, are becoming increasingly convinced that Archilochus' invective poetry was part of an oral tradition of *iambus*, or Greek blame poetry, possibly cultic in origin and in performance and at least as old as the epic tradition, which used stock characters and the first-person persona in a conventional way. If this is true, Archilochus' "lyricism" in the modern sense of "expressing individual emotions" is much more formal and limited in scope than has heretofore been realized.

Archilochus' meters and style were imitated by later monodic Greek poets, including Alcaeus and Anacreon, but ancient admiration of Archilochus' skilled manipulation of meter was balanced by the poet's perhaps unjustified reputation for violent and abusive verse. The fifth century lyric poet Pindar himself criticized Archilochus for such violence in a *Pythian* ode. There is a suggestion that Archilochus was the butt of some later Greek comedy. Archilochus' poetry was evidently very influential on the iambics of the Hellenistic poet Callimachus, on the satirical poems of Catullus, and especially on the *Epodes* of Horace. The poet was also the subject of several pieces in the *Palatine Anthology*. Archilochus' influence on more modern poets has been limited by the fragmentary preservation of his poetry.

Biography

A general biographical sketch of Archilochus can be drawn from the extant fragments, as well as from ancient sources which were clearly dependent for information on Archilochus' poetry. Particularly informative are several third and first century B.C. inscriptions which were recently found on Archilochus' native Paros and which are usually called the *Monumentum Archilochium*. These inscriptions were mounted in a sanctuary of Archilochus, the Archilocheion, founded in the third century B.C., and are evidence of the poet's posthumous appeal to the inhabitants of his birthplace. Unfortunately, nearly all the available biographical information concerning Archilochus must be qualified by its ultimate poetic source. While Archilochus does use the first-person persona and often provides apparent autobiographical information in his poetry, there is little that can be verified by independent sources. Modern scholars tend to argue that many of Archilochus' personal statements, especially in *iambus*, are actually conventions of the genre and provide little information about the life of the poet himself.

Even the dating of Archilochus is much debated. The poet's reference to a full eclipse of the sun in poem 74 D. suggests a date of either 711 or 648 B.C. The recent discovery in Thasos of the late-seventh century tombstone of Archilochus' friend Glaucus (see, for example, poem 56 D.) makes the later period more likely for the poet's floruit. It is, therefore, probably safe to assume that Archilochus lived during the mid-seventh century B.C., perhaps from 680 to 640 B.C.

Traditionally, Archilochus is said to have been the son of Telesicles, a Parian aristocrat, and a slave woman, Enipo, but this bastard status may be a fictional poetic stance ("Enipo" may be derived from *enipe*, an epic word for "rebuke" or "invective"). It is fairly certain, however, that both Archilochus' life and his poetry reflect the history and rich Ionian tradition of Paros, the Aegean island on which he grew up. In the seventh century B.C., Paros organized a colony on the gold-rich island of Thasos, and it is probable that both Archilochus' father and the poet himself were involved in this venture. Mention of both islands occurs frequently in the surviving fragments. Archilochus' common martial themes mirror the military concerns of the Greek Archaic Age, when colonization and intense rivalry between city- and island-states led to frequent warfare. The tradition that Archilochus was a mercenary soldier may be a misinterpretation of his own poetry, but the evidence suggests that he was often called upon to fight, both for Paros and Thasos, against the Thracians, Euboeans, and Naxians. He is said to have been killed in battle by a Naxian named Corax, but this name, too (which means "crow"), may be derived from the invective tradition. The bulk of Archilochus' extant fragments do not support the antimilitaristic sentiment which some have noted in such poems as "On My Shield," but rather suggest the patriotic sentiments of an archaic Greek who knew his human weaknesses on the battlefield. Archilochus does not reject the martial world, but rather sees himself as a "soldier-poet."

The *Monumentum Archilochium* provides the mythic tale of how Archilochus as a boy met the Muses, who gave him a lyre in exchange for the cow which his father had sent him to sell. This etiology of Archilochus' poetic inspiration may have been derived from the poet's own work and is almost certainly an imitation of Hesiod's encounter with the Muses.

The best-known portion of Archilochus' poetry is concerned with his aborted engagement to Neobule, the daughter of Lycambes. According to tradition, Lycambes, said to have been an acquaintance of the poet's father, agreed to a match between Neobule and Archilochus. For unknown reasons, Lycambes later changed his mind, and Neobule married someone else. Much of Archilochus' invective poetry is directed against Lycambes and two of his daughters (the Lycambides), who are said to have hanged themselves as a result of the poet's bitter attacks. The entire Neobule story has by many scholars come to be considered spurious autobiographical material, despite the apparent confirmation of the tale suggested by a Hellenistic epitaph poem for the Lycambides. The suicide theme could be the result of the "killing-satire" tradition. In addition, the morphological relationship between Lyc-*amb*-es, i-*amb*-os, and dithyr-*amb*-os suggests to some modern scholars, including Martin West, that Lycambes and his daughters were not historical personages but rather stock characters in a traditional *iambus*, or blame poetry, possibly with some original cultic link with Dionysus and Demeter. The establishment of the Archilocheion sanctuary on Paros gives some confirmation of the poet's possible cultic connections.

Analysis

Archilochus' poetry sprang from the rich oral poetic heritage of prehistoric and archaic Greece, and especially of Ionia. It was influenced not only by the impersonal, formulaic, epic tradition ending with Homer, but also by a parallel oral tradition of more personal expression which led, beginning with Archilochus in the mid-seventh century B.C., to Greek iambic, elegiac, and lyric poetry. It is probable that the invective mood, animated dialogues, and vivid expression of personal feelings which fill Archilochus' poems were not inventions of the poet, but rather his inheritance from the iambic and elegiac traditions, which Archilochus utilized in his own distinctive, usually unorthodox, manner. Interaction between the epic and lyric traditions is particularly evident in Archilochus' poetry, in which the poet not only uses but also often semantically transforms Homeric words, epithets, and even scenes. Archilochus' poetry is filled with metaphors which are often derived from Homeric, martial sources, but which are abrupt and violent in their poetic context; the much-discussed metaphor of a woman taking a town by storm through her beauty is one example. Archilochus can also be seen to use conventional themes in unconventional ways: for example, his "On My Shield," in which he revises traditional military values; his unorthodox *propemptikon* or "bon voyage" poem (fragment 79a D.), which is really a wish for an evil voyage upon a personal enemy; and his seduction poetry, which has, at least once, in the *Cologne Epode*, an unconventional climax. His poetry also shows a fondness for animal fables in the tradition of Aesop; Archilochus uses these fables, often in unusual contexts, as brief metaphors or extended allegories. The biographical Archilochus may lie hidden behind the persona of his poetry, but the poetry itself reveals the talents of an original and unorthodox mind whose contributions to the Greek iambic and elegiac traditions are monumental. There may have been a lost "lyric" tradition before Archilochus, but through his personal, first-person poetry a distinctive form of poetic expression developed which lies at the beginning of the European lyric tradition.

Fragment 67a D. is a trochaic tetrameter example of the hortatory poem usually expressed in elegiacs and forms part of a thematic group in Archilochus' poetry on *tlesmosyne* or "endurance" (fragments 7 D., 68 D., and 58 D.). Significantly, this group is not bound to a particular meter and is composed of both elegiac and trochaic tetrameter. The exhortative theme is distinctive in 67a D. in that it is an introspective address to the poet's *thumos*, his "heart," rather than to another person (such as Glaucus in 68 D.). Address to one's own *thumos* and reflection on one's own state of mind are found in such epics as the *Odyssey* (c. 800 B.C.), but Archilochus' adaptation of this epic trope to the first-person persona reveals the ability to distance oneself from one's poetic persona, an ability which is essential to the lyric mode. In 67a D., Archilochus addresses his heart in a military or nautical context, as if his heart is under siege or at sea: "thrown into confusion" (*kukōmene*); "ward off" (*alexou*). The vocabulary is Homeric, but the context is original. The poet's advice to his heart is climaxed in lines four through six with a pair of parallel imperative phrases. The first pair, "don't in victory openly gloat" and "nor in defeat at home fall in grief," is balanced not only in sentiment but also in word order, where Greek participial references to victory (*nikōn*) and defeat (*nikētheis*) are completed in meter and in sense by the imperative forms "gloat" (*agalleo*) and "grieve" (*odureo*). In the second pair of imperative phrases, the emphasis is not so much on the contradictory imperatives "rejoice" (*chaire*) and "give sorrow" (*aschala*) or on the objects of these actions, "good fortune" (*chartoisin*) and "evils" (*kakoisin*), but on the adverbial qualification of these commands at the beginning of the last line, "at least not excessively" (*mē liēn*). This plea for moderation in the expression of emotion was a traditional archaic Greek sentiment, best known in the form of the Apollonian dictum "nothing in excess" (*mēden agan*), but Archilochus sums up this concept, in the rest of the last line, by a final imperative phrase semantically charged in a striking way: "Recognize what a rhythm of order controls human life."

Archilochus' use of *rhusmos*, an Ionic form of the Greek word *rhuthmos*, is ambiguous. The primary meaning of this word is "measure" or "order," but eventually the word developed a secondary meaning of flux or change. Both meanings of the word may be operative in the poem and result in a paradoxical reading of the human situation: the order (*rhuthmos*) of human life is the constant change (*rhuthmos*) which Archilochus exhorts his heart to accept. Fragment 67a D. thus demonstrates Archilochus' original use of Homeric vocabulary and concepts as well as the hortatory mood of Greek elegy in a distinctive meter.

"On My Shield," composed of a pair of elegiac couplets, is Archilochus' best-known piece, in which he abandons his shield in battle. The shield, "untarnished by arms," that is, "brand-new," is left beside a bush where it is picked up by an enemy Saian (a Thracian). The poet's preference for saving his own life over keeping his shield (which he says he can always replace) has usually been interpreted as an outright rejection of epic, martial standards in favor of a more personal, self-centered attitude. Even in antiquity, this poem was contrasted with the Spartan woman's command to her man to return from battle "with his shield or on it," and Archilochus was known, derogatorily, as a *rhipsaspis*, or "shield-thrower," "deserter." Several later poets, including Alcaeus, Anacreon, and Horace, imitated this poem.

It should be noted, however, that, unlike some of his later imitators, Archilochus does not actually throw away his shield but rather hides it under a bush. Archilochus' act is not a frantic gesture in the midst of headlong flight, but a calculated attempt to save his life, and, possibly, his shield. The sentiment is certainly different from the Homeric battle standard, but only in emphasis. Archilochus, whose military adventures clearly speak through these lines, is not spurning martial values, but rather placing his emphasis on the preservation of life instead of gear.

The noble value which the shield possesses in epic (for example, the importance of the shield of Achilles in the *Iliad*, c. 800 B.C.) is certainly undermined by Archilochus, who says of his shield that he can buy a "better one" (*ou kakiō*), but the underlying implication of this purchase is that Archilochus is prepared to enter battle again in the future. On the level of language, there appears to be a contrast in the poem between standard Homeric expressions and their unconventional contexts. The poet's lighthearted attitude toward the loss of his shield is reinforced in several ways. First, he uses the derogatory Homeric word *erretō* (to hell with it) in an emphatic position in reference to the shield. The epithet *amōmēton* (blameless), used for the lost shield, is also significant, for the poet's preference for a rare Homeric form of "blameless" instead of the more common epic form *amumona* is perhaps deliberately and comically unorthodox. Archilochus uses an even rarer form (*amōmon*) of this epithet in the *Cologne Epode*. Finally, the contrast between loss of shield and saving of life may be underscored by the possible phonological pun, unintelligible in translation, of *Saion* and *exesaosa*.

Archilochus also expresses personal, unconventional views in an unconventional way in fragment 112 D., which is metrically an example of his asynartetic poems, using a combination of dactylic tetrameter, ithyphallic, and iambic trimeter catalectic. Here the poet is describing not a martial experience but an emotional one, but this personal theme is expressed in a vividly Homeric vocabulary: Eros (Passion), which in archaic Greek poetry was still an emotion rather than the anthropomorphic mythological figure (Cupid) of later periods, is "coiled beneath the heart" of Archilochus. The word *elustheis* (coiled) verbally recalls the epic scenes in which Odysseus was coiled beneath the Cyclops' sheep and Priam at Achilles' feet. In the second line, "Eros pours a thick mist over the poet's eyes," the words "pour" (*echeuen*) and "mist" (*achlun*) both invoke epic passages where the mist of death pours over a dying warrior. The Homeric vocabulary thus implies a vivid metaphor for Eros, which has a deathlike grasp on the poet and which is depicted, like death, as an external rather than an internal force. Archilochus continues this unconventional use of Homeric vocabulary in the last line, where Eros "steals the tender heart from his breast." Once again epic formulas for death are applied to Eros, but the epithet "tender" (*hapalas*) may be intentionally ambiguous; a secondary meaning of the word, "weak/feeble," is perhaps implied by Archilochus as a subtle transformation of the Homeric epithet into a significant expression of the poet's helplessness in the face of violent passion.

A recent papyrus find, the *Cologne Epode*, not only has added forty precious lines to the corpus of Archilochus but also has greatly advanced knowledge of the poet's epodic and invective style. This epode, a composition of iambic trimeters, hemiepes, and iambic dimeter, is most easily accessible in English translation in the work of John Van Sickle. The papyrus, the beginning of which is lost, appears to pick up in the middle of a dialogue between a man and a woman. The conversation is being narrated by the man. Only the last four lines of the woman's speech survive. The bulk of the extant poem is devoted to the man's response, "point by point," to the woman. The general background is an attempted seduction in which the woman argues against and the man for immediate physical union. The poem climaxes in a narration of sexual activity, the precise nature of which has been greatly debated. (Full intercourse and "heavy petting" are the apparent choices of interpretation.) A similar use of dialogue within narrative is employed by Archilochus in another recent papyrus find, which is also a seduction scene. The narrative in the *Cologne Epode* demonstrates Archilochus' skilled use of a structure well suited to the tone of Ionian *iambus*, the genre of personal expression and ridicule in which the poet is here operating.

The world of Homer is not far to seek, in both the vocabulary and themes of the *Cologne Epode*. The use of the matronym "daughter of Amphimedo" is good epic diction, and the phrase "I shall obey as you order" is another obvious example of Homeric phraseology. Thematically, the epode is a close iambic adaption of Hera's seduction of Zeus in the *Iliad*, book 14. The revelation in line 16 of the epode that Archilochus is probably talking to Neobule's sister makes the issue of autobiographical experience particularly pressing, but comparison of the epode to book 14 suggests that it is not so much the narration of a spontaneous and emotional event as it is an artistic, stylized variation of a Homeric seduction. The *Cologne Epode*, perhaps more than any other extant Archilochean fragment, suggests the presence of an artificial rather than an authentic first-person persona.

Formality is especially evident in the depiction of the female in a bucolic setting and the contrasting use of images from several archaic Greek professions and activities in an erotic context. While Archilochus' adaptation of the bucolic setting from Homer is evidenced by the fact that both poems accompany sexual union with wildly blooming flowers, Archilochus has integrated this association of the female with the fertility of nature in a more basic way, into the very fiber of his vocabulary and imagery. The woman herself is described as "beautiful and tender" (*kalē tereina*), while her sister Neobule feels the brunt of Archilochus' invective in her description as a withered flower (*anthos d' aperruēke*). The final stage of this natural process is represented by the woman's late mother, Amphimedo, "who now is covered by the mouldering earth."

The concept and vocabulary, originally Homeric, is manipulated by Archilochus here into an unorthodox and subtle metaphor arguing in favor of the masculine demand of immediate sexual gratification. At the same time, the narrator disguises his eroticism behind references to various professions: rhetoric ("answering point by point"); architecture ("the coping stone" and "architrave"); navigation or horse racing ("I'll hold my course"); war ("reconnoitering"); wrestling ("seizing her"); and animal husbandry ("hasty bitch, blind pups"). The last reference, to an old Greek proverb, also underscores Archilochus' fondness for the use of animal fables as exempla. The proverb, arguing against hasty action, is a subtle ploy on the part of the narrator to disguise his own ambitions.

The fragments of Archilochus' work thus reveal a dynamic poetry which creates, from the vocabulary and themes of the oral epic and iambic traditions, the impression of a personal voice upon which modern lyric poetry is ultimately based. It is especially through his unconventional use of standard words and concepts that Archilochus' style develops its forceful and unexpected turns of thought and expression. Although critical discussion of Archilochus' life and poetry may never be free from the controversies occasioned by the lack of primary evidence, enough of his work survives to show his original contributions to the European poetic tradition, especially in the areas of metrical experimentation, iambic or invective poetry, and lyric or first-person expression.

Bibliography
Campbell, David A. *Greek Lyric Poetry*, 1967.
Diehl, Ernst. *Anthologia Lyrica Graeca*, 1922-1925, 1940.
Kirkwood, G. M. *Early Greek Monody*, 1974.
Van Sickle, John. "Archilochus: A New Fragment of an Epode," in *Classical Journal*. LXXI (1975), pp. 1-15.
_____ , ed. *The New Archilochus*, in *Arethusa*. IX (1976). Special Archilochus issue.
West, Martin. *Studies in Greek Elegy and Iambus*, 1974.

Thomas J. Sienkewicz

LUDOVICO ARIOSTO

Born: Reggio Emilia, Italy; September 8, 1474
Died: Ferrara, Italy; July 6, 1533

Principal poem and collections

Orlando furioso, 1516, 1521, 1532 (English translation, 1591); *Satire*, 1534 (written in 1517-1525; *Ariosto's Satyres*, 1608); *Cinque canti*, 1545.

Other literary forms

Ludovico Ariosto was an influential verse dramatist of his time, following the form of the Latin comedies of Plautus and Terence and rigorously adhering to the unities of time and place, though setting the plays in Ferrara and using the society of that city for his plots. His plays include *La cassaria* (1508; *The Coffer*), *I suppositi* (1509; *Supposes*, 1566), *Il negromante* (1520; *The Necromancer*), and *La Lena* (1529; *Lena*). His final play, "I studenti," written in 1533, was completed posthumously by his brother Gabriele and retitled *La scolastica* (1547; *The Students*).

Achievements

Ariosto was one of the greatest Italian poets, his supreme achievement being the long poem *Orlando furioso*. Many writers and thinkers of the Renaissance regarded *Orlando furioso* as one of the greatest works ever composed, and its influence lasted well into the Romantic period, though it is little read today. Although Ariosto's patrons, the Este family, did not fully recognize the importance of the poet who was under their care, Ariosto's epic poem established a proud, if fictitious, line of descent for the Estensi, pleased the court at Ferrara, and spread Ariosto's name across Europe; even bandits were said to hold him in awe. *Orlando furioso* captured the essence of Renaissance thought in its dynamic combination of classical form, fantasy, chivalry, medieval romance, irony, morality, and style. Fiercely independent as an artist, Ariosto obsessively wrote and rewrote his epic until it became, along with the works of Michelangelo, Leonardo da Vinci, and Raphael, one of the supreme artistic expressions of the Italian Renaissance.

Biography

Ludovico Ariosto was the son of Niccolo Ariosto, captain of the guard of Reggio Emilia, and vassal of the Duke of Ferrara. Niccolo was a stern father and a harsh ruler who was hated by the people of Reggio Emilia. In 1484, he moved to Ferrara with his ten children and set Ariosto to the study of law, despite the boy's inclination toward poetry. Ariosto resisted and was eventually permitted to study literature with Gregorio de Spoleto, until 1499, when Gregorio left for France as the tutor of Francesco Sforza. Ariosto was fluent in Latin (Horace became his favorite poet, exerting a significant influence on his later poetic forms and style), but, as a result of Gregorio's departure and subsequent events, he never learned Greek, a failure which he regretted for the rest of his life. His first poetry was in Latin and earned the praise of Pietro Bembo, who urged him to continue writing in Latin. Ariosto, however, with his taste for simple things, preferred the vernacular and soon wrote only in Italian.

In 1500, Ariosto's father died and the young man was forced to take up the management of his mother's dowry and put aside his studies in order to care for his four brothers and five sisters. His dream of a simple life filled with Humanistic studies was shattered; he found himself preoccupied with the banal tasks of finding positions for his younger brothers and administering the estate, an experience on which he would comment bitterly in his *Satire*. In 1502, he wrote a long Latin poem in honor of the marriage of Alfonso d'Este to Lucrezia Borgia and was rewarded with a captaincy in Reggio. He worked his way up to gentleman-in-waiting to Cardinal Ippolito d'Este, the brother of Duke Alfonso, and was sent on various diplomatic missions for the Este family. In 1509, for example, he went to Rome to seek the aid of Pope Julius II against Venice. On two other occasions, he visited the Pope, trying to tighten the relationship between Julius and the Estensi, who were allied by marriage to Louis XII of France. Julius, however, became instrumental in driving the French from Italy with the League of Cambrai. Indeed, Ariosto irritated Julius so much that the Pope threatened to have him tossed into the Tiber; he was forced to flee over the Apennines with Duke Alfonso in order to escape the consequences of Julius' fury.

In 1513, Ariosto visited the new Pope, Leo X, who had been his friend as a cardinal, expecting the Pope to become his patron. Leo, however, was a Medici (son of Lorenzo de' Medici), and that family hated the Estensi, so Ariosto went home empty-handed. In the same year, on his way home from a diplomatic mission in Florence, he began a long romantic attachment to Alessandra Benucci. He had carried on a number of previous romances, several leading to the birth of illegitimate children. One son, Virginio, born in 1509 to Orsolina Catinelli, became Ariosto's favorite and resided with Ariosto until the old man's death, even after Ariosto married Alessandra.

In 1516, Ariosto completed his first version of *Orlando furioso* and dedicated it to his unappreciative patron, Ippolito. (The Cardinal coarsely asked Ariosto where he had come up with all that foolishness.) Ariosto was thoroughly disillusioned with his patron, who, he suspected, gave him his pension to compensate the poet only for his life-threatening duties as a diplomatic messenger and not at all for his poetry. Furthermore, Ariosto was irregularly paid. A year later, when Ippolito was appointed Bishop of Budapest, Ariosto pleaded ill health, the poor health of his mother, and the desire to continue with his studies, and refused to accompany Ippolito to Hungary. The poet was not disappointed when the angry Cardinal released him from his service and even denied him an interview. Ariosto proudly said that if the Cardinal had imagined he was buying a slave for a miserable seventy-five crowns a year, he was mistaken and could withdraw the pension.

Ariosto entered the service of Duke Alfonso and became Governor of Garfagnana, a wild area between the provinces of Modena and Lucca, and claimed by the Luchesi, Pisans, and Florentines. It had surrendered to the Estensi, however, and though given only halfhearted support by the Duke, Ariosto proved himself a capable, honest, and diligent administrator. His letters to the Duke from his headquarters in Castelnuovo show that, despite his feeling of being in exile, he was a wise ruler in meting out justice, exacting tribute, and controlling the bandits. He was constantly called upon to settle squabbles, feuds, and complaints and to coax one faction to make peace with another. There is a story of his having been captured by bandits and taken to their chieftain. When the bandit leader discovered that he was addressing the author of *Orlando furioso*, he humbly apologized for his men's failure to show Ariosto the respect which he deserved, a respect not shown even by his patrons. Ariosto did his best in extraordinarily difficult circumstances and was delighted when, after three years, he was allowed to return to Ferrara. One critic has observed that sending the gentle Ariosto to Garfagnana could be compared to Queen Victoria sending Tennyson to subdue a rebellion in Afghanistan; such were the absurdities of the patronage system.

Seeking a tranquil existence, Ariosto bought a vineyard in the Mirasole district with money he had set aside. He had always been frugal, and he built a small, simple house with a Latin motto on the facade: "Parva sed apta mihi, sed nulli obnoxia, sed non/ Sordida, parta meo sed tamen aere domus" ("A little house, but enough for me; to none unfriendly, not unclean, and bought with my own money"). Living with his son Virginio and his lame brother Gabriele, he was married to Alessandra Benucci (secretly, so that he could still collect his ecclesiastical income) and spent his time gardening, reading the Latin classics, writing comedies, and superintending their performance and the construction of a theater. He also made his third revision of *Orlando furioso*, increasing the number of cantos from forty to forty-six. When this task was completed, he traveled to Mantua to present a copy to Emperor Charles V, to whom the Estensi had become allied after abandoning the French. Charles appreciated the arts; allegedly, he once stooped to pick up Titian's brush, and there was a rumor that he intended to crown Ariosto in a special ceremony. This never came about, however, and the poet died of tuberculosis a year after his trip to Mantua. He was buried in the church of San Benedetto, though his remains were later transferred to the Biblioteca Comunale of Ferrara.

The posthumous success of Ariosto's great epic was extraordinary. It went through 180 editions in the sixteenth century, often in expensive illustrated formats. It was translated into all the languages of Europe and imitated in all of them.

Analysis

About 1494, Ludovico Ariosto began writing poetry, and, for about ten years, he wrote almost exclusively in Latin, primarily using the poetic forms of Catullus and Horace but influenced by many classical poets as well, including Albius Tibullus and Sextus Propertius. Although his verse in Latin is not equal in technical skill to that of Giovanni Pontano or Pietro Bembo, it has distinctive qualities, particularly its sincerity, which caused Bembo to urge Ariosto to continue writing in Latin. Ariosto's first published Latin ode, of 1494, is an Alcaic (the form most frequently employed by Horace), "Ad Philiroen" ("To Philiroe"). Written just as Charles VIII of France was about to invade Italy, it extols the blessings of peace and love. Catastrophe threatens, but it is good to lie under the trees gazing at Philiroe and listening to the murmur of a waterfall. Critic Francesco De Sanctis observes that Ariosto, in his Latin verse, thinks, feels, and writes like Horace. Political upheavals are not worth worrying about as long as one can wander in the fields in pursuit of Lydia, Lycoris, Phyllis, Glaura, or any other woman given a Latin pseudonym.

In these lyrics, such as "De puella," "De Lydia," "De Iulia," "De Glycere et Lycori," "De Megilla," and "De catella puellae," one immediately perceives the personality of Ariosto and the general aspiration of artists in the Renaissance to transcend ordinary events for the higher realms of art. Despite his diplomatic career, Ariosto always preferred a simple existence in unpretentious surroundings, but not until late in his life was he able to settle in his little house near Ferrara, where he could spend his time on poetry and gardening. His preference for this type of life is apparent even in his earliest works. He found no satisfaction in the complexities of court and politics, and attempted to achieve classical serenity in the pleasures of nature, love, and poetic form. It hardly mattered to him whether Italy was tyrannized by a French king or an Italian one: Slavery is slavery.

Despite Bembo's advice, Ariosto preferred to write in the vernacular, though his lyrics in Italian are a great deal less sensuous than are their Latin counterparts. Heavily influenced by Petrarch, the passions become Platonic, and the physicality of kisses and embraces is replaced by worshipful comparisons of the love object with divinity and the sun. Most of these poems are respectable, but workmanlike, imitations of Petrarch and are far from Ariosto's greatest work. The poet himself showed a great deal of indifference to the scattering of lyric poems he wrote throughout his life, never collecting and publishing them. He wrote in a number of forms: elegies, sonnets, canzones, madrigals, *capitoli,* and one eclogue. In the case of many poems ascribed to Ariosto, there are serious questions of authenticity. His most famous lyric poem is the sonnet "Non so s'io potro ben chiudere in rima" (I know not if I can ever close in rhyme), which touches on his falling in love with Alessandra in Florence on St. John's Day as the accession of Leo X was being celebrated.

Between 1517 and 1525, Ariosto wrote seven verse epistles in tercets, modeled after Horace's *Sermones* (35 B.C.). Published posthumously, as *Satire*, because of the real people and situations mentioned in them, these poems reveal much of what is known of Ariosto's personality. Written to friends and relatives such as Bembo and Ariosto's brothers Alessandro and Galazio, the satires are autobiographical and use his personal experiences and observations to make larger moral generalizations. The writer's need for independence is expressed, corruption in the Church and court is exposed, and the dangers of ambition are shown in an Aesop-like fable of a pumpkin that climbs a pear tree. Other poems express Ariosto's regrets at not having completed his education, his views on marriage, his love for the simple life, and his unhappiness at being separated from his family by his patrons' business.

Frequently witty, the satires lack the aristocratic sophistication of Horace and often seem rambling and coarse. Instead of offering incisive observations on human weakness and foolishness, Ariosto often seems to be using the satires as a device to release his pent-up frustrations with a world that will not leave him alone. Nevertheless, the satires do tell a reader much about the atmosphere of the Italian Renaissance, especially the obsessive scrambling for power among noble families.

Were it not for his great epic poem *Orlando furioso*, Ariosto would be regarded as no more than a minor poet whose lyrics influenced the French Pléiade and whose Roman-style comedies made a mark on Renaissance English drama through George Gascoigne, who adapted *Supposes* for the British stage, and William Shakespeare, who used part of it for the subplot of *The Taming of the Shrew* (c. 1594). *Orlando furioso*, however, is one of the great works of the Renaissance, dwarfing the numerous romances of other writers of that period. It served as a model for Cervantes' *Don Quixote* (1605, 1615) and Edmund Spenser's *The Faerie Queene* (1590, 1596). It influenced Bernardo Tasso's *Amadigi* (1560) and Torquato Tasso's *Gerusalemme liberata* (1581; *Jerusalem Delivered*, 1594, 1600). Robert Greene wrote a play entitled *The History of Orlando Furioso* (1594), and Shakespeare's *Much Ado About Nothing* (c. 1598) derives from an episode in Ariosto's epic. John Milton made some use of the poem, and *Orlando furioso* left its mark on the Romantic period as well, particularly on the poetry of Lord Byron. Sir Walter Scott faithfully read through *Orlando furioso* every year and relished the epithet bestowed upon him by Byron, who called him "the Ariosto of the north." Though not widely read in the twentieth century, *Orlando furioso* is nevertheless considered one of the masterpieces of the Italian Renaissance.

Ariosto's great poem began with his desire to complete the *Orlando innamorato* (1483, 1495; Roland in love) of the "Homer of Ferrara," Matteo

Maria Boiardo. The Orlando of Boiardo's poem is descended from the hero of the Carolingian epic *Chanson de Roland* (eleventh century). Boiardo merged the traditions of the Arthurian romance with those of the Carolingian, and in his hands Orlando becomes much more than a warrior battling Saracens. The love theme of Arthurian romance assumes a dominant role, as the title reveals. The epic is complex, with supernatural events, subplots, battles with infidels and dragons, strange people and islands, fairies, giants, and the rescues of fair maidens. In the latter part of the poem, Boiardo intended to have the Saracen knight Ruggiero convert and marry Bradamante and to make them the ancestors of the Este family. Boiardo, however, died in the same year the French invaded Italy, and his Ruggiero remains Moslem and unmarried.

In 1506, Ariosto began *Orlando furioso* to complete Boiardo's epic, and over a lifetime of writing and revising, he proved himself the best Italian poet of the genre. As his predecessor had integrated the Carolingian and Arthurian traditions, so Ariosto added to them the classical tradition. Many critics have commented that the title of Ariosto's epic echoes Seneca's *Hercules furens* (first century A.D.). Ariosto's opening words, "I sing of knights and ladies, of love and arms, of courtly chivalry, of courageous deeds . . . ," are very close to the opening words of Vergil's *Aeneid* (29-19 B.C.): "Of the arms and the man I sing." In fulfilling Boiardo's intention to establish an illustrious lineage for the Estensi, Ariosto was also paralleling Vergil's attempt to establish a great ancestry for Augustus Caesar. The following line, "I shall tell of the anger, the fiery rage of young Agramante their king . . . ," is reminiscent of the opening of Homer's *Iliad* and the "wrath of Achilles." Critics have also noted the influence of Ovid, Lucan, and Statius on Ariosto's epic.

To summarize the story line of *Orlando furioso* would take many pages. The poem is longer than the *Iliad* (c. 800 B.C.) and the *Odyssey* (c. 800 B.C.) combined, and simply cataloging its characters is a major task. Some critics have therefore asserted that the poem is episodic and lacks unity. Most, however, point to the story of Ruggiero and Bradamante as the central plot around which the themes revolve, although many episodes seem to have no explicit connection with the conflicts between duty and love which constantly interfere with their relationship. Bradamante refuses to marry Ruggiero unless he converts to Christianity, and Ruggiero hesitates to do so while his lord Agramante is in danger. Later, Ruggiero becomes the friend of Leo, the man Bradamante's father had chosen to be her husband, and, out of loyalty, agrees to fight Bradamante in disguise, as Charlemagne has proclaimed that only he who defeats Bradamante in combat may marry her. Leo, however, asks Charlemagne to give his rights over her to Ruggiero (yet another act of selfless friendship and chivalry). As Ruggiero and Bradamante are being married, however, Rodomonte, a Moslem African king, calls Ruggiero an apostate, and they fight a duel. The poem ends with Rodomonte's condemned soul, in typical Renaissance style, blaspheming on its way to Hell.

Besides recounting the difficulties which Ruggiero and Bradamante must overcome in order to establish the Este line, *Orlando furioso* tells the story of Orlando, driven to madness by his love for Angelica, daughter of the Emperor of Cathay, who has been sent to destroy the court of Charlemagne. Despite the title of the poem, his story seems secondary to that of Ruggiero. After Angelica flees Paris, Orlando searches the world for her, like a knight of the Round Table in quest of the Holy Grail, encountering various adventures along the way but always one step behind her. He rescues a woman from being sacrificed to a monster, for example, just after Ruggiero has lifted Angelica off the same island by means of the hippogriff, a flying horse.

Midway through the epic, Orlando goes mad—God's punishment for abandoning the Christian armies—and rampages naked across France. He stumbles across Angelica as she is about to set sail, but because of his state, they do not recognize each other, and Angelica sails out of the poem. Orlando swims across the Strait of Gibraltar to Africa and does not recover his senses until another madman, Astolfo, travels with St. John in Elijah's chariot of fire to the Moon, where all the things mankind has lost are collected. Astolfo recovers his own senses and puts Orlando's in a jar, so that he can transport them to Orlando. Restored, the knight devotes himself to the Christian cause and kills Agramante and several others in battles at Bizerta and Lipadusa.

This brief outline of the action of *Orlando furioso* can give only a partial idea of the epic's complexity. The range of Ariosto's imagination is enormous, and that the poem manages to maintain any coherence at all, considering its myriad characters and supernatural intrusions, is testimony to Ariosto's genius. Besides being unified by its major plots, the poem is unified by its warning to Christendom that its internecine troubles can only increase the Islamic threat. The Turkish advance into Europe was stopped only in 1529, four years before Ariosto's death, when the siege of Vienna was abandoned. The poet did not live to see the Battle of Lepanto in 1571, which ended the Ottoman threat to Europe, and throughout his life, the Turks seemed to be growing in power, while Christians squabbled among themselves.

Many critics argue that *Orlando furioso* is unified primarily by its style and tone rather than by its plot. With fantastic episodes occurring in every canto, Ariosto sustains the suspension of disbelief by deft use of details, imbuing scenes with the texture of familiar reality. He avoids the bombast and overt rhetorical flourishes that damage the style of so many epic poems of the period.

As De Sanctis points out, there are many tales concerning Ariosto's absent-mindedness while composing the epic. It is said, for example, that he once walked halfway to Modena before remembering that he was still in his slippers. Few works of art in any age have been created with the intensity that Ariosto brought to *Orlando furioso*. As his satires prove, Ariosto took the role of the artist very seriously. Art was his faith; religion, morality, and patriotism were secondary. Ariosto's incessant reworking of the poem shows his artistic obsession with finding the ideal form for his creation. Just as Dante had captured the essence of the end of the Middle Ages, so Ariosto synthesized the essence of the Renaissance, merging classical form with medieval romance and balancing the ironic detachment of a poetic craftsman with an earthy sense of reality.

Major publications other than poetry
PLAYS: *La cassaria*, 1508 (*The Coffer*); *I suppositi*, 1509 (*Supposes*, 1566); *Il negromante*, 1520 (*The Necromancer*); *La Lena*, 1529 (*Lena*); *La scolastica*, 1547 (*The Students*); *The Comedies of Ariosto*, 1975 (includes all Ariosto's plays).

Bibliography
Brand, Charles. *Ludovico Ariosto*, 1974.
Croce, Benedetto. *Ariosto, Shakespeare, e Corneille*, 1920.
De Sanctis, Francesco. *History of Italian Literature*, 1968.
Donadonio, Eugenio. *A History of Italian Literature*, 1969.
Fletcher, Jefferson Butler. *Literature of the Italian Renaissance*, 1934.
Gardner, E. G. *The King of Court Poets*, 1906.
Griffin, Robert. *Ludovico Ariosto*, 1974.
Symonds, John Addington. *Renaissance in Italy*, 1881.
Wilkins, Ernest Hatch. *A History of Italian Literature*, 1954.

J. Madison Davis

HANS ARP
Jean Arp

Born: Strasbourg, France; September 16, 1887
Died: Basel, Switzerland; June 7, 1966

Principal collections

Die Wolkenpumpe, 1920; *Der Pyramidenrock*, 1924; *Weisst du schwarzt du*, 1930; *Des taches dans le vide*, 1937; *Sciure de gamme*, 1938; *Muscheln und Schirme*, 1939; *Rire de coquille*, 1944; *Le Siège de l'air*, 1946 (as Jean Arp); *Beharte Herzen, Könige vor der Sintflut*, 1953; *Wortraüme und schwarze Sterne*, 1953; *Auf einem Bein*, 1955; *Unsern täglichen Traum*, 1955; *Le Voilier dans la forêt*, 1957 (as Jean Arp); *Worte mit und ohne Anker*, 1957; *Mondsand*, 1959; *Vers le blanc infini*, 1960 (as Jean Arp); *Sinnende Flammen*, 1961; *Gedichte, 1903-1939*, 1963; *Logbuch des Traumkapitäns*, 1965; *L'Ange et la rose*, 1965 (as Jean Arp); *Le Soleil recerclé*, 1966 (as Jean Arp); *Jours effeuillés*, 1966 (as Jean Arp); *Arp on Arp*, 1972 (poetry and prose); *Gedichte, 1939-1957*, 1974; *Three Painter Poets*, 1974.

Other literary forms

Hans Arp, in addition to his large body of poetry, also wrote a substantial number of lyrical and polemical essays, in which the metaphysical basis of his thought is given its clearest and most systematic expression. These essays are collected in *On My Way* (1948) and *Dreams and Projects* (1952). Arp also wrote about his fellow artists in *Onze peintres vus par Arp* (1949), a collection that helps to clarify the aesthetic values that influenced his own work as a ґlastic artist. Arp also published two works of fiction: *Le Blanc aux pieds de nègre* (1945), a collection of short stories, and *Tres inmensas novelas* (1935), short novels written in collaboration with the Chilean poet Vicente Huidobro.

Achievements

Hans Arp actually has two reputations: one as a plastic artist of long-standing international fame; the other, much less established, and of more recent origin, as a poet. It is only in recent years that Arp has been recognized as an important and original contributor to the twentieth century literary avant-garde, yet his reputation has continued to grow since the collected editions of his poetry in French and German began to appear in the 1960's.

As a literary artist, Arp is best known for his association with Dada and Surrealism. Together with Tristan Tzara, Hugo Ball, Richard Hülsenbeck, Marcel Janco, and Emmy Hennings, Arp was one of the earliest and most enthusiastic supporters of the Dada movement that began in Zurich in February of 1916.

Dada's principal target was man's overestimation of reason. Its aim, Arp said, was "to destroy the reasonable deceptions of man," to expose "the fragility of life and human works" through the use of Dadaist humor, which would reveal "the natural and unreasonable order" of things. The poems of Arp's first collection, *Die Wolkenpumpe* (the cloud pump), date from this period, as does "Kaspar ist Tot" ("Kaspar Is Dead"), perhaps the most famous of all Dada poems. The Dada use of humor to reorient modern man's attitude toward the world was followed by Arp in these poems, where he began to develop his decidedly personal "Arpian humor."

Dada's critique of modern man, however, was not entirely destructive, despite the commonly held belief that it was a totally negative response to the world. Arp's own work is one of the best testaments to this fact. In order to rectify modern man's mistaken view of his place in the universe, Arp offered the notion of a "concrete art" that could transform both man and the world. His intention was "to save man from the most dangerous of follies: vanity . . . to simplify the life of man . . . to identify him with nature."

It was through his participation in the Dada group that Arp became acquainted with the Paris Surrealists, and after he and his wife moved to the Paris suburb of Meudon in 1926, Arp frequently participated in Surrealist activities and contributed to their publications.

Biography

Hans Arp, also known as Jean Arp, was born in Strasbourg on September 16, 1887. At the time of his birth, Alsace-Lorraine, the region in which Strasbourg lies, belonged to Germany, although culturally it was tied to France, to which it presently belongs. Arp's bilingualism, his equal ease with both French and German, which was a product of the history of this region, helps to account for the confusion concerning his Christian name. As Arp explained it, when he wrote in French, he called himself Jean Arp; when he wrote in German, he called himself Hans Arp. In his view, neither name was a pseudonym—the change was made simply for convenience, as one shifts from speaking one language to the other according to the language of the auditor.

This mingled French and German heritage was also reflected in Arp's home and social environment. His father, Pierre Guillaume Arp, who operated a cigar and cigarette factory in Strasbourg, was of Danish descent. His mother, Josephine Köberlé Arp, was of French descent. At home, Arp recalled, French was spoken. In the state-operated primary and secondary schools he attended, however, standard High German was used, and taught, the Alsace-Lorraine being at the time under German annexation. With his friends he spoke the Alsatian vernacular, a dialect of different derivation from the standard German used in education and for official business.

Arp's first published poem appeared in 1902, when he was only fifteen. Like most of his earliest poetry, it was written in the Alsatian dialect, although only two years later he had completed, in standard High German, a manuscript volume of poems. This manuscript, entitled "Logbuch," was unfortunately mislaid by the publisher to whom it was sent. Three poems by Arp in German did appear the same year, however, in *Das Neue Magazin*.

About 1904, Arp's involvement with the plastic arts began in earnest. He visited Paris for the first time, and for the next five years he studied art not only at Strasbourg, but also in Weimar and Paris. In 1909, Arp, having served his artistic apprenticeship at various academies, moved with his family to Weggis, on the eastern shore of Lake Lucerne in Switzerland. In the five years Arp spent at Weggis, two important developments occured. Isolated from the influences of the academies and their avant-garde faddishness, Arp began to develop the personal aesthetic he called "concrete art," which was to influence the entire course of his career. In addition, he became acquainted with other artists who, like himself, were also pursuing personal aesthetics independent of the Paris academies. During this period, Arp exhibited his work with some of these artists, including Wassily Kandinsky and Paul Klee.

In 1914, Arp returned to Paris only to discover that war had been declared. Because his German money was suddenly valueless in France, and his German citizenship unwelcome, he promptly returned to neutral Zurich, and in order to avoid the draft, persuaded the authorities at the German consulate that he was mentally ill. In Zurich, Arp exhibited the abstract collages and tapestries which are the earliest examples of his work extant. In November of 1915, at an exhibition of his work with his friend and fellow artist Otto Van Rees, he met his future wife, Sophie Taeuber, an artist who was a native of Zurich.

In 1916, Arp and Taeuber participated in the activities of the newly formed Dada group which met regularly at the Cabaret Voltaire. At this time, Arp produced bas-relief sculptures and woodcuts reflecting the developing aesthetic that he termed "concrete art." Unlike the earlier geometric productions of his abstract period, these reliefs and woodcuts were composed of asymmetrical curvilinear and bimorphic forms; they were, as Arp later explained, "direct creations," truly "concrete" art, not abstract representations of already existing forms. In 1921, Arp married Sophie, and together they collaborated on cut-paper collages and other plastic works. Arp also returned to writing poetry, producing a great number of poems in German which were collected in *Die Wolkenpumpe*, *Der Pyramidenrock*, and *Weisst du schwarzt du*.

After the demise of Dada in 1924, Arp formed an increasingly close association with the Surrealist movement, and in 1926, he settled permanently in the Paris suburb of Meudon. Arp's first poem written directly in French was published in 1933, in the Surrealists' journal *Le Surréalisme au service de la révolution*, and his first collection of poems in French, *Des taches dans le vide* (splotches in space), appeared in 1937. At this time, Arp also began to create the free-form sculptures that he called "concretions," and that were to bring him international acclaim as a sculptor. He also began to experiment with a new type of "torn-paper" collage; his comments on these collages have often been linked to the Surrealist technique of "automatic writing." From this time on, Arp published poetry in both French and German, often translating originals from one language into the other, and in the process frequently introducing substantial changes.

In 1940, with the outbreak of World War II, the Arps fled south from Paris to Grasse to escape the German occupation, later managing to reach Zurich, in neutral Switzerland, in 1942. It was there that Sophie met with an accidental death on January 13, 1943, sending Arp into a deep depression that lingered for many years. Some of his most moving poems are beautiful evocations of Sophie's transforming influence upon his life.

After the war, Arp's growing fame as an important modern sculptor, as well as the increasing demand for exhibitions of his plastic works, allowed him to travel widely. During this period, he visited the United States, Mexico, Italy, Greece, Jordan, Israel, and Egypt.

In 1959, Arp married Marguerite Hagenbach, who had been a friend of Sophie in Zurich and had long admired Arp's work. In the remaining seven years of his life, Arp and Marguerite spent part of the year at their home in Meudon, and the remainder at a second home near Locarno, in southern Switzerland. On June 7, 1966, Arp died at the age of seventy-eight, while away from home, in Basel.

Analysis

Two important characteristics of Hans Arp's poetry distinguish it from the work of other Dada and Surrealist poets: his highly personal humor, and the metaphysical philosophy that underlies all his mature work.

Arp's humor achieves its effect by combining opposites: the celestial with the terrestrial, the eternal with the transitory, the sublime with the mundane among others. That which comes from above—the celestial, the eternal, the sublime—sustains and nourishes man, while that which comes from below—the terrestrial, the transitory, the mundane—confuses and intoxicates him. Thus, Arp's conception of humor is connected with his metaphysical philosophy, which aims to restore the lost balance of forces in man. Arp uses humor in his work to destroy "the reasonable deceptions of man," which lead him to believe that he is "the summit of creation."

In Arp's view then, humor and metaphysics are not mutually exclusive, and elements of both are often present in a single work. A good example of this is the early poem "Kaspar Is Dead." The poem is written in the form of an elegy, and begins, as is customary in the genre, with a lament for the dead. The poem then proceeds to describe the remarkable accomplishments of the deceased, which seem superhuman in character: "who will conceal the burning banner in the cloud's pigtail now . . . who will entice the idyllic deer out of the petrified bag . . . who will blow the noses of ships umbrellas beekeepers ozone-spindles and bone the pyramids." It seems as if some golden age has passed: the link between man and nature has been broken by the death of Kaspar. At this realization, the speaker resumes his lament, but this time it seems even more self-conscious, and it includes a note of facetiousness: "alas alas alas our good kaspar is dead. goodness gracious me kaspar is dead." In the second half of the poem, the speaker turns to more generalized metaphysical speculation: "into what shape has your great wonderful soul migrated. are you a star now or a chain of water . . . or an udder of black light?" He despairs once again at the realization that, wherever he is and in whatever form, Kaspar can no longer reestablish for man the broken link between himself and nature. He has ceased to be human, and has thus been liberated from the tragic condition of temporal consciousness that the speaker still suffers. The speaker concludes with resignation that it is man himself who is obligated to reestablish a proper relationship with nature; he cannot rely on anyone or anything else to do this for him, even such a heroic figure as Kaspar.

One of Arp's most successful attacks on the reasonable deceptions of man is a poem of his early maturity entitled in German as "Ich bin ein Pferd," in French as "Je suis un cheval," and translated into English as "I Am a Horse." It is not man himself that is under attack but his vain rationality. The speaker of the poem is a reasoning horse, who resembles Jonathan Swift's Houyhnhnms. Investing a subhuman creature with the proud vanity of rational man creates an ironic situation reminiscent of the fable, in which talking animals are used to satirize particular forms of human folly. In this poem, however, it is the human beings who behave instinctively, emotionally, and impulsively—much to the disgust of the dignified horse, who observes the action from a detached perspective.

As the poem begins, the equine speaker is riding in a crowded passenger train, and "every seat is occupied by a lady with a man on her lap"—a most unpleasant sight to the snobbish, socially respectable horse. In addition to being crowded, the compartment is unbearably hot, and all the human passengers "eat nonstop." When the men suddenly begin to whine, unbuttoning the women's bodices and clutching their breasts, wanting to be suckled, the horse alone resists this primitive, uncivilized impulse, maintaining his proud composure. Yet at the end of the poem, the detachment of the speaker, his feeling of superiority relative to the weak-willed humans with whom he shares the compartment, is revealed as a mere pose which disguises the same basic impulses behind the mask of rationality, for when he neighs loudly, "hnnnnn," he thinks proudly of "the six buttons of sex appeal" on his chest—"nicely aligned like the shiny buttons of a uniform." Through the agency of a reasoning horse, Arp presents a Dadaist fable which exposes the foolish vanity and isolation that has resulted from man's overestimation of his greatest creation—reason.

Arp's work consists of more than attacks on the reasonable deceptions of man and satires of his vain pride. Arp devoted a substantial portion of his mature work to communicating, in poetic images and symbols, his distinctive metaphysical philosophy, which has been called variously Platonic, Neoplatonic, Romantic, and Idealist. Arp's worldview eludes these categories; it is personal and intuitive in character, not critical and systematic.

When Arp spoke about the formation of his worldview, he associated it with two particular experiences. The first was the period of isolation he spent at Weggis, which gave him the opportunity to cast aside the aesthetic of abstraction and formulate his theory of "concrete art." The second experience was his meeting Sophie Taeuber, whose work and life expressed in an intuitive way, free from self-consciousness, the reorientation of human values that Arp had been seeking.

Arp's metaphysical beliefs, transformed into poetic images and symbols, appeared with increasing frequency in his poetry in the years following Sophie's death. One of the best of these metaphysical poems is "Dans le vide" ("In Space"), a moving imaginative elegy written after the death of Arp's friend and fellow artist, Theo van Doesburg. In this poem, death is treated as cause for celebration, not mourning. When the poem begins, the soul of Arp's beloved friend—after having sojourned for a time in the transitory material world below—is preparing to leap out into the unknown, the eternal realm of unbounded space above. The soul, freed from the physical body, realizes that death is a return home, not an exile. This is reinforced by the fact that he enters space, the Above, in the fetal position—which is also the crouch he assumes in order to leap into space.

Refusing to see this death as a loss, Arp focuses on the freedom his friend is now able to enjoy for the first time, as he is joyously liberated from the demands of others. Doesburg now knows neither honor nor dishonor, censure nor obligation; he dwells blissfully alone, in an eternal realm of light. Arp had already described this state of blissful eternal existence in a much earlier poem entitled "Il chante il chante" ("He Sings He Sings"). It is in later poems such as "In Space" that Arp reached the height of his powers as a highly distinctive, imaginative, and lyrical poet.

Major publications other than poetry

SHORT FICTION: _Tres inmensas novelas_, 1935 (with Vicente Huidobro); _Le Blanc aux pieds de nègre_, 1945.

NONFICTION: _On My Way_, 1948; _Onze peintres vus par Arp_, 1949; _Dreams and Projects_, 1952; _Arp on Arp_, 1972 (poetry and prose); _Collected French Writings_, 1974.

Bibliography

Last, R. W. _Hans Arp: The Poet of Dadaism_, 1969.
Matthews, J. H. _Surrealist Poetry in France_, 1969.

Motherwell, Robert, and Jack D. Flam, eds. *The Dada Painters and Poets*, 1951.

Read, Herbert. *The Art of Arp*, 1968.

Richter, Hans. *Dada: Art and Anti-Art*, 1965.

Rimbach, Guenther C. "Sense and Non-Sense in the Poetry of Jean Hans Arp," in *German Quarterly*. XXXVI (1963), pp. 152-163.

Steven E. Colburn

KOFI AWOONOR
George Awoonor-Williams

Born: Weta, Ghana; March 13, 1935

Principal collections

Rediscovery and Other Poems, 1964; *Night of My Blood*, 1971; *Ride Me, Memory*, 1973; *The House by the Sea*, 1978.

Other literary forms

Kofi Awoonor has shown a lifelong interest in the oral poetry of his Anlo people, publishing his own translations of three contemporary traditional Ewe poets in *Guardians of the Sacred Word* (1974). In his introduction to these translations, Awoonor refers to himself as "a child of the soil, a poet who is striving to make some relevant statements on the contemporary African's condition, eager to absorb the sounds, rhythms, and rituals that nurtured him." An important contribution to the body of African oral poetry available in print, *Guardians of the Sacred Word* includes Vinorkor Akpalu, who exercised a significant influence on Awoonor's early verse.

Awoonor's *The Breast of the Earth* (1975) is a sensitive survey of the history, culture, and literature of Africa south of the Sahara. Its careful consideration of all the factors, both indigenous and Western-introduced, influencing the growth of contemporary African literature, makes it a landmark volume. Awoonor is also a capable writer of fiction, with a number of unpublished manuscripts and several short stories in print; his only published novel, *This Earth, My Brother*, appeared in 1971. The conflicts that haunt its lawyer-protagonist—between European ways and the culture of his homeland of Keta, between the wealthy suburbs of the capital city and the poverty of its slums—are expressions of the central theme that unifies all of Awoonor's works: the search for a new tomorrow in a recently independent Africa still confused by its bitter colonial past, a search for a synthesis of Western values and technology with the basically humanistic African culture that holds Awoonor's first allegiance.

Achievements

Generally acknowledged as one of Africa's most exciting poets, Awoonor has been a significant presence since the publication in 1963 of his first poems, in Gerald Moore and Ulli Beier's *Modern Poetry from Africa*. His work is included in every anthology of contemporary African literature and has been translated into many languages, including Russian, French, Chinese, and German. His presence at various international forums on African literature and the awards he has won to encourage his continued study of oral traditions and contemporary African literature attest his stature, and he has been invited to read his poetry and discuss his work at colleges and universities throughout the United States, England, and Europe.

Although he is one of the most widely traveled contemporary African writers, Awoonor has maintained and continued to explore those links to his Ewe culture and language that make his poetry effective and unique. He has captured the feel and rhythms of traditional oral poetry in an English which, unlike that of such African poets as Christopher Okigbo and Wole Soyinka, is seldom obscure. In the words of one of Africa's foremost literary critics, Ezekiel Mphahlele (in his introduction to Awoonor's *Night of My Blood*), Awoonor's verse is "the truest poetry of Africa." As Mphahlele says, "Although Awoonor's poetry is packed with ideas, his gentle diction carries us there with its emotional drive, its traditional speech patterns. For all that, the poetry stays on the ground, avoiding any intellectual horseplay."

Whereas Christopher Okigbo (born in Nigeria in 1932 and killed in action with the Biafran Army in 1967), the most critically acclaimed African poet of Awoonor's generation, said that he wrote for other poets, Awoonor has sought a much broader audience, emulating in the context of African and world literature the role of the Ewe oral poets among their own people.

Awoonor has led a life exemplary of the committed writer, saying once that he "thrives on opposition and conflict" and stating early in his career that his pet aversions are "poseurs and hypocrites and righteousmen." Always political but never doctrinaire or propagandistic, he speaks with passion about the inequities of the world in a voice that avoids stridency. Indeed, his voice is often as gentle as a lover's, but his vision is unclouded by romanticism. His stance is closest, perhaps, to that of another well-traveled poet who addressed his verse to the common people—Pablo Neruda.

Awoonor's greatest accomplishment may lie in his synthesis of African ideas and Western experience. He reveres the philosophy of Africa yet moves in the technological world of the late twentieth century with ease, drawing from both cultures to forge a literary voice at once genuinely African and distinctly modern. Awoonor's language effects a similar synthesis, carrying the strong music of his native Ewe into English. (He continues to write in his native language, often doing first drafts in Ewe and producing both Ewe and English final versions.) Ewe is a highly tonal language, sung as much as spoken, with tonality determining the meaning of innumerable words. That Awoonor has made the transition from Ewe to English without sounding strained, stilted, or incomprehensible is almost an act of magic.

Awoonor's synthesis of language and ideas strengthens his expression of that "conflict between the old (traditional) and the new (foreign)" that the Nigerian critic Romanus Egudu rightly sees as characteristic of Awoonor's poetry. Awoonor, however, unlike many of his contemporaries, does not stop at that point of conflict. Instead, he works toward a resolution, building a bridge to a new land which may not yet exist but which his work foresees, shaped from both past and present and based on the soil where ancestors are buried but never truly dead.

Awoonor's eloquent exhortation at the end of *The Breast of the Earth* serves as a concise statement of his poetic stance:

> Those who call for a total Europeanization of Africa are calling for cultural suicide. Those who are asking for a pure and pristine journey into the past are dreamers who must wake up. For in the center, somewhere between those two positions, lies the only possibility.

It is in that center, a center which *does* hold, that the poetry of Kofi Awoonor lives.

Biography

Kofi Awoonor's childhood was spent in the Volta region of Ghana near the seacoast town of Keta. Long a meeting place for the East and the West, both through agricultural commerce and the slave trade, the Keta area is also known for the strength of its traditional customs and the eloquence of its oral poets. Such poems of Awoonor's as "Night of My Blood" and "My Uncle, the Diviner Chieftain" show how deeply and personally the history and culture of his Anlo people influenced his formative years, despite the European surname Williams once appended to his African name (indeed, his first poems were published under the name George Awoonor-Williams). Though highly educated, Awoonor has never turned his back on the culture and beliefs that shaped his early years. In a 1975 interview, he said:

> As society progresses, this whole technological society in which we are living today, we tend to forget about those other mysterious areas of human experience. But hocus-pocus is part of our waking world. I believe strongly, very, very strongly, that I am never alone.

In a way, then, Awoonor's biography is that of a tribal man and cannot be separated from the history of his people. An understanding of his life should include an awareness of the traditions, for example, of the Ewe migration from the town of Notsie in present-day Togo, where the Ewe were held captive by an African tyrant, as well as some knowledge of how deeply the drumbeat penetrates every aspect of life in Anlo. While recognizing the holistic virtues of the "African way," Awoonor grew up knowing that all the evils of African life could not be attributed to colonialism.

Awoonor received his secondary education at the famous Achimota Secondary School near the capital city of Accra. At the University of Ghana at Legon, he won his first major literary recognition, the university's Gurrey Prize for the best original creative writing. After graduation, he lectured in English at the university from 1960 to 1963 before taking an appointment as a research fellow and lecturer in African literature at the university's pioneering Institute of African Studies. During the years that followed, he was constantly active, traveling to China, Russia, and Indonesia, editing the literary review *Okyeame*, acting as the managing director of the Ghana Film Corporation, and founding the Ghana Playhouse, where he worked as both producer and actor.

The overthrow of Kwame Nkrumah in 1966 coincided with Awoonor's decision to study abroad. In 1967, with the aid of a Longmans fellowship, he went to the University of London, where he obtained a master's degree in modern English, focusing on the linguistic features of English in West Africa. A Farfield fellowship brought him in 1968 to the University of California at Los Angeles. In 1969, he accepted a position at the State University of New York at Stony Brook, where he eventually obtained his doctorate and became chairman of the comparative literature program. Aside from brief trips to Europe and Africa, Awoonor was not to leave the United States until 1975, when he ended his eight years of exile at the invitation of the Ghanaian head of state, Colonel Acheampong, to become the chairman of the English department at the University of Ghana at Cape Coast. Awoonor's years in the United States were most productive: He published two volumes of poetry, a novel, a critical study of African literature, and an anthology of Ghanaian poets which is also a seminal work on traditional oral poets. (It should be noted that various internal crises suffered by one of his publishers, Nok Books, have delayed for more than half a decade an edition of his selected poems.)

Awoonor returned to Ghana with a number of ambitious projects in mind, including the launching of a publishing company, but political turmoil in Ghana interfered with his plans. The Ewe have a long history of nationalistic aspirations (because of arbitrary colonial boundaries, they are divided almost evenly between the present-day nations of Ghana and Togo), and Awoonor was linked to an Ewe military officer's alleged plot to overthrow the government of Ghana. On December 31, 1975, Awoonor was arrested for "harboring a fugitive" and placed in detention in Ussher Fort. His imprisonment lasted more than a year. His poems written during that period (later published in *The House by the Sea*) were smuggled out of prison and sent in letters to America, to one of his publishers, signed with such pseudonyms as I. H. A Birdcry. Following an international outcry and efforts by Amnesty International, Awoonor was released and, in 1977, was sent as Ghana's representative to the International Festival of African Arts and Culture (FESTAC) in Nigeria. In 1978, however, his home was surrounded by troops, and he escaped in the night, slipping over the border to Togo.

From 1978 to 1982, political turmoil continued in Ghana, with elections, coups, and the execution for political corruption of no fewer than three of Ghana's former heads of state, including Acheampong. During this period, Awoonor returned to Cape Coast as dean of the faculty of arts. In 1981, he was awarded a Rockefeller Foundation fellowship to further a study of "the moral perspective in the folktale and the modern novel in Africa." Currently, he is again living outside his native land, as Ghanaian ambassador to Brazil; the relatively modest demands of his post permit him the time to work on new poems and to study the links between Afro-Brazilian culture and the traditions of his homeland.

Analysis

A useful key to understanding Kofi Awoonor's poems may be found in his own description in 1971 (published in *Palaver: Interviews with Five African Writers in Texas*, 1972) of his poetic development to date, which he divides into three phases "punctuated by my relationship to technique and my relationship to theme." The first phase, which Awoonor calls his apprenticeship, saw the creation of work that drew heavily on the tradition of the Ewe song, especially the dirge form. These laments—which have, as Awoonor puts it, a "lyrical structure with the repetitions of sections, segments, lines, along with an enormous, a stark and at times almost naive quality"—shaped his often anthologized "Songs of Sorrow" and "Song of War."

In the traditional Ewe dirge, the poet usually sings from the point of view of a man overwhelmed by the weight of life and by the enormity and inevitability of death. One should be careful, however, not to mistake this tone for one of total despair or hopelessness. An awareness of death is linked in African philosophy with an understanding that the departed ancestor's spirit still cares for the living left behind, and the bridge between life and death, or—to use a metaphor that both the Romans and the Ewe understand well— the ferry that crosses the river from the land of the living is a much more visible presence to the Ewe than to a contemporary Westerner. Awoonor's early poems fall squarely within that tradition and have images and even whole lines that are direct translations from the dirge poets of Anlo. Thus, it is with a distinctly Ewe voice that Awoonor speaks in "Songs of Sorrow" when he writes:

> My people, I have been somewhere
> If I turn here, the rain beats me
> If I turn there the sun burns me
> The firewood of this world
> Is only for those who can take heart
> That is why not all can gather it.

The poem's proverbial message is that suffering must be expected in any human life. It is only those who are able to "take heart," who continue to strive in the face of adversity, who can collect the firewood of the world, not merely surviving within the often hostile environment but husbanding it for their good and the good of others. The catalog of woes that follows—the loss of children, the extinction of great households, the fall of leaders ("the tree on which I lean is fallen")—is thus intended as a realistic appraisal of the worst events that might befall one. Knowing that these things can happen, the person of resolve should be inspired to strive that much harder.

"The Sea Eats the Land at Home" also draws on the tradition of the lament, but it is a more original poem, one that points toward Awoonor's mature style. Blending wide personal experience with ancestral rhythms, the poem describes with photographic accuracy the erosion that has so often threatened the existence of the town of Keta. It captures the living presence of the sea, a capricious deity which men may propitiate but can never control. Awoonor has witnessed its capriciousness more than once (there are destroyed remnants of half a dozen breached seawalls in front of Fort Prinzenstein in Keta), and he has made it visible even to those who have never been to the coast. There is nothing vague or unclear in the poem. It moves with a slow, inexorable dignity that echoes the movement of the sea, ending with lines that resound like the ebb and flow of the waves: "In the sea that eats the land at home,/ Eats the whole land at home." It was a remarkable achievement for a young poet.

Awoonor's poems never operate on a single level. As in the traditional Anlo poems, where a leopard is never merely a leopard but may also be a number of other things, including death, an enemy, or the Yewe cult, Awoonor's references to nature are symbolic. Nowhere is this more clear than in "The Weaver Bird." These birds are found throughout Africa. In Ghana, they are brightly colored and raucous birds that make large colonies of finely constructed hanging nests. Beautiful yet obstreperous, creative yet crowding out the other birds in the environment—what better symbol for the colonizing European? At first, in Awoonor's poem, the weaver seems little more than a bird, even though it "built in our house/ And laid its eggs on our only tree." When the bird begins "Preaching salvation to us that owned the house," however, it is obvious that it represents the Christian missionary presence in Africa, a source of confusion for the true owners of the house. Awoonor's poem offers a powerful image of that clash of cultures in which the African is forced to conform to a European value system: "Its sermon is the divination of ourselves/ And our new horizons limit at its nest." Nevertheless, though their traditional ways have been sullied by the invaders, the poet and his people have not been defeated; indeed, the last lines of the poem might serve as an anthem for postcolonial Africa:

> We look for new homes every day,
> For new altars we strive to rebuild
> The old shrines defiled by the weaver's excrement.

The second phase of Awoonor's poetry is hinted at by "The Weaver Bird." Influenced by his study of Western literature, and particularly by the poetry of T. S. Eliot, Gerard Manley Hopkins, and William Butler Yeats, Awoonor began to write poems which embody in their linguistic texture as well as in their themes the collision of Western and African values. In this second phase, Awoonor has said, he dealt "continuously with the theme of the conflict of cultures." The poetry is meant to be a commentary on the way the poet was torn in two by his allegiance to that side and his allegiance to this side, without this conflict ever being resolved. "The Years Behind" and "We Have Found a New Land" are two excellent examples. The former begins with lines that have the tone and diction of an English lyric, flowing with an almost artificial ease: "Age they say cannot wither the summer smiles/ nor will the trappings of our working clothes/ change into the glamour of high office./ Twenty-eight seasons have passed/ and the fleshy flushes of youth are receding/ before the residuary worm's dominion/ in the house of the fire-god." At that point, though, one third of the way into the poem, something begins to happen; the imagery leaves England far behind: "On the sacred stone with the neglected embers/ the cock-offering has fluttered and gone./ The palm-oil on the stone gods has turned green/ and the gods look on concerned and forgotten." The focus of the poem, then, is not on the poet's own approaching age, but on the condition of his people and their gods, their culture. Though still alive, that culture is in neglect, while the speaker himself is in exile "among alien peoples whose songs are mingled with mine." What, then, can be done? The answer comes in the last four of the poem's twenty-three lines, with the beat and the wording of a traditional Anlo song. Neither working clothes nor the robes of high office are the proper garb for the poet. He must have a garment that is at once traditional and newly made, much as the famed Ewe weavers make kente cloth from the fine imported threads of England, embroidering it with old symbols that have proverbial connotations:

> Sew the old days for me, my fathers,
> Sew them that I may wear them
> for the feast that is coming,
> the feast of the new season that is coming.

A similar movement can be traced in "We Have Found a New Land," with its ironic image of "smart professionals in three piece" who find this Western costume inappropriate for their tropical homelands and begin "sweating away their humanity in driblets." They think they have "found a new land/ This side of eternity/ Where our blackness does not matter/ And our songs are dying on our lips." In their view, it is the poet—who wears traditional dress and speaks of the old ways, despite his Western education—who has "let the side down," their language reflecting their British overlay. The poet weeps for them—and for that part of himself which has not yet been reborn, for those who "have abjured the magic of being themselves." The conclusion of the poem again holds out a hope for a renewed future by looking to the past: "Reaching for the Stars we stop at the house/ of the Moon/ And pause to relearn the wisdom of our fathers."

The third stage in Awoonor's poetic development, beginning around 1970 and continuing to the present, has been marked by a preference for the long poem. In the works of this period, the struggle expressed in his earlier poems has found a resolution. This does not mean that the world around the poet has achieved equilibrium. Africa is still torn by internal strife, and the ordinary people of the world for whom the poet attempts to speak (*all* the ordinary people of the world, not just those of his native continent) still suffer under oppression. As Awoonor says in his powerful poem "The Wayfarer Comes Home," written while he was being detained in Ussher Fort, "You know/ our gods are maimed/ by native and foreign cudgels." Awoonor's vision of the future, however, is stronger than the disillusionment of the present.

In the more than four hundred lines of "The Wayfarer Comes Home," the imprisoned poet looks far beyond the borders of his native Ghana to witness to a worldwide struggle for human dignity. Like Awoonor's other long poems, "Night of My Blood" (which retells the story of the Ewe migration), "I Heard a Bird Cry," and "Hymn to My Dumb Earth," "The Wayfarer Comes Home" makes great use of Ewe rhythms, at times even breaking into the native language itself. Like "Hymn to My Dumb Earth," the poem modulates between a prose rhythm tone and a stress rhythm, but this is not a departure from Awoonor's traditional roots. Interestingly enough, this seemingly modern structure, with something like reportage flowing into song (reminiscent of the works of Robert Duncan and Allen Ginsberg), characterizes the Ewe technique in poetry, whereby the cantor makes his address to the audience and then swings into the story.

The unifying image of "The Wayfarer Comes Home" is the "evil animal," the creature that has been created by colonialism, by the misuse of power, by human greed. The poet sees his mission as destroying that beast and prophesies its demise. At the end of the poem, when the poet-hunter—whose vision has ranged throughout the world seeking that empowering feminine presence that is his one true love and his native land—predicts his eventual triumph, it is a triumph for all humanity, one which all human beings should strive for and celebrate.

Major publications other than poetry
NOVEL: *This Earth, My Brother*, 1971.

NONFICTION: *Guardians of the Sacred Word*, 1974 (translation); *The Breast of the Earth*, 1975.

Bibliography
Egudu, Romanus. *Four Modern West African Poets*, 1977.

Lindfors, Bernth, ed. *Palaver: Interviews with Five African Writers in Texas*, 1972.

Morrell, Karen L. *In Person: Achebe, Awoonor, and Soyinka*, 1975.

Roscoe, Adrian A. *Mother Is Gold*, 1971.

Zell, Hans, and Helene Silver. *A Reader's Guide to African Literature*, 1971.

Joseph Bruchac

MIHÁLY BABITS

Born: Szekszárd, Hungary; November 26, 1883
Died: Budapest, Hungary; August 4, 1941

Principal collections
Levelek Irisz koszorújából, 1909; *Herceg, hátha megjön a tél is!*, 1911; *Dante komédiája*, 1913, 1920, 1923, 1939 (translation); *Recitativ*, 1916; *Pávatollak: Műfordítások*, 1920; *Összegyüjtött munkái*, 1937-1939; *Jónás könyve*, 1940; *Hátrahagyott versei*, 1941; *Vlogatott művei*, 1959; *Összegyüjtött versei*, 1963. Only a few of Babits' poems have been translated into English, and these have appeared in the *Hungarian Quarterly*, *The New Hungarian Quarterly*, and the *Slavic and East European Review*.

Other literary forms
Although best known for his lyric poetry, Mihály Babits was also among the outstanding essayists of modern Hungary, and his novels and short stories were important expressions of the Hungarian intellectuals' search for their place in a changing society. Equally familiar with the history of European and Hungarian culture, the formal and contextual problems of literature from Homer to the moderns, and the literary struggles of his own times, Babits wrote essays on topics ranging from Henri Bergson and Friedrich Nietzsche to folk literature. Especially revealing of his attitude toward the responsibility of creative artists is his 1928 essay, *Az írástudók árulása* (the treason of the intellectuals), which took its topic as well as its title from Julien Benda's *La Trahison des clercs* (1927). Babits' awareness of the intellectual and artistic ferment of the twentieth century is evidenced by the numerous reviews and critical essays he published.

Babits' novels and short stories are marked by the lyrical approach to prose characteristic of his generation. His short novel *A gólyakalifa* (1916; *The Nightmare*, 1966) is heavily garlanded with the Freudian trappings of the period, particularly with notions concerning dreams and split personalities. The novel *Timár Virgil fia* (1922; the son of Virgil Timár) is closer to the author's own experiences, as it deals with the life of a teacher-priest whose conflict with the urban world ends in tragic isolation, while *Kártyavár* (1923; house of cards) offers a repulsive picture of modern Budapest and its corrupting influence on human character. Babits' best novel is *Halálfiai* (1927; the condemned), an obituary-like tableau of his own generation, a Hungarian *Buddenbrooks* in which embezzlers, small-town curmudgeons, susceptible wives, and representatives of the emerging urban bourgeoisie are masterfully presented. *Elza pilóta vagy a tökéletes társadalom* (1933; Elza the pilot, or the perfect society) is a witty, stylistically elegant, though somewhat anemic utopian novel which takes place in "the forty-second year of the next war," and which is graced by an emphasis on two lasting human values: peace and decency.

Babits' translating activities began as mere philological excursions into other literatures, in part to satisfy his curiosity, and in part to assist him in finding his own voice. In time, however, he developed into one of the most significant modern Hungarian translators, with a range that included classical Greek drama and medieval Latin verse as well as the works of Dante, William Shakespeare, Johann Wolfgang von Goethe, George Meredith, Edgar Allan Poe, Oscar Wilde, and Charles Baudelaire. The impressionistic ease of Babits' early translations was replaced by a disciplined striving for precision and faithfulness.

It should be mentioned among the lasting contributions of Babits that, as the curator of the Baumgarten Foundation and as the editor of the journal *Nyugat*, he exercised great refining, moderating, and encouraging influence on his contemporaries and on younger generations of writers as well—an influence still vital today.

Achievements

Babits, the lyric poet of "restless classicism," embodied the modern synthesis of the Hungarian spirit with the great European values. While his humanistic orientation and moral stand remained consistent throughout his life, the marginal nature of his background, combined with the events of his times, presented him with a weighty dilemma: His liberal erudition made him break with the provincialism of the late nineteenth century and urged him to lead his culture toward an acceptance of Western European trends, but his innate idealism made him lean toward conservatism and reinforced his view of literature as an "elite function," independent of any social utility. His writings represent the highest level of urban liberalism in Hungarian literature. Standing on the ground of a humanism which was declared anachronistic and unrealistic by many of his contemporaries, Babits defended the cultural values he considered timeless, against all onslaughts, from Right and Left alike. His experimentation with form and his meticulous craftsmanship enabled him to become one of the most accomplished masters of Hungarian literature. During his declining years, Babits became a living cultural symbol in his country: He dared to produce intellectual writings in an age when the cult of spontaneous life-energy was approaching its peak and young geniuses openly raged against the artistic validity of intellect.

Biography

Mihály Babits was born the only son of an intellectual Roman Catholic family. His father, a circuit judge, was assigned to Budapest and the city of Pécs before he died in 1898. Thus, young Babits became acquainted with various parts of Hungary, but always considered Transdanubia (or, as he preferred to call it, Pannonia, after the ancient Roman territory) as his home region. From 1901, he studied at the University of Budapest, majoring in Hungarian and Latin. During his school years, he began to write poetry, and among his best friends he could count Dezső Kosztolányi and Gyula Juhász, who were also to become outstanding poets. After receiving his diploma in 1906, Babits taught in high schools in Szeged, in Fogaras (Transylvania), and in one of the workers' districts of Budapest. His poems were first published in 1902, and by 1908 he was one of the chief contributors to the new literary journal *Nyugat*. During the years preceding World War I, he published several volumes of poetry, read voraciously to acquire a broad European background, and began to translate the classics. He was opposed to the war from its beginning, and his pacifism became ever more outspoken. The nationalist press of the period attacked him, and one of his poems, "Fortissimo," provoked the confiscation of the journal in which it appeared.

Although decidedly apolitical, Babits welcomed the Revolution of 1918, seeing in it the end of Hungary's participation in the war and the birth of a national republic. As the revolution was quickly taken over by Hungary's handful of Bolsheviks, however, he became disappointed and aloof, even though the short-lived Republic of Councils appointed him professor of world literature at the University of Budapest. His acceptance of this position was harshly criticized in certain quarters during the subsequent years of counter-revolutionary backlash, but by that time his position as one of the central figures in Hungarian cultural life was established.

In 1921, Babits married Ilona Tanner, who (under the name Sophie Török) was herself an accomplished poet. At their summer home, in one of the most picturesque parts of Hungary, they entertained many of the country's best writers and poets. In 1927, Babits was appointed curator of the prestigious Baumgarten Foundation, which had as its aim the aiding of impoverished young writers and artists. This meant not only that his financial situation improved, but also that he became perhaps the preeminent literary arbiter in the country—a role that was confirmed when he became the editor of *Nyugat*.

The 1930's brought a series of painful and destructive illnesses to Babits: first, polyarthritis, later cancer of the larynx. The frail man underwent dangerous operations which proved to be only half successful. During the last years of his life, he was able to communicate only with the aid of his "talking notebooks." In spite of his illnesses, however, he remained active. In 1940, he was awarded the San Remo Prize by the Italian Government for his translation of Dante's *La divina commedia* (c. 1320) and subsequently he was elected a member of the Hungarian Academy of Sciences.

Analysis

The first volumes of the young Mihály Babits, *Levelek Irisz koszorújából* (leaves from Iris' wreath) and *Herceg, hátha megjön a tél is!* (prince, what if the winter comes?), contain poems representing the best of Hungarian *fin de siècle* aestheticism and secessionist tendencies. Babits rejected both the lyrical approach of his contemporaries—who, in the tradition of Hungarian populism, relied on the anecdotal retelling of subjective experiences—and the pathos of the neo-Romantics. The most frequent object of his early poetry is a cultural experience treated in an intellectualized manner; his own feelings appear only indirectly and in a highly generalized form. Another notable trait of Babits' youthful poetry is its playful richness and variety of tone. The poet refuses to reveal his feverish inner turmoil, his painful loneliness, and his internal conflict between thought and action. He hides behind a number of veils: now a scene from Hindu mythology, now a figure of the Roman Silver Age, now an episode from modern life—many worlds, many styles, many ways of looking at human existence. The poet's touch makes the rather ponderous Hungarian words dance in exciting configurations. Babits' verse can be read in a number of ways, not only because of the virtuoso arrangement of rhyme and rhythm, but also because of the shimmering sound and sense of every word within the lines. Perhaps more than any of his Hungarian predecessors, Babits maintained a strong connection with the fine arts, not merely in his themes and images, but also in his approach to literature. His stance as a craftsman was consciously chosen to distinguish himself from the multitude of spontaneous and pseudospontaneous versifiers.

Despite his experimental playfulness, Babits' poems are always thoughtful, often philosophical; they are also among the most eloquent expressions of the *fin de siècle*'s characteristic moods: nostalgia, dissatisfaction, and a superstitious, almost mystical *Weltangst*. There are also powerful streaks of Satanism and sin consciousness in his poetry. This strain in Babits' work is not attributable to the poet's personal experience, for he led a quiet, almost ascetic life; rather, it can be viewed as an expression of "preventive guilt," resulting from the purity of his soul: While he recoiled from the touch of the vulgar, he was at the same time attracted by it.

Babits considered himself one of the last descendants of the great Hungarian poets of the nineteenth century and refused to bow to the "vulgar" democratism of his age. His sentences, therefore, remain among the weightiest in Hungarian literature; the poet crammed them with colorful and unusual words, arranged so that the reader is forced to read the lines rapidly, without relaxing his intellectual excitement. If they are to yield their full meaning, though, the sentences have to be broken down and dissolved, somewhat like those of the English sonneteers. As in the work of his great contemporary, Endre Ady, the sentences in Babits' verse have a larger function than simply conveying the idea: With their solidity or elusive airiness, their zig-zagging speed or ponderous pace, they are meant to express the atmosphere and the emotional content of the poetic text.

There was a perceptible conflict between the young poet and the culture of Hungary under a dual monarchy, but this was scarcely manifested in writings of social or political content. The overwhelming presence of subjective elements, the almost total exclusion of reality, the adoration of the past, and an emphatic cultivation of Nietzschean individualism are all indicative of Babits' desire to evade having to deal with the present, even at the risk of becoming isolated.

The years of World War I brought significant changes in Babits' poetry. "The cool glitter of classical contemplation" is gone from the poems written during this period. The style is now simpler and closer to everyday experience, while the poet's active pacifism also forced him to discontinue his flirtation with irrationalism. Babits remained immune to the radical fervor which infected many of his contemporaries, but his desire for peace was passionate, and, at times, militant. After he claimed, in one of his poems, that he would rather shed blood for the little finger of his beloved than for any flag or cause, the nationalistic press of the period attacked him sharply. This did not stop the poet from repeating his cry for peace: "Let it end!" The signs pointing toward a great social upheaval in Hungary filled him with hope and enthusiasm: "The world is not a plaything! Here, one must see and create!" Soon, however, it became obvious that he viewed the events of 1919 (the "mud and blood of the revolution," in the words of a Hungarian historian) with increasing apprehension. Hope in the passing of the chaos permeates his writings after 1919, and, in a characteristically bitter image, he compares political ideologies to "slow-acting poisons."

In words as well as deeds, Babits put a distance between himself and public affairs during the post-World War I decades. "Fence in your property!" was his *ars poetica*; he sought to preserve his islandlike independence and remain aloof from politics, which interested him only as "a threatening force, which may seriously interfere with my life." Nevertheless, Babits' withdrawal into the shell of love (as represented by his 1921 marriage, and by the frequent get-togethers with a small circle of friends) cannot be classified as a frightened retreat. In stating his conviction that it is "better not to understand one's age and to be left behind" (repeated later as "noble souls do not pay obeisance to their immediate environments"), Babits remained consistent with his elitist conception of art. As the spiritual leader, later editor, of *Nyugat*, and as the curator of the prestigious Baumgarten Foundation, he remained uncompromising in upholding the highest artistic standards, and he refused to treat literature as a social force, or as a propaganda tool. At the same time, there were anticapitalist pieces among his poems ("The Mice of Babylon") and, realizing that the age of *fin de siècle* individualism was ended, he was enthusiastic about the rise of a socially and politically active neopopulist trend in Hungarian literature. Even his hitherto dormant nationalism was aroused, and in several poems he eloquently pleaded the cause of his nation.

The form of Babits' poetry now changed. The craftsman gave up strict rhyme and rhythm, and assumed the freer style of Expressionism, while his sentences became more puritanical, almost "democratic" in their spareness. He became more aware of the dominance of concrete experience, and registered this with sad resignation, because he could never become a vitalist. The main motive of his poems remains the primacy and freedom of the human spirit over matter, a message he often conveyed with the resignation of a wounded combatant.

With Europe shifting toward the Right and the ascent of Fascism, even Babits found it impossible to remain aloof. He was forced to take sides for moral and intellectual reasons. His condemnation of anything cheap, low-grade and vulgar—which had made him lose faith in the Bolshevik experiment—was turned against the rising tide of another ideological madness, foreboding new horrors for his continent. He began to revise his views but had no time to complete this task; illness and suffering—which are the topics of several late works in Babits' oeuvre—sapped his energy during his final years. In *Jónás könyve* (the book of Jonah), a confessional allegory on the biblical theme, Babits appears chastened and repentant of his earlier idealism and aloofness: "The wicked find their cronies among the silent!" The most eloquent testimony of the poet, however, is perhaps best summed up in these lines from one of his essays: "I still believe in human reason. I am still convinced that, as far as it reaches, it faithfully serves that which it cannot comprehend, . . . and that the poem will not suffer but improve if it is constructed by human intellect (as long as the Owner watches over the Architect!). Europe has experienced years of mindless horror: Let the age of reason come forth!"

Major publications other than poetry

NOVELS: *A gólyakalifa*, 1916 (*The Nightmare*, 1966); *Timár Virgil fia*, 1922; *Kártyavár*, 1923; *Halálfiai*, 1927; *Elza pilóta vagy a tökéletes társadalom*, 1933.

NONFICTION: *Az írástudók árulása*, 1928; *Esszék, Danulmányok*, 1978 (2 volumes).

MISCELLANEOUS: *Összegyüjtött munkai*, 1937-1939 (collected works, included prose and poetry).

Bibliography

Cushing, George F. *Hungarian Prose and Verse*, 1956.
Czigány, Lorant. *The Oxford History of Hungarian Literature from the Earliest Times to the Present*, 1983.
Grosz, Joseph. *Hungarian Anthology: A Collection of Poems*, 1963.
Kirkconnell, Watson. *A Little Treasury of Hungarian Verse*, 1947.
Klaniczay, Tibor, ed. *History of Hungarian Literature*, 1983.

Lengyel, Balázs. "A Poet's Place: Mihály Babits," *The New Hungarian Quarterly*. XXIV, no. 90 (Summer, 1983).

Menczer, Béla. *A Commentary on Hungarian Literature*, 1956.

Reményi, József. *Hungarian Writers and Literature*, 1964.

Tezla, Albert. *Hungarian Authors: A Bibliographical Handbook*, 1970.

András Boros-Kazai

INGEBORG BACHMANN

Born: Klagenfurt, Austria; June 25, 1926
Died: Rome, Italy; October 17, 1973

Principal collections

Die gestundete Zeit, 1953; *Anrufung des grossen Bären*, 1956; *Gedichte, Erzählungen, Hörspiel, Essays*, 1964; *Werke: In 4 Bänden*, 1978.

Other literary forms

In addition to her poetry, Ingeborg Bachmann published two radio plays, three volumes of short stories, and a novel. Much of her prose concerns the role of women in search of their own identity. Bachmann also collaborated with the composer Hans Werner Henze, writing the librettos for his operas *Der Prinz von Homburg* (1960; the prince of Homburg) and *Der junge Lord* (1965; the young lord). She was praised by critics as a librettist of great talent. Bachmann's other publications include essays in which she discusses her poetic theory.

Achievements

Bachmann attracted and fascinated readers and critics alike during her short life and has continued to do so since her untimely death in 1973. Bachmann's work has been praised as great and pure poetry, and she has been compared with such towering figures of German poetry as Friedrich Gottlieb Klopstock, Friedrich Hölderlin, and Rainer Maria Rilke. At the same time, the critic Peter Demetz has charged that her verse is marred by a "gauche combination of high polish and utterly sentimental *Kitsch*," and her metaphors have been labeled vague, justifying almost any interpretation.

It cannot be denied that Bachmann's personality and her life, shrouded in mystery to this day, have attracted at least as much attention as her work. After her appearance in 1952 at a meeting of Gruppe 47 (group 47), an influential circle of postwar writers, followed in turn by a story about her in *Der Spiegel*, Germany's mass-circulation newsmagazine, Bachmann could never rid herself of her image as a beautiful blonde who had become, of all things, a writer—sensuous yet intellectual, a cosmopolite from a provincial town in Austria, succeeding in a world traditionally dominated by males. When, after her death, her colleagues Günter Grass, Uwe Johnson, and Max Frisch began writing about her, Bachmann, who had already become a legend of sorts, gained increasing recognition as a significant figure in postwar German literature.

Bachmann's appeal derived from a happy fusion of traditional and modern elements. The older generation of readers, reared on Hölderlin and Georg Trakl, appreciated her classical German, while the younger critics welcomed her linguistic experiments, controlled as they were, and what Peter Demetz has called her "hard, dry poems in the manner of the older Brecht." It was, however, mainly because of their themes that Bachmann's poems struck the nerve of their time. In a period when Germans were busy reconstructing their country and enjoying the fresh fruits of the so-called economic miracle, she sent out warning signals of approaching doom. In imploring tones, she attempts to remind her readers that the end of time is near—the titles of her first two volumes, *Die gestundete Zeit* (borrowed time) and *Anrufung des grossen Bären* (evocation of the great bear), are such signals. The poems in these collections clearly define the situation: "Borrowed time, now recalled, grows visible on the horizon"; the "creature of cloudlike fur . . . with tired flanks, and the sharp, half-bared teeth stands threateningly in the sky." In the same breath, however, Bachmann exuberantly announces her readiness for life: "Nothing more beautiful under the sun than to be under the sun. . . ." Bachmann's combination of apocalyptic vision and lyrical affirmation compelled the attention of her generation.

While Bachmann's poems must be understood as products of their time and seen in their historical and cultural context, they have universal and timeless appeal. Bachmann's existential concern, her warnings not to succumb to comfortable adjustment, and the unique poetic quality of her language will continue to capture the imagination of readers.

Biography

The daughter of a schoolteacher, Ingeborg Bachmann grew up in her native Klagenfurt, the capital city of Austria's southernmost province, Carinthia. If the fictional account of *Jugend in einer österreichischen Stadt* (1961; youth in an Austrian town) is any indication, Bachmann's childhood and youth were not particularly happy. Perhaps this accounts for her reticence concerning that period of her life. She does mention the traumatic days of March, 1938, when Adolf Hitler annexed Austria, and the German army triumphantly marched into Klagenfurt with most of her countrymen applauding enthusiastically. Otherwise, very little is known about Bachmann's life before the age of twenty-three.

Bachmann initially studied law but soon took up philosophy at the universities of Innsbruck, Graz, and Vienna. In 1950, she received her doctorate with a dissertation on the critical reception of Martin Heidegger's existential philosophy. In 1950 and 1951, she traveled to London and Paris. For two years, she was a member of the editorial staff of Radio Rot-Weiss-Rot, the American-sponsored radio station in Vienna. In 1952, she gave her first reading at a meeting of Gruppe 47.

After the success of her first two books of poetry, Bachmann chose to take up the life of a free-lance writer, residing in Rome for many years. Her visit to the United States in 1955, at the invitation of Harvard University, provided the background for the American setting of her highly successful radio play, *Der gute Gott von Manhattan* (1958; the good god of Manhattan). From 1959 to 1960, Bachmann was the first guest lecturer in poetics at the University of Frankfurt. She was awarded many of the important literary prizes of her time, including the Great Austrian State Prize in 1968. Bachmann died in 1973, following a somewhat mysterious fire in her Rome residence. Five years later, her collected works were published in four volumes by Piper Verlag in Munich. The tenth anniversary of her death sparked renewed interest in Bachmann and was the occasion for many symposia throughout the world on her work.

Analysis

With love and joy, departure and death as her prevalent themes, it seems safe to say that Ingeborg Bachmann stays well within the conventions of poetry. Nor is her message novel; after all, the end of the world has been proclaimed many times before in poetry. Bachmann tells her readers solemnly that "the great cargo of the summer" is ready to be sent off and that they must all accept the inevitable end. Time is only borrowed, if one is to believe the ominous title of her first collection of poems. The titles of many of her poems are ciphers of farewell: "Ausfahrt" ("Departure"), "Fall ab, Herz" ("Fall Away, Heart"), "Das Spiel ist aus" ("The Game Is Over"), "Lieder auf der Flucht" ("Songs in Flight"). Indeed, Bachmann's poetry constitutes a "manual for farewells," as George Schoolfield has put it.

Images of night, darkness, ice, and shadow abound in Bachmann's verse. Upon closer inspection, however, one also discovers an entirely different set of images: warmth, summer, sunlight, plant growth. While all these images too may look conventional at first glance, one soon discovers that Bachmann has a very private mythological system and that most of her images have meaning only within that system. Many critics have attempted to decode Bachmann's verse; perhaps the most persuasive reading is that of Hans Egon Holthusen, who sees two basic attitudes reflected in Bachmann's poetry. One must agree with his diagnosis that there is a tension between hope and despair or joy and anguish in the fabric of nearly every poem by Bachmann.

Bachmann's "dark" or "negative" images are ciphers for what Holthusen calls her "elegiac" consciousness (in contrast to her "panegyric" consciousness, as reflected in her "positive" imagery). Images of ice, snow, cold, or barren landscape represent restricting elements in life, such as the impossibility of communication between lovers. Particularly in her first volume, *Die gestundete Zeit*, Bachmann frequently writes about the coldness of time. The poem "Curriculum Vitae," for example, evokes a winter landscape. In it, life is imaged as a quest for a path laid between ice skeletons. Even in Bachmann's love poems, there are repeated images of snow, ice, and cold.

Such imagery must be related to Bachmann's worldview. Although there are those who see her poems as reflections of a blurry *Weltschmerz* trimmed in beautiful language, her pessimism was earned by experience and reflected a concrete historical situation. Bachmann herself protested frequently against the mere culinary enjoyment of her poetry. Rather, she wanted her poems to be understood as a reaction to the unprecedented horrors of World War II. This intention is clear in "Früher Mittag" ("Early Noon"), a major poem of her first collection. In this poem, there are numerous references to Germany's recent past. Having been offered a platter on which is displayed the German heart, Bachmann's lyrical traveler opens the heart, looks inside, and reflects on what he finds: Germany's misuse of idealism and its efforts to disguise the past with what George Schoolfield has called the "simple heartiness of the beer-garden." Fragments of a song by Franz Schubert and a poem by Johann Wolfgang von Goethe, cherished treasures of the German musical and literary heritage, are interspersed with Bachmann's lines reminding the reader, all too painfully, of the aesthetic component of the German mind. In their context, these quotations sound like parodies, for Germany, in the poem, is a beheaded angel, and yesterday's hangmen drink from the golden goblet of Goethe's "Der König in Thule"—who, one must know, was "faithful unto the grave." The message could not be lost on the German (or Austrian) reader of the poem. After all, loyalty was a key word with which many of Hitler's henchmen defended their actions. Later in the poem, Bachmann conjures up Dostoevski's *Zapiski iz myortvogo doma* (1861-1862; *House of the Dead*), provoking visions of Germany as a Siberian labor camp, with all the old jailers still in power—a not-so-subtle reminder that many of Germany's war criminals went free, had their civil rights and privileges restored, and even, in some cases, once again enjoyed positions of power.

"Early Noon" clearly demonstrates that Bachmann did not wish to retreat into a realm of private memories or to hide behind fairy tales, as some critics have charged. On the contrary, it should be mentioned here that even many of her love poems are not so private as they may at first appear. Love, too, is shown as a victim of the modern age. Communication is no longer possible. The poem "Nebelland" ("Fog Land"), for example, is set in the winter. The lost lover is seen as a fish. The speaker is being driven away by ice floes, symbols of despair and desolation.

Although her poems can be related to their historical situation, Bachmann was not, strictly speaking, a political poet. Her methodological approach to language was based on her study of the philosopher Ludwig Wittgenstein. Attempting to discover the limits of human understanding, Bachmann, in "Early Noon," questions the effectiveness of the poetic word. "Where Germany's soil blackens the sky," she writes, "the cloud searches for words and fills the crater with silence. . . . " Silence, the ultimate vanishing point of a poem? In "Early Morning," Bachmann clings to the hope that the unspeakable may still be said. The poem concludes with the words: "The unutterable, gently uttered, goes over the land: it is already noon." As Schoolfield explains, "unutterable" is an abstract noun with two implications. Unspeakable crimes and unutterable beauty come to mind, and beyond these connotations lies a hint that there are problems the complexity of which defies expression.

It should be pointed out that Bachmann's skeptical attitude toward language reflects an Austrian tradition whose roots lie in the linguistic and philosophical dilemmas of the turn of the century. Hugo von Hofmannsthal, in his celebrated *Brief des Lord Chandos* (published in a journal as "Ein Brief" in 1902, published in book form in 1905; *Letter of Lord Chandos*, 1952), expressed his despair at the ineffectiveness of poetic language. In "Early Noon," an echo of the famous last sentence of Wittgenstein's *Tractatus Logico-Philosophicus* (1922) can be heard: "What one cannot speak of, one must keep silent about."

Many of the poems in Bachmann's first collection read—in the apt formulation of George Schoolfield—like a *vade mecum* of instruction for dealing with a brief phase of European history. One such poem is "Herbstmanöver" ("Autumn Maneuvers"). In it, Bachmann addresses German readers of the 1950's. They may find personal pleasures by traveling to the most exotic lands, but they will still be afflicted by twinges of guilt—guilt that they will not be able to dispel by claiming that they are not at home.

Another such poem is "Die gestundete Zeit" ("Borrowed Time"). When time actually does run out and appears on the horizon, "your beloved," Bachmann writes, "sinks into the sand, which rises to her wandering hair, choking her into silence and finding her mortal, willing to part after each embrace." Once again, the imagery of this poem and its symbols, drawn from nature, should not be regarded as mere ornamentation but rather as integral elements in a "complex totality operating on the outer boundaries of meaning." Again, an individual is shown as being incapable of communication and falling into silence.

One of Bachmann's best-known poems is "Anrufung des grossen Bären" ("Evocation of the Great Bear"). It has been anthologized many times and has provoked numerous interpretations. In spite of its fairy-tale-like introduction and atmosphere, it suggests many parallels with contemporary history. In the first stanza, the image of a shaggy bear blends with that of the Ursa Major of the stars. The mighty old bear is about to break loose and destroy all of those shepherds, representatives of mankind who have, maliciously or mischievously, invoked him, knowing full well that he would destroy them and their flock, thus bringing about their predicament. In the second stanza, the bear becomes a symbolic bear, and the Earth itself becomes a pinecone with which he plays, testing it between his teeth, rolling it between the trees, and grabbing it with his paws—all this symbolizing man's precarious position. A warning follows in the last two stanzas: Contribute to the church and keep the blind man (who shows the bear at carnivals) happy, so that he will not let the beast loose. The bear could still crush all cones, all worlds that have fallen from the trees of the universe. Biblical parallels suggest themselves here: the story of the Last Judgment, the Fall of Man. In the final analysis, no single interpretation is possible. The total effect of Bachmann's symbolic vocabulary in this poem is to leave the reader in doubt about its exact meaning. Bachmann's entire oeuvre can be interpreted as a transformation of inner conflict into art. In a speech of thanks to the donors of an award she received, Bachmann spoke in the following terms of the function of the poet: "We extend our possibilities in the interplay between the impossible and the possible. It is important for us to create this tension, we grow on it, we look toward a goal, which becomes more distant the closer we get."

In this speech, Bachmann expresses a certain ambivalence about the role of the poet. She vacillates between a firm belief in the eternal value of poetry and poetic language and a sense of its ultimate futility. In the end, the latter prevailed, and she virtually gave up poetry. The few poems that Bachmann wrote after 1956 and published in various magazines all revolve around her doubts about the validity of poetic language. The final poem of her collection *Anrufung des grossen Bären*, entitled "Ihr Worte," ends with two ambiguous lines that are indicative of her crisis: "Kein Sterbenswort, Ihr Worte!" (not one more death-prone word, you words!).

Ingeborg Bachmann has been called a poet-thinker. As such, she made heavy demands upon herself, and her work likewise demands much from her readers. Bachmann's readiness to confront, using exemplary lyric language, the issues of Germany's dark historical past as well as the universal problems of modern man has secured for her a permanent position among the great poets of German literature.

Major publications other than poetry
NOVEL: *Malina: Roman*, 1971.

SHORT FICTION: *Das dreissigste Jahr*, 1961 (*The Thirtieth Year*, 1964); *Jugend in einer österreichischen Stadt*, 1961; *Simultan: Neue Erzählungen*, 1972.

PLAYS: *Die Zikaden*, 1955 (radio play); *Der gute Gott von Manhattan*, 1958 (radio play); *Der Prinz von Homburg*, 1960 (libretto); *Der junge Lord*, 1965 (libretto).

Bibliography
Bareiss, Otto, and Frauke Ohloff. *Ingeborg Bachmann: Eine Bibliographie*, 1978.

Bender, Wolfgang. "Ingeborg Bachmann," in *Deutsche Literatur seit 1945 in Einzeldarstellungen*, 1970. Edited by Dietrich Weber.

Benn, M. B. "Poetry and the Endangered World: Notes on a Poem by Ingeborg Bachmann," in *German Life and Letters*. XIX (October, 1965), pp. 61-67.

Demetz, Peter. "Ingeborg Bachmann," in *Postwar German Literature: A Critical Introduction*, 1970.

Lyon, James K. "The Poetry of Ingeborg Bachmann: A Primeval Impulse in the Modern Wasteland," in *German Life and Letters*. XVII (April, 1964), pp. 206-215.

Marsch, Edgar. "Ingeborg Bachmann," in *Deutsche Dichter der Gegenwart*, 1973. Edited by Benno von Wiese.

Mechtenberg, Theo. *Utopie als ästhetische Kategorie: Eine Untersuchung der Lyrik Ingeborg Bachmanns*, 1978.

Pausch, Holger. *Ingeborg Bachmann*, 1975.

Schoolfield, George C. "Ingeborg Bachmann," in *Essays on Contemporary Literature*, 1966. Edited by Brian Keith-Smith.

Jürgen Koppensteiner

CHARLES BAUDELAIRE

Born: Paris, France; April 9, 1821
Died: Paris, France; August 31, 1867

Principal collections

Les Fleurs du mal, 1857, 1861, 1868 (*Flowers of Evil*, 1909); *Eureka*, 1864 (translation); *Les Épaves*, 1866; *Petits Poèmes en prose*, 1869 (also known as *Le Spleen de Paris*; *Paris Spleen*, 1869); *Oeuvres complètes*, 1868-1870, 1961.

Other literary forms

Collections of Charles Baudelaire's essays on literature, art, aesthetics, and drugs appeared under the titles *Les Paradis artificiels* (1860), *Curiosités esthétiques* (1868), and *L'Art romantique* (1868). Baudelaire also published translations of several volumes of the prose works of Edgar Allan Poe. The most convenient edition of most of his works is the Pléiade edition, *Oeuvres complètes* (1961), edited by Yves Le Dantec and Claude Pichois.

Achievements

Although Baudelaire was close to the major Romantic artists and poets, his work announced something new and difficult to describe. Baudelaire did not introduce a fundamentally new aesthetic principle but made important changes in the proportions of idealism and realism, formal beauty and attention to ideas, social commitment and alienation from society—all categories through which the Romantic poets had expressed their conception of literary art. More than most Romantics, he wrote poetry based on the ugliness of urban life and drew an intense beauty from the prosaic and the unspeakable. Although major Romantics, including Victor Hugo, had broken down many restrictions on subjects that could be treated in poetry, Baudelaire went further, choosing such topics as crime, disease, and prostitution as his points of departure. While many Romantics suggest a transcendent redemptive quality in art, a spiritual enlightenment that gives the readers a kind of religious or social pathway to liberation, Baudelaire tantalizes the reader with religious hope but then pulls it away, suggesting that all hope is in the moment of artistic insight and not in the real future.

The image of the poet as prophet or spiritually superior dreamer, typical of Hugo or Alfred de Vigny, flickers occasionally through Baudelaire's work, but it generally yields to an image of the poet as a sensitive and marginal individual whose only superiority to his contemporaries is his consciousness of his corruption and decadence, something Baudelaire expressed as "conscience [or consciousness] in the midst of evil." Baudelaire thus prepared the way for the decadent poets, and for those poets of the twentieth century who conceived of their work as primarily individual and not social. In this regard, it is significant that Baudelaire introduced Edgar Allan Poe to the French. Poe subsequently came to be a major influence on Stéphane Mallarmé and Paul Valéry and has even played a role in contemporary French psychoanalysis.

In terms of poetic form, Baudelaire's major innovation was undoubtedly in the prose poem, which existed before him but achieved status as a major form principally through *Paris Spleen*. In his verse, Baudelaire often used the highly restrictive "fixed forms" with their set repetition of certain verses, such as the *pantoum*, in which the second and fourth verses of one stanza become the first and third of the following four-verse unit. Such forms were common among the Romantics, but Baudelaire's combination of this formal perfection with surprising and even shocking subjects produces a dissonant and unforgettable music. Baudelaire thus avoids the pitfalls of the school of "art for art's sake," which he denounced for its exclusive attachment to surface beauty.

Although Baudelaire is sometimes grouped with the Symbolists, a movement that constituted itself more than a decade after his death, Baudelaire himself neither belonged to nor founded a school. It is probably fair, however, to designate him as the earliest exponent of modernism. He constantly sought, in both literature and painting, works that expressed a beauty specific to the reality of the moment, even if that reality was unpleasant or bizarre.

Biography

Charles-Pierre Baudelaire was born in Paris on April 9, 1821. His father, Joseph-François, was of modest origin but well educated, for he attended seminary and became a priest before the Revolution. Well connected, he became preceptor to the children of the Duke of Choiseul-Praslin and, as a painter, was personally acquainted with Enlightenment figures such as Condorcet and Cabanis. After the Revolution, having left the priesthood, Joseph-François Baudelaire worked on the administrative staff of the French senate. Caroline Archenbaut-Defayis, Baudelaire's mother, was thirty-four years younger than his father. Widowed, she remarried when her son was six years old. Baudelaire's stepfather, Jacques Aupick, was a career military officer who had him placed in a series of boarding schools, first in Lyons, when the child was nine, and then in Paris, at fifteen. The choice of schools permitted Baudelaire to be near his mother as the Aupick household moved in response to the officer's promotions.

As an adolescent, Baudelaire was friendly, religious, and studious. He won prizes in Latin verse composition (one of the poems in *Flowers of Evil* is in Latin). He seems to have had few serious disputes with his stepfather until after obtaining the *baccalauréat* in 1839. After that, however, the now successful general became progressively the object of Baudelaire's dislike and even hatred. Disapproving of the young man's friends and conduct, the general sent him on a long boat trip toward India, but Baudelaire, once embarked, refused to go farther than Mauritius. When Baudelaire reached legal majority in 1842, he broke with the Aupicks and lived prodigally on the money he inherited from his father. The life of ease of the young literary dandy lasted only two years, however, for the Aupicks had Baudelaire placed under conservatorship in 1844 on the grounds that he was incapable of managing his money. This deprivation of his full personal freedom had a devastating effect on Baudelaire, who attempted suicide the following year. Upon his recovery, he apparently resolved to write copiously and seriously, contributing to various reviews, especially *L'Artiste* and *Le Corsaire-Satan*.

Baudelaire was widely acquainted with important Romantic authors, including Charles Sainte-Beuve, Theóphile Gautier, Hugo, Gérard de Nerval, Théodore de Banville, Petrus Borel (the Wolf-man), and Champfleury. He was also close to the active painters of his day and spent much of his time in their studios. His essays on expositions and on individual artists, especially Eugène Delacroix and Constantin Guys, actually occupy twice as many pages in the complete works as his literary criticism. More intermittently, Baudelaire was involved in the political life of his day, manning the barricades in the 1848 Revolution and distributing political tracts. His love of order, or rather his aspiration to order and hatred of disorder, kept him from fitting into the Revolutionary cause, and his hatred of the bourgeoisie prevented him from siding with the conservatives.

By 1845, Baudelaire was already announcing a forthcoming volume of poetry, under the title "Les Lesbiennes." In 1848, he claimed to be working on a volume called "Les Limbes." Finally, in 1855, he settled on the title *Flowers of Evil*. When it appeared in 1857, the collection provoked a scandal that led to the prosecution of the poet and the publisher. Six of the poems were suppressed, and the poet was fined.

The death of General Aupick a few months before the appearance of *Flowers of Evil* led Baudelaire to a reconciliation with his mother. Although he never succeeded in putting his life in what he called "order," living within his means and avoiding debts, his attempt to heal his rift with his respectable middle-class origins may explain the increasingly Christian and even Catholic orientation of his ideas in the last decade of his life. In 1866, while visiting Brussels, Baudelaire was stricken with partial paralysis and became aphasic. He died in Paris after more than a year of suffering.

Analysis

Charles Baudelaire insisted that *Flowers of Evil* should be read as a structured whole and not as a random collection of verse. Whatever one may think about the authority of such claims, the six major divisions of the book, beginning with the longest section, eighty-five poems, entitled "Spleen et idéal" ("Spleen and Ideal"), and ending with the six poems of "La Mort" ("Death"), seem to outline a thematic and perhaps even chronological passage from aspirations toward a transcendence of pain, suffering, and evil (in the earliest section) through the exploration of various kinds of intoxication or escape—glimpsed in the sections "Le Vin" ("Wine"), "Flowers of Evil," and "Révolte" ("Rebellion")—only to end in death, seen itself as a form of escape from the disappointments or boredom of this world.

Throughout *Flowers of Evil*, a major theme is the uncovering of man's own contradictions, hypocrisies, desires, and crimes: all the aspects of life and fantasy that the respectable middle-class hides. In the very first poem of the book, "Au lecteur" ("To the Reader"), Baudelaire establishes an unusual relationship with his public. The poem begins with a list of vices—stupidity, error, sin, and stinginess—but instead of reproaching humanity and urging the reader to reform, the poet finishes the sentence with an independent clause containing a remarkable simile: "We feed our nice remorse,/ As beggars nourish their lice." Over this humanity presides the Devil, described two stanzas later as the magician, not Hermes but Satan Trismegistus (three-times great), who turns the rich metal of the will into vapor like an alchemist working backwards. Building toward what will apparently be a crescendo of vice, Baudelaire, in stanza 7, lists sins that man would commit if he had the courage (such as rape, poisoning, stabbing, and arson) and then points to a still greater vice, which he names only three stanzas later in the conclusion: boredom (*ennui*). In the poem's striking concluding lines, Baudelaire claims that the reader knows this "delicate monster," and then calls the reader "Hypocritical reader, my likeness, my brother!"

This strange poem, borrowing so much of its vocabulary and rhetoric from the tradition of religious exhortation, does not choose between good and evil. Instead, it promotes a third term into what is usually a simple dilemma: boredom, as the greatest of vices, is an aesthetic concept that replaces traditional moral concepts of evil as that which must be avoided at all costs, a vice which "could swallow the world in a yawn." In religious verse, the address to the reader as a brother is part of a call, first to recognize a common weakness and, second, to repent. Baudelaire does make an avowal of similarity but calls for an aesthetic rather than an ethical response.

The largest part of *Flowers of Evil* evokes a struggle against boredom through the artistic use of the ugliness of everyday life and ordinary, even abject, passions. The poem "Les Phares" ("Beacons") is an enumeration of eight great painters, including Peter Paul Rubens, Rembrandt, and Michelangelo, not as a celebration of human greatness but as a testimony to human sentiment and sensation, predominantly in the negative. Rubens is described, for example, as a "Pillow of fresh flesh where one cannot love" and Rembrandt as a "sad hospital full of murmuring." The last three stanzas seem at first to point to a religious purpose in this art which depicts a swarming, nightmare-ridden humanity, for Baudelaire uses terms from religion: malediction, blasphemy, *Te Deum*. Mankind's art is called a "divine opium," but this drug is not offered upward as incense to the Deity. It is, rather, an opium for human hearts. The purpose of art is ambiguous in this conclusion, for it is the best testimony to human dignity but is destined to die at the edge of God's eternity. In the historical context of French Romanticism, this vision of art serves at least to set Baudelaire apart from the partisans of "art for art's sake," a movement that Baudelaire himself called the "Plastic school." Clearly, the visual beauty of the paintings alluded to is not their primary characteristic in "Beacons." These works of art are great because of their representative quality and for the tension between their beauty and the suffering on which they are based.

The paradoxical search for an art that draws its beauty from ugliness and suffering appears in a spectacular way in another of the early poems of *Flowers of Evil*, entitled "Une Charogne" ("A Carcass"). Baudelaire's particular delight in the shocking combination of refined form with a crude and repugnant subject is noticeable in the very organization of the stanzas. There are twelve units of four lines each: the first and third lines of each stanza are rhyming Alexandrines (twelve-syllable lines), while the second and fourth lines are rhyming octosyllables. This division imposes a rhythm that heightens the contrast between refined gentleness and sickening sensations. As a whole, the poem is a monologue addressed to a person or character whom the speaker calls "my soul." Although there is a certain ambiguity about the significance of the term (it could represent a division of the self into two parts, a common Baudelairean theme), the poet's "soul" assumes the role of a woman to whom he speaks in words of endearment. He also recalls, however, the discovery, one summer morning, of a carcass lying near a pathway.

The opening stanza illustrates the way in which a tension is created between contrasting tones. The first two lines are addressed to the soul in terms that allow one to expect some pretty image, something that would fit the context of a beautiful, mild summer morning. The end of the second Alexandrine however, names the object: a "foul carcass." The discovery occurs as the speaker and his soul are coming around a bend in the path (*détour*) which parallels the transition from the first half of the stanza to the somewhat startling second half. The next eight stanzas continue to tell about the discovery of this cadaver in a tone that alternates, sometimes within stanzas and sometimes from one stanza to the next, between a distant aesthetic contemplation and a crude and immediate repulsion. The fourth stanza starts with a presentation of the point of view of the sky witnessing the "blossoming" of the carcass as if it were a flower, while the next two lines ("The stench was so strong that you thought you would faint on the grass") take a distinctly human point of view, even rather sadistically delighting in the soul's weakness. The speaker's reaction is represented as quite different, much closer to that attributed to the sky. In stanza 7, he compares the sounds coming from the carcass, eaten by organisms of decomposition, to flowing water and wind and to the sound of grain being winnowed. Not only does this comparison permit the poet to find beauty in ugliness, but it also permits him to pay homage to the bucolic poetry of the Renaissance (exemplified in such poems as Joachim du Bellay's "D'un vanneur de blé aux vents" ("From a Winnower to the Winds"), showing that classical themes can be presented in a thoroughly modern way.

In the following stanza, the speaker's drift continues from a purely aesthetic contemplation of the object to a comparison of the carcass to an artist's preliminary sketch in the artist's memory. This reverie is broken off in the ninth stanza by the return to the supposed summer morning scene and the recollection that a dog was waiting for the couple to leave so that she could get her meat.

The last three stanzas are quite different, for they depart from the scene, which is in the past, and look forward to the future of the speaker's beloved "soul," foreseeing the time when she will be like that carcass. Yet, even in this section (a form of *envoi*, a traditional closing message to the addressee of a poem), the alteration of tone continues. In the tenth stanza, where the speaker declares "You will be like this filth," he still continues to refer to her as "my angel and my passion." This contrast leads toward the final stanza in which Baudelaire, again recalling the poetry of the French Renaissance, proclaims the immortality of his poetry ("I have kept the form and divine essence/ Of my decomposed loves") in contrast to the fleshly mortality of his "soul," his beloved.

It is impossible to assert that this conclusion is a straightforward poetic doctrine. Perhaps the poet, after having cast the "soul" in the paradoxical role of decomposition, is exercising a final irony toward his own poetry. In any case, it is clear that "A Carcass" represents Baudelaire's reworking of traditional texts from classical and Renaissance tradition. His way of using the tradition sets him apart from those Romantics he called the Pagan school, who preferred to assume the posture of outright return to pre-Christian belief by denying historical evolution. One reason Baudelaire objected to this position was that he himself possessed a deeply tormented Christian character— described by some as Jansenist, that is, as belonging to the most severe, pessimistic, and ascetic form of seventeenth and eighteenth century French Catholicism—penetrated by the sense of sin and guilt. He could not imagine a simple return to classical "innocence." Baudelaire also had an acute sense of the passage of time and of historical change. In calling the work of the neopagans "a disgusting and useless pastiche," he was implicitly drawing attention to his own use of antiquity in a resolutely modernist manner, one that did not copy the ancients but assimilated their ideas into a representation of the reality of modern life.

The poignancy that Baudelaire achieves with such an approach can be seen in his "Le Cygne" ("The Swan"), dedicated, like two other poems in the section "Tableaux parisiens" ("Parisian Pictures"), to Victor Hugo, a deep believer in the historical movement of poetry. "The Swan" is divided into two numbered parts, one of seven and the other of six stanzas. In the first section, the speaker begins by addressing the legendary figure Andromache, the Trojan Hector's widow, captive in the city of Epirus. The Parisian speaker's memory, he says, has been made pregnant by the thought of the "lying Simoïs swelled by your tears." This allusion to the legends of Troy is the key to understanding the rest of the first part of the poem, most of which seems merely to tell of an event in the speaker's own life, an event without apparent connection with Andromache. He was walking across the new Carrousel Square when he recalled a menagerie that once stood on that spot. A swan had escaped from its cage and was bathing its wings in the dust of a gutter.

The allusion to Andromache is now clearer, for the "lying" Simoïs was a replica in Epirus of the small river that once flowed at the foot of the walls of Troy. In an attempt to make the widow happier, her captors had constructed this imitation, described by Baudelaire as "lying" because it is not only false but actively and disappointingly deceitful. It can never replace the Simoïs but can only remind Andromache of the discrepancy between past and present. In the second part of the poem, Baudelaire explains the multiple analogy that had been left implicit in the first part. Returning to the present (the first part had been composed of three chronological layers: the legendary past of Andromache, the moment when the speaker saw the swan, and the approximate present in which he recollects the swan), he exclaims, "Paris changes! but nothing in my melancholy/ Has moved!"

What had seemed in the first part to be a comparison only between the widow and the swan now includes the speaker. Each of the three has an immovable memory on the inside—the speaker compares his to rocks—which cannot match the mutable outside world. This dissonance between mind and world is expressed not only in the image of the swan but also, more subtly and pathetically, in the temporal organization of the poem. Between the time he saw the swan and the time of the creation of the poem, the swan has vanished and the old Carrousel has been changed into the new. The chronological layering of the text has the same function as the simile. Furthermore, the changes in Paris, composed of monumental constructions of carved stone, give the city an ironic and metaphoric significance. Monuments, like the palace of the Louvre near which the menagerie stood, are usually associated with memory. They are meant to last longer than individuals. Here, however, the city represents change. Baudelaire has thus united a commonplace of certain Romantic poets (the indifference of nature to man's suffering) with a classical poetry of cities (Troy, Epirus, Rome) to produce a thoroughly modern poetic idiom.

The conclusion of "The Swan" continues the interplay of literary allusion, for it opens still further the analogy involving Andromache, the swan, and the poet to include an African woman exiled in a northern climate, sailors, captives, and the conquered. There is a decidedly epic quality to this expansion of the analogy to include vast numbers of modern exiles. Baudelaire did not, unlike many Romantics, believe in long poems, and he seems here to be condensing the grandeur of the epic into the brevity of the personal lyric. The many components of this epic analogy, stretching from Andromache to the suggestively open-ended last line ("Of captives, of the conquered . . . of still others!), are reminiscent of the multiple symbolic figures (the artists) of "Beacons." With this latter poem "The Swan" also shares the vision of suffering as a defining characteristic of life, for exiles "Suck at the breast of Sorrow as if she were a good wolf." This image is a way of tying in the Roman epic of Romulus and Remus while emphasizing the voluntary or consoling aspect of pain and suffering.

Suffering, inflicted on others or on oneself, is a frequent theme in *Flowers of Evil* and is linked to learning and self-awareness. In the "Heautontimoroumenos" (a Greek term for "The Executioner of Oneself," borrowed from a comedy of Terence), the speaker declares himself a "dissonance in the divine symphony" on account of the irony that eats away at him. In the most remarkable stanza, he declares in part, "I am the wound and the knife!/ I am the blow and the cheek!" In the poem immediately following, "L'Irrémédiable" ("The Irreparable"), after briefly tracing the fall of an ideal being from Heaven into Hell, Baudelaire evokes a "Somber and clear tête-à-tête/ A heart become its own mirror!" This division of the self into two sides, each looking at the other, is then described metaphorically as a "Well of truth, clear and black/ Where a pale star trembles." Although, here, knowledge is stressed more than the pain that is so fiercely displayed in "Heautontimoroumenos," pain must be the outcome of self-examination in this "well of truth" because the inward discovery is the sentiment of a fall from a higher state, an "irreparable" decadence. Yet, there is a tension here between the claim to total clarity and the image of the well, for the latter promises depths which can never be coextensive with the mirroring surface. Working back from this tension, one can see that the whole poem is full of terms for depth, darkness, and entrapment. The lucidity toward which the poem tends will never be complete, for consciousness can only discover the extent, apparently infinite, of its deprivation.

The concluding note of *Flowers of Evil*, the section called "Death," is a reminder of this perpetual quest for new discovery, even at the price of horror. In fact, the last stanza of the concluding poem, "Le Voyage" ("The Trip"), is based on the concept of depth that had already appeared in "The Irreparable": "Plunge into the deeps of the abyss, Hell or Heaven, that difference/ Into the depth of the Unknown to find something *new*!" Here the preoccupation with boredom as supreme evil in "To the Reader" appears coupled with the themes of knowledge and discovery that constitute much of the other sections. "The Trip" is a kind of summary in dialogue of *Flowers of Evil*, beginning with the childlike hope of discovery in the exploration of the real world. When asked later what they discovered, the travelers say that no city they discovered was ever as interesting as the cities they imagined in the shapes of clouds. Then, in passages that seem to recall the "Parisian Pictures," "Wine," and "Rebellion," the world of human sin is sketched out as a monotonous mirror in which man sees his own image, "An oasis of horror in a desert of boredom!" The only hope is in death itself, addressed in the last two stanzas as a ship's captain. He alone holds out a balm for our boredom, which itself results from an irresolvable tension between the aspirations of the heart and the outside world, ostensibly a mirror but actually an incomplete reflection because it can capture only actions and not intentions.

Baudelaire's collection of prose poems, *Paris Spleen*, is thematically very similar to *Flowers of Evil*. The prose pieces, however, have greater means to establish a situation for the poetic speaker and to accumulate aspects of life that seem "realistic" but serve ultimately to reveal figurative meanings in the most ordinary surroundings, a process sometimes called "correspondences" after the title of one of Baudelaire's verse poems. Frequently, as in "Le Gâteau" ("The Cake"), Baudelaire dramatically alters the situation of the poetic speaker so that he is not a representative of dissatisfaction with the world but an amazed spectator of the subjectivity of desire. In "The Cake," a traveler finds himself in a country where his plain bread is called "cake," unleashing a fratricidal war for its possession. In "Le Joujou du pauvre" ("The Poor Child's Plaything"), he discovers two children playing on opposite sides of a fence. One child is rich and has a meticulously crafted doll while the other holds his toy in a little cage. It is a living rat. Although these texts include elements of diction, characterization, and setting typical of fiction in the realist or Naturalist vein, Baudelaire always suggests a larger significance that makes the scene or incident figurative. In "The Poor Child's Plaything," the fence between the children is referred to as a symbolic barrier, and the rat is described as a toy drawn from life itself. Baudelaire specifies the metaphoric meaning much less in the prose poems than in his verse. One can, however, easily view the rat as a synecdoche for Baudelaire's aesthetic, based on drawing beauty from those aspects of life that are most repulsive.

Baudelaire's corrosive irony, his suggestive understatement of the metaphoric sense of his images, and his aggressive use of material drawn from the prosaic side of life have had a lasting success and influence. Movements as diverse as Symbolism, Dadaism, and the Italian neorealist cinema have claimed descent from his work.

Major publications other than poetry

NOVEL: *La Fanfarlo*, 1847; *Adventures d'Arthur Gordon Pym*, 1858 (translation).

SHORT FICTION: *Histoires extraordinaires*, 1856 (translation); *Nouvelles*

Histoires extraordinaires, 1857 (translation); *Histoires grotesques et sérieuses*, 1864 (translation).

NONFICTION: *Les Paradis artificiels*, 1860; *Curiosités esthétiques*, 1868; *L'Art romantique*, 1868; *Mon coeur mis à nu*, 1887 (*My Heart Laid Bare*, 1950); *The Mirror of Art*, 1955; *The Painter of Modern Life and Other Essays*, 1964.

MISCELLANEOUS: *Oeuvres complètes*, 1868-1870, 1961 (Pléiade edition).

Bibliography
Bandy, W. T., comp. *Baudelaire Judged by His Contemporaries*, 1933.

Bersani, L. *Baudelaire and Freud*, 1977.

Carter, A. E. *Charles Baudelaire*, 1977.

Gilman, Margaret. *Baudelaire the Critic*, 1943.

Peyre, H., ed. *Baudelaire: A Collection of Critical Essays*, 1962.

Poulet, G. *Who Was Baudelaire?*, 1969.

Sartre, Jean-Paul. *Baudelaire*, 1947.

Symons, Arthur. *Baudelaire: A Study*, 1920.

John D. Lyons

SAMUEL BECKETT

Born: Foxrock, Ireland; April 13, 1906

Principal poems and collections

Whoroscope, 1930; *Echo's Bones and Other Precipitates*, 1935; *Poems in English*, 1961; *Zone*, 1972 (translation); *Collected Poems in English and French*, 1977.

Other literary forms

Samuel Beckett is far better known for his fiction and plays than for his poetry, even though it was as a poet that he began his writing career. In fact, Beckett has explored almost every literary form, writing in English and in French. His early fiction, the collection of stories *More Pricks than Kicks* (1934) and the novels *Murphy* (1938) and *Watt* (1953), were written originally in English, but his best-known fictions, including the trilogy of *Molloy* (1951; English translation, 1955), *Malone meurt* (1951; *Malone Dies*, 1956), and *L'Innomable* (1953; *The Unnamable*, 1958), *Comment c'est* (1961; *How It Is*, 1964), and *Le Dépeupleur* (1971; *The Lost Ones*, 1972), were written and published originally in French. Beckett continues to write fiction, and, from the beginning, his greatest strength has been as an innovator, writing prose works which do not seem to fit easily into traditional categories but which extend the possibilities of contemporary fiction and which have had a profound influence on the writers who have followed him.

Beckett is also a writer of plays, and, when his name is mentioned, most people think of *En attendant Godot* (1952; *Waiting for Godot*, 1954). This difficult theatrical work met with astounding success on stages thoughout the world, and it is still Beckett's best-known and most-discussed piece. Other works for the stage, *Fin de partie* (1957; *Endgame*, 1958), *Krapp's Last Tape* (1958), *Happy Days* (1961), and *Rockaby* (1981), to name only a few, have extended the possibilities of live theater.

Never content to restrict himself to a single medium, Beckett has demonstrated that radio and television can serve as vehicles for serious drama with radio plays such as *All That Fall* (1957), *Cascando* (1963), and *Words and Music* (1962) and with television scripts such as *Eh Joe* (1967). Beckett also wrote the filmscript for the short movie *Film* (1966), produced and directed by Alan Schneider and starring Buster Keaton. Like the novels and the plays, these works for the mass media tapped new possibilities and pointed out new directions which other, younger writers are only now beginning to explore.

Early in his career, Beckett also showed that he was a brilliant critic of the arts, writing on the fiction of James Joyce and Marcel Proust and on the paintings of his longtime friend Bram van Velde. Also, in addition to translating his own works, he has translated other writers, including Robert Pinget, Paul Éluard, Alain Bosquet, and Sebastien Chamfort from the French and *An Anthology of Mexican Poetry* (1958) from the Spanish. His English version of Arthur Rimbaud's "Le Bâteau ivre" ("The Drunken Boat"), done in the 1930's but lost for many years and rediscovered and published for the first time only in the 1977 *Collected Poems in English and French*, is masterful, but best known is his 1972 translation of Guillaume Apollinaire's "Zone," a long poem that addresses many of Beckett's own themes and which opens with a line that could well characterize Beckett's efforts in all forms: "In the end you are weary of this ancient world."

Achievements

When the Swedish Academy selected Beckett to receive the Nobel Prize for Literature in 1969, the award only confirmed what critics and readers had known for some time: that he is one of the most important literary figures of the late twentieth century. Few authors in the history of literature have attracted as much critical attention as Beckett, and with good reason: he is both an important figure in his own right and a transitional thinker whose writings mark the end of modernism and the beginning of a new sensibility, postmodernism. The modernists of the early twentieth century—James Joyce, W. H. Auden, Virginia Woolf, Marcel Proust, and others—were stunned by the absurdity of their world. Previous generations had filled that world with philosophical, religious, and political meanings, but whose orderly visions of reality no longer seemed to apply to life in the early 1900's. The modernists lacked the faith of their forebears; they had experienced the chaos of the modern world with its potential for global war and the destruction of civilization, and they believed that the order of reality was a fiction, that life was unknowable. In response to their doubts, they turned literature in upon itself, separating it from life, creating an art for its own sake. These writers trusted in language to create new meanings, new knowledge, and a separate, artistic human universe.

As a young man, Beckett also experienced this sense of absurdity and meaninglessness in the modern world, but, unlike his modernist predecessors, he could not even muster faith in his art or in language. Thus, while Joyce could revel in the possibilities and textures of the written word, Beckett could not. Instead, he reduced his fictions, his plays, and his poems to the barest elements, and, throughout his career, he has tried to rejoin art and life in his own way. For the premodernists, art imitated the world beyond the human mind. The modernists rejected this idea of imitation, and so has Beckett. Instead, his art reflects the inner world, the world of the human voice, the only world men can ever really experience. In the premodern era, art was successful if it depicted some truth about the world. For the modernists, art succeeded only on its own terms, regardless of the world beyond the scope of the arts. For Beckett, art never succeeds. It is a necessary failure which never manages to link the inner mind to outer reality. As such, art is an exercise in courage, foredoomed to failure, like human life itself. Man is man not because he can give meaning to the world or because he can retreat into aesthetics but because he can recognize that his world is meaningless and that his life is leading him only toward death; yet he must continue to live and strive. As a philosopher of failure, Beckett is the first thinker of our own age.

Biography

Samuel Barclay Beckett grew up in a suburb of Dublin, Ireland, a Protestant in a Catholic country and therefore something of an exile in his own land. He attended Trinity College in Dublin, where he discovered his talent for languages and studied English, French, and Italian. He taught for two terms at Campbell College in Belfast and then, in 1928, traveled to Paris, where he lectured in English at the École Normale Supérieure. It was during this tenure that he met his countryman James Joyce. Beckett returned to Ireland to teach four terms at Trinity College, but, in 1932, after much consideration, he left the teaching profession, convinced that he could not survive as a writer in academe. For the next five years, he wandered through Europe, settling permanently in Paris in 1937.

There are probably many reasons for Beckett's self-imposed exile and for his decision to write in a language that is not his by birth, but surely one reason is the influence of Joyce, who recommended exile for artists. It would be difficult to overestimate the effect that Joyce had on Beckett's life and work. In the late 1930's, the younger Irishman was an intimate member of Joyce's inner circle. He worked on a translation of Joyce's "Anna Livia Plurabelle" into French, took dictation for his friend, wrote a critical study of Joyce's writings, ran errands for the Irish master, and even attracted the romantic interest of Joyce's daughter, Lucia. Apparently, Joyce thought a great deal of Beckett, and Beckett looked upon Joyce as a consummate master, so that it is possible he decided to write in French in order to avoid the language which, in his own mind, Joyce had all but exhausted.

As Beckett grew older and developed as a writer, Joyce's influence began to weaken, and, in many ways, Beckett's later style—spare, flat, reduced to the barest elements—is the antithesis of Joyce's rich, punning, heavily textured prose. Beckett also rejected Joyce's "Irishness" in favor of characters and settings without specific nationality or history. In the early poetry, however, the influence of Joyce and Ireland is still strong; in fact, it is in his poems that Beckett began to work through Joyce's voice and to discover his own.

Analysis

Whoroscope was Samuel Beckett's first major publication. It is a long poem, written originally in English and published in book form by the Hours Press after winning a prize offered by the publisher for the best poem on the subject of time. The first-person narrator of the work is René Descartes, the seventeenth century French philosopher, mathematician, and scientist, and the poem is so full of obscure allusions to his life and times that, at the publisher's request, Beckett added a page and a half of notes to the ninety-eight-line piece. In fact, the notes are almost as interesting as the poem itself, and, without them, it is unlikely that the average reader would even recognize Descartes as the speaker.

Whoroscope is an important poem, not only because it marked Beckett's official entry into the literary world but also because it introduced the basic themes that continued to occupy him as a writer and thinker. Clearly, Beckett himself has recognized this fact, because he has chosen to keep this early work intact in the subsequent collections of his poetry, *Poems in English* and *Collected Poems in English and French*, which include all the works discussed here. In many ways, *Whoroscope* is quite unlike the author's later writings. The structure of the piece is open, without rhyme or regular meter. The poem shows the influence of the French Surrealists in its associative juxtaposition of images, but the influence of Joyce is also apparent in the punning title and in the body of the text.

On first reading, it is not at all obvious that this is a poem about time. From the opening line, Descartes rambles on, apparently at random, about various events in his life, without respect for chronology or even historical accuracy. In the closing section, it becomes clear that the philosopher is on his deathbed and that his ramblings are the result of illness and fever. In a sense, his life is flashing before his eyes. He is trying to grasp the fullness of time at the moment of his death, and a closer reading shows that the sequence of memories is not random at all but associative, each a memory leading to the next—not in chronological order but in the order dictated by Descartes' subjective thought process.

In fact, the poem is very much about time—the time of a man's life and the attempt to recapture lost time in the instant before time runs out. The Joycean influence in Descartes' stream-of-consciousness narrative is evident, but it is also obvious that Beckett has learned a great deal from Marcel Proust's *À la recherche du temps perdu* (1913-1927; *Remembrance of Things Past*, 1922-1931), which the young Beckett knew well—so well, in fact, that in 1931 he published *Proust*, a book-length study of this French masterwork.

Whoroscope, then, is about time as the great destroyer, time that eats up a man's life and leads only to death. It is important to remember, however, that this poem is about the lifetime of a particular man, Descartes, and there is good reason for Beckett's choice of this philosopher as his narrator. Like Beckett himself, Descartes was a transitional figure, the father of modern philosophy and the opponent of Aristotelian Scholasticism. He and his contemporaries initiated a new age in Western civilization, an age that is only now passing away, and, in his poem, Beckett pays tribute to other great thinkers, such as Galileo and Francis Bacon, who directed Western thought into the era of science and rationalism.

Descartes was a great builder, but he was also a great destroyer of the philosophies of the past, and, in the poem, he speaks with pride of "throwing/ Jesuits out of the skylight." He devoted his life to the development of a new system of thought, but, in so doing, he also undermined the Aristotelian metaphysics that had served as the basis of European philosophy for centuries. Ironically, while Descartes was destroying his predecessors, the time of his own life was destroying him.

This is one of the key themes of Beckett's work: the fact that death comes to all living things, without reason, without justice, regardless of whether one is innocent or guilty. As Beckett writes in a later, untitled poem, man lives "the space of a door/ that opens and shuts." He is born to die; he is dying even in the womb, losing time from the moment of conception, and there is nothing that can stop or even delay this process. Each man's life cancels itself, moment by moment.

The historical Descartes died while in the service of Queen Christina of Sweden, a harsh woman who forced the aging philosopher to call upon her at five o'clock each morning, although he had been in the habit of staying in bed until midday all his life. This change in his routine, coupled with the northern weather, led to his final illness. In the poem, the fictional Descartes refers to Queen Christina as "Rahab of the snows." Rahab was a biblical harlot mentioned in *La divina commedia* (c. 1320; *The Divine Comedy*) of Dante (whom Beckett has called "the only poet"), and so it would seem that the Queen is the whore of the title. In his notes to the poem, Beckett points out that Descartes kept his birthday secret so that no astrologer could cast his horoscope. The philosopher was opposed to such mysticism, not only because it was unscientific but also because he felt that many people let their entire lives be dictated by astrology; he even knew of two young men who had allowed themselves to die simply because their horoscopes had predicted death for them. With this knowledge, the Joycean pun of the title becomes clear. Queen Christina, the harlot, has cast Descartes' death, which was present from the moment of his birth. His "whoroscope" is her prediction of his inevitable end.

This theme of the inevitability of death, of death as a necessary function of birth, runs through the poem in the form of a motif. Again in the notes, Beckett explains that Descartes liked his morning omelet to be made from eggs that had been hatched from eight to ten days—that is, eggs in which the embryo was partially developed. Time and again in the poem he asks about his morning eggs: "How long did she womb it, the feathery one? . . . How rich she smells,/ this abortion of a fledgling!"

For Beckett, the egg is the symbol of the fetus conceived only to die, its brief life span lived out in the instant between nonexistence and nonexistence. The time of the egg is the time of the philosopher as well. Like all men, Descartes is dying before he has lived, and, like the fledgling in the egg, he is dying for no purpose, simply because that is the way things are.

Beckett has explored the themes of the inevitability of death and the meaninglessness of life time and again in his works, but he has always coupled these themes with another: the necessity of going on, of raging against the inevitable, of refusing to accept man's fate. In the poem "Serena III," he insists that man must "keep on the move/ keep on the move," and, in *Whoroscope*, he depicts Descartes first as angry, cursing his fate, then as begging for another chance at a life he has never managed to understand, a "second/ starless inscrutable hour." There is no reason for him to go on, and yet, as a human being, he must.

For Beckett, man must die, but he must also live and think and speak, as Descartes does, even to the last possible instant. He must live in his own inner world, which is always dying, and he must also live in the outer world, which will live on after him and which, therefore, is not his. This theme of the conflict between the inner and the outer worlds which runs through Beckett's later work is present in *Whoroscope* as well. The very structure of the poem, which follows the philosopher's associative thinking, places the narrative within Descartes' mind, although in the end it moves to the outer world, to "Christina the ripper" and to her court physician, Weulles, who is attending to Descartes in his last moments. In his inner world, Descartes is alive and reliving his past, but it is the outer world which is leading him to inevitable death. Descartes devoted his life to trying to understand the outer world, but the very foundation of his thought, the dictum "cogito, ergo sum" ("I think, therefore I am"), trapped him within his own subjectivity, and generations of later philosophers have tried to understand how one can move from the certainty of the "cogito" to the world beyond which is not oneself. The "cogito," the single point of certainty in the Cartesian philosophy of doubt, is the fulcrum of modern Western philosophy, and yet it restricts the thinker to his own inner world, to what Beckett, in his poem "The Vulture," calls "the sky/ of my skull."

For Beckett, it is impossible for man to come to know the world beyond his skull, that very world in which he must live and die. In the play *Endgame*, the characters Hamm and Clov live within a skull-like structure; Hamm is blind, and Clov can see the world only through two eyelike windows which restrict his vision. In the short novel *The Lost Ones*, an entire society lives and passes away within a huge white dome, a skull. In *Whoroscope*, Descartes can know his inner world, but the outer world remains "inscrutable." He knows that he thinks and, therefore, that he is, but he does not know why. He wants to know the truth and to speak it, but the "cogito" cannot lead him to knowledge of the outer world. In the poem, he mentions St. Augustine, who also sought a single point of certainty in a world in which everything was open to question and found that the only thing he could be sure of was that he could be deceived. The Descartes of the poem states the Augustinian dictum as "Fallor, ergo sum!" ("I am deceived, therefore I am"). At the moment of death, this certainty seems truer to the philosopher than his own "cogito." To be a man is to be deceived, to fail, and, for a human being, courage is the courage to fail. Man is man only insofar as he knows that failure is inevitable and yet keeps going in spite of that knowledge.

There is another important Beckett theme which surfaces only briefly in *Whoroscope* but which becomes the main focus of the author's second collection of poems, *Echo's Bones and Other Precipitates*: the theme of the impossibility of love in the face of absurdity and death. For Beckett, love is another of man's basic needs, as important as the quest for meaning, and as futile. The Descartes poem touches on the theme only briefly, in the philosopher's memory of a little cross-eyed girl who was his childhood playmate and who reminds him of his only daughter, Francine, who died of scarlet fever at the age of six. The implication is that love always ends, if not now, then later; like the rest of life, love is both essential and hopeless, necessary and frightening. Knowing that love is impossible, pretending that it is not, man loves, and that love is the source of his pain but also of his life.

The poems of *Echo's Bones and Other Precipitates* differ from *Whoroscope* not only because they focus on love but also because the narrator is not a fictional version of a historical character but the author himself. The title of the collection comes from Ovid's *Metamorphoses* (before A.D. 8), from the story of Echo, who, after being spurned by Narcissus, lets herself wither away until only her bones and voice remain. The connection between Ovid's tale and Beckett's theme of love is clear, but the story of Echo also provides the poet with two of his favorite images: the inevitability of death and the survival of the voice.

Most of the titles and forms of the poems in this collection are based on the songs of the troubadours, which Beckett knew well and which attracted him no doubt because they were songs of love and, often, of loss, and also because the troubadours were usually wanderers and exiles, like Beckett himself and like the narrators of most of these poems. The work "Enueg I" draws its title from the traditional Provençal lament or complaint, and, as might be expected, it is a complaint of love. In the poem, the narrator leaves the nursing home where his beloved is dying of tuberculosis ("Exeo in a spasm/ tired of my darling's red sputum") and wanders through Dublin, traveling in a wide circle. He finds that the world is full of images of death ("a dying barge," "the stillborn evening," "the tattered sky like an ink of pestilence") and that he cannot forget his beloved or the fate of their love. Of course, these signs of death are not really present in the outer world; they reflect the narrator's inner life, the only life he can know, and, like Descartes, he rages against what he knows to be true as his own blood forms a "clot of anger."

There is no romance in Beckett's lament, only the all-encompassing awareness of mortality. Love and romance are like "the silk of the seas and the arctic flowers/ that do not exist," figments of the imagination that lose all sense of reality in the face of "the banner of meat bleeding."

The narrator keeps moving, however, and throughout the poem he has contact with others, with a small boy and "a wearish old man," an archetypal Beckett character, "scuttling along between a crutch and a stick,/ his stump caught up horribly, like a claw, under his breech, smoking." These meetings show the continuing possibility of human contact, even in a dying world; and they also make clear the need for going on even in the face of futility. Perhaps the others, like the narrator, are also moving in circles, but circular movement is still movement, and even the old man, crippled and in pain, does not remain motionless, does not give up.

"Sanies I" is also modeled on a Provençal form; the title is derived from a Latin term meaning "morbid discharge." For Beckett, writing is such a discharge, a residue, a "precipitate." It is a by-product of living and dying, but it is also that which remains, like Echo's voice.

Like the narrator of "Enueg I," the narrator of "Sanies I" is a wanderer in the process of completing a circle; in this case, he is returning home to Ireland after traveling in Europe, apparently in Germany, for his speech is full of Germanic terms. Like later Beckett protagonists, he rides a bicycle, and he describes himself as "a Ritter," a German knight, and, therefore, a somewhat ironic hero, although perhaps the only kind of hero who remains in the postmodern age: the hero who keeps moving. He has been wandering for a long time, and he says that he is "müüüüüüüüde now." The German *müde* means "tired," but the extended *ü* sound also gives a sense of boredom, an essential element in most of Beckett's work. Clearly, the narrator is both tired and bored, and, as a result, he is "bound for home like a good boy." Thinking about home and his parents, he recalls his birth and longs for that sweet oblivion of the womb: "Ah to be back in the caul now with no trusts/ no fingers no spoilt love."

This is a key passage. "The caul" to which the narrator would like to return is a fetal membrane covering the head, and, according to folklore, the child who is born with a caul is born to good luck. The implication here, however, is that the best of luck is never to have been born at all and, therefore, to avoid "trusts" and "spoilt loves," those exercises in futility. The unborn child also has "no fingers," and one without fingers cannot, and therefore need not, travel on a bicycle, as the narrator does. Even better, one without fingers cannot write, no matter how strongly he might feel the need to do so.

Of course, the narrator no longer has the option of not being born. He is "tired now hair ebbing gums ebbing ebbing home," and yet he approaches his hometown like a *Stürmer*, German slang for "lady-killer." It would seem that, despite his "spoilt loves," he is prepared for love again, and, indeed, he sees his beloved waiting for him. "I see main verb at last/ her whom alone in the accusative/ I have dismounted to love." In German, the "main verb" comes at the end of the sentence, and in this sentence that word is "love." At the last moment, however, the narrator sends the girl away ("get along with you now"), refusing to make the mistake his parents made by bringing another being into the world. Although one cannot return to the peace of the womb, one can at least refuse to pass on the curse of life to another.

If "Sanies I" is about nonexistence in the womb (the Cartesian egg), and if "Enueg I" is about nonexistence in the tomb, the title poem of the collection brings these two notions together. "Echo's Bones" is a short lyric that restates Beckett's key themes in capsule form. The first word of the poem is "asylum," a reference to the womb, but this is an "asylum under my tread," a shelter underground, a tomb. Like those in the womb, those in the tomb are beyond the confusions and pains of living now that they have run the gauntlet of life, "the gantelope of sense and nonsense." Only now, in death, are they free to be themselves, "taken by the maggots for what they are," and what they are is fleshless bone, without love or dreams and without the need to keep striving. The title of the poem, however, is a reminder that something more than bone remains: the voice. The words may be only a "morbid discharge," but, like Echo's voice, they survive.

Leaping ahead four decades to "Something There," a poem composed in 1974, the reader finds that the author's voice has changed, although his key themes remain. Here the lines are short and direct, flat and prosaic. There are no obscure allusions, no Joycean puns. The "something there" of the title is "something outside/ the head," and this contrast of inner and outer worlds returns the reader to *Whoroscope* and to the Cartesian dilemma of subjectivity which cannot reach beyond itself. The poem tries to reach that "something" in the only way it can, through words, but "at the faint sound so brief/ it is gone." The reality beyond the inner mind disappears as soon as the words of the mind try to grasp it, and so language, in the end, describes only the inner world which becomes something like a womb and a tomb in the midst of life. The inner world is not life, and yet, despite the fact that man cannot reach beyond his inner self to comprehend the "something outside/ the head," still he must try to do so, and the sign of his failure is language, the voice which always remains.

One can argue that Beckett's view of existence is largely negative. On the other hand, however, it is important to remember that he has been influenced greatly by the medieval theologians who argued that truth, in the person of God, is beyond positive statement and that man can know the truth only in the negative, by describing what it is not. Beckett seems to have taken the same approach. It is true that he writes about the curse of life, but he does so beautifully, raging against the inevitability of silence. The beauty of his work is the beauty of the human will to live in the face of death. Beckett sings the praises of those who say, with the nameless, formless, faceless narrator of *The Unnamable*: "I can't go on, I'll go on."

Major publications other than poetry

NOVELS: *Murphy*, 1938; *Molloy*, 1951 (English translation, 1955); *Malone meurt*, 1951 (*Malone Dies*, 1956); *L'Innomable*, 1953 (*The Unnamable*, 1958); *Watt*, 1953; *Comment c'est*, 1961 (*How It Is*, 1964); *Le Dépeupleur*, 1971 (*The Lost Ones*, 1972).

SHORT FICTION: *More Pricks than Kicks*, 1934; *Stories and Texts for Nothing*, 1967; *First Love and Other Shorts*, 1974; *Fizzles*, 1976.

PLAYS: *En attendant Godot*, 1952 (*Waiting for Godot*, 1954); *Fin de partie*, 1957 (*Endgame*, 1958); *All That Fall*, 1957 (radio play); *Krapp's Last Tape*, 1958; *Happy Days*, 1961; *Words and Music*, 1962 (radio play); *Cascando*, 1963 (radio play); *Film*, 1966 (screenplay); *Eh Joe*, 1967 (television script); *Sans*, 1969; *Not I*, 1974; *Rockaby*, 1981.

NONFICTION: *Proust*, 1931.

ANTHOLOGY: *An Anthology of Mexican Poetry*, 1958.

Bibliography

Alvarez, A. *Samuel Beckett*, 1973.

Bair, Deirdre. *Beckett: A Biography*, 1978.

Esslin, Martin, ed. *Samuel Beckett: A Collection of Critical Essays*, 1965.

Friedman, Melvin J., ed. *Samuel Beckett Now*, 1970.

Harvey, Lawrence E. *Samuel Beckett: Poet and Critic*, 1970.

Hassan, Ihab. *The Literature of Silence*, 1967.

Kenner, Hugh. *Samuel Beckett: A Critical Study*, 1961.

Robinson, Michael. *The Long Sonata of the Dead*, 1969.

Welch D. Everman

GUSTAVO ADOLFO BÉCQUER

Born: Seville, Spain; February 17, 1836
Died: Madrid, Spain; December 22, 1870

Principal collection
Rimas, 1871 (*The Rhymes*, 1891, 1898, 1908).

Other literary forms
Although Gustavo Adolfo Bécquer's fame rests mainly on his only volume of poetry, *The Rhymes*, he was also a notable prose writer. Bécquer demonstrated his talent at an early age with the publication of *Historia de los templos de España* (1857; a history of Spain's temples), an ambitious project of which only the first volume, a study of the churches of Toledo, was completed. Posterity has recognized the greater value of a variety of prose works which appeared in Madrid's newspapers and magazines during Bécquer's lifetime. Outstanding among these works are the newspaper letters published under the heading *Desde mi celda* (1864; *From My Cell*, 1924). They were written from Veruela's monastery in Aragón, where the author had gone to seek relief for his failing health. In these "letters," Bécquer pours out his moral biography, revealing himself to be a religious man who is both aware of the problems of his surroundings and sensitive to the legends and traditions he hears from shepherds and rovers in the northeast of Spain.

Also of great importance among Bécquer's prose works are the four "Cartas literarias a una mujer" (1871; "Letters to an Unknown Woman") and the prologue to the book *La Soledad* (1861) by his friend Augusto Ferrán. In these works, Bécquer expresses his ideas about love, literature in general, and, above all, poetry. In his prologue to Ferrán's book, Bécquer categorizes his own poetic production as the kind that is "natural, brief, dry, that which germinates in the soul like an electric spark, touches the feelings with a word and flees. . . . "

Bécquer's most celebrated prose works were his more than twenty legends, "Leyendas" (1860-1864). The themes of these prose tales do not differ substantially from those of the tales in verse typical of the Romantic movement in Spain and throughout Europe; they reveal a taste for the macabre, for medieval settings and exotic lore. What differentiates Bécquer's legends from the verse narratives and plays of the Duque de Rivas and José Zorrilla is their greater emphasis on the mysterious, the uncanny, the supernatural.

Achievements
Bécquer achieved fame only after his death. Although in his last years he was beginning to be recognized as a good journalist and an excellent prose writer, he was virtually unknown as a poet; only a handful of his poems were

published during his lifetime.

Bécquer's recognition as a poet began with the publication of *The Rhymes* one year after his death. By 1881, when the third edition of his poems was published, Bécquer was acknowledged as an important poet, and his fame was spreading throughout the Hispanic world. Since that time, Bécquer's reputation has grown steadily; his verse has achieved both critical acclaim and an extraordinary popular appeal. Indeed, after Miguel Cervantes' *Don Quixote de la Mancha* (1605, 1615), no literary work has had as many editions in Spanish as Bécquer's *The Rhymes*. In the last 150 years, no Spanish poem has touched as many hearts or has been recited and memorized as often as "Rime of the Swallows," and in that period, no poet has surpassed Bécquer's influence on Hispanic poetry. All the movements, groups, and poetic generations that have come after Bécquer in Hispanic literature have been indebted, directly or indirectly, to his innovations.

Biography

Gustavo Adolfo Bécquer was born in Seville, in the south of Spain, on February 17, 1836, the son of José María Domínguez Insausti, a painter, and Joaquina Bastida Vargas. The surname Bécquer had come to Spain from Flanders during the seventeenth century as Becker. Although the direct line of the name had ended with the poet's great-grandmother, the whole family was still known as the Bécquers. One month before young Bécquer turned five, his father died, and four years later his mother died also, leaving Bécquer and his seven brothers to the responsibility of their surviving relatives. While under the care of his mother's uncle, Don Juan de Vargas, Bécquer began to study at the Colegio de San Telmo in Seville, in order to become a sea pilot. When this school was closed a short time later, he went to live with his godmother, Doña Manuela Monchay. It was decided that Bécquer should take up his late father's profession, and he began to study painting at the school of the Sevillian artist Antonio Cabral Bajarano. Bécquer devoted his free time to reading in his godmother's library, where he developed his preference for Horace and for the Spanish Romantic José Zorrilla and where he became fond of literary studies in general.

Bécquer also studied painting with his uncle Joaquín Domínguez Bécquer. Nevertheless, his interest in literature had continued to grow, and when his uncle expressed doubts about Bécquer's potential to become a great artist, Bécquer decided, in 1854—against his godmother's advice—to go to Madrid and seek his fortune as a writer.

If in Seville Bécquer had found little happiness, he found even less in Madrid, where he always had economic difficulties and where he was soon diagnosed as having tuberculosis, the sickness that would take him to an early grave. Bécquer quickly ran out of the little money he had brought from Seville, and when he could no longer pay rent in the boardinghouse of Doña Soledad, she generously allowed him to continue residing there anyway. During his early years in Madrid, he worked in collaboration with various friends, turning out translations from French and writing original dramas and *zarzuelas* (musicals). These pieces for the stage, largely hackwork, did not command good payment, and some were not even produced. Needing to find another source of income, Bécquer obtained an insignificant position as a public servant, but he was soon fired, after being caught during working hours drawing a picture of William Shakespeare's Ophelia. In those days, he also contributed to a number of Madrid's newspapers and magazines, and he even tried, unsuccessfully, to found some new ones. These activities neither produced sufficient income for a comfortable life nor contributed to Bécquer's fame, since his works were often published without his name.

In the year 1858, Bécquer began to publish his "legends" in the newspapers of Madrid; in the same year, he met Julia Espín, a beautiful girl who later became an opera singer. It is said that, although Bécquer's love for this girl was unrequited, she inspired many of the entries in *The Rhymes*. It was at this time that Bécquer experienced his first health crisis. In 1859, a poem later included in *The Rhymes* was published under the title "Imitación de Byron" ("Imitation of Byron"); it was the first of fifteen of *The Rhymes* that appeared in Madrid periodicals during Bécquer's lifetime.

In 1860, Bécquer published his "Letters to an Unknown Woman" and met Casta Esteban Navarro, his doctor's daughter, whom Bécquer married the following year; the marriage would eventually produce two sons. In that same year, Bécquer's brother, Valeriano, a notable painter, came with his two children to live in Madrid and soon moved in with Gustavo and his wife. Throughout his married life, the poet and his wife spent several periods near Soria, where his father-in-law had a house. Between 1863 and 1864, Bécquer spent eight months living in the monastery of Veruela, where he wrote the letters in *From My Cell*. On several occasions, Bécquer and Valeriano took long trips to various parts of Spain, during which the artist would paint typical local scenes while the writer would take notes for his own works or would write articles for newspapers.

The year 1864 marked a change in Bécquer's life. He was appointed to a higher civil-service position with a better salary, but a change in the government caused him to lose the job a year later. Soon, however, yet another change in the government resulted in his reappointment to the job, where he worked until 1868, when the revolution that dethroned Isabella II took place. In the same year, Bécquer separated from his wife. Taking his two children, he went to live with Valeriano in Toledo, where he supposedly wrote the last poems for the book *The Rhymes*. A year later, they all returned to Madrid, and Bécquer resumed his journalistic work for the newspaper *La ilustración de Madrid*, where he was appointed editor in 1870. In September of that year, Valeriano died, and almost immediately Bécquer's wife repentantly returned to live with him and their children. Soon, the poet's health took a turn for the worse, and he died on December 22, 1870, at the age of thirty-four.

After Bécquer's death, his friend appointed a committee to publish his works. The committee collected his prose works which had appeared in the periodicals of Madrid and published them with the seventy-six poems from the manuscript of *The Rhymes*. This first edition of Bécquer's works was published in 1871, one year after his death.

Analysis

The poems that made Gustavo Adolfo Bécquer famous, and that make up practically his entire production, are those included in his book *The Rhymes*. Only eight or ten other poems have been found, almost all juvenilia and not of high quality. When Bécquer's friends published the first edition of his works in 1871, *The Rhymes* consisted of seventy-six untitled poems as well as the previously published prose works. Another manuscript of the collection was later found, containing three more poems, for a total of seventy-nine. The discovery and publication of other poems raised the number to ninety-four, but later it was proved that many of the new poems actually had been written by Bécquer's contemporaries or had been fraudulently attributed to him.

The single most important influence on Bécquer's poetry was Heinrich Heine, whose impact on Bécquer is universally acknowledged. In addition, critics have pointed out a wide variety of lesser influences, ranging from Lord Byron and Edgar Allan Poe to the German poets Johann Wolfgang von Goethe, Friedrich Schiller, and Anastasius Grün (pseudonym of Anton Alexander, Count of Auersperg) and the Spanish poets Eulogio Florentino Sanz (the translator of Heine into Spanish), José María de Larrea, and Augusto Ferrán. Nevertheless, Bécquer's poetic genius was so powerful that he was capable of fusing these influences with that of the popular Andalusian tradition to create his own distinctive style.

The most important characteristics of Bécquer's poetry are its simplicity and its suggestive, ethereal inwardness. It should be noted that the great majority of his poems are very short; his verse lines are generally short as well, and he prefers assonance to rhyme. Bécquer's language is elegant but simple, lacking exotic and high-sounding words, and he uses a minimum of rhetorical techniques. His preference for suggestion rather than explicit state-ment is reflected in his frequent use of incorporeal motifs such as waves of light, the vibration of air, murmurs, thoughts, clouds, and sounds. Anecdotes are absent from his poetry, except for some extremely short ones that are indispensable to the communication of emotions. Nature appears in his poems impressionistically, mirroring the poet's interior drama. Above all, Bécquer is an eminently subjective poet who uses his poetry to express his inner feelings with almost complete indifference to the objective reality of the world.

The above-mentioned characteristics, as well as others, place Bécquer as a precursor of the Symbolist movement. Traditionally, he has been considered a late Romantic, and to a certain extent this classification is correct. In Bécquer's poetry, it is easy to observe the cult of the individual, the exaggerated sensitivity, the centering of the world on the subjectivity of the poet—all typical of the Romantic movement. Nevertheless, these characteristics appear in Bécquer in conjunction with others that typify the Symbolism of Stéphane Mallarmé, Paul Verlaine, and Arthur Rimbaud. For Bécquer, emotions or feelings are the true object of poetry. Feelings cannot be expressed with exact and precise words, and to represent his interior world, the poet must rely on suggestion and evocative symbolism. In the first poem in *The Rhymes*, Bécquer says that he would like to express the "gigantic and strange hymnal" that he knows, by "taming the rebel, and miserly language,/ with words that are at the same time/ sighs and laughs, colors and notes." In these lines, it can be seen that Bécquer conceived of the possibility of the correspondence of sensations, also typical of Symbolism. For him, as for the Symbolists, there is an ideal, absolute, and perfect world, of which the familiar physical world is an imperfect representation, significant not for itself but only for the impressions of a higher reality that it conveys. Finally, Bécquer, like the Symbolists, made frequent allusions to music and struggled to make his language as musical as possible.

In the manuscript of *The Rhymes*, the poems do not follow a chronological order; indeed, they seem to follow no logical order at all. The most widely accepted critical opinion is that, having lost the original manuscript (which he gave to a friend for publication right before the revolution of 1868), Bécquer had to reconstruct the collection from memory, adding some new poems. It is speculated that in the new copy, the majority of the poems appear in the order in which the poet remembered them, interspersed with those newly created. In any case, when Bécquer's friends decided to publish his works, they rearranged the poems, placing them in the order in which they have appeared in all of their subsequent publications.

The sequence imposed on the poems, justifiably or not, gives the collection a "plot." Early poems in the sequence reflect the enthusiasm of a young poet who seeks to explain the mystery of his art and who discovers the mysterious connections between poetry and love. In later poems, however, celebration of love gives way to disillusionment with the beloved. In the final poems in the sequence, the poet is increasingly preoccupied with death.

Thus, with few exceptions, the poems collected in *The Rhymes* can be divided into four sequential groups. The first group consists of poems that consider the poet per se and the nature of poetry; the second, of poems dealing with love; the third, of poems expressing disillusionment with love; and the fourth, of poems dealing with anguish and death.

Included in the first group are poems 1 through 8—except for Poem 6 (a pathetic description of Shakespeare's Ophelia)—and Poem 21. In poems 2 and 5, Bécquer focuses his attention on the poet per se, trying to explain what it means to be a poet and to describe the intimate nature of the poetic spirit. In the first of these two poems, Bécquer employs a series of similes to define himself both as a poet and as a human being. To suggest the narrow limits of man's control over his own destiny, Bécquer imagines himself to be an arrow, a dry leaf, a wave, and a ray of light, saying in the last stanza that he is crossing the world "by accident," "without thinking/ where I am coming from nor where/ my steps will take me." In Poem 5, Bécquer portrays the poet as a vase containing the poetic spirit, described as an "unknown essence," a "mysterious perfume." Throughout the poem, Bécquer tries to determine the nature of that spirit. He identifies it in another series of beautiful similes where the objects of comparison are almost always immaterial and vague, with the clouds, the waking of a star, the blue of the sea, a note from a lute, and so on. This poem introduces an important idea in Bécquer's poetics: Poetry is the marvelous reduction of ideas and feelings to words and verbal forms. The poetic spirit is described as the "bridge that crosses the abyss," as "the unknown stair/ that connects heaven and earth," and as "the invisible/ ring that holds together/ the world of forms with the world of ideas."

The remaining poems of the first group attempt to explain the mystery of poetry. Poem 1 declares that poetry is "a hymn" that cannot be confined by words and that the poet can communicate fully only with his beloved. Here again, one notes the identification of poetry with feelings and the insistence that feelings cannot be explained but can be communicated only emotionally. These same notions lie behind the succinct affirmation of Poem 21, repeated by countless lovers of the Hispanic world since it was first published: Bécquer answers his beloved's question, "What is poetry?" with the simple statement, "Poetry is you."

The second group of poems, those dealing with love, includes poems 9 through 29, except for 21 (already placed in the first group) and 26 (which is closely related to the poems in the third group). Some of these poems can be considered as a series of gallant phrases forming beautiful madrigals appropriate for address to young ladies. Among them are Poem 12, written to a green-eyed girl; Poem 13 (the first of Bécquer's poems to have appeared in a newspaper, entitled "Imitation of Byron"), composed for a blue-eyed girl; and Poem 19, addressed to a girl who has the purity of a white lily. Some of the poems in this group have the charm, brevity, and sparkling shine of the *coplas* (ballads) from the Andalusian region; among these are poems 17 and 20.

In almost all the remaining poems of the second group, Bécquer appears as the poet of love, but of love as a superior and absolute feeling. Poems 9 and 10 show the universality of love. The former attempts to present all of nature as loving, and the latter describes how everything is transformed when love passes by. In poems 11 and 15, Bécquer realizes that love and the beloved for whom he searches are ideal entities of an absolute perfection and beauty that cannot exist in tangible reality. In the first of these two poems, two girls appear, one brunette and the other blonde, and each in turn asks the poet if it is she for whom he is looking, to which he answers no. Then comes an unreal girl, "a vague ghost made of mist and light," incorporeal and intangible, who is incapable of loving him; immediately, the poet shows his preference for this ethereal firgure, crying "Oh come, come you!" In Poem 15, the ideal beloved is a "curled ribbon of light foam," a "sonorous rumor/ of a golden harp," and the poet runs madly after her, "after a shadow/ after the fervent daughter/ of a vision."

The beloved becomes corporeal in only a few poems of the second group. In Poem 14, the poet sees "two eyes, yours, nothing else," and he feels that they irresistibly attract him. In Poem 18, the entire physical woman appears "fatigued by the dancing" and "leaning on my arm," and in Poem 29, the poet and his beloved are reading the episode of Paolo and Francesca in Dante's *La divina commedia* (c. 1320; *The Divine Comedy*) when suddenly they turn their heads at the same time: "our eyes met/ and a kiss was heard." Finally, in this second group, there is a poem that expresses the realization of love. In a typical series of incorporeal images, Bécquer says that his and his beloved's souls are "two red tongues of fire" that reunite and "form only one flame," "two notes that the hand pulls at the same time from the lute," "two streams of vapor" that join to form only "one white cloud," "two ideas born at the same time," and "two echoes that fuse with one another."

The third group of poems in *The Rhymes*, those expressing disillusionment with love, includes poems 30 through 51 as well as Poem 26. Although in these poems Bécquer continues talking about love, the ideal and sublime love of the poet has decayed, ending in failure and producing great disappointment, disenchantment, and sorrow. Bécquer speaks scornfully of feminine inconstancy in a few poems, but without the note of sarcasm characteristic of Heine. In Bécquer, sorrow produces only a fine irony, which at times leads him to insinuate that women are valuable only for their physical beauty. In Poem 34, after describing in detail the beauty of a woman, the poet faces the fact that she is "stupid." Bécquer resolves this conflict by saying that, as long as she stays quiet, her intelligence is of no concern to him, since "what she does not say, will always be of greater value/ than what any other woman could tell me." Similarly, in Poem 39, the poet enumerates the character flaws of a woman, only to end up stressing his preference for physical beauty by saying, "but . . . / she is so beautiful!"

The most interesting and intense poems of this third group are those in which the poet expresses his sorrow at the failure of his love. Some of them also seem to be the most autobiographical, although the impression given by the poems of *The Rhymes* is that all of them were the result of experiences lived by their author. Poem 41 appears to allude to the incompatibility between

Bécquer and his wife, although it could refer to another woman. Its three brief stanzas present the poet and his beloved as opposing forces: the hurricane and the tower, the ocean and the rock, the beautiful girl and the haughty man. In each instance, the conclusion is the desolate phrase, "it could not be." The next poem, number 42, describes the moment when "a loyal friend" tells the poet a piece of "news" not mentioned in the poem. The last lines, in which the poet expresses his gratitude, would seem rather prosaic if the author had not earlier shown the intensity of his sorrow by saying, "then I understood why one cries,/ and then I understood why one kills."

The fourth and last group of poems in *The Rhymes*, those preoccupied with anguish and death, includes poems 52 through 76. In general, the poems of this group seem to be more detached from autobiographical experience, less charged with emotional intensity. Perhaps for this very reason, they are pervaded by a haunting lyricism.

One of the most famous poems ever written in Spanish is Poem 53, the so-called "Rime of the Swallows," which has been read and memorized by one generation after another. The poem expresses the brevity and the irreversibility of life and the unique value of every experience. The poet admits that the "dark swallows will return," but not "those that learned our names," "those . . . will not return!" He acknowledges that there will be flowers again on the honeysuckle tree, but not "those decorated with dew/ whose drops we used to see trembling," "those . . . will not return!" Finally, he concedes that "the fervent words of love/ will sound again in your ears," but "as I have loved you, . . . do not deceive yourself/ nobody will love you like that!"

The last poems in the collection are dominated by the theme of death. When the poet asks himself about his origin and his end in Poem 66, he ends his expression of radical loneliness by affirming that his grave will be "where forgetfulness lives." In Poem 71, he hears a voice calling him in his sleep, and he concludes that "somebody/ whom I loved has died!" In another of his most famous poems, which is also the longest in the book, Bécquer describes the funeral of a girl, repeating at the end of each stanza, "my God, how lonely stay the dead!" The same experience may have inspired poems 74 and 76. In Poem 74, it seems that he sees a dead woman, and at the spectacle of death his soul is filled with "a fervent desire": "as the abyss attracts, that mystery/ was dragging me towards itself." At the same time, the angels that are engraved on the door seem to speak to him: "the threshold of this door only God trespasses." In Poem 74, which concludes the volume, Bécquer again describes the funeral of a woman and expresses his own wish to rest from the struggles of life: "oh what love so quiet that of death/ what sleep so calm that of the sepulchre."

Major publications other than poetry
SHORT FICTION: "Leyendas," 1860-1864.

NONFICTION: *Historia de los templos de España*, 1857; "Prologue" to *La Soledad*, 1861 (by Augusto Ferán); *Desde me celda*, 1864 (*From My Cell*, 1924); "Cartas literarias a una mujer," 1871 ("Letters to an Unknown Woman").

MISCELLANEOUS: *The Infinite Passion: Being the Celebrated "Rimas" and the "Letters to an Unknown Woman,"* 1924 (includes *The Rhymes*, *From My Cell*, and "Letters to an Unknown Woman").

Bibliography

Alonso, Dámaso. "Originalidad de Bécquer," in *Poetas españoles contemporáneos*, 1969.

Alonso, Martín. *Segundo estilo de Bécquer: Ensayo biocrítico del poeta y de su época*, 1972.

Balbín Lucas, Rafael de. *De poética bécqueriana*, 1969.

Bousoño, Carlos, and Dámaso Alonso. "Las pluralidades paralelísticas de Bécquer," in *Seis calas en la expresión literaria española*, 1963.

Brown, Rica. *Bécquer*, 1963.

Díaz, José Pedro. *Gustavo Adolfo Bécquer: Vida y poesía*, 1964.

Díez Taboada, Juan María. *La mujer ideal: Aspectos y fuentes de las rimas*, 1965.

Rogelio A. de la Torre

PIETRO BEMBO

Born: Venice, Italy; May 20, 1470
Died: Rome, Italy; January 18, 1547

Principal collections

Gli Asolani, 1505 (includes poems and prose; English translation, 1954);
Rime per festa carnascialesca, 1507; *Rime*, 1530; *Carmina*, 1533; *Opere*, 1729;
Prose e rime di Pietro Bembo, 1960.

Other literary forms

Pietro Bembo's second major work, *Prose della volgar lingua* (1525; essays
on the vulgar tongue), was a dialogue dedicated to Cardinal Giulio de' Medici,
later Pope Clement VII, and set at the home of Bembo's brother, Carlo, in
Venice. The interlocutors are Carlo Bembo, Bembo's mouthpiece; Giuliano
de' Medici, Duke of Nemours; Federigo Fregoso; and Ercole Strozzi. In
book 1, it is established that Italian is preferable to Latin for current literary
use and that the language of Florence as used by Petrarch and Giovanni
Boccaccio is more appropriate for this purpose than the language of contemporary Florentine writers, the special brand of Italian spoken at the Papal
Court, or any other dialect. Bembo's approach to language is solely literary;
a spoken language unconsecrated by use as a literary medium was for him
not a language. When Giuliano suggests that literature should approach modern usage, Carlo Bembo makes the declaration that the more the literary
language approaches popular usage, the more it loses *gravità* (seriousness)
and *grandezza* (loftiness). Book 2 deals with the choice and placement of
words and the means by which the primary qualities of literary style—*gravità*
and *piacevolezza* (pleasantness)—may be achieved. There are etymologies
(for example, it is suggested that *madrigal* derives from *mandria*, meaning
"flock," and originally designated a song composed by shepherds while tending their flocks, even today a reputable hypothesis) and observations on the
poetic value of the various vowels and consonants. There is a review of early
Italian writers; Bembo points out that it is best not to imitate Dante's vocabulary, because he used words that are "rozze e disonorate" (rough and dis-
graceful). Practical advice for writing prose and verse follows, and then book
3 expounds upon grammatical rules. Its many examples are taken from Boccaccio and Petrarch, but it also includes quotations from Dante, from the
minor works of Boccaccio, and from such thirteenth century poets as the
Florentine Giovanni Villani and the Sicilian Guido delle Colonne of Messina.
Addressing writers, Bembo shows them how to achieve elegance by imitating
the greatest writers of Italian. He uses the terms *fiorentino* (Florentine),
toscano (Tuscan), and *volgare* (vernacular) indiscriminately; the polemic over
the designation of the language described and prescribed by Bembo had not

yet erupted, and even after it did erupt, Bembo refused to be drawn into it.

Bembo was searching for a pure Italian language, and he was not a Latinizer in the sphere of his Italian studies. If a word was closer to Latin but had not been used by the greats of the Italian literary tradition, that word was as distasteful to him as a non-Latin word or one grossly distorted from its Latin antecedent. In this he differed from Baldassare Castiglione, author of *Il cortegiano* (1528; *The Courtier*, 1561), who favored the eclectic or courtly solution to the language problem of Italy and preferred more Latinate forms, even if non-Tuscan, and the more recent borrowings from Latin such as *populo* to *popolo* or *onorevole* to *orrevole*. It was Bembo's philosophy that, as all reputable Latin should be modeled upon Cicero, all Italian should be verified first within the canon of Petrarch and Boccaccio. Even while he was papal secretary, he advised his colleague Jacopo Sadoleto to avoid reading the Epistles of Saint Paul, lest their unpolished language mar his style. In the words of John Addington Symonds, Bembo's "piety toward the mother-tongue was generous; his method of rehabilitation was almost servile."

Achievements

The influence of Bembo on his contemporaries and on the Italian language far outstripped his talent as a writer. The literary dictator of Italy for more than fifty years, he was dubbed the foster father of the Italian language, and authors whose names are today more familiar than his sent him their manuscripts for corrections and improvements. Bembo did not fail to partake of the best his era had to offer. He lived in the Florence of Lorenzo de' Medici, the Venice of Aldus Manutius, and the Rome of Pope Leo X. Bellini and Titian painted portraits of him. He was a friend of Lucrezia Borgia, Isabella d'Este, Raphael, Poliziano, Ludovico Ariosto, Desiderius Erasmus, and Pietro Aretino, and both friend and literary mentor to Gaspara Stampa, Vittoria Colonna, and Veronica Gambara. Giangiorgio Trissino, Colonna, and Ariosto, among many others, wrote sonnets to him. He wrote two of the most famous essays of his century and the best Petrarchan verse.

Bembo's poems were borrowed, translated, and clearly plagiarized by subsequent generations of European writers. Among Italian poets, his greatest disciple was Giovanni Della Casa. In England, Sir Thomas Wyatt paraphrased "Voi me poneste in foco" ("Lady, You've Set Me All Afire") from *Gli Asolani*, representing it as his own work, and Thomas Lodge included translations from Bembo in his *Phillis* poems. Because the principles of scansion are the same in Italian as in Spanish, Spanish poets such as Torres Naharro, Juan Boscan, and Luis de Léon were especially avid imitators of Bembo's verse, and Bembo's poem "Quand'io penso al martire" ("Madrigal") found its way into no less a work than *Don Quixote de la Mancha* (1605, 1615). Francisco de Sá de Miranda, who spent time in Italy in the 1520's and became acquainted with Bembo, introduced Petrarchan imagery in Portugal and ultimately influ-

enced the style of Luis de Camões. The epitaph Bembo wrote for Jacopo
Sannazzaro, "De sacro cineri flores. Hic ille Maroni/ Syncerus, musa proximus
ut tumulo" (Give to the sacred ashes flowers. Here Maro/ In Muse Sincerus
neighbors as in tomb) was copied on Edmund Spenser's tomb in Westminster
Abbey.

Bembo is also credited with having heterosexualized the concept of Platonic
Love. For the ancient Greeks, Platonic Love was not love between the sexes
but a philosophical idea based on heroic friendship, and what was so called
by the Neoplatonists was still essentially the same as, for example, the relationship of Marsilio Ficino and Guido Cavalcanti, or of Giovanni Pico della
Mirandola and Girolamo Benivieni. The Neoplatonic idealism that inspired
Bembo and his style of balanced moderation determined an important pattern
in the Renaissance poetry of several countries until the early Baroque.

Bembo restored Petrarchanism to its original luster and form by providing
an unmistakably elegant standard by which the excesses of such conceitful
poets as Il Chariteo, Antonio Tebaldeo, Serafino Aquilano, and Panfilo Sasso
(who stressed the obvious and inferior elements of Petrarch's poetry rather
than its deeper and less readily imitable perfections) could be judged as
inferior. The prose style of *Gli Asolani* is equally elegant. Bembo was always
an imitator, but he could judge better than others who and which elements
were worthiest of imitation. As his poetry is modeled after Petrarch, his prose
is modeled on the classicizing prose of the *Ameto* of Boccaccio. The Italian
of *Gli Asolani* is indeed a new classic language, as if its author had been
writing in Latin.

If readers did not become familiar with the Neoplatonism, the revised
Petrarchanism, and the lapidary stylistics of Bembo from *Gli Asolani*, they
read the words put into his mouth in the fourth book of Castiglione's *The
Courtier*, a work of deeper insight than Bembo's, and his name was subsequently associated with all the characteristics that Castiglione attributed to
him. Bembo, who is present in all the dialogues of *The Courtier*, assumes a
leading role when the Duchess asks him to expound on what kind of love is
appropriate for a courtier. Despite what his American translator Rudolph B.
Gottfried calls the raillery and worldliness apparent in *Gli Asolani*, Bembo
waxes almost mystical as he defines the Neoplatonic doctrine of love for
Castiglione. He speaks of the divine origin of beauty, the distinction between
the worlds of sense and intellect, and the various steps by which sensual love
for a woman is finally transformed into spiritual love for God.

Perhaps Bembo at the age of fifty-eight simply allowed himself to appear
more Platonic than he had been in his earlier years. The fifty *Rime per festa
carnascialesca* that he composed for the Carnival at Urbino in 1507 (reworked
by the Spaniard Juan Boscan in his own long poem, *Octava rima*, omitting
certain stanzas whose licentiousness was unsuited to Spanish taste) urge Duchess
Isabella Gonzaga and her sister-in-law Emilia Pia not to deny themselves the

joys of love and are anything but Platonic. Even in *Gli Asolani*, published some twenty years before *The Courtier*, Perottino's attack on, and Gismondo's eulogy of, earthly love are more convincing than Lavinello's shorter Platonic resolution of the problem in book 3. While Castiglione uses some of the same arguments that are advanced in *Gli Asolani*, he also adds material that makes Bembo more Platonic than he appears in his own works; indeed, Bembo's Platonism in *Gli Asolani* is more literary than philosophical. The fact remains, however, that without Bembo, the finer art of Castiglione might never have emerged.

As a native Venetian and an affiliate of the Papal Court who endorsed the Florentine dialect, Bembo did not see himself as a pacesetter. He had observed that the majority of older exemplary writers were native Tuscans, but he mistakenly considered himself the successor of such non-Tuscan writers as Pietro de Crescenzi and Guido delle Colonne of Messina. Actually, their works had been composed in Latin and translated anonymously by Tuscan scribes. It was not until the decision of Jacopo Sannazzaro, a Neopolitan, to write his highly successful *Arcadia* (1504) in Tuscan that the precedent of the Tuscan dialect as a vehicle for non-Tuscan writers was set. In the wake of Sannazzaro, Bembo proclaimed the preeminence of fourteenth century Tuscan; his views prevailed, and the influence of his prescriptive attitude on the subsequent development of Italian literature can hardly be exaggerated. Ludovico Ariosto, for example, undertook a massive revision of *Orlando furioso* (1516, 1521, 1532) after the appearance of Bembo's *Prose della volgar lingua*. He attempted to bring his Italian closer to the precepts of Bembo by doubling consonants, modifying his use of the article (*il* for *el*, *lo* before impure *s*), and revising verb forms. In a letter to Bembo dated February 23, 1531, Ariosto announced his intention of coming to Padua to consult him on stylistic matters. Ariosto gave Bembo a permanent tribute in the body of his masterpiece:

> I see Pietro Bembo here,
> Him who our pure and dulcet speech set free
> From the base vulgar usage, and made clear
> By his example what it ought to be.

Biography

Pietro Bembo, the son of Venetian vice-doge and senator Bernardo Bembo and his wife, Elena Morosina, was born in Venice in 1470. Bembo acquired a more thorough knowledge of Tuscan than would have otherwise been possible, because his father, a member of Ficino's Academy, took him to Florence when he was eight years old. Proud of the boy's facility with languages, his father sent him to Messina to study under Constantine Lascaris in 1492. Bembo stayed in Sicily for two years, years of intense study which he fondly remembered all of his life. Later, he studied philosophy at Padua under Pietro Pomponazzi, for whom Bembo would later intercede to save him from condemnation by the Lateran Council.

In 1498, Bembo's father went to Ferrara as Venetian coruler and took Pietro with him, hoping to acquaint him at long last with affairs of state. There he became intimate with Jacopo Sadoleto and Ercole Strozzi, and was appreciated by Duke Ercole of Ferrara. When Duke Ercole's son and heir Alfonso married Lucrezia Borgia in 1502, Bembo became friendly with her as well, and there developed between the two of them a deep friendship that may or may not have been Platonic.

On leaving Ferrara, Bembo returned to Venice, where he helped the printer Aldus Manutius form a learned academy and, in 1501, prepared for him the text of Petrarch's *Canzoniere* (written 1374, published 1470), as well as the first Aldine copy of *La divina commedia* (c. 1320; *The Divine Comedy*), published under the title *Terza rima* in 1502. Bembo and Aldus are credited with establishing the use of the apostrophe, the period, and the comma in modern printing.

Tall and handsome, witty and learned, a writer of verse in three languages (Italian, Latin, and Greek), Bembo was in his prime when he moved to Urbino in 1506. Until 1511, he was a member of the court circle of Urbino, which, under Duke Guidobaldo Montefeltro and his wife Elisabetta Gonzaga, rivaled Ferrara in social, artistic, and literary brilliance and which included such figures as the dramatist Bernardo Bibbiena, Giuliano de' Medici, Ottaviano Fregoso (later doge of Genoa), Louis of Canossa (later papal nuncio to France), and sundry other poets, musicians, and visitors. It was this refined circle that Castiglione idealized in *The Courtier*, and it was to Bembo that he gave the most distinguished role in the dialogue to discourse upon the nature of Platonic Love.

In 1512, Bembo accompanied Giuliano de' Medici to Rome, and when Giuliano's brother became Pope Leo X in 1513, Bembo was given duties as Leo's secretary, a post he shared with his old friend and fellow student Sadoleto. Bembo was precisely the man to make Leo's life more agreeable by flattering his superficial tastes and by directing the faculties of his highly cultured mind to frivolous, if intellectual, amusements. The position afforded Bembo the opportunity to display his greatest talent, composing papal documents and letters in very polished Latin. It was also during these papal years that Bembo was most aggressively Ciceronian in his controversy with Poliziano and Erasmus.

In 1519, Bembo's debt-ridden father died, and Bembo left the Vatican to spend most of the next year between Venice and Padua. In April, 1521, wearied after nearly thirty years of continual court life, harried by illness, and depressed by the deaths of many of his good friends in Rome the previous year (Raphael, the banker Agostino Chigi, and Bibbiena had all died in 1520), he resigned his secretaryship and retired to his villa Noniamo near Padua. There, he entertained himself collecting manuscripts (his library, particularly rich in the works of the Provençal poets and Petrarch, passed after his death to Urbino and thence to the Vatican), experimenting with horticulture, and following the example of Horace and Vergil in appreciating the charms of country life. He was living with Morosina (Ambrogia della Torre), whom he had met in Rome in 1513 when she was barely sixteen (his ecclesiastical responsibilities and aspirations had precluded marriage), and was much concerned with the education of their three children, Lucilio, Torquato, and Elena. In 1530, he was appointed historiographer of the Venetian Republic, succeeding Andreas Navigero, and later, librarian of St. Mark's.

After the death of his beloved Morosina in August, 1535, Bembo embraced a more austere life, gave up his classical interests, and devoted himself to scriptural and patristic readings. Pope Paul III made him a cardinal in 1539, when he was sixty-nine years of age. In 1541, he was given the bishopric of Gubbio, where he moved in 1543. In 1544, he was given the rich see of Bergamo, but he never moved there. During these last years of life, Bembo seems to have taken great interest in the reforming views of Cardinal Pole and Vittoria Colonna at Viterbo—so much so that after his death, his name was found on the list of suspects of the Roman Inquisition.

In March of 1544, Bembo moved back to Rome, where he lived until his death in 1547 after a fall from his horse. He was buried in the Church of the Minerva between Popes Leo X and Clement VII. Olimpia Morata wrote the following words for him in Greek: "Bembo is no more. . . . He dies, and with him, disappears the splendid genius of eloquence; Cicero seems to have passed away a second time into the dark shadows."

Analysis

Gli Asolani is a treatise on love in three books, with sixteen poems (canzones, canzonets, and one double sestina) interspersed in the text. The canzonets do not qualify as madrigals, even by Pietro Bembo's own broad definition in *Prose della volgar lingua*, but in *Italian Poets of the Renaissance*, Joseph Tusiani nevertheless gives to one of them, "Quand'io penso al martire," the title "Madrigal." The treatise takes its name from the Castello d'Asolo, belonging to Caterina Cornaro, the former queen of Cyprus, in the mountains north of Venice, which also served as the poetic inspiration of Robert Browning, who made it the scene of "Pippa Passes" and finished there the collection of lyrics entitled "Asolando." Bembo wrote the treatise between 1497 and 1502, recast the work in 1503 and 1504, and published it in 1505, with a dedication to Lucrezia Borgia. The three principal speakers are three young Venetian gentlemen, Perottino, Gismondo, and Lavinello, and their ladies, Lisa, Sabinetta, and Berenice, all members of the court under fictitious names. Praises of the Asolan circle run through the work, and the picture of the six novices, sauntering through shade and sunlight under the vines of a leafy pergola or seated on the grass listening to a deftly stroked lute, retains its freshness even for the modern reader.

The discussion revolves around the question of whether love is a good or a bad thing. Gismondo maintains that it is good, and Perottino counters that it is bad with an argument that occupies the entire first book. Berenice refuses to accept his conclusion, whereupon Perottino recites a list of love's casualties (Pyramus and Thisbe, Murrha and Byblis, Medea, Tarquin) and supports his argument by singing songs of his own composition. Perottino's tale of sighs and wretchedness is also punctuated with questions on punning etymologies, such as the relationship of *amare* (to love) and *amaro* (bitter), *donna* (lady) and *danno* (damage), *giovani* (young men) and *giovano* (they help).

One of the poems he recites, translated by Tusiani as "Madrigal," is "Quand'io penso al martire," which traces how the lover is forced by Love to stand before the sea of bitterness, where, once facing death, he is so happy to be relieved of his first burden that he feels like living again. In another, which Perottino recites in a voice "which would move stones," "Lady, You've Set Me All Afire," the poet admits that he is not as angry at the lady who caused his discomfort as he is at Love and at himself for allowing himself to be in Love's thrall.

In book 2, Gismondo refutes the arguments of Perottino, concluding that love is not only good but also the source of all that is good in life. In the canzonet "Non si vedrà giammai stanca né sazia" (O love, my lord, faint and forworn this pen), Gismondo thanks Love for leading him to seek the skies and for giving his speech a music sweet. It is to Love that the poet owes his happy life and his pure and joyous thoughts.

On the third afternoon, the Queen and some other guests join the six, and Lavinello assumes a conciliatory position between Perottino and Gismondo, arguing that love can be good if it is worthy love of a good object; that love is evil if it is love of an evil object and evil as well if it is unworthy love of a good object. Love is the search for beauty, and beauty, physical or mental, is a grace, which derives from good proportion, compatibility, and harmony of the various elements. Halfway through Lavinello's argument and after he recites three poems, he introduces a conversation he claims to have had with a hermit that morning. If love is to be good, the hermit tells Lavinello, it must arise from true beauty, beauty that is divine and immortal.

All in all, *Gli Asolani* has little that is original. From Petrarch, Bembo derived the first and second books and the first half of the third book, while the hermit's conversation is mainly from Dante; despite the Neoplatonic label attached to Bembo, only a few tidbits are borrowed from Platonic theory. Although some of its individual passages are beautiful, on the whole the work holds little appeal for the modern reader. Bembo makes no attempt to develop an independent philosophy apart from Ficino's theory of Platonism, nor does

Bembo, except in the second book, try to relate it to practical problems, regarding it as a thing beautiful in itself, a charming abstraction shining in its distant and rarefied air.

The poetry in *Rime* is thoroughly Petrarchan in form (sonnets, canzones, *ballate*), phrasing (eyes brighter than the sun, the calming smile, the ivory hands), imagery (love as the impious lord, the lover as the ship battered by the storm, the song of birds expressive of the pain of love), and content (the request to God for the power to resist love, lamentation for the ruthlessness of love, regret for allowing oneself to be caught by love). Bembo's poetry demonstrates a more refined taste than that of earlier imitators of Petrarch, but it still lacks originality by modern standards. Bembo's most famous sonnet, "Crin d'oro crespo" ("A Curly Hair of Gold"), is a catalog of his lady's attributes that ends with a line taken almost verbatim from Petrarch: "Grazie, ch'a poche il ciel largo destina" ("Graces that on few women heaven freely bestows").

While Petrarch was keenly and painfully aware of both the transitory nature of man's existence and the profane power of love to deflect him from his true devotion to God, these themes did not particularly interest Bembo. There is some religious poetry among his sonnets, but it is rather facile; indeed, Bembo wrote to the Duchess of Urbino on March 20, 1504, that the thought of heavenly things had never occupied him much and did not occupy him then at all. He is supposed to have undergone a conversion after the death of Morosina, but until then he had blithely accumulated ecclesiastical benefits without in the least renouncing earthly pleasures. In his sonnet, "O Sol, di cui questo bel sol è raggio" (O sun, of whom this beautiful sun is a glimmer), written probably in 1538, he asks God to look upon his soul, "to sweep away the ancient fog," and to keep his soul safe from the injuries of the world. In "Signor, quella pietà, che ti constrinse" (Lord, that mercy which bound you), the reader is impressed with the familiarity that Bembo affects in order to bargain for his salvation, which may be due to the earlier date of its composition (1510). In "Signor, che per giovar si chiama Giove" (Lord, who for your help, are called Jove), written in 1528, he plays flippantly upon the similarity of the verb *giovare* (to help) and the name of the pagan deity *Giove* (Jove).

Bembo wrote many occasional poems, such as to celebrate the birth of a friend's son or the exploits of an unidentified "conqueror of Naples." He had a knack for converting an ordinary incident into a subtle vignette. In "Ove romita e stanca si sedea" (where tired and alone she sat), the poet, like a thief burning with hope and fear, surprises his beloved as she is lost in thought and perhaps even talking to herself. She is mildly upset that he has seen her so absorbed, and he is possessed by tenderness to have seen her so. His elegies on the death of persons dear to him are counted among his best poems; unlike so many of his Petrarchan exercises, they do not lack spontaneous emotion. "Donna, di cui begli occhi alto diletto" (lady, whose beautiful eyes gave such delight) is one of his many sonnets on the death of his mistress Morosina, and "Adunque m'hai tu pur, in sul fiorire" ("On the Death of His Brother") was penned in memory of his brother Carlo, who died at the age of thirty-two in 1503.

Bembo also wrote Latin poetry. His hexameter poem "Benacus" is a description of Lago di Garda, and he also wrote epitaphs in Latin for many of his contemporaries. In his epitaph for Poliziano, whose death in 1494 followed close upon that of his patron, Lorenzo de' Medici, Bembo tells how death struck him while he wept, breaking his heartstrings in the middle of his sighs, and dubs him in the last line as "master of the Ausonian [Italian] lyre." Two elegiac poems, "Priapus" and "Faunus ad nympheum flumen," are remarkable for their pagan approach to morality; his masterpiece in elegiac meter is "De Galeso et Maximo," about a boy, Galesus, who wrongs his master, Maximus, who, as the epigraph explains, is a great man in Rome and may possibly represent Pope Leo X himself. When Maximus is confronted with the boy's misdeed, the boy does not apologize but rather runs to clasp the neck of his angry master, raining kisses upon him. Bembo concludes: "Still doubting, Maximus? Change place with me:/ Gladly I'd bear such infidelity."

The influence of Bembo was so strong that an entire half century (1500-1550) has been designated by many critics as the "Bembist period." His support of the vernacular as the equal of Latin, and his support of the Florentine dialect over competing dialects, determined in no small way the course of Italian literature. As a poet, he refurbished the Petrarchan tradition, and he was instrumental in the spread of Neoplatonism. While it is true that his influence on literature was out of proportion to the value of his literary output, Bembo inspired a fierce loyalty in his contemporaries, and his precepts commanded a vigorous authority long after his death.

Major publications other than poetry

NONFICTION: *De Aetna*, 1496; *Prose della volgar lingua*, 1525; *De Guidobaldo liber* or *De Urbini ducibus*, 1530; *Rerum Venetarum historiae libri XII*, 1551.

MISCELLANEOUS: *Gli Asolani*, 1505 (includes prose and poetry; English translation, 1954); *Epistolarum Leonis X nomine scriptarum libri XVI*, 1535; *Epistolae familiares libri VII*, 1552; *Lettere*, 1548-1553 (4 volumes).

Bibliography
Dionisotti, Carlo, ed. "Introduction," in *Prose e rime di Pietro Bembo*, 1960.
Durant, Will. *The Story of Civilization*, 1935.
Fletcher, Jefferson Butler. *Literature of the Italian Renaissance*, 1934, 1964.
Forster, Leonard. *The Icy Fire: Five Studies in European Petrarchism*, 1969.

Hare, Christopher. *Life and Letters in the Italian Renaissance*, 1915.
Migliorini, Bruno. *The Italian Language*, 1966.
Robb, Nesca A. *Neoplatonism of the Italian Renaissance*, 1935, 1968.
Symonds, John Addington. *The Renaissance in Italy*, 1886.
Tusiani, Joseph. *Italian Poets of the Renaissance*, 1971.
Wilkins, Ernest Hatch. *A History of Italian Literature*, 1962.

Jack Shreve

GOTTFRIED BENN

Born: Mansfeld, Germany; May 2, 1886
Died: Berlin, East Germany; August 7, 1956

Principal collections

Morgue und andere Gedichte, 1912; *Söhne*, 1913; *Fleisch*, 1917; *Schutt*, 1924; *Spaltung*, 1925; *Betäubung*, 1925; *Gesammelte Gedichte*, 1927; *Aus-gewählte Gedichte, 1911-1936*, 1936; *Gedichte*, 1936; *Zweiundzwanzig Ge-dichte*, 1943; *Statische Gedichte*, 1948; *Trunkene Flut*, 1949; *Fragmente*, 1951; *Destillationen*, 1953; *Aprèslude*, 1955; *Gesammelte Gedichte*, 1956; *Primäre Tage, Gedichte und Fragmente aus dem Nachlass*, 1958; *Primal Vision*, 1958; *Gedichte aus dem Nachlass*, 1960; *Gottfried Benn: Selected Poems*, 1970; *Gottfried Benn: The Unreconstructed Expressionist*, 1972.

Other literary forms

Gottfried Benn was primarily a poet, but he did write some significant works in other genres, most notably a collection of novellas, *Gehirne* (1916; brains); his novel, *Roman des Phänotyp* (1944; novel of the phenotype); his essay *Goethe und die Naturwissenschaften* (1949; Goethe and the natural sciences); his autobiography, *Doppelleben* (1950; double life); and his theo-retical treatise, *Probleme der Lyrik* (1951; problems of lyric poetry). His writings also include other prose and dramatic works.

Achievements

No other German poet exemplifies as fully as Benn the emergence of the modern tradition within postwar German literature. His radical aesthetic as well as his political affiliations have made Benn a controversial figure. He was the "phenotype" of his age—that is, the exemplary representation of the intellectual and spiritual condition of his times. As such, Benn can be viewed not only as a remarkable poet, but also as an important figure of twentieth century German *Geistesgeschichte*.

Benn's early work (until about 1920) was known only to a relatively small circle of readers. Indeed, it was only after World War II, in the last decade of his life, that Benn achieved fame. His achievements were acknowledged in 1951, when he was awarded the Georg Büchner Prize in literature. For years prior to this time, Benn had been blacklisted, as it were, as a result of his short-lived infatuation with Nazism. Because of the public commentary to which he had been subjected, Benn was reluctant to reenter public life. He did publish again, however, and in the years before his death a generation of poets in search of a tradition flocked around him like disciples around a master. What were the reasons for Benn's appeal?

The years of Nazi control had yielded a vast wasteland in German literature.

Indeed, the historical events of the twentieth century, in particular as they affected Germany, intensified the general philosophical disorientation of the immediate postwar period. Marxism was no real alternative for the West; Existentialism prevailed instead, based in large measure on the writings of Martin Heidegger and Jean-Paul Sartre. In this context, Benn's theory of art as a metaphysical act had considerable authority. For postwar poets in search of a new way of writing, Benn provided a transition from the various offshoots of French Symbolism and German Expressionism to contemporary modernism.

Biography

Gottfried Benn was born on May 2, 1886, the son of a Protestant minister. He studied philosophy and theology at the University of Marburg and later studied medicine at the University of Berlin. He completed his medical degree in 1910 and was awarded first prize for his thesis on the etiology of epilepsy in puberty. Benn worked as a pathologist and serologist in Berlin, where he became friends with several Expressionist poets, the most important of whom was Else Lasker-Schüler. Benn also set up medical practice in Berlin, and his first volume of poetry, *Morgue und andere Gedichte* (morgue and other poems), clearly shows the influence of his scientific and medical training: the cold and unforgiving objectivity and precision of medical and surgical technique inform these poems, with their shocking portrayal of brutality and morbidity.

In 1914, Benn traveled briefly to the United States. Upon his return, he was drafted into the military medical corps, serving as an officer in Belgium before returning to Berlin in 1917. These years, contrary to what one might expect, were extremely productive for Benn as a writer, and he later noted that during the following years, on the whole relatively uneventful for him, he constantly drew for inspiration on his experiences in Belgium.

In 1933, Benn filled the position of which Heinrich Mann had been relieved, section president of the Prussian Academy. Later, Benn became director for the Department of Literature. In April of the same year, he gave a radio talk, "Der neue Staat und die Intellektuellen" ("The New State and the Intellectuals"), clearly in response to a letter from Klaus Mann, the son of Thomas Mann, who wrote from the south of France. It is true that Benn initially embraced National Socialism in 1933. He greeted the political doctrines of the Nazis as a means for overcoming the stagnation and nihilism of Western civilization, but he soon regretted his participation and withdrew into silence.

In 1935, Benn left Berlin and headed for Hannover. It was Benn's early poetry which gave rise to the debate on Expressionism carried in the émigré paper *Das Wort*, printed in Moscow. In the ensuing years, Benn had a run-in with W. Willrich, a party loyalist who labeled Benn a "cultural Bolshevist" and tried to have Benn effectively "removed" from public life. Ironically, only the intervention of Heinrich Himmler himself stayed Willrich's attempts.

Benn remained in the army medical service from 1935 until the end of the war. After 1948, he enjoyed a new phase of poetic creativity, and his poetry eventually achieved recognition throughout Europe.

Analysis

Both poetically and existentially, Gottfried Benn resided at the crossroads of two significant traditions. At the turn of the century, the natural sciences exercised a substantial "claim to truth" and provided influential paradigms of thought. For many of Benn's generation, however, scientific study had entered a rapid phase of entropy—it was seen no longer to answer questions meaningfully from the humanist point of view. In fact, one could even say that the "scientific approach" was seen by many to "explain" the universe inadequately, precisely because it did not pose the right questions. In Germany, the most significant manifestation of this dissatisfaction with the scientific paradigm took place under the rubric of "Expressionism," which in many respects carried on the tradition of German Romanticism. The tension exemplified in the conflict between Benn's scientific training and his early intoxication with Expressionism came to play an important role in the development of his aesthetic theory and poetry.

A concept basic to Benn's thought was his conviction that humankind necessarily "suffered consciousness." He attributed this suffering to modern overintellectualization: "The brain is our fate, our consignment and our curse." The modern consciousness fragments the totality of the world into its conceptual categories; reality is particled past meaningful comprehension; and the loss of man's capacity to perceive relationships points ineluctably in the direction of nihilistic resignation. During the years from 1921 to 1932, Benn studied the works of Johann Wolfgang von Goethe, Friedrich Nietzsche, Oswald Spengler, Carl G. Jung, Ernst Troeltsch, and Gotthold Lessing, and through his study of prehistory, paleontology, and myth, he developed his own notions of art, reality, and the self.

In Benn's conceptual framework, the inner space once occupied by the premodern sense of harmony and totality is now filled with a kind of nostalgic longing. By somehow penetrating and deactivating the rational consciousness, Benn hoped to return (momentarily) to archetypal, primal, and prelogical experience. Benn identified this act as "hyperemic metaphysics"—that is, an intensified state of perception (such as that induced by intoxication, dream visions, or hallucinations), which he then applied exponentially to derive his "hyperemic theory of the poetic," or primal moments of poetic creativity.

It is necessary to see how Benn viewed the creative process in order to understand his poetry. According to Benn, the creative process required first "an inarticulate, creative nucleus, a psychic substance"; second, words familiar to the poet which "stand at his disposal" and are "suited to him personally"; and third, a "thread of Ariadne, which leads him with absolute certainty out of this bipolar tension"—that is, the tension between the psychic substance and the "word." This amalgam constitutes the basic creative situation for Benn.

One of his first poems, "Schöne Jugend" ("Beautiful Youth"), perhaps best illustrates Benn's early cynicism. The poem describes the dissection of the body of a young (and possibly at one time "beautiful") girl, whose decomposed mouth and esophagus are perfunctorily noted, as is the nest of young rats discovered beneath the diaphragm, "one little sister" of which lay dead while the others lived off the liver and kidneys—"drank the cold blood and had/ spent here a beautiful youth." A quick death awaits the rats: "They were thrown all together in the water. Ah, how their little snouts did squeal!" It becomes obvious that the "beautiful youth" to which the title refers is not that of the young girl, as the reader is intended to assume, but rather of the rats.

A good example of Benn's preoccupation with the capacity of language to "fascinate," and in so doing to give momentary vision to meaning within meaninglessness (form from chaos), is his poem "Ein Wort" ("One Word"). This poem is about the fact that words and sentences can be transmuted into *chiffres*, from which rise life and meaning. The effect can be such as to halt the sun and silence the spheres, as everything focuses for the moment on the primal catalyst, the single word. The word, however, is transitory, brilliant but short-lived, and already in the second and last strophe of this brief poem it is gone, leaving behind it the self and the world once again apart and distinct, alone in the dark, empty space surrounding them. Perhaps this paraphrase of Benn's poem gives an idea of how Benn viewed the magic of the poetic word, its unique ability to stand (and consequently place the reader/ listener) outside the "normal" conceptual categories of time and space. It communicates truth as a bolt of lightning momentarily illuminating the sky.

The radical dissolution of meaning with the evaporation of the word's spellbinding aura, as this last poem illustrates, aligns with Benn's view of the disintegration of reality in general. Nowhere are the consequences of this loss of reality for the individual given more poignant expression than in Benn's poem "Verlorenes Ich" ("Lost Self"). Benn applies the terminology of modern science as an explanation of the radical alienation of the modern self. The strictly scientific explanation of the universe does not adequately explain the vicissitudes of human existence. Benn does not envision a return to a previous form of existence, since that is an impossibility, nor does he seek refuge in a Christian answer, positing God as the source of an otherwise incomprehensible universe. Neither, however, is his stance one of resignation or of *l'art pour l'art*, even though he is often reproached for both. Instead, his predicament always centers on the struggle for human meaning and significance. The solution to this existential dilemma, he finds, is manifested in the intellectual and spiritual acts that human beings can perform, among these the creative act of giving form. "The artist," wrote Benn, "is the only one who copes with things, who decides their destiny."

It is true that Benn felt that all good poetry is "addressed to no one," and that he expressly refuted the possibility of poetry having any public function. To castigate Benn for an unconscionable aestheticism, though, would not be accurate or just. He does not cast aside the question of ethical responsibility; if he did, one would not expect to find such an obsession with what constitutes the essence of humanity, above all with the existential-poetic confrontation with Being. To explore this problem further, it is illuminating to consider a highly autobiographical poem of Benn, "Abschied" ("Departure"), contained originally in a cycle of poems Benn referred to as "Biographische Gedichte" ("Biographical Poems") and first published in *Zweiundzwanzig Gedichte* (twenty-two poems). Formally, the poem is a classic example of artistic control: four strophes of eight lines each in iambic pentameter, with alternating feminine and masculine rhymes in an *ababcdcd* scheme. Structurally, the poem constitutes a tightly organized unit: its formal principles interact with its themes—namely, the schizophrenic existence of the persona and the acknowledged taking leave from the old Self.

The topos of parting (*Abschied*) is itself an interesting one within German poetry; one may recall the significant example of Goethe's "Willkommen und Abschied" ("Greeting and Parting"). Benn's poem, however, does not deal with the separation of two individuals—two lovers, for example. Instead, it describes a separation of the persona, a division of the Self into a former "You" and a present "I." The You represents the part of the individual which belongs to a world of the past, while the I attempts to grasp and develop within the poem the process of alienation to which it has been subjected. The first strophe outlines the relationship of the former to the present Self by employing a series of metaphors, while the second strophe probes the cause of the schism and relates the sole recourse as perceived by the persona. The link between past and present—memory—becomes the topic of the third strophe, and finally the poem moves toward a further degree of estrangement, concluding with a note of sadness and melancholy typical of Benn.

The subject of each independent clause in the first strophe is the pronoun "you," and initially it is the active subject, while the "I" remains the passive object. The relationship is established via a metaphor: "You fill me as does blood the fresh wound,/ and run down its dark path." The image of the wound operates on the physical plane to suggest impairment, disease, decay. Later, in the third strophe, this physical affliction is seen to be present on a psychological plane as well. The adjective describing the wound, "fresh," can be read two ways. On the one hand, it accentuates the grotesque nature of the wound by showing it in its first moments when blood flows most freely. On the other hand, "fresh" can suggest "recent." The reader is thus made privy to the suffering of the persona as it takes place. The metaphor of the wound encompasses the first two lines of the poem. The dark trace of the blood is more than merely graphic realism; it evokes an aura of mysterious origin. Blood is the life-sustaining fluid, and its escape from the wound enacts the kind of exposure that the "deep self" of the persona endures. Its dark hue contrasts with the "day of minutiae," the "heavenly light" of the third strophe, and "a high light" in the third line of the last strophe. Its opaqueness suggests obscurity and impregnability. The persona's flight into silence at the end of the second strophe ("you must take your silence, travel downward/ to night and sorrow and the roses late") gives image to the inexpressibility of the "deep self."

The night setting maintains the motif of darkness found in the "dark path" on the second line. The hour corresponds to dusk and evinces the twilight of the former self, the You. The atmosphere of darkness surrounding the You continues to dominate, although it retreats for the moment with the appearance of roses in the following line. While this imagery is initially perplexing (because it does not seem to cooperate with the earlier metaphor of the wound), under the assumption that the You represents a former state of naïve harmony and quietude, the rose will be seen to bloom now only with difficulty, indicating the suffering connected with the memory of the persona's previous unified existence.

In the second strophe, the self-reflection intensifies, resulting in a kind of linguistic breakdown: the abstract nouns lack contact with reality and no longer illustrate the tendency toward analogous thought, as in the first five lines; no finite verb appears from lines six to eight, leaving the explication static and ineffective. Significantly, it is the second strophe which introduces the idea of alienation. Its cause is seen as the absence of a homogeneous reality, as a craze of pluralities (Benn speaks of "realities"). Resistance against this disembodying centrifugal force is sustained within the act of composing the poem itself, in the creative act which circles around the "deep self" in an attempt to describe it with more accuracy than simple, or even scientific, language can yield. "The form *is* the poem," Benn wrote elsewhere, stating the crux of his aesthetic.

In spite of the alienation from the "deep self," it is only this region that can satisfy the needs of the persona. This part of the Self, however, is (linguistically) impregnable, and silence represents the only alternative. The poem ends as "a last day" (Benn's own advancing age), which "plays its game, and feels its light and without/ memory goes down—everything is said." Such a poetic stance is rooted in the modernist poetic tradition. Benn acknowledges that no word or sign can now reveal that for which he searches; they are but symbols of the essential thing.

Had the persona no memory of itself, then no tension or conflict would result. The plague of consciousness is such, however, that it disrupts the fluidity of expression. This is represented throughout the poem by frequent dashes, colons, and question marks. Sentences and thoughts are left incomplete, fragmented; punctuation replaces words and becomes itself a frustrated sign or symbol of the inexpressible. The "deep self" evades all intellectualization.

In his epoch-making address, *Probleme der Lyrik*, Benn postulated that "not one of even the great poets of our time has left behind more than six or eight complete poems. The rest may be interesting from the point of view of biography and the author's development, but only a few are content in themselves, illuminating from within themselves, full of lasting fascination—and so, for these six poems, [there are] thirty to fifty years of asceticism, suffering, and struggle." Even according to Benn's own stringent definitions, he deserves to be acknowledged as a great poet.

Major publications other than poetry
NOVEL: *Roman des Phänotyp*, 1944.
SHORT FICTION: *Gehirne*, 1916.
NONFICTION: *Goethe und die Naturwissenschaften*, 1949; *Doppelleben*, 1950; *Probleme der Lyrik*, 1951.

Bibliography
Grimm, Reinhold. *Gottfried Benn*, 1958.
Hamburger, Michael. *Reason and Energy*, 1957.
Lohner, Edgar. "Gottfried Benn," in *Deutsche Dichter der Moderne*, 1975.
_____ . *Passion und Intellekt: Die Lyrik Gottfried Benns*, 1961.
Meyer, Theo. *Kunstproblematik und Wortkombinatorik bei Gottfried Benn*, 1971.
Schünemann, Peter. *Gottfried Benn*, 1977.

Richard Spuler

THOMAS BERNHARD

Born: Heerlen, Netherlands; February 10, 1931

Principal collections

Auf der Erde und in der Hölle, 1957; *In hora mortis*, 1957; *Unter dem Eisen des Mondes*, 1958; *Die Irren-die Häftlinge*, 1962.

Other literary forms

Thomas Bernhard's reputation rests primarily on his fiction and his memoirs. His first novel, *Frost* (1963), won critical acclaim, and his subsequent novels, novellas, and stories have brought him most of the significant literary prizes awarded in the German-speaking world. Among Bernhard's novels are *Verstörung* (1967; *Gargoyles*, 1970—literally translated, the title means "derangement"); *Das Kalwerk* (1970; *The Lime Works*, 1973); and *Korrektur* (1975; *Correction*, 1979). Bernhard's memoirs, regarded by many critics as semifictional, present autobiographical material in the monomaniacal voice of his fictional narrators. This ongoing sequence includes *Die Ursache* (1975; the cause), *Der Keller* (1976; the cellar), *Der Atem* (1978; the breath), *Die Kälte* (1981; the cold), *Ein Kind* (1982; a child), and *Wittgenstein's Neffe: Eine Freundschaft* (1983; Wittgenstein's nephew: a friendship).

The premiere of Bernhard's first play, *Ein Fest für Boris* (1970), created a small sensation, and since then more than ten of his plays have been produced, some of them at the Salzburg Festival; among them are *Die Macht der Gewohnheit* (1974; *The Force of Habit*, 1976) and *Über allen Gipfeln ist Ruh: Ein deutscher Dichterag um 1980* (1981).

Achievements

Critic George Steiner has described Bernhard as "the most original, concentrated novelist writing in German." The locution "writing in German" is significant, for Bernhard's achievements must be seen in the context of the Austrian literary tradition. Bernhard occupies a special position in contemporary Austrian literature. Unlike most Austrian writers of recent fame, he does not belong to a group, such as the Wiener Gruppe or the group at the Forum Stadtpark in Graz, nor can he be identified with any of the prevailing literary factions. Yet if Bernhard is a nonconformist—in his personal life as well as in his writing—he is nevertheless a typical Austrian author, rooted in the Austrian literary tradition, despite the fact that he rejects "Austria" as a political and ethnic abstraction and even blames her for much of his existential anguish. This distinctively Austrian tradition is characterized by several features, the foremost of which is a morbid preoccupation with death, and in particular with suicide.

Another facet of this tradition can be traced to the Baroque period and manifests itself as an inclination to give form preference over substance—to value the way something is expressed more highly than what is said. Other Baroque contributions to the Austrian tradition clearly visible in Bernhard's work are the *memento mori* theme and the typically Austrian response to this reminder of the imminence of death, the *carpe diem* motif. Yet another Baroque ingredient is the recurring metaphor of the *theatrum mundi*—the notion that the world is a stage upon which all humans must perform their roles. It is no accident that Bernhard has increasingly devoted himself to the theater in the 1970's and 1980's and that critics have noted in his works affinities with Hugo von Hofmannsthal and Franz Kafka.

Austrian literature has a long tradition of complaining about the conservative artistic attitudes of the Austrians and about the narrowness of the country's intellectual life. This complaint, which is surely not exclusively Austrian, appears in the works and in the private utterances of Wolfgang Amadeus Mozart, Franz Grillparzer, Sigmund Freud, and Arthur Schnitzler, to name only a few, and a frighteningly large number of Austrian artists and intellectuals were driven to suicide or into exile by this feeling of rejection and claustrophobia. Bernhard expresses this notion with obsessive force in many of his works. He does not grant interviews and lives in virtual isolation on a farm in a secluded valley, rejecting most involvement in the social life of the Austrian literary scene.

Lastly, Bernhard is firmly entrenched in an Austrian tradition of language skepticism associated with Hofmannsthal, Ludwig Wittgenstein, and Theodore Mauthner. Bernhard's entire oeuvre is informed by a profound distrust of language as an efficacious artistic or communicative tool. The influence of Wittgenstein, most explicit in the novel *Correction*, in which one of the characters is modeled after him, and in the memoir *Wittgenstein's Neffe*, is of particular significance in Bernhard's development. Bernhard treats Wittgenstein with a mixture of reverence and savage irony, and the philosopher's ideas are implicit in all Bernhard's works. One of the key phrases in *Gargoyles* is an implicit response to the famous aphorism which concludes Wittgenstein's *Tractatus Logico-Philosophicus* (1922); Bernhard writes: "The words we use really do not exist any longer. . . . But it is also no longer possible to be completely silent." Bernhard shares this belief with many contemporary Austrian writers, including Peter Handke.

While Bernhard's verse is not his most significant contribution to Austrian literature—four slim volumes containing some 150 poems are an insufficient basis for such a claim—it did provide Bernhard with an early testing ground for his literary talent. Critics so far have not paid much attention to Bernhard, the poet, although this neglect is not justified. At their worst, the poems are a youthful testimony to early poetic influences and to eclectic readings in nineteenth century European philosophy. At their best, they are lyrical precursors of Bernhard's fiction, foreshadowing the linguistic experiments of his early prose and introducing the themes of his mature work, such as death, the desertion of God, impotence in the face of suffering, the world as prison and insane asylum, rural decay, urban decadence, and the impossibility of communication. Bernhard's poetry is sure to be given increased critical attention.

Biography

Biographical data, particularly of Thomas Bernhard's early life, must be considered with some caution, as many of these "facts" have been excerpted from the author's autobiographical writings and from a letter to the editor of an anthology, published in 1954—a letter which Bernhard had not intended to make public.

Bernhard was born on February 10, 1931, the illegitimate son of an Austrian carpenter. Bernhard's mother was the daughter of an eccentric Austrian writer, Johannes Freumbichler. In the strictly Catholic, rural Austrian environment, an illegitimate birth would have created quite a stir, and so Bernhard was born in a convent near Maastrich, Netherlands, where his mother had to remain in service to defray the cost of the birth of her son. Much of Bernhard's childhood was spent with his maternal grandparents near Salzburg. He formed a strong attachment to his grandfather, who became the dominating personal and intellectual influence of his early life, as described in Bernhard's memoir, *Ein Kind*. In Freumbichler's house, the young Bernhard met Ödön von Horvath and Carl Zuckmayer; Zuckmayer later wrote encouraging and thoughtful reviews of the young man's first volumes of poetry. Bernhard's grandfather, who had received the highest Austrian literary award, mainly for his novel *Philomena Ellenhub* (1937), was an avid reader of the German writers and philosophers of the later nineteenth century and was particulary fond of Michel de Montaigne. Bernhard claims to have read Arthur Schopenhauer in Freumbichler's study and to have discovered then for the first time "the impossibility of saying the truth and the inability of transcending human existence."

In 1938, Bernhard's family—his mother was then married to a man who was not Bernhard's father—moved to Traunstein, Bavaria, where the boy had his first music lessons. Music has played an important part in Bernhard's life; much of his literary vocabulary is taken from musical terminology, and he speaks in terms of the theory of musical composition when he discusses the structure of some of his works. In 1943, the boy was sent to a Nazi-sympathizing boarding school in Salzburg. After the war, the school was taken over by the Roman Catholic Church, but Bernhard claims not to have noticed any difference. In his memoir *Die Ursache*, he deals extensively with this depressing period in his life.

In 1946, Bernhard's family was forced to leave Germany and moved to

Salzburg. Soon after that, Bernhard quit school and apprenticed himself to a grocery merchant. His relationship with his stepfather deteriorated, and finally the working conditions in the wet storage cellar of his employer (described in his memoir *Der Keller*) caused Bernhard to contract first pleurisy and then a severe lung disease. The next four years, a hellish period described in the memoirs *Der Atem* and *Die Kälte*, were spent being shuttled between hospitals and sanatoriums; in 1949, Bernhard's grandfather was taken to the same hospital where the young man himself lay in a bathroom in the section for the terminally ill. During the following year, both Bernhard's grandfather and his mother died, and he also learned that his natural father had died in 1943 in the turmoil of the war. It was at this time, while confined to the bed of a hospital for pulmonary diseases, that Bernhard began to write. He is convinced that this activity prevented him from succumbing to insanity or suicide and eventually cured him of his illness.

In 1951, Bernhard received a scholarship to attend the music academy in Vienna, but since the stipend covered only his tuition, he was forced to work as garbage collector, luggage porter, and attendant to a seventy-year-old insane woman whom he cared for until her death. He often slept in railroad cars and in abandoned air-raid shelters; his move to the Mozarteum in Salzburg in 1952 was a welcome change. At the Mozarteum, he did considerable acting and directing in addition to his musical studies and earned his way by working for a local newspaper, mainly as a court reporter and an art critic. In the period from 1952 to 1956, Bernhard also submitted his first poems and short stories to various publishers and to literary contests, but with no success. In 1955 and 1956, he interrupted his studies at the Mozarteum to travel around Europe; he was graduated in 1957 after completing a thesis on Antonin Artaud and Bertolt Brecht. In that year, Bernhard also published his first two volumes of poetry, followed by his third collection in 1958. During the next five years, he tried to make his living as a free-lance writer in Vienna and Carinthia; he traveled frequently and also spent a short time as librarian at the Austrian Cultural Institute in London.

Discouraged by his continuous failure to gain recognition as a writer— again and again his submissions did not find favor with the judges of literary contests awarding prestigious and lucrative prizes—Bernhard decided to emigrate to South Africa. Allegedly on the very day he was ready to embark from Venice, he received notice that his first novel, *Frost*, had been accepted for publication. Official recognition and prizes followed in rapid succession, most notably the Austrian State Prize in 1968, when he shocked the dignitaries with his polemical acceptance speech.

Analysis

Thomas Bernhard's biography offers a temptation to the critical reader of his work. It is easy to conclude—as many critics have—that his chaotic, parentless childhood, the rootless life of his adolescence, the loss of all of those he loved, and his own near-fatal illness are the direct causes of the grim worldview expressed in his novels and plays, and are responsible for the melancholy tone of his poems. Such a view is contradicted by the fact that Bernhard's journalistic work, which is chronologically closest to the period from 1950 to 1952, the most depressing years of his life, shows few traces of this pervasive pessimism. The articles and reviews of that time are full of praise for contemporary artists; they speak of the regenerative beauty of the Salzburg region and comment favorably on the value of regional Austrian culture. The tone of these articles is low-key, often a little sad, but still full of *joie de vivre* compared to that of his early poems, which appeared in 1957. Further study of Bernhard's life and his published and unpublished work of the years from 1950 to 1957 is needed to explain the struggling author's change in outlook.

Bernhard's first collection of poems, *Auf der Erde und in der Hölle*, was published in 1957 in an edition of one thousand. It contains seventy-one poems grouped into five thematic sections; many of these poems have since been included in anthologies of contemporary German and Austrian poetry. Bernhard himself claims to have been influenced mainly by Walt Whitman, Georg Trakl, and Charles Péguy—the latter supplies the motto for the volume—but one also hears echoes of Paul Celan and Charles Baudelaire, as well as of William Blake's more hellish visions.

"Der Tag der Gesichter" appears as a separate poem before the first section and sets the tone for the entire volume: the "Earth" and the "Hell" of the title are not to be understood as separate locations but as identical places. The poet acknowledges his complicity in the decay, suffering, and death that are all around him. He anticipates shudderingly the apocalyptic "day of visions" when he will be shown Hell, reproduced for the reader in the following seventy poems. It is the Earth as Inferno that the poet sees. *Auf der Erde und in der Hölle* offers a vision of Hell without any glimpses of Heaven. The five sections of the volume systematically deny any relief from this view and reject any traditional redemptive imagery.

The journey through Hell—the reluctant reader is led by the guilt-ridden poet—begins in the traditional "dark wood," the rural region of Bernhard's ancestors. There is no pastoral tranquillity, however, in this "other world behind the trees." This area has changed drastically since the time of the poet's great-grandfather. Now, there is decay, despair, and other harbingers of death in the form of frost, crows, and blackbirds. The black farm soil prophesies a wintry death; schnapps, fame, and love are insufficient anesthesia for loneliness and the sense of complicity in the sad state of the world. What is the poet to do, cast out from this destroyed Eden into the night? The brave front he puts up at times—as in the great poem "Crows," which ends with the line "But I am not afraid"—cannot be maintained for long, and he crosses the river to find "another world."

There, he finds the "burnt-out cities" of the second section—Vienna, Paris, Venice, Chioggia—cities which one can no longer shore against one's ruins. Wherever the journey leads, the poet encounters night, death, the pale, unapproachable ghosts of his ancestors, and anterooms to Hell. Attempts at cleansing through penitence on Ash Wednesday (Bernhard knows T. S. Eliot very well) are ineffectual.

In the last section, "Rückkehr in eine Liebe," the poet expresses the wish to be able to return to his "love," represented by his rural village, the memory of his parents, and nature, but even the first poem of the section, "Yeats war nicht dabei," indicates that he cannot go home again. The fields do not accept his name, the trees withdraw their roots, and no one offers him a bed and a jug with drink.

Auf der Erde und in der Hölle is a remarkable first collection of poems. Clearly, there are literary debts, but Zuckmayer's judgment, that these poems show the mark of the great modern artists and originate from the same artistic background as the music of Béla Bartók, is accurate.

Bernhard's second collection of poems, *In hora mortis*, also appeared in 1957. The title is taken from the Latin text of the "Hail Mary," in which the Holy Virgin is asked to intercede for all sinners in the hour of death. The volume, much slimmer than *Auf der Erde und in der Hölle*, is dedicated to "my only and true friend G. L. whom I met at the right moment." "G. L." is almost certainly the young Austrian composer Gerhard Lampersberg, who had apparently taken in the despondent writer for some time between 1957 and 1959. Bernhard always speaks in negative terms of the Church and of religion, but it appears that the time he spent in a Catholic boarding school left him with the wish to come to terms with that facet of his childhood. It is even more likely that his self-confessed interest in Blaise Pascal's *Pensées* (1670; English translation, 1688) and his early acquaintance with the writings of Schopenhauer and Montaigne are responsible for the persistent religious stratum in his early work.

In hora mortis has the structure of a prayer—it is quite possible that Pascal's "Prayer in Sickness" is the model—and employs frequent direct appeals to "my God" and "my Lord." These appeals are not always submissive in tone; the first line of the collection, "Wild grows the flower of my anger," indicates the mood of the poet. Rebellion, outrage, and disappointment in an elusive God dominates the early parts of the volume; later, the tone changes to hopelessness and to the Schopenhauer-like recognition that redemption is only possible when the rebellious will to live has been subdued. It can be assumed that the poetic experience in this slim volume closely parallels Bernhard's wrestling for a spiritual and intellectual position during the time of his near-fatal illness.

In these poems, Bernhard does not as closely identify himself with his literary models as in *Auf der Erde und in der Hölle*. His poetry here approaches that of his contemporaries Ingeborg Bachmann, Christine Busta, and Christine Lavant in its imperious appeals to a *Dieu abscondit*. Bernhard's early verse depicts a desolate universe through which man is condemned to wander aimlessly, incapable of bringing any relief to the universal suffering, unable to stop the general decay, but also unable to resign himself completely to this condition. The language is emotional, the imagery flowery, and the tone still echoes the plaintive cries of the Expressionists. Bernhard's next collection of poems, however, published in 1958, marked a transition from subjective lyrical Expressionism to the maniacal "objectivity" of his prose.

In *Unter dem Eisen des Mondes* (under the iron of the moon), Bernhard broke completely with his poetic models. The fifty-seven untitled poems in this volume severely reduce the use of the first person in an attempt to objectify the lyrical "I" of *Auf der Erde und in der Hölle* and *In hora mortis*. The title is taken from Georg Büchner's play *Woyzeck* (1879; English translation, 1927), from the scene in which the protagonist is about to stab his fiancée; to her observation, "How red the moon rises!" He replies with the words "like a bloody blade" (*Eisen*).

This bloody moon casts a grim light; there is not even the elusive hope for redemption still expressed in *In hora mortis*, nor the faint prospect of a "return to love." Images are no longer used as objective correlatives of the poet's subjective feelings but take on a physical and metaphysical reality of their own. The reader can no longer escape by rejecting Bernhard's night visions as sentimental exaggerations of a paranoid, tortured soul but must deal with an intellectual position. The symbolism of the four seasons which runs through the whole volume further serves this purpose.

Unter dem Eisen des Mondes was the penultimate step in Bernhard's development from lyric poet to novelist. The symbolic code of these poems and their syntactic structure anticipates the forms of his early prose, particularly of his first novel, *Frost*. Apart from some poems published in the magazine *Akzente* in 1968, but probably written before 1963, Bernhard published only one more, very small volume of poetry before abandoning verse after the success of his first novel.

Published in 1962 by a small Klagenfurt publisher in an edition of only 120 copies, *Die Irren-die Häftlinge* does not appear in many Bernhard bibliographies. The critic Manfred Mixner considers it the last and most important stage of Bernhard's early creative period. The left-hand pages of this collection contain "Die Irren," a poem of fifteen stanzas; on the right-hand pages appears "Die Häftlinge," a poem of twenty-two stanzas. Both are interrupted by aphoristic prose sentences which appear to be quotations, but no source is indicated. Some of these sentences seem like remarks by a distant observer concerning the "madmen" and "prisoners" who are the subjects of these two long poems.

Madmen and prisoners (their prisons are often metaphorical) are the central characters of Bernhard's novels and plays. In his later work, Bernhard reiterates his conviction that the human condition is best defined as incarceration. Most of his characters are trapped by the narrowness of their physical, cultural, or geographical prisons. Only "insane" people are sensitive enough to recognize the inevitability of their fate as prisoners, from which they try to find relief in interminable cascades of tautological ruminations. The "sane" people live as animals, unthinking, trapped in lies and clichés.

In *Die Irren-die Häftlinge*, Bernhard anticipates the recurring themes of his prose. The madmen are anonymous, deprived of their individuality by being addressed only by the symptoms of their condition. Their fate is not presented from their subjective standpoint as lyrical narrators; instead, they are viewed by an impersonal observer who registers their hate, their torture, and their indignation as if seen through the peephole of their cells and who punctuates his observations with aphorisms on rationality. With this virtually forgotten volume, Bernhard found the logical transition from poetry to the novel; he abandoned the emotive stance of the lyrical "I" and assumed the role of an omniscient, clinical observer who presents the twitchings of his tortured madmen and prisoners in the manner of a painstakingly arranged medical report.

The small but growing number of Bernhard scholars have devoted themselves almost exclusively to his fiction, his memoirs, and his plays, neglecting his journalism and paying scant attention to his poetry. Bernhard's verse deserves to be read for its own considerable achievements rather than as a mere preface to his fiction.

Major publications other than poetry
NOVELS: *Frost*, 1963; *Verstörung*, 1967 (*Gargoyles*, 1970); *Das Kalwerk*, 1970 (*The Lime Works*, 1973); *Korrektur*, 1975 (*Correction*, 1979).

PLAYS: *Ein Fest für Boris*, 1970; *Die Macht der Gewohnheit*, 1974 (*The Force of Habit*, 1976); *Über allen Gipfeln ist Ruh: Ein deutscher Dichterag um 1980*, 1981.

NONFICTION: *Die Ursache*, 1975; *Der Keller*, 1976; *Der Atem*, 1978; *Die Kälte*, 1981; *Ein Kind*, 1982; *Wittgenstein's Neffe: Eine Freundschaft*, 1983.

Bibliography
Barthofer, Alfred. "Berge schwarzer Qual: Zur thematischen Schwerpunktstruktur der Lyrik Thomas Bernhards," in *Acta Germanica*. IX (1976), pp. 187-211.
Domandi, Agnes, ed. "Thomas Bernhard," in *Modern German Literature*, 1972.
Mixner, Manfred. "Vom Leben zum Tode: Die Einleitung des Negationsprozesses im Frühwerk Thomas Bernhards," in *Bernhard: Anäherungen*,

1981. Edited by Manfred Jurgensen.

Schwedler, Wilfried. "Thomas Bernhard," in *Handbook of Austrian Literature*, 1973. Edited by Frederick Ungar.

Sorg, Bernhard. *Thomas Bernhard*, 1977.

Franz G. Blaha

WOLF BIERMANN

Born: Hamburg, Germany; November 15, 1936

Principal poems and collections

Die Drahtharfe: Balladen, Gedichte, Lieder, 1965 (*The Wire Harp: Ballads, Poems, Songs*, 1968); *Mit Marx- und Engelszungen: Gedichte, Balladen, Lieder*, 1968; *Für meine Genossen: Hetzlieder, Gedichte, Balladen*, 1972; *Deutschland: Ein Wintermärchen*, 1972; *Nachlass I*, 1977; *Poems and Ballads*, 1977; *Preussischer Ikarus: Lieder, Balladen, Gedichte, Prosa*, 1978; *Verdrehte Welt—das seh' ich gerne: Lieder, Balladen, Gedichte, Prosa*, 1982.

Other literary forms

Nearly all of Wolf Biermann's published work consists of poems and songs. This fact reflects his conviction that poetry, especially song, provides the most appropriate and effective means of conveying the intensely personal and political content of his work. Biermann's other writings reinforce this strong political emphasis. These writings include numerous commentaries, interviews, letters, and autobiographical accounts, as well as a children's book, *Das Märchen vom kleinen Herrn Moritz* (1972; the tale of little Mister Moritz), a number of translations of poetry and songs, and a single play. The play, Biermann's only major nonpoetic work, is entitled *Der Dra-Dra: Die grosse Drachentöterschau in acht Akten mit Musik* (1970; the dra-dra: the great dragon-killer show in eight acts with music). An adaptation of the fairy-tale comedy *Drakon* (1943; *The Dragon*, 1963), by the Russian playwright Yevgeny Schwartz, the play concerns the fate of a city-state ruled by a dragon; in Biermann's hands, it becomes a political parable about the still-powerful specter of Stalinism in Eastern Europe.

Achievements

Biermann is perhaps the best-known living German-language poet. The success of his books—*The Wire Harp* is the best-selling book of German poetry in the postwar era—and the popularity of his more than one dozen recordings provide ample evidence of this.

Several factors have contributed to Biermann's renown. There is, first, the political controversy which has surrounded him since he first fell into disfavor with cultural authorities in East Germany in the early 1960's. While his problems with the party bureaucracy led very quickly to an absolute publication and performance ban in the East, his identification with opposition forces in East Germany served to increase his notoriety, particularly in the West. It is ironic that, although Biermann's work was never to reach a large audience in the Socialist East—depending as it did upon the circulation of underground manuscripts and tapes—his poetry and recordings have been widely distributed and discussed in capitalist West Germany.

Another factor has played an even more central role in Biermann's popularity as a poet. He is a people's poet in every sense of the word, a fact which is reflected in the everyday language, themes, and imagery of his poetry. His preference for simple, traditional forms, such as the German folk song and the ballad, and his use of music as a vehicle for his texts have enhanced the strong populist appeal of his work.

Biermann's strong identification with the traditions of the German folk song and the political song places him somewhat outside the mainstream of contemporary German-language poetry, with its greater emphasis on sophisticated aesthetic and literary values. Nevertheless, the strength and vitality of Biermann's language and imagery effectively rebut the notion that the populist orientation of his work lessens its significance in any way, and his poems are clearly among the most provocative being written in Germany today.

Biermann has been awarded numerous prizes, including the prestigious Berlin Art Prize for Literature (the Fontane Prize) in 1969, and the Jacques-Offenbach Prize given by the city of Cologne in 1974. The latter award specifically recognized Biermann's achievement as a composer, writer, and performer of the contemporary political song.

Biography

Wolf Biermann comes from a Communist, working-class family tradition. His father, Dagobert Biermann, a Jewish worker on the Hamburg docks, joined the Communist Party in 1921 and was active in the anti-Fascist resistance of the early and mid-1930's. Arrested in 1937 for his role in sabotaging arms shipments to Francisco Franco's Spain, he was sent in 1942 to Auschwitz, where he was put to death in 1943. Although Biermann hardly knew his father, he was reared by his mother and grandmother, both active Communists, in the spirit and image of the elder Biermann. This legacy of political activism and Communism has had a profound effect upon Biermann's life.

In the spirit of his father, Biermann left his native Hamburg in 1953 to join in the Socialist experiment under way in East Germany. There, he finished his high school education and, from 1955 to 1957, studied political economy at Humboldt University in East Berlin. In 1957, he interrupted his studies to take a position as a dramatic assistant at Bertolt Brecht's theater, the *Berliner Ensemble*. Although Brecht had died the previous year, this confrontation with his work was of great importance in Biermann's development. During this period, too, he met Brecht's friend and collaborator, the composer Hanns Eisler, whose musical influence is readily apparent in Biermann's songs.

The years from 1960 to 1964 represent a particularly significant period in Biermann's life. He had returned to the university in 1959 to study philosophy and mathematics, but his studies were gradually replaced by an ever-greater emphasis upon his artistic interests. In 1960, at the relatively late age of twenty-three, he began to write and compose his first songs. The songs written after the building of the Berlin Wall in 1961 concentrated more and more upon the discrepancy between the promise and the reality of socialism in East Germany and quickly drew the attention of cultural authorities.

In 1961-1962, Biermann helped to found the Berlin Worker and Student Theater and wrote his first dramatic effort for its scheduled opening. His unpublished play "Berliner Brautgang," a love story set amid the political tensions of the newly divided city, was never performed. Before its premiere, the theater was closed by authorities and Biermann was placed under a performance ban. The ban was lifted again in 1963, but Biermann was excluded from the Socialist Unity Party, in which he had been a candidate for membership.

During a brief period of relative cultural freedom in 1964, Biermann began to make a name for himself as a writer and performer of political songs. He was allowed to undertake a concert tour of West Germany, which established his reputation there as one of East Germany's leading young poets, and which led subsequently to the 1965 publication in the West of his first book of poems, issued by a Leftist publishing house. This brief cultural thaw, however, ended for Biermann as abruptly as it had begun; at the Eleventh Party Congress in 1965, his poetry was attacked for its "dangerous" subjectivity and its "anti-Communist" slant, and he was placed under a second absolute publication and performance ban.

For the next eleven years, Biermann lived as a "nonperson" in his homeland: there was no possibility for public discussion or performance of his work, much less publication; he was under constant surveillance; his friends were subjected to various forms of official intimidation. Surprisingly, during this period he was allowed to continue to publish and record his work for release in the West. His reputation grew as he, together with his close friend, the physicist and philosopher Robert Havemann, became the focus and primary symbols of intellectual opposition in East Germany.

As early as 1972, Biermann was offered the chance to emigrate to the West, but he was adamant in his refusal to leave his chosen land. Unexpectedly, Biermann was allowed in 1976 to accept an invitation from West German unionists for a concert tour of several major cities. Following the first concert, in Cologne, he was notified that his East German citizenship had been revoked and that he would not be allowed to return home. This calculated move by the Party resulted in an unprecedented protest among artists and intellectuals in the East, the repercussions of which are still being felt in East German cultural policy today.

Since his expatriation, Biermann has steadfastly resisted the tendency in the West to cast him in the role of an anti-Communist dissident. Even today, he maintains that his problems with the Party in East Germany are problems among Socialists, and he remains true to the Communist ideals of his father.

Analysis

Wolf Biermann is a political poet. He follows in the tradition of François Villon, Heinrich Heine, Kurt Tucholsky, and Bertolt Brecht, with whom he shares both an acute political awareness and a biting, aggressive wit. As with these forerunners, art, life, and politics are virtually inseparable in Biermann's work. He is, as one collection of critical essays refers to him in its title, a "Liedermacher und Sozialist," both a "maker of songs" and a dedicated Socialist; his poetry records with great feeling his own political struggle as a Socialist poet and his personal political fate as a renegade and exile.

Biermann's connection with the tradition of Heine and Brecht is apparent. He is the prototypical "troublesome" poet, unwanted and rejected by his homeland—a homeland which he "loves" and "hates" in nearly equal degree. In a recurring image in his poetry, Biermann portrays himself as the embattled but unrelenting poet caught in the no-man's-land between East and West, as the poet balanced precariously on the Wall—neither understood nor at home in either Germany. He is torn as Germany itself is torn, not between socialism and capitalism—for his political position as a Socialist is clear—but torn by the disparity between Germany's promise and its reality. He is both the victim and the uncompromising critic of this disparity, which is given concrete form in his poetry in the image of the Berlin Wall.

This intense intermingling of the personal with the political is central to all Biermann's poetry and provides the key to its understanding. One cannot separate the poetry from the man and his experience, or hope to understand it fully outside the political and historical context of his personal struggle. The focus of the poetry is always the political reality of contemporary German life and the poet's response to it.

Although his poems and songs display a rich variety of themes, Biermann's central concerns may be summarized under three broad headings: the division of Germany; the yet-unfulfilled promise of socialism; and the poet's celebration of life in spite of a harsh and hostile reality. As these themes suggest, the poetry often exhibits an antithetical structure built upon the contradictions and antagonisms which Biermann perceives around him—antagonisms between the real and the possible, between that which exists and that which remains to be done, and, ultimately, between the forces of quiescence, stagnation, and death and those of life. The conflict expressed in the major themes is mirrored in Biermann's own mixed feelings regarding the world around him. These reactions are expressed in a broad range of tones, from anger and bitterness to ecstatic celebration. Biermann's poems are alternately sad and accusatory, aggressive and subdued, but there remains in them always a determined optimism and a fundamental affirmation of life.

Biermann's first collection of poetry, *The Wire Harp*, introduces many of the central themes and formal hallmarks of his work. His preference for a simple lyrical style and for everyday rather than literary language is clearly demonstrated here, as is his reliance upon traditional lyrical forms and rhymed verse. He reacts in these poems both to the broader world—as in his critically optimistic picture of socialism in the "Buckower Balladen" ("Buckow Ballads") and in his indictment of American racism in the "Ballade von dem Briefträger William L. Moore" ("Ballad of the Letter-Carrier William L. Moore")—and to the more immediate personal world of his loves, his joys, and sorrows, as illustrated in the "Berlin" poems of this volume. Included under the heading "Portraits" are tributes to both Brecht and Eisler, as well as the well-known "Ballade auf den Dichter François Villon" ("Ballad on the Poet François Villon"). Here, Biermann celebrates the rude and drunken Frenchman with whom he so obviously identifies. He, like his "brother" Villon, is always in trouble with the authorities, and he never tires of ridiculing their petty fears. In this poem, Biermann is at his provocative best, and he revels in the impudent, mocking tone of his great predecessor.

In the group of poems entitled "Beschwichtigungen und Revisionen" ("Reassurances and Revisions"), Biermann addresses his ambivalent relationship to the Communist Party. He alternately asserts his role as the critical outsider in "Rücksichtslose Schimpferei" ("Reckless Abuse") and affirms his solidarity of purpose with his comrades in "An die alten Genossen" ("To the Old Comrades"). These poems characteristically illustrate Biermann's defiant subjectivity and his refusal to accept the Party's demand for artistic and political conformity. In the poem "Tischrede des Dichters" ("The Poet's Table Speech"), Biermann presents his criticisms by means of a simple culinary metaphor: he complains that his comrades reject his rich and varied cuisine, preferring instead their bland "single-course dinner of happiness." The tone of the poem is assertive and yet conciliatory as Biermann defends his role as critic and argues for greater artistic tolerance.

In the poems and songs of his second collection, *Mit Marx- und Engelszungen* (with the tongues of Marx and Engels—or angels) Biermann continues his attack upon the blandness of officially sanctioned literature. There is, however, a discernible difference in tone in these poems. Although the poet's voice is no less insistent here, the tone has become more earnest and betrays some hint of the bitterness and frustration which have come of Biermann's prolonged isolation. In the love songs included in this volume, Biermann celebrates life and love, combining traditional images of spring and hope with good-humored earthiness. The poems express the poet's hope against the background of his personal political struggle, and they represent an attempt to counteract his growing sadness.

In one of the last songs in the collection, Biermann finds the source of this sadness in the deep division of Germany itself. He concludes his poem "Es

senkt das deutsche Dunkel" ("The German Darkness Falls") with the paradoxical assertion that, though he lives in the "better half" of this divided land,
he feels "double the pain." This doubly intense pain is the pain of hopes
betrayed, a theme which comes to play an ever-greater role in his work.

The idea for Biermann's long narrative poem *Deutschland: Ein Wintermärchen* (Germany, a winter's tale) was taken from Heine's verse satire of
the same title, which appeared in 1844. Biermann's poem was written in 1965
shortly after a visit to his native Hamburg, where he had stopped during his
Western concert tour the year before. Biermann uses the occasion of his trip,
as Heine had done more than one hundred years earlier, to reflect satirically
upon Germany's current political "misery" as mirrored now in the country's
political division. He has retained both the tone and the simple folk-song
verse (four-line stanzas rhyming *abab*) of the original, and he consciously
imitates and parallels Heine's masterpiece at every turn.

The return to this "foreign" homeland evokes a mixed response in Biermann. Though he views the "German question" from the perspective of a
Socialist, critical of Western capitalism, he does not gloss over the present-
day heritage of Stalinism in Eastern Europe. He concludes his "winter's tale"
with the important programmatic poem "Gesang für meine Genossen" ("Song
for My Comrades"), which summarizes the political focus of his entire work,
a work which he characterizes here as "das Lied von der verratenen Revolution" (the song of the revolution betrayed). The poem illustrates a central
paradox of Biermann's work: the fact that he devastatingly criticizes that
which he loves. The Party is simultaneously the object of his love and his
hate, for it represents both the future hope of socialism and its current dogmatic inflexibility and bureaucratic stagnation.

The poetry of Biermann's third collection, *Für meine Genossen* (for my
comrades), documents the "crimes" of which he was accused in East Germany.
Organized under five headings corresponding to sections of the East German
penal code, the poems are presented as evidence of his "misdemeanors,"
"slander," "agitation," and "irresponsibility," but also of the "extenuating
circumstances." Biermann defends his "crimes" by placing them in the context
in which he prefers to view them: each section of the collection begins with
an appropriately "heretical" quotation from Karl Marx, Lenin, or Rosa Lux-
emburg that supports Biermann's view of revolutionary art and its function
in socialist society.

The poems and songs of *Für meine Genossen* continue in the vein of Biermann's earlier collections. The theme of betrayal—the betrayal of the Revolution by the Party, and the betrayal of hope by the friends who have given
up the fight—is especially prominent and is recorded in emotions ranging
from impatience and anger to profound sorrow. The melancholy undertone,
present to some extent in the earlier poetry, is more pronounced here, and
the songs have lost much of the playfulness of the early years. The ballad, in

Biermann's view a proper instrument of "agitation," maintains its formal preeminence in his work, but is complemented here by highly self-conscious and reflective poems that expand his range of expression.

Biermann's experimentation with new forms and themes alongside the old is carried a step further in the book *Preussischer Ikarus* (Prussian Icarus). This volume was the first to be published after Biermann's expatriation in 1976, and includes both poems written in the East and others written in and from the perspective of his Western exile. Together with the familiar East German motifs of the earlier collections, there are a variety of new, specifically Western themes. Biermann responds here not only to the problem of his exile, but to the Western German political scene as well—to the misdirected terrorism of the Baader-Meinhof era and the disarray and ineffectiveness of the West German Left.

The title for the collection is taken from the "Ballade vom preussischer Ikarus" (ballad of the Prussian Icarus), which closes the first half of the book. In the poem, Biermann projects himself into the role of a modern Icarus weighed down by the heavy iron wings of Prussian tradition—a tradition of authoritarianism and unquestioning obedience that continues to throttle the socialist revolution in the East. The West, however, offers Biermann no solace; the poems that close the second half of the volume portray the ostensibly "free" and "democratic" West as merely the other side of the same German coin.

In the West, Biermann remains the critical outsider he has always been. Nevertheless, the poetry which he has published since 1976 indicates that he has been able to adapt to the challenge of his new circumstances, a fact which is illustrated by his exploration of new thematic material in place of the specifically East German subject matter of the earlier work.

Major publications other than poetry
    PLAY: *Der Dra-Dra: Die grosse Drachentöterschau in acht Akten mit Musik*, 1970.
    CHILDREN'S LITERATURE: *Das Marchen vom kleinen Herrn Moritz*, 1972.

Bibliography
Arnold, Heinz Ludwig, ed. *Wolf Biermann*, 1975.
Flores, John. "Wolf Biermann," in *Poetry in East Germany*, 1971.
Hermand, Jost. "Biermanns Dilemma," in *Basis: Jahrbuch für deutsche Gegenwartsliteratur*. IV (1973), pp. 175-191.
Jäger, Manfred. "Der Zorn des Zufrühgekommenen. Wolf Biermanns Reflexionen über Wort und Tat," in *Sozialliteraten*, 1973.
Rothschild, Thomas, ed. *Wolf Biermann: Liedermacher und Sozialist*, 1976.

James R. Reece

ALEKSANDR BLOK

Born: St. Petersburg, Russia; November 16, 1880
Died: Petrograd, U.S.S.R.; August 7, 1921

Principal poems and collections

Stikhi o prekrasnoy dame, 1904; *Nechayannaya radost*, 1907; *Snezhnaya maska*, 1907; *Zemlya v snegu*, 1908; *Nochyne chasy*, 1911; *Skazki*, 1912; *Krugly god*, 1913; *Stikhi o Rossii*, 1915; *Solovinyy sad*, 1918; *Dvenadtsat, Skify*, 1918; *Dvenadtsat*, 1918 (*The Twelve*, 1920); *Iamby: Sovremennye stikhi 1907-1914*, 1919; *Sedoe utro*, 1920; *Za granyu proshlykh dnei*, 1920; *Poems of A. B.*, 1968; *Selected Poems*, 1972.

Other literary forms

Aleksandr Blok wrote three lyrical plays, the first of which, *Balaganchik* (1906; *The Puppet Show*, 1963), was staged immediately and widely. The second, *Korol na ploshchadi*, written in 1906 (*The King in the Square*, 1934) remained unpublished in his lifetime, although its material was absorbed into other works. *Roza i krest* (1922; *The Rose and the Cross*, 1936), was popular in print, had more than two hundred rehearsals at the Moscow Art Theater, but was never publicly staged. Several additional dramatic monologues failed before presentation. Blok also wrote critical essays on poetry and drama, a series of articles dealing with the role of the intelligentsia in Russian cultural development, translated several plays from French and German for stage production, and edited his mother's translation of the letters of Gustave Flaubert. Much of his work was reissued in various collections during his lifetime, and posthumous editions, including diaries, letters, and notebooks, have appeared regularly. A scholarly collected works in nine volumes has been completed in the Soviet Union.

Achievements

Aleksandr Blok was the leading Russian Symbolist and is universally regarded as one of the most important Russian poets of the twentieth century. The Symbolists were interested in poetic reform in order to reshape the partly sentimental, partly social-oriented poetic idiom of the second half of the nineteenth century. They favored a return to mysticism, albeit with modern overtones, free from the rational tenor of the scientific age. The movement's early exponents, notably Konstantin Balmont and Valery Bryusov, incorporated French Symbolist ideas into their work, but when Blok began to write at the turn of the century, Symbolism was no longer a single unit. It had disintegrated into literary factions which reflected the movement's precepts in their own way. Though Blok paid homage to the search for spiritual values, his mysticism owes as much to the writings of his uncle, the religious philosopher Vladimir Solovyov, as to Stéphane Mallarmé, with whom he shared the striving to give shape to the "music of the spheres," the elusive entities beyond reality.

In contrast to his eccentric fellow Symbolists and the equally whimsical linguistic experimenters of other movements, Blok stood out as a contemplative, sincere individual whose philosophical concerns were as important as the language used to express them. He attached an almost metaphysical significance to the creative power of the poet, and this belief in the transcendental quality of art led him to reach beyond the partisan interests of his contemporaries to create a solid, coherent poetical system reminiscent of the "Golden Age" of Alexander Pushkin, Mikhail Lermontov, and Fyodor Tyutchev almost a century earlier. Blok's considerable talent and natural sense of rhythm facilitated the realization of these aspirations, resulting in an amazing output during twenty years of literary activity. Thematically, Blok brought the cult of the Eternal Feminine to Russia, using the concept as focal point in his search for spiritual unity. The immense range of this vision, incorporating, among others, the Virgin Mary, Holy Sophia, Mother Russia, Blok's wife, and St. Petersburg prostitutes, permitted the poet to extend early mystical longings to the concrete realities of his own life and to revolutionary changes. His verse cycles dedicated to his native land, his perceptive essays on the role of the intelligentsia, and his refusal to emigrate during the famines of the Civil War brought him deference from all segments of the Russian public. Stylistically, he honored the conventions of the past by building on existing rhyme schemes in much of his work, even as he changed from the traditional counting of syllables in a metric foot to modern tonic verse patterns.

Blok's poetry appealed to fellow poets, critics, and the public at large alike. He managed to avoid censorial confrontations with both prerevolutionary and postrevolutionary regimes to emerge as the most esteemed writer of the Silver Age, at once a preserver of tradition and a precursor of modern poetry. His work is widely translated and discussed abroad, while he remains a respected literary figure in the Soviet Union.

Biography

The artistically, academically, and socially illustrious family into which Aleksandr Blok was born on November 16, 1880, contributed significantly to his poetic development and success. His maternal grandfather was the prominent botanist and rector of St. Petersburg University, Andrey Beketov, and his grandmother was an editor and translator—from English, French, and German—of artistic and scientific works. Blok's mother, one of the prime influences on his life, wrote poetry herself and established a reputation as a translator of French literature. Several other female members of the family were also engaged in literary activity, especially the interpretation of French writers to the Russian public, thus exposing Blok early to the ideas of Euro-

pean literature. The Blok side of the family consisted of outstanding professional people, though tainted with a strain of insanity which affected Blok's
father, a law professor at Warsaw University. Blok believed that his father's
mental instability contributed to his own frequent despondency. Blok's parents, highly individualistic and incompatible in personality, did not remain
together for long. The poet was born in his mother's ancestral home and
reared by a household of solicitous women, who nourished both his physical
and artistic development until age eleven, when he was finally enrolled in a
boys' school. By that time, he had already written poems, coedited an informal
family journal, and taken part in domestic theatricals. Blok's lifelong attachment to the feminine principle in his poetry, and his first book of verse
specifically devoted to that concept, may well reflect the influence of the
women in the Beketov household.

In 1898, Blok entered the Law School of St. Petersburg, but changed three
years later to the philology department, from which he was graduated in 1906.
In 1903, he published his first verses and married the daughter of the scientist
Dmitry Mendelyev, a family friend. He had also become interested in mystic
philosophy, contributing essays to the Religious-Philosophical Society, of which
he was a member. By the time his first verses were printed, he had amassed
more than six hundred poems, most of which found ready acceptance after
his debut. From this point on, a steady stream of poems, dramas, and essays
issued from Blok's pen with seeming effortlessness. In 1904, the collection
Stikhi o prekrasnoy dame appeared, to be followed in 1907 by his second
book, *Nechayannaya radost*, and several plays. Under the influence of his
mystical beliefs, Blok had transferred the cult of a divine feminine vision to
his wife Lyubov, an aspiring actress, to whom many of the "Beautiful Lady"
poems were dedicated. Blok's close friend and fellow mystic, the poet Andrey
Bely, carried this adoration to extremes, causing family disharmony. Blok's
wife rejected all mysticism, lived a life of her own, and bore a short-lived son
conceived in an extramarital liaison. Nevertheless, the couple remained
together as trusted friends. Blok to the end admired, needed, and relied on
Lyubov's strong, earthy personality, as he had earlier relied on his mother
and grandmother.

The shattered idealism of Blok's marriage and the miscarried 1905 uprising
drew the poet away from the otherworldly themes of his early work. As he
developed a more skeptical, practical outlook, he immersed himself in the
street life of St. Petersburg, giving himself up to several passions. His infatuation with Natalia Volokhova, an actress in his play *The Puppet Show*,
inspired the verse cycles *Snezhnaya maska* (the snow mask) and "Faina,"
which are among his finest works. A happier love affair with the opera singer
Lyubov Delmas in 1914 engendered the cycle "Karmen."

Blok made five journeys abroad. As a young man, he accompanied his
mother twice to Germany. Later, in 1909, he traveled with his wife to Italy

and transformed his impressions of that country into the group of "Italyanskie stikhi." In 1911, the Bloks toured Europe, which provided inspiration for the verse tale *Solovinyy sad* and the play *The Rose and the Cross*, reflecting experiences on the Basque coast and in Brittany respectively. A nagging feeling of guilt about having neglected his father is reflected in the unfinished epic "Vozmezdie" (retribution).

Blok's political involvements were minor, though controversial. His ideas on the state of the country were published in *Rossia i intelligentsia* (1918), a series of essays spanning a decade. Blok accuses his own upper class of having created a cultural schism by looking to Europe while slighting its own people and heritage. This negative attitude toward the existing ruling circles encouraged him not to condemn the revolution, though he did not welcome it enthusiastically. A stint at the front contributed to his unhappiness, as he saw the philosophical unity sought in his work disappear in the ravages of war and revolution. He served briefly on a provisional government commission investigating suspect czarist officials, then composed his best-known and most controversial poem, *The Twelve*, which depicts a murderous Red Army detachment as disciples to an ineffectual, effeminate Christ. The equally provocative *Skify* (the Scythians) followed a few days later. Between 1918 and his death on August 7, 1921, Blok wrote little, though he continued work on "Vozmezdie." The Bolshevik government, grateful for his conciliatory stance, printed and reissued many of his works and appointed him to several literature boards and artistic commissions. Through these activities his material circumstances were less desperate than those of his fellow citizens, but his health declined quickly just the same. Depression and doubts about the future of his country hastened his end. Russia's artistic, literary, and governing elite and more than a thousand people followed his coffin in recognition of his cultural contributions.

Analysis

Aleksandr Blok sought to give a metaphysical dimension to his poetry by creating a persona that pays homage to a supernatural ideal, in his own words "an essence possessed of an independent existence." This ideal is usually represented by the concept of the Eternal Feminine, which takes on a range of embodiments in the various stages of Blok's development. Initially, he depicted an ephemeral, distant spirit, "the Beautiful Lady," whose presence the poet perceives in almost every poem, but who is never made manifest. As Blok matured, his mental discipline, inquiring mind, and sensuous disposition prompted him to alter the image, until it became more of a literary device and less of a religious inspiration. While the vision retained some of its ethereal, purifying characteristics in later works, it also assumed demoniac, physically alluring aspects. In many other poems, desperate city women, whose misfortunes Blok ascertained from newspapers, represent the feminine ideal, as do the poet's female friends and relatives. The persona's attitude to the changing image is ambiguous. He is inexplicably and fatally drawn to some embodiments, observing others wistfully and indifferently. Eventually, social pressures, war, and revolution drew Blok further from the transcendental sphere, causing him to blend his vision with the concept of Mother Russia. Blok then saw "the Beautiful Lady" in the lined faces of praying peasant women and urban prostitutes, and even in the Russian landscape. A final attempt to revive the religious dimension of the image occurs in the revolutionary poem *The Twelve*, in which an effeminate, Christ-like ghost silently and gently accompanies marauding Bolshevik revolutionaries.

Although the Eternal Feminine is a constant in Blok's work, it does not exhaust his poetic themes. After witnessing the bloodbath of the unsuccessful 1905 uprising in St. Petersburg, he devoted an entire cycle, "Gorod," to his hometown. Only a few of these poems express political observations; most of them deal with the darker aspects of street life. Feelings of impending catastrophe, both personal and societal, pervade the poetic atmosphere. The later cycle "Strashny mir" (a terrible world) extends this theme of urban degradation and misery. In one of the sections of the cycle, "Plyaski smerti" (dances of death), which echoes Charles Baudelaire's "Danse Macabre," Blok evokes the disintegration of his society, which the persona views in the shape of a corpse, no longer believing in transcendence, while soulless St. Petersburg citizens dance their own deaths through empty lives. In the seventy-two-poem cycle "Arfy i skripki" (harps and violins), Blok endeavors to link poetry to music, and several of his verses were later set to music. He manages to reproduce the rhythm of ballads, romances, and factory and folk songs in these and many other poems. Finally, the unfinished epic "Vozmezdie" is a lyrical chronicle of his family's and nation's destiny. Blok's general poetic mood ranges from mystical belief and idealistic expectation to false rapture, skeptical, even cynical visions of life, and eventually sadness, despair, and critical aloofness.

Stylistically, Blok stands between the traditional syllabic meter and modern tonic patterns. In his earlier work, metric regularity and exact rhyme dominate, to be followed by syllabotonic verse and experiments with vers libre. His rhymes become approximate, until he evolves a very modern, conversational style. Typically, his line has three stresses, interrupted by one or two unstressed syllables, but his rather extensive output shows great stress and syllable diversity within the line. He favors lexical repetition and occasionally repeats the first stanza as the last, with slight lexical change, to achieve a musical effect. Not the least of his skills is to transform vague, mystical notions into concise, elegant verse. Blok's poetry is more accessible than the linguistic experiments of the Futurists and other innovators, and theme or thought are not as completely subordinated to technique. This accessibility, achieved with no loss of artistic quality, and the generally held belief that he re-created the great poetic traditions of the nineteenth century, give him a fame and exposure not matched by other modern Russian poets.

Blok's celebration of a feminine ideal is a twentieth century version of earlier cults, encompassing the Gnostic image of Holy Sophia, the adoration of the Virgin Mary in its various guises, Dante's devotion to Beatrice, and Johann Wolfgang von Goethe's evocation of the Eternal Feminine in *Faust* (1808). Blok was not directly influenced by Western manifestations of the concept, though he employed all of them. His interest in the symbol came from the writings of the mystic philosopher Vladimir Solovyov, who incorporated Holy Sophia into his ideological system. Blok called his ideal more generally "The Beautiful Lady," devoting not only his first collection, *Stikhi o prekrasnoy dame*, to her, but extending the vision in diverse guises in all major subsequent work. His choice of an ancient symbol was influenced by the belief that familiar, even proverbial concepts, call forth deeper emotions than newly created metaphors. The more than three hundred poems of his first collection portray the Beautiful Lady as a godlike essence which can never assume concrete, earthly shape, but is accessible in spirit to the perceptive poetic persona. The image thus appears in fleeting poses, in the flickering of a candle, the rustle of a curtain, a breeze, or simply as a felt presence. Particularly prominent is Blok's evocation of a distant shadow: "I waited for You. But Your shadow hovered/ In the distance, in the fields . . ." or "You are leaving into crimson sunset/ Into endless circles."

In this semblance, the Beautiful Lady is sometimes an elemental, an almost pagan spirit, enveloped in mists and twilight, floating by in a snowflake or glistening in a star. She appears as a figure in a song and is herself a song, perceived in snatches of distant melodies. In line with traditional symbolism, she is frequently represented by a radiant light: "I wait. Unexpectedly a door will open,/ And vanishing light will fall on me." The association with light extends naturally to religious settings, in which the Beautiful Lady is an incarnation of the Virgin. She is anticipated by the persona at the temple entrance: "The church steps are illuminated/ Their stones alive—and waiting for Your steps," and immediately perceived within: "Holy Lady, how caressing the candles,/ How comforting Your features." The poems tend to follow a rigid scheme: a physical setting empty of other people, the persona's anticipation, his ritualistic incantations, resulting in perception of the vision.

Blok often used dark/light contrasts to separate image from persona and the rest of the world. In a well-known poem of this type, "I Go into Darkened Temples," the worshiper waits in the dim edifice, contemplating the flickering candle before the icon of the Virgin. The intense longing produces a state of excitement, in which real or imaginary creaks, rustles, and movements translate into a perception of her presence. The icon seems to come alive as the worshiper falls into a trance, engulfed by dreams and fairy-tale images. The final impression is an instant of joy and relief. These verses are not so much a lyrical diary, though Blok designated them as such, as they are a glimpse of his spiritual search. The intensity of his emotions carries a hint of immaturity, even sentimentality, which is redeemed, however, by the careful transmutation of the ecstasy into a restrained poetic idiom, and by the gossamer quality of the dreamlike reflections.

Several factors led the poet to change the image and thus extend the range of his spiritual odyssey. The idea of constant longing and expectation, interrupted only by vague, insubstantial moments of revelation, failed to satisfy the poet on a permanent basis. Doubt in the validity of his adoration, even in the existence of the Beautiful Lady and impatience with her remoteness already appear in the first collection. Blok sees himself as her "Obscure slave, filled with inspiration/ Praising You. But You don't know him." He also reproaches her: "You are different, mute, faceless,/ Hidden away. You bewitch in silence." In the end, he challenges the symbol more directly: "You are holy, but I don't believe You." In one of Blok's most quoted poems, "I Have a Premonition of You," he fearfully anticipates other embodiments: "The entire heaven is on fire, and Your appearance near,/ But I am terrified that You will change your visage." The changes were inevitable in the light of the poet's determination to transfer some of the mystique to his fiancée Lyubov, who became his wife in 1904. This attempt at earthly incarnation miscarried, for while he implored Lyubov to serve as his inspiration, addressing her with the same capitalized "You" often lavished on the Beautiful Lady, she refused all mysticism and insisted on an ordinary flesh-and-blood relationship.

Blok's second book, *Nechayannaya radost* (unexpected joy), features an altered image of the Beautiful Lady. The thirteen-poem lead cycle "Puzyry zemli" identifies the symbol with the Macbethian witches, described by William Shakespeare: "The earth has bubbles, as the water hath/ And these are of them." Religious adoration is here replaced by riotous cavorting amid the demons of the St. Petersburg marshes. The second cycle of the book, "Nochnaya fialka," a fantastic tale composed in 1905-1906, expands this underground involvement. A new version of the Eternal Feminine appears in the form of a graceful but lethally poisonous flower princess. The dreamer-poet leaves his city and friends to venture far into a swampy netherworld, where he encounters a faceless, ageless vegetable female. This sweet-smelling woman flower eternally spins, casting her devastating marsh breath over others, while she herself blooms in the poisonous atmosphere. The sleepy hero perceives distant echoes of a happier land, now forever lost to him. The style of "Nochnaya fialka" demonstrates Blok's increasing technical mastery. Though he preserves traditional regular rhythm, he uses free verse and uneven rhyme and syllable schemes. This poem is considered one of Blok's best.

In Blok's subsequent collections, the Eternal Feminine assumes whatever aspect suits the poetic theme. When casting his unrequited love for Natalia Volokhova into verse in the cycle *Snezhnaya maska*, the vision becomes a glacial force, indifferently condemning the persona to a frozen wasteland. In "Faina," she is a cruelly teasing gypsy. Blok's most famous poems feature other embodiments of the ideal. In "The Stranger," she is a prostitute, uncannily reflecting the purity and mystery of the Beautiful Lady, and in "A Girl Sang in a Church Choir," she is a young singer transformed into a ray of light, promising salvation, while the piercing cries of a child reveal her deception. When the poet does make contact with his vision, the encounter is usually unsatisfactory or violent, as in "Humiliation," where the persona wrestles with a prostitute and shouts in despair: "I am neither your husband, nor bridegroom, nor friend!/ So go ahead, my erstwhile angel and plunge/ Your sharp French heel into my heart."

Blok's most controversial manifestation of a divine vision occurs in the final stanza of his revolutionary poem *The Twelve*. Technically, *The Twelve* is a masterpiece. It pits the icy, howling snowstorm of the revolution against the vulnerable population, seen as unsure of its footing and slipping on the ice. All segments of society confront and attempt to hurdle the Bolshevik snowdrift. A fur-clad upper-class lady fails and lies prostrate; a fat-bellied priest attempts to squeeze by furtively; a bourgeois stands undecided at the crossroad; an intellectual shouts his dissent; a peasant woman, not understanding the political event, succeeds in clambering across the snowdrift. Prostitutes using incongruous political jargon establish union fees for their services. These scenes are background for the main drama dealing with twelve Red Army men who think they safeguard the revolution, but really loot and kill. One of them murders his lover in a jealous rage, only to be overcome by religious scruples and feelings of guilt. At poem's end, the revolutionaries continue on their violent path, boldly asserting their freedom from religion, but—unknown to them—they are led by the shadowy, gentle, garlanded figure of an effeminate Christ, whose unexpected appearance transmutes the marauders into the twelve disciples. Blok was vilified by both the Left and the Right for this inexplicable ending, but insisted that his poetic instinct dictated it. The controversy over this image for a long time obscured appreciation of the poem's exquisite artistic craftsmanship. Blok wrote very little after *The Twelve*.

Blok was the forerunner of modern Russian poetry. He replaced the realistic, low-quality verse of the second half of the nineteenth century with a new lyricism, to which he gave a mystical dimension. In much of his work, he pursued the cult of the Eternal Feminine, investing it first with a religious aspect, then adapting it to the needs of his poetic themes. Technically, he freed Russian verse from rigid meter and led the way to modern tonic patterns. The social upheavals of his era are reflected in his work, but always subordinate to artistic requirements. Blok appealed to all segments of the public and continues to be popular at home and abroad.

Major publications other than poetry

PLAYS: *Balaganchik*, 1906 (*The Puppet Show*, 1963); *Korol na ploshchadi*, written 1906 (*The King in the Square*, 1934); *Pesnya sudby*, 1919 (*The Song of Fate*, 1938); *Roza i krest*, 1922 (*The Rose and the Cross*, 1936).

NONFICTION: *Rossia i intelligentsia*, 1918; *Katilina*, 1919; *O simvalizme*, 1921; *Pis'ma Aleksandra Bloka*, 1925; *Pis'ma Aleksandra Bloka k rodnym*, 1927; *Dnevnik Al. Bloka 1911-1913*, 1928; *Dnevnik Al. Bloka 1917-1921*, 1928; *Zapisnye knizhki Al. Bloka*, 1930; *Pis'ma Al. Bloka k E. P. Ivanovu*, 1936; *Aleksandr Blok i Andrey Bely: Perepiska*, 1940.

Bibliography

Freiman, I. *The Spirit of Music*, 1946.

Hackel, Sergey. *The Poet and the Revolution: Aleksandr Blok's "The Twelve,"* 1975.

Muchnic, Helen. *From Gorky to Pasternak*, 1961.

Poggioli, Renato. *The Poets of Russia*, 1960.

Pyman, Avril. *The Life of Aleksandr Blok*, 1979, 1980.

Reeve, F. D. *Aleksandr Blok: Between Image and Idea*, 1962.

Margot K. Frank

JOHANNES BOBROWSKI

Born: Tilsit (Sowjetsk), East Prussia; April 9, 1917
Died: East Berlin, East Germany; September 2, 1965

Principal collections

Sarmatische Zeit, 1961; *Schattenland Ströme*, 1962 (*Shadow Land*, 1966); *Wetterzeichen*, 1966; *Im Windgesträuch*, 1970.

Other literary forms

Although Johannes Bobrowski is remembered primarily for his poetry, he did publish two critically acclaimed experimental novels: *Levins Mühle: 34 Sätze über meinen Grossvater* (1964; *Levin's Mill: 34 Statements About My Grandfather*, 1970) and *Litauische Klaviere* (1966; Lithuanian pianos). He also wrote several short stories, which are collected in the following volumes: *Boehlendorff und andere Prosa* (1965; Boehlendorff and other prose), *Mäusefest und andere Erzählungen* (1965; festival of the mice and other stories), and *Der Mahner* (1967; *I Taste Bitterness*, 1970). Working as a reader at an East German publishing house, he had the opportunity to edit books by others, including collections of legends and poetry. Recordings of several of his poems are available.

Achievements

Bobrowski belonged to that generation of East German poets who matured late artistically, since their creative development was interrupted by the events of World War II and the founding of a new state. When Bobrowski finally published his first slender volumes in the early 1960's, they caused a great deal of excitement in both East and West Germany, for he was recognized as a major talent. His thematic concerns were new and provocative, and his unique style, based in part on classical German modes yet stripped to the bare linguistic essentials, was rich in metaphor and allegory. For his poetic accomplishments he was awarded the prestigious prize of the Group 47 in 1962, a prize given only to the most promising new authors in the German-speaking world. In the same year, he won the Alma-Johanna-Koenig Prize in Vienna. For his novel *Levin's Mill*, he was awarded the Heinrich Mann Prize of the East Berlin Academy of the Arts and the international Charles Veillon Prize from Switzerland, both in 1965. He was posthumously granted the East German F. C. Weiskopf Prize in 1967.

Together with Erich Arendt and Peter Huchel, Bobrowski is credited with giving a new direction and inspiration to East German poetry, which until his time was rather bogged down in the principles of Socialist Realism and the Brechtian tradition. Bobrowski showed his own generation and younger, emerging poets that artistic integrity and genuine creativity and diversity were possible within the framework of a Socialist state. He also called attention to the great classical German heritage, which had been largely forgotten in the postwar years, and to the most recent developments in West German and foreign poetry. About ten years later, in the early 1970's, his name was again invoked by younger authors in East Germany who sought a new means of aesthetic expression. Although Bobrowski was notably absent from literary anthologies and histories in East Germany immediately after his death, he is today given a place of honor in the literary canon there and is recognized as a humanitarian author who strove for Socialist ideals. In West Germany, more emphasis is placed on an appreciation of his style. He is often mentioned in connection with Günter Eich and Paul Celan, who, like Bobrowski, employed a reduced and concentrated lexical inventory, to the point of being hermetic or even opaque, and who at the same time did not shy away from combining mythological elements with autobiographical and contemporary references.

Biography

Johannes Bobrowski was born in a German town in East Prussia, not far from Lithuania; his father was a German railroad employee of Polish descent. Bobrowski spent his childhood in the small village of Mozischken and frequently visited his grandparents on their farm in the country. It was at this time that he learned much about the culture and history of the Slavic peoples who lived across the border. In 1928, the family moved to Königsberg (now called Kaliningrad), where Bobrowski attended a college-preparatory high school. In school, he was particularly attracted to the disciplines of music and painting; one of his teachers there was the writer Ernst Wiechert. In 1937, the family moved again, this time to Berlin, where Bobrowski began to study art history.

In 1939, Bobrowski was conscripted into military service. During World War II, he served as a soldier in France, Poland, and northern Russia, but he was also a member of the Bekennende Kirche (the confessing Church), a Protestant resistance group. He was taken prisoner of war in 1945 and remained in Russian captivity until 1949; he was held in the regions of the Don and middle Volga rivers and did forced labor as a coal miner. He returned to East Berlin in 1949, and in 1950 he began working as a reader at the publishing house Union Verlag, affiliated with the Lutheran Church. He remained there until his death, resulting from complications after an appendicitis operation, in 1965.

Bobrowski began writing poetry in 1941, when he was stationed at Lake Ilmen, and a few of his poems were published in the "inner emigration" magazine *Das innere Reich*. He did not write much again until the early 1950's. His first poems after the war appeared in 1954 in the East German literary magazine *Sinn und Form*, which was edited by his friend Peter Huchel. Bobrowski continued to write sporadically after this literary debut, but he did not feel that his style had matured sufficiently until the early 1960's, when he published his first two volumes of poetry. He completed work on his third volume, *Wetterzeichen* (signs of the weather), but it did not appear until after his death. A fourth volume, *Im Windgesträuch* (in the wind bushes), appeared in 1970, containing poems of lesser quality which were written between 1953 and 1964.

Analysis

Many of Johannes Bobrowski's poems, as he often stated, have as their central theme the relationship between the Germans and their neighbors to the East, the Slavic peoples. Because he grew up along the river Memel, where these two cultures merge, Bobrowski was particularly sensitive to this issue. From the days of the Order of the Teutonic Knights in the Middle Ages, the Germans had treated these people very badly, and the history of their relations is marred by war, repression, and murder. Bobrowski the poet recalls these atrocities, lest contemporary Germans forget to atone for their past misdeeds. To accomplish this goal, Bobrowski uses the concept of "Sarmatia," a vague term applied by ancient historians and geographers to the area that he has in mind—namely, the territory between Finland and southern Russia from the Baltic to the Black Sea. He populates his Sarmatia with a host of various personages: ancient gods, legendary figures, and historical personalities. Bobrowski thus creates a mythology of sorts in order to come to terms with the German past, but it is not a well-defined mythology, and one can discern its full richness only by studying his poems as a totality. Thus, when one reads about the ancient gods Perkun and Pikoll in "Pruzzische Elegie" ("Prussian Elegy"), about the great Lithuanian ruler Wilna in "Anruf" ("Appeal") or in "Wilna," about the legendary sunken city of Kiteshgorod in "Erzählung" ("Story"), or about Russian writer Isaac Babel in "Holunderblüte" ("Elderblossom"), one confronts only one aspect of Bobrowski's poetic world. History is treated as myth and myth as history. The reader must be willing to mingle and combine past and present, the real and the fictional, in order to form a coherent concept of the historical development Bobrowski has in mind.

This historical dimension of Bobrowski's poetry offers a key to understanding his works. His poems contain five intertwined temporal layers: ancient times, in which the Slavic or Sarmatian tribes were free to determine their own existence and live in close harmony with nature; past centuries of conflict with the German invaders; the horrors of World War II, which Bobrowski had personally experienced; the present time, in which one must rectify old wrongs; and a future era, in which all men will live in communion with one another. It is often difficult to separate these layers, particularly when the reader finds many confusing temporal references within a single poem, yet this very ambiguity accounts for the richness of Bobrowski's verse; the various layers illuminate one another and promote an understanding of historical and cultural processes. Moreover, these poems transcend their historical occasion, offering profound general insights into man's inhumanity to man on a global scale and forcefully arguing the need for reconciliation and the end of barbarism. They can thus be read and appreciated by persons from various cultural backgrounds and different eras. This rich philosophical content of the poems also explains how Bobrowski, as a Christian non-Marxist, was able to survive and publish in East Germany. He was seen as a seer or prophet who pointed out the errors of the past and the way to achieve the future brotherhood of all men—one of the proclaimed goals of the Communist state. In a manner similar to the historical process he was describing, Bobrowski's poetry underwent a noticeable thematic development or progression: His first poems are concerned primarily with the fantastic landscape of Sarmatia; later poems include historical events and persons from the recent and distant past; and finally, Bobrowski arrives at a discussion of the problems of his present-day Berlin.

Not all Bobrowski poems deal with Sarmatia. A few treat the themes of love and death, not with any specificity, but in general philosophical terms. Two other categories, however, must be discussed in greater detail. The first contains poems written in honor or in memory of other artists with whom Bobrowski feels some affinity, such as François Villon, Joseph Conrad, Dylan Thomas, Marc Chagall, Johann Georg Hamann, Friedrich Gottlieb Klopstock, Gertrud Kolmar, Friedrich Hölderlin, Else Lasker-Schüler, Nelly Sachs, Wolfgang Amadeus Mozart, Johann Sebastian Bach, Christian Domelaitis, and J. R. M. Lenz. These "portrait poems" are not biographical or artistic summaries, but rather impressions of the artists or their lives. Bobrowski merely takes one aspect or feature of the artist and explains why he admires it or considers it important for his work. Thus, in the poem "An Klopstock" ("To Klopstock"), Bobrowski praises Klopstock's notion that one must recall the past and atone for former transgressions. (Bobrowski considered Klopstock to be his "taskmaster," both stylistically and thematically.) In "Hamann," he praises the eighteenth century poet for collecting and preserving ancient tales and legends. (Bobrowski was greatly influenced by Hamann while still in school and felt that Hamann's life's goals were similar to his own. He had been collecting material for years for a monograph on Hamann but was unable to complete it because of his premature death.) In the poems "Else Lasker-Schüler" and "An Nelly Sachs" ("To Nelly Sachs"), Bobrowski points to the suffering these poets endured because they were Jewish, a suffering similar to that of the Jews living in Sarmatia. Bobrowski shared with all of these artists a deep humanistic commitment to his fellowman and a concern for suffering in the world.

Another significant category of Bobrowski's poems, though by no means large, could be termed "metapoetry." In these poems, Bobrowski describes his concept of poetic language and poetic communication. Two of these poems are especially paradigmatic: "Immer zu benennen" ("Always to Be Named") and "Sprache" ("Language"). Here, Bobrowski shows that he believes in an almost mystical relationship between the word and the thing named, that the word somehow captures the spirit of the thing or the person to which it refers. This idea plays an important role in Bobrowski's mythology, for objects, particularly from nature, take on a new significance: They become part of man, part of his past and his relationship to other men. Thus, not only history is important for an understanding of man's advance into the future, but also words and nature, for by means of these two elements men can communicate with one another and prepare themselves for what is to come. This is for Bobrowski the highest sense of poetry—it speaks to the reader on several levels and raises his degree of consciousness. Poetry does not, Bobrowski claims, move the reader to bold political or social acts.

Because of his emphasis on man's relationship to nature through language, and because he believed that man's harmony with nature, which was somehow lost in the past, must be regained in order to save the human race, Bobrowski's work has often been referred to as nature poetry. This description is valid only to a certain extent. It is true that Bobrowski does employ a great number of recurring nature motifs in his poetry, most frequently rivers, birds, trees, fish, stones, wolves, light, and darkness. These motifs, however, are not an evocation of nature per se. They do not merely conjure up the beauty of landscapes to be admired and enjoyed, but rather they function as symbols within the overriding thematics of the poem. Although they have varying connotations, Bobrowski generally uses these motifs to connect man to nature and to show how man is part of the natural historical process. The objects of nature remain constant throughout historical change, says Bobrowski, and so, too, does man's soul. If man can rid himself of the barbarous acts of war and violence and return to his primeval natural state, he will have reached his ultimate goal. This strong concern for the human and communal element is what sets Bobrowski's poems apart from traditional nature poetry.

Bobrowski's symbolic treatment of nature is only one aspect of his laconic style. The most striking feature of his poetry is the reduction of the linguistic material to an extreme minimum. Frequently, lines consist of merely a word or two each, and the length of the line is very irregular. Bobrowski often employs sentence fragments consisting of a single word, and longer syntactic units are usually broken up into several lines, interrupting the semantic flow. The breaking of the poem into small phrases gives primacy to the individual word and lends the poetic message an aspect far different from what it would possess were it written in prose or even conventional poetic style. The free rhythms are sometimes fairly regular, so that the reader is often reminded of the odes and elegies of previous centuries. Bobrowski's concentrated and abbreviated style demands the active participation of the reader, who must fill in the missing material and make the appropriate associations and connections, a process similar to that through which one tries to remember events of the distant past. Such a difficult procedure tends at times to weaken the thematic impact of the poem, but as Fritz Minde points out in an article on Bobrowski, the poems can indeed be decoded with the help of published biographical and historical material; their difficult construction mimics the deformed and incoherent structure of reality.

In *Poetry in East Germany*, John Flores suggests a method by which this decoding can be performed. He believes that most of Bobrowski's poems have three parts or stages. In the first, or introductory, part, the author relies chiefly on nouns, employed in an uncertain, staccato fashion. He is setting the mood for the poem by using the naming process described above. The reader is uncertain and somewhat confused. In the second stage, spatial and temporal connections begin to appear. The style is more reflective and narrative, and nouns are linked with verbs. The thematic thrust of the poem begins to take shape. In the final stage, the staccato mode is reintroduced, but here the verb prevails. The author unleashes his thoughts and ideas in a torrent of words. These thoughts have been building in intensity throughout the poem, and they all come together in the end in a desperate cry for recognition.

The difficult and cryptic nature of many of Bobrowski's poems raises the question of his place in literary history. Was he a true member of the avant-garde, a forerunner of or participant in the reductive "linguistic" movement of contemporary German poetry? No, he did not use language as a collection of building blocks devoid of meaning. Instead, he can be seen as part of the movement toward radical reduction of language that began around 1910 with the Expressionists in Germany and that insisted on a language free of all decadent cultural encrustations. Such a purification of language became all the more necessary after the abuses of the Nazi years. At the same time, however, Bobrowski went beyond this essentially negative program, offering in his verse substantive arguments in favor of a new and better world.

Major publications other than poetry

NOVELS: *Levins Mühle: 34 Sätze über meinen Grossvater*, 1964 (*Levin's Mill: 34 Statements About My Grandfather*, 1970); *Litauische Klaviere*, 1966.

SHORT FICTION: *Boehlendorff und andere Prosa*, 1965; *Mäusefest und andere Erzählungen*, 1965; *Der Mahner*, 1967 (*I Taste Bitterness*, 1970).

Bibliography

Bridgwater, Patrick. "The Poetry of Johannes Bobrowski," in *Forum for Modern Language Studies*. II (1966), pp. 320-334.

Flores, John. *Poetry in East Germany*, 1971.

Glenn, Jerry. "An Introduction to the Poetry of Johannes Bobrowski," in

The Germanic Review. XLI (1966), pp. 45-56.

Hoefert, Sigrid. *West-Östliches in der Lyrik Johannes Bobrowskis*, 1966.

Minde, Fritz. "Johannes Bobrowski," in *Die deutsche Lyrik 1945-1975*, 1981. Edited by Klaus Weissenbürger.

Streller, Siegfried. "Johannes Bobrowski," in *Literatur der DDR in Einzeldarstellungen*, 1972. Edited by Hans Jürgen Geerdts.

Titel, Britta. "Johannes Bobrowski," in *Schriftsteller der Gegenwart*, 1963. Edited by Klaus Nonnenmann.

Robert Acker

EDWARD KAMAU BRATHWAITE

Born: Bridgetown, Barbados; May 11, 1930

Principal poems and collections

Rights of Passage, 1967; *Masks*, 1968; *Islands*, 1969; *The Arrivants*, 1973 (a trilogy including *Rights of Passage*, *Masks*, and *Islands* in revised form); *Other Exiles*, 1975; *Days and Nights*, 1975; *Black & Blues*, 1976; *Mother Poem*, 1977; *Sun Poem*, 1982.

Other literary forms

Edward Kamau Brathwaite has published scores of books, articles, and reviews as a historian and literary critic. Among his historical studies are *The Development of Creole Society in Jamaica, 1770-1820* (1971), one chapter of which was expanded and published as *Folk Culture of Slaves in Jamaica* (1970); *Contradictory Omens* (1974); and *Caribbean Man in Space and Time* (1975). His historical studies have delineated the pressures that have shaped present-day Caribbean life. He is particularly interested in the transmission of African culture to the New World, the "'little' tradition of the ex-slave," and its promise to serve as a "basis for creative reconstruction" in postemancipation, postcolonial Creole society. His literary criticism has sought out the presence of African traditions in Caribbean literature and has helped to develop a vigorous, indigenous school of West Indian criticism. Brathwaite's work as poet, critic, and historian has made available to a wide audience the rich cultural heritage of Caribbean people.

Achievements

Brathwaite is one of the most popular and critically acclaimed writers to emerge in the West Indies during the remarkable period in the region's history and literature following World War II. He epitomizes the intensified ethnic and national awareness of his generation of writers—including Derek Walcott, Wilson Harris, Michael Anthony, Martin Carter, Samuel Selvon, John Hearne, and Austin Clarke, to name several of the more prominent—whose writing seeks to correct the destructive effects of colonialism on West Indian sensibility. Brathwaite's aim, as he has described it, is to "transcend and heal" the fragmented culture of his dispossessed people through his poetry, reexamining the whole history of the black diaspora in a search for cultural wholeness in contemporary Caribbean life.

Brathwaite offers his poetry as a corrective to the twin problems of the West Indian: dispossession of history and of language. The West Indian writer labors in a culture whose history has been distorted by prejudice and malice, the modern version of which is the commonplace notion, after James Anthony

Froude and V. S. Naipaul, that nothing was created or achieved in the West Indies. The Afro-Caribbean's history is the record of being uprooted, displaced, enslaved, dominated, and finally abandoned. Brathwaite's reclamation of racial pride centers on rectifying the significance of the Middle Passage not as the destroyer but as the transmitter of culture.

The second problem that the writer confronts, that of language, is an aspect of cultural dispossession. The diversity of Creole languages, hybrids of many African and European tongues, reinforces the insularity of the individual and devalues the expressively rich languages that the people use in their non-official, personal, most intimate lives. Brathwaite's poems in Bajun dialect extend the folk traditions of Claude McKay and Louise Bennett and ground his work in the lives of the people for and about whom he writes.

The problem of language, however, is not a matter of choosing the Creole over the metropolitan language. It is a deeply political and spiritual problem, since, as Brathwaite writes, it was with language that the slave was "most successfully imprisoned by the master, and through his (mis-)use of it that he most effectively rebelled." With nearly all other means of attaining personal liberty denied, the slave's last, irrevocable instrument of resistance and rebellion was language. For the West Indian writer, Caliban in William Shakespeare's *The Tempest* (1611), written at the beginning of England's experiment in empire, is the archetype of the slave who turns his borrowed language against his master. To turn his instrument of rebellion into one of creation is Brathwaite's task. Accordingly, in his poem "Caliban" (in *The Arrivants*), Brathwaite's persona begins by celebrating the morning of December 2, 1956, the start of the Cuban Revolution, which remains a symbol of the regions self-determination. In the second section of the poem, Brathwaite adapts Shakespeare's "'Ban Ban Caliban,'/ Has a new master" curse-chant to the hold of a slave ship, articulating a spirit of resistance which turns in the final section into an assertion of endurance. At the end of the poem, the slaves' nightly limbo on deck becomes the religious ceremony—the seed of African culture carried to the New World—of the assembled tribes, who are able to raise their ancestral gods and be for the moment a whole people. What Brathwaite achieves in "Caliban" he achieves in his poetry at large: He uses his languages, both Creole and metropolitan English, to define the selfhood of the group in positive terms, contrary to the negations of the colonizers. "Within the folk tradition," Brathwaite writes, "language was (and is) a creative act in itself; the word was held to contain a secret power." In his poetry, the power of the word is to conjure, to evoke, to punish, to celebrate, to mourn, to love. He uses language boldly as one who seeks its deepest power: to reveal and heal the wounds of history.

Biography

L. Edward Kamau Brathwaite, the son of Hilton Brathwaite and Beryl Gill

Brathwaite, was born in Bridgetown, Barbados, on May 11, 1930. He enrolled at Harrison College in Barbados but won the Barbados Scholarship in 1949, enabling him the next year to read history at Pembroke College, Cambridge University, England. He received an honors degree in 1953 and the Certificate of Education in 1955.

His earliest published poems appeared in the literary journal *Bim*, beginning in 1950. The poems of that decade, some of which are collected in *Other Exiles* and, in revised form, in *The Arrivants*, portray an estranged world fallen from grace, a world that can be redeemed through poetic vision—a creative faith that sustains the more complex fashionings of his later work. Brathwaite shared with other West Indian writers of his generation a strong sense of the impossibility of a creative life in the Caribbean and of the equal impossibility of maintaining identity in exile in England or North America. That crisis of the present he understood as a product of his island's cultural heritage fragmented among its several sources: European, African, American Indian, and Asian.

His reading of history at Cambridge heightened both his sense of the European culture, which had been the dominant official culture of the West Indies, and his need to understand the African culture that had come with the slaves on the Middle Passage. His search led him to Africa, where from 1955 to 1962 he served as an education officer in Kwame Nkrumah's Ghana. His career in Ghana (and in Togoland in 1956 and 1957 as United Nations Plebiscite Officer) provided the historical and local images that became *Masks*, the pivotal book of *The Arrivants*. In Ghana, he established a children's theater and wrote several plays for children (*Four Plays for Primary Schools*, 1964, and *Odale's Choice*, 1967). He married Doris Welcome in 1960, and he has a son, Michael Kwesi Brathwaite.

Brathwaite returned to the West Indies after an exile of twelve years to assume a post as Resident Tutor at the University of the West Indies in St. Lucia (1962-1963) and to produce programs for the Windward Islands Broadcasting Service. His return to the Caribbean supplied the "center" that his poetry had lacked:

> I had, at that moment of return, completed the triangular trade of my historical origins. West Africa had given me a sense of place, of belonging; and that place . . . was the West Indies. My absence and travels, at the same time, had given me a sense of movement and restlessness—rootlessness. It was, I recognized, particularly the condition of the Negro of the West Indies and the New World.

The exploration of that sense of belonging and rootlessness in personal and historic terms is the motive for Brathwaite's subsequent work in poetry, history, and literary criticism. He began in 1963 as lecturer in history at the University of the West Indies at Kingston, Jamaica, where he became Senior Lecturer. He earned his Ph.D. at the University of Sussex in England from

1965 to 1968. His dissertation became *The Development of Creole Society in Jamaica, 1770-1820*, a study of the assimilation of cultures by various groups within the colonial hierarchy.

His poetry continues to explore the cultural heritage of the West Indies in historical and personal terms. *The Arrivants*, begun upon his return to the West Indies in 1972, represents a turning away from the introspection of his early poems toward a larger historical perspective on the Caribbean, as well as the beginnings of a personal solution to the problems of exile and cultural fragmentation.

Analysis

Edward Kamau Brathwaite's early poetry in *Bim*, collected later in *Other Exiles*, with its themes of anxiety and alienation, changed under the search for racial and cultural identity while the poet was in exile. Brathwaite became surer of his European heritage while he was a student in England and recovered the remnants of his African heritage while working in Ghana. Those two great cultures, in conflict in the New World for the last four centuries, are the forces that shape Brathwaite's personal and racial history and the poetics through which he renders his quest for wholeness.

He is equally indebted to the Euro-American literary tradition through the work of T. S. Eliot and to the Afro-West Indian tradition through the work of Aimé Césaire. Brathwaite draws upon Eliot's musical form in *Four Quartets* (1943) for his own use of musical forms developed in stages of the black diaspora—work song, shanto, shango hymn, spiritual, blues, jazz, calypso, ska, and reggae—for his poetic rendering of historic and lyric moments. He also draws his aesthetic for rendering modern industrial and mercantile society in the United States and the Caribbean from Eliot's *The Waste Land* (1922). From Césaire's *Cahier d'un retour au pays natal* (1939; *Return to My Native Land*, 1968), Brathwaite derives the epic and dialectical structure of his trilogy as well as the surrealistic heightening of language that propels the movement from the reality of the Caribbean as wasteland to the vision of the Caribbean as promised land.

That movement can be discerned in the three books of *The Arrivants* through the poet's reconstruction of racial history and his tracing of his personal history. *Rights of Passage*, the first book of the trilogy, contains the restless isolation of his early life in Barbados that sends him into exile in England and Africa, as well as a recollection of the first phase of the black diaspora, the advent of the slave trade and the Middle Passage. The original dispersal of tribes from Ethiopia to West Africa, as well as his own search for his African origins, is the subject of *Masks*. In *Islands*, racial and personal history merge in the exile's return to the West Indies.

Readers of *The Arrivants* who focus on its historical dimension figure Brathwaite as the epic poet of the black diaspora, while those who focus on the autobiography make him the hero of the poem. Taking both approaches as valid, with the binocular vision that the poem requires, one can see that the central figure of the rootless, alienated West Indian in exile and in search of home is the only possible kind of hero for a West Indian epic. That questing poet's voice is, however, often transformed into the voice of a precolonial African being fired upon by a white slaver; the Rastafarian Brother Man; Uncle Tom; a *houngan* invoking Legba; or some other historic or mythic figure. Brathwaite's use of personas, or masks, derives equally from the traditions of Greek drama (dramatic monologue) and African religious practice (chant or invocation). One communal soul speaks in a multiplicity of guises, and the poet thereby re-creates not only his own quest as victim and hero, but also the larger racial consciousness in which he participates. The poet's many masks enable him to reconstruct his own life and the brutal history that created "new soil, new souls, new ancestors" out of the ashes of the past.

Combining racial history and personal quest in *The Arrivants*, Brathwaite has fashioned a contemporary West Indian myth. It is not the myth of history petrified into "progress," but that of a people's endurance through cycles of brutal oppression. Across centuries, across the ocean, and across the three books of this poem, images, characters, and events overlay one another to defy the myth of progress, leading in the poem only to heaven swaying in the reinforced girders of New York, and to the god of capitalism floating in a soundless, airtight glass bubble of an office, a prisoner of his own creation. For the "gods" who tread the earth below, myth is cyclical, and it attaches them to the earth through the "souls" of their feet in repetitions of exodus and arrival.

The trilogy begins with one tribe's ancient crossing of the Sahara desert, their wagons and camels left where they have fallen, and their arrival at a place where "cool/ dew falls/ in the evening." They build villages, but the cattle towns breed flies and flies breed plague, and another journey begins, for across the "dried-out gut" of the riverbed, a mirage shimmers where

> trees are
> cool, there
> leaves are
> green, there
> burns the dream
> of a fountain,
> garden of odours,
> soft alleyways.

This is the repeated pattern of their history: exodus across desert, savannah, ocean; in caravan, ship, or jet plane; visitations of plague, pestilence, famine, slavery, poverty, ignorance, volcanoes, flood. The promised land is always elsewhere, across the parched riverbed ("Prelude") or in the bountiful fields of England, not in Barbados ("The Cracked Mother").

The connections between history and biography and the difficult process of destroying the colonial heritage in favor of a more creative mode of life are evident in the six poems forming the "Limbo" section of *Islands*. In "The Cracked Mother," the first poem of "Limbo," the dissociation of the West Indian's sensibility (regarding his attitudes toward self, race, and country) threatens to paralyze the poet's dialectical movement toward a sustaining vision. The poet's rejection of his native land in favor of England is an acceptance of the colonial's position of inferiority. That attitude is instilled in young West Indians, such historians as Walter Rodney, Frantz Fanon, and Brathwaite have argued, by the system of colonial education that taught an alien and alienating value system. The debilitating effects of such an education are the subject of "The Cracked Mother." The three nuns who take the child from his mother to school appear as "black specks . . . / Santa Marias with black silk sails." The metaphor equates the nuns' coming with that of Columbus and anticipates the violence that followed, especially in the image of the nuns' habits as the sails of death ships. With her child gone, the mother speaks in the second part of the poem as a broken ("cracked") woman reduced to muttering children's word games, which serve as the vehicle for her pain:

> See?
> She saw
> the sea . . .
> I saw
> you take
> my children . . .
> You gave your
> beads, you
> took
> my children . . .
> Christ on the Cross
> your cruel laws teach
> only to divide us
> and we are lost.

History provides the useful equation of nuns' habits with sails and the nun's rosary with beads that Columbus gave to the inhabitants of his "discovered" lands, but it is Brathwaite's own biography that turns metaphor into revelation in the last two parts of the poem, showing how ruinous the colonial mentality is, even to the point of rejecting the earth under one's feet (another "cracked mother") because it is not England.

Brathwaite's corrective begins in "Shepherd," the second poem of the "Limbo" section. Having recalled the damage of his early education and having felt again some of the old abhorrence of the colonial for himself, the poet returns to the African drumbeats of *Masks* to chant a service of possession or reconnection with the gods of his ancestors. The poet then addresses his peers in proverbs, as would an elder his tribe:

> But you do not understand.
> For there is an absence of truth
> like a good tooth drawn from the tight skull
> like the wave's tune gone from the ship's hull;
> there is sand
> but no desert where water can learn of its loveliness.

The people have gifts for the gods but do not give them, yet the gods are everywhere and waiting. Moving in *Islands* toward the regeneration promised in *Masks*, Brathwaite continues with "Caliban" to explore the potential for liberty inherent in the Cuban Revolution, then moves at the moment of triumph back into the slave ship and the limbo that contained the seeds of African religion and identity.

The "Limbo" section ends with the beautiful poem "Islands," which proposes the alternatives that are always present in every moment of Caribbean history: "So looking through a map/ of the islands, you see/ . . . the sun's slums: if you hate/ us. Jewels,/ if there is delight/ in your eyes." The same dichotomy of vision has surrounded every event and personage in the poem, all enfolded upon the crucial event of the Middle Passage: Did it destroy a people or create one? Brathwaite's account of the voyage in "New World A-Comin" promises "new words, new waters, new/ harbours" on the one hand, and on the other, "the flesh and the flies, the whips and the fixed/ fear of pain in this chained and welcoming port."

The gods have crossed with the slaves to new soil, and the poet has returned to the origin of his race to discover his communal selfhood in African rite, which requires participation by all to welcome the god who will visit one of them. *The Arrivants* is a long historical and autobiographical poem, and it is also a rite of passage for the poet-priest who invites the god to ride him. Brathwaite's incantatory poems in *Masks* are his learning of the priest's ways, which restores his spirit in *Islands*. The refrain "Attibon Legba/ Ouvri bayi pou'moi" (in "Negus") is the Voodoo *houngan*'s prayer to the gatekeeper god Legba to open the door to the other gods. The prayer is answered in the final poem "Jou'vert" ("I Open"), where Legba promises

> hearts
> no longer bound
> to black and bitter
> ashes in the ground
> now waking
> making
> making with their
> rhythms some-

thing torn
and new.

In *Mother Poem*, the first book of Brathwaite's planned second trilogy, the
central figure is not the restless poet but the mother he has left and returned
to, the source of his life. The types of motherhood established in "The Cracked
Mother" are reiterated here as the poet's human mother and his motherland,
Barbados. Both "mothers" are established in the first poem, "Alpha," the
origin. Barbados is the mother island of porous limestone (thus absorbing all
influence of weather and history), cut by ancient watercourses that have dried
up in sterility. Her dead streams can be revived only by the transfigured
human mother, who "rains upon the island with her loud voices/ with her
grey hairs/ with her green love." The transfiguration that occurs in the last
lines of the book must wait, however, for the woman to endure the dream-
killing, soul-killing life of the island that is dominated by "the man who
possesses us all," the merchant, the modern agent of bondage.

The mother is his victim, no matter whether she "sits and calls on jesus
name" waiting for her husband to come home from work with lungs filled
with jute from the sugar sacks, or whether she goes out after his death to sell
calico cloth, half-soled shoes, and biscuits, or persuades her daughter to sell
herself to the man who is waiting: "It int hard, leh me tell you/ jess sad/ so
come darlin chile/ leh me tell he you ready you steady you go" ("Woo/Dove").

She gets no help from her men, who are crippled, destroyed, frightened,
or sick from their lives of bondage to the merchant. In "Woo/Dove," one
man goes to Montreal to work for nine years and sends back nothing; in
"Milkweed," another goes to work for life in the local plantation, brings
nothing home, and loses three fingers in the cane grinder. Nor does she receive
comfort from her children, "wearing dark glasses/ hearing aids/ leaning on
wine" ("Tear or Pear Shape"), who were educated by Chalkstick the teacher,
a satirical composite of the colonial educator whose job is to see that his
pupils "don't clap their hands, shake their heads, tap their feet" or "push
bones through each others' congolese nostrils" ("Lix"). Nor does her help
come from her sisters ("Dais" and "Nights") or from her Christianity ("Sam
Lord").

Rather, the restoration of her powers as life-giver begins in the guttural,
elemental, incantatory uttering of "Nametracks," where, as a slave-mother
beaten by her owner, she reminds herself and her huddled children, in dark
monosyllables like the word game of "The Cracked Mother," that they will
endure while "e di go/ e go di/ e go dead," that despite all his power, he
"nevver maim what me." Her eyes rise from the plot of land she has bought
with her meager earnings, the land that has sustained her and her children,
to the whole island and a vision of revolutionary solidarity with her people:
"de merchants got de money/ but de people got de men" ("Peace Fire").

With full realization that her child will be born to the life of "broken islands/ broken homes" ("Mid/Life"), the human mother in "Driftwood" still chooses to suffer the "pour of her flesh into their mould of bone." "Driftwood" ends with the mother re-created in clay by the potter who can work again, in stone by the sculptor whose skill has returned, and in her words gathered by the poet as rain, gathering in the dry pools, flows once more past the ruins of the slave and colonial world, refreshing and renewing the ancient life of the island.

Major publications other than poetry

PLAYS: *Four Plays for Primary Schools*, 1964; *Odale's Choice*, 1967.

NONFICTION: *Folk Culture of Slaves in Jamaica*, 1970; *The Development of Creole Society in Jamaica, 1770-1820*, 1971; *Contradictory Omens: Cultural Diversity and Integration in the Caribbean*, 1974; *Caribbean Man in Space and Time*, 1975.

Bibliography

Baugh, Edward, ed. *Critics on Caribbean Literature*, 1978.

Brown, Lloyd W., ed. *West Indian Poetry*, 1978.

Cudjoe, Selwyn R. *Resistance and Caribbean Literature*, 1980.

King, Bruce, ed. *West Indian Literature*, 1980.

Moore, Gerald. *The Chosen Tongue: English Writing in the Tropical World*, 1969.

Rohlehr, Gordon. *Pathfinder*, 1981.

Robert Bensen

BERTOLT BRECHT

Born: Augsburg, Germany; February 10, 1898
Died: East Berlin, East Germany; August 14, 1956

Principal collections

Hauspostille, 1927 (*Manual of Piety*, 1966); *Lieder, Gedichte, Chöre*, 1934 (*Songs, Poems, Choruses*); *Svendborg Gedichte*, 1938 (*Svendborg Poems*); *Selected Poems*, 1947; *100 Gedichte*, 1951 (*A Hundred Poems*); *Gedichte und Lieder*, 1956 (*Poems and Songs*); *Gedichte*, 1960-1965 (9 volumes; includes collections published during Brecht's lifetime plus collections reconstructed after his death, such as *Lieder zur Klampfe von Bert Brecht und seinen Freunden*, 1918, *Songs to the Guitar by Bert Brecht and His Friends*; *Psalmen und Episteln*, 1920-1922, *Psalms and Epistles*; *Lesebuch für Städtebewohner*, 1926-1927, *Reader for Those Who Live in Cities*; *Gedichte aus dem Messingkauf*, 1930-1950, *The Messingkauf Poems*; *Die Steffinische Sammlung*, 1938-1940, *The Steffin Collection*; *Gedichte im Exil*, 1944, 1948, *Poems in Exile*; *Buckower Elegien*, 1953, *Buckower Elegies*); *Bertolt Brecht: Poems 1913-1956*, 1976 (includes the collections already mentioned).

Other literary forms

An exhibit of the Brecht archive, on display in the poet's final residence, includes more than thirty works for the theater and a number of dramatic fragments, about thirteen hundred poems and songs, three novels and several fragments of novels, numerous film scripts, more than 150 nonfiction works, and many articles, short stories, and speeches.

Bertolt Brecht first became known as a dramatist when he won the distinguished Kleist Prize in 1922 for his plays *Baal* (1922; English translation, 1970); *Trommeln in der Nacht* (1922; *Drums in the Night*, 1966) and *Im Dickicht der Städte* (1923; *In the Jungle of Cities*, 1961). His other well-known dramas include *Mutter Courage und ihre Kinder* (1941; *Mother Courage and Her Children*, 1948), *Der gute Mensch von Sezuan* (1943; *The Good Woman of Setzuan*, 1961), and *Leben des Galilei* (1943; *Galileo*, 1947). His operas, *Die Dreigroschenoper* (1928; *The Threepenny Opera*, 1955) and *Aufstieg und Fall der Stadt Mahagonny*, 1930 (*Rise and Fall of the City of Mahagonny*, 1957), are well-known and widely performed. His longer prose works include the novels *Der Dreigroschenroman* (1934; *The Threepenny Novel*, 1937, 1956) and *Die Geschäfte des Herrn Julius Caesar* (1956; the affairs of Mr. Julius Caesar). Brecht also wrote about eighty short stories, not to mention the essays in his *Arbeitsjournal* (1938-1955, 1973; work journal). The complete edition of his works (published by Suhrkamp) runs to twenty volumes. A prolific writer, Brecht experimented with several literary forms and subjected nearly everything he wrote to painstaking revision.

Achievements

Just as he would have it, Brecht remains today a controversial figure. His literary works, his politics, and his biography spark disagreement, but one thing is clear: Brecht belongs among the great writers of the twentieth century, and certainly among the great modern poets. When Brecht died, Lion Feuchtwanger praised him as the only originator of the German language in this century.

Brecht was a bit of a showman (he was immediately recognizable in Berlin with his leather jacket, his proletarian cap, and his nickel-rimmed glasses), but he was always more interested in what people thought of his work than in what they thought of him. Eric Bentley, for example, has called Brecht's *Manual of Piety* "one of the best of all books of modern poems." Brecht's initial success on the stage in 1922 was echoed in 1928 with the sensational premier of *The Threepenny Opera* in Berlin. Toward the end of his life, Brecht was awarded the East German National Prize (1951), the highest distinction conferred by the German Democratic Republic on one of its citizens. In 1954, he became vice president of the East German Academy of Arts. One year before his death, he traveled to Moscow to accept the Stalin Peace Prize.

Without a doubt, Brecht is best known for his concept of the epic theater and his staging and acting technique of *Verfremdung* (alienation). He sought the intellectual rather than the emotional engagement of the audience, and his propensity for didactic structure rather than sentimental discourse is evident in his poetry as well. Brecht embraced Karl Marx's thesis that "it is not a matter of interpreting the world, but of changing it." His anti-Aristotelian theater concentrated on the factual and sober depiction of human and social conflicts, but with humorous alienation and alienating humor. To do serious theater today without acknowledging Brecht in some way is nearly impossible.

An assessment of Brecht's achievements cannot overlook his relation to literary tradition. Brecht "borrowed" freely from his predecessors, and he frequently chose the forms of parody or satire to make his readers aware of historical change and social contradictions. His candid speech did not always win favor: Because of his antiwar poem "Legende vom toten Soldaten" ("Legend of the Dead Soldier"), which was appended to his play *Drums in the Night*, Brecht was high on the Nazis' list of undesirables. It must be ranked among Brecht's accomplishments that, with his pen, he fought doggedly against the forces of evil and injustice which he saw embodied in the figure of Adolf Hitler and in the Nazi regime. The intensity and range of Brecht's voice as an essayist and dramatist have long been recognized; in contrast, because of the publication history of his poetry, it is only since Brecht's death that the power and scope of his lyric voice have begun to be appreciated.

Biography

Eugen Bertolt Friedrich Brecht was born into a comfortable middle-class home. His father, the manager of a paper factory, was Catholic; his mother, Protestant. Brecht was reared in the Lutheran faith. Before long, he turned strongly against religion, but the language of Martin Luther's translation of the Bible continued to influence Brecht throughout his life. A local Augsburg newspaper carried his first poems and essays in 1914, under the pen name "Berthold Eugen." Brecht dropped the mask in 1916 with the publication of his poem "Das Lied der Eisenbahntruppe von Fort Donald" ("Song of the Fort Donald Railroad Gang"), in the same local paper.

A restless and arrogant student ("I did not succeed in being of any appreciable help to my teachers"), Brecht enrolled in the University of Munich in 1917. There, he claimed to study medicine (as his father wished) and learned to play the guitar (less to his father's liking, no doubt). He completed a brief term of military service in 1918 as a medical orderly in a hospital for patients suffering from venereal disease. (It was in this year that Brecht wrote the "Legend of the Dead Soldier.") In Munich, Brecht soon became more interested in the local cabarets than in the study of medicine. He especially enjoyed the comedian Karl Valentin, who, along with Frank Wedekind, became an important influence on Brecht's literary development. He turned increasingly to literature and began taking seminars at the university with Professor Arthur Kutscher in 1918; he wrote the first version of *Baal* between March and June of the same year. Brecht traveled to Berlin in 1920; the city impressed him, but he returned to Munich after failing to make substantial literary contacts.

Brecht was to make one more trip to Berlin before finally moving there in 1924. From then until 1933, he spent his time in the capital and cultural center of Germany. The surging pulse of this modern city fascinated Brecht and prompted his *Reader for Those Who Live in Cities*. In 1926, he first became acquainted with the writings of Marx; in its profound impact on his work, Brecht's discovery of Marx could be compared to Friedrich Schiller's reading of Immanuel Kant. At the time, Brecht was working on the play "Wheat" (to be staged by Erwin Piscator), and he wanted to understand how the exchange market worked. In the short run, his effort proved futile: "From every point of view," he wrote, "the grain market remained one impenetrable jungle." The consequences of his study, however, were far-reaching. His planned drama was never completed. Instead, he began to read Marx intensely: "It was only then that my own jumbled practical experiences and impressions came clearly into focus." Brecht's conversion to the principles of Communism had begun. What followed in its literary wake were the operas and several strongly didactic plays in the early 1930's. Brecht, the eminent political poet, wisely left Germany on February 28, 1933, the day after the burning of the Reichstag. Several years of exile ensued.

"Changing countries more often than shoes," as Brecht reflected once, he eventually found his way to a place near Svendborg in Denmark, after traveling through Prague, Zurich, Lugano, and Paris. In Denmark, Brecht was—

for the time being, anyway—relatively settled. Still, he remained acutely sensitive toward "escape routes" (images of doors are frequent in the poetry of his exile). He traveled to Moscow and New York in 1935, to London in 1936, and to Paris in the next year. With the threat of Nazi invasion looming large, Brecht left Denmark for Sweden in 1939 and settled near Stockholm. Before long, this sanctuary, too, appeared endangered by the Nazis. Brecht fled to the United States in 1941.

Brecht's life in exile, coupled with his fascination for the exotic, drew him in particular to the Chinese poet, Po Chü-yi, whose work he had come to know through the translation of Arthur Waley. In America, Brecht was particularly conscious of his displacement; having settled in Santa Monica near Hollywood, he never felt comfortable in the "tinsel town." His productivity slackened somewhat during his American years, though he collaborated with artists of the stature of Fritz Lang and Charles Laughton. On October 30, 1947, the day after he appeared before the House Un-American Activities Committee, Brecht flew to Paris and shortly thereafter moved to Switzerland.

Brecht's second wife, the accomplished actress Helene Weigel, was an Austrian citizen, and it is most likely for this reason that Brecht acquired Austrian citizenship as well, even though he finally settled in East Berlin in 1949. There, until his death in 1956, Brecht worked with the Berlin Ensemble. Meanwhile, his Austrian citizenship allowed his work to remain accessible to all the German-speaking countries (Brecht was also shrewd about the business and politics of publication). As he wished, Brecht's death was accorded a quiet ceremony. He lies buried in an old cemetery not far from his apartment, near the graves of G. F. W. Hegel and Johann Gottlieb Fichte.

Analysis

It is important to note that Bertolt Brecht's creativity as a poet resulted less from any inclination toward introspection than from his desire to communicate with others. Against the prevailing tone of German poetry in the 1920's, at least as it was represented by Rainer Maria Rilke, Hugo von Hofmannsthal, and Stefan George, Brecht's poetic voice startled and shocked his readers. "These poems [of Rilke et al.] tell ordinary people nothing, sometimes comprehensibly, sometimes incomprehensibly," he wrote in his youth. One of Brecht's main objections to this style of poetry was that its sense of artistic order hid rather than disclosed the chaos he saw in modern life. For this reason, Brecht eventually came to see rhyme and rhythm as obstructive and to prefer "Rhymeless Verse with Irregular Rhythms," as the title of an essay in 1939 reads. As basic to Brecht's poems as their consideration of the reader is his notion of functionality. He first articulated this concept in 1927 when asked to judge a poetry contest which had brought more than four hundred entries. Brecht read them all and awarded no prize. Instead, he acknowledged an unsubmitted poem from a little-known writer, appreciating its simplicity, its engaging choice of topics, its melodiousness, and its documentary value. The notion that "all great poems have the value of documents" was central to Brecht's thought. Writing poetry was, for Brecht, no "mere expression," but a "social function of a wholly contradictory and alterable kind, conditioned by history and in turn conditioning it."

Brecht wrote his poems in, as he called it, "a kind of Basic German." His sensitivity for the "gestic" power of language was nurtured by his fondness for Luther's Bible (the term Brecht uses, _Gestus_, is difficult to render adequately in English: John Willet identifies it with "gesture" and "gist," attitude and point). At the root of Brecht's poetry, indeed all of his work, are the notions of clarity ("The truth is concrete" was Brecht's favorite maxim from Hegel) and functionality. Form, of which Brecht was a master and not a slave, was a means toward an end, that being enlightenment. In tracing Brecht's poetic development, one can see how the forms and motifs change against the backdrop of these guiding concepts.

One attribute of the term "gestic" is that of performance. Brecht was always concerned with delivery (it is central to his theory of the epic theater), and his early poetry is characterized by its close links with song. Indeed, most of Brecht's early poems were written to be accompanied by the guitar. Verse and melody often came about simultaneously, the rhythm of the words combining with the flow of the song. It is not surprising that Brecht's early poems acknowledge such traditional forms as legends, ballads, and chronicles. He was aware that no poet who considered himself important was composing ballads at that time, and this fact, too, may have intrigued the young iconoclast. What drew Brecht to these older poetic forms was their attention to adventure, to nature, and to the role of the heroic individual. Brecht rejuvenated a tired literary tradition by turning to the works of François Villon and Rudyard Kipling. Brecht's ballads mark a decisive turning point in the history of that genre.

"Song of the Fort Donald Railroad Gang," written in 1916, exhibits Brecht's youthful keenness for the frontier spirit. It relates the struggle and demise of a railroad crew laying track in the wilderness of Ohio. The portrayal of nature as rugged and indifferent marks a distinct switch for Brecht from the mediocre war poems he had been writing earlier. A common denominator, however, was the element of destructive force. This poem leads, step by inevitable step, through six strophes toward the culminating catastrophe. Initially, nature tolerates the intruders, who can be seen as pilgrims of modern progress pitted against the dense forests, "forever soulless." With the onset of torrential rains, the tolerance of nature becomes indifference, but the railroad gang forges on. Striking up a song within a song, they take to singing in the night to keep themselves awake and posted of the dangers posed by the downpour and the swelling waters. For them, escape is not an option. Death simply comes, and comes simply, leaving only the echo of their melody: "The trains scream rushing over them alongside Lake Erie/ And the wind at that spot sings a stupid melody." A stupid melody? What has happened to these modern "heroes"? There are no modern heroes, Brecht answers—and this in the poetic form which traditionally extols them. Brecht debunks their melody, uses the ballad to put an end to the balladesque hero. Death and nature prevail.

Death and nature, along with murder and love, are the elemental themes distinguishing Brecht's early poems. He was wont to treat these perennial subjects, though, in nontraditional ways. He does this with great effect in what is ostensibly a love poem, "Erinnerung an die Maria A." ("Remembering Marie A."), written in 1920 and later included in *Manual of Piety*. It is more lyrical than the balladesque forms Brecht had already mastered, but it does not get lost in sentimentality. Instead, Brecht achieves a parody of the melancholy youth remembering an early love, and in its attitude it is quintessential Brecht. What the speaker in the poem actually recalls is less his "love so pale and silent/ As if she were a dream that must not fade," than it is "a cloud my eyes dwelt long upon/ It was quite white and very high above us/ Then I looked up, and found that it had gone." Not even the woman's face remains present for Brecht's persona, only her kiss, and "As for the kiss, I'd long ago forgot it/ But for the cloud that floated in the sky." The idyllic atmosphere of the first strophe turns out to be nothing but cliché.

What Brecht does with the element of time in this poem is essential to its overall effect. He establishes an internal relationship on three levels: first, the love affair, located in the past; second, the passage of time, the forgetting which wastes all memory; third, the making present, by means of the cloud, that September day long ago. The tension Brecht succeeds in creating between these different levels has ironic consequences. For one, his use of verb tenses renders as present what is actually narrated in the past tense, while the grammatical past tense functions on the level of present time. The hierarchy of experiences is also switched: the backdrop of nature, the embodiment of everything transitory, can be remembered, while the primary experience (or what convention dictates should be the primary experience)—namely, the relationship between the lovers—falls prey to bad memory. Ultimately, it is a poem about the inconstancy of feeling and the mistrust between people which renders meaningful and lasting relationships problematic. It treats an old theme originally; where others write poems directed toward those lovers in the present, those passed away, those absent, or even those expected in the future, Brecht writes of the lover forgotten.

"I, Bertolt Brecht, came out of the black forests." So begins Brecht's famous autobiographical poem, "Vom armen B.B." ("Of Poor B.B."), first written in 1922, later revised when he was preparing *Manual of Piety* for publication. It was composed during a period when Brecht had his feet mostly in Augsburg and Munich, but his mind mostly in Berlin. The poem marks a turning point for Brecht. He leaves behind the ballad form and takes up the theme of the city. Nature in the raw yields to the irrepressible life of the big city, although neither locus is ever idealized. Written literally while under way (apparently on a train to Berlin), the poem is about where one feels at home, "one" in this instance being no one but Brecht himself. "In the asphalt city I'm at home," he admits, and he goes on to describe the daily routine of city dwellers, situating himself in their midst: "I put on/ A hard hat because that's what they do./ I say: they are animals with a quite peculiar smell/ And I say: does it matter? I am too." The poem is full of cynicism and despair. The poet admits that he is undependable and remains convinced that all that will remain of the cities is what passed through them—that is, the wind: "And after us there will come: nothing worth talking about." Thematically, the change of emphasis in "Of Poor B.B." prepares the way for the poems collected in *Reader for Those Who Live in Cities*. Formally, the delivery of the poem is less dependent upon melody (song) and relies on the premise of conversation between poet and reader.

Brecht's poems of the 1930's reveal a heightened awareness of the function of the poet with regard to his readership. He had made this point quite polemically already in 1927 as the judge of the poetry contest noted above. The poem, he claimed, had functional value. Looking for the functional lyric caused Brecht to seek a new style and idiom. The often-quoted poem "In finsteren Zeiten" ("In Dark Times"), written in 1937 during Brecht's exile in Denmark, attests his self-conscious task as responsible poet. Brecht imagines what people will later say about these "dark times." "They won't say: when the child skimmed a flat stone across the rapids/ But: when the great wars were being prepared for." History, in other words, will ride along on the backs of the little people—as Brecht makes clear in "Fragen eines lesenden Arbeiters" ("Questions from a Worker Who Reads")—but what remain visible are only the "great powers." In the face of this adversity, Brecht remarks with chagrin: "However, they won't say: the times were dark/ Rather: why were their poets silent?"

Brecht refused to be silent. His "Schlechte Zeit für Lyrik" ("Bad Time for Poetry"), written in 1939, is a personally revealing poem about his own internal struggle to reconcile aesthetic demands with demands of social responsibility: "In my poetry a rhyme/ Would seem to me almost insolent." Still, as Brecht wrote in his essay on poetry and logic, also from the 1930's, "we cannot get along without the concept of beauty." The poem "Bad Time for Poetry" thus concludes:

> Inside me contend
> Delight at the apple tree in blossom
> And horror at the house-painter's speeches.
> But only the second
> Drives me to my desk.

Brecht seldom mentioned Hitler by name, preferring to call him only "the house-painter," ridiculing Hitler's artistic pretentions.

To appreciate Brecht's aesthetic sensitivities, one must realize that he saw the felicitous poem as one in which "feeling and reason work together in total harmony." For Brecht, too, there was no distinction between learning and pleasure, and thus a didactic poem was also cause for aesthetic pleasure. The sensual pleasure derived from knowledge is an important aspect of the title figure of Brecht's play *Galileo*. What to do with knowledge and wisdom was another question which, for Brecht, followed inevitably. He answered it in his poem "Legende von der Entstehung des Buches Taoteking" ("Legend of the Origin of the Book Tao-Tê-Ching on Lao-tzû's Road into Exile") written in 1938 and included in the *Svendborg Poems*.

This poem is a highly successful combination of Brecht's earlier fascination with legends, the balladesque narrative, and the aesthetics of functional poetry. It relates the journey of Lao-tzû, "seventy and getting brittle," from his country, where "goodness had been weakening a little/ And the wickedness was gaining ground anew" (a topic of immediate interest to the exile Brecht). Brecht does not puzzle over Lao-tzû's decision to leave; it is not even an issue. He states simply: "So he buckled his shoe." (One recalls Brecht's line that he had "changed countries more often than shoes.") Lao-tzû needs little for the journey: books, pipe, and bread (note here the relation between knowledge and sensual pleasure). After four days, he and the boy accompanying him come across a customs official at the border: "'What valuables have you to declare here?'/ And the boy leading the ox explained: 'The old man taught'/ Nothing at all, in short." The customs official, however, is intrigued by the boy's modest assertion that the old man "'learned how quite soft water, by attrition/ Over the years will grind strong rocks away./ In other words, that hardness must lose the day.'" The official shouts to them before they are able to move on and requires them to dictate what it was the old man had to say about the water: "'I'm not at all important/ Who wins or loses interests me, though./ If you've found out, say so.'" The old man obliges him ("'Those who ask questions deserve answers'"), and he and the boy settle down for a week, the customs man providing them with food. When the dictation is finally done, "the boy handed over what they'd written./ Eighty-one sayings." This is the wisdom of Lao-Tzû, for which posterity has been grateful, but Brecht is quick to point out that "the honor should not be restricted/ To the sage whose name is clearly writ./ For a wise man's wisdom needs to be extracted./ So the customs man deserves his bit./ It was he who called for it."

Brecht's return to rhyme in this poem is consistent with its ballad form. Where rhyme no longer sufficed for what was to be said, Brecht applied his theory of rhymeless verse with irregular rhythms. He had already used this style occasionally in the 1920's but mastered it fully in the poetry of the 1930's and 1940's; the form corresponded to Brecht's perception of a society at odds with itself, and it dominated his later lyrical writings.

Brecht's later poetry tends to be at once more intimate and more epigrammatic than his earlier work. This late style is best illustrated in his last volume of poems, the *Buckower Elegies*, written in 1953. The poems are concise evidence of Brecht's fascination with the fragmentary nature of the lyric, which he viewed as an appeal to the reader. Many of the poems mimic the open form of the riddle, with a strong central image, as in "Der Radwechsel" ("Changing the Wheel"). In six brief lines, Brecht observes how a driver changes a wheel. He voices his own dissatisfaction with his course in life ("I do not like the place I have come from./ I do not like the place I am going to"). Brecht characteristically leaves this poem open toward the future: "Why with impatience do I/ Watch him changing the wheel?"

The critic Joachim Müller has written that "In all its phases and in all its forms, Brecht's poetry is neither exclusively subjective confession, nor simply an agitator's call to arms; every confession becomes an appeal to human activity, and every appeal, however it may alienate us by its satire or its polemics, springs from the deep emotion of a rational heart that sees all conditions in the world dialectically and that always sides with what is human against every inhumanity."

Major publications other than poetry

NOVELS: *Der Dreigroschenroman*, 1934 (*The Threepenny Novel*, 1937, 1956); *Die Geschäfte des Herrn Julius Caesar*, 1956.

SHORT FICTION: *Geschichten von Herrn Keuner*, 1930, 1958.

PLAYS: *Baal*, 1922 (English translation, 1970); *Trommeln in der Nacht*, 1922 (*Drums in the Night*, 1966); *Im Dickicht der Städte*, 1923 (*In the Jungle of Cities*, 1961); *Die Dreigroschenoper*, 1928 (libretto; *The Threepenny Opera*, 1955); *Aufstieg und Fall der Stadt Mahagonny*, 1930 (*Rise and Fall of the City of Mahagonny*, 1957); *Mutter Courage und ihre Kinder*, 1941 (*Mother Courage and Her Children*, 1948); *Der gute Mensch von Sezuan*, 1943 (*The Good Woman of Setzuan*, 1961); *Leben des Galilei*, 1943 (*Galileo*, 1947); *Der kaukasische Kreidekreis*, 1949, 1956 (*The Caucasian Chalk-Circle*, performed 1948, revised version published 1960); *Collected Plays*, 1970-1979 (9 volumes).

NONFICTION: *Arbeitsjournal*, 1938-1955, 1973; *Kleines Organon für das Theater*, 1948 (*Brecht on Theater*, 1964); *Schriften zum Theater*, 1964-1967 (7 volumes).

Bibliography

Dickson, Keith. *Towards Utopia: A Study of Brecht*, 1978.
Ewen, F. *Bertolt Brecht: His Life, His Art and His Times*, 1969.
Fuegi, J. *The Essential Brecht*, 1972.
Gray, Ronald. *Brecht*, 1961.
Grimm, Reinhold. *Bertolt Brecht*, 1975.

Hill, Claude. *Bertolt Brecht*, 1975.
Morley, Michael. *Brecht: A Study*, 1977.
Schuhmann, Klaus. *Der Lyriker Bertolt Brecht, 1919-1933*, 1974.
Spalter, Max. *Brecht's Tradition*, 1967.
Weideli, Walter. *The Art of Bertolt Brecht*, 1963.

Richard Spuler

ANDRÉ BRETON

Born: Tinchebray, France; February 19, 1896
Died: Paris, France; September 28, 1966

Principal poems and collections

Mont de piété, 1919; *Clair de terre*, 1923; *L'Union libre*, 1931 (*Free Union*, 1982); *Le Revolver à cheveux blancs*, 1932; *L'Air de l'eau*, 1934; *Fata Morgana*, 1941 (English translation, 1982); *Pleine marge*, 1943; *Young Cherry Trees Secured Against Hares*, 1946; *Ode à Charles Fourier*, 1947 (*Ode to Charles Fourier*); *Poèmes*, 1948; *Poésie et autre*, 1960; *Selected Poems*, 1969; *Poems of André Breton*, 1982 (includes *Free Union* and *Fata Morgana* among other selected poems).

Other literary forms

Breton published many experimental works during his career, some of which were written in collaboration with friends. *Les Champs magnétiques* (1921; magnetic fields), the first Surrealist text to employ the technique of "automatic" writing, was done with Philippe Soupault. *L'Immaculée Conception* (1930; immaculate conception), an attempt to simulate the thought processes of various types of insanity, was written with Paul Éluard. Among the basic Surrealist documents were several works by Breton alone, such as *Poisson soluble* (1924; soluble fish) and *Les Vases communicants* (1932; the communicating vessels), which mixed lyrical elements with philosophical speculations cast in the form of prose, as well as the numerous polemical manifestos such as *Manifeste du surréalisme* (1924; *Manifesto of Surrealism*) and *Second Manifeste du surréalisme* (1930; *Second Manifesto of Surrealism*). Breton's numerous essays were also collected in three volumes: *Les Pas perdus* (1924; the lost steps), *Point du jour* (1934), and *Perspective cavalière* (1970). Convenient selections from Breton's prose in English translation have appeared in *Manifestoes of Surrealism* (1969), translated by Richard Seaver and Helen R. Lane, and *What Is Surrealism? Selected Writings* (1978), edited by Franklin Rosemont.

Achievements

Above all, André Breton will be remembered as the founder and leader of the Surrealist movement. Of all the avant-garde movements which rocked the foundations of the arts at the beginning of the twentieth century, Surrealism has had perhaps the greatest and longest-lived impact. Surrealism, created in Paris in 1924 by André Breton and a small group of friends, was the last inheritor of a long series of "isms," including Dadaism, German Expressionism, French and Spanish Cubism, Italian Futurism, and Anglo-American Imagism and Vorticism, which attempted to transform modern man's conception of the world through artistic innovation. Under the leadership of Breton, Surrealism became the most mature expression of this developing sensibility, not only because of its relatively well developed underlying philosophy—which was both far-reaching and systematic in nature—but also because it eventually came to have the greatest international scope of all of these movements and because it stimulated the production of a vast body of work of great diversity in all the major artistic genres—poetry, fiction, drama, philosophy, painting, sculpture, and film.

Biography

André Breton was born on February 19, 1896, in Tinchebray, a small inland town in the old French province of Normandy. The family soon moved, however, to the fishing port of Lorient, in Brittany, on the Atlantic coast of France. This seaside environment was particularly important later in the poet's life. When Breton first began to write in 1914, his highly imaginative lyrical poems expressed the wondrous abundance of nature and were often filled with images of sea life and other details evoking the maritime setting of his youth—which contrasted sharply with his life in Paris.

Breton was an only child, and his parents seemingly had an unusually strong influence on his personality. His father, who was a merchant, seems almost a prototype of the complacent, self-satisfied bourgeois that the Surrealists were later to attack as the epitome of the social conformity they rejected. Breton's mother, whom he described as straitlaced, puritanical, and harsh in her response to any suggestion of impropriety, must have also been responsible, to a large degree, for his later hatred of restraint and his provocative attitude toward anything he considered conventional.

Being the only child of a comfortably situated family, Breton had much attention lavished on him, and, naturally, his parents had great ambitions for him. He attended school in Paris from 1907 until his graduation in 1912, entering the Sorbonne in 1913 to study medicine. This contact with medicine was also important for the later development of the poet and is reflected in Breton's diverse poetic vocabulary. Even more important, however, was the experience which resulted when Breton was sent to work at the neurological center of the hospital at Nantes during World War I instead of into combat. Breton's experiences as a medical assistant during the war—first at Nantes and later at the psychiatric center at Saint-Dizier, to which he was transferred in 1917—introduced the young, impressionable poet to the bizarre aberrations of mental illness.

During this period, Breton was exposed not only to the diverse forms of mental illness from which the soldiers suffered but also to the theories upon which the practical measures used to treat them were based. Among the most important of these theories were those of Jean-Martin Charcot, Sigmund Freud, and Pierre Janet, each of which contributed an important element to the formulation of Breton's view of the operation, structure, and purpose of the human mind. From Charcot's work, Breton learned of the unlocking of the will through the use of hypnosis and saw some of the dramatic cures it was able to effect. From Freud's work, he learned about the existence of the unconscious, its role in determining mental health, and the method of dream interpretation by which one could reveal its secrets to the dreamer. From Janet's work, he learned about the existence of "psychic automatism" and the means by which it might be evoked—which eventually resulted in his own experiments with automatic writing.

These influences were reflected in three important ways in Breton's later work. First, they resulted in the two important prose experiments in automatic writing that he produced: *Les Champs magnétiques*, written with Philippe Soupault, and *Poisson soluble*, which Breton created alone. The second product of his wartime experience was the novel *Nadja* (1928; English translation, 1960), which describes the encounter of an autobiographical persona with a mysterious woman who suffers a bizarre and debilitating psychosis. The third product of these influences was *L'Immaculée Conception*, a series of writings undertaken with Paul Éluard, with the purpose of simulating, in verbal form, the thought processes of various types of insanity.

Following the war, Breton came under the influence of Dadaism, which by then had moved its base of operation from Zurich to Paris. The heyday of Dada in Paris was brief, however, lasting from January of 1920 until July of 1923. In the meantime, beginning in May of 1921, Breton and some of his friends were forming a new group whose optimistic attitude toward life, experiments with new methods of literary composition, and increasingly systematic philosophical orientation was in marked contrast to Dada's attitude of nihilistic despair. Breton later called this period, which extended from May of 1921 until October of 1924—when the first *Manifesto of Surrealism* was published—the "intuitive phase" of Surrealism. The publication of this first manifesto established, in an explicit way, a new aesthetic and a profoundly optimistic, imaginative conception of the world which its author, André Breton, named "Surrealism." The intense period of Surrealist creative activity, which began at that time and continued unabated until the appearance of the *Second Manifesto of Surrealism* in 1930, Breton was later to call the "reasoning phase" of Surrealism. This period culminated in the appearance of *Les Vases communicants*, a series of lyrical philosophical discourses expressing in mature, fully developed form the central ideas of the Surrealist philosophy and aesthetic.

The period following 1930, the year of the second manifesto, was characterized by two developments. One of these was the Surrealists' increasing involvement with the Communist International movement. The second development was, in a direct sense, an outgrowth of the first, for it was also during this period that Surrealism was disseminated on a worldwide scale and gained adherents outside Western Europe in many places where it was seen as the artistic concomitant of Marxist revolutionary philosophy. This period, which might be called, with some small injustice, the "dogmatic phase" of Surrealism, lasted until the outbreak of World War II. In 1941, Breton left France and lived for five years in New York. When he returned to Paris in 1946, Surrealism was effectively dead, although with those few friends of the original group who still remained, and with the growing support of countless other self-acknowledged "Surrealists" in many other countries where their dream had been carried, André Breton lived on as the universally acknowledged magus of Surrealism until his death on September 28, 1966, in Paris.

Analysis

André Breton's poetry forms a relatively small though important part of his total literary output, being dwarfed in quantity by his lengthy experiments in prose and his numerous polemical writings. His poetry, from the first published collection, *Mont de piété* (mount of piety), to his last major poetic work, *Ode to Charles Fourier*, shows a remarkable consistency of style. As a poet, Breton is best known for his remarkable imagery—which, at its best, expresses the powerful ability of the imagination to reconcile basic human drives and desires with the material conditions of reality and, at its worst, lapses into bizarre forms of irrationality which are incomprehensible to all but the poet himself.

In general terms, Breton's poetic imagery is characterized by comparisons which yoke together extremely disparate objects, by the sudden, sometimes violent shifting of context as the poet moves from one image to the next, and by an extremely indirect method of expressing comparisons between objects. It is these three qualities, above all, which give his poetic imagery the appearance of being spontaneous rather than deliberate. As recent critics have shown, however, much to Breton's credit as a poet, this initial impression is a misleading one.

Breton's imagery is reinforced by other prominent aspects of his style, one of which might be called "devices of syntactic derangement." These devices range from the use of simple paradoxes involving logical and semantic contradictions, to syntactic ambiguity involving multiple or imprecise grammatical modification, to much more unsettling contradictions of reference—where the referent of a speech act is left unidentified, is deliberately misidentified, or is made ambiguous.

One other important element of Breton's style which helps to support the dramatic effect of his poetic images on his readers is his diction, which is characterized by two principal traits. The first of these is the extremely wide range of his vocabulary, which frequently includes the use of words from anatomical, zoological, botanical, and technical contexts that are unfamiliar to most readers of poetry. The second important trait of his diction is the tendency to use words in specialized, atypical ways that emphasize (and often create) their figurative meanings over their denotations. These qualities have two important effects on Breton's work: The first helps make possible his imagery of violent contrasts, and the second is, to a large degree, responsible for the great difficulty his readers and translators encounter searching for paraphrasable or translatable meaning in his work.

Another element of Breton's style which deserves mention is his use of recurring themes and symbolic motifs, such as the revolver as a synecdochic image for rebellion or revolt of any kind. As critics have recently discovered, these recurring thematic and symbolic elements in Breton's work can frequently be used as contextual clues for interpreting his most difficult works.

The poetry of André Breton expresses three key ideas—the liberating power of the imagination, the transformation of the material world into a utopian state, and the exploration of human potentiality through love between the sexes—which recur, with increasing elaboration, throughout the course of his work and constitute the essence of his Surrealist vision.

Breton's faith in the liberating power of the human imagination, although suggested and influenced by his contact with modern psychoanalytic thought, especially that of Freud on the operations of the unconscious, goes far beyond the notion of simply releasing the bound or "repressed" energies which is the therapeutic basis of psychoanalytic practice. For Breton, the unconscious is not an enclosed inner space, or reservoir, of trapped energy; it is, rather, the way out of the everyday world of material reality into the realm of the surreal. According to the Surrealists, this realm—where human reason and imagination no longer struggle against each other but function in harmony—is the ultimate reality, and man's goal in life is to seek out continually the signs of this reality, which, when directly experienced, is capable of transforming the life of the person. Although Breton envisioned the realm of the surreal as accessible to all men who seek it, it was especially important for the artist, whose goal was to capture the fleeting traces of *le merveilleux* (the marvelous) in his writing.

The Surrealists recommended a number of different methods for attaining this experience. Two, in particular, are frequently used and referred to in Breton's work: the surrendering of the person to the *hasard objectif* (objective chance) of the universe, and the evocation of the "primary processes" of the unconscious through such procedures as automatic writing. The first of these methods is illustrated well in "Au regard des divinités" ("In the Eyes of the Gods"), one of Breton's early poems from *Clair de terre* (the light of Earth):

> 'Shortly before midnight near the landing-stage
> If a dishevelled woman follows you, pay no attention.
> It's the blue. You need fear nothing of the blue.
> There'll be a tall blonde vase in a tree.
> The spire of the village of melted colors
> Will be your landmark. Take it easy,

> Remember. The dark geyser that hurls fern-tips
> Towards the sky greet
> Greets you.'

This poem reads like, and in fact is intended to be, a set of instructions for encountering the marvelous through the technique of objective chance.

Breton's other primary technique for evoking the marvelous—using the unfettered association of ideas in the unconscious to produce automatic writing—is illustrated by "Au beau demi-jour" ("In the Lovely Half-light"), a poem from *L'Air de l'eau* (air of the water):

> In the lovely half-light of 1934
> The air was a splendid rose the colour of red mullet
> And the forest when I made ready to enter it
> Began with a tree that had cigarette-paper leaves
> For I was waiting for you. . . .

Not only did Breton believe in the power of the creative imagination to transform the life of individual men, but also he believed in the possibility of transforming society itself into a Socialist utopia, and he came to believe that the Communist International movement was a means to that end. Breton's association with the Communist Party, which began about 1930, was an increasingly divisive force among the French Surrealists. Many who were willing to accept Surrealism's aesthetic and philosophical premises did not believe that this view of life could ever transform the material world of nations and societies. Breton saw this resistance toward political involvement as an indication of insufficient commitment, while those who resisted engagement countered by emphasizing the restrictive nature of the Communist Party, its repressive disciplinary practices, and its hostility to artistic activity that did not directly further the interests of the Party itself. Regardless of the problems it created for him, Breton never gave up this utopian faith, as the choice of subject for his last major poetic work, *Ode to Charles Fourier*, makes clear.

The third key idea that informs Breton's poetry is one which, like his belief in the liberating power of the imagination, was shared by many of the Surrealists: the belief that romantic love was the means by which man might establish an enduring link between the mundane world of material reality and the limitless, eternal world of surreality. At times, the mere presence of the beloved is enough to evoke such a response, and some of Breton's most moving poetry deals with this experience. The idea is expressed in two principal forms in Breton's love poetry. The first is the belief in woman as muse: The beloved becomes the source of contact with the realm of surreality, where, Breton's friend Paul Éluard (the greatest of the Surrealist love poets) wrote, "all transformations are possible." This belief is clearly expressed in two of Breton's best poems: the famous "catalog-poem" *Free Union*, which celebrates the magical connection between the poet's beloved and the unspoiled world of nature, and *Fata Morgana*, which celebrates the ecstatic elation of the poet at the advent of a new love. The second form taken by this belief in the magical power of love is the equation of poetic creation itself with sexual love, as in "Sur la Route de San Romano" ("On the Road to San Romano"): "Poetry is made in a bed like love/ Its rumpled sheets are the dawn of things."

It was these three ideas—together with the support of countless writers, scattered across the world, who identified themselves with the Surrealist ideal—which sustained Breton throughout a career that lasted more than fifty years. Although Breton died in 1966, the beliefs that he helped to formulate and that he expressed so brilliantly in his own poetry continue to exist.

Major publications other than poetry

NOVEL: *Nadja*, 1928 (English translation, 1960).

NONFICTION: *Les Champs magnétiques*, 1921 (with Philippe Soupault); *Manifeste du surréalisme*, 1924 (*Manifesto of Surrealism*); *Les Pas perdus*, 1924; *Poisson soluble*, 1924; *L'Immaculée Conception*, 1930 (with Paul Éluard); *Second Manifeste du surréalisme*, 1930 (*Second Manifesto of Surrealism*); *Les Vases communicants*, 1932; *Point du jour*, 1934; *Manifestoes of Surrealism*, 1969 (includes the above manifestos plus other prose writings); *Perspective cavalière*, 1970; *What Is Surrealism? Selected Writings*, 1978.

Bibliography

Balakian, Anna. *André Breton: Magus of Surrealism*, 1971.

_____ . *Surrealism: The Road to the Absolute*, 1959.

Benedikt, Michael. *The Poetry of Surrealism: An Anthology*, 1975.

Browder, Clifford. *André Breton: Arbiter of Surrealism*, 1967.

Carrouges, Michel. *André Breton and the Basic Concepts of Surrealism*, 1974.

Caws, Mary Ann. *The Poetry of Dada and Surrealism*, 1970.

_____ , ed. *About French Poetry from Dada to Tel Quel*, 1974.

Fowlie, Wallace. *Age of Surrealism*, 1950.

Raymond, Marcel. *From Baudelaire to Surrealism*, 1949.

Steven E. Colburn

JOSEPH BRODSKY

Born: Leningrad, U.S.S.R.; May 24, 1940

Principal collections

Stikhotvoreniia i poèmy, 1965; *Ostanovka v pustyne*, 1970; *Selected Poems*, 1973; *Konets prekrasnoi èpokhi*, 1977; *Chast' rechi*, 1977 (*A Part of Speech*, 1980); *Rimskie elegii*, 1982.

Other literary forms

Joseph Brodsky's essays and reviews, some of which have been collected in *Less Than One* (1984), are valuable in their own right; brilliant, arrogant, and idiosyncratic, they establish Brodsky as one of the finest poet-essayists of the twentieth century. Among Brodsky's subjects are Osip and Nadezhda Mandelstam, Marina Tsvetayeva (unlike most of his prose, his two essays on Tsvetayeva, one brief and one extended, were written in Russian, the language Brodsky normally reserves for his poetry), W. H. Auden, Constantine Cavafy, and Eugenio Montale; the essay "Less Than One" is an extraordinary meditation on the city of Leningrad, part memoir and part cultural history.

Achievements

Brodsky is generally recognized as one of the most gifted poets writing in Russian; for many, there is little question of his having any rivals. Perhaps Brodsky's most remarkable "achievement" has been his ability to continue writing poems in Russian despite the hardships of political persecution within the Soviet Union and, later, the alienation from the everyday rhythms of the Russian language imposed by his exile to the United States. Brodsky matured as a poet in a Leningrad devoid of poetic "movements"; indeed, the sense of being alone as a poet pervades his work to an unusual degree. It is difficult to assess Brodsky's generation of poets. The work of contemporaries whom he has praised, poets such as Evgeni Rein and Anatol' Naiman, is available only sporadically in the West, and then in the limited distribution of the émigré presses.

Brodsky's poems have been translated into many languages, including French, German, Italian, Swedish, Czech, and Hebrew, but it is the English translations which have won him high regard and a rather wide audience in the West. Brodsky's participation in the translation process, given his own fine skills as a translator, have ensured high-quality versions which sound like anything but adaptations from another language. Brodsky has been accorded many honors, including Guggenheim and MacArthur Foundation Fellowships, an honorary doctorate from Yale University, and membership in the American Academy of Arts and Letters.

Biography

Joseph Aleksandrovich Brodsky was born in Leningrad on May 24, 1940. Brodsky's mother worked as a translator, an occupation her son was to take up as well; his father worked as a news photographer. During the German blockade of the city, Brodsky spent some time with his grandparents. He has recalled a somewhat later time of fear during the government-orchestrated anti-Semitic hysteria of 1953, when it seemed that his family might be "resettled" far from Leningrad. During these last years of Stalinism, Brodsky was an unenthusiastic student; he left school in 1955 to pursue independent studies in various languages and literatures. In 1956, he began learning Polish, a language which gave him access to Western literature not available in Russian; he has recalled that he first read the works of Franz Kafka and William Faulkner in Polish translation, and he encountered the poetry of Czeslaw Milosz, whom he has called "one of the greatest poets of our time, perhaps the greatest."

The year 1956, when Brodsky was only sixteen, was crucial in establishing his sense of himself and of Russia. When Brodsky refers to himself as a member of the "generation of 1956," he has in mind the shock of recognition forced by the invasion of Hungary, a recognition of his status as a poet in a totalitarian state. If Brodsky saw Stalinism less as a political era than as a "state of mind," then the events of 1956, three years after the death of Stalin, proved the ugly endurance of a repressive regime which soon began to harass Brodsky personally.

Brodsky made several trips away from Leningrad on geological expeditions, traveling throughout the Soviet Union to the Amur River near China, Central Asia, the Caspian Sea region in the South, and the White Sea area in the North, where he was to spend nearly two years in exile a few years later. These travels exposed Brodsky to a variety of landscapes and may in part account for the powerful, if unattractive, natural descriptions in his mature verse. His travels permitted him a great deal of freedom, but his vaguely unorthodox movements and affiliations eventually drew the attention of KGB officials. Brodsky was first arrested in 1959 and twice confined to mental hospitals. These visits provided the setting for his most ambitious long poem, a dialogue between "Gorbunov i Gorchakov" ("Gorbunov and Gorchakov"). Brodsky had begun writing poems as early as 1958, though he now dates his first serious work from about 1963 (the year of his elegy to John Donne).

Arrested again and tried in 1964, Brodsky was sentenced in March to five years exile and hard labor; the charge was "parasitism." In effect, Brodsky was put on trial for identifying himself as a poet without "proof" in the form of a university degree or membership in the Writers' Union. The notes from his trial, smuggled out of Leningrad and excerpted often in articles about Brodsky, make for perverse evidence for his belief that the spiritual activity of writing poetry cannot be tolerated by a state which defines writing as a political act. Many Soviet cultural figures of international renown, including Dmitri Shostakovich and Kornei Chukovskii, testified on Brodsky's behalf and agitated for his early release, often at great professional and personal risk. As a result, Brodsky served only twenty months of his term, doing agricultural work in a small "village"—actually just a few huts in the wilderness—near Arkhangel'sk. He continued reading and writing; his first acquaintance with the works of W. H. Auden came in 1965, in translation. (He had known Robert Frost's poems as early as 1962 and was astonished by Frost's "hidden, controlled terror.")

Auden's influence is apparent in Brodsky's poem written on the occasion of T. S. Eliot's death in 1965; the lament looks ahead to the mature verse that Brodsky was writing on his return to Leningrad that year. It was at this time that his friends succeeded in shortening the length of his prison term. Anna Akhmatova, whom Brodsky had first met in 1960, was chief among this group of friends. Though he does not recall initially feeling an affinity with Akhmatova, Brodsky and she became close friends. His work owes more to the style and preoccupations of Osip Mandelstam than to Akhmatova, but Brodsky found in Akhmatova a living link to Russia's great poetic tradition, a poet who had known Mandelstam well, a poet who incarnated in her life and in her verse Russia's great upheavals.

Brodsky matured a great deal as a poet between 1965 and 1972. He gave readings to small groups of students, and even managed to have four of his poems published in 1966 and 1967 in official publications of Soviet cultural organs. A first volume of his poems had appeared without his authorization in the United States in 1965; a revised version, which included new poems, came out in 1970. Brodsky supported himself in Leningrad as a translator during these years, producing Russian versions of writers ranging from Andrew Marvell and John Donne to Tom Stoppard. Brodsky did nothing, however, to become more acceptable to the Soviet regime during these seven years in Leningrad. In 1972, he was exiled from the Soviet Union; he was not even told where the plane he was boarding would take him—to Siberian exile, or to freedom in the West. The plane landed in Vienna, where Brodsky was met by an American Slavicist, Carl Proffer, with an invitation to teach in Ann Arbor, Michigan. In Vienna, Brodsky sought out W. H. Auden, who arranged for him to participate in the Poetry International in London and generally smoothed his way for his introduction to the West.

Settling in the United States, Brodsky slowly began a life of teaching, writing, giving readings and meeting fellow poets. He has taught at the University of Michigan, Queens College, the Five Colleges (Amherst, Hampshire, Mount Holyoke, Smith, and the University of Massachusetts), New York University, and Columbia University. Since 1981, he has been the Five College Distinguished Professor of Literature, with tenure at Mount Holyoke College; he spends each fall teaching at Columbia as well. Brodsky became an American citizen in 1977. He continues writing poetry in Russian (he collaborates on his English translations) and essays and reviews in English.

Analysis

In describing his poetry, Joseph Brodsky has said that his "main interest is the nature of time," a theme which also recurs with obsessive frequency in his essays. Beginning even before his exile to Arkhangel'sk in 1964 and persisting in his most recent works, there is a preoccupation with endings, with concluding moments which illuminate with sudden new depth the meaning of all that has come before. Brodsky, whose stance as a poet is that of a watcher and listener rather than that of a participant and speaker, records his sense of a period of time in a manner that is more transcendental than teleological. In a 1962 poem, "Ogon', ty slyshish' . . ." ("The Fire Is Dying Down"), Brodsky observes how the room and objects around him absorb the shifts in time marked by the changing fire. A sense of lateness advances on the poet "from the corners"; he finds himself "suddenly at the center." Time has paused so palpably that the "clock hands have completely disappeared." The fire dies by the end of this twenty-line poem, but its brightness does not abandon the attentive watcher, who remains behind in the room's darkness. Just as it is important that the clock hands are not only invisible but also *silent*, silence being the analogue of time's halt, so it is crucial in the last line that the fire glows not in the poet's eyes, but in the room itself. The encroaching darkness of the dying fire becomes an external event that marks the inner fact of the poet's eyes growing cold, "motionless."

In another short lyric of 1962, a poem of fourteen lines with only a few near-rhymes and simply entitled "Sonet" ("Sonnet"), Brodsky explores a moment defined by a different kind of ending. Speaking to a loved woman, the poet envisions a new eruption of Vesuvius which will someday cover their dusty city with ash. He hopes that when the eruption begins, he will be able to set off for her house, so that future excavators will find them still embraced. The poem stops time in that final embrace, preserved by a layer of ash. The embrace and the ash are equally sustaining for the poet, who notes the passing clouds, a frequent emblem for the passing of time in Brodsky's poems. It is typical of Brodsky's poems that the very moment which destroys a city and all life in it also contains the possibility of preservation against decay.

The poem mirrors this contrast between the threat of change and the saving power of volcanic ash in its formal arrangement. As in many early Brodsky poems, the unit of division in the poem is the line. Without enjambments and virtually without rhyme (there is some sound interlocking in the first four lines), the poem's ordering principle is the sequence of its thoughts, expressed at the even pace of one clause per line. The exception is line twelve, "then I would like for them to find me," a single thought in two clauses (in Russian), the crucial turning point of the poem. The meter of the poem is iambic, mostly feminine pentameter, five-footed iambs being the commonest line length in Brodsky's repertoire in the 1960's, and the most successful. The sonnet feels experimental, though, because there are two lines of two and four metric feet, respectively, and virtually no rhyme, as if it were testing the boundaries of its own timing. Like Brodsky's many unrhymed sonnets, the poem shows how time can be controlled, slowed or hurried, within the conventions of meter and rhyme; the final picture of an unending embrace literally suspends time, so that the poem challenges, visually as well as verbally, the unspoken condition of all Brodsky's work, the effect of time on man.

The tender lyrics of early, as well as later, Brodsky, are balanced by verses of ironic distance and glittering wit. In some poems, such as the famous "Pamiatnik" ("Monument"), the serious if slightly mocking tones of the first lines ("Let's build a monument/ at the end of a long city street") turns toward a sarcastic finale—in this case prepared for by the poem's accumulation of petty details from Leningrad life: "Let's build a monument to lies." That final sentence indicts monument building as yet another hypocritical activity in a society whose public life proves inevitably false. In a longer poem, "Dva chasa v rezervuare" ("Two Hours in a Reservoir"), Brodsky mixes German and Yiddish phrases into a running monologue. The speaker pronounces his thoughts as they furiously charge past him in whatever language comes to his lips: "Enter and *exeunt* devils, thoughts./ Enter and *exeunt* guests, years." Narrative fragments about Faust and Johann Wolfgang von Goethe, Dr. Faustus and Thomas Mann, interrupt speculations about God and poetry and the fact that man is hurtling toward his death. The poem extends Brodsky's preoccupation with time, quoting Faust's famous desire to seize and hold one beautiful moment, a line Brodsky might be expected to appreciate—indeed, one he uses more than once. The poem's pace, though, is breakneck, the puns (particularly between languages) rampant, and the humor of the piece as pungent as it is inventive. Brodsky's search for ways to understand the passing of time, often defined by its endpoints, emerges in poems as varied as the witty "Odnoi poetesse" ("To a Certain Poetess"), where a relationship has outlived love, or the delicate "Aeneas i Dido" ("Aeneas and Dido"), where the moment of parting is captured poignantly by details—passing clouds, the hem of a tunic, a fish chasing after a ship at sail.

"Aeneas and Dido" deals with the end of a myth, and the poem concludes with a memorable picture. Dido watches Aeneas looking through a window, both of them realizing that the new gusts of wind will make it possible for Aeneas to set sail and leave Dido behind. Windows appear frequently in Brodsky's poems, often framing a landscape seen from within a room. Indeed, space becomes almost the conceptual framework through which time is explored in Brodsky's poems: his remark that literature shows what time does to a man was made in a talk entitled "Language as Otherland," and the titles of his poems often locate lyrics spatially as well as temporally. Examples of this can be found in each stage of his career, including "Zimnim vecherom v Ialte" ("A Winter Evening in Yalta"), "Dekabr' vo Florentsii" ("December in Florence"), and "Osen' v Norenskoi" ("Autumn in Norenskaia").

Brodsky's settings are occasionally interiors; small rooms become intimate settings for discovering the world outside and, always, oneself. In "Sumev otgorodit'sia . . ." ("Now that I've walled myself off from the world"), glimpses of puddles and fir trees merge with the domestic drama of a poet studying his face in a mirror. Brodsky has moments of self-description, framed by mirrors and windows, reminiscent of the later works of Akhmatova, though Brodsky always seems in search of some truth deeper than the self-image a piece of glass presents him. Self and other, interiors and landscapes interpenetrate one another in Brodsky's poems; as furiously as he seeks boundaries, walling himself off spatially, or describing endpoints in time, spaces and periods of time run into one another, and the confusions press the poet all the more in his attempt at self-definition.

Brodsky's landscapes are inseparable from the homesickness which pervades his verse. There *is* no place called "home" which is exempt. While he was in internal exile in Arkhangl'sk, Brodsky compared himself to Ovid; in the West, he has described scenes as diverse as Cape Cod and Cuernavaca, hills and lagoons and sluggish rivers, stopovers in St. Mark's Piazza or along Roman roads. Brodsky loves Venice, a city which glows through his poems like Leningrad, but there is not any landscape, any visual image of indoor or outdoor space with which the poet is not somehow at odds.

New places provide fresh scenes for seeing, new ways to show what one must see. If the goal of his poetry is, as Brodsky said in 1972, "to show man the true scale of what is happening," then landscape and cityscape finally offer a figurative vocabulary for philosophical apperceptions. The "scale" for Brodsky is never political but always personal, a fact which made him politically suspect in the Soviet Union.

Brodsky's philosophical preoccupations (the nature of "reality," and what it means for time to pass) and figures of expression (mythological plots, interior and exterior landscapes) are constants in his poetry, of which he continues to find new variations. There is, however, a more distinct sense of development in the prosodic features of Brodsky's poems, and these changes provide the clearest indications of his battle with Russian poetic tradition. Certain Brodskian themes resemble those of poets whom he is known to admire: the parting and exile of Mandelstam, the meditations on death of Evgeni Baratynskii, the monuments of Alexander Pushkin if not of Gavrila Derzhavin, the epistolary acts of self-definition of Dmitry Kantemir. In the case of Brodsky's verse forms, however, there are only a few poems with rather self-conscious and specific models, the most notable being his poem on the death of Eliot, written in the form and spirit of Auden's "In Memory of W. B. Yeats."

Brodsky's early poems strive to carve their own prosodic molds, using simple, assertive sentences, and a structuring free-verse line the firm closure of which allows few enjambments. The rhymes are experimental, often only hints at sound repetitions. In the early 1960's, Brodsky experimented with the placement of the line in such poems as "Ryby zimoi" ("Fish in Winter") and "Stikhi pod èpigrafom" ("Verses with an Epigraph"). Poems such as these make the most startling break with Russian prosodic tradition, spread over a page in complex patterns of indentation like those of E. E. Cummings (whom Brodsky admired in his youth). More deeply radical, though, and more difficult to sustain, are poems with very long verse lines, such as "Proplyvaiut oblaka" ("Clouds Swim By"). Here Brodsky repeats and interweaves similar phrases to break up long lines, while subtly binding them more tightly one to another. In later poems, Brodsky has used refrains to the same effect: the word "stifling" recurs as a one-word sentence in "Kolybel'naia Treskovogo Mysa" ("Lullaby of Cape Cod"). The long line has led Brodsky to explore ternary meters (several poems use anapest pentameter); in some cases, various kinds of ternary meters appear fleetingly with rhymes or near-rhymes structuring the poem. The impression in "Clouds Swim By" is one of fluidity which is being formidably if flexibly shaped, perhaps the most appropriate form for a poem that describes the changing shapes of clouds overhead.

Longer verse lines have come into Brodsky's work with complex sentences, as well as enjambments more abrupt than those previously found in Russian poetry. Regular meters are usually used, though they are the less common meters of iambic pentameter (not the common meter in Russian as it is in English; Russian depends far more on iambic tetrameter) and anapest pentameter. There are striking ventures in stanzaic form, the most remarkable in "Gorbunov and Gorchakov." In this long poem, Brodsky limits himself to an *ababababab* sequence in each ten-line stanza; the poem contains fourteen sections of ten such stanzas and is actually a conversation, sustaining the rhythms and dictions of colloquial speech within its very demanding form.

With these additional formal complexities, Brodsky has entered a grammatical universe adequate to the expression of his metaphysical questions. As has been noted by Richard Sylvester, Brodsky's complex sentences convey an ever-changing nexus of logical relationships, where words such as "because," "despite," "when," "where," and "if" become the all-important links in sentences dependent on several semantic fields. In such late poems as the cycle "Chast' rechi" ("A Part of Speech"), subject matter, diction, even stylistic level may change in such quick succession as to seem arbitrary: one poem in the cycle begins "A list of some observations." Yet Brodsky's poetry has become anything but inscrutable; his complex forms provide myriad vehicles perfectly suited for exploring themes of fragmentation, decay, solitary observation, and intense recollection.

In Brodsky's well-received collection, *A Part of Speech*, images and underlying questions extend the issues raised in his earlier poems. The desire to focus on particular points in time finds him often retreating into memory. The orientation toward the past was felt keenly in poems from the 1960's; one of Brodsky's best-known poems is "Ostanovka v pustyne" ("A Halt in the Wilderness"), where the razing of an Orthodox church is witnessed as a gesture of senseless modernization. Time as a category has tragic dimensions for Brodsky, as he himself has said. Near the end of "A Halt in the Wilderness," he speaks acerbically of "the relay race of human history." That poem looks ahead to ask what sacrifices the new era might demand, but there is no redeeming belief in progress for Brodsky. In his essays, Brodsky has dwelt on the evils of the twentieth century; he offers his readers little consolation and certainly no respite from personal responsibility in the dogmas of ideology or religion. In "Lullaby of Cape Cod," Brodsky defines his sense of human knowledge and its limitations in lines that resonate beyond his experience of emigration: "Having sampled two/ oceans as well as continents, I feel that I know/ what the globe itself must feel: there's nowhere to go."

Akhmatova found that in Brodsky's first poems the speaking voice was extremely solitary. The sense of bearing a unique vision is undiminished in Brodsky's recent poems, ranging from the varieties of quantification in "Lullaby of Cape Cod" to the equation that acts as a fluctuating refrain in "Èkloga IV-ia (Zimniaia)" ("Winter Eclogue: IV"): "Time equals cold." The more nearly oxymoronic Brodsky's declarations, the more finely he has sharpened his sense of the metaphysical conceit into an instrument for measuring a vision which is always just evading the poet's means of expression.

There is no expectation of finding the "right" metaphor, as frequent images of echoless space imply. "A glance," wrote Brodsky in "A Part of Speech," "is accustomed to no glance back." Brodsky's poems are less a relief from solitude than a journey forth, a journey deeper and farther into the "otherland" of language. To say that the journey is "merely long" is to say nothing, and to say everything. Brodsky writes in "Lullaby of Cape Cod":

> Far longer is the sea.
> At times, like a wrinkled forehead, it displays
> a rolling wave. And longer still than these
> is the strand of matching beads of countless days;

> and nights.

To observe that the break between "days" and "nights" is radical in terms of syntax and prosody is to describe Brodsky's poetics; to add that the break is unbearably long, that it expresses a discontinuity central to his metaphysical premises, is to initiate an examination of Brodsky's underlying themes at the level on which he deserves to be understood.

Major publication other than poetry
NONFICTION: *Less Than One*, 1984.

Bibliography
Birketts, Sven. "The Art of Poetry XVIII: Joseph Brodsky," in *Paris Review*. LXXXIII (Spring, 1982), pp. 82-126.
Lamont, Rosette C. "Joseph Brodsky: A Poet's Classroom," in *Massachusetts Review*. XV (1974), pp. 553-577.
Lòsev, Aleksei. "Niotkuda s liubov'iu: Zametki o stikhakh I. Brodskogo," in *Kontinent*. XIV (1977), pp. 307-331.
Sylvester, Richard D. "The Poem as Scapegoat: An Introduction to Joseph Brodsky's *Halt in the Wilderness*," in *Texas Studies in Literature and Language*. XVII (1975), pp. 303-325.
Verheul, Kees. "Iosif Brodsky's *Aeneas and Dido*," in *Russian Literature Triquarterly*. VI (1973), pp. 490-501.

Stephanie Sandler

PEDRO CALDERÓN DE LA BARCA

Born: Madrid, Spain; January 17, 1600
Died: Madrid, Spain; May 25, 1681

Principal poem and collections

Psalle et sile, 1741; *Poesías*, 1845; *Obra lírica*, 1943; *Sus mejores poesías*, 1954; *Poesías líricas en las obras dramáticas de Calderón*, 1964; *Los sonetos de Calderón en sus obras dramáticas*, 1974.

Other literary forms

Pedro Calderón de la Barca is known primarily as a verse dramatist, an occupation to which he was dedicated during his entire life. He wrote more than one hundred plays, most of which were published during his life or soon after his death. Some of the better known include *Amor, honor, y poder* (1623; love, honor, and power); *El sitio de Breda* (1625; the siege of Breda); *El príncipe constante* (1629; *The Constant Prince*, 1853); *La dama duende* (1629; *The Parson's Wedding*, 1664); *Casa con dos puertas mala es de guardar* (1629; *A Tutor for the Beaus: Or, Love in a Labyrinth*, 1737); *La devoción de la Cruz* (1633; *Devotion to the Cross*, 1832); *Los cabellos de Absalón* (1634; the hair of Absalom); *La vida es sueño* (1635; *Life Is a Dream*, 1830); *El mayor encanto, amor* (1635; love, the greatest enchantment); *A secreto agravio, secreta venganza* (1635; *Secret Vengeance for Secret Insult*, 1961); *El mágico prodigioso* (1637; *The Wonder-Working Magician*, 1959); *El mayor monstruo, los celos* (1637; jealousy, the greatest monster); *El alcalde de Zalamea* (1637; *Nobility: Or, The Alcalde of Zalamea*, 1885); *El médico de su honra* (1650; *The Physician of His Own Honour*, 1853); *El pintor de su deshonra* (1650; *The Painter of His Dishonour*, 1853); *La hija del aire* (1653; *The Daughter of the Air*, 1831); *Las tres justicias* (1661; *Three Judgements at a Blow*, 1853); and *Ante que todo es mi dama* (1662). Calderón also wrote more than seventy Eucharist plays, or *autos*, including *El gran teatro del mundo* (1633; *The Great Theatre of the World*, 1946); *La cena de Baltasar* (1634; *Belshazzar's Feast*, 1903); *La nave del mercader* (1674; the merchant's ship); *No hay más fortuna que Dios* (1677; God, the only fortune); *El gran mercado del mundo* (1677; the great market of the world); and *El día mayor de los días* (1678; the greatest day of all times). Calderón also wrote four *zarzuelas* (which might be considered musical comedies): *El jardín de Falerina* (1648; the garden of Falerina); *El golfo de las sirenas* (1657; the gulf of the Sirens); *El laurel de Apolo* (1658; the laurel of Apollo); and *La púrpura de la rosa* (1660; the blush of the rose).

Achievements

Pedro Calderón de la Barca lived during Spain's Golden Age, his death marking the end of that most productive period of Spanish letters. He was known as a poet and dramatist in his teens, and in his early twenties he took several poems to the poetic jousts held in 1620 and 1622 to commemorate the beatification and canonization of Saint Isidro. He was awarded a prize in the second contest, and Lope de Vega, who was the organizer of the two events, praised the young poet highly on both occasions. Indeed, throughout his life, Calderón continued to write lyric poetry, the great bulk of which, however, is incorporated into his plays. His first dated play, *Amor, honor, y poder* is from 1623, and subsequently he established himself so well in the theatrical scene that, when Lope de Vega died in 1635, Calderón became the official court dramatist, a position he held until his death. Calderón proved a worthy successor of Lope de Vega, for he wrote more than two hundred dramatic pieces, a total second only to that of Lope de Vega. Calderón produced several masterpieces, including *Life Is a Dream*, one of the great works of Spain's Golden Age. In addition, he was the supreme master of the *auto* or Eucharist play, a dramatic form which he refined and improved progressively and to which he was dedicated almost exclusively during the last years of his life.

Biography
   Pedro Calderón de la Barca was born in Madrid into a family of some nobility. His father, Diego Calderón de la Barca, came from the valley of Carriedo, in the mountains of Santander, and was a secretary to the treasury board under Philip II and Philip III. Calderón's mother, Ana María de Henao, was from a noble family of the Low Countries that had moved to Spain long before. Calderón was their third child.
   Soon after Calderón was born, his family moved to Valladolid, following the transfer of the court, and there the boy learned his first letters. When the court returned permanently to Madrid, and with it his family, Calderón, then nine years old, was placed in the Colegio Imperial of the Jesuits, where he studied Latin and humanities for five years.
   Calderón's mother died in 1610, and his father married Juana Freyre four years later, only to die himself the following year. His death was followed by a bitter and costly lawsuit between Juana and the Calderón children, ending favorably for Juana. Calderón had entered the University of Alcalá de Henares in 1614, but, after his father's death, he transferred to the University of Salamanca to be under the supervision of his uncle. In Salamanca, he studied canon law and theology, planning to become a priest and take charge of a chaplaincy endowed by his maternal grandfather. Calderón abandoned his studies in 1620, however, and returned to Madrid, where for some time he led a turbulent life. He and his brothers, Diego and José, were engaged in a fight which resulted in the murder of Diego de Velasco. The father of Velasco demanded retribution, and the Calderón brothers settled the case by paying

six hundred ducats (a substantial sum in those days).

While in Salamanca, Calderón had started writing poetry and drama; in Madrid, he entered the poetic competitions of 1620 and 1622, organized to celebrate the beatification and canonization of Saint Isidro. Calderón's entries won the praise of Lope de Vega, judge of the contests and editor of its proceedings. The works that Calderón presented to these jousts are of interest not only because they are his earliest extant poems but also because they are among his few surviving nondramatic poems.

The next few years took Calderón away from Spain. He enlisted in the Spanish army and went to Northern Italy and to Flanders, where he probably witnessed the defeat that the Spaniards inflicted on the Flemish, an event that he dramatized so well in *El sitio de Breda*. The poet returned to Madrid around 1625, and soon afterward he entered the service of Duke Frías. From that time on, Calderón fully committed himself to the theater, constantly writing new plays and staging them with all the available machinery and scenery. According to Pérez de Montalbán, Calderón had written many dramas by 1632—all of which had been acted successfully—as well as a substantial body of lyric verse. Consequently, he was enjoying an enviable reputation as a poet.

About that time, the dramatist was involved in another unhappy event. Pedro de Villegas wounded one of Calderón's brothers very seriously, and in pursuit of Villegas, Calderón, accompanied by some police officers, violated the sanctity of the Trinitarians' convent. The entire court reacted negatively to this event, including Lope de Vega, who protested violently because his daughter Marcela was in the convent. Calderón was reprimanded for his actions, but nothing more, and he even made fun of the affair in *The Constant Prince*. His popularity was already larger than the gravity of his actions, and, therefore, he came out of it free.

In 1635, the Retiro Gardens and Palaces were opened with great festivities, and Calderón's play, *El mayor encanto, amor*, was staged for the occasion. Lope de Vega died that same year, and Calderón became officially attached to the court, furnishing dramas for the exclusive entertainment of the Royal Palace. In recognition of his services, King Philip IV made Calderón a knight of the Order of Santiago in 1637. As such, he participated in the liberation of Fuenterrabía that same year, and with the army of Count Duke Olivares, he took part in the pacification of Catalonia, serving loyally and courageously until 1642, in recognition of which he was awarded a monthly pension of thirty gold crowns.

The war of Catalonia made an impact on Calderón, aggravated by the fact that his brother José lost his life in the conflict. Nevertheless, he went back to Madrid and continued his occupation as court dramatist, increasingly enjoying the favor of the King, who put in his hands the arrangement of the festivities for the arrival of the new Queen, Mariana de Austria, in 1649.

During these years, Calderón, about whose intimate life little is known, fathered a son out of wedlock. This son, born around 1647, died before reaching adulthood, while his mother died soon after his birth. Calderón, who had been contemplating the idea for some time, determined to become a priest. He was ordained in 1651, and two years later Philip IV appointed him to the chaplaincy of the New Kings in the Cathedral of Toledo. Calderón moved to that city, but he kept in contact with Madrid, supplying the court with new plays and *autos* on a regular basis. While in Toledo, and inspired by the inscription of the cathedral's choir, he wrote the poem *Psalle et sile* (sing and be silent), an unusually self-revealing work.

Calderón returned to Madrid in 1663 as the chaplain of honor to Philip IV, who had created that position to ensure Calderón's presence in the court. Later that year, Calderón joined the Natural Priests of Madrid, and he became head of the congregation afterward, remaining in that position until his death. He led a quiet life during that time, dedicated to his priestly duties and restricting his literary activity to the writing of Eucharist plays and an occasional drama for the court. He still enjoyed an immense popularity, and his plays were staged frequently. Three volumes of his *Partes* (1636-1684; collected plays) appeared during this period (two had been published in 1636 and 1637), although he disowned four dramas of the last volume, and one of the Eucharist plays. Preparation was under way to publish his entire dramatic production, a task that was undertaken by Juan de Vera Tassis after Calderón's death.

Calderón died on May 25, 1681; his death marked the end of the Golden Age of Spanish literature. Following his desires, the dramatist was buried during a simple ceremony, but a gorgeous one took place a few days later to satisfy the many admirers who wanted to pay homage to the playwright for the last time.

Analysis

There are extant only about thirty nondramatic poems by Pedro Calderón de la Barca. Most of them are short poems, composed for a particular occasion, usually in praise of someone in whose collection they would appear.

As he did in his plays, Calderón employed a variety of verse forms in his nondramatic poems, but the sonnet is the prevalent form. The sonnet had been an important part of Spanish poetry since Juan Boscán and Garcilaso de la Vega assimilated the Italian poetic form into Castilian verse, but it was losing popularity during Calderón's time, as he observes in one of his plays, *Ante que todo es mi dama* (my lady comes before everything else). Fifteen of Calderón's nondramatic poems are sonnets; added to the sonnets that he included in his dramatic works, and the one inserted in the longer poem *Psalle et sile*, they make a total of eighty-six sonnets, collected in a single volume by Rafael Osuna in 1974.

Calderón's sonnets reflect the main poetic currents of his times; Gongorism and *conceptismo* are both present, with a preference for the latter. In general, Calderón's sonnets reveal the poet's desire for a poetry of geometric perfection, evident in the parallel constructions, the *enumeratio* of concepts and *recopilación* or recapitulation of them in the final line, and other rhetorical techniques. They are also filled with the rich imagery that the poet uses in all of his literary production. The nondramatic sonnets are, in general, less convincing than those found in the plays, given their occasional character, but some of them are well constructed and worthy of praise. Among these are the sonnet dedicated to Saint Isidro, beautiful in its simplicity; the one written in honor of Saint Teresa de Ávila, which shows a fervent respect for the reformer of the Carmelitans; the one inserted in *Psalle et sile*, which hails the Cathedral of Toledo as a symbol of faith; and the one praising King Philip IV's hunting skills, the best of all, according to Osuna.

Another poetic form that Calderón used with great skill is the romance. He gives a particular lightness to this traditional verse form, making the poem flow with ease, always adapting it appropriately to the theme he is poeticizing. In this meter, Calderón wrote his only two extant love poems, an ascetic composition, and a self-portrait in verse that reveals his comic genius. This last is, unfortunately, incomplete, yet the 173 lines of the fragment are rich in wit. Calderón first describes his physical appearance—not forgetting any part of his body—in a very unflattering manner. He proceeds to tell the reader about his studies in Salamanca, referring to his mother's desire that he become a priest, his dedication to the theater, and his days as a soldier, adding jokingly that none of these occupations enabled him to find a decent woman who would marry him. The poet, however, does not let this situation affect him, for he has learned that "As a philosopher says, it makes good sense to adapt to the times." Based on this thinking, he involves himself with two women because he prefers two ugly maids to a beautiful lady. The poem ends abruptly in an argument against Plato's concept of love. The sarcastic tone of the opening lines informs the entire composition; for example, when referring to his lack of responsibility, the poet observes that his peccadilloes are excused by everyone because he is a Salamanca graduate. The tone of the poem is far from Calderón's characteristic sobriety, although it is possible that he wrote other poems of this nature which have not survived. Because of the reference to the time he spent in the army, the poem must have been written sometime between 1625 and 1637, for he became very disappointed with the reality of war during the Catalonian uprising.

It is in his serious compositions that Calderón shows his best abilities as a poet. In them, as in some of his philosophical plays, Calderón is preoccupied with the reality of death. The best poem of this type is "Décimas a la muerte" ("Decima"), the tone of which is reminiscent of Jorge Manrique's *Coplas por la muerte de su padre* (1492; *Ode*, 1823), although it is less impressive than that fifteenth century masterpiece. Its themes include the brevity of life; the justice of death, which ends every man's life equally; and the *ubi sunt* topos. Absent from it is the theme of fame, so strong in Manrique and present elsewhere in Calderón's works. Here, the poet is deeply pessimistic: "Everything resolves to nothingness,/ all comes from dirt, and dirt becomes,/ and thus it ends where it began." This sense of pessimism is heightened by the fact that there is only a vague reference to eternal life at the end of the poem. The emphasis is placed on the "end" of everything and the absurdity of life, on a pervasive lack of meaning.

A similar attitude is expressed in another poem, "Lágrimas que vierte un alma arrepentida" (1672; tears of a repentant soul). Written in Calderón's old age, "Lágrimas que vierte un alma arrepentida" reveals his strong religious sentiments. The poet presents himself with humility, declaring that he is a sinner, full of vices, and asks God to forgive him. The poem is an expression of love for Christ; it recalls Saint Teresa of Ávila and the anonymous "Soneto a Cristo crucificado" ("Sonnet to Christ Crucified").

Calderón's longest poem is *Psalle et sile*, written in Toledo while the poet was in charge of the chaplaincy of the New Kings (1653-1663). The 525-line poem was inspired by the words inscribed at the entrance of the cathedral's choir. Calderón tries to explain the meaning of the inscription, which, because of its location, implies a request or command to those who enter the choir. How is it possible to sing and be silent at the same time? The poet praises silence as the greatest moderation and as the language of God, with Whom one can communicate only in the silence of one's soul. Calderón adds, however, that "he who speaks with propriety does not break silence." To speak with propriety, one has to concentrate on the subject of the conversation. In the same manner, one needs to concentrate when conversing with God, which can be done only by meditating. If one is immersed in meditation, then one is speaking the language of God—that is, one is truly silent. At the same time, one could sing songs without interrupting the mental conversation with God. Following this reasoning, it is possible to sing and to be silent simultaneously, utterly absorbed in spiritual communication with God.

Major publications other than poetry

PLAYS: *Amor, honor, y poder*, 1623; *El sitio de Breda*, 1625; *Casa con dos puertas mala es de guardar*, 1629 (*A Tutor for the Beaus: Or, Love in a Labyrinth*, 1737); *La dama duende*, 1629 (*The Parson's Wedding*, 1664); *El príncipe constante*, 1629 (*The Constant Prince*, 1853); *La devoción de la Cruz*, 1633 (*Devotion to the Cross*, 1832); *El gran teatro del mundo*, 1633 (*The Great Theatre of the World*, 1946); *Los cabellos de Absalón*, 1634; *La cena de Baltasar*, 1634 (*Belshazzar's Feast*, 1903); *A secreto agravio, secreta venganza*, 1635 (*Secret Vengeance for Secret Insult*, 1961); *El mayor encanto, amor*, 1635; *La vida es sueño*, 1635 (*Life Is a Dream*, 1830); *Partes*, 1636-1684; *El alcalde de Zalamea*, 1637 (*Nobility: Or, The Alcalde of Zalamea*, 1885); *El mágico prodigioso*, 1637 (*The Wonder-Working Magician*, 1959); *El mayor monstruo, los celos*, 1637; *El jardín de Falerina*, 1648; *El médico de su honra*, 1650 (*The Physician of His Own Honour*, 1853); *El pintor de su deshonra*, 1650 (*The Painter of His Dishonour*, 1853); *La hija del aire*, 1653 (*The Daughter of the Air*, 1831); *El golfo de las sirenas*, 1657; *El laurel de Apolo*, 1658; *La púrpura de la rosa*, 1660; *Las tres justicias*, 1661 (*Three Judgements at a Blow*, 1853); *Ante que todo es mi dama*, 1662; *La nave del mercader*, 1674; *El gran mercado del mundo*, 1677; *No hay más fortuna que Dios*, 1677; *El día mayor de los días*, 1678; *Autos sacramentales*, 1717 (6 volumes).

Bibliography

Hesse, Everett W. *Calderón de la Barca*, 1967.

Hillborn, Harry W. "Calderón's Quintillas," in *Hispanic Review*. XVI (1948), pp. 301-310.

_____ . "Calderón's Silvas," in *PMLA*. LVIII (1943), pp. 122-148.

Osuna, Rafael. *Los sonetos de Calderón en sus obras dramáticas*, 1974.

Parker, Jack H., and A. M. Fox. *Calderón de la Barca Studies, 1951-1969*, 1971.

Ticknor, George. *History of Spanish Literature*, 1849.

Wilson, Edward M. "Calderón and the Décimas a la muerte," in *Bulletin of Hispanic Studies*. XLVIII (1971), pp. 301-313.

Wilson, Edward M., and Jack Sage. *Poesías líricas en las obras dramáticas de Calderón: Citas y glosas*, 1964.

Juan Fernández Jiménez

CALLIMACHUS

Born: Cyrene, a Greek colony in North Africa; c. 305 B.C.
Died: Alexandria, Egypt; c. 240 B.C.

Principal poems and collections

Callimachus is said to have written eight hundred books, an astonishing output even if one takes into account the generally shorter length of the ancient scroll. Of his poetry, only the six *Hymns* (ranging from one hundred to three hundred lines, all but one in dactylic hexameter) and the *Epigrams* (sixty-four short poems, most of them in elegiac couplets) survived from antiquity more or less intact in the manuscript tradition. The *Aetia* (causes— originally seven thousand lines in four books) *Iambi*, *Hecale* (an *epyllion* or "little epic"), *Lock of Berenice*, and a handful of lyric poems are extant only in fragmentary form as they were discovered on papyri found in Egypt or were partially quoted by later ancient authors.

In addition, nearly four hundred fragments, ranging from one line to fifty, which cannot be placed for certain in any larger context, attest the wide range and varied content of Callimachus' otherwise unknown verse. Only the titles of these other compositions survive to tantalize modern scholars. For Callimachus' *Hymns* and *Epigrams*, the numerical systems of A. W. Mair in his book *Callimachus: Hymns and Epigrams* (1955) are used. For Callimachus' *Iambi*, the numerical system of C. A. Trypanis in *Callimachus: Aetia, Iambi, Hecale, Minor Epic and Elegiac Poems and Other Fragments* (1958, 1975) is used.

Other literary forms

Callimachus himself was a scholar and literary critic as well as a poet and wrote prose monographs on subjects as diverse as the names of tribes, rare words, barbarian customs, and marvelous occurrences throughout the world. Unfortunately, none of the prose is extant.

Achievements

Callimachus is the preeminent "Alexandrian" poet, the most daring, technically skilled, and prolific among the writers practicing their art in that Hellenized Egyptian city during the third century B.C. Like his contemporaries Theocritus and Apollonius Rhodius, Callimachus wrote allusive, learned, yet dramatic poetry; unlike these two fellow Alexandrians, however, he seems to have mined deliberately the widest variety of genres. Moreover, he alone among the poets whose work survives from this period crafted and refined throughout his career a poetic dogma, a highly developed notion of what a poem should be. In this, one could compare him with Ezra Pound among modern poets, continually urging his colleagues to "make it new" and exerting a powerful influence on subsequent generations of poets. Callimachus, who was also like Pound in being a scholar of poetry, renewed the Greek poetic tradition in two ways: he cultivated forms that had fallen into disuse (such as the hymnic) and he infused traditionally nonpersonal poetry with allusions to his own time and condition. A hymn, for example, could become a vehicle for praise of the patron monarch Ptolemy and for pronouncements on style, while purporting to praise Zeus or Apollo; a funerary epigram might be turned in the poet's hands to serve as a sophisticated joke. It was Callimachus' achievement to compose poetry that satisfied a discerning, restricted audience—the royal court at Alexandria and other scholar-poets—without becoming hopelessly obscure or dated. Instead, his poetry in all genres usually attains the ideal he set: lightness of tone is wedded to brevity, urbane manner, erudite content, and exclusive allusions. That these qualities were prized in poetry is evidenced by the many papyrus fragments later discovered to contain works by Callimachus—far more than those of any other author, including the very popular Euripides. Ironically, this "exclusive" poet obtained a far-from-exclusive audience, perhaps because his verse challenged the reader as it simultaneously offered rare pleasures. His influence extended even beyond the Greek-speaking lands; the verse of the Roman poets Ennius, Catullus, Horace, Vergil, and Propertius, and the poetic stance which each assumes, would be unthinkable without the example of Callimachus.

In turn, from the poets writing during the reign of the Emperor Augustus, the English "Augustans" inherited the Callimachean poetic ideal; Alexander Pope's *The Rape of the Lock* (1712, 1714) echoes the Alexandrian poet's *Lock of Berenice*, although Pope added the mock-epic tone. Indeed, Callimachean aesthetic principles are so much a part of the European literary tradition that they may be taken for granted. Yet, whenever a new poetic movement (Imagism, for example) challenges outworn canons of taste, jettisons tedious narrative, and turns instead to highly crafted "small" verse forms, the creators of the new poetry are treading the path first cleared by the Alexandrian poet.

Biography

Callimachus was not a native Alexandrian; he grew up and seems to have begun composing poetry in Cyrene, a Greek city of North Africa. From a commentary on a lost portion of his long poem, the *Aetia*, it appears that Callimachus represented himself as once dreaming that he was transported from his boyhood home in Libya to Mt. Helicon, the place on the mainland of Greece which was considered the traditional home of the Muses. He thus alludes to an early initiation into his art.

Neither his date of birth nor his parentage is known, but Callimachus' family apparently prided itself on being descended from Battus, the legendary eighth century B.C. founder of Cyrene. From this assumption it may be deduced that his education was that of an aristocrat. On moving to Alexandria, however, which was one of the main cultural centers of Hellenistic Greek civilization, Callimachus was initially a marginal figure; family connections did not help. He held the position of schoolmaster in the suburb of Eleusis, which was not a lucrative job. Several of his epigrams that mention his poverty have been thought to date from this period (c. 280-270 B.C.); nevertheless, it should be remembered that the topic of poverty (*penia*) was a convention in Greek literature as early as Hesiod (fl. 700 B.C.), a poet whom Callimachus admired and imitated. When, therefore, the poet addresses a lover in Epigram 34 M. "You know that my hands are empty of wealth . . ." and proceeds to beg affection, the words are most likely those of a persona rather than of the poet himself.

At some later point, Callimachus received an appointment to the great library at Alexandria, perhaps after an introduction to Ptolemy II Philadelphus, the library's royal patron (who ruled from 285 to 246 B.C.). Callimachus' ground-breaking compilation of the 120-volume *Pinakes* (tablets), a catalog of the library's hundred thousand or so papyrus scrolls of Greek literature, entailed far more than merely listing titles, involving him in decisions about genre, authorship, authors' biographies, and the arrangement of sections within each work. This extensive piece of literary history provided the poet with a wealth of material—often obscure—from which to fashion learned verse.

Despite his important contributions there, Callimachus was never appointed head of the library. Some controversy may have been involved, as literary infighting was surely a part of his life, but the details of his arguments with various contemporaries remain vague. Ancient commentators mention a feud between Callimachus and Apollonius, the author of the epic *Argonautica* (third century B.C.). Callimachus' preference for brevity and disdain for pseudo-Homeric epic apparently prevailed for a time: Apollonius is said to have left, humbled, to live on the island of Rhodes. Callimachus' *Ibis*, now lost, a piece of darkly worded invective which Ovid later imitated, may have hastened its victim's departure from Alexandria. Other personal enemies apparently were attacked through allusions in the revised prologue of the *Aetia*.

While much of his poetry continues such artistic debates, several of Callimachus' poems might best be understood in a different light—as responses to occasions at the royal court which demanded expression on the part of an "attached" poet. The *Lock of Berenice*, for example, commemorates an actual event, the dedication of a wife's lock of hair to petition the gods for the safe return of her husband, Ptolemy III, as he departed for war in 247 B.C. (This is the only datable poem extant.) Again, court happenings might be alluded to in that portion of the *Hymn to Zeus* that mentions Zeus's rule over his older brothers; the entire composition may be an elaborate, half-veiled praise of Callimachus' patron. It is surely not a real hymn meant for ritual recitation.

Unfortunately, nothing is known of the poet's relation with the royal family other than that their patronage extended until his death at an advanced age. This social situation in its broader implications must be kept in mind: what appears to be Callimachean allusive indirection often might have resulted from politic discretion.

Analysis

Since the legacy of Callimachus lies so much in his theory of style, it is best, first, to examine several of his extended metaphors describing the ideal style; then his major works can be evaluated according to his own aesthetic standards.

In most cases, Callimachus' pronouncements about poetry are blended skillfully with other topics. Epigram 30 M. is a good example. The seven-line poem builds on the poet's exclusive tastes:

> I hate a cyclical poem, take no delight in the road
> That carries many to and fro. I detest
> A lover that wanders, nor do I drink from a well;
> All held in common I abhor. . . .

Then the poet dramatically changes tack. What began as a literary manifesto ends abruptly as a bitter personal love poem:

> Lysaniē, you are beautiful, beautiful . . .
> But before Echo speaks this, someone says
> "Another possesses him."

The reader is left in suspense, yet he could eventually conclude that the poet, true to his lonely principle in life as in art, is here abandoning the one thing he does *not* hate.

The long, undistinguished epic poems called "cyclic," because they complete the Trojan War myth cycle, represent for Callimachus all that one should avoid in verse. Even though his *Hymn to Apollo* uses the centuries-old Homeric meter and epic diction, the poem in praise of the god is startlingly fresh and compresses details of geography, ritual, history and myth, into a dramatic framework. The final lines, which express Callimachus' aversion for the epic form, are spoken by the god of poetry himself, using the images of Epigram 30 M. again—wide thoroughfares and water. To "Envy" (Callimachus' unnamed detractors), whispering in Apollo's ear like a court sycophant about the hateful poet "who does not sing as many things as the sea" (that is, vast epics), the god replies with a kick. He cites the filthiness of the "great stream" Euphrates; in an oracular tone, he says that Demeter's shrine is watered by "bees" (priestesses of the goddess) that carry water only from pure, undefiled streams. Envy is thus defeated.

Purity of water, insectlike artisanship—these are metaphors for Callimachus' light, unencumbered verse. The two images are combined once more in the combative prologue to the "collected poems" edition of the *Aetia*. After acknowledging the objection that he has not written "one long poem," Callimachus again uses the dramatic mask of Apollo to defend his own application of *techne* (skill) rather than bulk and big noises: as a youth, he saw the god, who instructed the poet to "nourish a slender Muse," to imitate the cicada. Callimachus' final prayer to become "the light one, the winged," living on dew, takes on a more personal note, for now he desires the insect's levity in order to shake off burdensome old age.

How does Callimachus in his verse attain this cicadalike freedom of expression? The *Aetia* itself can show. Although nearly half the length of the *Iliad* (c. 800 B.C.) when extant in full, this was certainly not "one long poem" but rather an episodic meandering through every sort of Greek ritual lore, a poem that explained (like the poet's prose works) curious customs—why the Parians, for example, sacrifice without flute music, or why the Lindians honor Heracles with blasphemy. A scholar's poem, the *Aetia* has the dramatist's voice behind its narrative, choosing exact details and often breaking into direct speech. Here Callimachus' novel narrative technique appears to be built on deliberate random changes of topic, like the flitting of an industrious insect.

The story of Acontius and Cydippe, one of the longer, completely separable stories within the *Aetia*, illuminates the Callimachean method very well. An introduction, sprinkled allusively with obscure proper names, relates the legendary beauty of this pair of lovers and tells how Acontius by means of an inscribed apple contrived to bind Cydippe on oath to love him, so that her attempts to marry others are all divinely thwarted. Then the poet focuses on one such attempt at marriage with another. Seeming to lose the narrative thread, however, he begins to describe the history of the ritual prenuptial sleep which Cydippe and her husband-to-be must take; but the poet breaks off: "Hold back, shameless soul, you dog!" Such rituals are too holy to tell; "having much knowledge is bad for one who does not control the tongue," he says. Clearly, the aposiopesis (falling silent) technique is employed only to show off, in elegant manner, a vast erudition, and at the same time it is a technique that prevents the reader from being bored with the extraneous details of the digression. Finally, the poet makes his transition to another topic by a surprising bibliographical reference, an unheard-of device in serious epic poems: "Cean, your clan, the Acontiadae, dwell in honored numbers at Iulis still. This love-match we heard from old Xenomedes, who set down once the entire island in a mythological history." At one stroke, the scholar-poet gives the *aetion* (cause) which he set out to tell—the origin of this clan—and turns his narrative to other Cean myths with a librarian's remark.

The "levity" of Callimachus can be appreciated in other ways; it is not merely narrative flightiness. Indeed, he sometimes employs old conventions for the sake of elaborate jokes. A few of his epigrams have their origin in this technique. There were generic social precedents for these short poems: the inscription-verses on tombs and on dedicated shrine offerings. The poet subverts both. A four-line poem poses as a tombstone epitaph to commemorate a youth who allegedly was putting garlands on his stepmother's tomb ("thinking now that she had changed life and her nature as well") when the woman's *stēlē* toppled and killed him. The last line is both traditional in its address to passersby, and humorous: "O step-sons, shun even a step-mother's grave." In imitation of a dedicatory object, Callimachus wrote another poem which plays on the similarity in Greek between the word for sea and the word for salt. Like a shipwrecked sailor who traditionally offered an oar or clothing to the gods who saved him from drowning, the speaker, Eudemus, in Epigram 48 M. dedicates his saltcellar: now he has become rich and no longer eats frugally, and so is "saved from the salt."

Lest it be thought that the poet only plays, one other epigram might be mentioned to acknowledge the elegiac strain and the ability to evoke intense feeling also to be found in Callimachus. Perhaps his most famous short poem, Epigram 2 M., is that addressed to Heraclitus:

> Someone told me of your death, Heraclitus, and put me
> In tears; I remembered the many times we both
> By conversing put the sun to sleep. . . .

Although his friend has been "ashes long since now," Callimachus in recalling him affirms the love of the art of poetry which the two friends shared:

> But your nightingales are still alive;
> Hades, who snatches all, will not put hand on them.

The light touch—of tone, as in many epigrams, of allusiveness and narrative pace, as in the *Aetia*—characterizes Callimachus' approach to other genres as well. Never satisfied with remaining at work in any single verse form, he seems to have intended to appropriate all, even writing tragedy and comedy (now lost). Doubtless this approach was criticized by his contemporaries as evidence of a lack of staying power; it was scorned as *polyeideia* (writing in many forms). Today, one sees this method as the prime virtue of Callimachean art. Three other works—*Iambi*, *Hymns*, and *Hecale*—show the advantages which Callimachus derived from this stylistic tenet.

The thirteen poems of the *Iambi* present a much modulated form of the invective traditionally associated with the genre of poetry written in this meter as practiced by Archilochus and Hipponax in archaic Greece. Attacks on personal enemies are replaced in these compositions by a mild correction of received opinion: the true story of a well-known proverb occupies Iambus 11 T., and similar antiquarian interests take up the description of statues, the origin of a footrace on Aegina, the reason that sows are slaughtered in a certain Aphrodite cult. These *Iambi* show Callimachus, as in the *Aetia*, crossing prose genres of historiography and mythology with disused poetic forms to create something new. In the few *Iambi* which mention contemporaries, the names in question are tangential to the poem. Thus, Iambus 2 T. relates one of Aesop's fables about the way in which animals lost their voices to men; only at the end does the poet intrude: "Eudemus, therefore, has a dog's voice, Philton a donkey's. . . ." Such a technique, distancing the original purpose of the iambic form, allows Callimachus to expand its range. He adapts it thereby to the changed social conditions of the third century B.C., in which the cosmopolitan court, rather than the tightly knit city-state, is the intended audience.

The *Hymns* and *Hecale*, finally, allow Callimachus' light handling to be traced through two interrelated effects. First, there is once again generic innovation; second, the innovation is tied to narrative methods of compressing, arranging, and ordering point-of-view, all of which are new.

The hymn, since the time of Homer, was a narrative commemorating the deeds of a particular divinity; it was framed by praises of the god. Callimachus, however, in the *Hymn to Apollo* and other hymns re-creates dramatically the god's epiphany at his shrine. The poem adopts a second-person narrator, rather than the more distant, epic-sounding third-person narration. Immediately noticeable, too, is the way in which Callimachus allies poetry with secret and holy ritual: to hear the poem, one must be an initiate, like the worshipers of Apollo. It is not far from such poetry to the Roman lyricist Horace's claim to be "priest of the Muses."

The *Hecale*, on the other hand, rather than being a reworking of a very old genre, is a completely new form, the *epyllion*, which arose in the Alexandrian period of Greek literature. Who its exact inventor was, is not known with certainty. Theocritus wrote several; Callimachus may simply have perfected the use of this form. The purpose of the "little epic" is not to tell all the deeds of a hero, for that ambition would require the scope of the detested "cyclic" poem. Instead, only one, often little-known episode in the life of a hero, one with plenty of local-color possibilities, is selected. In the case of the *Hecale*, it is Theseus' capture of a destructive bull which has been ravaging Marathon, near Athens. The scale of the narrative is further reduced by the poet's intense focus on the events of the night before the heroic feat, rather than on the deed itself. Theseus' visit to the rustic hut of an old woman named Hecale, the simple supper she prepares for him, their conversation—all are described in painstakingly realistic detail. There is pathos (the hero returns later to find the woman has died), erudition (the origin of the Hecale-feasts is explained), and a good deal of stylistic tour de force (into the "heroic" hexameter the poet fits the words "bread-box," "baking oven," and other commonplace terms). Although most of the poem survives in fragments, it was intact and widely imitated from Vergil's time to the thirteenth century. Fragmentary as the *Hecale* remains, it is nevertheless a fitting testament to its author's lifelong urge to distill, renew, and perpetuate essential and lively poetry.

Bibliography

Clausen, W. "Callimachus and Latin Poetry," in *Greek, Roman, and Byzantine Studies*. V (1964), pp. 181-196.
Meillier, Claude. *Callimaque et son temps*, 1979.

Richard Peter Martin

LUÍS DE CAMÕES

Born: Lisbon, Portugal; c. 1524
Died: Lisbon, Portugal; June 10, 1580

Principal collections

Os Lusíadas, 1572 (*The Lusiads*, 1655); *Cancioneiro*, 1580; *Rimas*, 1595 (*The Lyrides*, 1803, 1884).

Other literary forms

Although Luís de Camões does not seem to have tried to compete with his great compatriot, the dramatist Gil Vicente, Camões did write three short *autos* (short plays). *Enfatriões* (1587; amphytrions), an adaptation of Plautus' comedy, was probably staged in 1540 as a scholar's exercise or for an academic celebration at Coimbra University. The *Auto del-Rei Seleuco* (1644; the play of King Seleuco), based on Plutarch, was performed in the home of Estácio da Fonseca, one of the King's officials, perhaps on the occasion of a wedding, very likely in 1542 during the poet's sojourn in Lisbon and at court. Finally, *Filodemo* (1587), the longest, most classical, and most mature of Camões' plays, was presented in Goa in 1555 to honor the newly appointed governor of India, Francisco Barreto.

Achievements

No Iberian lyric poet has been more successful than Camões in the expression of feeling. Indeed, he represents all of Peninsular poetry at its peak. Lord Byron, whose inspiration introduced new emotion into literature, admired the authenticity of Camões' lyricism and understood the human truth in his verse. In all of his work, Camões was able to combine native Portuguese traditions with the classical influences and with the vital spirit of the Renaissance.

Camões is probably best known for his epic poem, *The Lusiads*. The focal point in this work is not Vasco da Gama, realistically characterized as the uncultivated captain that he was, but the Portuguese conquistadores as a whole—who, in the tradition of their ancestors, set out to create the vast Portuguese Empire for themselves and posterity. Although Camões wrote his propaganda to glorify the nation at its peak, he recognized the weakness of the imperial structure for the future. Such objectivity regarding the Empire— and the honesty to express his views to the King, to whom he dedicated his poem—bespeak Camões' faith in the best principles of the Renaissance and his confidence in himself as the poet most representative of his time.

Biography

Although he has had many biographers, little is known for certain of the adventuresome life of Luís de Camões, who represented so well in his life and works the Renaissance man and the Portuguese conquistador. The son of Simão Vas de Camões and Ana de Macedo or Sá, Camões was possibly related, through his paternal grandmother, to Vasco da Gama, as well as to other Portuguese notables dating as far back as 1370. Camões was a gentleman, then, although always of scant financial resources. It is clear, too, that he possessed a vast erudition. Because of the quantity and quality of Camões' learning, it is likely that he studied at Coimbra University and therefore that he was born in Coimbra, as he probably would have been too poor to move there from Lisbon.

With some reputation as well as noble birth, Camões went to Lisbon between 1542 and 1545, to frequent the court and enjoy the greater activity of the capital. His enjoyment was short-lived, unfortunately, for in 1546 or 1547 he was banished to Ribatejo because of his passion for a lady of the court whose parents did not approve. It is known that during the years from 1547 to 1549, Camões was in Ceuta, Morocco, winning his spurs as a proper young nobleman but losing an eye, probably in combat with the Moors. In 1549, he was back in Lisbon, where he led a Bohemian existence until 1553, when, in a brawl, he injured his adversary so seriously that he was jailed.

Camões was released only on the condition that he depart for India, which he did on March 7, 1553, after having been enlisted as a soldier for three years. His ship, the splendid *São Bento*, commanded by Fernão Alvares Cabral, capsized at the Cape of Good Hope but arrived at Goa in September, 1554. Despite his constant involvement in numerous military expeditions, Camões wrote regularly, presenting his short play *Filodemo* to the governor of India, Francisco Barreto, on the occasion of his installation in 1555. In 1556, the poet was in Macao, perhaps in the capacity of the governor's "officer for deceased and absentees," perhaps in prison for embezzlement, perhaps composing portions of *The Lusiads*. Internal evidence does reveal that, shipwrecked near the mouth of the Mecon River on his return to Goa, Camões swam to safety with his epic poem, albeit his Chinese sweetheart, Dinamene, drowned. Back in Goa in 1559 or 1560, he was imprisoned for debt.

After sixteen difficult years in the Orient, the weary poet decided in 1568 to return to Portugal with Pero Barreto Rolim, who, for an unknown reason, left Camões, without resources, in Mozambique. There Camões remained until 1569, when the well-known chronicler Diogo do Couto rescued him and took him back to Lisbon on the *Santa Fé* in 1569 or 1570. Camões had all but completed his great epic as his country was about to engage in the bloody Battle of Alcácer-Quibir (1578). The Inquisition's approval to publish *The Lusiads* was signed by King Sebastian on September 24, 1571, and two editions, one authentic, the other plagiarized, appeared in 1572. Pensioned by the King, the greatest of Portuguese poets struggled to survive—but probably without the rumored need to beg—until his death in 1580.

Analysis

During his lifetime, Luís de Camões never published his complete works. Many of his lyric poems were circulated as *separata* from admirer to admirer; many others were printed in the collective *cancioneiros* (songbooks), both during his day and posthumously. Those that the poet had collected in his personal *Parnaso* (Parnassus) were stolen from him. The first complete collection of Camões' lyrics appeared under the editorship of Fernão Rodrigues Lobo Soropita in Lisbon in 1595; the first critical edition, prepared by José Maria Rodriques and Alfonso Lopes Vieira, did not appear until 1932.

Camões' life was a continual *via dolorosa*, filled with love but also with sorrow and disaster. It was a life that taught him the entire gamut of tragic emotions, which his destiny called him to express in his lyrics. With very rare exceptions, Camões' songs, odes, elegies, *redondilhas*, and sonnets are composed of the passion and anguish caused him by his misadventures throughout a considerable part of the then vast Portuguese Empire and transmitted by him directly and sincerely to his sensitive readers of all time. It is not surprising that such an unfortunate lyric poet should so ably and faithfully interpret the human heart. He does not move the reader with sensuous images or brilliant technique alone. Constantly transformed and vibrant in his pain, Camões pours the wealth of his own varied experiences and tormented soul into each well-constructed stanza. Seldom capable of stirring the reader with their cold, almost inert poetics, Sá de Miranda, António Ferreira, and other contemporary poets pale before Camões, whose language is clear, grave, profound, dramatic, moving, and always harmonious.

Many were the women loved by Camões. Chief among them were Isabel Tavares, or "Belisa," the cousin whom he won in his youth in Coimbra; Catarina de Ataíde, or "Natércia," a lady of the court on whose account he was banished; Dinamene, the Chinese slave girl lost at sea; and Barbara, another slave woman about whom little is known. Although he treats other themes, often combining those of Portuguese tradition and those of the Renaissance, Camões' lyrics center on love—as do those of the great Petrarch, whom he emulated, cited, and sometimes paraphrased. Indeed, the Italian poet's influence was keenly felt by virtually all European lyric poets in the fifteenth and sixteenth centuries—in the Platonic transformation of erotic love, beyond the grave as well as in life, and in the quality of his imagery and mellifluous rhythms. Not only does Camões represent the apotheosis of the angelic beloved—framing her in all the attributes of incorruptible grace and revering her with feelings of purest chastity—but also all of nature shares in the poet's joy or anguish. Further, Camões uses metric forms—sonnets, songs, tercets, sestinas, and decasyllables—identical to those of Petrarch. The latter, however, was conscious of having made Laura's name famous through his work, whereas Camões' convulsive passion and pain seem more genuinely felt, more dramatic, and more human.

Platonism transformed Camões' emotion, tenderly sublimating it. Apart from Petrarch, Camões knew something of Plato's idealism, as may be seen in the *redondilhas maiores* beginning "Sobolos os rios que vão" ("Over the Rivers That Flow"). Written in despair when the poet was still in Goa or Mozambique, this long poem quivers with his painful longing for home and inner peace: Suffering the evils of Babylon, Camões weeps and moans nostalgically for the joys of Zion and glimpses the Promised Land. It may be said that Camões was more comprehensive than Petrarch in the matter of form, for he excelled in the traditional *redondilha* of the *cancioneiros* and in the inventions of the Renaissance alike. Doubtless first influenced by the graceful verse of Sá de Miranda, as were all the contemporary practitioners of the Italian style in Portugal, Camões learned as well, not only directly from Petrarch and Jacopo Sannazzaro (not to mention Vergil), but also from the Spanish Italianate poets Juan de Boscán and Garcilaso de la Vega. Ultimately, Camões rivaled Dante and Petrarch in the sonnet and song of Sicilian origin. Moreover, no lyric poet in Portuguese before or since has achieved Camões' transparency, plasticity, harmony, and taste in language, whether in the expression of abstract thought, concrete nature, or personal feeling.

Although it is Camões' lyric poetry that holds the greater interest for today's reader, it is *The Lusiads* that made its author universally famous. The idea of creating an epic poem concerning Portuguese expansion had existed from the fifteenth century, both in and out of Portugal. The Italian Humanist Poliziano, whose work later inspired Camões to a degree, had offered his services to João II to sing of his deeds in Latin verse. In the prologue to the *Cancioneiro general* (1516; general songbook), Garcia de Resende laments that the accomplishments of the Portuguese have not been properly glorified. Despite his repeated aversion to the military life on land and sea, António Ferreira encouraged his colleagues to write such an epic, and he himself attempted the epic style in several odes. This aspiration on the part of the Humanists was related to their ambition to revive the classical genres, including the epic; the voyages of the Portuguese could easily be compared to those of Ulysses and Aeneas.

Camões, too, sought to meet the challenge of the Homeric model that so engaged other Humanists. The maritime setting of the *Odyssey* (c. 800 B.C.) and other ancient poems was indeed appropriate for the central theme of a Portuguese epic, as was the nationalism of the *Aeneid* (29 B.C.-19 B.C.) for the official ideology of the Portuguese expansion, according to which the nation was fulfilling a divine mandate by extending both the Empire and the Faith. In the midst of wars between Protestants and Catholics—not to mention between rulers of the same religion, such as Charles V and Francis I—and above all in the face of the Turkish onslaught in the Mediterranean, the Lusitanians accepted their sacred mission as had the Crusaders before them.

It is unknown precisely when the young Camões set about writing *The

Lusiads, although it was probably composed between 1545 and 1570, but there is evidence in his collection of lyric poetry of early intentions to glorify the great deeds of his people. Camões' title, signifying "the Portuguese" (descended, according to legend, from Luso, a companion of Bacchus), incorporated a term created and used in several works by André de Resende, a scholar famous throughout Europe and a consummate Humanist. *The Lusiads*, first published in 1572, comprises ten cantos of ottava rima; the lengths of the cantos vary, ranging from eighty-seven stanzas (canto 7) to 156 stanzas (canto 10).

The poet begins by explaining the subject, invoking the Muses of the Tagus to grant him the proper sublime tone and flowing, grandiloquent style, and dedicating the poem to King Sebastian. The remainder of the work is divided between two main story lines, the first relating the history of Portugal prior to King Manuel (cantos 3, 4, and 8) and the second, the voyage of Vasco da Gama to India (cantos 1, 2, 5, 7, 9, and 10). Imitating Vergil, who has Aeneas narrate the history of his people and his own nautical adventures to Dido, Camões imagines Vasco and Paul da Gama telling different parts of their story to other characters. With this device, it was possible for Camões to introduce the historical narratives of the Lusos, ancient and modern, derived from the nationalistic works of João de Barros, into the description of the extraordinary voyage of Vasco da Gama, based on several written accounts as well as oral tradition, and at the same time maintain the structural balance of the poem. Thus, the history of past heroes seems related to that of current ones, with no interruption in the logical sequence of the action. The poem concludes with a sorrowful, poignant censure of the nation's decadence and with the poet's firm exhortation to the King to conquer Morocco.

Da Gama's voyage was insufficient to give artistic unity to the poem, however, for a work of art requires unity of action—that is, the convergence of the events in a dramatic situation and its denouement. Camões found no plot in the voyage, only a chronological sequence of events. Moreover, human characters and passions are indispensable in motivating the action of a narrative poem. Camões, however, failed to find these qualities in his historical figures—so much so that his characters more often resemble statues in a procession than human beings. It is perhaps for these reasons that, in keeping with the rules of the genre and, once more, with Vergil as his chief model, Camões invented a mythological plot of impassioned gods. The psychological interest, then, does not reside in the difficulties and complications of da Gama's voyage, but in the rivalry between Venus, patron of the Portuguese, and Bacchus, who is their enemy. This rivalry accounts for the obstacles that the fleet encounters on the eastern coast of Africa (the fictitious storm occurring at the end rather than the beginning of the trip) and for the intrigues that create enemies for the Portuguese. Disguised, Bacchus makes trouble for the protagonists, provokes mistrust of the newcomers, and stirs up the gods of the sea to unleash the storm against them. On the other hand, Venus intercedes on their behalf with Jupiter, who enlists the nymphs to weaken the efforts of the sea gods.

In general, the gods are more human than the humans, and the action depends on and revolves about them. The poet, however, strives for a realistic interpretation, at least within the realm of Christian miracle. The contacts between the gods and humans take place in dreams or through incarnations. Furthermore, the gods could be interpreted as angelic, demonic, or astrological forces—all very acceptable to the poet's contemporaries. At the end of the poem, the mythological fiction dissipates, and on the Isle of Love, the sea nymphs grant the returning sailors every favor, even immortality. Da Gama replaces Adamastor and Neptune as the lover of Thetis, who herself declares the use of mythology allegorical.

As a Humanist, Camões combined a reverence for the classical world with the passionate exploratory spirit characteristic of the Renaissance. Thus, his epic is a compendium of lore—geographical, nautical, and otherwise—much of which he acquired at first hand on his far-flung travels.

Indeed, the vigor of the Renaissance is consistently reflected in Camões' brilliant verse. Certain episodes reveal his genius in the dramatic description of the concrete. His accounts of the Battle of Aljubarroto (canto 4) and of the tourney of the Twelve English Peers (canto 6) are extraordinarily vivid portrayals of war. The poignant assassination of Inês de Castro (canto 3) is a scene worthy of Euripides, while the Old Man of Restelo, weeping and cursing at da Gama's departure (canto 6), and Adamastor, threatening the Lusitanian heroes and sobbing at the disappearance of the beautiful nymph (canto 5), are pathetic figures drawn with the realistic power of Dante. The furious waves and ominous winds (canto 6) and the "bloodsucking" waterspout (canto 5) are remarkable in their exact representational qualtiies, rivaling the naturalism of Albrecht Dürer or Michelangelo. Finally, the Isle of Love (canto 9) is a typical scene of pagan sensuality that depicts most vividly the voluptuousness to which the men of the Renaissance were so susceptible.

At the same time, Camões excelled in making his form follow its function. Many of his concise formulas have become engraved in the collective memory of the Portuguese people. Despite transpositions and other syntactical liberties modeled on Latin and despite an excess of mythological allusions, Camões' phrases are usually clear and precise. The prodigious sense of rhythm characteristic of his verse is sometimes adapted to the movement and sounds of battle, with much onomatopoeia, sometimes to the tedious calm of the doldrums on the equator, sometimes to the aroused ardor of desire, sometimes to the crystalline lyricism of Venus' island paradise. Coupled with a capacity for picturesque imagery, these devices make Camões the foremost exponent of the sensuous Renaissance.

The explicit ideological content of *The Lusiads* is of much less interest today than its artistic realization. The notion of Portugal as a model for the disunited Christian nations of Europe, already expressed by Gil Vicente and others, was perhaps advanced more eloquently and strikingly by Camões. That Portugal represented Western culture as opposed to the barbarism of the rest of the world, however, is not borne out by the bloodthirsty tale of Portuguese history as told by the poet. The noble warriors of *The Lusiads* faithfully reflect the ideology of the class to which Camões himself belonged. His sword in one hand and his pen in the other, he expressed a way of life— aristocratic, warlike, and highly individualistic.

Camões' influence on the Baroque period, which in some respects he fore-shadowed, was substantial. The term "poet" was said to be synonymous with his name. Editions of his lyric poetry began to appear immediately following his death, and new editions of the lyrics and *The Lusiads* were published throughout the seventeenth century—so enthusiastically that many works were incorrectly attributed to Camões. Biographies, commentaries, and criticism soon followed. Camões' first editors, André de Resende and Soropita, were his first disciples in the lyric as well, and because of Camões' prestige at court, Francisco de Portugal, more an imitator than a genuine poet, enjoyed considerable favor. As for narrative or didactic epics in Portuguese, more than thirty were composed between 1572 and 1656 alone, each exploiting different aspects of Camões' work and attempting to resolve the problems of the genre; as the Portuguese ideology of expansion deteriorated, the epic became a historical novel in verse. Although the importance of *The Lusiads* remains great, Camões' influence as a lyric poet has been more fruitful.

Major publications other than poetry
PLAYS: *Enfatriões*, performed 1540, published 1587; *Auto del-Rei Seleuco*, performed 1542, published 1644; *Filodemo*, performed 1555, published 1587.

Bibliography
Bismut, Roger. *La Lyrique de Camões*, 1971.
Bowra, Cecil M. *From Virgil to Milton*, 1945.
Braga, Theophilo. *Camões: Epoca e vida*, 1907.
Cidade, Hernani. *Luís de Camões*, 1952-1956 (3 volumes).
Saraiva, Antonio J. *Luís de Camões*, 1959.

Richard A. Mazzara

GIOSUÈ CARDUCCI

Born: Val di Castello, Italy; July 27, 1835
Died: Bologna, Italy; February 16, 1907

Principal collections

Rime, 1857; *Juvenilia*, 1863; *Giambi*, 1867 (later published as *Giambi ed epodi*, 1882); *Levia gravia*, 1868; *Decennalia*, 1871; *Poesie*, 1871; *Nuove poesie*, 1872; *Odi barbare*, 1877 (*Barbarian Odes*); *Nuove odi barbare*, 1882 (*New Barbarian Odes*); *Ca ira*, 1883; *Rime nouve*, 1887 (*Rime nouve of Carducci*, 1916; *The New Lyrics*, 1942); *Terze odi barbare*, 1889 (*Third Barbarian Odes*); *Rime e ritmi*, 1899 (*The Lyrics and Rhythms*, 1942); *Opere*, 1889-1909; *A Selection of His Poems*, 1913; *A Selection from the Poems*, 1921; *The Barbarian Odes of Giosuè Carducci*, 1939, 1950 (includes *Barbarian Odes*, *New Barbarian Odes*, and *Third Barbarian Odes*); *Opere complete*, 1940 (30 volumes; includes Carducci's nonfiction in addition to his poetry).

Other literary forms

Giosuè Carducci had a long career as a scholarly critic as well as a poet and combined the two activities well. He wrote many volumes of literary history and criticism and edited several editions of Italian authors, including Petrarch and Politian. His two volumes on Giuseppe Parini have been called "the most impressive monument of his indefatigable industry." His best-known essays include "Di alcune condizioni della presente letteratura," "Dello svolgimento della letteratura nazionale," "Del rinnovamento letterario in Italia," and "Confessioni e battaglie." The major fault in his prose, as in his poetry, is a tendency toward bombast, though at his best he was the finest essayist of his time. Often asked to speak on public occasions, he displayed disciplined classical eloquence, speaking on Vergil, Dante, Petrarch, Giovanni Boccaccio, Alessandro Manzoni, and Giacomo Leopardi. His greatest speech, delivered in Bologna on June 4, 1882, was his extemporaneous eulogy for Giuseppe Garibaldi, who had died two days previously: "Per la morte di Giuseppe Garibaldi" (on the death of Giuseppe Garibaldi). All of his nonfiction, as well as his poetry, is collected in his complete works, *Opere complete*.

Achievements

The first Italian to win the Nobel Prize for Literature, which he received in 1906, Carducci synthesized two great literary traditions to create a distinctive, original body of work. Although he came to maturity in the Romantic era, Carducci adhered to and helped maintain the values of the classical tradition; indeed, he became the outstanding exponent of the classicism which lay beneath the surface of Romanticism throughout the 1800's. Unlike his contemporaries, who looked nostalgically back to the Middle Ages, Carducci turned his attention toward ancient Rome and Greece. His fusion of a classical aesthetic with essentially Romantic sentiments exerted a powerful influence, particularly in the last decades of the century. Poets such as Enrico Panzacchi, Lorenzo Stecchetti, Giovanni Marradi, and Severino Ferrari were all part of Carducci's circle. Both for his influence and for his work, Carducci is recognized as the major Italian poet of the late 1800's.

Biography

Giosuè Carducci was born to Dr. Michele Carducci and Ildegonda Celli in Val di Castello, a small town near Viareggio, in Tuscany. Carducci's father was greatly affected by the patriotism which would lead to the Risorgimento. An active Carbonaro (a member of a secret society seeking the unification of Italy), he was confined for a year in Volterra because of his participation in the Revolution of 1831. When Carducci was three, his family moved to Bolgheri, in the wild and desolate Maremma region south of Pisa. Maremma, with its Etruscan tombs, became the emotional landscape of Carducci's later poetry, appearing in such poems as "Idillio maremmano" ("Maremma Idyll") and "Traversando la Maremma Toscano" ("Crossing the Tuscan Maremma"). Carducci's mother reared him on the tragedies of Vittorio Alfieri, a writer in the French neoclassical style who had sought to revive the national spirit of Italy. For his part, Carducci's father attempted to impart to his son his own fervent enthusiasm for the writings of Manzoni, but Carducci, always an independent thinker, never acquired a taste for Manzoni. The boy was also taught Latin by his father and delighted in the works of Vergil and other ancient authors. He avidly read Roman history and anything dealing with the French Revolution. His first verse, satirical in nature, was written in 1846.

In 1848, the Carduccis were obliged to move when the attempt at independence failed. The threat of violence became too great for Carducci's father, and the family relocated first to Laiatico, then to Florence. Carducci went to religious schools until 1852, and was influenced by his rhetoric teacher, Father Geremia Barsottini, who had translated into prose all the odes of Horace. The boy became further impassioned in the cause of Italian reunification and discovered the works of Ugo Foscolo and Giuseppe Mazzini. After completing his education, Carducci followed his wandering father to Celle on Mount Amiata, but soon after won a scholarship to the Normal School of Pisa. In 1855, he published his first book, *L'arpa del populo*, an anthology, and a year later he received his doctor's degree and a certification for teaching. He took a position as a rhetoric teacher in a secondary school at the *ginnasio* in San Miniato al Tedesco.

With several friends, among them Giuseppe Chiarini, Carducci founded a literary society, Amici Pedanti, a group that was essentially anti-Romantic and anti-Catholic. They believed that Italy's only hope for the future was in the revival of the classical, pagan spirit of the ancient world, which was emphasized as still existing in the Italian land and blood. Such opinions naturally provoked violent objections, both from Romantics and from those who favored the status quo. Carducci freely and ferociously responded in prose to the attacks many times. His first collection of poetry, *Rime*, appeared in July, 1857.

Although Carducci won a competition for the Chair of Greek in a secondary school in Arezzo, the granducal government did not approve his appointment, so, in 1857, he returned to Florence and eked out a living by giving private lessons. In November, his depression became worse when his brother Dante killed himself for unknown reasons. A year later, Carducci's father died, and Carducci became the head of his impoverished family. In 1858, he moved his mother and brother Walfredo into a very poor house in Florence, continuing his private lessons and editing the texts of the Bibliotechina Diamante of publisher Gaspare Barbèra. Together with Barbèra, he founded a short-lived periodical, *Il poliziano*. Despite his financial situation, Carducci married Elvira Menicucci in March, 1859.

With the union of Tuscany and Italy, Carducci's fortunes turned for the better. First, he was offered the Chair of Greek in the secondary school of Pistoia, where he remained for nearly a year; then, the Minister of Education, Terenzio Mamiani, appointed him to the Chair of Italian Eloquence at the University of Bologna. Carducci was somewhat ambivalent toward his professorial role and its traditional philological orientation and fretted about its effect on his poetry, but the position allowed him to deepen his acquaintance with the classics and with the literature of other nations. His political views also changed. Under Victor Emmanuel II, Carducci had been an idealistic monarchist in support of the union of Italy, but after Garibaldi was wounded and captured by government troops at Aspromonte in 1862, Carducci allied himself with the democratic republicans and became more pronouncedly Jacobin and anti-Catholic, venting his intense feelings in aggressive poetry.

Carducci published his *Giambi* (iambics; later *Giambi ed epodi*), a collection of polemical poems, under the pseudonym "Enotrio Romano"; the poems reveal Carducci's affinities with Victor Hugo and Heinrich Heine. "Inno a Satana" ("Hymn to Satan") was in a similar vein and became one of his most famous poems, though his work suffered in quality as he became more vituperative. By 1872, however, he had begun to control his polemical instincts, and some of his finest poems, later collected in *The New Lyrics*, were written in the 1870's. *Barbarian Odes*, begun in 1873, became his most influential work.

Indeed, following the publication of the collection *Barbarian Odes*, Carducci became an object of adulation for younger poets throughout Italy. Periodicals such as *Fanfulla della Domenica*, *Cronaca bizantina*, and *Domenica letteraria* helped spread his fame. *New Barbarian Odes* solidified his reputation, and he assumed the role of national poet.

In part, Carducci's position as a leader of young Italian poets was the result of the efforts of Angelo Sommaruga, who had founded *Cronaca bizantina* to encourage native Italian writing and gathered newcomers such as Marradi, Matilde Serao, Edoardo Scarfoglio, Guido Magnoni, and Gabriele D'Annunzio for its pages. Sommaruga sought out Carducci to give credibility to the group, and Sommaruga's encouragement spurred Carducci to intense activity in verse and prose. During this period, Carducci's political and philosophical views shifted; he resigned himself to the monarchy and acquired a more religious attitude, with some appreciation of the Church's mission, though he remained fundamentally anticlerical.

The last two decades of Carducci's life were filled with misery. In 1885, he became ill. Five years later he was made a senator, but in 1899, a stroke paralyzed his hand and nearly deprived him of speech. He continued working, despite the setbacks, publishing his last volume of poetry in 1899 and collecting his works from 1850 to 1900. In 1904, he resigned from teaching. He received the Nobel Prize for Literature the year before he died.

Analysis

When granting Giosuè Carducci the 1906 Nobel Prize, the Swedish Academy stated that the award was given "not only in consideration of his deep learning and critical research, but above all as a tribute to the creative energy, freshness of style, and lyrical force which characterize his poetic masterpieces." Carducci's works are exceptional in their synthesis of literary qualities often seen as opposites. Though his life coincided with the height of Romanticism in Italy, he took the classical mode as his paradigm of artistic creation. This might have made him a curious anachronism, but his passion and his agility with classical form kept his works free of the servility which mars much neoclassical poetry. Carducci had too great a heart to let formal considerations neuter him, and too much poetic skill not to exploit the opportunities of form.

Indeed, Carducci's great learning gave him the ability to scrutinize his own work, to evaluate and revise it with a living sense of literary history. Full of the passions of the Risorgimento and the nationalism of the new Italian state, he nevertheless viewed his work as part of a long historical tradition; whatever the Romans had been in essence was still in the Italian landscape, soil, and blood. Though Italy had drifted from the unity and glory of its past, it was always possible to restore those qualities, which were not dead but merely submerged. Classicism thus became a way of restoring to the Italian nation and people their rightful identity and heritage. Carducci himself wrote:

> Great poetry aspires ceaselessly to the past and proceeds from the past. The dead are infinitely more numerous than the living, and the spaces of time under the Triumph of Death are incomparably more immense and more tranquil than the brief moment agitated by the phenomenon of life.

Carducci collected his earliest poetry (that written between 1850 and 1860, including that published in *Rime*) in *Juvenilia*. In these early poems, the young Carducci was searching for his voice, but he had already adopted many of the values which inform his mature work. *Juvenilia* reveals a familiarity with Greek and Latin models as well as with Italian poetry; the values that antedate Romanticism are stressed, along with a natural humanism free of the sentimentality and egotistic aberrations of Romanticism. *Juvenilia* is highly patriotic in tone and often violently anti-Catholic because of the Church's opposition to the reunification of Italy. Carducci revives the memory of ancient poetry and pagan strength by saluting the ancient gods; he praises ancient Greece, "Mother Rome," and "free human genius." He reminds Italy of the greatness of Rome and the heroic example of the French Revolution. He salutes the heroes of Italian unity, such as Garibaldi, Mazzini, and Victor Emmanuel II, the latter in a joyous celebration of the imminent war with Austria in 1859. Many of the poems are violently emotional: Carducci attacks those whom he perceives as the enemies of Italy and plunges into depression over the contemporary state of the country and its people.

One of Carducci's most famous and controversial poems was "Hymn to Satan." Later in his life, the poet would disavow the poem and call it "vulgar sing-song," but he stood defiantly behind it when it was published, astounding the public and causing great outrage at the University of Bologna and elsewhere. The critic Querico Filopanti, for example, asserted that it was not a poem at all, but an intellectual orgy. In it, Carducci gives full vent to his anticlerical feelings, seeking to shock Italians out of their spiritual apathy. Satan becomes the symbol of nature and reason: He is Lucifer, carrier of light, enemy of asceticism and of a Church which denies the natural rights of man. Free thought, progress, and physical vitality are Satan's promises. Curiously, the poem praises Girolamo Savonarola for his defiance, ignoring the religious reformer's own asceticism. Carducci's Satan has been likened to Charles Baudelaire's in *Les Fleurs du mal* (1857, 1861, 1868; *Flowers of Evil*, 1909), but a more fruitful comparison can be drawn with the English Romantics' interpretation of John Milton's Satan in *Paradise Lost* (1667) as a Romantic hero. Carducci's Satan is clearly more Promethean than Satanic.

Levia gravia (light and heavy) has a tone of somberness and bitter disappointment, reflecting the events of the 1860's. During this time, the conquest of Rome was delayed, the disaster at Aspromonte occurred, and Carducci himself was drifting from his belief in the monarchy. The largely political inspiration and the tendentiousness which characterize *Levia gravia* also mar *Giambi ed epodi*, in which Carducci's combative nature overcomes his sense of poetry. "Canto dell'amore" ("Song of Love"), the last poem in *Giambi ed epodi*, provides a departure from this combativeness and reveals a depth greater than that of many of his earlier works. Most of this collection simply attacks and satirizes Pope Pius IX and the problems of the newly formed

Italian government. "Song of Love, " however, expresses a simple, robust view of life. Looking from Perugia, where the fortress of Paolina (a symbol of tyranny razed by the people in 1860) once stood, the poet is filled with the beauty of spring and lifted above the level of ordinary human struggle. The song of love fills him. The ancient Etruscans and Romans and foreign invaders of the Umbrian plain are evoked as symbolic of the ongoing cycles of nature. The poet even invites his enemy the Pope to drink a glass of wine to liberty with him. He hears a chant rising from the hills, the voice of people of the past saying, "Too much we hated, suffering. So love!/ Holy and fair the world shall be always."

Some critics, such as Eugenio Donadoni, remark on the gracefulness of images and rhythms in *Levia gravia* and date Carducci's beginnings as a major poet from this volume. Others, however, would delay his "arrival" as a major poet to the more mature *Nuove poesie*, four years later. One notable poem from the latter is "I poeti di parte bianca" ("Poets of the White Faction"), which makes reference to the factions in Dante's Florence and evokes that moment in history as well as the poetry of the fourteenth century. "Francesco Petrarca" celebrates the great sonneteer and speaks of raising an altar to him in the deep, green woods, combining Carducci's sense of landscape with his love for the tradition of Italian poetry.

At the center of Carducci's oeuvre is the highly influential and original sequence comprising *Barbarian Odes*, *New Barbarian Odes*, and *Third Barbarian Odes*. "I hate the outworn meters," Carducci proclaimed, and he began to adapt such classical forms as the Alcaic, the Asclepiad, and the Sapphic, all commonly used by Horace.

Carducci's adaptations of classical meters are extraordinarily successful; the demanding requirements of the ancient forms are satisfied gracefully and unobtrusively. When, late in life, he returned to modern forms, the musicality and facility of his verse were markedly enhanced.

Among the most successful poems of the *Barbarian Odes* is the pensive love poem "Alla stazione in una mattinata d'autunno" ("To the Station on an Autumn Morning"), in which Carducci evokes the melancholy feeling of the autumn season. "Miramar," the title of which is derived from the name of the castle near Trieste from which Maximilian began his voyage to Mexico, also conveys a tragic, pensive mood, using vivid natural imagery of the Adriatic Sea in the context of the story of the ill-fated Emperor Maximilian of Mexico. "Alla fonti del Clitunno" ("At the Sources of the Clitumnus"), a protest against Christianity, lacks the sharp edge of Carducci's earlier poems on the same topic. The poet celebrates the peasants who live along the quiet river, condemns the fanatic humility of medieval life, and hails the fecund vitality of Italy: Italy, mother of crops, laws, arts, and industry. "Presso l'urna di P. B. Shelley" ("Near the Urn of P. B. Shelley") is one of Carducci's many poems making reference to great persons, living or dead. Written in elegiac distichs (a dactylic hexameter followed by a pentameter), the poem portrays a faraway island where mythical and literary figures meet. Siegfried and Achilles walk along the sea; Roland and Hector sit together under a tree; Lear tells his story to Oedipus. Ophelia and Iphigenia, Cordelia and Antigone, Durendala and Andromache, Helen and Iseult, Lady Macbeth and Clytemnestra are paired. Shelley, the only modern poet present, has been brought to 'the island by Sophocles. The narrator speaks: "The present hour is in vain; it but strikes and flees;/ only in the past is beauty, only in death is truth." Like many classicists, Carducci believed that it is possible to cheat death only by the immortality of art.

In *The Lyrics and Rhythms*, his final book of poetry, Carducci abandoned the classical meters of *Barbarian Odes* and returned to modern forms. Many of the poems in this volume were composed in the Alps and have a clear, wide-ranging vision, as if written in imitation of the clear, broad expanses visible from the mountains. Standing on the "mount of centuries," the poet looks deeply into the past in order to see the future. The landscape is rich with associations from his memory, from history, from ancient myth and legend. The tone of the collection is generally solemn, as if Carducci, who had been obsessed with death since his brother's suicide and the death of his infant son, were contemplating his own end. In the gravity of its tone and the sweep of its vision, this last book of poems offers a fitting valediction.

Major publications other than poetry

NONFICTION: *Opere*, 1889-1909 (includes prose and poetry); *Opere complete*, 1940 (30 volumes; includes all of his prose and poetry).
ANTHOLOGY: *L'arpa del populo*, 1855.

Bibliography

Bailey, J. C. *Carducci*, 1926.
Busetto, N. *Giosuè Carducci: L'uomo, il poeta, il critico, e il prosatore*, 1958.
Chiarini, Giuseppe. *Memorie della vita di Giosuè Carducci*, 1903.
Croce, Benedetto. *Giosuè Carducci*, 1920.
Donadoni, Eugenio. *A History of Italian Literature*, 1969.
Galletti, A. *L'opera di Giosuè Carducci*, 1929.
Jeanroy, A. *Giosuè Carducci: L'homme et le poète*, 1911.
Saponaro, M. *Carducci*, 1940.
Scalia, E. *Carducci: His Critics and Translators in England and America*, 1937.
Wilkins, Ernest Hatch. *A History of Italian Literature*, 1954.
Williams, Oro. *Giosuè Carducci*, 1914.

J. Madison Davis

ROSALÍA DE CASTRO

Born: Santiago de Compostela, Spain; February 24, 1837
Died: Padrón, Spain; July 15, 1885

Principal collections

La flor, 1857; *A mi madre*, 1863; *Cantares gallegos*, 1863; *Follas novas*, 1880; *En las orillas del Sar*, 1884 (*Beside the River Sar*, 1937); *Poems of Rosalía de Castro*, 1964; *Obras completas de Rosalía de Castro*, 1966.

Other literary forms

Rosalía de Castro was a novelist as well as a poet. Her five novels—*La hija del mar* (1859; the daughter of the sea), *Flavio* (1861), *Ruinas* (1866; ruins); *El caballero de las botas azules* (1867; the knight with the blue boots); and *El primer loco* (1881; the first madman)—span the transition from Romanticism to realism. Although Rosalía herself put considerable stock in her novels, she is remembered only for her poetry.

Achievements

Rosalía de Castro has been called Spain's foremost woman poet; Gerald Brenan has gone further, asserting that if she had written more in Spanish than in her native Galician dialect, she would be recognized as the greatest woman poet of modern times. Her unabashedly heartthrobbing lyrics are saved from mawkishness by her disciplined style. Rosalía's poetry, along with that of Gustavo Adolfo Bécquer, is the most representative of Spanish poetry at the time of its transition from Romanticism to the modern lyric. Some critics believe that she interacted with Bécquer—that in fact she lent him in 1857 a copy of Gérard de Nerval's translation of Heinrich Heine's *Tragödien, nebst einem lyrischen Intermezzo* (1823), a book said to have influenced Bécquer. It was not until the second decade of the twentieth century, when Azorín (José Martínez Ruiz) and Miguel de Unamuno y Jugo recommended her to the public, that her reputation as a poet became assured. Later, even poet Luis Cernuda, who found her work uneven and sentimental, recognized the rare timelessness of her observations. Antonio Machado borrowed images from her poetry, Juan Ramón Jiménez referred to her as "our Rosalía," and Gerardo Diego used her name as a metaphor in his own poetry. Her Galician poetry inspired Federico García Lorca to write his own "poemas gallegos," including a "Canzón de cuna pra Rosalía Castro, morta" ("Lullaby for the Late Rosalía de Castro").

With her contemporaries Manuel Curros Enríquez (who wrote an elegy for her) and Eduardo Pondal, Rosalía made up a triad of Galician poets who effected a renaissance of their provincial literature. Using the folk songs of Galicia as her models, she bonded modern Spanish poetry to oral forms that would have otherwise been lost. She led the way for subsequent poets to utilize folk tradition, and her work tolled the death knell for urban Romanticism. Modernist poets availed themselves of the revolutionary meters used by Rosalía (her enneasyllabic verse in *La flor*—the flower—predates the so-called innovations of Rubén Darío), and her use of free verse heralded the boldness of contemporary poetry.

To a remarkable extent, Rosalía's Galician and Spanish poetry has been accepted into English-language anthologies of world verse, especially in those of women's poetry (such as *The Penguin Book of Women Poets*, 1979, and *A Book of Women Poets: From Antiquity to Now*, 1981).

Biography

Rosalía de Castro was born in Santiago de Compostela in 1837, the illegitimate child of María Teresa de la Cruz de Castro y Abadía. Her mother, who came from a once-wealthy family, was thirty-three when Rosalía was born; her father, Jose Martínez Viojo, was thirty-nine and a priest. Although her father could not recognize Rosalía as his daughter, he may have taken some interest in her welfare. Rosalía was brought up by Francisca Martínez, who, despite her surname, does not appear to have been the priest's sister. By 1853, Rosalía was living with her real mother, and there developed between them a deep bond. In Rosalía's eyes, her mother sanctified whatever sin she may have committed by reaffirming her obligation to her daughter in defiance of a hypocritical society.

A precocious child, Rosalía was writing verses by the age of eleven, and by sixteen she could play the guitar and the piano, had developed a fine contralto voice, and could draw well and read French. She read the foreign classics in translation and was fond of Lord Byron, Heinrich Heine, Edgar Allan Poe, and E. T. A. Hoffmann. Judging from the spelling errors in handwritten manuscripts of her poetry, however, her formal education may not have been extensive.

As a teenager, Rosalía was taken from Padron to Santiago, where she attended school and where she participated in the city's cultural life. At a young people's cultural society, she met Aurelio Aguirre, one of the most representative figures of the Romantic movement in Galicia, a man who was later to be the model of Flavio in her novel of the same name, and who dedicated to her a work called "Improvisation"—apparently an attempt to console her for the discrepancy between her enchanting poetry and her less than enchanting physical appearance. Perhaps it is too facile to attribute the characteristic wistfulness of her poetry to a failed love affair, but it has been suggested that the lost love recalled in her poems and her fiction was Aurelio Aguirre. Among the poems not included in her own collections but included in *Obras completas de Rosalía de Castro* is an elegy for Aguirre.

In 1856, Rosalía went to Madrid, where she stayed at the home of a relative.

It is generally said that she went "on family business," but it is possible she left home with the idea of becoming an actress in Madrid. Exposed to the cultural life of the Spanish capital, she devoted herself to writing and was able to meet other contemporary writers. In 1857, her first book of poetry *La flor* appeared and was favorably reviewed by Manuel Murguía in *La Iberia*. According to Murguía, he was not acquainted with the young authoress, but this is rather unlikely, not only because some of his comments presuppose a direct knowledge of Rosalía's personality, but also because he, too, had recently come from Galicia and, in fact, was Aguirre's best friend. Rosalía and Murguía were married in Madrid on October 10, 1858. Murguía, like Aguirre a Galician of Basque descent, was a journalist and historian destined to be honored in Galicia for his role in promoting regionalist literature. The couple had seven children. Their first child, a daughter, was born in 1859; their second child, also a daughter, was not born until ten years later. One of the twins Rosalía bore in 1871, Ovidio, was an accomplished painter of Galician landscapes but died young. Her youngest son died in his second year as the result of a fall, and her youngest daugher was stillborn in 1877.

In 1862, Rosalía's beloved mother died, and Rosalía honored her with a privately printed collection of poems, *A mi madre* (to my mother) of limited literary value but elegiac and emotional.

It remains unclear what kind of a marriage Rosalía had with Murguía. Gerald Brenan believes that Murguía, envious of his wife's talents, mistreated her; it is certain that Murguía destroyed his wife's correspondence after her death. Marina Mayoral, on the other hand, prefers to see in Murguía—who survived his wife by thirty-eight years and wrote lovingly and abundantly about her—one of the few mainstays of Rosalía's sad life. Despite the fulfillment of children and the security of family life, she was frequently bored, and in both her poetry and her fiction, she mourned lost happiness.

It is important, however, not to exaggerate the pathetic nature of Rosalía's life. She loved the arts and took great pleasure from her endeavors in the fields of music, drawing, and acting. She was a great success when she acted in Antonio Gil y Zárate's play *Rosamunda* (1839), and for the greater part of her life she enjoyed exchanging ideas with her friends. Her daughter Gala, who lived until 1964, was especially concerned that her mother not be remembered as morose. As Victoriano García Martí points out, people who are authentically sorrowful often develop a profound love of mankind and achieve a different kind of contentment. This was especially true of Rosalía, and after her death a legend grew concerning her generosity to others, endowing her with a kind of saintliness.

Between 1859 and 1870, the couple lived in Madrid and Simancas, where Murguía had a position as a government historian, and they traveled extensively throughout Spain. To Rosalía, any terrain that was not green, damp, and lush like her native Galicia was disappointing; thus, she disliked most of the rest of Spain. She became so consumed with nostalgia for her native land that she began her *Cantares gallegos* (Galician songs), written in Galician but given a Spanish title. In the 1870's, Murguía held positions in Galicia, and Rosalía spent much of her time at Padron, which she considered home. Having suffered from vague ill-health all of her life, she withdrew completely from society in her last decade; she died of uterine cancer in 1885. In the moments before her death, she received the Sacraments, recited her favorite prayers, and begged her children to destroy her unpublished manuscripts. With her last breath, she asked that the window be opened, for she wished to see the ocean—which in fact was not visible from her home.

Rosalía was buried near her mother in the peaceful cemetery of Adina in Padron, a place whose enchantment she had evoked in *Follas novas* (new leaves). On the very day of her death, accolades began to arrive, and as a result of the homage paid her in death, her remains were moved in 1891 to a marble tomb in the Convent of Santo Domingo de Bonaval in Santiago. In 1917, her compatriots, together with an organization of Galician emigrants in America, organized a campaign to raise a statue to their poet in the Paseo de la Herradura in Santiago, looking toward Padron. According to biographer Kathleen Kulp-Hill, this statue is faithful to portraits and descriptions of Rosalía. The figure is seated in a calm, pensive attitude, projecting an aura of strength and warmth.

Analysis

As Frédéric Mistral is to Provence and Joan Maragall to Catalonia, Rosalía de Castro is to Galicia, the northwest corner of the Iberian peninsula, linked politically with Spain but tied ethnically, linguistically, and temperamentally with Portugal. When Rosalía was nine years old, there was an unsuccessful insurrection in Galicia against the Spanish government. The unpleasant memory of the savage reprisals undertaken by the government may help explain her strong hostility toward Castile and Castilians, as in the lines, "May God grant, Castilians,/ Castilians whom I abhor,/ that rather the Galicians should die,/ than to go to you for bread."

Santiago de Compostela, Rosalía's birthplace, possesses the bones of Saint James the Apostle, for which reason Galicia became in the Middle Ages the third most holy shrine in Christendom (after Jerusalem and Rome). The steady stream of pilgrims traveling to Galicia from all parts of Europe made Santiago a medieval cultural center, and in the thirteenth century, Galician became the language of lyrical poetry throughout the Iberian peninsula. The Galician *jograles* (minstrels) sang characteristically of melancholy (designated in Spanish by its Galician and Portuguese name, *saudades*), as in, for example, their *cantigas de amigo*, the songs of women whose lovers were absent, either away at sea or fighting the Moors in Portugal. After the thirteenth century, however, there was an eclipse of Galician poetry, and it was not until the nineteenth century that an interest in the poetic potential of the Galician language was reawakened.

The poetry of Rosalía de Castro flows from line to line in a musical sequence and does not, as Gerald Brenan observes, condense well into a single epithet or phrase. She was not fond of metaphors, but rather relied heavily on repetition—in such lines as ("Breezes breezes, little breezes/ breezes of the land I come from")—and contrast—as in "To them those frosts/ are the promise of early flowers;/ To me they are silent workers/ weaving my winding sheet." In her earlier poems, she sometimes used the *leixa-pren*, a special feature of the medieval *cantigas de amigo*, whereby each new stanza begins with an echo from the last line of the previous stanza. Her diction is almost colloquial, her syntax uninverted (except in her earliest poetry and in some of her later poetry), and her adjectives are always the least ornamental possible. There abound words for the lushness of Galicia, names of animals and birds, and especially of trees (such as the oaks sacred to the ancient Celts of Galicia; giant chestnuts; and the cedars of "our own" Lebanon). In her somber moods, she draws repeatedly on Spanish adjectives such as *torvo* (grim), *amargo* (bitter), and *triste* (sad), and uses verbs such as *anonadar*, (to destroy), *agostar* (to wither up as in August), *hostigar* (to scourge), while she uses words such as *guarida* (liar), *nido* (nest), and *egida* (aegis) to express the security and coziness of home in Galicia. Galician, more than Spanish, is a nasal language (for example, Galician *min*, "my," as opposed to Spanish *mí*) and Rosalía uses its humming nasals as a tool to craft more sharply the gloom she suffers on Earth, as in the line "Pra min i-en min mesma moras" (for me and in myself you live), from "Cando penso que to fuche" (when I think that you have gone), in *Follas novas*.

One remarkable poem that reveals Rosalía's attitude toward sorrow is "Una-ha vez tiven un cravo" ("I Used to Have a Nail") in *Follas novas*. This painful nail, whether made of gold, iron, or love, leads the poet, weeping like Mary Magdalen, to entreat God to effect a miracle for its removal. When at last she gathers the courage to pluck it out, the void it leaves is something like a longing for the old pain. Some critics have speculated that without an abundant supply of sorrow for her to sublimate into poetry, Rosalía felt lost. This contradictory hunger for suffering cannot be reduced to the level of a personal neurosis, for it reflects the ideals of traditional Christianity. Rosalía believed that thistles, though harsh to the flesh, mark the road to heaven, and in "Yo en mi lecho de abrojos" ("I on My Bed of Thistles," from *Beside the River Sar*), avowedly preferred her destiny to a "bed of roses and feathers," which have been known to "envenom and corrupt."

Rosalía was conventionally religious; she needed God and sought Him everywhere, and she fought herself for her faith, as Unamuno did. There are biblical references in her poetry, as well as her marginally Christian *sombras* (shades), the souls of persons no longer living whom Rosalía "invokes" from time to time and who respond by intervening in the lives of the living. She also draws on Galician lore concerning the supernatural world. Witches (*meigas, lurpias*), warlocks, (*meigos*), and elves (*trasgos*) inhabit her forests, and the safety of the unwary nocturnal traveler may be jeopardized by the Host of Souls in Torment. In "Dios bendiga todo, nena" ("God Blesses Everything, Child," from *Cantares gallegos*, an old woman warns a young girl of the dangers of the world, whereupon the girl declares her intention never to leave her village without scapularies, holy medals, and amulets to protect her from witches. The fine line between religion and superstition is typified in "Soberba" ("Foolish Pride") in *Follas novas*, where a family frightened by a storm tries to placate God with candles, olive leaves, and prayers, and by scouring from their personal slates offenses that might have incurred His wrath. Nor is the imagery of the supernatural always to be taken literally. In an aubade, Rosalía has the heroine address her lover affectionately as "warlock" while he prepares to leave her bed, and elsewhere employs the same word to create a metaphor for sorrow: "N' hay peor meiga que un-ha gran pena" (there is no worse demon than a great sorrow).

Rosalía's first important book of poems was *Cantares gallegos*. In the prologue to this volume, she acknowledges the inspiration of *El libro de los cantares* by Antonio de Trueba, published the previous year, and apologizes for her shortcomings as a poet, claiming that her only schooling was that of "our poor country folk." The poems are dedicated to Fernan Caballero (Cecilia Böhl de Faber), the pioneer of the realistic novel in Spain, who won Rosalía's appreciation with her unprejudiced portrayal of Galicians. Working without a grammar, Rosalía apologizes for her Galician; indeed, it is not a pure dialect unaffected by Castilian influence, and lexical and orthographic inconsistencies abound. She attempted to imitate modern Portuguese in her use of diacritical marks, contractions, and elisions, and included a short glossary of Galician words for the sake of her Castilian readers.

Rosalía's usual procedure was to begin her poems with a popular couplet and then to elaborate it into a ballad. Her masterpiece is perhaps "Airiños, airiños, aires" ("Breezes, Breezes, Little Breezes") in which she portrays the nostalgia of a Galician emigrant, playing upon the dual meaning of *airiños* as "little breezes" and "little songs." Everywhere this unfortunate emigrant turns in the strange country of her destination, people peer curiously at her, and she longs for the sweet breezes of home, those "quitadoiriños de penas" (takers-away of sorrow) that enchant the woods and caress the land. Similarly as Galician poetry inspired the Castilian lyric of the fifteenth and sixteenth centuries, this poem influenced the revival of Spanish poetry that began thirty years after Rosalía's death. The *Romancero gitano* (1928; *Gypsy Ballads*, 1951, 1953) of Federico García Lorca, for example, with its themes and repetitions derived from folk tradition, owes much to this poem.

In "Pasa rio, pasa rio" ("Pass by, River, Pass By"), a disconsolate lover weeps tears into the ocean in hopes that they may reach her beloved in Brazil, where he has had to emigrate. The plight of the Galician emigrant forced to leave his homeland because of economic necessity troubled Rosalía deeply. There are many poems of praise for Galicia, such as "Cómo chove mihudiño" ("How the Rain Is Falling Lightly"), in which she describes Padrón, lulled by the river where the trees are shady, and reminisces about the great house owned by her humanitarian grandfather. She dares to ask the Sun of Italy if it has seen "more green, more roses,/ bluer sky or softer colors/ where foam stripes your gulfs with whiteness"; and is reminded by a wandering cloud of the sad shade of her mother wandering lonely in the spheres before she goes to Glory.

The poems of *Follas novas* are meant to be read and reflected upon, as opposed to the folk poems of *Cantares gallegos* with their marked oral quality. The 139 poems of *Follas novas* are more subjective and personal and bleaker than those of the ealier book, which radiate innocence and hope; they are also more innovative in form: Rosalía employed varying line lengths with metrical combinations then regarded as inappropriate for Spanish verse, such as combinations of eight with ten or eleven syllables or eight with fourteen. Dedicated to the Society for the Welfare of Galicians in Havana, the book was published simultaneously in Havana and Madrid in 1880. In her prologue, Rosalía expresses her concern for the suffering of Galicians in distant lands, and she also asserts her artistic independence as a woman. Certainly the successive deaths of her two youngest children within three months of each other in 1876-1877 did much to intensify her tragic sense of life, but many of the poems in this collection were written as long as ten years before the publication date.

Here, Rosalía's poetry is no longer concerned with aubades but rather with the departures of lovers and their separation. Love is no longer hopeful but rather furtive and anxious. In "¿Que lle digo?" ("What Should I Tell Her?") the emigrant may be plagued by *saudades* for his homeland, but may wax cynical about love as well: "Antona is there, but I have Rosa here." The landscape of Galicia is always in the background, but is no longer decorative and is now interwoven with more complex emotions. Death is seen as a cure for the disease of life, and the poet asks God why suicide must be deemed a crime.

Although she occasionally dedicated her poems to worthy persons (such as her husband and Ventura Ruíz de Aguilera), Rosalía did not often exalt either historical figures or living persons in her poetry. One notable exception, written in classical form, is her elegy on the tomb of Sir John Moore, the affable British general who led a retreat to Corunna that ended in the British victory over the Napoleonic forces there in 1809, but which cost Moore his life. *Follas novas* also includes a translation into Galician of the poem "Armonias d'a tarde" (harmonies of the afternoon), by Ventura Ruíz de

Aguilera, a contemporary poet who drew on the folk motifs of the Salamanca area.

As a result of complaints made by her Galician readers that some of her material was scandalous, Rosalía vowed never again to write in Galician, and it is to this decision and the Spanish poems of her last collection, *Beside the River Sar*, that she owes her prominence in Spanish literature. Not all the critics, however, proclaim the superiority of these poems. Gerald Brenan, who prefers the softer, more tender tone of her Galician verse, finds the aloofness of her Castilian poems chilling. Many of the poems collected in *Beside the River Sar* were written between 1878 and 1884 and were published in periodicals, some as distant as *La nación española* of Buenos Aires. These late poems reflect a greater concern with ideas; they are characterized by unusual combinations of lines and broken rhythms, with lines of as many as sixteen or eighteen syllables, and by a syntactical complexity not previously seen in Rosalía's work.

In *Beside the River Sar*, Galicia is no longer a focal point, assuming instead the role of a backdrop, and the folk element is even less in evidence. Rosalía continues to excel in nature poetry, displaying in "Los robles" ("The Oaks") a distinctly modern concern for ecology when she protests the wasteful destruction of trees in Galicia with an almost druidical reverence for arboreal vitality. The river Sar of the title, the beloved river of her homeland, is a symbol for the flowing of life toward its unknown and unknowable destination.

In what is possibly her most frequently anthologized poem, "Dicen que no hablan las plantas" ("They Say That Plants Do Not Speak"), Rosalía asserts the importance that natural phenomena such as plants, brooks, and birds have for her. Although it seems that these natural phenomena view her as a "madwoman" because of her outlandish dreams, she exhorts them not to poke fun at her, because without those dreams, she would lack the wherewithal to admire the beauty that they themselves so generously display.

In her valorization of dreams (*sueños* or *ensueños*) and her refusal to accept the pathetic constraints by which man is necessarily bound, Rosalía prefigures the concerns of the *generación del 98*, of poets such as Unamuno, Antonio Machado, and Azorín. Nevertheless, she must acknowledge that dreams can lead to folly, as they do in the poignant "La canción que oyó en sueños el viejo" ("The Song Which the Old Man Heard in His Dreams"), in which an old man, designated crazy in the poem, feels his blood pump and surge as his youthful passions return when in truth he should be reckoning with "infallible death" and "implacable old age."

In *Beside the River Sar*, the winter, symbolic of despair and the end of life in Rosalía's earlier work, is friendly, a herald, in fact, of spring, and is "a thousand times welcome." Even the desert of Castile, anathema in her earlier poetry and so drastically opposed to the lushness of Galicia, assumes a positive guise, coming to represent the realm beyond carnal suffering, lit by "another light more vivid than that of the golden sun."

One of the most interesting poems in the collection is the questioning and subsequently epiphanic "Santa Escolástica" ("Saint Scholastica"). In Santiago on a drizzly April day, the poet allows herself to absorb the dismal atmosphere. "Cemetery of the living," she exclaims, as she contrasts the gloom she sees around her with the city's medieval glory. This leads to her own rephrasing of that tortured question, "Why, since there is God, does Hell prevail?" She enters the Convent of San Martín Pinario in search of comfort. Her female soul begins to feel the sacred majesty of the temple as vividly as it has felt the satisfactions of motherhood. Suddenly, the sun strikes the statue of Saint Scholastica and brings into sharper focus the saint's ecstasy, which in turn produces an ecstasy in Rosalía, who exclaims exultantly, "There is art! There is poetry! . . . There must be a heaven,/ for there is God."

Kathleen Kulp-Hill contrasts this joyous poem from *Beside the River Sar* with a poem from *Follas novas* having the same setting, "N'a catedral" ("In the Cathedral"). In the latter, although the sun shines briefly into the dimly illuminated room, the shadows return, and the poet withdraws without consolation. As the contrast between the two poems suggests, Rosalía's last volume was a testament to hope.

In an age when poets declaimed, Rosalía de Castro had the courage to write honestly and realistically about issues that troubled her. She was unashamed to examine and interpret the feelings of the Galician peasantry, creating from their own forms and phrases a new poetry of rare beauty. As she explored her own hope and hopelessness and pondered the human condition in general, she translated her findings into poetry that speaks to all men.

Major publications other than poetry
NOVELS: *La hija del mar*, 1859; *Flavio*, 1861; *Ruinas*, 1866; *El caballero de las botas azules*, 1867; *El primer loco*, 1881.

Bibliography
Brenan, Gerald. *The Literature of the Spanish People*, 1957.
Chandler, Richard E., and Kessel Schwartz. *A New Anthology of Spanish Literature*, 1967.
Filgueira-Valverde, J. "Introduction," in *Poems of Rosalía de Castro*, 1964.
Kulp-Hill, Kathleen. *Rosalía de Castro*, 1977.
Madariaga, Salvador de. *Mujeres españolas*, 1975.
Mayoral, Marina, ed. "Introduction," in *En las orillas del Sar*, 1976.

Jack Shreve

CATULLUS
Gaius Valerius Catullus

Born: Verona, Italy; c. 85 B.C.
Died: Probably in Rome, Italy; c. 54 B.C.

Principal collections

Catullus was well-known to Augustan Rome, but he fell into obscurity as the Roman Empire declined. In the fourteenth century, a manuscript of his works was discovered containing 116 of his poems, varying from a short couplet to a long poem of more than four hundred lines. Catullus wrote in Latin. His Latin texts, edited by Elmer Truesdell Merrill with extensive notes and information about his life and works, are available in *Catullus* (1893). A good modern translation of his poems is that of Frank O. Copley, *Gaius Valerius Catullus: The Complete Poetry, a New Translation with an Introduction* (1957).

Other literary forms

Catullus is remembered only for his poetry.

Achievements

Catullus is one of the greatest lyric poets of all time. He lived in Rome when that city was the center of the world and when it was rocked to its foundations by political and social revolution. Catullus was in his early twenties when, in 62 B.C. under the consulship of Cicero, the Catiline Conspiracy occurred. The poet lived to see the coalition of Julius Caesar, Pompey, and Crassus form in 60 B.C., and Caesar's subsequent rise to power. Catullus had been dead only about five years when civil war broke out between Caesar and Pompey. Pompey's death at the battle of Pharsalus occurred in 48 B.C., and Caesar was assassinated in 44 B.C. References to Julius Caesar, Pompey, and Cicero appear in various poems of Catullus. He wrote during the stormy period when the Roman Empire was established, immediately prior to the reign of Augustus (27 B.C.-A.D. 14). Catullus bitterly attacked Caesar and his favorites in early poems but eventually came to support the Caesarian party. His poetry precedes the somewhat later literary wave of Vergil (Publius Vergilius Maro, 70-19 B.C.) and the Augustan poets.

Catullus was the leading representative of a revolution in poetry created by the *neoteroi* or "new men" in Rome. Rather than writing about battles, heroes, and the pagan gods, Catullus draws his subjects from everyday, intensely personal life. He writes about lovers' quarrels, arguments, indecent behavior, and his love for his brother and for his Italian countryside. Whatever he writes is marked by a high level of passion, rather than by the Augustan ideal of calm detachment. His poetry is personal, intense, and excited. His language is that of the street: slang, profanity, dialect. His poems are frequently dramatic monologues in which an aggrieved suitor addresses his mistress or an injured party pours malediction on his enemy. The reader must envision many of Catullus' poems as little one-act plays, with a persona speaking the lines, a dramatic audience listening to the speech, and a particular situation in which these words might be spoken appropriately.

Although the content, topics, and language of Catullus' poems were drawn from the seamy streets of Rome, his poetic forms were not. Catullus studied and imitated the meters of late Greek literature of the Alexandrian school; probably for this reason, he was called in ancient times the "learned" Catullus. The late Greek poets developed complicated metrical patterns which Catullus translated into the Latin language. (This subject is discussed extensively in Merrill's edition of Catullus.)

Catullus was a precursor of the Augustan age, a conveyor of the Alexandrian formal tradition into Latin poetry, with a genius for intense, passionate, personal poetry. Even in translation, he is funny and obscene, furious and touching.

Biography

Very little biographical information about Gaius Valerius Catullus is known with certainty. From references in his poetry and from legend, a series of traditional hypotheses about his life have evolved. Ancient sources indicate that he was born in what is now Verona. His family must have been wealthy and powerful, although he never mentions any family member except his brother. Catullus was probably a younger son who went at an early age to Rome to make his way. He owned a villa at Sirmio in the lake district of northern Italy and another in the Sabine Hills. It appears that he lived a life of ease and culture. The only documented fact about his career is that he traveled to the province of Bythinia on the staff of the Governor Gaius Memmius in about 57 to 56 B.C. The likely motive for such a trip would be to earn a fortune, but later unfavorable references in Catullus' poems suggest that the undertaking was not completely successful.

The poems of Catullus are often dramatic, like the sonnets of William Shakespeare: a lover sings the praises of his beloved or heaps scorn on a rival. While it is not accurate to consider such poems as directly autobiographical, it has become customary to assume that they reflect to some degree real happenings in the life of the poet. If the reader considers the poems to be mainly nonfiction, an emotional tale emerges about love and hate in Rome long ago. The poet falls in love with Lesbia, a married woman. She toys with his affection and keeps him in torment. She is unfaithful to him with many men. The poet attacks his rivals viciously in words, but he is nevertheless enslaved by Lesbia's charms, until he flees from Rome on his venture to Bythinia to escape her treacheries.

Modern scholars suggest that Lesbia is a pseudonym for a real woman, Clodia, the sister of Publius Clodius Pulcher and the wife of Q. Caecillius Metellus Celer, who was consul in the year 60 B.C. This hypothesis seems to be supported by several references in the poems and suggests that Catullus really was involved in an affair that followed the outlines suggested in his poems. Sophisticated readers of poetry, however, will hesitate to accept such easy equations of art and reality. It is equally possible that Lesbia and her lover are both merely fictional inventions of a clever writer.

Whether Catullus left Rome to forget his cruel beloved or to get rich, he apparently was unhappy with his experience as a follower of the Governor Memmius, who became an object of attack in several of Catullus' later poems. While in Bythinia, he wrote a tribute to his dead brother's grave, and he celebrated in poetry his own return to Italy. In Rome once again, the poet celebrated a new beloved, the boy Juventius, who also proved unfaithful. Catullus viciously attacked a character whom he called "Mentula"—the word literally means "penis" in Latin—thought to be based on Caesar's associate, Mamurra. Although critical of Caesar, Catullus eventually was reconciled with the Caesarian political group. He died in his thirtieth year.

It was probably an admirer who collected Catullus' poems in a book after his death and divided it into three parts according to the verse forms of the poems. The first group includes sixty poems on various themes, all in iambic or logaoedic rhythm. The middle group includes longer poems and begins with three epithalamia. The third group consists of shorter poems in elegiac meter. Gradually, the poems of Catullus fell out of favor, and he became an unknown figure until the fourteenth century when Benvenuto Campesino rediscovered the texts, probably in Verona. From that original, many copies were made, so that the works of Catullus were well-known to the great writers of the Italian Renaissance.

Analysis

Gaius Valerius Catullus was a master of erotic poetry. Modern attitudes toward sexual love derive from conventions of courtship which can be traced back to Catullus. Some of his sexual poems seem wholesome and agreeable to the modern "liberated" reader; others may seem "unnatural" or obscene. In either case, Catullus was one of the first writers to codify a set of conventions for courtship: the blazon or praise of the beloved, the lover's lament at his unfaithful love, the abasement of the lover captivated by his unworthy beloved, the vilification of the rival for the beloved's affection, the antiblazon or enumeration of the beloved's defects, the comparison of married to adulterous love. These topics or themes have become commonplace in Western literature, but Catullus was one of the first to invent and systematically explore them. The 116 poems of Catullus can be grouped into several categories: those celebrating sexual love; those that taunt and insult; travel and loco-descriptive verse; and mythological material such as the stories of Theseus and Ariadne, Peleus and Thetis, and Attis. Although these themes overlap, almost all of his verse fits into one or more of these categories.

Examples of his praise for sexual love include poems 5, 7, 8, 51, 70, 86, 87, 109, and others. Poem 5 is rightly famous as the prototype of the address of the lover to his beloved, "gather ye rosebuds while ye may." It is a poem of seduction in which the lover reminds the beloved that life is short, and time is fleeting, and she had better not delay too long in consenting to their union. The lover reminds the beloved that soon they will die and sleep one long eternal night; he asks for a thousand or a hundred thousand kisses. Carried away by the passion of these lines, the reader may fail to notice how contrary this erotic sentiment is to conventional morality. Rather than directing his attention to loftier matters, the lover elevates sexual union to a position of supreme importance. Such an exaltation of love is basic to the courtly tradition which developed later in the Renaissance.

Poem 70 introduces the notion that the beloved is not to be trusted, for lovers' promises are as fleeting as words written in dust or running water. Poem 109 expresses the lover's fervent wish that his beloved speak the truth when she promises to love him. Poem 86 presents a comparison or combat between the beloved Lesbia and another woman called Quintia. The poem is in the form of a blazon and begins by enumerating all of Quintia's outstanding physical features: her complexion, size, and shape. The lover grants that Quintia is physically well-made but argues that she lacks personality. Only Lesbia has the inner spark, the charm that can truly be called beautiful. A cruder but nevertheless amusing version of this kind of love poem, sometimes called antiblazon, is poem 43. The lover's rival is called Mentula; Mentula has a girl whom some might call pretty, but the lover systematically examines her nose, feet, eyes, fingers, lips, and tongue, concluding that only a country bumpkin would call such a girl pretty. In every way, Lesbia far surpasses his rival's girl.

To elevate the significance of physical love to that of a religion and to make the beloved a goddess of love turns the lover into a helpless suppliant at the mercy of an unpredictable deity. Poem 8 is the lover's lament. He knows that Lesbia is merely toying with him, and he resolves not to run after her, not to be a foolish slave to desire. The lover rages at his unfaithful mistress—for example, in poems 37 and 58 where he accuses her of becoming a common whore; in poem 38, however, he is begging her to take him back again. Strangely, the worse the beloved treats him, the more the lover desires her. Poem 72 explains that Lesbia's behavior breaks the lover's heart but inflames his lust for her. Catullus encapsulates the lover's lament in a couplet, justly called the best two lines of psychological analysis ever written, poem 85. The lover says that he hates and he loves her. If you ask him why, he cannot explain. He simply feels that he is crucified. The final word, *excrucior*, literally "to be crucified," is particularly well-chosen because the crossed feelings of love and hate catch the lover when they intersect and nail him, as it were, to a cross.

In addition to his passion for the woman Lesbia, Catullus also celebrates a homosexual love for the boy Juventius. The poet's addresses to the boy follow conventions of romantic love similar to those which govern his speeches to Lesbia. Poem 48 celebrates the boy's kisses much as poem 5 does the woman's. Poem 99 tells how the once-sweet kisses of the boy turn bitter because he is unfaithful. Poem 81 mocks the boy for having a new boyfriend, a country hick unworthy of him. Poem 40 threatens a rival who has stolen the affection of the lover's boy. In general, Catullus endorses wine, women (or boys), and song. Poem 27, for example, is a famous drinking song; but, there is always pain close beneath the revelry. Not only does he both love and hate Lesbia, but he is also crucified by conflicting feelings about Rome, about all of his acquaintances, about life in general. He sees the ugliness barely hidden beneath the fashionable woman's makeup, the betrayal lurking behind the hearty greeting of the politicians and lawyers of the capitol, and death everywhere—the death of a pet sparrow, death pursuing golden boys and girls, the death of his beloved brother.

Catullus is also the master of poetic taunts and insults. Seldom has a writer humiliated so many public figures so effectively, so obscenely, so inventively. There are too many poems of this sort to analyze them in detail. Mentula, the supposed rival for Lesbia's favors, heads the list of those in the poet's disfavor. Mentula's virility, wit, poetry, courage, and personal hygiene all come into question. Usually, Catullus uses some common Roman name, the equivalent of English names such as Jimmy or Wayne, as a pseudonym for a historical personage. Modern scholars have spent much effort trying to discover who the characters attacked in the poems really are. No doubt this provided sport for the Roman audience as well, as readers whispered about the true identity of the characters ridiculed or, perhaps, libeled in Catullus' lines.

Sometimes, however, he does not hesitate to name names. Poem 93, for example, is a couplet addressed to Caesar by name, and it says that the poet does not care what the great man thinks. Poem 29 names Mamurra, who was Caesar's prefect in Gaul. The poem accuses Mamurra of looting Gaul for his own profit and refers repeatedly and mockingly to Mamurra as the degenerate descendant of the founding fathers of Rome. After maligning Mamurra's sexual habits and his wasteful financial practices, the poem concludes that men like Mamurra have brought Rome to ruin. It is not necessary to know the exact identity of the unfortunate people who suffered the scathing attacks of Catullus. They are better understood as comic types, like caricatures. As such, they show the poet's ability to sketch a portrait of human deviance in a few biting lines. Thallus in poem 25 is the softest, most cunning, most delicate homosexual—and he steals personal belongings from the clothing of people at the public baths. Flavius in poem 6 has a new girl who is too spirited for him. Suffenus in poem 22 is the prolific poet who writes and writes, but who never rises above mediocrity. Furius in poem 23 is the poor man who toadies to the rich and powerful, not realizing that he is better off in poverty than he would be as a client. Egnatius in poem 39 is the ingratiating man who always smiles. In a court of law or a business deal, he remains smiling. Catullus speculates obscenely about how Egnatius polishes his shining teeth. Scatology and references to personal uncleanliness abound in these verses— for example, the attack on Rufus in poem 69. Unfaithfulness and lack of decency in small personal dealings also infuriate Catullus, as in poem 77. Sexual behavior is commonly ridiculed—for example, the poems numbered 88 and 91, which accuse Gellius of incest and other unusual practices. Usually these attacks are framed in the most offensive language imaginable, as the attack on Aemillius in poem 97.

A number of the poems are about travel and celebrate the Italian rural life. Poem 10 humorously explains that Catullus did not get rich on his trip to Bythinia. Poem 31 celebrates his return from the barbarian province to his beautiful villa in Sirmio. Even in modern times, this lake-dotted area in northern Italy is a delightful place to visit, but the poem by Catullus is not merely a reflection of the real peace of such a landscape. It is an example of the pastoral convention, a celebration of the virtues of the simple life. Not only is the barbarian province of Bythinia contrasted to the homely peace of Sirmio, but the poem also implies that the country life has a simplicity and virtue lacking in the nasty city. Catullus seems to have a contradictory set of attitudes in this regard. In some poems, his worst insult is to accuse someone in Rome of being a hick or a country bumpkin. At other times, the sexual rivalry and power struggles among greedy Romans seem to turn sour, and he longs for the simplicity and honesty of the farm. Poem 44 is an example of this longing for the rural life. Thus, Catullus turns at times to recall the few moments in his life where decency and faithfulness have appeared—for example, the touching references to his brother's death in poems 65 and 68, and especially the lovely elegy, poem 101.

The most important single poem by Catullus is poem 64, a wedding song or epithalamium for Peleus and Thetis, sometimes called his "little epic." It celebrates the marriage of two sets of mythical characters, Peleus/Thetis and Theseus/Ariadne. The poem actually consists of two legendary stories, one embedded within the other. The outer story concerns the wedding of the man Peleus with the goddess Thetis. According to the myth, from this union was born the great Greek hero Achilles. The inner story concerns Theseus and Ariadne. According to the myth, the island of Crete had exacted a tribute of youths and maidens from Athens who were to be sacrificed to a monster, the Minotaur. Prince Theseus of Athens goes to Crete and, with the help of the Cretan princess Ariadne, slays the Minotaur. He takes Ariadne with him back to Athens but stops along the way at the island of Naxos. There he abandons her and sails to Athens alone.

Ariadne's grief on Naxos is the topic of the embedded story in poem 64. The inner and outer stories are linked together by a clever device. The wedding bed of Peleus and Thetis is decked with an embroidered cloth which depicts the earlier legend of Theseus and Ariadne. As the poet describes the scene of the consummation of the marriage of Peleus and Thetis, he digresses to describe the embroidery, thus juxtaposing and contrasting the two pairs of lovers. Although the language and situation of this poem is much more elegant than the rough "street talk" of the poems concerning Lesbia and of the taunts and insults, there is a certain similarity in subject. The epithalamium celebrates sexual union in extremely frank terms. Both the legend of Peleus and Thetis and that of Ariadne on Naxos involve the mating of a human being with a divinity. Both, therefore, imply that love can elevate man to superhuman states of being.

Both poems also recognize that the joy of eros is all the more keen because it is fleeting and subject to change. The opening lines of poem 64 tell how Thetis, the daughter of Jupiter and princess of the sea, became enamored of Peleus, the mortal prince of Thessaly. Jupiter himself approves of the match. The wedding takes place in Thessaly, and the poet describes the gathering of the guests and the decoration of the house. Among the decorations of the wedding chamber there is a wonderfully designed cloth depicting the abandonment of Ariadne on Naxos by her careless lover, Theseus. About half of the poem, from line 50 to line 266, describes the embroidered scene, contrasting the unhappy love of Ariadne to the happy expectations of Peleus and Thetis on their wedding day. The story begins with a lush description of the aggrieved Ariadne wading in the wake of her departing lover's ship. The poet then digresses to tell how Ariadne came to this sorry situation, how Theseus set out from Athens to slay the Minotaur on Crete and free his people from the annual tribute, how Ariadne helped Theseus slay the Minotaur in its labyrinth and so left Crete with him. Although Ariadne had abandoned her family and friends to follow Theseus, he forgets her and sails away from Naxos. In a long speech, Catullus rehearses a theme common to his Lesbia poems: faithless love. Ariadne cries out her complaint to the faithless Theseus in a brilliant and heart-wrenching dramatic scene, but she realizes that Theseus is so far away that he cannot even hear her.

Ariadne is finally avenged, however. Her complaint echoes to heaven and Jupiter ordains a terrible revenge. Theseus had promised his father that, if he succeeded in slaying the Minotaur and returned alive from Crete, he would carry new white sails on his return voyage so that his father could see from afar his success; but, if he died in the attempt, the sails of his ship would be black. The gods see to it that Theseus' forgetfulness is total; he not only forgets Ariadne, but he also fails to hoist the new white sails, so that his father, watching from the headland for the return, imagines his son to be dead and commits suicide in despair. Thus, Theseus has cause to grieve for his forgetfulness exactly as Ariadne did. Moreover, the weeping of Ariadne inflames Bacchus, the god of revelry, with love for her. With luxuriant pomp and procession he comes to Naxos and takes Ariadne for his own. This apotheosis of Ariadne through love is depicted on the veil which decks the wedding bed of Peleus and Thetis. In addition to this wonderful fabric, other gifts come to the lovers. The centaur Chiron comes down from the mountains with woodland gifts. The Naiads, spirits of streams and springs, bring their greenery. Prometheus, too, who gave man fire, is a guest. At the wedding party, the three Fates sing, foretelling that a son will be born to the couple, a son who will be the great Achilles. The poem thus implies that the wedding will benefit all of Greece.

Catullus concludes by observing that the gods were once friends and guests at human events, such as this wedding, long ago. Since those ancient times, however, man has fallen on evil ways—greed, fratricide, incest, lechery of all sorts—and the gods no longer consort familiarly with mankind. This poem of 408 lines is not as massive an accomplishment as the *Aeneid* (c. 29-19 B.C.) of Vergil, which is the epitome of epic poetry in Latin. On the other hand, jewel-like perfection and economy characterize the little epic of Catullus, making it a glory of the Latin language.

Catullus is a major poet because he transmitted important features of the literary tradition which he received from earlier classical writers and, also, because he modified tradition and literally invented new styles, themes, and modes of thinking which are still used in modern poetry. The "traditional" Catullus learned from Greek models a number of lyric meters and stanzaic forms. He translated these into Latin, and from his experiments, the later vernacular poets of Europe were able to develop a formal richness in the short poem. He also reworked traditional stories from classical mythology and passed them on, enriched and embroidered more elegantly than they were before passing through his hands. The story of Theseus and Ariadne is ancient and common in classical times, but the modern reader remembers it in the words of Catullus' depiction of Ariadne on Naxos wading after her false lover's departing ship and crying out her grief. If Catullus had done nothing but purvey the poetic forms and stories of Greek culture to us by way of Latin, he would still deserve a major place in literary history. Catullus was more than a merely traditional writer, however. He exhibited a major, original, inventive power in several aspects of his work.

Catullus brought to his poetry an unusual sense of immediate, personal involvement. It is no accident that readers tend to look at his poems as if they were autobiographical. They are written so that it seems certain that they express some lived, deeply felt, personal experience: betrayed love, petty insult, grief at the loss of a brother. Such intense involvement in the poems is created in part by the use of a highly dramatized form of speaking, like the dramatic monologues of Robert Browning. When one reads Catullus, one is compelled to imagine the speaker of the lines as a character in a play. One is forced to construct a persona speaking, and one must imagine the dramatic circumstances under which these words might be uttered. The heightened immediacy of the lines supports Catullus' use of highly colloquial vocabulary and sentence structure. Many students of Latin, approaching Catullus for the first time, are baffled by his language—his use of profanity, slang, neologisms, and sentence fragments. Yet, to base poetry in language as it is really spoken by ordinary men rather than in some artificial "poetic" dialect was a remark-able achievement, well understood by modern writers.

Catullus invented, too, the introverted concentration of his lyric poetry. His poems almost all turn inward on the speaker's own feeling and attitudes. The speaker may be talking about X, but the poem's real focus is on how the speaker feels about X and not on the ostensible subject of the work. When Catullus writes about the Caesarian party, the reader is interested in how Catullus feels, not about what the Caesarians were or what they did. History tells readers the facts; Catullus understood that poetry tells readers how human beings respond to history.

Because Catullus turned inward and attempted to analyze human emotions, he naturally found himself talking mainly about love and hate. His poems externalize feelings, especially erotic feelings. He used traditional forms of poetry to express attitudes seldom defined before. His poetry, for the first time in Western literature, systematically developed the ideas and conventions of courtly love. When his poems were rediscovered in the Renaissance, writers such as Petrarch saw there a prototype for the conventions of courtly love. Contemporary attitudes toward the sexual relationship are so pervasive and powerful that one seldom stops to consider their origins. Turn on the popular radio stations, however, listen to a few songs and ask where these ideas come from: Why is erotic love elevated to such a high place in the contemporary system of values? Why is faithless love lamented so extravagantly? Why is erotic rivalry the source of so much hostility and anxiety? Why is the woman given a dominant position in the relationship, like a goddess giving her favors or denying them? Such modern attitudes toward erotic love were, in many cases, first stated in Catullus, transmitted through the courtly love-poets of Europe to emerge scarcely changed in lyrics from Nashville and Liverpool today.

Catullus' greatest accomplishment was to express intensely personal feelings in traditional poetic forms. Like all the greatest artists, he united a command of tradition with an individual talent which caused him to change and expand the possibilities he inherited.

Bibliography
Frank, T. *Catullus and Horace: Two Poets in Their Environment*, 1928.
Havelock, E. A. *The Lyric Genius of Catullus*, 1967.
Munro, H. A. J. *Criticisms and Elucidations of Catullus*, 1878.
Wheeler, A. L. *Catullus and the Traditions of Ancient Poetry*, 1934.

Todd K. Bender

CONSTANTINE P. CAVAFY
Kōnstantionos Petrou Kabaphēs

Born: Alexandria, Egypt; April 29, 1863
Died: Alexandria, Egypt; April 29, 1933

Principal collections

Constantine P. Cavafy cannot really be said to have published a collection of his poetry during his lifetime. Although he began writing as early as 1882, he first chose to circulate a privately printed pamphlet to friends in 1904, at the age of forty-one. This "first edition" of one hundred copies included only fourteen poems; he rejected, held for revisions, or destroyed the remainder of the some two hundred he had written to that time. In 1910, he reissued this group with seven poems added. After 1911, the year from which Cavafy himself dated his poetic maturity, he "promulgated his work" (in the words of the translator and critic Edmund Keeley) "largely by distributing folders that contained offprints or broadsheets held together by a huge clip, with a list of the contents in each kept up-to-date in his own hand. When the clips became overburdened, he would have some of the offprints withdrawn and sewn at his own expense into booklets to accompany the ever-expanding folders." The result was that at Cavafy's death, his "collected works" consisted of two sewn pamphlets containing sixty-eight poems thematically arranged and a folder containing sixty-nine other poems arranged according to date of publication. His heir and first editor, Alexander Singopoulos, thus became the first actually to publish a collection of Cavafy's poems, in 1935, two years after the poet's death. He chose to omit seventy-five poems that Cavafy had left among his papers in various stages of revision with the note "Not for publication but may remain here."

The following list, therefore, is of the principal Greek collections and English translations which have gradually extended Cavafy's published canon to its present 180 poems: *Poiēmata* (edited by Alexander Singopoulos, 1935; poetry); *The Poems of C. P. Cavafy* (translated by John Mavrogordato, 1951); *The Complete Poems of Cavafy* (translated by Rae Dalven, 1961); *Poiēmata* (edited by George Savidis, 1963; poetry); *K. P. Kabaphē: Anekdota poiēmata* (edited by George Savidis, 1968; unpublished poetry); *Passions and Ancient Days* (translated by Edmund Keeley and George Savidis, 1971); and *C. P. Cavafy: Collected Poems* (translated by Edmund Keeley and Philip Sherrard, edited by George Savidis, 1975).

Other literary forms

Except for a few essays on literary topics and short notes on language and metrics to be found in his papers, Constantine P. Cavafy did not work in any literary form other than poetry. Greek poet George Seferis, in *On the Greek*

Style (1966), quotes Cavafy as having said, near the end of his life, "I am a historical poet. I could never write a novel or a play; but I hear inside me a hundred and twenty-five voices telling me I could write history."

Achievements

Constantine P. Cavafy did not achieve public acclaim during his lifetime. The fortunes of war, however, marooned two English novelists—E. M. Forster and Lawrence Durrell—in Alexandria during World War I and World War II, respectively. Forster had one of Cavafy's best poems, "The God Abandons Antony," translated and printed in his *Alexandria: A History and Guide* (1922) and spread his name among such literary figures as T. S. Eliot, T. E. Lawrence, and Arnold Toynbee, so that after Forster's stay in Alexandria, Cavafy received many European visitors. Lawrence Durrell modeled aspects of Cavafy in the figures of the brooding old poet of the city and the homosexual physician, Balthazar, important characters in his masterwork *The Alexandria Quartet* (includes *Justine*, 1957; *Balthazar*, 1958; *Mountolive*, 1958; *Clea*, 1960). Thus, the Alexandria which tantalizes the imagination of the modern Western reader is to no small degree the city as imagined by Cavafy.

Cavafy remained almost unknown in Greece until after his death. In 1963, the centenary of his birth was marked by the publication of a collected edition of his works, including both his poetry and volumes of previously unpublished prose and other prose. The 1968 publication of seventy-five previously unpublished poems was the major literary event of the year in Athens.

Adding weight to Cavafy's reputation was W. H. Auden's statement in 1961 (in his introduction to *The Complete Poems of Cavafy*, translated by Rae Dalven) that Cavafy had influenced his writing for more than thirty years. Auden singled out for praise "the most original aspect of [Cavafy's] style, the mixture, both in his vocabulary and his syntax, of demotic and purist Greek," and paid tribute also to Cavafy's rich evocation of Alexandria and of Hellenic culture.

In the early 1880's, when Cavafy began to write, the official language of Greece—the language employed by the government and taught in the schools—was *Katharevousa* or purist Greek, "a language," in the words of Linos Politis in *A History of Modern Greek Literature* (1973), "based on popular speech, but 'corrected' and 'embellished' on the model of the ancient." At the same time, there were in Greece passionate advocates of the demotic or spoken tongue, who believed that it alone should be the language of Greek literature and the Greek state. Although this linguistic controversy persists in Greece even today, modern Greek writers have overwhelmingly adopted the demotic. The tension between a demotic base and borrowings from purist, classical, and the other evolutionary forms of the language accounts in part for the remarkable vitality of modern Greek poetry—a development in which Cavafy played a significant role. Cavafy himself said, "I have tried to blend the spoken with the written language . . . trembling over every word." The remarkable result was a poetic diction that not only draws on the traditions of Greek from its entire history but also, on occasion, is able to combine phrases and whole lines of ancient Greek with the modern, demotic language and yet remain entirely clear and understandable to any educated Greek reader.

Cavafy's distinctive language can be appreciated only in the original Greek, but even a reader who knows Cavafy's poems in translation can appreciate one of his principal achievements: the creation, in Auden's words, of a unique "tone of voice, a personal speech . . . immediately recognizable." Cavafy's poetic voice represents a "style of deliberately prosaic quality, simple, concentrated, almost dry, economical, unadorned, divested of every element which would cause it to deviate from the strictest austerity—at its best inevitable," as Petroula Ruehlen puts it in *Nine Essays in Modern Literature* (1965). It is above all Cavafy's *voice* that, in translation, has exercised a powerful influence on contemporary American poetry.

Biography

Constantine Peter Cavafy was born Kōnstantionos Petrou Kabaphēs, the youngest and most beloved son of a wealthy Alexandrian merchant; both Cavafy's father and his mother came from prosperous families in Constantinople. By the time of Cavafy's birth, his father's business in cotton, grain, and buffalo hides had benefited from the Crimean War and the family had settled in a luxurious house in the fashionable rue Cherif in Alexandria. The poet's first seven years were spent in a household accustomed to elaborate balls and parties and the company of wealthy business people and professionals of various nationalities. A generous man of European outlook who had lived for some time in England, Cavafy's father saw to it that the children were tended by an English nurse, a French tutor, and Greek servants. Unfortunately, he died in 1870 without leaving the family well provided for; though the family was always "respectable," and though the Cavafy brothers retained the cachet of a wealthy, upper-class milieu, the family fortune was severely reduced.

In 1872, Cavafy's mother, Haricleia, took the family to Liverpool. Because of the economic crisis of 1876 and the three eldest sons' inexperience and ill-advised speculation, the family farm had to be liquidated in 1879, whereupon the Cavafys returned to Alexandria actually impoverished. Cavafy had thus spent seven formative years, from the age of nine to the age of sixteen, in England, where he acquired an excellent facility with the English language and a lifelong love for the works of William Shakespeare, Robert Browning, and Oscar Wilde. For the rest of his life, Cavafy spoke Greek with a slight English accent and often spoke or corresponded in English with his brothers; in the position he held for thirty years immediately under British superiors in the Irrigation Department of the Ministry of Public Works in Alexandria, he was valued for his ability to teach Egyptian employees the English language.

Upon his return to Alexandria in 1879, Cavafy enrolled for three years in a business school, the Hermes Lyceum. In 1882, political and military disturbances by Egyptian nationalists seeking to end foreign rule and expel foreigners led to the bombardment of the city by British warships anchored in the harbor. Along with many other Europeans, the Cavafy family left, this time for Constantinople and the home of Haricleia Cavafy's father, George Photiades, a wealthy diamond merchant. While living in Constantinople from 1882 to 1885, Cavafy wrote his first poetry and had his first homosexual experiences. These two activities were to become the chief concerns of his life. He wrote both prose and poetry in French and English as well as in Greek. It was also during this period in Constantinople that Cavafy first became familiar with demotic Greek.

In 1885, Haricleia Cavafy moved the family back to Alexandria for the last time; Cavafy really never left the city again. He took several trips at odd intervals, once visiting France and England and a number of times journeying across the Mediterranean to Athens, but his attachment to Alexandria was profound. When asked late in his life to move to Athens, Robert Liddell reports Cavafy replied: "Mohammed Aly Square is my aunt. Rue Cherif Pacha is my first cousin and the Rue de Ramleh my second. How can I leave them?" He lived with his mother until her death in 1899, when he was thirty-six, then with his brother Paul, taking in 1907 an apartment on the third floor of 10 Rue Lepsius. This apartment was to remain Cavafy's residence until his death twenty-six years later.

In 1891, the death of Cavafy's second eldest brother led him to seek a permanent position in the Irrigation Department, where he had been working part-time for three years. At the same time, he began a chronological listing of all of his poems to date—a list that shows how many he wrote but did not publish. From 1892, Cavafy's life assumed the routine in which his poetry, work, and personality took their characteristic form. His hours as a bureaucrat were not long, from 8:30 in the morning until 1:30 in the afternoon, but the work was tedious and paid minimally; more often than not, Cavafy came to work as much as an hour late. He was reasonably dutiful, if often too scrupulous about his responsibility for all European correspondence; a "trifle overdeliberate" is the phrase cited in his record for 1913, and his subordinates complained that he was overly strict in requiring fastidiously correct records and translations. Cavafy recognized the cost to his art; Liddell quotes him from 1905: "How often during my work a fine idea comes to me, a rare image, and sudden ready-formed lines, and I'm obliged to leave them, because work can't be put off. Then when I go home and recover a bit, I try to remember them, but they're gone." He never forgot that he was the son of a rich man. Nevertheless, records show that regular increases in pay and annual leave (finally reaching twelve weeks) marked his path to the position of subdirector of his section. He also supplemented his income by speculation on the Egyptian Stock Exchange, occasionally with great success.

Away from his job, Cavafy's life centered on his apartment at 10 rue Lepsius, where friends and literary figures visited, and on his nocturnal activities in the cafés and shady quarters of Alexandria. While still living with his mother, Cavafy had bribed the servants or persuaded his brothers to ruffle up his bed so that it looked as if he had spent the night at home. Then he had to cross from the respectable section of the city where he lived with his mother to the area of taverns, bars, and brothels. Living alone after 1910, he enjoyed greater freedom; the old Greek quarter called Massalia, to which he had moved, gradually deteriorated, so that at some point a brothel occupied the ground floor in his building. Cavafy did not have a single long-standing relationship during his entire life; his closest friends, Pericles Anastassiades (as of 1895) and Alexander Singopoulos (whom he met in 1915), were both considerably younger. He did not dislike or avoid women, however, counting several among his closest friends.

Cavafy never published his most explicitly erotic poetry during his life. It is clear that he suffered some guilt concerning his homosexuality, perhaps in part because of his genteel background and his desire to maintain a certain social standing. A secretive man, an engaging poseur, Cavafy was extremely vain, about both his looks (cultivating his boyish demeanor past middle age) and his literary reputation, which he often urged others to spread, but he was also a lively and informed conversationalist. His method of distributing his poetry, with its calculated air of mystery, suggests the mixture of arrogance and reticence which characterized both his life and his work. Cavafy died on his seventieth birthday from cancer of the larynx and was buried in the family plot in the Greek cemetery in Alexandria.

Analysis

To enter the world of Constantine P. Cavafy's poetry is to embrace simultaneously the significance of historical, artistic, and erotic experience, to enter a world with an "atmosphere of refinement and passion . . . just perceptible pathos . . . reserve . . . mystery" in Marguerite Yourcenar's memorable phrasing. This is possible because, as C. M. Bowra points out,

> Cavafy risks no stunning effects. His is a great poetry strictly truthful and circumstantial and realistic, concerned above all to present human nature as it is and to make its presentation entirely convincing not merely to the imagination but to the intelligence. This quiet air, which looks so easy to maintain and must have in fact demanded the greatest self-control and critical judgment, is Cavafy's special triumph.

George Seferis, an important younger contemporary of Cavafy, explains how Cavafy's poetic language makes this possible: "Cavafy stands at the boundary where poetry strips herself in order to become prose." Because he is an "unpoetic" poet, his poetry is both easy and difficult to translate—that is, he rarely employs such devices as internal rhyme, alliteration, simile, or metaphor. Instead, he employs unadorned, factual description. His preference after 1900 for free verse reinforced the deliberately prosaic quality of his poetry.

Cavafy himself classified his poetry thematically into three categories: the historical, the artistic or philosophical, and the erotic, though it is essential to remember that these three kinds of experience often appear in the same poem. Many other divisions are also possible: sequences of poems sharing similar themes, drawn from the same historical period or incident, using the same real or similar imaginary characters. The sum of Cavafy's experience, however, as well as his own statement, make the poet's own classification illuminating.

Cavafy identified both one of the historical periods most important for his work and his own method of using history when he said that the Byzantine historians "cultivated a kind of history that has never been written before or since. They wrote history dramatically." These historians created a sense of the living presence of figures and events, transcending time and assuming eternal significance, just as the Byzantine mosaic artist represented life in timeless, two-dimensional forms. To read about the Alexandrians in 100 B.C. in the twentieth century, for example, is to compress the two thousand years between the two epochs and to share the experience of both periods simultaneously. Cavafy's method of dramatizing history is marvelously economical; he need not draw explicit comparisons between the past and present, for he makes the past present by depicting people and events of universal human significance.

In "Waiting for the Barbarians," for example, one of Cavafy's best-known poems, two imaginary citizens in an unspecified Roman city discuss events in the local senate on a day when the barbarians are coming to take power. No speeches are being given, no laws are being passed. All the political leaders have adorned themselves in their finest attire; bedecked with jewels, they have prepared a scroll to give to the barbarians. The poem is in the form of a dialogue between the first speaker, who asks naïve questions, and the second, apparently as worldly-wise as the first is unknowing, who answers in a dry, flat tone, matter-of-fact to the point of testiness, as if speaking to a child. Lacking any description of events in the third person, the poem creates a sense of live observation with its dialogic form. The naïve questioner is as awed by the splendid throne, garments, and jewelry he asks about as the seemingly more knowing speaker is unimpressed, but the poem's penetrating irony is that both are blind to the truth of their corruption—the first in refusing to see it, as his repeated "why" shows, the second in accepting it so readily with a self-conscious air of world-weary sophistication. Cavafy thus implies that the final truth of a historical situation can never be known, creating a double irony for the reader: The truth is that the truth cannot be known. Nevertheless, on the surface, the poem merely records a simple conversation.

The dialogue is not as common a form in Cavafy's poetry as the dramatic monologue, which offers him, in Yourcenar's words, "the possibilities of *acting* in every sense of the word . . . to have his own emotions confirmed by another mouth." Two such dramatic monologues are "Exiles," in which the speaker accepts the surface of political or historical events with the culpable naïveté of the questioner in "Waiting for the Barbarians," and "Phihellene," in which the speaker is another self-deluded sophisticate.

Exiled to Alexandria by political events in Constantinople in the ninth century, the speaker of "Exiles" is overly certain that he and his fellow exiles will be able to overthrow the Macedonian usurper Basil, who, in reality, ruled for twenty-two years after killing his co-emperor, Michael III. The activities of the exiles are a kind of game: Their use of fictitious names and their superficial enthusiasm in studying literature both suggest their immaturity. Their confidence that they will overthrow Basil is clearly unfounded, and much of the irony of the poem derives from the speaker's complacency, from his tone of voice.

Quite different is the cutting, ironic realism of the speaker of "Phihellene," who thinks he knows all the world's tricks. The speaker is the insignificant monarch of an unspecified territory on the eastern fringe of the Roman empire; the poem consists of his instructions to a subordinate concerning a coin that is to be minted in his honor. The inscription which will accompany his image on the coin, he specifies, should not be "excessive or pompous—/ we don't want the proconsul to take it the wrong way;/ he's always smelling things out and reporting back to Rome—/ but of course giving me due honor." For the obverse of the coin, he suggests a depiction of a "good-looking" discus-thrower, but above all ("for God's sake," he urges, "don't let them forget"), he is concerned that the inscription testify to his appreciation of Hellenic culture—"that after 'King' and 'Savior,'/ they add 'Phihellene' in elegant characters." The central irony of the poem is the consuming desire of this petty monarch to be celebrated as a man of culture, a desire that has its counterpart in the cultural pretensions of many twentieth century dictators.

In several poems on Mark Anthony, Cavafy further manipulates dramatic situation and point of view to present the unusual perspectives on historical figures for which his poetry is noted. The speaker of "In a Township of Asia Minor" has just dictated a lavishly flattering proclamation in honor of Anthony's anticipated victory at Actium. Learning that Octavius has defeated Anthony, the speaker merely instructs his amanuensis to substitute Octavius' name for Anthony's, adding "It all fits brilliantly." In "Alexandrian Kings" and "In Alexandria, 31 B.C.," Cavafy also shows the superficiality and triviality of politics, here in the third person. The Alexandrians, faced with the parade of Cleopatra's children, who all receive important titles, "knew of course what all this was worth,/ what empty words they really were, these kingships." Just as calmly, they allow a peddler from a nearby village to sell his perfumes for the celebration of Anthony's triumph because "someone tosses him the huge palace lie:/ that Antony is winning in Greece" ("In Alexandria, 31 B.C.").

In "The God Abandons Antony," Cavafy uses the second person to give Anthony advice. Whether the speaker lives in Anthony's or Cavafy's time does not matter; he tells Anthony right to his face to accept courageously his loss of Alexandria. Anthony should not mourn his luck or "say/ it was a dream"; rather, he should "go firmly to the window/ and listen with deep emotion" to the city's "exquisite music," confirming the city's delights and his pleasure in them. Here, Cavafy speaks in the poetic voice of an Alexandrian who has dignity, confidence, and self-knowledge.

In the second major category of his poems, Cavafy shows artists at work and presents some of his ideas on the artistic process. Although Cavafy cannot automatically be identified with the speakers of these poems, it is clear that many of them do, in fact, express his attitude toward his art. The need for craftsmanship and the relationship between art and reality are recurring themes in this group of poems.

Two poems concerning the relationship between art and life are "I've Brought to Art" and "Melancholy of Jason Kleander, Poet in Kommagini, A.D. 595." In the first poem, the poet says he has brought life to art, "desires and sensations/ . . ./ indistinct memories/ of unfulfilled love affairs," and art has known how "to shape forms of Beauty,/ almost imperceptibly completing life,/ blending impressions, blending day with day." In the second, in the voice of the poet Jason Kleander, he says that art has "a kind of knowledge about drugs:/ certain sedatives, in Language and Imagination," which relieve the pain of the "wound from a merciless knife" that age inflicts.

In many of the poems in this group, Cavafy reveals the sense of secrecy and isolation underlying his art. The first-person speaker in "Hidden Things" says he will be understood only "From my most unnoticed actions,/ my most veiled writing," but that "Later, in a more perfect society,/ someone else made just like me/ is certain to appear and act freely." "Walls," written as early as 1896 and printed as the first poem by Keeley and Sherrard in the authoritative *C. P. Cavafy: Collected Poems*, indicates just how isolated Cavafy may have felt. His oppressors, identified only as "they," have built walls around him: "But I never heard the builders, not a sound./ Imperceptibly they've closed me off from the outside world." In "The First Step," however, another early poem, he speaks of the necessary difficulty of art: Theocritos rebukes a young poet who says that he has "been writing for two years/ and . . . [has] composed only one idyll"; even the artist who has completed only one work is "above the ordinary world/ . . . a member of the city of ideas." Here, the artist's isolation from the "ordinary world" becomes a badge of pride.

The private world of Cavafy's art is nowhere seen more clearly than in the third division of his work, the erotic poems, the most explicit of which he never published himself. Cavafy perhaps believed that he could publish "Pictured" and "When They Come Alive" within three years of their composition because both justify imaginary erotic experience by the art which it helps to create and nurture. In "Pictured," a writer, discouraged by the slow progress of his work, gazes at a picture of "a handsome boy/ . . . lying down close to a spring." The picture revives the poet's inspiration: "I sit and gaze like this for a long time,/ recovering through art from the effort of creating it." Though it could be argued that there is little art in the picture, the image of the youth has nevertheless inspired the very poem which describes it. "When They Come Alive" is addressed to an unidentified poet (perhaps Cavafy, addressing himself?); the poem begins: "Try to keep them, poet,/ those erotic visions of yours,/ . . . Put them, half-hidden, in your lines." The poem concludes by urging the conscious cultivation of such erotic fantasies.

It is interesting to compare these two poems with another erotic poem "At the Theatre," written before them but never published in Cavafy's lifetime. Here, erotic reverie is not justified as a stimulus to artistic creation but is rather celebrated for its own sake. Addressed to a young man whose "strange beauty" and "decadent youthfulness" have aroused the speaker's "mind and body," the poem concludes: "in my imagination I kept picturing you/ the way they'd talked about you that afternoon." In "Half an Hour," another poem never published by Cavafy, the speaker recounts a "totally erotic" half hour at a bar in which the sight of "your lips . . . your body near me" were all his imagination needed. As the poet says, "we who serve Art,/ sometimes with the mind's intensity/ can create pleasure that seems almost physical"—as strong a statement of the power of imagination as could be asked for.

Another poem unpublished during Cavafy's lifetime, "And I Lounged and Lay on Their Beds," again justifies debauchery for the sake of art. The poet says that "When I went to that house of pleasure/ I didn't stay in the front rooms where they celebrate,/ with some decorum, the accepted modes of love"; instead, in "the secret rooms," he "lounged and lay on their beds"— a line more suggestive than any fuller description of the experience would be. It was a consummate artistic touch to begin the title with "And," here deliberately ambiguous: it may suggest that much more took place than is explicitly described in the title. In Cavafy's poetry, all experience takes on the sacred value of ancient and mysterious temple rites.

A final poem, "Craftsmen of Wine Bowls," serves to show how Cavafy combined erotic, artistic, and philosophical themes in a single poem. In a dramatic monologue, a silversmith describes how his memory, which he begged to help him, enabled him to see "the young face I loved appear the way it was"—a difficult achievement, because "some fifteen years have gone by since the day/ he died as a soldier in the defeat at Magnesia." Magnesia was the battle that established Rome's supremacy in the Hellenized East; thus, the trouble the silversmith takes to commemorate his fallen love seems justified by the nobility of the soldier's cause. Carved on what is only a small bowl, the figure is of a "beautiful young man,/ naked, erotic, one leg still dangling/ in the water," an appropriate image for Cavafy's delicate, refined, and passionate art.

Bibliography

Auden, W. H. "Introduction," in *The Complete Poems of Cavafy*, 1961.

Bien, Peter. *Constantine Cavafy*, 1964.

Bowra, C. M. *The Creative Experiment*, 1949.

Forster, E. M. "The Poetry of C. P. Cavafy," in *Pharos and Pharillon*, 1923.

Keeley, Edmund. *Cavafy's Alexandria: Study of a Myth in Progress*, 1976.

——————. "The 'New' Poems of Cavafy," in *Modern Greek Writers*, 1972. Edited by Edmund Keeley and Peter Bien.

Liddell, Robert. *Cavafy: A Critical Biography*, 1974.

Pinchin, Jane L. *Alexandria Still: Forster, Durrell, Cavafy*, 1977.

Ruehlen, Petroula K. "Constantine Cavafy: A European Poet," in *Nine Essays in Modern Literature*, 1965. Edited by Donald Stanford.

Seferis, George. "Cavafy and Eliot—A Comparison," in *On the Greek Style*, 1966.

Yourcenar, Marguerite. "An Introduction to Cavafy," in *Shenandoah*. XXXII (1980).

John M. Lee

GUIDO CAVALCANTI

Born: Florence, Italy; c. 1259
Died: Florence, Italy; August 27 or 28, 1300

Principal collections

Le rime, 1527; *The Sonnets and Ballate of Guido Cavalcanti*, 1912 (Ezra Pound, translator).

Other literary forms

Guido Cavalcanti is remembered only for his poetry.

Achievements

The extant poems of Cavalcanti number fewer than threescore; when taken together, however, they are compelling evidence that he was one of the finest Italian poets of his age. Ezra Pound, Cavalcanti's translator into English, even exalted him above Dante, noting in 1929 that "Dante is less in advance of his time than Guido Cavalcanti." While Pound's enthusiasm for Cavalcanti was perhaps excessive, there is little doubt that, except for Dante, Cavalcanti was the most outstanding member of the famous "school" of *il dolce stil nuovo* (the sweet new style). Although some critics question the existence of such a school in late-thirteenth century Italy, it is generally conceded that a number of poets of the period constituted an informal group defined by common linguistic and thematic concerns. In addition to Dante and Cavalcanti, this group included Guido Guinizzelli, the founder of the school, and several writers of love lyrics: Lapo Gianni, Gianni degli Alfani, Dino Frescobaldi, and Cino da Pistoia.

The major themes of *il dolce stil nuovo* are outlined in Guinizzelli's seminal canzone "Al cor gentil ripara sempre amore" ("To the Noble Heart Love Always Returns"). Foremost is a new concept of nobility, which is no longer tied to birth or social rank but rather to spiritual perfection or moral worth. Second is the identification of love with the noble heart, meaning that love is reserved for the heart of a truly noble soul (as defined above) and that the noble heart is likewise reserved for love. Last is the theme of the spiritualization of woman. Since women inspire love, and love in turn is the cause and product of a noble heart, women may prove to be instruments of moral perfection. Every lady is a potential *angelicata crïatura* (angelic creature), to use Cavalcanti's phrase and to employ terminology characteristic of the *stilnovisti*.

The phrase "the sweet new style" derives from *Purgatorio* (*Purgatory*) in Dante's *La divina commedia* (c. 1320; *The Divine Comedy*). It is Bonagiunta Orbicciani da Lucca's term for the poetics espoused by Dante, Cavalcanti, and several of their contemporaries. The "sweetness" of the new style refers primarily to the gentleness of the subject matter (love), the purity of the language (vernacular Italian), and the graciousness of the chosen poetic rhythms (implying an avoidance, for example, of harsh rhymes). The "newness" derives from the originality of the poets' inspiration—that is, an inner, emotional need to write verse as opposed to a purely intellectual decision to compose—and from the abundance of new expressions, rather than stereotypical phrases, designed to communicate the psychological state of the poet. Cavalcanti's careful depiction of the various states of his emotions, such as self-pity and bewilderment, is noteworthy for its innovative departure from timeworn clichés. An even more important achievement, however, was the remarkable influence Cavalcanti exerted on his onetime friend Dante, who early in his career referred to Cavalcanti as his *primo amico*, or "first friend," and to whom he dedicated *La vita nuova* (c. 1292). It was Cavalcanti who encouraged Dante to write his poetry in the vernacular instead of in Latin; Dante's decision to follow his friend's advice changed forever the course of Italian poetry.

Biography

Guido Cavalcanti was born in Florence, Italy, a few years prior to Dante's birth. The exact year of Cavalcanti's birth has never been established. While some have placed it as early as 1240, Natalino Sapegno and many others believe that the poet was born just before 1260. His father was Cavalcante de' Cavalcanti, a descendant of Guelph merchants and the same figure who appears next to the Ghibelline Farinata degli Uberti in one of the burning tombs of the heretics in the *Inferno*. Dante's treatment of Cavalcanti's father and father-in-law in this famous episode has led to much speculation about Cavalcanti's own philosophical and religious beliefs and was in part responsible for the depiction of Cavalcanti as a heretic in various stories by Giovanni Boccaccio and others. What is known of Cavalcanti's life comes in large part from the contemporary chronicles of Filippo Villani and Dino Compagni. At an early age, Cavalcanti was betrothed by his father to Beatrice (Bice) degli Uberti, daughter of Farinata. This was essentially a political marriage, one designed, like so many of the time, to put an end to the internecine wars between the Guelphs and the Ghibellines, who supported the papacy and the emperor respectively. Cavalcanti was among the Guelph representatives at the peace negotiations held by Cardinal Latino in 1280; he took part in the general council of the commune in 1284, together with Compagni and Brunetto Latini, and his friendship with Dante dates from this period. He was a fierce adversary of Corso Donati, leader of the Black Guelphs. Because of his hatred for Donati, he joined the opposing White Guelph faction. His allegiance to that faction led to his exile in Sarzana, Italy, on June 24, 1300. It was on that date that the priors of Florence, of which Dante was one, attempted to resolve the city's political strife by banishing the leaders of both factions. While banished, Cavalcanti contracted malaria. Although he was recalled to Florence soon thereafter, he never recovered, and he died in his native city on August 27 or 28 of the same year. His death was recorded on August 29, 1300, in the register of the dead in the Cathedral of Santa Reparata.

These meager facts about Cavalcanti's life and death shed little light on the poet's personality, which is largely shrouded in legend. Perhaps because Dante attributes *disdegno* (disdain) to him in a verse of the previously cited episode in the *Inferno*, other authors have also characterized Cavalcanti as haughty, aristocratic, and solitary. Dante's portrayal of his supposedly best friend as disdainful has led many to conclude that their friendship sharply diminished at some point during their later years. Some speculate that this happened because of conflicts over literary values, with Dante preeminently interested in ethical understanding and Cavalcanti in aristocratic expression. Others argue that the differences in their perception of love formed the basis for the breakdown of their friendship. A disagreement over political matters is yet another possible explanation, although both Dante and Cavalcanti were White Guelphs, and Dante's permanent exile followed Cavalcanti's temporary exile by only a year or so. Whatever the case, Compagni describes Cavalcanti as a "noble knight" and as "courteous and bold" but also as "disdainful and solitary and devoted to study." Villani writes that the poet was a "philosopher of antiquity, not a little esteemed and honored for his dignity." It is Villani also who outlines the rancor and bitterness that Cavalcanti felt toward Donati, who evidently attempted to assassinate Cavalcanti as he made a pilgrimage to Santiago de Compostela. Boccaccio, in his commentary on the *Inferno*, speaks of Cavalcanti as a "most well-bred man and wealthy and of a lofty intellect." Regardless of who paints the portrait, Cavalcanti always appears as intelligent but a man apart, a solitary person destined to exile by his temperament if not by his politics.

Analysis

Guido Cavalcanti's poetry, like that of other *stilnovisti*, may be viewed, in part, as a reaction to the poetry of Guittone d'Arezzo and his followers. Guittone's mid-thirteenth century poetry was largely imitative of the Provençal tradition: hermetic in nature, it also emphasized rhetorical, metrical, and verbal complexities. Poets of "the sweet new style," on the other hand, de-emphasized technical elements so that aspects such as meter and rhyme were generally subservient to meaning. Also, whereas Guittonian poetry covered a wide range of subjects, Guinizzelli and his disciples focused almost entirely on love and its effects. Cavalcanti, however, should not be seen as a mere conformist to Guinizzelli's dicta, for Cavalcanti in turn distinguished himself from many of his own school. In his concentration on love's psychology, he was philosophically more sophisticated than all other *stilnovisti* except Dante. He introduced, for example, the concept of *spiriti* (spirits) into his poetry in order to dramatize the conflicting emotions and behaviors that love elicits.

The term "spirit" is a technical term of Scholasticism; it refers, according to Albertus Magnus, to the "instrument of the soul" or the "vehicle of life." Spirits represent the essence of life. They shine in the eyes of the beloved and console the heart of the lover. They are forced to flee, however, when love invades. Their flight results in man's metaphorical death. It is not surprising, then, that closely related to the theme of spirits in Cavalcanti's poems is the theme of death.

If one facet of Cavalcanti's poetry may be characterized as highly philosophical, the other can be described only as profoundly lyrical. The preoccupation with love and death, for example, results in a melancholy portrayal of the poet's mercurial emotions: happiness is poignantly juxtaposed to sadness. Tears and sighs become appropriate symbols of the persona's ever-changing state of being because they can stand either for joy or sorrow, pleasure or pain. Love is always the culprit that renders the lover defenseless, a helpless observer. Love causes both agony and ecstasy; eventually, it generates a deep-seated desire for release via death. The poet's sense of helplessness before such an all-powerful conqueror is reflected in the presentation of the lover as spectator. This distancing technique leads to a highly dramatic tension and a beautiful lyric expression. It allows the poet to observe and record the effects of love but does not permit him to intervene.

Cavalcanti's known works include thirty-six sonnets, eleven ballads, two canzones, two isolated stanzas, and one motet. In addition, two ballads of questionable authenticity are occasionally attributed to him. The sonnets, because of their large number, seem to represent the poet's preferred form. The major theme of most of the sonnets relates, not unexpectedly, to the pain and weakness that love inflicts on the lover. Love, however, is not the only argument in the compositions. The sonnets of correspondence, for example, are the most important in the collection from a historical perspective, and they show the range of topics covered. These sonnets were dedicated or written to other men, including the poets Dante, Alfani, Guittone d'Arezzo, Guido Orlandi, and a certain Bernardo da Bologna (about whom very little is known).

The five sonnets addressed to Dante are either responses to rhymes on love by Dante or words of friendly encouragement. "Vedeste, al mio parere, onne valore" ("You Saw, in My Opinion, Every Valor") is a reply to Dante's famous call to love's faithful, "A ciascun' alma presa e gentil core" ("To Every Captured Soul and Noble Heart"). On the other hand, one sonnet to Orlandi, "Di vil matera mi conven parlare" ("Of a Vile Matter I Must Speak"), constitutes a rather caustic personal attack. Another sonnet, addressed to Guittone and entitled "Da più a uno face un sollegismo" ("From Many to One Makes a Syllogism"), falls in the tradition of the harsh literary criticism of Guittone also found in Dante's writings. A sonnet to Nerone Cavalcanti, "Novelle ti so dire, odi, Nerone" ("News I Know to Tell You, So Hear,

Nerone"), testifies to the fierce fight between the Cavalcanti and Buondel-monti families.

In the ballads, one finds themes such as that of exile in "Perch'io non spero di tornar giammai" ("Because I Hope Not Ever to Return") and of country delights in "In un boschetto trova' pasturella" ("In a Woods I Found a Shep-herdess"). As noted earlier, the theme of death often accompanies or weaves through the prevailing theme of love. This is seen in the ballad "Quando di morte mi conven trar vita" ("When I Must Take Life from Death"). On the poet's pilgrimage to Santiago de Compostela, he stops in Toulouse. There, in the Church of the Daurade, he imagines an encounter with Mandetta, a beautiful woman recalled in the ballad "Era in penser d'amor quand'io trovai" ("I Was Thinking of Love When I Found"). The beauty of Mandetta is also described in the sonnet "Una giovane donna di Tolosa" ("A Young Woman of Toulouse"). The young woman reminds him of his faraway lady, whom Cavalcanti never mentions by name in his poetry. Dante, however, refers to her as Vanna, short for Giovanna, and states in *La vita nuova* that she was also known, because of her beauty, as Primavera, or Springtime.

The poet's most famous poem, which is also his most difficult, is neither a sonnet nor a ballad. Perhaps the most-discussed canzone in all of Italian literature, "Donna me prega" ("My Lady Asks Me"), a poem of seventy-five lines, has been described by John Colaneri as "an intellectual, philosophical, and somewhat obscure exposition of the essence of love." Most scholars would agree with this description, especially the reference to the poem's obscurity. Interpretations of the work differ widely, drawing variously on Arab mysticism, Averroist thought, Arab-Christian Platonism, Thomist philosophy, and neo-Aristotelianism.

From a technical viewpoint, "My Lady Asks Me" is a virtuoso performance, offering unequivocal proof of the poet's exceptional rhyming ability. The poem is meant to be a treatise on the philosophy of love as well as a highly lyrical composition, however, and in the canzone's opening stanza, Cavalcanti raises the following questions: Where does love exist? Who creates it? What is its virtue, its power, and its essence? The answers to these queries are contained in the remainder of the poem, but in a rather complicated philosophical knot.

In most of his poetry, Cavalcanti has a great desire to render visible that within man which is invisible, such as the movements of the human soul. The poet transforms these actions into images of real beings. Thus, "spirits" (as the term was used in Scholastic philosophy, to designate the vital faculties of man) were introduced into love poetry. All of the *stilnovisti* made use of them for the purpose of artistic representation, but it was principally with Cavalcanti that the systematization of the spirits took place. Indeed, it was primarily because of Cavalcanti that spirits became an integral part of the literary expression of the amorous theme and that they remained there for centuries.

Bibliography

Contini, Gianfranco, ed. *Poeti del duecento*, 1960 (2 volumes).

Dronke, Peteı. *Medieval Latin and the Rise of the European Love Lyric*, 1969 (2 volumes).

Shaw, J. E. *Guido Cavalcanti's Theory of Love: The "Canzone d'amore" and Other Related Problems*, 1949.

Wilhelm, James J. *Dante and Pound: The Epic of Judgement*, 1974.

Madison U. Sowell

PAUL CELAN
Paul Ancel or Antschel

Born: Czernowitz, Romania; November 23, 1920
Died: Paris, France; April, 1970

Principal collections

Der Sand aus den Urnen, 1948; *Mohn und Gedächtnis*, 1952; *Von Schwelle zu Schwelle*, 1955; *Sprachgitter*, 1959 (*Speech-Grille and Other Poems*, 1971); *Die Niemandsrose*, 1963; *Atemwende*, 1967; *Fadensonnen*, 1968; *Lichtzwang*, 1970; *Schneepart*, 1971; *Selected Poems*, 1972; *Zeitgehöft*, 1976; *Paul Celan: Poems*, 1980.

Other literary forms

Paul Celan's literary reputation rests exclusively on his poetry. His only piece of prose fiction, if indeed it can be so described, is "Gespräch im Gebirg" (1959), a very short autobiographical story with a religious theme. Celan also wrote an introductory essay for a book containing works by the painter Edgar Jené; this essay, entitled "Edgar Jené und der Traum vom Traume" (1948), is an important early statement of Celan's aesthetic theory. Another, more oblique, statement of Celan's poetic theory is contained in his famous speech, "Der Meridian" (1960), given on his acceptance of the prestigious Georg Büchner Prize. (An English translation of this speech, "The Meridian," is available in the Winter 1978 issue of *Chicago Review*.)

Achievements

Celan is considered an "inaccessible" poet by many critics and readers. This judgment, prompted by the difficulties Celan's poetry poses for would-be interpreters seeking traditional exegesis, is reinforced by the fact that Celan occupies an isolated position in modern German poetry. Sometimes aligned with Nelly Sachs, Ernst Meister, and the German Surrealists, Celan's work nevertheless stands apart from that of his contemporaries. A Jew whose outlook was shaped by his early experiences in Nazi-occupied Romania, Celan grew up virtually trilingual. The horror of his realization that he was, in spite of his childhood experiences and his later residence in France, a German poet was surely responsible in part for his almost obsessive concern with the possibilities and the limits of his poetic language. Celan's literary ancestors are Friedrich Hölderlin, Arthur Rimbaud, Stéphane Mallarmé, Rainer Maria Rilke, and the German Expressionists, but even in his early poems his position as an outsider is manifest. Celan's poems, called hermetic by some critics because of their resistance to traditional interpretation, can be viewed sometimes as intense and cryptic accounts of personal experience, sometimes as religious-philosophical discussions of Judaism, its tradition and its relation to

Christianity. Many of his poems concern themselves with linguistic and poetic theory to the point where they cease to be poems in the traditional sense, losing all contact with the world of physical phenomena and turning into pure language, existing only for themselves. Such "pure" poems, increasingly frequent in Celan's later works, are largely responsible for the charge of inaccessibility which has been laid against him. Here the reader is faced with having to leave the dimension of conventional language use, where the poet uses language to communicate with his audience about subjects such as death or nature, and is forced to enter the dimension of metalanguage, as Harald Weinrich calls it, where language is used to discuss only language—that is, the *word* "death," and not death itself. Such poems are accessible only to readers who share with the poet the basic premises of an essentially linguistic poetic theory, a demand which is made by many works of modern literature.

In spite of all this, much of Celan's poetry can be made accessible to the reader through focus on the personal elements in some poems, the Judaic themes in others, and by pointing out the biblical and literary references in yet another group.

Biography

Paul Celan was born Paul Ancel, or Antschel, the only child of Jewish parents, in Czernowitz, Romania (now Chernovtsy, U.S.S.R.), in Bukovina, situated in the foothills of the Carpathian Mountains in what is today northern Romania. This region had been under Austrian rule and thus contained a sizable German-speaking minority along with a mix of other nationalities and ethnic groups. In 1918, just two years before Celan's birth, following the collapse of the Austro-Hungarian Empire, Bukovina became part of Romania. Thus, Celan was reared in a region of great cultural and linguistic diversity, the tensions of which energized his poetry.

Little is known of Celan's early childhood, but he appears to have had a very close relationship with his mother and a less satisfying relationship with his father. Positive references to his mother abound in his poems, whereas his father is hardly mentioned. After receiving his high school diploma, the young Celan went to study medicine in France in 1938, but the war forced his return in the following year to Czernowitz, where he turned to the study of Romance languages and literature at the local university. In 1940, his hometown was annexed by the Soviet Union but was soon occupied by the Germans and their allies, who began to persecute and deport the Jewish population. Celan's parents were taken to a concentration camp, where they both died, while the young man remained hidden for some time and finally ended up in a forced-labor camp. These events left a permanent scar on Celan's memory, and it appears that he had strong feelings of guilt for having survived when his parents and so many of his friends and relatives were murdered. After Soviet troops reoccupied his hometown, he returned there for a short time and then moved to Bucharest, where he found work as an editor and a translator. In 1947, his first poems were published in a Romanian journal under the anagrammatic pen name Paul Celan. In the same year, he moved to Vienna, where he remained until 1948, when his first collection of poetry, *Der Sand aus den Urnen*, was published.

After moving to Paris in the same year, Celan began to frequent avant-garde circles and was received particularly well by the poet Yvan Goll and his wife. Unfortunately, this friendship soured after Goll's death in 1950, when Goll's wife, Claire, apparently jealous of Celan's growing reputation as a poet, accused him of having plagiarized from her husband. A bitter feud resulted, with many of the leading poets and critics in France and Germany taking sides. During this period, Celan also began his work as a literary translator, which was to be a major source of both income and poetic inspiration for the rest of his life. He translated from the French—notably the writings of Rimbaud, Paul Valéry, and Guillaume Apollinaire—as well as the poetry of William Shakespeare, Emily Dickinson, and Marianne Moore from the English and the works of Aleksandr Blok, Sergei Esenin, and Osip Mandelstam from the Russian.

In the following years, Celan married a French graphic artist, Gisèle Lestrange, and published his second volume of poetry, *Mohn und Gedächtnis* (poppy and memory), containing many poems from his first collection, *Der Sand aus den Urnen*, which he had withdrawn from circulation because of the large number of printing mistakes and editorial inaccuracies it contained. *Mohn und Gedächtnis* established his reputation as a poet, and most of his subsequent collections were awarded prestigious literary prizes.

Celan remained in Paris for the rest of his life, infrequently traveling to Germany. During his later years, he appears to have undergone many crises both in his personal and in his creative life (his feud with Claire Goll is only one such incident), and his friends agree that he became quarrelsome and felt persecuted by neo-Nazis, hostile publishers, and critics. His death in April of 1970, apparently by suicide—he drowned in the Seine—was the consequence of his having arrived, in his own judgment, at a personal and artistic dead end, although many critics have seen in his collections *Lichtzwang*, *Schneepart*, and *Zeitgehöft*, published posthumously, the potential beginning of a new creative period.

Analysis

Paul Celan's poetry can be viewed as an expressive attempt to cope with the past—his personal past as well as that of the Jewish people. Close friends of the poet state that Celan was unable to forget anything and that trivial incidents and cataclysmic events of the past for him had the same order of importance. Many of his poems contain references to the death camps, to his dead parents (particularly his mother), to his changing attitude toward the

Jewish religion and toward God. In his early collections, these themes are shaped into traditional poetic form—long, often rhymed lines, genitive metaphors, sensuous images—and the individual poems are accessible to conventional methods of interpretation. In his later collections, Celan employs increasingly sparse poetic means, such as one-word lines, neologisms, and images that resist traditional interpretive sense-making; their significance can often be intuited only by considering Celan's complete poetic opus, a fact which has persuaded many critics and readers that Celan's poems are nonsense, pure games with language rather than codified expressions of thoughts and feelings which can be deciphered by applying the appropriate key.

Mohn und Gedächtnis, Celan's first collection of poetry (discounting the withdrawn *Der Sand aus den Urnen*), was in many ways an attempt to break with the past. The title of the collection is an indication of the dominant theme of these poems, which stress the dichotomy of forgetting—one of the symbolic connotations of the poppy flower—and remembering, by which Celan expresses his wish to forget the past, both his own personal past and that of the Jewish race, and his painful inability to erase these experiences from his memory. Living in Paris, Celan believed that only by forgetting could he begin a new life—in a new country, with a non-Jewish French wife, and by a rejection of his past poetic efforts, as indicated by the withdrawal of his first collection.

Mohn und Gedächtnis is divided into four parts and contains a total of fifty-six poems. In the first part, "Der Sand aus den Urnen" ("Sand from the Urns"), Celan establishes the central theme of the collection: The poet "fills the urns of the past in the moldy-green house of oblivion" and is reminded by the white foliage of an aspen tree that his mother's hair was not allowed to turn white. Mixed with these reflections on personal losses are memories of sorrows and defeats inflicted upon the Jewish people; references to the conquest of Judea by the Romans are meant to remind the reader of more recent atrocities committed by foreign conquerors.

The second part of *Mohn und Gedächtnis* is a single poem, "Todesfuge" ("Death Fugue"), Celan's most widely anthologized poem, responsible in no small part for establishing his reputation as one of the leading contemporary German poets. "Death Fugue" is a monologue by the victims of a concentration camp, evoking in vivid images the various atrocities associated with these camps. From the opening line, "Black milk of daybreak we drink it at sundown . . ."—one of the lines that Claire Goll suggested Celan had plagiarized from her husband—the poem passes on to descriptions of the cruel camp commander who plays with serpent-like whips, makes the inmates shovel their own graves, and sets his pack of dogs on them. From the resignation of the first lines, the poem builds to an emotional climax in the last stanza in which the horror of the cremation chambers is indicated by images such as "he grants us a grave in the air" and "death is a master from Germany."

While most critics have praised the poem, some have condemned Celan for what they interpret as an attempt at reconciliation between Germans and Jews in the last two lines of the poem. Others, however, notably Theodor Adorno, have attacked "Death Fugue" on the basis that it is "barbaric" to write beautiful poetry after, and particularly about, Auschwitz. A close reading of this long poem refutes the notion that Celan was inclined toward reconciliation with the Germans—his later work bears this out—and it is hard to imagine that any reader should feel anything but horror and pity for the anonymous speakers of the poem. The beautifully phrased images serve to increase the intensity of this horror rather than attempting to gloss it over. "Death Fugue" is both a great poem and one of the most impressive and lasting documents of the plight of the Jews.

"Auf Reisen" ("Travel"), the first poem of the third part of the collection, again indicates Celan's wish to leave the past behind and to start all over again in his "house in Paris." In other poems he makes reference to his wife, asking to be forgiven for having broken with his heritage and married a Gentile. As the title of the collection suggests, the poppy of oblivion is not strong enough to erase the memory of his dead mother, of his personal past, and of his racial heritage. In poems such as "Der Reisekamerad" ("The Traveling Companion") and "Zähle die Mandeln" ("Count the Almonds"), the optimistic view of "Travel" is retracted; in the former, the dead mother is evoked as the poet's constant travel companion, while in the latter, he acknowledges that he must always be counted among the "almonds." The almonds (*Mandeln*) represent the Jewish people and are an indirect reference also to the Russian Jewish poet Osip Mandelstam, whose work Celan had translated. The irreconcilable tension between the wish to forget and the inability to do so completely is further shown in "Corona," a poem referring to Rainer Maria Rilke's "Herbsttag" ("Autumn Day"). Whereas the speaker of Rilke's poem resigns himself to the approaching hardships of winter, Celan converts Rilke's "Lord: it is time" into the rebellious "it is time that the stone condescended to bloom."

The poems in *Mohn und Gedächtnis* are not, for the most part, innovative in form or imagery, although the long dactylic lines and the flowery images of the first half begin to give way to greater economy of scope and metaphor in the later poems. There is a constant dialogue with a fictional "you" and repeated references to "night," "dream," "sleep," "wine," and "time," in keeping with the central theme of these poems. Celan's next collections show his continued attempts to break with the past, to move his life and his poetry to new levels.

In *Von Schwelle zu Schwelle* (threshold to threshold), Celan abandoned his frequent references to the past; it is as if the poet—as the title, taken from a poem in *Mohn und Gedächtnis*, suggests—intended to cross over a threshold into a new realm. Images referring to his mother, to the persecution of the Jews, to his personal attitude toward God, and to his Jewish heritage are less frequent in this volume. Many German critics, reluctant to concentrate on Celan's treatment of the Holocaust, have remarked with some relief his turning away from this subject toward the problem of creativity, the possibilities of communication, and the limits of language. Indeed, if one follows most German critics, *Von Schwelle zu Schwelle* was the first step in the poet's development toward "metapoetry"—that is, poetry which no longer deals with traditional *materia poetica* but only with poetry itself. This new direction is demonstrated by the preponderance of terms such as "word" and "stone" (a symbol of speechlessness), replacing "dream," "autumn," and "time." For Celan, *Von Schwelle zu Schwelle* constituted a more radical attempt to start anew by no longer writing about—therefore no longer having to think about— experiences and memories which he had been unable to come to grips with in his earlier poems.

Speech-Grille is, as the title suggests, predominantly concerned with language. The thirty-three poems in this volume are among Celan's finest, as the enthusiastic critical reception confirmed. They are characterized by a remarkable discipline of expression, leading in many cases to a reduction of poetry to the bare essentials. Indeed, it is possible to see these poems as leading in the direction of complete silence. "Engführung" ("Stretto"), perhaps the finest poem in the collection and one of Celan's best, exemplifies this tendency even by its title, which is taken from musical theory and refers to the final section of a fugue. A long poem which alludes to "Death Fugue," it is stripped of the descriptive metaphors which characterized that masterpiece, such as the "grave in the air" and "the black milk of daybreak"; instead, experience is reduced to lines such as "Came, came./ Came a word, came/ came through the night,/ wanted to shine, wanted to shine/ Ash./ Ash, ash./ Night."

Celan's attempt to leave the past behind in *Speech-Grille* was not completely successful; on the contrary, several poems in this collection express sorrow at the poet's detachment from his Jewish past and from his religion. It is therefore not surprising that Celan's next collection, *Die Niemandsrose* (the no-one's rose), was dedicated to Osip Mandelstam, a victim of Joseph Stalin's persecutions in the 1930's. One of the first poems in this collection makes mention of the victims of the concentration camps: "There was earth inside them, and/they dug." Rather than concentrating on the horrors of camp existence, the poem discusses the possiblity of believing in an omnipotent, benevolent God in the face of these atrocities; this theme is picked up again in "Zürich, zum Storchen" ("Zurich, the Stork Inn"), in which Celan reports on his meeting with the Jewish poet Nelly Sachs: "the talk was of your God, I spoke/ against him." Other poems contain references to his earlier work; the "house in Paris" is mentioned again, and autumn imagery, suggesting the memory of his mother, is used more frequently. Several other poems express

Celan's renewed and final acceptance of his Jewish heritage but indicate his rejection of God, culminating in the blasphemous "Psalm," with its bitter tribute: "Praised be your name, no one."

Celan's poetry after *Die Niemandsrose* became almost inaccessible to the average reader. As the title *Atemwende* (breath turning) indicates, Celan wanted to go in entirely new directions. Most of the poems in Celan's last collections are very short; references to language and writing become more frequent, and striking, often grotesque, portmanteau words and other neologisms mix with images from his earlier poems. There are still references to Judaism, to an absent or cruel God, and—in a cryptic form—to personal experiences. In the posthumously published *Schneepart*, the reader can even detect allusions to the turbulent political events of 1968. The dominant feature of these last poems, however, is the almost obsessive attempt to make the language of poetry perform new, hitherto unimagined feats, to coerce words to yield truth which traditional poetic diction could not previously force through its "speech-grille." It appears that Celan finally despaired of ever being able to reach this new poetic dimension. The tone of his last poems was increasingly pessimistic, and his hopes, expressed in earlier poems, of finding "that ounce of truth deep inside delusion," gave way to silence in the face of the "obstructive tomorrow." It is the evidence of these last poems, more than any police reports, which make it a certainty that his drowning in the Seine in 1970 was not simply the result of an accident.

Celan's poetry can be understood only by grasping his existential dilemma after World War II as a Jewish poet who had to create his poetry in the German language. Desperate to leave behind everything which would remind him of his own and his people's plight, he nevertheless discovered that the very use of the German language inevitably led him back to his past and made a new beginning impossible. Finally, the only escape he saw still open to him was to attempt to abandon completely the conventions of German lyric poetry and its language, to try to make his poetry express his innermost feelings and convictions without having to resort to traditional poetic diction and form. Weinrich suggests that Celan, like Mallarmé before him, was searching for the "absolute poem," a poem which the poet creates only as a rough sketch and which the reader then completes, using private experiences and ideas, possibly remembered pieces of other poems. If this is true, Celan must have ultimately considered his efforts a failure, both in terms of his poetic intentions and in his desire to come to terms with his personal and his Jewish past.

Major publications other than poetry
  SHORT FICTION: "Gespräch im Gebirg," 1959.
  NONFICTION: "Edgar Jené und der Traum vom Traume," 1948; "Der Meridian," 1960 ("The Meridian," 1978).

Bibliography

Glenn, Jerry. *Paul Celan*, 1973.

Meinecke, Dietlind. *Über Paul Celan*, 1973.

Szondi, Peter. *Celan-Studien*, 1972.

Weinrich, Harald. "Paul Celan," in *Deutsche Literatur der Gegenwart I*, 1971, 1976.

Franz G. Blaha

LUIS CERNUDA

Born: Seville, Spain; September 21, 1902
Died: Mexico City, Mexico; November 5, 1963

Principal poems and collections

Perfil del aire, 1927; *Egloga, elegía, oda*, 1927; *Un río, un amor*, 1929; *Los placeres prohibidos*, 1931; *Donde habite el olvido*, 1934; *Invocaciones*, 1935; *La realidad y el deseo*, 1936, 1940, 1958, 1964; *Las nubes*, 1940; *Como quien espera el alba*, 1947; *Poemas para un cuerpo*, 1957; *Desolación de la quimera*, 1962; *The Poetry of Luis Cernuda*, 1971; *Poesía completa*, 1973; *Selected Poems of Luis Cernuda*, 1977.

Other literary forms

Although Luis Cernuda is best known for his poetry, he was also a prolific essayist and critic. He published several works in prose, three of which, devoted to criticism, appeared during his lifetime. In his *Estudios sobre poesía española contemporánea* (1957; studies on contemporary Spanish poetry), Cernuda analyzes the most important trends in Spanish poetry since the nineteenth century. He bestows upon Gustavo Adolfo Bécquer the distinction of having reawakened poetry after more than a hundred years of lethargy, and he lauds Miguel de Unamuno y Jugo as the most important Spanish poet of the twentieth century. Cernuda's *Pensamiento poético en la lírica inglesa (siglo XIX)* (1958; poetic thought in English lyricism), a study of the theory of poetry as practiced by nineteenth century British poets, reveals Cernuda's deep appreciation of and attachment to English verse of the Romantic and Victorian periods. Many of Cernuda's essays and magazine and newspaper articles—which appeared originally in such publications as *Caracola, Litoral, Octubre, Cruz y raya, Heraldo de Madrid*, and *Insula*—have been collected in the two-volume *Poesía y literatura* (1960, 1964; poetry and literature) and in *Crítica, ensayos y evocaciones* (1970; criticism, essays and evocations). *Variaciones sobre tema mexicano* (1952; variations on a Mexican theme), often referred to as poetic prose, is an affectionate reflection by the poet on the people of Mexico, their music, their art, their churches, and their poverty and misery. Mexico was the poet's adopted homeland, after some years in what he perceived to be alien environments, and he felt warmed by the Mexicans, their culture, and their climate, so reminiscent of his native Andalusia. *Ocnos* (1942, 1949, 1964) is a meditation upon time, a prose poem that becomes the lyrical confession of a poet writing about himself and his art. Because it contains Cernuda's analysis of his work, this volume is a useful companion to his poetry. Cernuda also undertook the translation into Spanish of the poetry of Friedrich Hölderlin, Paul Éluard, William Wordsworth, and William Blake, as well as plays by William Shakespeare. He did not devote much effort to fiction, leaving behind only three short pieces: "El indolente" ("The Indolent One"), "El viento en la colina" ("The Wind on the Hill"), and "El sarao" (the dancing party), all published in the collection *Tres narraciones* (1948; three narratives).

Achievements

While Cernuda is recognized as an important member of the *generación del 27* (considered by some a second Spanish Golden Age), he did not receive during his lifetime the acclaim and recognition extended to some of his contemporaries, such as Federico García Lorca, Jorge Guillén, Rafael Alberti, and Vicente Aleixandre. Furthermore, Cernuda never enjoyed financial or professional security. His position as a self-exile—he never returned to Spain, even for brief periods, after 1938—might explain his lack of popularity during the 1930's and 1940's; his political sympathies (staunchly Republican), his open homosexuality, his reticence, and even the seemingly simple structure and language of his poetry were all factors that may have distanced him from an entire generation of readers. More recently, Cernuda's audience has been growing: a number of important critical studies have appeared in the last fifteen years, a complete edition of his poetry has been published, and a collection of many of his extant essays was issued in 1970—clear indications that Cernuda is being reappraised by a new generation of Spanish poets and critics.

Even now, however, as Carlos-Peregrín Otero has observed, it might be premature to evaluate Cernuda's impact and his role as an innovator in Spanish letters. Cernuda displayed, first and foremost, a commitment to poetry and to the creative act. His work allowed him to express himself and served to sustain him. It was through his poetry that he came to understand himself and the world, and this understanding helped him to endure the solitude and melancholy of his alienated and withdrawn existence. Through his writing, he was able to objectify his desire, his passion, and his love and to liberate himself in ways that his social persona never could. He also used his poetry to battle against his obsession with time and its relentless passage. These were the principal themes of Cernuda's works. He expressed them with increasing clarity and simplicity of language, yet, toward the end of his life, his work began to acquire the quiet, meditative tone of a man who is confident in the knowledge that his art, if nothing else, will escape decay.

Biography

Born to a comfortable middle-class family of Seville, Luis Cernuda y Bidón was the youngest of the three children of Bernardo Cernuda Bousa, a colonel of a regiment of engineers, and Amparo Bidón y Cuellar. In Cernuda's poem "La familia" ("The Family"), which appeared in *Como quien espera el alba* (like someone awaiting the dawn), the domestic environment of his youth is portrayed as grave, dark, and rigid like glass, "which everyone can break but no one bends." The poet does not reveal any warmth or affection for his parents or his two sisters. His parents, he adds, fed and clothed him, and even provided him with God and morality. They gave him all: life, which he had not asked for, and death, its inextricable companion. From an early age, Cernuda displayed a timidity and reticence which were to characterize his social interaction throughout his life.

Cernuda first began to appreciate poetry at the age of nine, when he came across some poems by Gustavo Adolfo Bécquer (1836-1870), the Romantic poet whose remains were transferred from Madrid to Seville for permanent interment in 1911, causing excitement among the residents of the city and renewed interest in the poet's work. After completing secondary school in a religious institution, Cernuda enrolled at the University of Seville to study law in 1919. He received his law degree in 1925 but never practiced. His most important experience during his university years was his contact with Pedro Salinas, the eminent poet whose first year as a professor at the university coincided with Cernuda's first year as a student. Their association—at first formal, impersonal, and restricted to the classroom—developed in the course of the next few years, as Salinas encouraged Cernuda and other students to pursue their poetic inclinations. Salinas recommended that Cernuda begin to read French authors, among them Charles Baudelaire, Stéphane Mallarmé, and André Gide. Gide's works helped Cernuda to confront and to reconcile himself to his homosexuality. Through the influence of Salinas, Cernuda was able to publish nine poems in the prestigious magazine *Revista de occidente* when he was only twenty-three. Two years later, in 1927, Cernuda published his first collection, *Perfil del aire* (air's profile). In spite of the coolness with which it was received, with one or two notable exceptions, Cernuda had determined to devote his life to writing, putting an end to any professional indecision he had felt earlier.

Upon the death of his mother in 1928—his father had died in 1920—Cernuda left Seville for good, traveling first to Málaga and then to Madrid, and meeting a number of the writers and poets who would be known as the *generación del 27*, among them Manuel Altolaguirre and Emilio Prados (the editors of *Litoral*), Vicente Aleixandre, and Bernabé Fernández-Canivell (future director of the literary magazine *Caracola*, an outlet for Cernuda's poetry). He had met García Lorca in Seville in 1927. In the fall of 1928, through Pedro Salinas, Cernuda was offered an appointment as Spanish lecturer at the École Normale de Toulouse, a position that afforded the young poet the opportunity to spend some time in Paris. During his year in France, he immersed himself in the Surrealist movement and adopted a style and point of view to which he would adhere for the next four years.

The decade of the 1930's was one of steady productivity for Cernuda, marked by increasing recognition of his gifts among other writers of his generation. At the same time, it was a period of political instability that forced writers to take sides. Cernuda was a staunch supporter of the Spanish Republic, and for a brief period, around 1933, a member of the Communist Party, contributing several political articles to *Octubre*, a magazine edited by Rafael Alberti. In 1934, for a short time, he worked for Misiones Pedagógicas (pedagogic missions), an educational program sponsored by the Republican government to bring culture to remote areas of the country. Cernuda's job was to explain the great masterpieces of Spanish painting, presented to the audience in reproduction. Cernuda spent the first summer of the Spanish Civil War, in 1936, in Paris as a secretary to the Spanish ambassador to France, Alvaro de Albornoz, whose daughter Concha was a friend of Cernuda. Upon his return to Spain, Cernuda joined the Republican popular militia and fought in the Guadarrama. In the winter of 1938, he traveled to England to deliver a series of lectures arranged for him by the English writer Stanley Richardson. A few months later, while returning to Spain through France, Cernuda decided to go into exile permanently, first to Great Britain, where he taught in Surrey, Glasgow, Cambridge, and London, and then to the United States, where he arrived in the fall of 1947. His appointment as professor of Spanish literature at Mount Holyoke College, negotiated for Cernuda by Concha Albornoz, initiated the most stable and financially untroubled period of the poet's life. The New England climate and the isolation of the school, however, made Cernuda restless and caused him to explore the possibility of a teaching post at a university in Puerto Rico. In 1953, after several summers spent in the more hospitable Mexico, he resigned his tenure at Mount Holyoke and settled in Mexico, where he would remain—with only brief returns to the United States to teach at San Francisco State College and the University of California at Los Angeles—until his death from a heart attack in 1963. While in Mexico, he supported himself by his writing and by teaching several courses at the Universidad Autónoma in Mexico City.

Analysis

In the case of Luis Cernuda, it is impossible to separate the poet from the man—his personality from his literary production. As much as Cernuda himself protested that he loathed the intrusion of the person in the poem, he, much more than most of his contemporaries, can be said to have revealed himself through his writing. He offered readers a glimpse of his poetic world from one window only, as Jenaro Talens states, and that window is open to the main character, who is frequently—if not always—Cernuda himself. As a consequence, his poetic production reflects his development as a man and his awareness of himself. This, in turn, tends to focus most analyses of his work along closely chronological lines, as his poetry evolves from the vague and dreamy musings of youth to the bitter acceptance of the relentlessness of time and the inevitability of death. Beginning with the first book of poems,

Perfil del aire—published as a supplement to the magazine *Litoral* and edited by Manuel Altolaguirre and Emilio Prados in 1927—Cernuda embarked upon a journey of self-discovery. In this first collection, the youthful poet presents an indifferent, indolent attitude toward the world; he is there, but he dreams and is surrounded by emptiness. Dreams and walls protect him, provide him with a haven for his loneliness; there, he can savor his secret pleasures and his unfulfilled yearnings. This first major effort, retitled "Primeras poesías" and revised before reappearing in the first edition of *La realidad y el deseo* (reality and desire), was not well received. Cernuda was criticized sharply for imitating Jorge Guillén, and his production was judged unoriginal. More recent criticism, while acknowledging Cernuda's debt to Guillén, dismisses these charges as exaggerated, praising this early work for its fine sensibility and for the musical quality of its language.

The negative reception of his first book encouraged Cernuda to withdraw, at least personally, from what he considered the literary mainstream and, by his own admission, "to wish to cultivate that which is criticized by others." He began work on a second collection, *Egloga, elegía, oda* (eclogue, elegy, ode), a series of four poems patterned after classical and neoclassical models, particularly the works of Garcilaso de la Vega, whose meter and rhyme Cernuda imitated deliberately. Some years later, reflecting on his development as a writer, Cernuda said that, while this second work had permitted him to experiment with classical themes and strophes, its style did not satisfy him, for he was unable to find what he loved in what he wrote. Nevertheless, in *Egloga, elegía, oda*, the poet was able to express more forcefully some of the feelings first introduced in *Perfil del aire*. Vague yearnings have become a compelling attraction to beauty in all of its forms; the poet's need to satisfy his desires is confronted by the opposition of desire to such satisfaction. In this set of poems, he begins to remove his cloak of ennui, revealing a strong, sensuous nature. The pursuit of pleasure replaces indifference as the antidote for solitude and sadness. Desiring to express himself in a more daring fashion and to rebel against the constraints of bourgeois society, which misunderstood him and his sexuality, Cernuda gravitated toward the Surrealists. He read the works of Louis Aragon, André Breton, and Paul Éluard, whose poetry he translated into Spanish.

Cernuda's Surrealist stage began, not coincidentally, with his year in France (1928-1929) and resulted in two important works, *Un río, un amor* (a river, a love) and *Los placeres prohibidos* (forbidden pleasures). The most notable technical characteristic of *Un río, un amor* is Cernuda's use of free verse, which was also being adopted during this period by other Spanish poets, such as Aleixandre, García Lorca, and Alberti. Freed of external constraints, Cernuda's verse nevertheless retained a strong sense of meter, and the rhythm of his lines was preserved through accentuation and cadence. He also made use of reiteration, anaphora, and anastrophe. From this period onward, Cernuda began to experiment with longer lines, although they seldom exceeded eleven syllables. In *Los placeres prohibidos*, Cernuda continued to discard technical conventions, alternating between verse and prose poems. Thematically, Surrealism provided Cernuda with the opportunity to liberate himself from social restrictions. Asserting his linguistic and stylistic freedom, he wrote of "night petrified by fists," "towers of fear," "iron flowers resounding like the chest of man," "tongue of darkness," and "empty eyes."

Toward the end of *Un río, un amor*, Cernuda intimates what is expressed openly in *Los placeres prohibidos*; he accepts his homosexuality and admits to being possessed with love. This love takes the form of passionate physical desire, rendered no less glorious and pure because of its carnality; only the outside world tarnishes this love with its opprobrium. In *Un río, un amor*, love produces an emptiness and a vacuum. Man is like a phantom, without direction; he is indifferent to the world, as if he were dead. In *Los placeres prohibidos*, however, love ceases to be the object of dreams; it becomes something real, the primary goal of man's desire, the motive behind all he does and feels: To give in to this love, without reservation, is man's purpose. Its attainment is nevertheless elusive—except for some fleeting moments—and contains an element of pain; herein lies the source of the solitude and the impotence of man.

A third work published during this period, *Donde habite el olvido* (where oblivion dwells), closes out Cernuda's Surrealist phase. It was written after a failed love affair, one that the author naïvely had believed would last forever. This accounts for the bitterness of its tone, the poet's desire for death, and the harsh indictment of love, which, once it disappears, leaves nothing behind but the "remembrance of an oblivion." In the fourth poem of this collection, Cernuda retraces his personal history, as if it were a life already lived, replete with regrets and unfulfilled expectations. The first part of the poem exudes optimism, expansiveness, and anticipation, conveyed by the spring moon, the golden sea, and adolescent desire. The light, however, turns into shadows; the poet falls into darkness and is ultimately a living corpse.

With his next major publication, *Las nubes* (the clouds), Cernuda introduced two important new themes into his poetry: historical time, with its specific focus on Spain as the abandoned and beleaguered homeland, and man's spirituality and religiosity. Love, the recurring topic of much of Cernuda's work, plays virtually no role in this collection. In "Un español habla de su tierra" ("A Spaniard Speaks of His Homeland"), the poet writes nostalgically of the happy days of the past, before his land succumbed to the conquering Cains. The bitter days of the present find sustenance in the fond memories of years gone by, an idealized past that might someday be re-created yet to which the poet cannot return. When that day comes, and his homeland is free, it will come looking for him—only to discover that death has come to call first. Ironically, as one critic has pointed out, this poem was prescient in its chronology. In "Impresión de destierre" ("Impression of Exile"), the dislocated narrator—then in London—overhears a fatigued voice announce the death of Spain; "'Spain?' he said. 'A name./ Spain has died. . . .'"

Las nubes also contains the clearest expression of Cernuda's views on traditional religion. While his poetic use of belief in the supernatural has been described as a type of pantheistic hedonism based on Mediterranean mythology, his spiritual quest included attempts to find answers in more traditional Christian imagery by positing the existence of a God through Whom man can achieve love. Cernuda devoted four poems in this collection to the broad question of the existence of God: "La visita de Dios" ("God's Visit"), "Atardecer en la catedral" ("Dusk in the Cathedral"), "Lázaro" ("Lazarus"), and "La adoración de los magos" ("The Adoration of the Magi"). In the long poem "God's Visit," the protagonist, in a voice filled with anguish, confronts God with the terrible wreckage of what is now the speaker's country, the poet's paradise of years gone by, perhaps destroyed by the casual wave of His hand. As the last hope for renewal, the protagonist begs God to restore to the world beauty, truth, and justice; without these, he warns, God could be forgotten.

More firmly rooted in Christianity is the five-part poem "The Adoration of the Magi," in which Cernuda's debt to T. S. Eliot is clear. The poem opens with a meditation by Melchior on the existence of God, reaching the conclusion that if he himself is alive, God, too, might well exist. This knowledge does not fully satisfy Melchior. To reason the existence of God is not enough; some more evocative proof is needed. The second part of the poem, "Los reyes" ("The Kings"), presents the Magi, each with a distinctive voice which expresses the conflicting visions of a single character: Melchior the idealist, Gaspar the hedonist, and Balthasar the skeptic. Through their intertwined monologues, the pilgrim searches for proof of the existence of God. The next section, "Palinodia de la esperanza divina" ("Palinode of Divine Hope"), is perhaps the most inventive; in it, the author expresses the disenchantment and disappointment felt by the Magi upon arriving in Bethlehem after a long journey and finding nothing but a poor child, a life "just like our human one," after expecting ". . . a god, a presence/ radiant and imperious, whose sight is grace." In the fourth part, "Sobre el tiempo pasado" ("On Time Past"), the protagonist is the old shepherd (Father Time?) who remembers a period in his youth, long past, when three wise men came to look at a newborn child. The old man, however, has no recollection of a god; how can a humble shepherd, whose knowledge of man is so lacking, have seen the gods? The poem closes with a short fifth part "Epitafio" ("Epitaph"), wherein man, as searcher, is told that he once found the truth but did not recognize it; now he can console himself by living his life in this world, as a body, even though he cannot be free from misery.

The publication of *Las nubes* marked a new beginning for Cernuda, the man and the poet. He had departed from Spain; he was approaching the age of forty—an age which, for a man who associated beauty with youth and joy with youthfulness, must have created much anxiety. His prospects for recognition in Spain had been shattered by political events. Cernuda responded to this situation by creating a protagonist with a distinct identity; he created *the poet*, whose role it was to subsitute as the main character for the author and who would, when called upon, assume all responsibility for failure. Thus, Cernuda created what Phillip Silver calls his "personal myth" and entered into the mature stage of his poetic production. Poetry became a means to understand and preserve the past. The need to fulfill a grand passion was discarded; man must resign himself to a world that belongs to the gods, a world in which he cannot partake of paradise. If man can be made into a myth, however, his life will be eternal and his beauty everlasting. In poems such as "Noche del hombre y su demonio" ("A Man's Night and His Demon") and "Río vespertino" ("Evening River") from *Como quien espera el alba*, Cernuda expresses an attitude of acceptance, as if recounting a life already lived. He anticipates, without fear, the inevitability of death. There is but one small consolation: There is no ash without flame, no death without life. In the long poem "Apología pro vita sua" from the same collection, the poet gathers up all the suffering of his existence: his obsessions as a poet, the war, his agnosticism, and his need and hope for a personal, intimate God. From his bedside, the protagonist summons first his lovers—some of whom he loved—to help illuminate his world growing dim, for "Is passion not the measure of human greatness . . . ?" He then calls in his friends to help him renounce the light. As in a confessional, he admits to regrets, but only for those sins which he has not had the opportunity or the strength to commit. He asserts that he has lived without God because He has not manifested Himself to him and has not satisfied his incredulity. The protagonist maintains that to die, man does not need God; rather, God needs man in order to live. In an apparent contradiction, a few lines later, he asks God to fill his soul with the light that comes with eternity.

The past, that which has been, and the inevitble passage of time become the dominating theme of the remainder of Cernuda's poetic output. In his mature verses, he recounts his life and his loves with the pessimistic tone of one who knows that they will never come again. Splendor, beauty, passion, and joy are juxtaposed to solitude, old age, and death.

Major publications other than poetry

SHORT FICTION: *Tres narraciones*, 1948.

NONFICTION: *Ocnos*, 1942, 1949, 1964; *Variaciones sobre tema mexicano*, 1952; *Estudios sobre poesía española contemporánea*, 1957; *Pensamiento poético en la lírica inglesa (siglo XIX)*, 1958; *Poesía y literatura*, 1960, 1964 (2 volumes); *Crítica, ensayos y evocaciones*, 1970.

Bibliography

Capote Benot, J. M. *El surrealismo en la poesía de Luis Cernuda*, 1976.

Coleman, Alexander. *Other Voices: A Study of the Late Poetry of Luis Cernuda*, 1961.

Delgado, Agustín. *La poética de Luis Cernuda*, 1975.

Harris, Derek. *Luis Cernuda: A Study of His Poetry*, 1973.

Jiménez-Fajardo, S. *Luis Cernuda*, 1978.

Morris, C. B. *A Generation of Spanish Poets: 1920-1936*, 1969.

Otero, Carlos-Peregrín. *Letras*, 1966.

Paz, Octavio. "La palabra edificante," in *Cuadrivio*. 1965, pp. 167-203.

Silver, Phillip. *"Et in Arcadia Ego": A Study of the Poetry of Luis Cernuda*, 1965.

Talens, Jenaro. *El espacio y las máscaras: Introducción a la lectura de Cernuda*, 1975.

Wilson, E. M. "Cernuda's Debts," in *Studies in Modern Spanish Literature and Art Presented to Helen I. Grant*, 1972. Edited by N. Glendinning.

Clara Estow

AIMÉ CÉSAIRE

Born: Basse-Pointe, Martinique; June 26, 1913

Principal poem and collections

Cahier d'un retour au pays natal, 1939, 1947 (*Memorandum on My Martinique*, 1947; also as *Return to My Native Land*, 1968); *Les Armes miraculeuses*, 1946 (*Miraculous Weapons*); *Soleil cou coupé*, 1948 (*Beheaded Sun*); *Corps perdu*, 1950 (*Disembodied*); *Ferrements*, 1960 (*Shackles*); *Cadastre*, 1961 (revised editions of *Beheaded Sun* and *Disembodied*; *Cadastre: Poems*, 1973); *State of the Union*, 1966 (includes abridged translations of *Miraculous Weapons* and *Shackles*); *Aimé Césaire: The Collected Poetry*, 1983.

Other literary forms

Poet, dramatist, and essayist Aimé Césaire is recognized primarily for his poetry; the first major poem he wrote, *Return to My Native Land*, set the tone and thematic precedence for his subsequent writings. *Tropiques*, a cultural magazine of which the poet was one of the principal founders, featured Césaire's own poems, which were reprinted in the Gallimard edition of *Miraculous Weapons* in 1946. As well as a vehicle for literary content, the magazine was used to arouse the cultural and political consciousness that would continue to mark Césaire's personality throughout his life. While Césaire's poetry attests his exceptional talent as an artist, his polemical and historical works, *Discours sur le colonialisme* (1950; *Discourse on Colonialism*, 1972)—born out of the poet's disillusionment with the inferior role Martinique continued to play in its relations with France—and *Toussaint Louverture* (1960)—named after the black hero Toussaint-Louverture, who led the 1802-1803 revolution in Haiti—demonstrate the poet's effort to assail racism, colonialism, and the cultural alienation of blacks from all sides. He continued to explore the problems of the existence of blacks in the world and African culture, especially the issue of decolonization, in his drama—which is more accessible than his poetry. His plays include *La Tragédie du Roi Christophe* (1963; *The Tragedy of King Christopher*, 1969), *Une Saison au Congo* (1966; *A Season in the Congo*, 1968), and a reworking of William Shakespeare's play *The Tempest* (1611) entitled *Une Tempête* (1969; *The Tempest*, 1974).

Achievements

Césaire arrived in France in 1931, at a time when Surrealism had already begun to dominate the literary scene. Instead of an ideology, this movement provided Césaire with the poetic vision and creative license to set his own creative Muse into action. Fleeing the oppressive poverty of his native Martinique, Césaire was ripe for the ideals put forth by the Surrealists. He was attracted, in particular, to the notion of "écriture automatique" (automatic writing) and the Freudian concept of the self, hidden in the recesses of the subconscious, waiting only for a propitious moment to reveal itself. Armed with these two concepts, Césaire destroyed the poems he had written previously and began writing his epic poem *Return to My Native Land*, which would eventually gain for him great fame. More significant, he adopted the methods of the Surrealists in the service of a truly revolutionary cause.

Thus, Césaire's sojourn in France, originally envisioned as an escape from the hopeless conditions in Martinique, resulted instead in his own cultural and political awakening. While pursuing his studies in Paris at the Lycée Louis-le-Grand, he met Léopold Senghor (who later became the first president of Senegal). Thanks to their friendship, Césaire acquired a greater knowledge and appreciation of Africa. Together, they joined forces with Léon Damas, another young poet, to establish the journal *L'Étudiant noir*, which replaced a previous journal, *Légitime défense*, that had been silenced after its first publication. Thus, Césaire's cultural and political consciousness gradually began to take on a more concrete form. Before, racism and colonial exploitation were, in his perception, limited mainly to the geographical confines of the West Indies and, especially, to Martinique. Once in Paris, however, he began to realize that the suffering of blacks extended well beyond the boundaries of his homeland. For Césaire, Senghor, and Damas, the creation of *L'Étudiant noir* was an acknowledgment that blacks in the West Indies, Africa, and elsewhere underwent a common experience.

Although Césaire worked zealously to produce a poem that would express the range, depth, and complexity of his poetic vision, his efforts were not initially received with enthusiasm. The first publisher to whom he submitted *Return to My Native Land* refused to publish the poem. Césaire succeeded in having only excerpts from the poem published in the magazine *Volonté* in 1939. Consequently, both the poet and his work went unnoticed for the most part, but this did little to dampen his creative spirit. When Césaire finally returned to Martinique, where he founded the journal *Tropiques* with the aid of his wife, Suzanne Césaire, René Menil, and Aristide Maugée, he continued to bring to life his poetic inspirations. It was not, however, until Césaire met André Breton (who became aware of Césaire's poetic genius after having read, in *Tropiques*, the poems that make up *Miraculous Weapons*) that Césaire was reintroduced to France's reading public. Subsequent admiration of Césaire's work was not limited to writers or political figures. The 1950 deluxe edition of *Disembodied* contained thirty-two engravings by Pablo Picasso that richly illustrated the ten poems in the collection.

That poetic genius which caught the attention of Breton continues to be recognized by Césaire's critics. Césaire's contribution to literature goes beyond his exceptional use of Surrealist techniques, his extraordinary mastery of the French language, and his attempt to articulate the inhumane effects of racism and colonialism. By his example, Césaire helped to give impetus to the first great outpouring of written literature in Africa and the West Indies.

Biography

One of several children, Aimé Césaire was born on June 26, 1913, in Basse-Pointe, Martinique. Most of his childhood was spent in the midst of poverty, and as Césaire grew older, he became acutely aware of the oppressive conditions of the majority of the Martinicans. At the Lycée Schoelcher in Fort de France, he excelled in his studies, winning a scholarship to the Lycée L'ouis-le-Grand in Paris. Ironically, this sojourn in Paris paved the way for Césaire's political maturation. His friendship with Senghor, whom he met at Louis-le-Grand, was instrumental in changing Césaire's view of Africa, which would serve time and again as a source of inspiration for him. Once he completed his studies, he returned to Martinique with his wife, Suzanne, whom he married while he was still a student at the École Normale Supérieure.

Césaire's return to Martinique, a journey he had envisioned in his first poem, was as significant as his departure. He (as well as his wife) enjoyed a brief teaching career at his former *lycée* in Fort de France. As usual, Césaire left his mark, inspiring his students with his love of poetry and instilling in them an enthusiasm for learning. Like many of his black contemporaries, Césaire took on the dual role of artist and political leader. Elected mayor of Martinique and deputy to the National Assembly in France, Césaire worked diligently to improve the plight of the Martinicans. During his fourteen years of office in the National Assembly, he was a member of the French Communist Party, but he left the Party when he perceived its indifference to the particular interests of Martinique. In 1957, Césaire founded the Martinican Progressive Party, and, despite his disillusionment, he never ceased to play an active role in shaping the political life of his homeland.

Analysis

In his preface to the first complete edition of Aimé Césaire's *Return to My Native Land*, André Breton remarked that this poem represented the "greatest lyrical monument of the times." Indeed, Césaire's first major poem has left an indelible mark upon literature. Of all of his works, *Return to My Native Land* is, by far, the most criticized, analyzed, and quoted.

If poetry allows the human spirit to liberate itself from the bonds of reason, as the Surrealists suggest, then it becomes quite clear why Césaire's first major work has such a strong autobiographical tone. The ever-present "I" calls attention to the poet's desire to become rooted once again in his history and culture. Thus, *Return to My Native Land*, a poem of revolt, self-awakening, and "engagement," represents, first and foremost, the poet's personal testimony. From the start, it recalls the town where Césaire grew up, an image which seems both to attract and to repel him. He vividly evokes the stagnant existence of black peasants in Martinique, trapped in poverty and despair, resigned and silent. The emphasis placed on the geographical isolation of the island reinforces, as well, the idea of cultural alienation from the African sources of the black people.

Césaire presents a distressing picture of the poverty in which he and his six brothers and sisters lived. His father's health was being destroyed by an unknown illness, and his mother spent her days and nights pedaling a Singer sewing machine to help provide the family's daily sustenance. Yet poverty and illness were not the most tragic effects of colonialism and racism, for Césaire saw an entire race reduced to a state of intellectual and emotional apathy, convinced of their inability to build, to create, to take control of their own destiny. It was in response to this sense of apathy and self-contempt that Césaire developed the concept of *négritude*, emphasizing a very proud self-awareness of "blackness" and the distinctive qualities of black culture.

Césaire's recognition and acceptance of Martinique's history, which also represents his own as well, makes it possible for him to purge himself of his feelings of cultural inferiority and to begin his ascent toward a new sense of racial consciousness. From the abyss of despair there arises a magnificent cry of protest. In *Return to My Native Land*, Césaire undertakes what he envisions as a messianic mission: He becomes the voice of the downtrodden, the victims, the exploited, the oppressed—those who are unable to verbalize and articulate their own cry of protest. Critics often compare the poet to Christ, citing as examples the lines in which Césaire takes on himself the prejudices held against blacks. At one point, his account of the inhumanities suffered by blacks is reminiscent of the scourging of Christ. Césaire's acceptance of his Christ-like role strongly underscores the message of "engagement," the poet's role as a socially and politically committed artist.

The themes and motifs found in Césaire's first major poem recur throughout his oeuvre. *Shackles*, published in 1960, explores the vicissitudes of the black experience in Martinique and the evolution of African culture. The title, which denotes the forging of iron, suggests the era of slavery. Césaire recaptures this brutal moment in black history in the title poem, which is replete with nautical expressions used to evoke the voyage of the slave ship. He uses this image to draw a comparison between the agony suffered by the slaves and the misery which plagues the lives of the Martinicans, "arrimés de coeurs lourds" (stowing heavy hearts). It is with this new generation of slaves, who are not necessarily physically bound by chains, that Césaire is primarily concerned.

The poet recognizes the need to reconcile the present with the past, heretofore rejected and denied, before there can be any real and permanent cultural revolution. Therein lies the salvation of Martinique, cut off physically and emotionally from its African roots. The past represents, in Césaire's words, an old "wound" which has never healed, an "unforgettable insult."

Thus, Césaire, with other *négritude* writers, has finally been able to set the record straight, to place colonialism and slavery in their proper perspective. Like all the other sons and daughters of humanity, the black people were not destined to be slaves for all time.

African independence has signaled the beginning of a new phase in the history of blacks. Suddenly, it became apparent that the masters of colonialism were not entirely invincible. This is a positive sign for Césaire, who sees in these events a confirmation of the latent force among blacks—a force needed to overcome years of inferiority and submission. His poem "Pour saluer le Tiers Monde" ("Salute to the Third World") is above all one of praise and exaltation. The poet feels an immense sense of pride in the advent of a new African. Césaire punctuates the text, several times, with the emphatic words "I see," calling attention to the fact that he is a witness to these changing times. The image Césaire presents of Africa, unexpectedly standing upright, contrasts, significantly, with his image of Martinique, made powerless by its somnolence. Césaire laments the lack of racial and cultural consciousness among the Martinicans and celebrates Africa, the maternal source of his people. Indeed, to some degree, Césaire places the burden of leadership for the West Indies on Africa. The poet depicts a symbolic ritual in which he covers his body with the soil of Africa in such a way as to infuse himself with her strength. It is important to note that Césaire's treatment of Africa in *Shackles* recalls his original theme of the "return to his native land," which signifies not only a physical journey but also a return to his African heritage.

While he grapples with the larger problems of Martinique's fate, Césaire continues to confront his personal dilemma as a committed artist. His situation is not a unique one; it is one he shares with the educated elite of all Third World nations. With this privileged status comes the awesome responsibility to represent the voice of the masses. In his public life, Césaire does this through his active involvement in the political affairs of Martinique. In the same way, his poetry reaffirms continually his message of racial consciousness and commitment. There is no "art for art's sake" in Césaire's work; style and content are so closely intertwined that it is virtually impossible to talk about one without the other.

In *Return to My Native Land*, Césaire refers to the creative power of words, a power which enables the individual to alter reality. Poetry has allowed the poet the freedom to manipulate and violate the French language in ways that would not have been possible in prose. Thus, the very texture of his language is political; his style is a declaration of independence, shattering conventions associated with the oppressors of his people.

Despite the thematic consistency that characterizes Césaire's oeuvre, a certain movement can be traced from *Return to My Native Land* to *Shackles*. The former deals with the necessity to affirm and reclaim the dignity of blacks. It was the product of a period of intense soul-searching for the poet, who had to overcome his own sense of cultural and racial inferiority. In *Shackles*, on the other hand, Césaire seeks to reconcile the ideals of *négritude* with the existing realities in the West Indies. The masses do not appear to be ready to take their destiny into their own hands, and Césaire has come to realize that the effects of years of silent resignation will be reversed only gradually. In all of his works, however, Césaire is remained committed to his people, serving them as visionary, storyteller, historian, and poet.

Major publications other than poetry

PLAYS: *La Tragédie du Roi Christophe*, 1963 (*The Tragedy of King Christopher*, 1969); *Une Saison au Congo*, 1966 (*A Season in the Congo*, 1968); *Une Tempête*, 1969 (*The Tempest*, 1974).

NONFICTION: *Discours sur le colonialisme*, 1950 (*Discourse on Colonialism*, 1972); *Toussaint Louverture*, 1960.

MISCELLANEOUS: *Oeuvres complètes*, 1976.

Bibliography

Arnold, A. James. *Modernism and Negritude: The Poetry and Poetics of Aimé Césaire*, 1981.

Condé, Marse. *Profile d'une oeuvre: Cahier d'un retour au pays natal*, 1973.

Juin, Hubert. "Aimé Césaire, poète noir," in *Présence africaine*, 1956.

Kesteloot, Lilyan. *Aimé Césaire*, 1962.

Sartre, Jean-Paul. "Orphée noir," in *Situations III*, 1949.

Cherie R. Maiden

RENÉ CHAR

Born: L'Îsle-en-Sorgue, France; June 14, 1907

Principal poems and collections

Les Cloches sur le coeur, 1928; *Arsenal*, 1929; *Ralentir travaux*, 1930 (with Paul Éluard and André Breton); *Le Marteau sans maître*, 1934; *Moulin premier*, 1937; *Placard pour un chemin des écoliers*, 1937; *Dehors la nuit est gouvernée*, 1938; *Le Visage nuptial*, 1938 (*The Nuptial Countenance*, 1976); *Seuls demeurant*, 1945; *Feuillets d' Hypnos*, 1946 (*Leaves of Hypnos*, 1973); *Le Poème pulvérisé*, 1947; *Fureur et mystère*, 1948; *Les Matinaux*, 1950; *Lettera amorosa*, 1953; *Hypnos Waking*, 1956; *Cinq Poésies en hommage à Georges Braque*, 1958; *La Parole en archipel*, 1962; *Commune présence*, 1964; *Le Nu perdu*, 1971; *La Nuit talismanique*, 1972; *Aromates chasseurs*, 1976; *Poems of René Char*, 1976.

Other literary forms

Like many French poets, René Char has written a great number of prose poems and is considered one of the finest practitioners in this genre since Charles Baudelaire and Arthur Rimbaud, by whom he was heavily influenced. These works are scattered throughout Char's poetry collections, suggesting that he does not distinguish the prose poem as a separate form. Char has published several volumes of essays, including *Recherche de la base et du sommet* (1955; inquiry into the base and the summit) and *Sur la poésie* (1958; on poetry). He has also contributed a number of prefaces, introductions, and catalogs for art shows, such as the 1973 Picasso exhibit in Avignon. Char's lifelong interest in painting is reflected in essays on Georges Braque, Joan Miró, and other contemporary artists; he has also been active in other arts, writing the scenario for the ballet *L'Abominable homme des neiges* (1956; the abominable snowman), for example, and the play *Le Soleil des eaux* (1949). Char's work has been set to music by composer Pierre Boulez.

Achievements

Early in his poetic career, Char was deeply involved in Surrealism, co-authoring several works with Paul Éluard and André Breton and gaining some recognition for his work. Under that influence, he was encouraged in his taste for the fragment—the incomplete line and "broken" metaphor, which he called *le poème pulvérisé*. These Surrealist techniques led to his being identified with the movement but did not lead to serious individual recognition.

After World War II, Char dedicated his *Leaves of Hypnos* to Albert Camus, a fellow Resistance fighter, who called Char France's greatest living poet, praising his shift from the self-absorption of Surrealism to a more universal view. Char thereby became associated with the rising tide of Existentialism and achieved recognition as a major poet. Char also is credited with achieving a new validation for the prose poem, which, though it had a long tradition in France, was still regarded as a stepchild of "real" poetry.

Biography

René-Émile Char was born on June 14, 1907, the son of Émile Char, a manufacturer, and Marie-Thérèse-Armand Rouget of Cavaillon. Char's father, who served as the mayor of L'Île-en-Sorgue, was the son of a ward of the state who had been given the name "Charlemagne," later shortened to "Char-Magne" and, eventually, to "Char." Char spent his childhood in L'Île-en-Sorgue in the Vaucluse region in the south of France. The Vaucluse has a lush landscape ringed with mountains, the beauty of which would later fill his poetry. It is also an area of diverse industries, and the young Char became familiar with men of many occupations, especially craftsmen, peasants, and Sorgue River fishermen. Their rugged independence helped to instill in him a lifelong love of freedom. The boy had begun his education in the public schools when his father died in 1918. He then continued to the *lycée* in Avignon (the closest large city) for his *baccalauréat*. In 1924, he spent some time in Tunisia, where he developed a distaste for colonialism. He returned to study briefly at the École-de-Commerce in Marseilles, leaving from 1927 to 1928 for artillery service in Nîmes. In 1928, he published his first book of poems, *Les Cloches sur le coeur*.

Char sent a copy of his second collection, *Arsenal*, to Paul Éluard, the chief poet of Surrealism, in Paris. Éluard was impressed with Char's work and went to L'Île-en-Sorgue to meet him. They became lifelong friends, and Char moved to Paris, where Éluard introduced him to the leading figures of Surrealism, including André Breton. Char cowrote the poem *Ralentir travaux* (works slowed down) with Éluard and Breton and helped found the periodical *La Surréalisme au service de la révolution*. In 1933, Char married Georgette Goldstein (they were divorced in 1949) and a year later published *Le Marteau sans maître* (the hammer without a master). During the early 1930's, he resided sometimes in Paris, sometimes in L'Île-en-Sorgue, and made several trips to Spain.

By the mid-1930's, the political climate in Europe was changing, and Char broke with the Surrealists in 1934, as Éluard soon would, sensing a need for the kind of action hinted at in *Le Marteau sans maître*: the defense of the oppressed and the fight for justice. In 1935, Char accepted a job as manager of the chalk pits in Vaucluse, but he soon resigned. In 1936, he was seriously ill as a result of blood poisoning, and he spent a year—the same year the Spanish Civil War began—convalescing in Cannea. He published *Placard pour un chemin des écoliers* (sign for a bypath) and *Dehors la nuit est gouvernée* (somewhere night is ruled) in the late 1930's, both titles indicating his growing sense of commitment. As 1939 ended, Char found himself mobilized into the artillery in Alsace, where he fought until the French surrender.

Returning to L'Île-en-Sorgue, Char was suspected by the Vichy police of being a Communist because of his association with Surrealism. He fled with Georgette to the Alps and there began his activities as a *maquisard* in the Armée Secrète. Using the name Captain Alexandre from 1943 to 1945, Char became the departmental commander of the Parachute Landing Division of the Second Region of the *Forces françaises combattantes*, and deputy to the regional commander of the Free French operations network. He was wounded in combat against the Germans in June, 1944, and, after being cared for by Resistance doctors, he continued to Algeria in July, 1944, in response to a summons from the North Africa Allied Council. Subsequently, he was parachuted into France and participated in the battles to liberate Provence. Demobilized in 1945, he received several decorations for his service, including the Croix de Guerre and the Médaille de la Résistance.

From 1939 to the liberation of France, Char had not published any poetry. When *Seuls demeurant* (the only ones left) and *Leaves of Hypnos* appeared, he became famous. Georges Mounin's critique *Avez-vous lu Char?* (1947; Have you read Char?) praised Char's work and contributed to his success. Char again began to live part of each year in Paris and part in the Vaucluse; he did not, however, participate in the "official" literary life. He has generally declined the honors offered to him, although he was made a Chevalier de la Légion d'Honneur and received the Prix des Critiques in 1966, and he argues that poetry should not be considered a means of making a living. He also stood apart from the partisan political involvements which entangled many French writers of the time—especially those who shared Char's leftist sympathies.

One of Char's closest friends was the novelist Albert Camus, who, like Char, linked literature with the struggle toward freedom and human dignity. Char also exchanged letters with the Russian poet and novelist Boris Pasternak and, beginning in 1955, kept in close contact with the German philosopher Martin Heidegger.

Throughout the 1950's and 1960's, the audience for Char's poetry grew, and he was translated into numerous foreign languages. Beginning with his association with Georges Braque in 1947, Char has often published his poetry in beautiful editions, illustrated by celebrated contemporary artists such as Picasso, Nicolas de Stäel, Louis Broder, and Louis Fernandez. Char has also illustrated his poetry himself. His interest in philosophy has dominated his later poetry, and since the 1950's, Char has seen his role as poet as that of a commentator on society, a revolutionary in the service of humankind.

Analysis

Albert Camus once wrote that René Char's poetry was both ancient and new, subtle and simple, carrying both daytime and night: "In the brilliant landscape where Char was born, the sun . . . is something dark." Camus thus identified one of the predominant characteristics of Char's poetic method: the juxtaposition of opposites. According to critic Robert W. Greene, Char has rejected one of the fundamental concepts of Western thought: the Aristotelian principle that a thing cannot be anything other than what it is at one moment in time. Any poem working within different principles seems as obscure and vaporous as Eastern religions which deny the reality of the world. Char, however, deeply admires the fragments of Heraclitus—who believed in the unity of opposites—and sets up oppositions throughout his poetry. Similar concepts can be found in earlier poetry influenced by Eastern thought, such as Ralph Waldo Emerson's "Brahma," in which the slayer is simultaneously the one who is slain. Char's rejection of the identity principle, however, has different implications in its twentieth century context. It reflects the linguistic, subjective philosophies developing in the late nineteenth and early twentieth centuries, and though Char has a tendency toward the fragmentary aphorism (possibly influenced by the fragments of Heraclitus), he grapples with the problems of this century in a specific way. Thus, as Camus rightly observed, Char's poetry is both "ancient and new."

The concluding lines of Char's important early poem "Commune présence" are characteristic in their conjunction of opposites: "You have been created for extraordinary moments . . . Adjust yourself and disperse without regret." Here, a near-heroic proclamation of identity is immediately followed by a line advising assimilation. The following line, "According to a soft hardness," embodies yet another contradiction and illustrates Char's technique of opposing semantic units. It furthermore conveys Char's fundamental view of a world of unsynthesized opposites. Life is simultaneously total resistance and total acceptance. One is reminded of the Existentialist assertions that whatever a person does is completely absurd, yet that it is necessary to act as if each moment had meaning. The final two lines of the poem contain a command: "Swarm the dust/ No one will decelerate your union." The penultimate line is a contradiction because a swarm of bees is similar to a cloud of dust only in appearance. Dust moves at random, each mote in its own direction; bees move in rough unison. Dust dissipates into nothingness; bees have a vital purpose. The final line promises that nothing can oppose the eventual union, however—the union that comes from an initial scattering. In political terms, one sees the allusion to humankind as a collection of individual, meaningless units (like dust), which can gain new meaning by union (like a swarm). All those meaningless units (bees, motes, people), added together, become meaning. Metaphorically, darkness becomes the sun.

Char's early association with Surrealism might be regarded as an influence in that direction, or it may be seen as a reflection of what Char already was reaching for in his work. As Camus wrote, "No doubt he did take part in

Surrealism, but rather as an ally than as an adherent, and just long enough to discover that he could walk alone with more conviction." This is the general critical appraisal. Anna Balakian, however, asserts that Char carries on the tradition of Surrealism better than anyone else. As Char describes in *Le Poème pulvérisé*, he faces—like Breton and the others—"this rebellious and solitary world of contradictions" and cannot live without the image of the unknown before him. In this vast unknown, this world finally impossible to understand (hence the Surrealist's despair), one can only be an explorer, and poetry is the medium of exploration: words and meaning in conflict. Irrationality is crucial in setting aside the world of illusion and seeing beyond, to the more legitimate world of dreams. *The Nuptial Countenance* has been cited as exhibiting this trait in its mixing of objects that defy classification; it has many resemblances to the works of Breton and Éluard.

Critic Mechthild Cranston argues that Char took two important insights with him when he broke with Surrealism: He saw that the existing world order was in need of reexamination, along with the canons of art, and that violence and destruction would not solve the problems of his generation. The first idea has remained with him throughout his career, in his commitment to the Resistance and in his generally leftist politics. The second, however, has undergone modification. In Char's Surrealist period, he speaks of the need for violence, catastrophes, and crimes to help create a new concept of art. "Les Soleils chanteurs" mentions specific kinds of violence which will revitalize poetry. Char's poetry of this period is filled with images of chemicals, metals, and machinery, like the works of the Futurists, and has a similar purpose: to destroy the florid, false language of late Romanticism. Char's experience of the real—not metaphorical—violence of World War II changed his orientation. In his poetry published since the war, he has abandoned the rhetoric of the Surrealists, achieving a new humility and seeking the simplicity of a child's vision.

Char's later poetry is also distinguished by its moral intensity, particularly its commitment to freedom. In Char's view, anything that inhibits human freedom is immoral. The poet's duty is to do battle continually against anything that would restrict humankind's ability to seek meaning. This includes any preconceived ideas, even the idea of liberty itself. One might see in this stance a combination of the didactic nature of Surrealism and the call to action and freedom in Existentialism. Like the Existentialists, Char attempts to re-create ethics for modern man, yet in doing so he invokes the mystery so important to Surrealist art. Thus, for Char, poetry is an Existential stance, a *becoming*, an invitation to return to natural insights and to reject mechanical materialism.

Major publications other than poetry
PLAY: *Le Soleil des eaux*, 1949.

NONFICTION: *Recherche de la base et du sommet*, 1955; *Sur la poésie*, 1958.

Bibliography
Balakian, Anna. "René Char in Search of the Violent Man," in *World Literature Today*. LI (1977), pp. 380-384.
_____ . *Surrealism*, 1959.
Caws, Mary Ann. *The Presence of René Char*, 1976.
_____ . *René Char*, 1977.
Cranston, Mechthild. *Orion Resurgent: René Char, Poet of Presence*, 1979.
Greene, Robert W. "René Char, Poet of Contradiction," in *Modern Language Review*. LXVI (1971), pp. 802-809.
La Charité, Virginia A. "The Role of Rimbaud in Char's Poetry." in *PMLA*. LXXXIX (1974), pp. 57-63.
Lawler, James R. *René Char: The Myth and the Poem*, 1978.
Mounin, Georges. *Avez-vous lu Char?*, 1947.
Piore, Nancy Kline. *Lightning: The Poetry of René Char*, 1981.

J. Madison Davis

CHARLES D'ORLÉANS

Born: Paris, France; May 26, 1391
Died: Amboise, France; January 4, 1465

Principal poems and collections

Livre contre tout péché, 1404; *Retenue d'amours*, 1414; *Ballades*, c. 1415-1460; *Chansons*, c. 1415-1460; *Songe en complainte*, 1437; *Rondeaux*, c. 1443-1460; *The English Poems of Charles of Orleans*, 1941, 1946.

Other literary forms

In addition to his poetry, Charles d'Orléans left a long and partly autobiographical speech which he had presented in defense of the Duke of Alençon at the latter's trial. The speech, which dates from 1458, contains reminiscences of Charles's captivity and of his early life.

Achievements

Charles is by any measure one of the preeminent poets of the latter Middle Ages; most critics would in fact rank him second in France only to François Villon. They would, however, doubtless consider him a rather distant second, and that would represent both an accurate assessment and something of an injustice. He is by no means the literary equal of Villon, one of the world's great poets. Yet Charles is often underestimated, not only because he is inferior to Villon, but also because, quite simply, he is *not* Villon.

To many readers, Charles's poetry may seem somewhat dated, in contrast to the timeless texts of his contemporary. Indeed, Charles uses images, formulas, and conventions associated with the literature of courtly love, which enjoyed its greatest vogue during the twelfth and thirteenth centuries. His allegories and personifications have been dismissed as delicate and cultivated playthings, valuable witnesses to an age but of quite limited appeal to modern readers.

It is important, however, to meet Charles on his own terrain and on his own terms; there he is found to be an extraordinary poet. Charles was a wealthy and refined prince; for him and for many of his contemporaries, poetry was both a pastime and an art to be cultivated. A poem might be a witty rejoinder in a literary debate with friends, or it might be an artistic creation of the highest order, an artifact to be sculpted carefully and consciously. In such a system, Charles's use of traditional materials—his allegories and personifications and courtly images—was fully justified. An attentive reading, moreover, reveals that he was by no means a slave to tradition. What he borrowed he was able to renew, and his best poems derive much of their appeal from his subtle re-creation of traditional materials.

Re-creation occurs within the bounds of individual poems as well; there are, for example, few poets more adroit than Charles at leading gracefully into a refrain so as to alter its meaning slightly with each stanza. He is a master of style, of wit, of verbal color, yet he is sometimes considerably more than that. No sooner is the reader lulled by an extended series of abstractions and personifications than Charles suddenly shifts to an unadorned declaration of the pain he felt at his captivity, deprived as he was not simply of love but of his homeland and his freedom.

Charles engaged frequently in poetic contests and games, and poetry was for him avocation as well as art. Under the circumstances, repetition and unevenness are inevitable. More often than not, however, he proves himself to be an extraordinary practitioner of his art—that of the refined and delicate poem which deserves admiration for what it is rather than criticism for what it lacks.

Biography

Charles d'Orléans was born in Paris on May 26, 1391; his father was Louis, Duke of Orléans, whose brother was King Charles VI. In 1406, a marriage was arranged between Charles and his cousin Isabelle of France. The following year (in November, 1407), his father was assassinated by Jean-sans-Peur, Duke of Burgundy, and Charles himself became Duke of Orléans. Isabelle died in 1409, and the next year, following an alliance with the Count of Armagnac, he married eleven-year-old Bonne d'Armagnac. He spent several years trying to avenge his father's death, doing battle with the Burgundians, concluding more than one unsuccessful treaty, and occasionally seeking the aid of the English.

France's troubles were not limited to the regional struggles which occupied much of Charles's early life; he had, in fact, been born at the midpoint of the Hundred Years' War, and before his twenty-fifth birthday he was taken prisoner by the English in the Battle of Agincourt (October 25, 1415). He spent the next twenty-five years as a prisoner in England. It was a curious kind of imprisonment; although he was frequently moved from place to place, he was never held behind bars. He was allowed to receive visitors, money, and servants from France, and he had access to various amenities and pleasures, which (according to some reports) may have included female companionship. It was hardly a difficult existence, but Charles was nevertheless separated from his homeland and family, and many of his poems from the period bitterly lament his plight.

Changes in the political and military situation (along with the payment of a substantial ransom and a promise never again to take up arms against the English) secured Charles's release in November, 1440, and, his second wife having died five years earlier, he soon married Marie de Clèves, niece of the Duke of Burgundy. For the remainder of his life, he dabbled occasionally in military and political affairs but was largely content to devote his time to poetic pursuits, especially at his castles in Blois and Tours.

During the night of January 4, 1465, he died at Amboise, at the age of seventy-three.

Analysis

The subjects of Charles d'Orléans' poetry are love, his imprisonment in England, and the pain he suffers from both. These are not necessarily discrete subjects; they frequently overlap and merge. For example, in the courtly idiom adopted by Charles, love always entails the lover's loss of freedom. Accordingly, the poet often appears to have transformed his captivity into an amorous metaphor (without, however, diluting its literal force); he was the prisoner of the English in much the same way that his persona was the prisoner of love. His themes are also related in a more direct way, for his imprisonment deprived him not only of freedom but also of love and pleasure. Thus, even in one of his more clearly patriotic poems, "En regardant vers le pays de France," ("While Looking Towards the Country of France"), where the source of his suffering is his separation from his homeland, his pain is caused in part by the loss of "the sweet pleasure that I used to experience in that country," one of his specific pleasures obviously being that of love.

During his years in England, Charles often lamented the separation from "his lady." Critical efforts to identify that lady (with Isabelle, with Bonne d'Armagnac, or with an English acquaintance) have not met with success; this failure is both inevitable and appropriate. The fact is that courtly convention would be likely to preserve the anonymity of the lady, and also, more to the point, her identity is simply irrelevant. She may thus have been *any* woman or an amalgam of several women—or she may not even have existed except as an abstraction. Indeed, in some poems she appears to represent not a particular lady but France itself, for Charles uses the same general terms to describe his absence from his lady and his separation from his country. Again, Charles's emotion is his principal focus, and a shifting, ambiguous relation exists between the major causes of it. For a poet like Charles, given to persistent metaphorical associations, his lady and his country easily become almost interchangeable or doubled poetic referents throughout the period of his captivity.

There are many places where Charles makes explicit reference to his experiences in England. Even though his captors treated him comparatively well, his poems could hardly have conveyed more anguish and melancholy. His best-known work of the period is doubtless the poem "While Looking Towards the Country of France," in which Charles, from Dover, laments his fate and declares: "Peace is a treasure that cannot be praised too highly. I detest war, for it has long prevented me from seeing my beloved France." Later, he was to remark in another context that he would prefer to have died in battle rather than endure his English captivity. Other works express his sorrow at France's lot and his later exultation at the English defeat ("Rejoice, Noble Kingdom of France"). Such passages offer a good deal of interest for reasons both historical and biographical, and even though their artistic value is uneven, some of them are likely to appeal to modern readers more than do Charles's love poems.

On first reading, the love poems may appear dated—and, indeed, some of them are. Charles is generally thought of as a poet of courtly love, and that is the way he began his literary career. At that time, he cultivated (not always with much originality) all of the conventions of courtly love inherited from Guillaume de Lorris (in *Le Roman de la rose*, thirteenth century; *The Romance of the Rose*) and from others who wrote two centuries or more before Charles. Not only his ideas but also his modes of expression are traditional. Thus, in Ballade 29 he writes: "I do not fear Danger or his followers,/ For I have reinforced the fortress/ In which my heart has stored its goods/ . . . And I have made Loyalty mistress of it." Such passages are often ingenious, but the premises underlying them offer nothing new.

With time, however, his ideas evolved, and later he either turned against courtly love or (according to John Fox) simply found it largely irrelevant. Thus, while he had earlier noted without much apparent conviction that "Sadness has held me in its power for so long that I have entirely forgotten Joy," his protestations begin to assume a more personal and intense tone. He points out that "the poor souls of lovers are tormented in an abyss of sorrow" (Rondeau 140); he wonders if it is Fortune's desire that he suffer so much (Rondeau 217); he orders Beauty out of his presence, because "you tempt me too often" (Rondeau 236). In some cases, to be sure, the later poems are superficially indistinguishable from the traditional laments of the courtly lover, but one can generally discern a subtle shift of tone, and some texts go further and constitute a clear rejection of courtly premises. For example, replacing the traditional notion that suffering tempered by hope is adequate recompense for the lover is Charles's insistence (in Rondeau 65) that he can love only if his love is reciprocated, and in Rondeau 160 he states cynically that a medicine can surely be found to help those who are in love.

A revealing example of the evolution in Charles's thought is provided by the contrast between his two long poems, *Retenue d'amours* (love's retinue) and *Songe en complainte* (dream in the form of a complaint). The former, written prior to Agincourt, offers a traditional allegorical presentation of a young man's initiation into love: He leaves *Enfance* (childhood) and entrusts his life to Lady Youth. He is afraid, because Youth has long served the God of Love, and Charles has heard many men tell of "the pains that Love makes them endure." Considering himself unable to bear the torment, he is reluctant to expose himself to Love's power. Youth assures him that those who complain are not true lovers who know what joy is and that honor and great good come to those who love. After meeting other members of Love's retinue, he awakens to love in a traditional way: Beauty shoots an arrow into his heart through his eyes. Becoming Love's vassal, he swears to accept the ten commandments of Love (to remain honorable, loyal, discreet, and so on).

More than twenty years later, Charles composed *Songe en complainte*, which serves in one sense as a continuation of the earlier poem, but which also proves to be its converse, its mirror image. Here, noting that his heart requires repose, his purpose is to *disengage* himself from love, to reclaim his heart, long held captive by the God of Love. Whereas he had earlier emphasized the joy of love and had accepted its pain as a natural, even desirable phenomenon, the older Charles now finds pain too high a price to pay for love and desires release from his vows. His attitude toward love is now melancholy, heavily tinged with skepticism.

The two long poems are important as a dramatic illustration of Charles's evolution, but artistically they are not particularly impressive creations. They are straightforward and (especially in the former case) derivative, and emphasis remains primarily on the elaboration of theme to the virtual exclusion of expressive subtlety and poetic effect. In fact, it could be said, with little injustice to Charles, that his poetic temperament is reductive, not expansive. He is generally more successful in his shorter forms. Thus the ballades are usually better than the long poems, and the rondeaux are better still. His most successful pieces approach the status of Imagist poems, presenting a single, self-contained, vivid image, generally in the opening lines. The body of the poem is largely an elaboration of this image, often involving the subsidiary images derived from and supporting the principal one. Ironically, the elaboration may at times dilute the power of the image instead of intensifying it. Charles himself must have realized as much; he gradually began to abandon the ballade in favor of the shorter rondeau (a fixed-form poem containing three brief stanzas, usually of four or five lines each, with the beginning of the first stanza serving as the refrain of the other two). The dimensions of this form were ideally suited to Charles's talent and temperament, and his rondeaux present what John Fox describes as "an art form at its peak." Many of the themes, images, and personifications used in the long poems find their way into the shorter ones as well, although in the latter Charles molds them to his purposes with greater originality and flexibility.

Despite the fact that Charles is often considered to have made extensive use of allegory, it is essential to define his technique with more precision. Ann Tukey Harrison correctly suggests that Charles reduces allegories and personifications to metaphors tailored to his purposes. Often the narrative element in his poems is radically diminished or entirely eliminated, leaving him with *Esperance* (hope), *Beauté* (beauty), *Bon Acceuil* (welcome), or some other quality which appears to be a dramatized personification but in fact simply represents an aspect of his own experience. Thus, one of his famous poems, "La Forêt de longue actente" (the forest of long awaiting), provides not the locus of a sustained series of events (as it might have for Guillaume de Lorris, for example) but rather a simple indication of a psychological or emotional state.

Moreover, while Charles may appear to maintain a static set of personifications adopted from earlier tradition, his system is in reality remarkably flexible, each figure being freely fashioned to the need created by a particular poem and by a particular dramatic situation. Thus, Comfort (for example) may be specific or abstract, ally or foe, as the context dictates. Each figure exists within a rather wide range of possible functions, and, as a result, Charles's poetic cosmos is constantly shifting and developing with each text and with each artistic choice.

The stylistic pattern employed in "La Forêt de longue actente" (that is, the conjoining of a natural or architectural object with an abstraction) occurs in many of Charles's poems and pulls them in opposing directions, creating a tension between the concrete and the abstract: the Cloud of Sadness, the Ship of Good News, the Doorway of Thought, the Window of the Eyes. Such formulas are simple stylistic inversions that present a metaphor (thought is a doorway) as an apparent allegory. Charles is clearly fashioning a very personal version of allegory—or, rather, using the appearance of allegory to amplify and deepen the meaning of his images.

Several of Charles's images (castles, forests, ships) suggest confinement or containment, and the temptation to propose a biographical reading is not easily resisted. Obviously, such images reflect the poet's own imprisonment. Such a reading may seem plausible, but it ultimately does an injustice to Charles as a poet, because it reduces the text to an item of biographical evidence. Critical focus must remain on the poem itself, and instead of seeing the text as an index to his life, the critic should regard Charles's experience as material and inspiration for an autonomous series of texts. Some of his poems do indeed speak directly and explicitly of his captivity in England, yet loss of freedom is a familiar metaphor in the tradition of courtly love, to say nothing of love poetry of other ages.

As Charles had first been the willing poetic prisoner of love, and as he had later been imprisoned by the English, he gradually came to see himself as the captive of old age. He began to consider love an inimical force, and for him it was explicitly linked to the aging process. The culmination of this development is found in *Songe en complainte*. He notes that it ill befits an old man to make a fool of himself with regard to love, and he announces that "Love and Old Age are incompatible." Here the melancholy that characterizes many of his poems takes on a new tone; instead of a gentle melancholy presumably felt by all lovers (and accepted by Charles's persona during his earlier years), this poem offers a note of genuine sadness and almost forlorn resignation. Such an evolution is in one sense typical of his work. There are few themes or images that he either adopts or discards during the course of his career; rather, it is the use of them that changes, the tone of them that evolves. His originality thus lies not in the fashioning of new themes, but in the particular ways his persona comes to react to conventions borrowed from earlier poets.

Charles d'Orléans thus represents the continuation and culmination of a style and a tradition two centuries old or older, but he also represents their renewal. He puts a personal stamp on the allegorical method, and at the same time he manages to raise his poetry—which participates in venerable tradition—above the level of the personal. His poems do not present a broad and elaborate canvas; they are far closer to the refined art of the miniature: diminutive, delicate, intimate. In the rondeau, Charles found his ideal form and cultivated it extensively, leaving a body of work that not only presents unusual historical interest but also preserves a number of small and often exquisite masterpieces.

Bibliography

Fox, John. *The Lyric Poetry of Charles d'Orléans*, 1969.
Goodrich, Norma Lorre. *Charles of Orléans: A Study of Themes in His French and in His English Poetry*, 1967.
Harrison, Ann Tukey. *Charles d'Orléans and the Allegorical Mode*, 1975.
Planche, Alice. *Charles d'Orléans, ou la recherche d'un langage*, 1975.
Poirion, Daniel. *Le Poète et le prince*, 1965.

Norris J. Lacy

ALAIN CHARTIER

Born: Bayeux, France; c. 1385
Died: Avignon, France; c. 1430

Principal collection

The Poetical Works of Alain Chartier (1974; J. C. Laidlaw, editor). The editor of this recent and useful collection refers to previous critical studies and editions by André du Chesne, G. du Fresne de Beaucourt, Arthur Piaget, and Pierre Champion. The Laidlaw edition has filled gaps and corrected errors of former editions.

Other literary forms

Traditional literary history has judged Alain Chartier's poetry to be less important than his prose works. This evaluation is based on the fact that many of the poems are conventional, courtly creations, whereas the prose works deal with substantial moral and political issues. Modern scholars, however, have adopted a new perspective on Chartier's poetry, seeing in it a symbolic extension of the content found in the prose works. This new approach reveals a continuity and balance in Chartier's works.

Chartier wrote in both Latin and French. His major prose works in French are *Le Quadrilogue invectif* (1489; *The Invective Quadrilogue*, late fifteenth century), written in 1422, and *Le Traité de l'espérance: Ou, Consolation des trois vertus* (1489; *The Treatise on Hope: Or, The Comfort of the Three Virtues*; late fifteenth century) written about 1428. *The Invective Quadrilogue*, composed after the Battle of Agincourt, is a patriotic allegory in which France exhorts the orders of society—chivalry, the clergy, and the common people—to seek peace together. Chartier takes a firm stand in this work, which many critics consider his most important, for national unity, for the poor, and for the Dauphin Charles. The author's longest work and among his last, *The Treatise on Hope*, was inspired by Boethius. Allegorical and historical figures paint a vivid tableau of a country distressed by continual conflict and then offer a religious solution to national problems. The treatise is a combination of verse and prose, with prose predominating.

Chartier's Latin works include official diplomatic speeches and letters, personal letters to his family and friends and *De vita curiali* (1489; *The Curial*, 1888), the shortest of the prose works and of uncertain date. *The Curial*, written first in Latin, then translated into French, as *Le Curial*, is a vehement attack on the practices of court life. Because of the problems presented by the manuscript tradition, several theories on date of composition and authorship have been advanced. Scholars are not certain whether Chartier composed one or both parts.

Above all, Chartier's prose writings are distinguished by their eloquence.

Both his contemporaries and successors appreciated and imitated his conciseness and oratorical style. Modern scholars have appreciated the extent to which he consecrated his literary skill to addressing the problems of his times. One critic, Edward J. Hoffman, in his 1942 study, *Alain Chartier: His Work and Reputation*, sees in Chartier's literary contribution "a crusading spirit . . . an eloquence born of sincerity and genuine sympathy, all put to the service of a high moral purpose: the regeneration of a stricken, prostrate nation."

Achievements

Alain Chartier has been called the "Father of French Eloquence" and one of the first of France's great patriots. Literary history has admired him most for his patriotism, his humanism, and his erudition. During his lifetime and in the century that followed, Chartier was held in high esteem for his oratorical and poetic ability. Then, for many years, he fell out of critical favor and was rarely mentioned with judgment other than disdain for the excessively traditional aspects of his work. Modern critics have benefitted from the studies of Arthur Piaget, Pierre Champion, and Gaston Paris, as well as by the clarification of the confusing and extensive manuscript tradition. In addition to Hoffman, scholars such as J. C. Laidlaw, William W. Kibler, and C. J. H. Walravens have based their evaluations on more reliable texts and have viewed Chartier in his historical as well as his literary context. Chartier was an erudite author, trained in a traditional medieval background that profoundly influenced the formation of his poetic canon. His frequent use of allegory, personification, and courtly themes characterizes his poetry. Yet beyond mastery of conventional form and the expression of traditional themes, the poet devoted his scholarship and literary skill to communicating moral ideas to his readers. This aspect of his work issued from his observations of his contemporaries and his participation in the political events of his lifetime. Because he was deeply affected by conflict and suffering, Chartier moved from a purely aesthetic to a more realistic thematic conception.

Biography

Constructing an accurate biography of Alain Chartier has proved an arduous task for scholars. Biographers have had to deal with many problems—scarce information, variable spellings of the author's surname, and frequently contradictory references—in order to propose an approximate chronology. Account books, political and diplomatic documents, and the author's own works have been fruitful sources of information.

Chartier was born toward the end of the fourteenth century, probably 1385, into a property-holding family in Bayeux, Normandy, in France. His father was Jean Chartier. Alain was older than his two brothers, Guillaume and Thomas, and preceded them to high office. Thomas was to become a royal secretary and notary; Guillaume, Bishop of Paris and royal adviser. Although little information concerning Alain's youth and years as a student is available, it is known that he left his native province to study at the University of Paris. It may be assumed from his scholarly knowledge and ability to write well in Latin and in Middle French that Chartier was an able student and that he received an excellent classical education. In addition to his mastery of language, his works bear witness to a broad knowledge of ancient history, philosophy, and literature.

The artistically nourishing atmosphere of the Anjou court was pivotal in the development of the young Chartier's literary talent, and his courtly love poems must have found an appreciative audience in royal circles. Chartier entered royal duty about 1418 and continued in the services of the Dauphin after the latter was declared King Charles VII. No mention is made of Chartier in royal records after 1429. As royal secretary, it was Chartier's duty to act as spokesman, deliver speeches, and present credentials during diplomatic missions. His work involved him in negotiations in Hungary, Venice, and Scotland, where he distinguished himself as an orator. Chartier's embassy to Scotland in 1428 is remembered through a famous anecdote. According to the legend, the Dauphiness Margaret of Scotland, daughter of James I and future wife of the Dauphin Louis (later Louis XI), approached Chartier, who was asleep in a chair, and kissed him on the mouth, saying that she did not kiss the man but rather the mouth that had spoken so many virtuous and beautiful words.

Although it is not known if Chartier was a member of the clergy, it is known that he held several ecclesiastical titles, such as canon, curate, and archdeacon, which the French king could have bestowed on a public servant. The emphasis on religion in his works would substantiate his close affiliation with the Church. Furthermore, that he neither married nor had children supports the hypothesis that he became a priest.

Chartier's disappearance in 1429 has been a subject for scholarly research. It is possible that, because of the harshly critical nature of his writings about politics, he fell out of royal favor and was even exiled. It must be remembered that Chartier lived in disillusionment and despair over the moral and political corruption that he had witnessed at first hand. Sensitive to the plight of his beloved country and of his compatriots, Chartier reacted constantly to his times. At the height of his literary career, France was torn by conflict without and within: the Hundred Years' War (1337-1453), the Burgundian-Armagnac civil wars, and the troubled reign of Charles VI. Clearly, Chartier dedicated his life to calling his fellowman to return to the virtuous ways of the past. Scholars find no evidence to prove that he lived after 1430 and believe that he is buried at the Church of Saint-Antoine in Avignon, France.

Analysis

The 1974 Laidlaw edition of Alain Chartier's poetry is comprehensive in its discussion of the background and manuscript tradition of each poem and also in its review of previous critical editions and bibliography. Students of Chartier will benefit from this work. All of the poems discussed in this section are found in the Laidlaw edition.

Chartier's poetry, though begun in the courtly tradition, illustrates a maturing process and a consequent passage from less serious thematic concerns to moral and political issues. His earliest love poems are traditional in form and at times somewhat awkward. "Le Lai de plaisance" ("The Lay on Pleasure"), dating from about 1414, provides an example of the young poet's early tendency to concentrate on metrical complexity and accurate rhyme scheme rather than on subject matter. Although it is not difficult to identify the poem's theme—thoughts on pleasure on New Year's Day—nor to detect its sad tone, it is nevertheless somewhat perplexing to follow the thematic development through the forty-eight stanzas. The poet presents the subject in a courtly manner in the form of advice on how to be an honorable lover, yet the message is obscured at times by the poet's intention to fulfill all of the technical requirements of the lay's fixed form. Chartier engaged in technical exercises with other fixed forms as well. His poetry shows him respecting and occasionally mastering the stanzaic, metric, and rhythmic uniformity of the ballad, the rondeau, and the chanson. Although Chartier was not innovative in the fixed-form genres, his poems possess graceful movement and harmony.

Chartier's longest poetic work, "Le Livre des quatre dames" ("The Book of Four Ladies"), written after the Battle of Agincourt, about 1416, represents a transition between his idealized poetry and realistic prose. This work holds special interest because, though it was written shortly after the very traditional "The Lay on Pleasure," it contains political ideas that Chartier develops later in his prose. In addition, "The Book of Four Ladies" describes the poet's personal sentiments at some length in a prologue of twelve stanzas. While on a solitary spring walk to forget his sadness over a love affair, the narrator meets four women who in turn reveal their grief at having lost their lovers in battle; one has been killed, one has been captured, another is missing, and the last has fled. It is possible, according to Laidlaw, to speculate on the identities of the women, placing them in the historic context of the conflicts of the Burgundian-Orléanist. Through the sad lamentations of these women, Chartier expresses far more than grief. He criticizes energetically and eloquently those in power who allowed France to fall into ruin and those who refused to defend their country. Although structurally traditional in its description of an idealized landscape and its plan of debate, the poem is an impassioned patriotic work heralding Chartier's important prose works.

Another poem that gives evidence of Chartier's transition to serious subjects is "Le Débat patriotique" ("The Patriotic Debate"), written sometime between 1416 and 1420. The poetic form is a debate between two noblemen during the course of which the author expresses his scorn for the behavior of the nobility, particularly toward peasants. Thematically, the poem is in the same current as *The Invective Quadrilogue* and *The Curial* because of its attack on the noble class, which, according to Chartier, has lost its nobility of spirit. The poet exhorts members of the privileged classes to return to honor and to earn the respect of those who follow their directions and their examples— it is through valor, not wealth and position, that men acquire distinction. The structural plan of the work, too, reinforces its important message. Hoffman points out that for modern readers, the dramatic, playlike format of this poem is especially realistic and convincing. In addition, he notes, Chartier's vivid vocabulary and energetic movement produce an atmosphere that is radically different from the allegories and didactic debates that characterize many of Chartier's poetic works. Because of the effective manner in which form supports meaning, several critics have ranked "The Patriotic Debate" as one of Chartier's best poems.

Also in the category of moral poetry is "Le Bréviaire des nobles" ("The Breviary for Nobles"), written about 1424. In this work, Chartier is again concerned with honor and virtue, which the poet invites his noble readers to emulate. Although the structure of the poem is completely traditional, it conveys the high moral message that lies at the heart of Chartier's serious writings.

It is interesting that Chartier's oeuvre is not chronologically consistent in its development toward greater moral and political expression. One of his most famous and popular poems, "La Belle Dame sans merci" ("The Beautiful, Pitiless Lady"), written in 1424, shows the poet moving in a different direction. Although many of his love poems became increasingly more realistic and influenced by events in French history, in this poem the poet looks inward and seems touched by worldly happenings only in the desire to take refuge from them. Here, Chartier seems to reject contemporary reality in favor of creating a more satisfactory, even courtly universe. Yet, strangely enough, the poetic world that he envisions is not a happy one. The hero is a sorrowful and scorned lover; the heroine is skeptical and independent. The two of them never succeed in communicating with each other. The portrayal of the cruel heroine angered Chartier's courtly readers to the extent that they demanded, through a noble, pro-feminist institution called the Court of Love, that the poet explain his intentions in belittling both his heroine and love. Chartier answered their accusation in a second poem, "L'Excusation" ("The Excuse"), in which he claimed that Cupid had forgiven him and that he would always serve and respect women. Allusions by other French poets of the period suggest that Chartier was expelled from the poetic Court of Love. This suggestion has not been proved; taken symbolically, however, it can be interpreted as a reflection of Chartier's rupture with the traditional aesthetic system of his day.

Major publications other than poetry

NONFICTION: *Le Quadrilogue invectif*, written 1422, published 1489 (*The Invective Quadrilogue*, late fifteenth century); *Le Traité de l'espérance: Ou, Consolation des trois vertus*, written c. 1428, published 1489 (*The Treatise on Hope: Or, The Comfort of the Three Virtues*, late fifteenth century); *De vita curiali*, 1489 (*The Curial*, 1888).

Bibliography

Bourgain-Hemeryck, Pascale, ed. *Les Oeuvres Latines d'Alain Chartier*, 1977.

Busquet, R. "Une Épitaphe d'Alain Chartier," in *Mémoires de l'Institut Historique de Provence*. VI (1929), pp. 179-187.

Champion, Pierre. *Histoire poétique du XVe siècle*, 1923.

Hoffman, Edward J. *Alain Chartier: His Work and Reputation*, 1942.

Kibler, William W. "The Narrator as Key to Alain Chartier's 'La Belle Dame sans merci,'" in *French Review*. V (1979), pp. 714-723.

Paris, Gaston. *Chansons du XVe siècle*, 1875.

Piaget, Arthur. *Alain Chartier: La Belle Dame sans merci*, 1942.

Walravens, C. J. H. *Alain Chartier: Études biographiques, suivies de pièces justificatives, d'une description des éditions des ouvrages inédits*, 1971.

Ann R. Hill

CHRISTINE DE PISAN

Born: Venice, Italy; c. 1365
Died: Probably at the Convent of Poissy, near Versailles, France; c. 1430

Principal poems and collections

Le Livre du chemin de long estude, written 1402-1403, published 1881; *Le Livre de la mutacion de fortune*, written 1400-1403, published 1959; *Cent Ballades*, written c. 1410, published 1886-1896; "Le Dittié de Jeanne d'Arc," written 1429, published 1838; *Oeuvres poétiques de Christine de Pisan*, 1886-1896.

Other literary forms

Christine de Pisan's oeuvre was not limited to poetry but included an impressive number of prose works as well. Composed primarily between 1400 and 1418, these works cover a broad thematic range and bear witness to a powerful and erudite ability; they include letters, short narratives, memoirs, manuals, autobiography, treatises, allegorical psalms, and meditations. Many represent an expansion and development of ideas expressed initially in her poetry; her early poetic commitment to scholarship, political ethics, religious devotion, and women's rights was amplified in the prose works of her maturity.

Achievements

Christine de Pisan is rightly recognized as France's first woman of letters, professional writer, and feminist. Although scholars of the past acknowledged and respected her ability, modern scholarship has elevated Christine (as she is known by scholars) to a deserved place in world literature. If this recognition has been somewhat tardy, the delay has been the result of the general inaccessibility of her work, spread among dispersed manuscripts. In recent years, however, a number of modernized versions from the original Middle French, translations, editions, and critical studies have dramatically heightened interest in her work. Especially remarkable are her learned vocabulary, her knowledgeable use of mythological allusions, and her feminism.

Christine excelled thematically and structurally in both traditional and innovative forms. As an accomplished lyrical poet, she received acclaim from her contemporaries for her conventional courtly poetry. In this category, for example, she demonstrated mastery of the ballad, rondeau, lay, pastoral, and lover's lament. These poems were designed to please the aristocracy at court through an idealized concept of love. Her skill in writing traditional poetry earned the admiration and support of many important members of the nobility, such as the Dukes of Orléans, Burgundy, and Berry as well as King Charles V. Although she was composing in the conventional style, Christine often interjected her own personality by describing events in her life, by referring to a noble benefactor, or by expressing her opinions on the important issues of her day. In this regard, the works possess a documentary value.

Although Christine's poetry exhibits a high degree of technical mastery, she was never content with virtuosity for its own sake. Central themes of the necessity for justice and responsibility in government, concern for all women, and religious devotion imbue her writings. As a whole, Christine's works bear witness both to a vast knowledge of history and to a profound moral commitment to the age in which she lived.

Biography

Although Christine de Pisan ranks as France's first woman of letters, she was not of French but of Italian birth. Born about 1365 in Venice, she spent only her first years in Italy, leaving her birthplace when her father received the position of astrologer at the court of Charles V of France. Tommaso di Benvenuto da Pizzano, known as Thomas de Pisan after his arrival in France, brought his family to Paris around 1368, and it was there that Christine had an experience that was to shape the course of her lifework. With her father's encouragement, she received the kind of education usually reserved for boys in the Middle Ages. A precocious child, Christine was eager to learn, and this unique educational opportunity proved to be the single most important factor in her life, for it provided the young artist with the scholarly tools and knowledge upon which she was to draw during her entire career. On these early foundations in classical languages, literature, mythology, history, and biblical studies, Christine would build a rich and varied literary edifice. In addition, her educational background influenced her perspective by prompting her to view her subjects in a historical, comprehensive, and ethical light.

Because of her creative talent and her ability to please the court with her poetry, Christine became a favorite and never lacked noble patronage. Yet at age fifteen, in 1380, she married not a nobleman but a court notary from Picardy, Étienne de Castel. According to *Lavision-Christine* (written 1405, published 1969), an autobiographical work, it was a happy marriage, and the couple had three children.

Two extremely unhappy events sharply influenced Christine's life and career before she was twenty-five years old. The first of these was the death of Charles V in 1380 and the subsequent government during the minority of Charles VI. During the regency period of the Dukes of Bourbon and Burgundy, Christine's father lost his court position. This demotion meant a loss of prestige as well as severe financial losses from which the scholar and former court astrologer never recovered. A few years later, in 1385, Thomas de Pisan died. Then, in 1389 or 1390, a second, even more devastating, event occurred when Christine's husband died in an epidemic. Thus, her ten-year marriage came to an abrupt end, leaving her with the heavy responsibility of rearing three children alone.

Instead of lamenting the loss of those who had supported and encouraged her literary talents, Christine turned to her art as a source of income as well as a refuge from grief. She was successful in her literary pursuits and regained noble patronage, moving gradually yet not exclusively into prose and producing a wide range of works. Although it is difficult to reconstruct her biography for these years, it is thought that she entered the Dominican convent at Poissy around 1418, the time of the Burgundian massacres. Scholars base this hypothesis on the description of a visit to her daughter at Poissy in "Le Dit de Poissy" (the proverb of Poissy) in the second volume of *Oeuvres poétiques de Christine de Pisan* (poetic works of Christine de Pisan). She did not break the silence of her retreat until 1429, when she composed the poem "Le Dittié de Jeanne d'Arc" (Joan of Arc). Thus, Christine concluded her literary career appropriately, honoring a woman who, like herself, had risen above adversity to pursue her goals. The exact date of her death is not known.

Analysis

The most striking characteristics of Christine de Pisan's work are her breadth of knowledge and her active engagement of the social and political issues of her day. While these attributes would be considered typical rather than extraordinary in a modern writer, they are indeed intriguing in a woman living at the turn of the fifteenth century. Clearly, credit for the wealth of knowledge seen in her works must be given to the exceptional education which she received. Nevertheless, an analysis of the artist must include recognition of the artistic sensitivity and the reverence for life which she brought to her career. Because of the broadness of her vision, she transcended the traditional courtly style of poetry in which she was trained and began to include significant personal, political, and moral issues in her poems. Her works weave innovation into traditional background by passing from idealized medieval expression to realistic humanist concerns that are closer in spirit to the Renaissance.

Christine's first published works in verse reveal her conformity to the literary standards of the era. The aesthetic canon governing late medieval poetry did not accept expressions of individual joy or sorrow but instead required these emotions to be placed in a universal framework. Christine's early works demonstrate not only her respect for the existing literary system but also her mastery of it. In her ballads, lays, and rondeaux, there is a harmonious relationship between form and meaning. An example of the traditional mold can be seen in *Cent Ballades* (one hundred ballads). In Ballad 59, following the social code of the era, the poet advises young lovers to be noble, peaceful, and gracious. Written in decasyllabic lines, the ballad follows the prescribed form in stanzaic composition, regular rhyme, and refrain. The tone is appropriately elevated by the use of virtuous, abstract vocabulary, and verbs in the imperative and subjunctive moods. This ballad is typical of Christine's courtly love poems, which in their grace and elegance meet and even surpass the criteria of the times.

At the beginning of her career, Christine was dependent upon the approval of her patrons, and it was important to please them by adhering to acceptable forms and also to amuse them with clever versatility and occasional flattery. She accomplished this by writing a group of rondeaux, very brief poems in lines of two to four syllables in equally short stanzas. These poems on the chagrin of love are typical of the clever, though sometimes exaggerated, metric exercises with which late medieval poets experimented. Christine also excelled at occasional verse; several of her poems in this category go beyond flattery by conveying a secondary message which in the course of the poem emerges as the main theme. For example, in a series of poems honoring Charles d'Albret, a patriotic high constable, Christine salutes his royal lineage, then hastens to one of her favorite and most important themes, the defense of the honor of women, particularly those in need. Although Christine continues to observe the fixed form of the ballad, she transmits her intense interest in her subject through a passionate tone, a concrete vocabulary, and a rhythmic pattern that dramatically emphasizes key words. The contemporary theme is anchored to ancient history as the poet compares the champion of her sex to the virtuous Roman Brutus.

Many of Christine's poems are centrally concerned with women's rights. It would appear that the genesis of this theme in her work was twofold. First, as a woman who herself had to work for a living, Christine could identify with women who had suffered misfortune, most of whom did not have her advantages. Many times in her works, she pleads for widows and orphan girls. While Christine's feminism thus had its roots in her own experience, it was also given force by her rejection of widely accepted literary stereotypes of women. She abhorred, for example, the image of her sex in *Le Roman de la rose* (thirteenth century; *The Romance of the Rose*), where women are portrayed as greedy, inconstant, and egocentric.

Christine's final literary work provides an appropriate conclusion to a survey of her poetic career. In terms of both theme and structure, "Le Dittié de Jeanne d'Arc" represents a culminating point because in it, the poet restates and unites both forcefully and creatively the concerns that inspired her whole literary career. Of the inspirations, the most prominent is religious devotion. The poem, which extols Joan of Arc's mission to save France, is a pious work, praising God's grace and power. Joan is uniquely qualified to champion France because she is God's handmaiden: "Blessed is He who created you!/ Maiden sent from God," exclaims the poet in the twenty-second stanza. Two secondary themes, patriotism and political concern, are welded to the religious motif; they also give the poem documentary value.

The poem reflects the attitude of a nation already weary from what was to be known as the Hundred Years' War (1337-1453) yet exhilarated by the victory of Orléans and the coronation of Charles VII at Rheims in 1403.

Christine's sense of reality does not allow her to be swept away by optimism. Instead, realizing that there are further civil dangers to be faced, she encourages mutual cooperation between citizens and their King.

The final theme of the poem, yet certainly not the least in importance, is explicitly feminist: The heroine, supported and uplifted by the author's belief that women are able to do all things, confers unity and balance to this hymn of praise. In her enthusiastic expression of admiration for Joan as a woman, Christine employs a range of technical devices which convincingly reinforce her message. Written in sixty-one stanzas of eight octosyllabic lines each, the poem adheres to a traditional stanzaic structure, yet within the stanzas, all formality disappears; marked by exclamations, direct address, rhetorical questions, concrete and picturesque vocabulary, and conversational movement, the style is highly innovative. In this final work, Christine left an eloquent testimony to her accomplishments as a woman and as a poet.

Major publications other than poetry

NONFICTION: *L'Epistre d'Othéa le déesse à Hector*, written 1400, published 1970 (*The Epistle of Othea to Hector: Or, The Boke of Knyghthode*, c. 1470); *Epistres du débat sur le Roman de la rose*, written 1402, published 1976; *Le Livre des fais et bonnes meurs du sage roi Charles V*, written 1404, published 1936-1940; *Le Livre de la cité des dames*, written 1404-1405, published 1982 (*The Book of the City of Ladies*, 1521); *Lavision-Christine*, written 1405, published 1969; *Le Livre des trois vertus*, written 1405, published 1912; *Les Sept Psaumes allégorisés*, written 1409-1410, published 1965; *Le Livre des fais d'armes et de chevalerie*, written 1410, published 1488 (*The Book of Fayttes of Arms and of Chivalry*, 1489); *Le Livre de la paix*, written 1412-1413, published 1977; *L'Epistre de la prison de la vie humaine*, written 1416-1418, published 1924.

Bibliography

Bell, Susan Groag. "Christine de Pizan (1364-1430): Humanism and the Problem of a Studious Woman," in *Feminist Studies*. III (1975), pp. 173-184.

Bornstein, Diane, ed. *Ideals for Women in the Works of Christine de Pizan*, 1981.

Favier, Marguerite. *Christine de Pisan, muse des cours souverains*, 1967.

Gabriel, Astrik L. "The Educational Ideas of Christine de Pisan," in *Journal of the History of Ideas*. XVI (1955), pp. 3-21.

McLeod, Enid. *The Order of the Rose: The Life and Ideas of Christine de Pizan*, 1976.

Rigaud, Rose. *Les Idées féministes de Christine de Pisan*, 1911, 1973.

Solente, Suzanne. "Christine de Pizan," in *Histoire littéraire de la France*. XI (1974), pp. 335-422.

Ann R. Hill

PAUL CLAUDEL

Born: Villeneuve-sur-Fère, France; August 6, 1868
Died: Paris, France; February 24, 1955

Principal poems and collections

Connaissance de l'est, 1900, 1952 (*The East I Know*, 1914); *Art poétique*, 1907 (*Poetic Art*, 1948); *Cinq Grandes Odes*, 1910 (*Five Great Odes*, 1967); *Vers d'exil*, 1912; *Corona Benignitatis Anni Dei*, 1915 (*Coronal*, 1943); *La Messe là-bas*, 1921; *Poëmes de guerre*, 1922; *Feuilles de saints*, 1925; *Cent Phrases pour éventails*, 1927; *La Cantate à trois voix*, 1931; *Petits Poëmes d'après le chinois*, written 1939; *Dodoitzu*, 1945; *Poëmes et paroles durant la guerre de trente ans*, 1945; *Visages radieux*, 1947; *Premiers Vers*, written 1950; *Poésies diverses*, written 1952; *Autres poèmes d'après le chinois*, 1957; *Traductions de poèmes*, 1957; *Oeuvre poétique*, 1957 (includes first publication of *Petits Poëmes d'après le chinois*, *Premiers Vers*, *Poésies diverses*, and *Autres poèmes d'après le chinois*, as well as all other titles above); *Poèmes*, 1967.

Other literary forms

Although Paul Claudel's poetry occupies a prominent place in his writings, it was his theater which brought him a worldwide reputation. Gallimard published Claudel's *Oeuvres complètes* (1950-1967) in twenty-seven volumes. His *Théâtre* (1947-1948) has also been published, in two separate volumes, by Gallimard in the Bibliothèque de la Pléiade series. Claudel stated repeatedly that human drama is not complete unless a supernatural element enriches it and brings to it a vertical sense. From the day of his conversion to Roman Catholicism on December 25, 1886, the Bible became his daily companion. In his poetry, the influence of the Bible manifests itself in an exuberant lyric vein, while in his plays it is evident in his conception of the conflict between good and evil—not so much a question of metaphysics as a struggle that takes place within the soul, among Satan, man, and God. Claudel's study of the Bible also resulted in a series of exegetical works that constitute a third important part of his creative artistry. Finally, the numerous volumes of Claudel's correspondence and the two volumes of his journal are indispensable guides to his inner life.

Achievements

The literary fate of Claudel can be compared to that of Stendhal (Marie-Henri Beyle), who, despite the initial indifference and lack of enthusiasm with which people of his generation received his writings, predicted that his works would be understood and successful by the end of the nineteenth century. Stendhal even dedicated his novel, *La Chartreuse de Parme* (1839; *The Charterhouse of Parma*, 1895), not without irony, "to the happy few" who were able to understand his art and thought. Time has proved that Stendhal judged with perspicacity both his own work and the evolution of the literary taste of his country. In the same way, when Symbolism was giving clear signs of its vitality, Ferdinand Brunetière, very skeptical of the success of the new movement, in an article published by *La revue des deux mondes* on November 1, 1888, dared challenge all the members of it by saying: "Give us a masterpiece and we will take you seriously." Henri Guillemin is surprised that Brunetière did not recognize the signs that were pointing to the man who was to come: "He was there, the man of masterpiece," he says, and in less than two years Claudel would publish his play *Tête d'or* (1890; English translation, 1919). Yet, despite this and many other masterpieces, Claudel remained unknown to the general public until after World War II.

Claudel was too religious for the secular Third Republic of France; his poetry ignored the Alexandrine meter and largely did without rhyme, while his plays dramatized a soul-searching and soul-saving adventure in which the eternal destiny of man took priority over psychology. Above all, Claudel did not use the literary language most of the French cherished, and he was accused of writing French poetry in German.

Nevertheless, Claudel persisted on his solitary course, largely undistracted by the literary fashions of the twentieth century. By the end of his life, he was numbered among the preeminent poets and playwrights of modern France.

Biography

Paul-Louis-Charles-Marie Claudel was born in Villeneuve-sur-Fère (Tardenois), France, on August 6, 1868. He was the youngest of three children, with two sisters, Camille and Louise. Their father, Louis-Prosper Claudel, was a civil servant who came to Villeneuve-sur-Fère from La Bresse, a small town in the Vosges region. By nature, he was an unsociable and taciturn person. His profession as civil servant left him little time for his children. Claudel's mother, born Louise Cerveaux, came from a family that had its origins in Villeneuve-sur-Fère. Like her husband, she was an unaffectionate parent; according to Claudel, she never kissed her children. The difficult character of the oldest child, Camille, may have been responsible for the mother's attitude and, indeed, adversely affected all the relationships in the family. In 1882, after many years of following her husband from place to place—Louis-Prosper Claudel had held posts in Villeneuve-sur-Fère, Bar-le-Duc, Nogent-sur-Seine, Wassy, Rambouillet, and Compiègne—Louise Claudel yielded to the pressure of Camille and agreed to settle with her children in Paris. Camille was eighteen years of age, Louise sixteen, and Paul fourteen.

Contrary to what one might expect, Paris did not fascinate the young Claudel: The crushing feelings of loneliness and boredom from which he suffered became even more frightening in the big city. Nor did Paris offer a respite from the endless family quarrels. In the restless atmosphere of the country's capital and under the pressure of his anarchist instincts, Claudel at one time contemplated suicide. Fortunately, as he grew into adulthood, he saw the positive side of Parisian life. He discovered the "mystical" beauty of Richard Wagner's music; at the age of nineteen, he was admitted to Stéphan Mallarmé's circle; and while still in the *lycée*, he enjoyed the company of classmates who were to become leading figures in French cultural and political life in the first half of the twentieth century. In 1886, purely by accident, Claudel discovered Arthur Rimbaud, in the June issue of *La Vogue* magazine, when he read Rimbaud's *Les Illuminations* (1886; *Illuminations and Other Prose Poems*, 1932) and *Une Saison en enfer* (1873; *A Season in Hell*, 1932).

On December 25, 1886, Claudel went to Notre-Dame of Paris, and there, during the early afternoon Office of Vespers, his "heart was touched" and he "believed." The nightmares that had haunted his youth were banished; his life and his obvious talent acquired a purpose. A creative enthusiasm inspired him to "evangelize" all the layers of his being. The process of this evangelization was to be reflected in his writings, both poetry and drama; he was to remain forever a poet committed to God and men.

After passing the examination for the Ministry of Foreign Affairs, Claudel entered into a diplomatic career that lasted until 1935. His first consular assignment took him to New York City and Boston in 1893. By that time, he had published *Tête d'or* and *La Ville* (1893; *The City*, 1920). His visit to the United States inspired him to write *L'Échange* (1901, 1954; the exchange), a masterpiece that presents a realistic image of American life and civilization. His diplomatic life took him next to China; between 1895 and 1900, Claudel held posts in Foochow, Shanghai, and Hankow. It was at this time that he turned to poetry. Upon his return to France, in 1900, Claudel thought of abandoning poetry and becoming a monk, but he was not accepted in either Solesmes or Ligugé. He decided then to pursue his diplomatic career, which took him back to China.

It was in 1900, on shipboard en route to China, that he met a married Polish woman, "Ysé" (Rose Vetch). They shared an adulterous affair which lasted four years. In 1906, while on vacation in France, Claudel married Reine Sainte-Marie Perrin, daughter of the architect of the Basilica of Fourvière in Lyons. Three days after his marriage, Claudel returned to China, accompanied by his wife. From that year on, Claudel's professional life never knew an eclipse; from China, he went on to Prague, Frankfurt, Rome, and Brazil. Finally, as ambassador, he served in Japan, the United States, and Belgium.

The last years of Claudel's life were filled with honors and recognition. Even the Académie Français reversed its 1936 rejection of him, and in 1946 Claudel was elected one of the Immortals of France. Perhaps the most striking symbol of Claudel's success is the fact that, on the night of his death in February, 1955, the Comédie-Française was rehearsing *L'Annonce faite à Marie* (1912; *The Tidings Brought to Mary*, 1916).

Analysis

One of the outstanding characteristics of Claudel's work is its cosmic dimension. His poetry does not form an exception to this general rule, for Claudel chose as its subject the visible world, enriching it with the invisible things of his faith. He was tempted neither to sacrifice the visible for the sake of the spiritual nor to do the opposite.

When he refers to his poetry in "La Maison fermée" ("Within the House") of *Five Great Odes*, Claudel uses this analogy: "The Word of God is the way that God gives himself to mankind. The created word is that way by which all created things are given to man." The universe of Claudel, one might say, is a man-centered world, but certainly not to the exclusion of God. In an analogous sense, the poet is called upon to redeem visible things from the corruption of time and to elevate them, by his created word, to the heights of eternity. "To name a thing," Claudel says in his *Poetic Art*, "means to produce it inextinguishable, for it is to produce it in relationship to its principle, which does not include cessation." In a sense, therefore, the peculiar vocation of the poet is to be a *pro*phet in the etymological sense of the word: He speaks *for* the visible universe.

However ironic it may sound, one has the impression that Claudel, after his conversion, wanted to "convert his conversion" to his own powerful nature, to the splendor of visible things, and to invite God Himself to join him in his celebration of this world. By embracing nature and by calling things by their names, however, the poet determines their place in the intention of their Creator. There is nothing that horrified Claudel more than the idea of a material infinite; he considered it a "scandal of the reason." Speaking of Dante's poetic endeavor, Claudel reminds himself that a true poet does not need "greater stars" or "more beautiful roses" than those nature furnishes. His task is to use words, those "resonant phantoms," to produce an enjoyable and intelligent picture of the universe.

If it is true that Claudel attained in *Five Great Odes* the summit of his poetic creation, it is because his genius had reached a level of synthesis where painful experiences and poetic inspiration were molded into a harmonious unity. Yet this synthesis was achieved only after a lengthy poetic development, beginning with Claudel's assimilation of Rimbaud and Mallarmé.

When, in June, 1886, Claudel discovered in *La Vogue* Rimbaud's *Illuminations* and *A Season in Hell*, he recognized in these poems the sign of his own deliverance. Rimbaud's poetic language fascinated Claudel; the simplest term Claudel could find to describe the fascination was "bewitchment." In an age marked by secularism and aggressive materialism, a young poet dared to speak of the nostalgia of the soul for freedom and of the reality of invisible things. Claudel was not naïve; he could hear blasphemy and cursing in the desperate cries of Rimbaud, but he was happy to inhale that "living and almost physical impression of the supernatural" that the poems of Rimbaud communicated to his soul. Claudel learned much from Rimbaud, not least the daring juxtaposition of images with no clear link among them. Above all, however, Rimbaud made Claudel aware that the material world, when it comes into contact with the spirit, becomes very fragile. Upon reading Rimbaud, Claudel said, he had the impression of hearing the voice of the most authentic genius of his time.

Like most poets of his generation, Claudel was also influenced by Mallarmé. As early as 1887, Claudel was among those who went to listen to the master of the Symbolist movement. It was a great privilege to be admitted to Mallarmé's salon; in the quasi-religious ambience of the Symbolists, to be recognized by Mallarmé was to be consecrated. Little is known of the extent of their personal relationship, but, while on his first diplomatic mission in China, Claudel was eager to continue his correspondence with the "master"; he even dared to express his reservations concerning Mallarmé's aesthetic principles. In his "La Catastrophe de l'Igitur," published in *Positions et propositions I* in 1928, Claudel recognizes that Mallarmé was the first poet to place himself in front of an object and ask the question, "What does that mean?" Claudel acknowledges that Mallarmé's way of trying to infuse the lifeless object with life was worthy of admiration, but he also underscores Mallarmé's failure to give the necessary answer to, or explanation of, his own question.

According to Claudel, if things and objects mean something, the poet has the obligation to speak for them. Mallarmé, on the contrary, hoped to condense in his verse the whole reality of things, by transferring them from the realm of "sensibility" to that of "intelligibility." The difference, then, between Claudel and Mallarmé is that, whereas Mallarmé believed that poetry is the ultimate forum of intelligibility and that there is nothing else to be understood beyond it, Claudel said that *through* the poetic word the visible reality becomes a key to another reality, that which is *meant* by the first one. In other words, and to paraphrase a thought of Claudel, the world is indeed a text that speaks "humbly and joyfully" of its own "absence" and of the presence of its Creator. Claudel rightly calls the adventure of Mallarmé a "catastrophe." One has but to remember the experience of Rimbaud, who, having tried to reach the ultimate and absolute power of the creative word, was forced to abandon poetry altogether, for absolute power pertains only to the absolute Word.

The prose poems of *The East I Know*, the composition of which was spread out over a period of ten years, were written under the influence of Mallarmé. Claudel at first called them "impressions," later "poems in prose." In some cases, they are less impressions than precise descriptions of the emotional significance that various elements of the Chinese universe held for him. Some aspects of the descriptiveness that one finds in *The East I Know* do not, it is true, have their origin in Mallarmé; they derive, rather, from one of Claudel's contemporaries, Jules Renard. In 1896, Renard sent a copy of his recently published book, *Histoires naturelles*, to his friend Claudel in China. It was in this book that Claudel found what he considered the ideal manner of describing nature. He states delightedly that the book is "full of nature"; he also found that Renard's sentences were better balanced than those of Mallarmé. Yet Mallarmé's distinctive sentences, composed entirely of subordinate clauses (main clauses were indicated by their absence), continued to excite Claudel with their suggestive juxtapositions. Ultimately, *The East I Know* led Claudel to a fusion of the two trends; that is, he had to learn how to harmonize the sentence with the message it contained and the exterior world with the spiritual world of which it offered signs. In achieving this synthesis, Claudel found his voice as a poet.

Claudel's achievement in *The East I Know* is exemplified in "L'Heure jaune" ("The Golden Hour"). The title signifies both the ripeness of the wheat field and the sunset hour. As the poet walks through the wheat field, a path opens in it. Suddenly, the wheat field turns into a table (a bread table) at which the poet can rest. He is invited by God to this universal banquet table, which is illuminated by the sun. Before the sun sets, the poet, raising himself above the table, takes a last look over the universe, which has reached the last phase of its maturity. Indeed, the whole universe has become like the sun, and the only wish the poet can utter is that he not perish before he reaches the "golden hour": "I wander through the lanes of the harvest, up to the neck in gold. . . . All is ripe. . . . Suddenly, to my eyes, the earth is like a sun. Let me not die before the golden hour!"

With *The East I Know*, Claudel completed his poetic apprenticeship. Having done so, he undertook a new genre, the ode. In 1900, he made two important literary discoveries: Thanks to his friend André Suarès, he read Pindar, whose odes he savored for their rhythmic invention and absolute freedom of form. In the same year, while he was seeking admittance to monastic life in Solesmes, his attention was called to the English poet Coventry Patmore, a convert to Catholicism who enjoyed an extraordinary vogue late in the nineteenth century but whose works are scarcely read today. Claudel liked Patmore so much that he translated some of his poems into French. Patmore furthered Claudel's knowledge of the art of the ode; he also taught Claudel how to use the theme of love in poetry—as both a profane subject and a mystical reality expressing the only possible relationship between man and God. A third element that greatly contributed to the making of *Five Great Odes* was Claudel's visit to the Louvre in 1900, during which he noticed for the first time a Roman sarcophagus with the nine Muses.

These three sources furnished him with sufficient material for the new work. Suddenly, as if a new revelation had filled his being, he realized with exuberant joy that he had something to say, that he possessed the words he needed to speak in the name of the silent universe. It is not surprising that he began to write the first of the odes, "Les Muses" ("The Muses"), in the monastery of Solesmes. He felt at the same time that he was "all alone," "detached, refused, abandoned, without a task, without vocation, an outcast in the middle of the world," yet called to something that he could not fathom. As if in answer to the question that Mallarmé addressed to things, Claudel affirms in the odes that he has found the secret; he knows now how to speak and how to tell what each thing *means*. It is not a slight change that has occurred: He has regained his voice, has recovered his poetic health, and, having been told that he has no religious vocation, is now free to return to his poetic one. He walked out of the monastery in Ligugé, "The Muses" yet to be finished; soon, he boarded a ship to China to resume his diplomatic post. On the ship, he met Ysé, the great love of his life, and he completed "The Muses." The joy that the muse inspired had turned into a question that he would make explicit in his play *Partage de midi* (1906; *Break of Noon*, 1960): "Why suddenly this woman on the ship?" Claudel could not answer the question; instead, for six years he kept silent. It was not until 1906 that he started to work on the second ode. He wrote about his illicit adventure in *Break of Noon* and ended his relationship with Ysé. The crisis of conscience that had paralyzed him for six years had finally come to a happy resolution. The illicit love had a purpose: Having discovered the "other" embodied in Ysé, Claudel was able to see the world anew, a "world now total" because it was seen with the eyes of the "other" as well as with his own. It was therefore fitting that Claudel should have transformed his love into an imperishable rose.

From the time of his meeting with Ysé, the rose is used in his poetry both allegorically and as a proper name, for Rose was the true name of Ysé. In a sense, his is a "roman de la rose," with the difference that Claudel possessed not so much the rose as the "interdiction." Because of this restraint, the rose brought him neither happiness nor fulfillment; knowing it was like knowing the "source of thirst." The rose, then, in *Five Great Odes*—it is presented throughout the poem—is a mystical rose with all the symbolism associated with it in the Western literary tradition. Claudel exploits this traditional symbolism and adds to it his own interpretation of the rose's perfume as the very essence of the flower. When inhaled (*respiré*), this perfume gives in an instant a sense of the fullness of eternity. The message of the rose is that, time having been abolished, one lives in eternity.

In "La Muse qui est la grâce" ("The Muse Who Is Grace"), Claudel continues the theme of the rose, although not without a certain irony. Having spent so many years meditating on the meaning of love, the poet realizes that it would be easier to live without woman, but then he must also realize that the Muse herself is a woman—a woman with the face of Wisdom. It is therefore perfectly orthodox to say that in the fifth ode, "Within the House," Claudel substitues Wisdom for the mystical rose. In doing so, he closed one of the major circles of his poetic and spiritual evolution. The night of his conversion on December 25, 1886, when he went home and opened his sister Camille's Bible, his eye fell on the passage in Proverbs that speaks of Wisdom.

Finally, he was led back to this Wisdom through the power of the mystical rose, which is Love.

Wisdom also taught Claudel that Creation is finite. "We have conquered the world," he says in "Within the House," "and we have found that Your Creation is finite." It appears contradictory that, while on the one hand Claudel never ceases looking for signs of phenomena to prove that eternity is available to human understanding and is anxious to replace the signifying with the signified, on the other hand he berates the idea of indefinite and infinite within the realm of Creation. According to Claudel, if there is a contradiction, it is certainly not going to surface in the right relationship between the world and God; on the contrary, it is always found in the deification of the finite universe. He believes that God so planned the world that everything should return to Him. Claudel thus conceives of the universe not as an automatic machine blindly traveling toward an undetermined goal, but as an entity within a perfect circle in which the vocation of the poet is to remind rational as well as irrational beings of the primordial unity their universe must achieve. That is why, in the midst of his joyous celebration in "Magnificat," he raises his voice against Voltaire, Joseph Ernest Renan, Jules Michelet, Victor Hugo, and all of those who continue to have nightmares or dream of a self-sufficient, man-created world. In his essay "Introduction à un poème sur Dante" (*Positions et propositions I*), Claudel takes issue with Hugo's cosmology, as expressed in the poem "Plein Ciel" ("Up in the Sky"), in which the Romantic poet imagines "Un Fini sans bornes" ("A Finite Without Limits"). Claudel does not hesitate to call this idea "a scandal for the reason, a disaster for the imagination." In contrast to these figures, he offers the portrait of Christopher Columbus, who, when he sailed to the West in order to reach India, was not led by any thought of discovery; he was, rather, led by the desire to prove that the Earth was a "circle," having its existence within the orbit of God. Thus, Columbus resembles the poet, who by vocation is the "sower of the measure of God," and the symbolism of the last ode's title becomes intelligible: "Within the House" is a perfect "circle," the movement of which is determined by the creative act of God and the redemptive charity of His Son.

The very form of Claudel's verse was biblical in inspiration. He employed from the beginning of his poetic career a form that has come to be known as the *verset claudélien*. Among the influences that shaped this distinctive form, the most significant was the Bible, as Claudel was quick to acknowledge—in particular, the Psalms and the books of the prophets. In the long swell of the Claudelian verset, the cadence and the length of the lines are determined by units of breath, which in turn are conditioned by the nature of the thought that is being expressed. The lyric breath demands a more regular form, and it may even take rhyme and assonance, whereas drama, which is charged with interior struggles and tensions, demands a less regular form.

In 1917, Claudel was charged with a new diplomatic mission, this time to Brazil. The journey there was more painful than previous ones: Claudel had to leave his wife, his children, and his country behind in the midst of a raging war and all of its uncertainties. The poem *La Messe là-bas*, written during this period, reflects his sense of exile. There is, however, another equally important theme in the poem—perhaps new at this point in Claudel's life—in the images of bread and wine as they become symbols in a liturgical and sacramental sense.

It should be remarked that the whole poem in its exterior form corresponds to the structure of the Catholic Mass and, as such, is a celebration of Communion. The question, then, can be raised in the following fashion: Communion with whom—and under what species? The first part of the question does not present any major problem; the poet has been separated from his family, and it is fitting that he should attempt to stay in communion with them in some way. On a deeper level, communion is reestablished between the two lovers, Claudel and Ysé. After all, they met on a ship that took both of them into exile, where they were to experience for years the desert of their love. On yet another level, Claudel savors communion with Rimbaud, whose poetry reminded him of the voice of the prophet in the desert announcing the breaking of the dawn. Finally, on the deepest level of his thought, Claudel celebrates that Communion with God which Rimbaud was unable to reach, for neither the method of Mallarmé nor the desire of Rimbaud proved capable of containing the Absolute in the poet's word. Faith, on the contrary, assures Claudel that, since God made Himself available to the understanding of the human soul in His own Word, the Catholic Mass is the only worthy celebration of this Communion: God instituted the Mass to commemorate His Communion with mankind. That is the reason Claudel selected the frame of the Mass to signify both poetry and communion.

It would be quite absurd to state that in Claudel's symbolism a tree, say, refers to man, or that bread represents an invisible celestial food. An object never refers to another object, only to itself. Claudel does not deny that there is something to be signified. In his system, whether aesthetic or spiritual, the physical and the spiritual realms coexist. What Claudel wants to say is that the bread and wine convey something in addition to the reality constituted by their molecular structure; their reality consists also in man's hunger and thirst for them. In the same way, one could say that light is provided because of man's need to see. Now, human hunger and thirst, if they are authentic, constitute a desire for something absolute—indeed, nothing but the absolute can satisfy them. In the Eucharistic celebration, the bread and wine lend, first of all, their physical appearance, but they are more than that: The word of the poet raises them into that region where the "object" can convey what the human desire is seeking. The poet can tell Ysé that they cannot satisfy their mutual desire and love unless they give priority to the Absolute Who is All in all. Rimbaud is recalled (as Mallarmé might have been) because he, too, was tempted to use the sacramental and liturgical symbolism of the Word without accepting the need for perfect communion.

Claudel believed that every poet enters this world with one purpose. "The thing of beauty" which is ultimately the message of all poets, while gaining shape and identity, traces its own history. In the case of Claudel, this poetic message evolved and developed like a seed—the word is found even on his tombstone—which goes through death and resurrection before producing new life. At the beginning of his poetic career, he gave way to his sentiments of exile: He found himself far from home and from Heaven; at the other end of his career, in a peaceful recognition, he humbly bowed before the solidity of the universe of God. Between these two points, Claudel seems to have run a double itinerary: While he poured into his drama all of his joys and sorrows, he reserved for his poetry the history of a rose, as if his life had been a "roman de la rose." In his poetry, however, this rose is transformed into a person, "Rose," who, in turn, having given the poet the joy of loving, is transfigured into a "mystical rose." In Claudel's poetry, love is a blessing when it arrives, but it is also meant to signify the absence of what it promises. Love therefore leads to Wisdom, which alone holds the keys to the mystery of the universe and the destiny of man; totality is found neither in woman's love nor in the fascination of the created universe, but in the eternal love of God.

Major publications other than poetry

PLAYS: *Tête d'or*, 1890 (English translation, 1919); *La Ville*, 1893 (*The City*, 1920); *L'Échange*, 1901, 1954; *La Jeune Fille Violaine*, 1901, 1926; *Le Repos du septiéme jour*, 1901; *Partage de midi*, 1906 (*Break of Noon*, 1960); *L'Otage*, 1911 (*The Hostage*, 1917); *L'Annonce faite à Marie*, 1912 (*The Tidings Brought to Mary*, 1916); *Protée*, 1914 (*Proteus*, 1921); *La Nuit de Noël*, 1915; *Le Pain dur*, 1918 (*The Crusts*, 1945); *L'Ours et la lune*, 1919; *Le Père humilié*, 1920 (*The Humiliation of the Father*, 1945); *Le Soulier de satin*, 1928 (*The Satin Slipper: Or, The Worst Is Not the Surest*, 1931); *Le Livre de Christophe Colombe*, 1933 (*The Book of Christopher Columbus*, 1930); *Jeanne d'Arc au bûcher*, 1939 (English translation, 1939); *L'Histoire de Tobie et de Sara*, 1942 (*Tobias and Sara*, 1962); *Théâtre*, 1947-1948 (2 volumes); *La Lune à la recherche d'elle-même*, 1948; *Le Ravissement de Scapin*, 1949.

NONFICTION: *Jacques Rivière et Paul Claudel*, 1926 (*Letters to a Doubter: Correspondence of Jacques Rivière and Paul Claudel*, 1929); *Positions et propositions I*, 1928; *L'Oiseau noir dans le soleil levant*, 1929; *Écoute, ma fille*, 1934; *Positions et propositions II*, 1934 (*Ways and Crossways*, 1933); *Conversations dans le Loir-et-Cher*, 1935; *Un Poète regarde la Croix*, 1935; *Figures et paraboles*, 1936; *Toi, qui es-tu?*, 1936; *Les Aventures de Sophie*, 1937; *L'Épée et le miroir*, 1939; *Contacts et circonstances*, 1940; *Présence et pro-*

phétie, 1942; *Seigneur, apprenez-nous à prier*, 1942; *Le Livre de Job*, 1946; *L'Oeil écoute*, 1946 (*The Eye Listens*, 1950); *Discours et remerciements*, 1947; *Du côté de chez Ramuz*, 1947; *La Rose et le rosaire*, 1947; *Paul Claudel interroge le Cantique des Cantiques*, 1948; *Sous le signe du dragon*, 1948; *Accompagnements*, 1949; *André Gide et Paul Claudel, 1899-1926*, 1949 (*The Correspondence, 1899-1926, Between Paul Claudel and André Gide*, 1952); *Emmaüs*, 1949; *Une voix sur Israël*, 1950; *André Suarès et Paul Claudel*, 1951; *l'Évangile d'Isaïe*, 1951; *Francis Jammes-Gabriel Frizeau et Paul Claudel*, 1952; *Introduction au Livre de Ruth*, 1952; *Paul Claudel interroge l'Apocalypse*, 1952; *Le Symbolism de la Salette*, 1952; *J'aime la Bible*, 1955 (*The Essence of the Bible*, 1957); *Conversation sur Jean Racine, qui ne souffre pas*, 1958; *Darius Milhaud et Paul Claudel*, 1961; *Aurélien Lugné-Poe et Paul Claudel*, 1964; *Au milieu des vitraux de l'Apocalypse*, 1966; *Jacques Copeau-Charles Dullin-Louis Jouvet et Paul Claudel*, 1966; *Journal I*, 1968; *Journal II*, 1969; *Mémoires improvisés*, 1969.

MISCELLANEOUS: *Oeuvres complètes*, 1950-1967 (27 volumes).

Bibliography
Chaigne, Louis. *Vie de Paul Claudel*, 1961.
Chiari, Joseph. *The Poetic Drama of Paul Claudel*, 1954.
Griffiths, Richard. *Claudel: A Reappraisal*, 1968.
Guillemin, Henri. *Le "Converti" Paul Claudel*, 1968.
Knapp, Bettina L. *Paul Claudel*, 1982.
Lioure, Michel. *L'Esthétique dramatique de Paul Claudel*, 1971.
Madaule, Jacques. *Le Drame de Paul Claudel*, 1964.
Vachon, Andre. *Le Temps et l'espace dans l'oeuvre de Paul Claudel*, 1965.
Watson, Harold. *Claudel's Immortal Heroes: A Choice of Deaths*, 1971.

Moses M. Nagy

JEAN COCTEAU

Born: Maisons-Laffitte, France; July 5, 1889
Died: Milly-la-Forêt, France; October 11, 1963

Principal poems and collections
La Lampe d'Aladin, 1909; *Le Prince frivole*, 1910; *La Danse de Sophocle*, 1912; *Le Cap de Bonne-Espérance*, 1919; *L'Ode à Picasso*, 1919; *Escales*, 1920; *Poésies, 1917-1920*, 1920; *Discours du grand sommeil*, 1922; *Vocabulaire*, 1922; *Plain-Chant*, 1923; *Poésie, 1916-1923*, 1924; *L'Ange heurtebise*, 1925; *Cri écrit*, 1925; *Opéra*, 1927; *Morceaux choisis*, 1932; *Mythologie*, 1934; *Allégories*, 1941; *Léone*, 1945; *Poèmes*, 1945; *La Crucifixion*, 1946; *Le Chiffre sept*, 1952; *Appogiatures*, 1953; *Clair-obscur*, 1954; *Poèmes, 1916-1955*, 1956; *Gondole des morts*, 1959; *Cérémonial espagnol du phénix*, 1961; *Le Requiem*, 1962.

Other literary forms
Jean Cocteau was a formidable artist in many genres and awesomely prolific. Among his seven novels, little read today, the most important is *Les Enfants terribles* (1929; *Enfants Terribles*, 1930, also as *Children of the Game*, 1955). Among his many plays, some of the most notable are *Orphée* (1927; *Orpheus*, 1933), *La Voix humaine* (1930; *The Human Voice*, 1951), *La Machine infernale* (1934; *The Infernal Machine*, 1936), *Les Parents terribles* (1938; *Intimate Relations*, performed 1952, published 1956), and *La Machine à écrire* (1941; *The Typewriter*, 1962). In the opinion of many critics, Cocteau's greatest achievements were in the cinema. His masterpieces—which he both wrote and directed—include *Le Sang d'un poète* (released 1932, published 1948; *The Blood of a Poet*, 1949), *La Belle et la bête* (released 1945, published 1946; *Beauty and the Beast*, 1950), *Les Parents terribles* (released 1948, published 1949; *Intimate Relations*, 1952), *Les Enfants terribles* (released 1950), *Orphée* (released 1949, published 1951), and *La Testament d'Orphée* (1959; *The Testament of Orpheus*, 1968). Cocteau also wrote scenarios for ballets by various composers, notably for Erik Satie's *Parade* (1917), for Darius Milhaud's *Le Boeuf sur le toit* (1920), and for *Les Mariés de la Tour Eiffel* (1921) which had music by "Le Six." Cocteau also collaborated on two opera-oratorios, *Oedipus-Rex* (1928) with Igor Stravingsky, and *Antigone* (1927; English translation, 1961) with Arthur Honegger. Cocteau's nonfiction includes a variety of idiosyncratic autobiographical and critical works.

Achievements
Cocteau was one of the most remarkable figures in twentieth century art. Extremely versatile, he unified his diverse interests by seeing them as merely different aspects of *poésie*: *poésie de roman* (poetry of the novel), *poésie de*

théâtre (poetry of the drama), *poésie cinématographique* (poetry of the film), and even *poésie graphique* (poetry of drawing). Curiously, with poetry as the metaphorical center of Cocteau's artistic achievement, critics are still uncomfortable with his accomplishment as a poet. Some consider him a central figure through whom the major currents of art in the early 1900's passed, while others regard him as a dilettante, interested only in stylishness and facile demonstrations of his considerable talents, lacking substance under the sparkling façade. Many of his contemporaries were uncertain of his importance because he remained always on the periphery of "serious" art. Looking back, however, it is clear that, at the very least, Cocteau's poetry is another brilliant aspect of one of the most versatile artistic minds of the century, and that it has been underrated largely because of the difficulty in grasping Cocteau in all his variety.

Biography

Jean Cocteau was born in a prosperous suburb of Paris to Georges and Eugénie Lecomte Cocteau, a cultivated bourgeois couple who exposed Jean, his brother Paul, and their sister Marthe to the fine arts. When at their suburban home, the children played on the grounds of a nearby castle designed by François Mansart. When in Paris—Cocteau would always consider himself a Parisian above all—his family lived with his grandparents, whose house contained classical busts, vases, a painting by Eugène Delacroix, and drawings by Jean-Auguste-Dominique Ingres. Cocteau's grandfather was a cellist and would often be visited by the renowned violinist Pablo de Sarasate. Some of Cocteau's fondest memories of his early life were of trips to the circus, the ice palace, and the theater, especially the Comédie-Française. Years later, in his own drama, he would attempt to duplicate the lighting or brilliancy of theatrical events in his memory and would discover from lighting technicians that it had been technically impossible to do such things when he was a child. Time had increased the splendor of his memories, including those of the castle and of his grandparents' house. He thus began to perceive his own life as having mythological dimensions, as even his personal experiences had become exaggerated and distorted over time.

In 1899, Cocteau's father committed suicide as a result of financial problems. Cocteau became an indifferent student at the Petit Lycée Condorcet and, later, at the Grand Condorcet. Like many creative personalities, he found the institutional atmosphere oppressive. Besides having a weak constitution, which often led to legitimate absences, he was frequently truant. During his illnesses, he often had his German governess stitching doll clothes for his model theater. One of his closest childhood friends was Réné Rocher, later to become a director, who spent much time with Cocteau and his miniature theaters. After a trip with his mother to Venice, Cocteau began study for his baccalaureate, had his first love affair (with Madeleine Carlier, ten years his senior), and became more involved with the theater—meeting Edouard de Max, who acted opposite Sarah Bernhardt. Quite naturally, with all this to entertain him, Cocteau failed the examination.

On April 4, 1908, de Max sponsored a reading of Cocteau's poetry, by de Max, Rocher, and other prominent actors and actresses, at the Théâtre Fémina. Because the event was attended by many of the elite of Paris, including several leading literary critics, Cocteau became instantly well-known. Subsequently, he became acquainted with such literary notables as Edmond Rostand, Marcel Proust, Charles Péguy, Catulle Mendès, and Jules Lemaître. He became quite enamored of Comtesse Anna de Noailles and tried to write poetry like hers, with a refined sensibility and enhanced sensuality. He was one of three founders of a literary magazine, *Schéhérazade*, which was dedicated to poetry and music, and rented a room at the Hôtel Biron, where Auguste Rodin and his secretary, Rainer Maria Rilke, were also staying.

When Cocteau was introduced to the great impresario Sergei Diaghilev of the Ballets Russes, he begged Diaghilev to permit him to write ballets. Diaghilev eventually said "Étonne-moi!" ("Astonish me!"), and Cocteau took this injunction as an order to give shape to the rest of his life's work. His first ballet, *Le Dieu bleu* (1912), was not successful, though Diaghilev produced it for the coronation of George V. Convinced the music was at fault, Cocteau began to associate with Igor Stravinsky, living with him for a while. During this period, Cocteau was also trying to defend himself against the accusation of Henri Ghéon in the *Nouvelle Revue française*, who charged that he was an entirely derivative poet. Around 1914, Cocteau underwent what he called a "molting," breaking free of the influence of Rostand and the Comtesse de Noailles and moving toward his eventual association with Max Jacob and Guillaume Apollinaire.

As World War I broke out, Cocteau attempted to enlist but was rejected for health reasons. Illegally, he became an ambulance driver on the Belgian front, but after being discovered, he was sent back to Paris. These experiences would later form a large part of his novel *Thomas l'imposteur* (1923; *Thomas the Impostor*, 1925). Back in Paris, he met Amedeo Modigliani and Pablo Picasso and introduced the latter to Diaghilev, thereby creating the association which would produce Erik Satie's 1917 ballet *Parade*, with scenario by Cocteau, costumes and set by Picasso, and choreography by Léonide Massine. *Parade* created a scandal with its atonal music and extraordinary set and costumes. Only the presence of Apollinaire, in uniform and wearing a bandage over his head-wound, kept the outraged spectators from attacking the creators of the ballet. Cocteau responded vigorously, attacking the musical influences of Claude Debussy, Richard Wagner, and Stravinsky and linking himself with the composers known as "Les Six" (Georges Auric, Louis Durey, Arthur Honegger, Darius Milhaud, Francis Poulenc, and Germaine Tailleferre).

In 1919, Cocteau met and fell in love with Raymond Radiguet, who was fifteen, handsome, and a poetic genius—or so Cocteau believed. Radiguet caused Cocteau to re-evaluate his aesthetics and move toward a simpler, classic style; thus inspired, he found new energy and created a number of new works, including *Le Grand écart* (1923; *The Grand Écart*, 1925) and the volume of poems *Plain-Chant*. Radiguet, however, died of typhoid in December, 1923, and Cocteau was devastated. Diaghilev tried to shake Cocteau from his despair by taking him on a trip to Monte Carlo. The trip itself did little good, however, and the discovery of opium there proved to be Cocteau's only solace. His addiction eventually provoked his friends and family to persuade him to enter a sanatorium in 1925. There, he came under the influence of Jacques Maritain, the Catholic philosopher, who briefly restored Cocteau's faith in religion. He was able to pick up the pieces of this life and create such works as *L'Ange heurtebise*, *Orpheus*, and *Children of the Game*. He even patched up his friendship with Stravinsky and wrote the words for Stravinsky's oratorio *Oedipus-Rex*.

In the 1930's, Cocteau seemed inexhaustible, even though he suffered a bout with typhoid in 1931. Plays, poems, songs, ballets, art criticism, and even a column for *Ce soir* poured forth from his pen. He took a trip around the world in imitation of Jules Verne's *Le Tour du monde en quatre-vingt jours* (1873; *Around the World in Eighty Days*, 1873). He became the manager of the bantamweight boxer Alphonse Theo Brown. Perhaps the most important of his activities during this period was his first attempt at *poésie cinématographique*, when he wrote and directed *The Blood of a Poet*.

Cocteau, always controversial, found himself squeezed between his artistic enemies and new political ones during the Nazi occupation of France. He was viciously attacked in the press. His play *La Machine à écrire* (1941; *The Typewriter*, 1962) was banned. He never backed off, however, even when beaten by a group of French Fascists for failing to salute the flag.

After the war, Cocteau found himself a "grand old man" of the artistic world, but he refused to rest on his laurels and continued arousing controversy. He traveled and wrote plays, journals, and films. He made recordings and designed frescoes for the city hall at Menton, the Chapel of St. Pierre at Villefranche-sur-Mer, the Chapel of Notre Dame in London, the Church of Saint Blaise-des-Simples in Milly-la-Forêt, and the Chapel of Notre-Dame-de-Jerusalem at Fréjus. He also designed fabrics, plates, and posters. He was made a member of the Royal Belgian Academy and the Académie Française in 1955 and received an honorary doctorate of letters from Oxford University in 1956. He died on October 11, 1963, shortly after hearing of the death of his friend Edith Piaf.

Analysis

Jean Cocteau's first three books of poetry enjoyed the kind of success which works that essentially flatter the prevailing literary establishment are prone to have. He was instantly praised and compared to various great poets, present and past, yet never aroused the outrage or bewilderment provoked by significant breakthroughs. Very much a salon poet and dandy, Cocteau had yet to discover his own voice. *La Lampe d'Aladin* contained poems dedicated to the various actors and actresses who had read them at Cocteau's "debut" in the Théâtre Fémina. Like much of the poetry of the early 1900's, the poems of this first volume seem self-serving, overly and insincerely emotional, and very immature, though occasionally some charming cleverness may emerge.

Cocteau's second collection, *Le Prince frivole* (the frivolous prince), is little better than the first. Its title came to be applied to its author, and Cocteau would later refer to the book as elevating him to the "Prince du Ridicule." The creation of poetry here is still an amusing game. Cocteau rather dutifully insists on melancholy in many of the works, but it comes off as posing, even though it may be indicative of an indefinable feeling that all the praise he was receiving was undeserved. After the publication of *La Danse de Sophocle*, the inadequacy of Cocteau's artistic commitment was brought home to him in a review by Henri Ghéon in *Nouvelle Revue française* (André Gide may have had a hand in its authorship). Ghéon pointed out the derivative qualities of Cocteau's three books and implied that the poet was immature, frivolous, and greatly overestimated. Ghéon said that Cocteau was undeniably gifted but that he had not devoted himself to his gift. The review was more important in Cocteau's life than the book itself, though one can see in *La Danse de Sophocle* the beginning of Cocteau's lifelong interest in the eternal truths found in ancient Greek mythology and literature. The review provoked Cocteau to understand "that art and poetry aren't a game, but a descent into a mine, down toward the firedamp and danger. . . . "

Cocteau did not publish another collection of poetry until seven years later, after working for the Ballets Russes, associating with a more radical set of artists, and after his experiences in World War I. Later, when republishing his works, he ignored the earlier three books and dated his beginnings as a poet from *Le Cap de Bonne-Espérance* (the Cape of Good Hope), which was inspired by his association with the aviator Roland Garros. Garros would take Cocteau on daily flights from Villacoublay. He performed numerous acrobatics with Cocteau in the plane, and the poet was inspired by the sensation of flying and the view of Paris from the air. In 1918, after a remarkable escape from a German prison, Garros was shot down and killed. A proof copy of Cocteau's long poem dedicated to Garros was found in his cockpit. In the book, the airplane symbolizes the modern era: It frees mankind from earthly considerations, putting the pilot or passenger into a realm of new visions and solitude, where he can find his soul. At the same time, he faces death.

The poems in *Le Cap de Bonne-Espérance* are extremely sensual, despite the abstract element, and attempt to re-create the physical sensations of flying with fragmented lines and onomatopoeic vowels. These techniques were not original to Cocteau; the typographical effects had been used by Stéphane Mallarmé, Apollinaire, and Pierre Reverdy, and the *lettriste* effects by Pierre Albert-Birot. Yet, as Adrienne Monnier points out, it was daring of Cocteau to employ these still-radical devices. André Breton, among others, considered the collection not radical enough and had a sour expression the whole time Cocteau was reading it in Valentine Gross's apartment. Cocteau is said to have called his work old-fashioned, in an effort to charm Breton, but many see the reading as the beginning of Cocteau's long battle with the Surrealists. The book also provoked a letter from Proust, who gently asked whether it did not display a certain indiscriminate use of images.

Discours du grand sommeil (discourse of the great sleep) consists of eleven poems written between 1916 and 1918 and was inspired by Cocteau's experiences with the Fusiliers Marins, among whom he lived, illegally wearing the Marine uniform until discovered by an officer. A day after Cocteau was ejected from the front, most of the Fusiliers Marins were killed. Cocteau attempted in these poems to end once and for all his role as the "prince of frivolity." Though flippancy was always part of Cocteau's demeanor, he once asserted that it was the bourgeois way of dealing with catastrophe—that what appeared to be frivolity to others was actually Cocteau's way of dealing with his profound sadness. *Discours du grand sommeil*, writes Wallace Fowlie, is "a plunge downward," "a contact with the grim presence of death." The poems are quite effective in conveying the horror of war, of the exhausting marches, the screams of the dying, and the endless suffering. There is also an awakening sense of the soldier as symbolic of the tragedy of human existence and a movement toward a more classical style and attitude. The volume clearly points toward Cocteau's later aesthetic.

Vocabulaire also reveals a cleaner, purer style than that of Cocteau's youthful works, yet still betrays the inordinate influence of the artistic movements of the war years, such as Dadaism, Futurism, Imagism, and Cubism. Cocteau's fixation upon certain images (such as snow turning to marble) is notable throughout his career. In this collection, the rose appears often, with obvious allusions to Pierre de Ronsard, in clear homage to French classicism. One finds Cocteau in search of himself, struggling as he had since the Ghéon review to achieve originality. The poems consist largely of philosophical speculations on the nature of change and the poet's role in metamorphosis. The endless flow of change is represented by the changes in clouds, aging, swans, the dissolution of salt statues, death, and snow. Cocteau's private mythology is fully developed here; several poems, such as "Tombeaux" (tombs) and "Oiseaux sont en neige" (birds are in snow), connect homosexuality to the themes of change and death. In these poems, Cocteau seems to be taking stock of his life, trying to find a direction and meaning to it.

Under Radiguet's influence, Cocteau was moving toward the tradition of

French literature that employs the brief, clear, precise sentence. Cocteau renewed himself with this classicism and rediscovered the themes of classical antiquity. In *Poésies, 1917-1920*, Cocteau introduced a new set of topics, themes, and motifs, such as the clown, circus, angel, sailor, and athlete. Perhaps the most significant poem in the collection is *L'Ode à Picasso* (ode to Picasso), an attempt to grasp the complexity of the painter and artist whom Cocteau often watched at work for hours on end. The poem reveals Picasso as a man possessed by an inner fire, an embodiment of the concept, expressed by Socrates in Plato's *Ion*, of the madness of the poet. Painting, sculpture, film, and any other expression of art are therefore merely facets of the same thing: *poésie*. Cocteau sees in Picasso a man in constant contact with the Muses, free of mundane considerations. The poem expresses much of what Cocteau would attempt to be, would have the courage to be, after being inspired by Radiguet. The final poem of *Poésies, 1917-1920*, "Mouchoir" (handkerchief), bids farewell to influences of the past and sets the poet out on a voyage into the unknown. To be a poet is thus to move ahead relentlessly, to be uncertain of the results, to follow no one.

Plain-Chant reveals in its title a further move toward simplification and, in Fowlie's view, is central to the work of Cocteau. It is classically metered and uses the imagery of Angel, Muse, and Death, symbolism which recurs in much of the rest of Cocteau's oeuvre. The Angel in this lyric poem is clearly Radiguet, and the poem expresses Cocteau's great love for him and also his fear of the death which will inevitably separate them. The Angel is his guide through the mysteries of poetic art and also his protector when the Muse leaves him or Death presses in on him. As Bettina Knapp has observed, however, Death becomes a restorative power, a bridge to another world: "He burrowed within and reached new depths of cognition, with beauty of form and classical restraint." The poem was also strangely prescient, as Radiguet died in 1923, emotionally shattering Cocteau.

Cocteau's discovery of his identity as a poet under the guidance of Radiguet was not lost in his plummet into despair brought about by the young man's death. The collection *Opéra* mixes Cocteau's visions induced by opium with lucid language and precise control. Even in his agony, he rigorously adheres to a classical detachment, a coolness that enhances the feelings and mythological dimensions of the works. A blending of Christian and pagan mythology points toward Cocteau's extensive revising and adapting of works of classical mythology for the stage and film. "L'Ange heurtebise" in *Opéra* is usually thought to be one of Cocteau's most significant poems. It explores the question of angelism, which he had discussed in an essay, *Le Secret professionnel* (1922). The poet is stuck on an earthly plane, struggling to understand a larger reality, while the Angel stands above. The Angel reappears in work after work of Cocteau, inspiring poets and urging them to look upon the human predicament with detachment.

Cocteau did not cease writing poetry until his death, but most critics seem indifferent to the large number of his works after *Opéra*. Perhaps his work in film and prose detracted from his development in poetry, though Cocteau himself saw all of his artistic works as facets of the same creative impulse: It was all poetry to him. His influence on the literary scene waned, perhaps because he had finally found his own unique path, and artists and critics found it difficult to categorize and thus assess the measure of Cocteau's achievement. His variety contributes to the difficulty of an overall assessment: He began each mature collection of poems as if he had only recently become a poet.

At the very least, Cocteau's poetry exhibits many of the primary traits of twentieth century poetry in its clean, precise form, its development of personal mythology, and its exploitation through adaptation of traditional mythological and literary themes. These traits are significant elements of the mainstream of modern poetry, and Cocteau is clearly in the middle of it.

Major publications other than poetry

NOVELS: *Le Potomak*, 1919; *Le Grand écart*, 1923 (*The Grand Écart*, 1925); *Thomas l'imposteur*, 1923 (*Thomas the Impostor*, 1925); *Le Livre blanc*, 1928 (*The White Paper*, 1957); *Les Enfants terribles*, 1929 (*Enfants Terrible*, 1930, also as *Children of the Game*, 1955); *Le Fantôme de Marseilles*, 1933; *Le Fin de Potomak*, 1939.

PLAYS: *Romeo et Juliette*, 1926 (translation); *Antigone*, 1927 (libretto; English translation, 1961); *Oedipus Rex*, 1928 (libretto); *Orphée*, 1927 (*Orpheus*, 1933); *La Voix humaine*, 1930 (*The Human Voice*, 1951); *La Machine infernale*, 1934 (*The Infernal Machine*, 1936); *L'École des veuves*, 1936; *Les Chevaliers de la table ronde*, 1937 (*Knights of the Round Table*, 1963); *Les Parents terribles*, 1938 (*Intimate Relations*, performed 1952, published 1956); *Les Monstres sacrés*, 1940 (*The Holy Terrors*, performed 1953, published 1962); *La Machine à écrire*, 1941 (*The Typewriter*, 1962); *Renaud et Armide*, 1943; *L'Aigle à deux têtes*, 1946 (*The Eagle Has Two Heads*, 1948); *Bacchus*, 1952 (English translation, 1955).

SCREENPLAYS: *Le Sang d'un poète*, released 1932, published 1948 (*The Blood of a Poet*, 1949); *Le Baron fantôme*, released 1943; *L'Eternel retour*, released 1943, published 1948; *La Belle et la bête*, released 1945, published 1946 (*Beauty and the Beast*, 1950); *Ruy Blas*, 1947; *Les Parents terribles*, released 1948, published 1949 (*Intimate Relations*, 1952); *L'Aigle à deux têtes*, released 1947; *Les Enfants terribles*, released 1950; *Orphée*, released 1949, published 1951; *Le Testament d'Orphée*, 1959 (*The Testament of Orpheus*, 1968).

NONFICTION: *Le Coq et l'arlequin*, 1918 (*Cock and Harlequin*, 1921); *Le Secret professionnel*, 1922; *Lettre à Jacques Maritain*, 1926 (*Art and Faith*, 1948); *Le Rappel à l'ordre*, 1926 (*A Call to Order*, 1926); *Opium: Journal d'une désintoxication*, 1930 (*Opium: Diary of a Cure*, 1932); *Essai de la critique indirecte*, 1932 (*The Lais Mystery: An Essay of Indirect Criticism*, 1936); *Portraits-souvenir, 1900-1914*, 1935 (*Paris Album*, 1956); *La Belle et la bête: Journal d'un film*, 1946 (*Beauty and the Beast: Journal of a Film*, 1950); *La Difficulté d'être*, 1947 (*The Difficulty of Being*, 1966); *The Journals of Jean Cocteau*, 1956; *Poésie critique*, 1960.

Bibliography

Brown, Frederick. *An Impersonation of Angels: A Biography of Jean Cocteau*, 1968.

Crosland, Margaret. *Jean Cocteau: A Biography*, 1956.

Fowlie, Wallace. *Jean Cocteau: History of a Poet's Age*, 1966.

Fraigneau, André. *Cocteau par lui-même*, 1957.

Knapp, Bettina L. *Jean Cocteau*, 1970.

Lannes, Roger. *Jean Cocteau*, 1945.

O'Brien, Justin. *Contemporary French Literature*, 1971.

Sprigge, Elizabeth, and Jean-Jacques Kihm. *Jean Cocteau: The Man and His Mirror*, 1968.

Steegmuller, Francis. *Cocteau*, 1970.

Stewart, D. "Cocteau: The Last Imagist Poet," in *Shenandoah*. IX (1958), pp. 36-41.

J. Madison Davis

SOR JUANA INÉS DE LA CRUZ
Juana de Asbaje y Ramírez de Santillana

Born: San Miguel Nepantla, Mexico; November 12, 1651
Died: Mexico City; April 17, 1695

Principal collections

The writings of Sor Juana Inés de la Cruz were first published in Spain toward the end of the seventeenth century. The initial volume of her works appeared in 1689; the second volume was printed in 1690; and there was a third and final volume in 1700. With the exception of several printings of those texts between 1700 and 1725, no attempt was made to edit and unify her works until Alfonso Méndez Plancarte produced his definitive study and compilation, *Obras completas de sor Juana Inés de la Cruz*, between 1951 and 1957. The four volumes of that collection include a number of selections omitted from the early editions as well as essays that reassess Sor Juana's place in literary history. Méndez Plancarte divides the works into four main sections, each given a separate volume: I, *Lírica Personal* (poetry); II, *Villancicos y letras sacras* (poetry); III, *Autos y Loas* (drama); IV, *Comedias, sainetes y prosa* (drama and prose).

Other literary forms

Sor Juana Inés de la Cruz's most readable prose work, the *Respuesta de la poetisa a la muy ilustre Sor Filotea de la Cruz* (1700; reply of the poetess to the illustrious Sister Filotea de la Cruz) is an appealing autobiographical defense of her precocious interest in learning, an emotional plea for acceptance as a woman and a scholar, and an obsessive declaration of faith. Sor Juana tries to convince her superiors that, despite her lifelong curiosity about the material world, theological concerns are still the most important to her.

El divino Narciso (1690; the divine Narcissus), a religious one-act play, is a tasteful and imaginative treatment of divine love in which Narcissus, as a figure of Christ, falls in love with human nature as a reflection of himself. With this short play, the fantasy of desire which takes so many forms throughout Sor Juana's work finds its ultimate synthesis of eros and agape.

Achievements

Sor Juana Inés de la Cruz was a Mexican literary virtuoso who was called the "tenth muse" during her lifetime, and who is generally considered the most important writer of colonial Spanish America. Although she wrote more than four hundred poems, twenty-three short plays, two full-length *comedias*, and various prose works, Sor Juana's reputation rests on a handful of poems (about two dozen in all), *El divino Narciso*, and *Respuesta de la poetisa a la muy ilustre Sor Filotea de la Cruz*. Although a reassessment of her works begun in the 1950's promises a more extensive list of her most important writings, it is likely that, with the exception of her extremely complex "Primero sueño" (first dream), the few pieces which earned her the admiration of Marcelino Menendez y Pelayo one hundred years ago will continue to be the ones that will assure her a place of prominence in Spanish letters.

At her best, Sor Juana was able to manipulate the often unwieldy and intricate language of the Spanish Baroque, with its rich heritage from the Golden Age, into expressions of delicate, feminine vision and sensibility. Her aesthetic documentation of the search for knowledge, love, and God is the most complete personal and artistic record of any figure from the colonial period. Sor Juana's love poetry appears to reflect frustrating and painful experiences prior to her entry into the convent at about the age of seventeen. Few of the poems are concerned with fulfillment or the intimate communication of personal feelings; most are, instead, variations on the themes of ambivalence and disillusionment in love. Sor Juana's philosophical poems are linked to her amatory verse by a sense of disenchantment. An exception to her general pessimism is "Primero sueño," in which the poet takes delight in depicting the joys and dangers of her intellectual explorations. More of Sor Juana's writings bear witness to her theological concerns. Although some of her religious lyrics express the same kind of anguish about God's love that she expressed about human love, she clearly attempted in her *villancicos* to use her poetic talent in the service of the Church.

Biography

Juana de Asbaje y Ramírez de Santillana was born on November 12, 1651, in San Miguel Nepantla, some sixty kilometers southeast of Mexico City. She was the illegitimate child of a Spanish captain and a Creole mother. In the charming *Respuesta de la poetisa a la muy ilustre Sor Filotea de la Cruz*, she tells how she learned to read at the age of three, and tagged along with one of her sisters to La Amiga, an elementary school, where she took her first formal lessons. She says that, at the age of eight, she begged her mother to let her cut her hair and dress like a boy so she could attend the university. That being denied her, she continued her self-education by reading the classics she found in her grandmother's house. Around 1659, she was allowed to go to Mexico City and live with the family of one of her aunts. Although not enrolled in the university, Juana privately continued her studies, which included twenty lessons in Latin. Twenty was apparently sufficient, for subsequently she was able to write Latin poetry as well as anyone in the viceroyalty.

By 1664, Sor Juana was a member of the viceregal court and was the darling of the vicereine. She so impressed the viceroy, the Marques de Mancera, with her knowledge, that he arranged for forty professors from the university to give her tests. Sor Juana passed them all, amazing the local elite. Her several years of court life must have been intense, emotional years. She was a beautiful woman and was doubtless wooed by gentlemen of some wealth and position. Nevertheless, by 1669, she had entered the convent and had taken religious vows, as much from aversion to marriage as from attraction to the celibate life. It was her desire to be free to learn, she states in the *Respuesta de la poetisa a la muy ilustre Sor Filotea de la Cruz*, that was the primary motivation for her vocation.

For the next twenty-three years, Sor Juana was the major literary figure in colonial Spanish America, composing everything from love sonnets to a treatise on music, almost all of her writing being done on request from high-ranking officials of the Church or the state. She wrote elaborate pieces for performance at liturgical functions, occasional verse for political events, and scenarios and scripts for afternoons of royal entertainment. Not long after the brilliant defense of her studies in *Respuesta de la poetisa a la muy ilustre Sor Filotea de la Cruz*, and at the height of her career, when her collected works were beginning to be published and acclaimed in Spain, pressures by her religious superiors induced her to give away her library of more than four thousand volumes and all of her scientific and musical instruments, and to abandon her writing altogether. Several years later, on April 17, 1695, she died in an epidemic that swept Mexico City.

Analysis

Although most of the compositions have merit, the lyric poems, in the order of their treatment here, are usually considered to be the best, and they may be used as a point of departure for delineating a canon of Sor Juana Inés de la Cruz's most significant writings.

Sor Juana Inés de la Cruz was a deeply passionate and intelligent woman who dedicated her life to knowledge and spiritual perfection. On the one hand, she seems to have renounced love for intellectual freedom, and from her amatory and philosophical writings, it appears that her renunciation of the world, along with her commitment to learning, paradoxically caused an obsession with intimacy and a profound disillusionment with any reality except that of spiritual intimacy. On the other hand, judging from her other prose and verse, Sor Juana was also a writer engaged with her society, closely involved with its institutions and its native culture. An anthology of Sor Juana's most popular compositions may slight this more social side of her personality, but it is important to remember as one reviews her major poems of love and disillusionment that the poetess wrote more concerning religion than about any real or imaginary love, and that she was as adept at elaborate versification about current events and visitors to the viceroyalty as at revealing her most private feelings. It is not difficult to dwell on the more romantic side of the "tenth muse," to use certain of her poems to enhance the image of a jilted, precocious, disenchanted teenage intellectual sequestering herself in a convent and spending her life in extremely elaborate sublimation. Her most famous pieces contribute to such an image, but as the reader is exposed to a wider spectrum of her talents, a more balanced picture emerges; a trajectory of maturation becomes visible in which Catholicism and the Baroque are means to the self-fulfillment and self-expression originally thwarted in her youth by her lack of social position and her fascination with scholarship.

If one reads Sor Juana's writings to observe a progression from human to divine love, it is appropriate to begin with the sonnet "Esta tarde, mi bien" (this afternoon, my love). The poem is one of the few in which she relates a moving encounter with another person, and it contrasts the impotency of words with the efficacy of tears in the communication of love. Here, there is none of the love-hate dialectic which colors most of her amatory poems; instead, one finds the description of a delicately feminine, sensitive, and formidably talented personality in a moment of unguarded abandon. It is only a slight exaggeration to say that after "Esta tarde, mi bien," one sees in Sor Juana's verse the psychological effects of an unhappy affair rather than the experience of love itself. Even the tender *lira* "Amado dueño mio" (my beloved master), while documenting in a poetic sense the dimensions of intimacy, is a conventional lament of the lover separated from the beloved. The lover, like a Renaissance shepherdess, tells her misfortunes to the wind, which carries her complaints, her passion, and her sadness to the distant partner. Alfonso Méndez Plancarte states that the poem contains some of Sor Juana's finest lines, and that it may surpass the eclogues of Garcilaso de la Vega. The comparison with Garcilaso is appropriate, and poetry in his likeness is fitting to express the absence of consummation rather than its presence; significantly, the *lira* keynotes a thematic transformation from completion to emptiness.

The sonnet "Detente, sombra de mi bien esquivo" (stay, shadow of my scornful love) can be considered an introduction to a series of poems which admit both the positive and negative effects of passion as well as the inconclusive status of unconsummated love. In "Detente, sombra de mi bien esquivo," the beloved himself eludes the poet, but his image cannot escape the prison of her fantasy. Important in this and the poems under discussion below is the counterpoint of conceits and emotions about the love "por quien alegre muero" (for whom I would happily die), but also "por quien penosa vivo" (for whom I live in agony), which develops to an extreme in the sonnet "Al que Ingrato me deja, busco amante" (I seek the one who spurns me) and "Que no me quiera Fabio, al verse amado" (that Fabio does not love me as I love him), and the *redondilla* "Este amoroso tormento" (this torment of love). In the latter piece, as in the other poems of this group, the poet never finds fulfillment, "porque, entre alivio y dolor, hallo culpa en el amor y disculpa en el olvido" (because between relief and pain, I find blame in love and exoneration in forgetfulness).

Beyond frustration and the love-hate duality which the poet attributes to romantic feeling lie disillusionment and bitterness. The sonnets "Silvio, yo te aborezco" (I hate you, Silvio), "Amor empieza por desasosiego" (love begins uneasily), and "Con el dolor de la mortal herida" (with the pain of a mortal wound) are among Sor Juana's strongest denunciations of the men she once might have loved, as well as of herself for having given in to loving them: "no solo a tí, corrida, te aborrezco,/ pero a mí por el tiempo que te quise" (not only do I abhor you/ but myself for the time that I loved you). Here the bittersweet of "Este amoroso tormento" turns to anger. The image of the lover purposely retained in "Detente, sombra de mi bien esquivo" is repeatedly banished, and it is a logical movement from such rejection to the *sátira filosófica*, "Hombres necios" (foolish men), one of Sor Juana's more popular denunciations of men as the source of all women's problems. In these feminist *redondillas*, the poet exposes the ways in which men "acusan lo que causan" (blame us for the things they cause). Why, she asks, do men want women to be good if they tempt them to be bad? Who, she questions, is the greater sinner, "la que peca por la paga o el que paga por pecar" (she who sins for pay or he who pays for sin)?

Since Sor Juana's poems are not usually dated, there is no way of knowing whether the progression from the delicate, loving "Esta tarde, mi bien" to the sarcastic "Hombres necios" reflects the sequential effects of an increasingly unhappy situation. In any case, these poems of erotic experience do fit a pattern which begins with brief reciprocal affection and degenerates into ambivalence, then finally into contempt. There are, at the same time, a great number of poems written to women which do not fit this generalization. Sor Juana apparently had very meaningful relationships with the wives of two of the Mexican viceroys, and her many verses to Lysi show a far more consistent emotional response than that depicted in poems of male-female interaction. Certainly the Lysi poems, perhaps especially the ornate "Lámina sirva el cielo al retrato" (the sky is lamina of your portrait), are a moving contrast to her more widely read poems' heterosexual canon.

Sor Juana's philosophic poems complement her negative attitude toward worldly love. "Verde embeleso de la vida humana" (green charm of human life) rejects illusions and hope as deceptive: "solamente lo que toco veo" (I only see what I can touch). It represents the repression of vain dreams, the acceptance of life without romance or even platonic fantasy. "Diuturna enfermedad de la Esperanza" (lasting infirmity of hope) reiterates this concept, and "Este que ves, engaño colorido" (this painted lie you see), a sonnet on her portrait, is an intense affirmation of the Catholic view that the flesh is "polvo, es sombra, es nada" (is dust, is a shadow, is nothing). Her "Rosa divina" (divine rose) is a variation on the universal theme of the brevity of beauty and life. Perhaps her most powerful renunciation is "Finjamos que soy feliz" (pretend that I am happy), in which she denies the validity of knowledge and maintains that because man can know nothing for certain, ignorance is preferable to imperfect knowing: "aprendamos a ignorar" (let us learn to not know). This poem is a moment of despair within the context of Sor Juana's self-confessed lifelong passion, the pursuit of knowledge. Her monumental "Primero sueño," the only work which she admitted to writing for her own pleasure and not to please someone else, is far more balanced in presenting her attitude toward learning.

The "Primero sueño," which is among the best philosophic poems in Spanish, is the height of Sor Juana's exploration of the Baroque. The poem begins with a description of nightfall, in which the entire physical world eventually succumbs to sleep. The human spirit, freed from the constraint of the body, soars upward to find a persepctive from which it can comprehend the immensity of the universe. Once it glimpses the overpowering dimensions of creation, the soul retreats to the shadows. Finding a mental shore on the sea of knowledge, it decides to approach the challenge of learning by dividing things into categories and mastering each division separately. In spite of doubts that the mind can really know anything, echoes of the dark vision of "Finjamos que soy feliz," the soul continues its search for truth. Dawn arrives, however, and the dream ends inconclusively. Universal knowledge has eluded the soul, but the dreamer has not despaired.

Once considered to be on the fringe of literature because of its purposeful Gongorism, "Primero sueño" is enjoying the positive reconsideration accorded the entire Spanish Baroque, in the course of which Luis de Góngora y Argote himself has been reinstated into the canon of major Spanish poets. Accepting the style of this poem as not only valid but also essential to its meaning, one can better appreciate Sor Juana's most mature and complex statement about the human condition. It is the culmination of a lifetime of study and reflection.

Sor Juana's religious writings include several "sacred ballads," among which "Amante dulce del alma" (sweet love of my soul), "Mientras la Gracia me exita" (while Grace moves me), and "Traigo conmigo un cuidado" (I have a deep concern) are generally held in high regard. All three attempt to express the effects of divine love. "Amante dulce del alma" asks why Christ might have willed to visit the poet in Holy Communion: has He decided to be present from love or from jealousy? She decides for the former, reflecting that since God knows all things, He can see into her heart and has no reason to be jealous. "Mientras la Gracia me exita" tries to clarify some of the feelings involved in the inner struggle between "la virtud y la costumbre" (virtue and habit). Like "Amante dulce del alma," this is a poem of scruples rather than a meditation of universal religious significance. "Traigo conmigo un cuidado" carries the analysis of spiritual love further and contrasts it with the poet's experience of human love. "La misma muerte que vivo, es la vida con que muero" (the same death that I live is the life in which I die), she writes at the end of the poem, attempting to sum up her contradictory mental state. Even though it is divine love which causes her to feel the way she does, there are parallels between the contrarias penas (contradictory anxieties) of "Este amoroso tormento" and those expressed in "Traigo conmigo un cuidado."

It is more fruitful to look for a developed sense of religious experience in Sor Juana's *villancicos* and her play *El divino Narciso* than in her personal religious lyrics. Although these works have generally been neglected, Méndez Plancarte and others have made convincing defenses of their genres as well as of the verse itself. *El divino Narciso* contains some of Sor Juana's best writing, and, with the *loa* (or one-act play) which precedes it, shows how she introduced Indian themes into her work. The most significant element of the play, however, is the successful depiction of divine love, sufficiently anthropomorphized to give it comprehensible human beauty. Here is also the full evolution of a spiritual maturity which finally quiets the older, worldly concerns.

Sor Juana is easily anthologized, but such selectivity does not provide a proper perspective from which to view her talents or interests. The genius of the "tenth muse" offers almost unlimited fare for those who would dwell on the poems and techniques in themselves; similarly, the literary historian will hardly want to limit his reading to Sor Juana's "best," but will find the richest commentary on colonial Mexico as well as the soul of the poet herself within the diversity of her complete works. There, instead of a facile trajectory from personal rejection to religion, one finds a maze of subtle Rococo revelations.

Major publications other than poetry

PLAY: *El divino Narciso*, 1690.

NONFICTION: *Respuesta de la poetisa a la muy ilustre Sor Filotea de la Cruz*, 1700.

MISCELLANEOUS: *Obras completas de sor Juana Inés de la Cruz*, 1951-1957 (4 volumes). Edited by Méndez Plancarte.

Bibliography
Abreu Gómez, Ermilo. *Sor Juana Inés de la Cruz: Bibliografía y Biblioteca*, 1934.

Chávez, Ezequiel A. *Ensayo de psicologiá de sor Juana*, 1931.

Menéndez y Pelayo, Marcelino. *Historia de la poesía hispanoamericana*, 1911-1913.

Mistral, Gabriela. "Silueta de sor Juana," in *Abside*. XV (1951).

Nervo, Amado. *Juana de Asbaje*, 1910.

Pfandl, Ludwig. *Sor Juana Inés de la Cruz*, 1963.

William L. Felker

GABRIELE D'ANNUNZIO

Born: Pescara, Italy; March 12, 1863
Died: Gardone, Italy; March 1, 1938

Principal collections

Primo vere, 1879, 1880; *Canto novo*, 1882, 1896; *Intermezzo di rime*, 1884 (later as *Intermezzo*, 1896); *Isaotta Gùttadauro ed altre poesie*, 1886, 1890; *Sari Pantaleone*, 1886; *Elegie romane*, 1892; *Poema paradisiaco—Odi navali*, 1893; *Le laudi*, 1899-1949 (*Laudi del cielo del mare della terra e degli eroi*, 1899; work was expanded to create *Maia*, 1903; *Elettra*, 1904; *Alcyone*, 1904, English translation, 1977; *Merope*, 1912; *Asterope*, 1949).

Other literary forms

In addition to poetry, Gabriele D'Annunzio's literary production encompasses many other genres: short stories, novels, autobiographical essays, political writings, and several plays, in Italian and in French.

The whole of D'Annunzio's production is available in three major editions: *Opera omnia*, (1927-1936); *Tutte le opere*, (1931-1937); and *Tutte le opere*, (1930-1965), which also includes D'Annunzio's notes under the title, *Taccuini*. Only a few sections of his vast correspondence have been published.

Achievements

D'Annunzio dominated the Italian literary scene from 1880 until the end of World War I. His literary work and his personal conduct challenged existing models with such an exuberant vitality that even the less positive aspects of his art and life have been influential, if only for the reaction they have provoked.

Extremely receptive to foreign influences, D'Annunzio, through a series of experiments with new forms and styles of composition, evolved an original poetic language. Replacing traditional grammatical links with paratactic constructions, he forged a style in which assonance, onomatopoeia, and alliteration prevail, achieving enthralling effects of pictorial and musical synesthesia.

Historically, D'Annunzio's most original achievement was to help to break the highly academic literary tradition which had been dominant in Italy for centuries and to reintegrate Italian culture into the mainstream of European intellectual life. He was the first modern Italian writer. His literary work in its amplitude and variety served as an invaluable source of motifs, themes, and suggestions for the brilliant generation of poets who came to maturity in the 1920's. As Eugenio Montale has observed, an Italian poet who has learned nothing from D'Annunzio is truly impoverished.

Biography

Gabriele D'Annunzio was born in Pescara, a small port city in the Abruzzi region, on March 12, 1863, to a well-to-do family. He received a solid classical education at the Liceo Cicognini, in Prato, and when he was only sixteen years old, he published his first collection of verses, *Primo vere* (early spring).

In 1881, D'Annunzio moved to Rome, where he registered at the university in the department of Italian literature, but he never completed his university studies. He chose instead to pursue a writer's career, consolidating his fame as a young poetic genius in the literary and aristocratic circles of the capital. During that time, he contributed verses, short stories, and articles to several publications, while enjoying an intense social life punctuated by love affairs, intrigues, and scandals. His second collection of verses, *Canto novo* (new song), was both more accomplished and more personal than its predecessor.

D'Annunzio's Roman period, interrupted by adventurous cruises and occasional sojourns in the Abruzzi region, lasted until 1891. By that time, he had already gained national recognition, sealing his social and literary success with his marriage to Maria Hardouin, Duchess of Gallese, and with the publication of a novel. These were fruitful years for D'Annunzio, as witnessed by the production of numerous novels and collections of short stories. D'Annunzio led an extravagant and magnificent life, a life of debts and scandals, of new loves and adventures. At the same time, he maintained an unrelenting rhythm of work. Indeed, all of his activities were encompassed and absorbed by a total engagement in literature.

D'Annunzio also nourished political ambitions. In 1896, he published *Le vergini delle rocce* (*The Maidens of the Rocks*, 1898), a novel whose antidemocratic message is emblematic of the writer's political choices. One year later, he entered the political arena and was elected as a representative to the Italian parliament. His activity there was unremarkable until 1900, when, during the controversy over the exceptional laws proposed by Pelloux's government, he theatrically shifted to the left wing, declaring: "I am going toward life." In the same year, he presented himself as a candidate in the Socialist list but was not elected; with this defeat, D'Annunzio closed his parliamentary experience.

In 1894, D'Annunzio had met Eleonora Duse, the great actress, who played a considerable part in his sentimental life and had a substantial influence on his literary activities. This union of love and art gave rise to a period of great literary achievements. At "La Capponcina," a villa in the hilly countryside of Florence, surrounded by horses, dogs, and works of art, D'Annunzio wrote another novel, a number of plays, and the first three volumes of *Le laudi*, which represent the highest expression of his poetic art. His relationship with Duse was interrupted in 1903 by new temptations. After a few years of extravagant expenses, D'Annunzio, driven by his taste for luxury and his passion for cars and planes, was insolvent. In 1909, "La Capponcina" was seized by the creditors, and one year later D'Annunzio left Italy for France, choosing what he pompously called a "a voluntary exile." There, he split his time between his residence in Arcachon and Paris, where he was soon introduced into the literary and social circles. To this period belong several works in Old French, the most prominent of which is *Le Martyre de Saint Sébastien*, a theatrical text with music by Claude Debussy, which was presented in Paris in 1911.

The French period came to a close at the outbreak of World War I. Faithful to the idea of traditional alliance between France and Italy, D'Annunzio returned to Italy to campaign in favor of Italy's intervention in the war against Germany. D'Annunzio's political speeches were a clamorous success, significantly contributing to the victory of the interventionist party.

As soon as Italy entered the war, D'Annunzio enlisted as a volunteer; he fought first on the front line and then participated in several actions on the sea and in the air. In January, 1916, as a result of a plane accident, he lost his right eye and had to spend three months immobilized and in darkness. During this period of forced inactivity, he painfully scribbled notes which were to become *Il notturno* (1921), a work in prose without a precise narrative line, in which he registered impressions and notations in a stream of consciousness in which past and present are intertwined.

The end of the war and the peace negotiations, quite unsatisfactory for Italy, found D'Annunzio in the role of the poet-prophet, the voice of the people demanding their rights. The polemics over the peace negotiations reached their height when it appeared that the city of Fiume would not be annexed to Italy. With his famous "Marci dei Ronchi," D'Annunzio, at the head of a group of volunteers, entered Fiume and established a temporary government. His action interrupted the diplomatic negotiations between Italy and Yugoslavia; the Italian government first ordered D'Annunzio to leave the city, and then sent the fleet to force him out.

Fiume was officially annexed to Italy in 1924. D'Annunzio's action may have had some weight in this decision, but its immediate result was a failure. Meanwhile, in Italy, D'Annunzio's prophetic role had been assumed by Benito Mussolini. D'Annunzio, disillusioned, retired to a large estate on Lake Garda which he renamed "Il Vittoriale." There, he spent the rest of his life, surrounded by a rich library and by the mass of disparate objects which he had collected with obsessive passion.

The relations between D'Annunzio and the Fascist government were respectfully cold. The poet, while subscribing to certain principles of Fascism, considered Benito Mussolini a poor imitator of his own style; Mussolini, for his part, chose to keep D'Annunzio at a proper distance while bestowing on him honors and subsidies.

When he was not traveling, D'Annunzio led a quiet life at "Il Vittoriale," devoting his time to editing his *Opera omnia*. In 1924, under the title *Le faville del maglio*, he gathered and published some of his previous writings which had appeared in *Il corriere della Sera*; a second volume appeared in

1928. D'Annunzio's *Le cento e cento e cento pagine del libro segreto di Gabriele D'Annunzio tentato di morire* (1935), clearly referred to a strange accident in 1922 (he had fallen from a window) which could have been a suicide attempt. He died in 1938.

Analysis

The "D'Annunzio phenomenon" has stirred a century-long argument between his admirers and detractors, and his reputation has endured alternating periods of favor and disfavor, often related to historical circumstances. Lately, under the impetus of a D'Annunzio revival both in Italy and abroad, his works have begun to be reevaluated in the light of new critical methods.

Considering the number of Gabriele D'Annunzio's poetry collections, novels, plays, and memoirs, it would be unrealistic to expect a consistent artistic level throughout his oeuvre, but it should be recognized that, in its vastness and diversity, his work is an invaluable documentation of half a century of European intellectual life. In this perspective, it is difficult to isolate certain verse collections from the context of his entire production. The pattern of receptivity and experimentation that characterizes D'Annunzio's poetry can only be appreciated by following the arc of his poetic achievement from *Primo vere* to *Laudi del cielo del mare della terra e degli eroi*, where the voice of the poet reaches the plenitude of his expressive means.

In *Primo vere*, the choice of language, images, and versification is clearly inspired by Giosuè Carducci's model. A second edition of the work in 1880, enriched with fifty-nine new poems, offers greater insights. The delicate musicality of certain verses, the attention devoted to the description of landscapes as the privileged scenery for love encounters, anticipate the distinctive tone which D'Annunzio was to achieve in *Canto novo*. The driving inspiration of this collection is the poet's yearning for identification with nature. A pervasive pagan sensuality saturates the atmosphere as nature and man vibrate with the same impulses: A woman's breath has the perfume of the forest, and her haunches are like those of an antelope; lovers are entwined like "virgin trees interlacing their branches." The metaphors unify Earth, sea, and man in a vitalistic élan in which all forms merge.

Canto novo establishes the alternation between two themes which constitutes a favorite pattern of D'Annunzio's dialectic: an unresolved conflict between the vitalistic impetus and a *fin de siècle* introspection and sadness. The tendency to magnify the elegiac and melancholic component in the poet's writings is evident in the prevalent interpretation of the collection's most celebrated poem, "O falce di luna calante" (oh, sickle of waning moon), which has often been read as an expression of weariness and consuming despair; as Barberi Squarotti has noted in *Invito alla lettura di D'Annunzio*, this interpretation takes the poem out of its context in the collection, for the next poem is an invitation to another day of joyous life and love.

D'Annunzio's negative note decidedly does prevail, however, in *Intermezzo di rime*, which was later revised and published under the shorter title *Intermezzo*. This new collection presented a sharp change in versification, tone, and inspiration. Influenced by the French Parnassian school, D'Annunzio abandoned Carducci's versification for the traditional meters of sonnets and ballads. The volume also reveals a renewed taste for mythological reminiscence, while the polished elegance of the compositions suggests a new concern with aestheticism. Here, closed gardens substitute for natural landscapes, bucolic pagan eroticism gives way to a refined experimentation with morbid sensuality, and vitalism turns into sadistic cruelty. The entire collection is informed by a spirit of willful transgression. The protagonist, "l'Adolescente," dissipates his vital energies in enervating lust. His attempt to achieve full control of life through the exaltation of the senses results in failure, as the satisfaction of pure sensuality rapidly wears out in disgust.

Several other important themes make their first appearance in this collection: the promenade, a privileged moment for erotic emotions; woman, the luxurious female whose castrating power destroys man's energies; art, the fruit and carrier of corruption; the poet, the supreme artificer, the jeweler chiseling the hard, resistant metal of language. Other, less significant sections of *Intermezzo* reveal a taste for the macabre and the sadistic, quite in fashion at that time.

Following several collections of poems which refined the manner of *Intermezzo*, *Poema paradisiaco* (published as part of *Poema paradisiaco—Odi navali*) introduced a new style. Here, following the French Symbolists and influenced as well by Giovanni Pascoli's *Myricae* (1891; tamarisks), D'Annunzio proposes a new musicality studiously built on a rhythm of verses broken by enjambments and interrupted by exclamations, questions, and invocations, where rhymes are hidden and assonance prevails. Memory, contemplation, and melancholy govern this poem of gardens (from the Greek *paradeisos*, "of the garden"), where "gardens" signify the closed space of interiority and meditation away from intellectual and sensual turmoil.

Poema paradisiaco evokes the languid melancholy of things that are no more, of sentiments that could have been. The memory of a brief encounter rouses a longing for an opportunity forever lost. The poet recalls flowers that have not been gathered, loves that have not been lived, privileged moments that have not been enjoyed. In "La passeggiata," the poet prefers a sweet and melancholy relation with a woman to the ardor of love, concluding with a subtly ironic comment: "o voi dal dolce nome che io non chiamo!/ perchè voi non mi amate ed io non vi amo" ("You, with the sweet name I do not call!/ because you do not love me and I do not love you"). *Poema paradisiaco* remains one of the fundamental works of nineteenth century Italian poetry for its innovative language and rhythm and for its influence on the following generation of poets.

While all the preceding poetic works of D'Annunzio have provoked contrasting critical opinions, *Laudi del cielo del mare della terra e degli eroi* has by general agreement been recognized as the poet's masterpiece. This vast work was to include seven books dedicated to the seven stars of the Pleiades, but only four books of the projected seven were published during D'Annunzio's lifetime: *Maia*, *Elettra*, *Alcyone*, and *Merope*. A fifth book, *Asterope*, published posthumously in 1949, includes the poems which D'Annunzio wrote during World War I.

Maia is mainly devoted to "Laus vitae," a long poem based on D'Annunzio's voyages in Greece in 1898 and 1899. In this poem, he celebrates the creative power of the classical world, comparing the vital drive of Greek civilization with the sterility of contemporary society. Hymns to Hermes, the creator, alternate with descriptions of modern cities where corruption and vice dominate, culminating with a vision of the "Great Demagogue," a mass leader who preaches the destruction of everything that is beautiful and noble. The populace is portrayed as an instinctively violent and somehow innocent animal, exploited by demagogues and sacrificed without pity. Destruction and suffering, the poet-prophet predicts, will be followed by the birth of a new society in which work and beauty will be equally respected and loved.

In these fiery images, D'Annunzio expresses his antidemocratic and aristocratic sentiments, inspired by Friedrich Nietzsche, but the complex system of the philosopher is narrowed down to serve a limited political program. The poem concludes with an invocation to Nature, the immortal Mother, who is the source of creation and renewal.

Elettra, named for the second star in the constellation, is divided roughly into two parts. In the first part, the celebrative and commemorative inspiration of many of the poems and their oratorical manner reveal D'Annunzio's ambition to create a new mythology, to become the epic bard of the new Italian nation. This effort is not always sustained by authentic inspiration, and in many poems rhetoric and artificiality prevail. The second part, "Le città del silenzio," is a celebration of the old Italian cities, silent and forgotten in the enclosure of their glorious past. Evocations of ancient events and descriptions of splendid monuments and palaces, dissolve into a subdued musicality tinted with melancholy.

In the third volume of the series, *Alcyone*, D'Annunzio reached his highest lyric expression. After the heroic tension of *Maia* and *Elettra* and their fervid affirmations and denunciations, *Alcyone* stands as a pause, a moment of total participation in the joyous blossoming of nature in its fullest season. The book opens with "La tregua," an invocation to "il magnanimo despota" (the generous despot), Nietzsche, the master of willpower. After a period of intense commitment to the fight against brutal ignorance, corruption, and vulgarity, the poet asks for a respite. He wants to be reinvigorated, forsaking public squabbles for the pure sources of life. The poem concludes with a celebration of pagan nature, the realm of fauns, nymphs, and satyrs.

In the following poems, a series of mythological passages translates the introductory hymn to nature into the apotheosis of poetry. In the poem "Il fanciullo," the divine flute player who modulates the most delicate murmurs of nature is the image of the youthful god of poetry: Here, poetry is the privileged activity where art and nature meet and merge. In "Lungo l'Affrico nella sera di giugno dopo la pioggia," a description of the fresh calm of nature in the twilight after a summer rain evolves into a meditation on the power of poetry. Nature offers itself like ductile clay to the poet, who shapes it into a durable work of art. In the following poem, "La sera fiesolana," this concept evolves into a conception of poetics which is central to an understanding of the collection. The landscape vibrates with a secret urge to express itself; hills and rivers, leaves and drops of rain, all of nature utters silent words that only the poet can hear. The voice of nature is the language of poetry itself. "La spica" and "Le opere e i giorni" carry the message even further, affirming that all forms of nature live only as a function of the poetic word, which, by naming them, calls them into existence.

After *Alcyone*, D'Annunzio was chiefly concerned with other literary genres. He seldom returned to poetry and then only for occasional lyric fragments. *Merope*, the fourth book of *Le laudi*, includes ten *canzones* composed on the occasion of the Italo-Turkish war. These poems do not add anything to D'Annunzio's reputation, the flamboyant rhetoric of the volume betrays its essentially political function.

With *Alcyone*, D'Annunzio's poetic inspiration achieved its fullest expression. The feeling of joyful participation in nature which informed his early verse reappeared in *Alcyone*, decanted, refined, and enriched by the variety of D'Annunzio's painstaking experiments with new forms and techniques and by his unrelenting meditation on poetry. Themes, motifs, and discoveries of the preceding collections merge in *Alcyone*, mythology, no longer an artificial ornament, is integrated with nature, which speaks through myths and transfers to the poet its creative force. In this world created by poetic language, everything harmonizes in a unique song celebrating the eternal beauty of life and nature in their multiform aspects.

D'Annunzio's art, based on classical culture yet renewed by the European avant-garde, represents the link between traditional and modern forms of poetry. Like all great writers, D'Annunzio created a personal poetic language to give life to his imaginative world; at the same time, his verse transcended personal concerns to serve as a testing ground for modern Italian poetry.

Major publications other than poetry

NOVELS: *Il piacere*, 1889 (*The Child of Pleasure*, 1898); *Giovanni Episcopo*, 1892 (*Episcopo and Company*, 1896); *L'innocente*, 1892 (*The Intruder*, 1898); *Il trionfo della morte*, 1894 (*The Triumph of Death*, 1896); *Le vergini delle rocce*, 1896 (*The Maidens of the Rocks*, 1898); *Il fuoco*, 1900 (*The Flame of Life*, 1900); *Forse che si forse che no*, 1910; *La Leda senza cigno*, 1916.

SHORT FICTION: *Terra vergine*, 1882, 1884; *Le novelle della Pescara*, 1892 (*Tales from My Native Town*).

PLAYS: *La citta morta*, 1898 (*The Dead City*, 1900); *La Gioconda*, 1899 (*Gioconda*, 1902); *La gloria*, 1899; *Francesca da Rimini*, 1902 (English translation, 1902); *La figlia di Iorio*, 1904 (*The Daughter of Jorio*, 1907); *La fiaccola sotto il moggio*, 1905; *La nave*, 1908; *Fedra*, 1909; *Le Martyre de Saint Sébastien*, 1911; *Le chevrefeuille*, 1913 (*The Honeysuckle*, 1916); *Parisina*, 1913; *La Pisanelle*, 1913; *Il ferro*, 1914 (Italian version of *Le chevrefeuille*).

NONFICTION: *L'armata d'Italia*, 1888; *L'allegoria dell'autunno*, 1895; *Contemplazione della morte*, 1912; *Per la piú grande Italia*, 1915; *Il notturno*, 1921; *Le faville del maglio*, 1924, 1928 (2 volumes); *Il libro ascetico della giovane Italia*, 1926; *La penultima ventura*, 1919, 1931 (2 volumes); *Le cento e cento e cento pagine del libro segreto di Gabriele D'Annunzio tentato di morire*, 1935; *Teneo te, Africa*, 1936.

MISCELLANEOUS: *Opera omnia*, 1927-1936; *Tutte le opere*, 1930-1965; *Tutte le opere*, 1931-1937.

Bibliography
Barberi Squarotti, G. *Il gesto improbabile*, 1971.
_____ . *Invito alla lettura di D'Annunzio*, 1982.
Croce, B. "Gabriele D'Annunzio," in *Letteratura della Nuova Italia*, 1964.
_____ ."L'ultimo D'Annunzio," in *Letteratura della Nuova Italia*, 1957.
De Felice, Pampaloni, E. Paratore, and Mario Praz. *Gabriele D'Annunzio*, 1978.
Devoto, L. "La musicalita dannunziana," in *Studi di stilistica*, 1950.
Flora, F. *D'Annunzio*, 1935.
Gullace, Giovanni. *Gabriele D'Annunzio in France: A Study in Cultural Relations*, 1966.
Jullian, P. *D'Annunzio*, 1971.
Noferi, A. *L' "Alcyone" nella storia della poesia italiana*, 1946.
Pancrazi, P. *Studi sul D'Annunzio*, 1939.
Paratore, E. *Studi dannunziani*, 1967.
Petronio, G. *D'Annunzio*, 1977.
Praz, Mario. *The Romantic Agony*, 1970.
Raimondi, E. "G. D'Annunzio," in *Storia della letteratura italiana*, 1969.
Rhodes, A. *The Poet as Superman: G. D'Annunzio*, 1960.
Rossi, A. "Stratigrafia di 'La pioggia nel pineto,'" in *I metodi attuali della critica in Italia*, 1975.
Woodhouse, J. R. *Alcyone*, 1978.

Luisetta Elia Chomel

DANTE
Dante Alighieri

Born: Florence, Italy; May, 1265
Died: Ravenna, Italy; September 13 or 14, 1321

Principal poem and collection
La vita nuova, c. 1292 (*The New Life*); *La divina commedia*, c. 1320 (*The Divine Comedy*).

Other literary forms
Dante's prose works are not usually taken as major literary achievements in themselves, although they provide many useful sidelights and clarifications to a reader of *The Divine Comedy*. Dante entitled the work *Commedia*. It was Boccaccio, forty years after Dante's death, who called the work *La divina commedia*, the name by which it is commonly known. *Il convivio* (c. 1307; *The Banquet*, 1909) was probably written between 1304 and 1307. An unfinished work of some seventy thousand words in Italian prose, it is a commentary on three canzones or odes in which the poet proposes a theory of allegory for moral readings of his poetic compositions, so that it will be clear that virtue, not passion, is the topic. A digressive apologia, *The Banquet* is a mine of information about medieval literary culture. *De vulgari eloquentia* (c. 1306; English translation, 1890), a Latin prose work of nearly twelve thousand words, was probably composed in the period from 1304 to 1306. It is believed to be the first study ever written about vernacular language and poetic style and contains fascinating conjectures about the origin of language, Romance linguistics, verse forms, metrics, and poetic sounds. *De monarchia* (c. 1313; *On World Government*) is a Latin prose work of nearly eighteen thousand words, probably written in 1312 and 1313; it is a series of arguments for world rule unified under the Holy Roman Empire. Dante's explanations of his ideas about the separate but complementary functions of Church and State are particularly valuable. Only a few of Dante's letters survive, but several of them contain seminal passages of Dantean thought.

Many of Dante's lyrics are probably lost forever, but if the eighty or so miscellaneous ones attributed to him are a fair sampling of his efforts, he put his finest in *The New Life*. Many of these smaller poems show only average craftsmanship and are interesting because they reveal a poet who actively participated in his society. Some of the sonnets are exchanges of opinions with friends; six are part of an invective, a contest both socially and intellectually (which was common then), between Dante and Forese Donati. There are love poems to various ladies, some of them real individuals, others clearly allegorical. The lyrics show a very human poet, playful and experimental, heated by anger and love, embittered by exile.

Achievements

Dante is among the greatest and most influential figures in the long history of Western literature, and no brief summary can do justice to the scope of his achievements. Perhaps his most enduring legacy has been the astonishing supply of signs and symbols for describing and evaluating inner experience which succeeding generations of readers have found in *The Divine Comedy*. Dante was ultimately a mystic in his approach to God, but he wrote with systematic clarity about every spiritual event, stopping only at the point where language and reason had to be abandoned. Probably the most learned, articulate voice in the Christian West since Saint Augustine, Dante created a powerful mindscape able to reflect every movement of the soul. He did this without subjectivism and narcissism. Dante's vision is both a mirror of the self and a window onto the outside world, the cosmos, and the divine. His inward journey is recounted with great intensity and variety, but with no surprises, for that inner world is no more ambiguous or mysterious than the outer world, and Dante did not confront either world in a metaphysical void. His vision is not a hallucinatory refuge, but a site where the interconnectedness of all things can be rationally presented and the consequent need for spiritual discipline and social duty can be argued.

Dante responded to two primary imaginative impulses. One drove him to put all of his experiences into an ordered relationship: eros, history, politics, faith. Behind these ideal forms and schematizations lies a genuine love of the created world in all its density. Dante insists that experience be known as actual *and* metaphorical, and that virtue be attained through historical processes. The other impulse moved him continually beyond each part of his creation, always ascending, so that each epiphany becomes a curtain to be drawn back to reveal a higher one. One reads Dante with an awareness of the elaborations of each part and the upward movement of the whole.

Dante was the most important voice in the vernacular love lyric before William Shakespeare. Dante's mastery of lyric form and meter was unparalleled, and he used the intellectually demanding conventions of *dolce stil nuovo* (sweet new style) with simplicity and ease. Had he taken Holy Orders, he could have given the world a pastoral voice worthy of John Donne or George Herbert. Dante's vocational decision was singular and uncompromising. He decided to be a citizen and a philosophical poet. The pains of citizenship fired the creator in him, so that he ultimately became the grandsire of Italian literature and indeed of much of Western literature written since his time. Dante excelled in the poetry of direct statement, in making thought melodic. He found ways to energize moral knowledge, so that it could both persuade and delight. He never wrote to be obscure or ambiguous, but it is important to remember that he was addressing keen, well-educated medieval minds. His mastery of narrative technique and symbolic detail encourages some readers to evaluate his art for its own sake, but Dante always wrote to make the reader look beyond his words to the vision that they served.

Biography

Dante Alighieri was a citizen, and his city was Florence. Medieval Italian cities were for the most part independent states, free of feudal allegiances, with power based not on land, but on harbors, commerce, and industry. The nobility within these cities had gradually yielded power to the new bourgeois interests, but the traditional lines of that struggle were still evident, the nobles seeking support from the Emperor and the bourgeois and popular elements tending to oppose the Empire and join with the Pope.

Those in the imperial faction were called Ghibellines, and the Papal, or at least the anti-imperial faction, were known as Guelphs. The faction one chose to support often had more to do with current and particular needs and where one's friends and enemies were, than with hereditary considerations. Dante's Florence was Guelph, which was enough to make rival cities support the Ghibelline cause—not that the Florentine Guelphs were able to live peaceably for long among themselves. A feud between two branches of a family in Pistoia, who called themselves "Whites" and "Blacks," spread to the Florentine upper classes. The Whites attracted the older families and Papal supporters, while the Blacks tended to attract the newly rich commercial classes.

Little is known of Dante's youth in Florence. It is clear that he read widely among Provençal and contemporary Italian poets as well as classical Latin writers; his writing also reveals a practical knowledge of music and painting. He may have attended the University of Bologna. He fought in the Florentine army and seems to have enjoyed many friendships throughout his city. The most important event in his life occurred at a May Day festival when he was nine years old. There he first saw Beatrice Portinari, who was eight at the time. They did not see each other again until nine years later, but Dante's devout fascination with her image and its significance lasted throughout his life. When she died in 1290, Dante diverted his grief by plunging into the difficult politics of the city and the study of philosophy. Between 1296 and 1301, the government of Florence entrusted him with high responsibilities in politics, finances, and diplomacy. His election as one of the city's six priors in the summer of 1300 exemplifies the public trust he enjoyed, a trust he justified when he validated the banishment of his close friend, the poet Guido Cavalcanti.

The year 1300 brought a convergence of several crises, political, spiritual, and economic, in the poet's life. So far as Dante's personal misfortunes are concerned, there are few details in the historical records. The larger event involved Charles de Valois, whom Pope Boniface had invited into Italy to help with the reconquest of Sicily. Charles was permitted to enter Florence with all of his troops, after assurances that he would not take part in the struggle between the Whites and the Blacks. Almost immediately, Charles allowed the Blacks to have the upper hand, at which point they began severe reprisals against the Whites. Dante was in Rome at the time as part of a delegation sent to secure guarantees from the Pope that the French forces would not interfere in Florentine politics. Dante was accused in absentia of barratry, extortion, impiety, and disloyalty, accusations which ultimately carried with them the death sentence. Dante never returned to Florence. As an exile, he drew closer to the exiled Whites and Ghibellines, but neither negotiations nor armed conspiracy succeeded in restoring them to power in Florence. Dante became disenchanted and impatient with his fellow exiles, who resented him, and may even have blamed him for the military reversals they were suffering.

A restless Dante may have spent time in at least a half dozen Italian cities and perhaps Paris at one point. He was unable to right things between himself and Florence, so that he might return. When Henry VII was elected Emperor, Dante envisioned an Italy unified under the Empire, with an end to the destructive rivalry between Church and State, but several key cities, aided by Florentine money, resisted Henry. When Dante angrily urged the Emperor to conquer Florence, he probably eliminated his last chance of entering the city alive. Florence excluded him from the general amnesty offered to the Whites, and then withstood the Emperor's assault; Henry died shortly thereafter. In 1315, probably because it needed talented citizens to help against a rival army, Florence declared itself willing to have Dante return, but he proudly rejected the terms. He was in Verona shortly after that, at work on *The Divine Comedy* under the patronage of Can Grande della Scala and his family. He spent his last days in Ravenna at the court of Guido da Polenta. In 1321, da Polenta sent him on a diplomatic mission to Venice. On his return, Dante fell desperately ill and did not recover. He was buried in Verona wearing Franciscan dress.

Analysis

Dante wrote *The New Life* to give an essential history of his own spirit, which was first aroused, then illuminated by his love for a woman. Here together are the narcissism and ecstasy of youth with the intricate design and perceptions of an older, uncompromising intelligence. The work consists of forty-two passages of prose commentary in which thirty-one poems are set at varying intervals. There are twenty-five sonnets, five canzones, and one ballad. The reader is not meant to abide the prose patiently until he reaches the next poem. Medieval poets believed that it should be possible to state in prose the core idea of any poem they created. Furthermore, no poem existed for its own sake—that is, solely for an aesthetic purpose. The prose keeps the reader in touch with the invisible realities and spiritual implications which were far more important to Dante than personal expression or artistic technique. The poems of *The New Life* describe and deal with romantic and sexual passion. Within the close boundaries and strict internal laws of poetic form, they either exemplify the point Dante is making in prose, or give way to a prose examination of the meanings beneath their surfaces. The poetic voice contains the original turmoil; the prose voice carries the more complete understanding of later personal reflection. The reader is thus able to share in the warmth of the original feelings and the sequence of epiphanies about them.

The topic of *The New Life* is love-suffering, which the poet will complain about but never abandon, for love-suffering is a way of life—indeed, part of the credentials of a noble person. The nobles whom Dante addressed constituted an elite, intelligent group who shared a sensitivity about love and who communicated easily with one another about its subtle doctrines. Traditionally, the medieval love poet did not concentrate on the real presence of the lady so much as on his own feelings about her. The poet would cry out against the upheavals his passions were causing and voice his fear and resentment of her coldness and elevated distance. Despite it all, he would vow to continue his martyrdom. These conventions of refined love were distorted and exaggerated, but they proved fit equipment for capturing the values of romantic experience. They take the reader past appearances into mental and spiritual realities which a camera eye can never see. The new ideas about love, which began emerging less than a century before Dante was born, caused a revolution in the sensibilities of Western European culture. Dante mastered them, then added a revolution of his own. He transcended the devouring egotism of his predecessors by identifying his own erotic drive and the mental processes it stimulated with the Divine Love which beckons to every soul. The lady thus becomes not merely the outer boundary of the lover's consciousness but a mediating presence between self and Deity. No longer a mirror of the poet's feelings, she stands as a window onto the infinite beauty of the Divine Presence and the way of salvation. *The New Life* records Dante's discovery of what he owed to several "God-bearing" ladies whom he encountered on his journey, Beatrice foremost among them.

The work begins with the intelligent and chastened voice of experience: Dante has learned to read the book of Nature, and he knows that the mystical significance of numbers can validate his spiritual discoveries. He has found a *vita nuova*, a new and miraculous life epitomized by the number nine, which the word *nuova* also signifies. Nine is the square of three, a number which, to the medieval imagination, represented perfection and the spiritual life. Dante explains how he first saw Beatrice when she was in her ninth year of life, and not again until nine years later, at the ninth hour of the day. Numbers are the clues to what Heaven has planned for him, so that when Dante writes this book of personal memory, made according to the laws of sequence and cause and effect, the reader is also aware of the perennial present of an unchanging ideal realm. For example, in section 3 of *The New Life*, Dante has a dream which is not only an erotic fantasy but also a prophecy. After he has seen Beatrice for the second time, the God of Love appears in a fiery cloud carrying Beatrice, who is asleep and flimsily clothed. Love wakens her and skillfully makes her eat of Dante's burning heart. Then the God begins to weep, folds his arms around her, and the two ascend heavenward. Dante notes that he had this dream at the first of the last nine hours of the night. Thus, the historical event of the lady's death, through the significance of numbers, reflects eternity.

The structure of Dante's book of memory suggests infinite harmony and reconciliation, particularly through the numbers three and nine. The thirty-one poems of *The New Life* fall into three groups, each group attached to one of the three canzones, or longer poems. At the center of the second or middle group is a canzone with four poems on either side of it. The first and third groups each have ten poems and one canzone; in the first group the poems precede the canzone, and in the second they follow it. Besides the obvious symmetry of the entire structure, there are nine poems in the middle group. If Dante had intended the first poem to be an introduction and the thirty-first to be an epilogue, the numbers nine and one would dominate the plan, although this is only a reasonable conjecture. Of more significance is the merger of numerical sign and literary idea in the middle group: the canzone which is at the exact center of the work refers to Beatrice's possible death with imagery traditionally associated with the Crucifixion of Christ. Thus, the center of the poet's book of memory and the center of Christian history are connected, through the analogy drawn between Beatrice and Christ.

The cast of *The New Life* is small, and the narrative is almost without setting and background. There are really only two actors: the poet, and the feminine presence who provides all the imaginative milestones in his life. Some women are useful distractions to prying eyes, so that he can conceal his true love's identity. The death of one of them tunes his grief for the eventual death of Beatrice, as does the death of Folco Portinari, Beatrice's father. If one takes this little history of a pilgrim's soul as an analogy for God's created time, where events can be understood either to anticipate or to look back toward Christ's Passion, death, and Resurrection, one immediately appreciates the suggestiveness of the format. When Dante contemplates the possibility of Beatrice's death, it seems to him that the sun grows dark and violent earthquakes occur. The next dream presents Beatrice following her beautiful friend, Giovanna, just as Christ followed John the Baptist. Her death will be comparably momentous and fruitful for his own life and later ages. Not that these insights enabled the poet to bear the actual death of Beatrice; the sonnets and canzones which follow that event are almost all to which a lyric poet can aspire, fusing intellect and pathos so perfectly that readers are reminded how imperfectly united their own souls are; at the same time, they are uplifted by the unity Dante has found. For long moments, the reader can believe that the alleged incompatibility between poetry and philosophy is but a jealous rumor.

As Dante decorates his own love story with signs of what he would come to understand about it in retrospect, he also means to show the progress of his own mind as events teach and shape him. He remembers himself as a self-preoccupied courtly lover, more educated and intellectually demanding than the troubadour poets from whom he learned, but, like them, emaciated by love-suffering, anxious, easily embarrassed, inclined to enjoy nursing his wounds in private, and completely under the rule of his master, Love. When, out of concern for her good name, Beatrice refuses to recognize him, he takes to his bed like a punished child. Then he begins to realize the limitations of this infantile mode. That night in a dream, the god appears and tells Dante that not he, but Love, is at the center of things, equidistant from all points on the circumference. Until he can accept the possibilities of this subtler and more comprehensive definition, the paradoxically painful and pleasurable qualities of his subjective experience will continue to vex him. Then, some town women, gently ridiculing his emaciated condition, suggest logically what Love had put more mysteriously: Happiness can come from the words he uses to praise Beatrice, not the words which concentrate on his own condition. With this nobler theme, his new life begins.

The famous canzone from section 19 which begins "Donne ch'avete intelletto d'amore," or "Ladies who can reason out Love's ways," describes the source of the lady's nobleness and perfection, which make all in Heaven want her with them, so that Heaven itself can be more perfect. On Earth, her glance can banish an evil intention or transform it to a noble one, and the worthy will feel salvation from having looked at her, for God has granted that whoever has talked with her will not come to a bad end. Having shifted his attention to a site outside himself, and having identified Beatrice as an emissary of Divine Love (able like It to create something where nothing has existed), Dante now has a talismanic axiom that will help him meet all future experience—even Beatrice's death, for everything coming to him from her will lead heavenward.

After Beatrice's death, a disconsolate Dante is temporarily distracted by the earthly beauty and compassion of a lady who looks at him sympathetically, but a vision of Beatrice resolves his inner struggle between reason and sensuality, and from then on the image of Beatrice is all he contemplates. The last sonnet of *The New Life* tells how his sigh passed the world's outermost sphere, moved by a new intelligence to the radiance of Beatrice in Heaven. When the sigh tries to report what it saw, its words are too subtle for Dante's comprehension; he is certain only that he hears Beatrice's name again and again. The highest and most serene image of the poet's renewed life is, paradoxically, beyond words. In the final section, Dante tells of a miraculous vision which included sights so profound that he made the resolution to say no more about Beatrice until he could find a suitably elevated vehicle. He closes with the wish that the Lord will grant him a few more years, so that he can compose a work about her which will contain things never said about any woman.

A diary unlike any written before it, *The New Life* was the work of a poet ready for sublime tasks who chose to review the development of his spiritual vision and poetic powers as the first step in the direction of carrying out those tasks. A finished masterpiece in its own right, it also served as a prelude to the greatest sustained poetic achievement in the West since Homer.

There probably never has been a piece of literary imagination as great in scope, as intricate in relationships among its parts, as fastidiously shaped to the smallest detail as Dante's *The Divine Comedy*. Besides the exacting challenge of maintaining poetic intensity for some fourteen thousand lines, there were the perils of dealing with interpretations of religious doctrine and Holy Writ in a fictional context. Even more perilous was the interpretation of Divine Justice, as it applied to specific historical incidents and individuals. Dante's genius and pious imagination flourished among these boundaries and obstacles. He used the appearances of the created world to describe the human heart in a theocentric universe. The three-part narrative pictures the soul deprived of God, in hope of God, and with God. Dante needed a design to mirror the unchanging realities beyond time and space, and he needed an action which would be an imitation of the soul's movements toward these realities. The symmetrical design of the entire work reflects divine perfection, as does its threefold narrative division and three-line stanzas. Each part, *Inferno*, *Purgatorio* (*Purgatory*), and *Paradiso* (*Paradise*), is divided into thirty-three cantos. With the introductory canto, these total one hundred, a number which also traditionally suggested divine unity and perfection.

The world of Dante's *The Divine Comedy* is vertical. The reader always moves downward or upward with the poet: the spiral descent into Hell, the climb up the purgatorial mountain, then up through the various planetary spheres, until the notions of movement up and down are no longer pertinent. The medieval model of the universe was similarly vertical, with Heaven above, Earth at the middle, and Hell below. Everything in God's creation was located at some point or other on a chain or ladder of being, which descended from His divine presence to the lowest form of inert matter. Each being was put at a particular step or degree on this scale, so that it could realize whatever purpose the Creator intended for it, but each thing or being was also understood in terms of what was above it and what was below it. The three realms of Dante's *The Divine Comedy* are vertically related, and each realm has its own vertical plan. The reader is continually urged to compare each spectacle with the one viewed previously and to ponder in retrospect its connection to the spectacle which follows it.

Writing a comedy was also imitating the world, at least as Dante used the term "comedy." In the medieval conception, comedy presented the happy resolution of a difficult situation. Thus, time and history could be seen as parts of a comic action, because Providence, working behind the superficial chaos of Fortune's wheel, would ultimately turn every earthly change to good. Human time and all of its pains began with the Fall of Adam, but that Fall looked forward to Christ's redemptive sacrifice. The sacrifice of Christ, who is often referred to as the "Second Adam," made it possible for the pattern of each life to be comic—that is, for man to conquer sin and win salvation. Dante's *The Divine Comedy* takes place at the end of Holy Week, during the most spiritually intense hours of the Christian year. For a time, darkness appears to triumph, as the God-Man is slain and buried, but out of seeming defeat comes a victorious descent into Hell and a resurrection which is the archetype of every spiritual rebirth which will come after it. When Dante descends into Hell on Good Friday and reaches Purgatory on Easter morning of the year 1300, the reader contemplates that holier comedy thirteen hundred years before.

The Divine Comedy offers more than structural symmetry and Christian values. It is also an imitation of the swarming variousness of the world of time and space: dreams, boasts, accusations, haunting beauties and catastrophes, wisdom, and reconciliation. The opening words hurry the reader into the narrator's dilemma and impasse, until, ninety-nine cantos later, the vision moves beyond human language and sensation. In his treatment of things invisible, Dante makes the reader touch with understanding almost every texture of earthly existence. To the medieval mind, the world was a book to be read, but a book could imitate the world by being an exhaustive compendium of information about geography, history, the nature of flight, even the spots on the moon. Dante's imagination is alert and curious, not satisfied with building a warehouse of facts. Dante further wishes the reader to visualize and experience the logistics of every step of the journey, feeling the heat, smelling the foulness, seeing different kinds of light and darkness, confronting the monstrosities, and struggling along the broken causeways.

The Divine Comedy is Dante's report of a journey he took into the anagogical realm of existence—that is, the afterlife—to witness the rewards and punishments which God's justice apportions to mankind on the basis of choices freely made in life. Dante himself said this much about his masterpiece. The reader learns while watching him learn, and because of that, even in the *Inferno*, moving toward the center of the Earth, the place farthest from God, there is a sense of the intelligence and soul expanding. The journey around which the narrative is constructed is also about the movement of every individual life. It intended to provide equipment for living in a City of God on Earth until the grander city of Jerusalem can be attained.

Although the meticulous physical detail encourages the reader to imagine himself on a journey in time and space, he is moving in a mindscape, a spectacle of the sinful human heart. Nowhere in Hell is he shown an attitude or act of which every living soul is not capable. Dante's descent involves a lowering of self through the admission of fault and capacity for fault, and the realization that the difference between man's sin and Satan's sin is one of degree rather than kind. Self-accusation and contrition make cleansing and regeneration possible, so that the climb to salvation can begin. Dante makes himself fall so that he may rise a stronger man, but his is a controlled fall. The vision of Hell could lead to despair and insane fascination, but with a guide who has been there before, Dante can have this terrible knowledge and survive. Having a second individual on the journey is also a useful narrative strategy, because the guide can interact dramatically with Dante the pilgrim and provide a normative presence, so that Dante the poet need not stultify the narrative with endless digressions about what the pilgrim cannot see.

That Dante should choose Vergil, the greatest of all Latin poets, to accompany him is not surprising. In one way or another, Vergil's writings had nourished every medieval poet. In his epic, the *Aeneid* (29-19 B.C.), Vergil had described a hero's visit to the underworld, and in that sense had been there once himself. His medieval admirers believed him to be a saint, a moralist, a prophet, even a magician. He was also a pagan and, as Dante strictly reasoned, had not been saved, but he was thought to embody natural wisdom unaided by revelation, which would make him a fit companion for a trip into the region of the damned. Vergil was also a poet of the Empire. He used the story of the fall of Troy to celebrate the founding of Rome and all the achievements of the divinely favored nation which followed it. Vergil predicted an era of world order and prosperity under Roman imperial rule. Many Christians believed that he foresaw in one of his pastorals the coming of the Redeemer and the Christian era. In his essay *On World Government*, Dante had argued that the Empire and the Church were two discrete but complementary modes by which divine purposes could be realized in human history, one emphasizing reason, the other revelation. Vergil epitomizes both the grandeur and the limitations of that gift of natural reason. He travels with Dante as far as he—that is, reason—can, and then is replaced by Beatrice, who personifies the light of divine revelation denied to pagans.

The world of *The Divine Comedy* is so wide and various that a comprehensive introduction to it is not possible in a brief essay, but canto 1 of the *Inferno* is a useful place to begin observing how Dante's composition works. It is Maundy Thursday night, the day before Good Friday in the year 1300. The poet's first words are about personal time, the midpoint of life at which he awakened to discover himself in a dark wood, with no idea where the right road was. Because the very first line refers to a stage of life, the reader is not likely to imagine a search through a literal wood for an actual road. A few lines later, as Dante painfully recalls the harshness and recalcitrance of the forest, it becomes clear that he is talking about his own former willfulness. As horrid as this time of error was, says Dante, good came of it. This mixture of fear and optimism sets the tone perfectly for the *Inferno* and for the rest

of *The Divine Comedy*. The opening lines involve the reader in the experiences
of another being as though they were his own (which, in a sense, they are).
Eschewing biographical or historical detail, Dante presents only the essential,
the elementary: At a crosspoint in life, another human realized that he had
lost touch with an important part of himself.

The poet does not know exactly how he lost his way in that wood, but the
torpor from which he suffered at the time was obviously spiritual. Struggling
out of the wood, he is aware of a steep mountain, and as he looks up at the
sun which lights the ways of men, he feels some comfort. Somehow, his
awareness of his own poor spiritual state and the grace of a loving God have
helped him through a dangerous maze, a place, he notes, from which no one
has escaped, once entrapped there. Clearly, the forest is a form of spiritual
death, or sin, but all the pilgrim has done so far is avoid the worst. To climb
the mountain and achieve the spiritual perfection it implies, he will need to
gain control of the complicated forces within himself.

A quick-stepping leopard first impedes his progress, but a look at the
morning sun, as beautiful as it was during the first moments of Creation,
restores Dante's hopes, which are again shattered when a lion, head held
high, approaches menacingly. Most intimidating is a gaunt, ravenous wolf,
which Dante says has conquered many men. The wolf begins to edge Dante
back down the path into the dark forest. Dante does not say what each of
these beasts symbolizes, but probably they represent types of sinful living.
This notion exists because, to the medieval mind, beasts usually stood for the
lower or unreasonable parts of the personal hierarchy. The leopard seems to
have the flair and energy of youth, the lion the more powerful intellectual
pride which can dominate later years, and the wolf the avarice for possessions
which comfort advanced years. Any one of these sins could weigh down a
traveler throughout life. Dante makes the point that inability to deal with the
three brings despair and spiritual disaster. The light of the sun offers encouragement; grace is available, but it has to be used. As he stumbles downward,
Dante sees a shadow. Although it seems unaccustomed to speaking, the shadow
answers when Dante calls to it for help, just as the way out of the woods
appeared when Dante admitted to himself that he was lost. The shadow is
Vergil, who stands for the natural good sense that Dante had allowed to lie
dormant.

Vergil does not want Dante to take on the she-wolf directly, for she has
been the ruin of many. There is another way out of the wood, Vergil says.
The person who confronts his own demons without a guide or a strategy is
inviting failure. Dante first needs to use his reason to understand the nature
of unforgiven sin and its punishment. Then he can visit the purgatorial realm,
where the vestiges of forgiven sins are removed, and finally a worthier guide
will show him the vision of ultimate reward. Vergil also cautions Dante against
becoming preoccupied with the sins of his fellow countrymen. In time, says

Vergil, a greyhound will come to chase the avaricious wolf from Italy. Whether this greyhound represents a great earthly prince or some divine apocalypse is not clear. The central point of this first canto is that, beginning with his own conscience, then using the legible signs in the book of the natural world and the revival of his own rational faculty, Dante is ready to journey toward whatever perfection he can hope to attain.

The above remarks are not an ambitious reading of obscure material. Dante saw clearly and wrote to be understood. He did, however, believe that it was natural and beneficial to require an audience to be alert to more than the literal in what he said. An extremely sophisticated tradition of biblical interpretation had prepared his audience to do that and to take pleasure in understanding more than surface meanings in a piece of writing. If the created world was a fair field of symbols, and if the revealed word could be read on several metaphorical levels, why not a story of the mind's journey to God? Thus, Dante wrote allegorical fiction, in which what is said is frequently intended to mean something else. The "literal" aspect of allegorical narrative is usually the least important, for it is the sense of the figurative and the symbolic which the author wants to exercise. The reader needs a fine set of interchangeable lenses in order to see the multiple levels.

Dante's Hell is in the center of the Earth, which was thought to be the center of the created world, but in a theocentric universe, the Earth was really on the outside looking in. The lowest point in Dante's Hell is therefore the farthest possible point from God; it is frozen, signifying the total absence of human or divine love. This Hell is fashioned from religious tradition and popular belief. Spectacular as some of the punishments are, the chief source of pain is indescribable: the eternal loss of the sight of God.

Although many modern readers reject the idea of eternal punishment, medieval Christian thinkers had concluded that an all-perfect Being had to embody justice as well as mercy. When an individual died, the reign of mercy ended and that of justice began. In this view, the damned have willfully rejected the power of grace, the teachings of the Church, and the Sacraments. If after this, God relented, He would be unjust. Justice also determines the nature of the punishments and the consequent degree of suffering. The punishment Dante imagines for each sin is a symbolic definition of the sin itself, which the sinner has to repeat for eternity. Only the living can learn from this infernal repetition. For all the uproar and movement in Hell, nothing changes. A medieval definition of change would be the movement of things toward the ideal form which God intended for them; not a single gesture in Hell does that.

Dante's Hell is an inverted hierarchy, with each level revealing a more serious sin below. Hell has nine circles, in addition to an outer vestibule. The upper five circles contain punishments for sins committed through misdirected or uncontrolled emotions; they reflect the perils of natural vitality and appetites, as the image of the leopard suggested. Next, behind the walls of the city of Dis, are crimes which require a stronger determination of the will to disrupt the plan of existence. The violence which appears here (circles six and seven) may be connected with the lion which threatened Dante earlier. The eighth circle is a long sheer drop below this and contains the violators of the various kinds of promise-keeping which make social life possible. The more complicated frauds of treason and betrayal in the ninth and lowest circle may be related to the ravenous wolf. Far more ingenious than the schematic layout of Hell is Dante's ability to keep a sense of spontaneity and discovery in what could have been merely a dutiful walk through a catalog of sin. Dante's skill at variation, which every medieval poet would have coveted, is perhaps the chief source of the poem's excellence. Even in *Purgatory*, where the treatment of each sin runs to a pattern, Dante somehow handles every section uniquely.

One of the sources of variety and sense of forward movement in the *Inferno* is the interaction between Dante and Vergil. Vergil chides, encourages, and revives his pupil as they travel through Hell. The pilgrim Dante becomes stronger and more sure of himself, less frightened by the nightmarish circus about him and more able to despise intelligently the evil he sees. At first, Dante does not believe himself to be fit for such a journey, but when Vergil tells him that Beatrice wills it, he immediately agrees to follow. Two cantos later, in Limbo, the greatest pagan poets are welcoming him to their company. Whenever he has need of Reason, Vergil is always there—even literally at one point—to lift and carry him out of danger. The danger and inhospitableness increase as the two proceed deeper. Everything they see is an inversion or distortion of Charity, the love of God and neighbor in which every Christian act is rooted. At the start, Charon, the underworld boatman, refuses to ferry Dante and Vergil across the river Acheron; in the ninth and lowest circle, Count Ugolino devours the head of the bishop whose betrayal caused the Count and his sons to be starved to death. The reader becomes increasingly aware of Dante's obsession with the two Florences: the City of God on Earth that he wanted it to become and the ungrateful zone of corruption it had been to him. In his darkest hour, Dante was nearer to Beatrice and all that she stood for than Florence would ever be to Jerusalem. Almost until the final instants of *Paradise*, Dante rails against the city that nourished and exiled him.

Somewhat like a Gothic cathedral, *The Divine Comedy* is a huge structural support covered with crafted sections of varying size and content, each section somehow finding a place in the totality. A very limited sampling of sections might begin with Upper Hell, where the sins of the incontinent are punished. It may be surprising to find that lust is the first sin viewed here, which makes it the least serious offense in Hell. Medieval moralists tended to treat sexual love as a natural behavior in need of a supernatural perspective. This is quite different from treating sexuality as a taboo, as later ages would. Even so, the reader should consider the mixture of feelings within Dante—who began as a lyric poet in the tradition of erotic courtship—as he watches the souls of the lustful tossed on a roaring black wind, an image of the uncontrollable passion to which they surrendered their reasoning power. They are like flocks of starlings and cranes borne up and down forever, shrieking as they go. The scene conveys the restlessness of human passion and the crowded commonness of the sin itself. The world's most famous lovers are in those flocks: Dido, Helen, Paris, Tristram. Seeing them, Dante grows dizzy with sympathy.

Two of the lovers are still together, dovelike as they waft along hand in hand. They are Paolo and Francesca, who suffered and died for love at the hands of Francesca's husband. Francesca delivers a courtly lyric celebrating the power of love which brought her and Paolo together, a lyric which ends with the assurance that damnation awaits the one who murdered them. Deeply moved by the lovers' tragedy, Dante asks to know more. What he hears is not the spell of romance but a rather ordinary process of young lechery: leisure time, suggestive reading, and the knowing glances which precede coupling. Dante has to be true to the old conventions of love here, the ones he transformed in *The New Life*; he also has to maintain the clear-eyed antiromanticism of Christian morality. It is all too much for the pilgrim, who falls into a dead swoon, until he awakes to find himself in the third circle, with the Gluttonous.

Like the Lustful, the Gluttonous have allowed themselves to be controlled and distortd by a natural urge. The image Dante uses to describe the punishment here is startling in the manner of a metaphysical conceit. First, he describes a cold, heavy rain soaking a putrid earth. Cerberus, the three-headed watchdog of the Underworld, is there, each head gorging on the souls of the Gluttonous as they wallow in the mud. To distract the monstrous beast, Vergil throws filthy mud down its throats. Cold rain seems to have no connection with excessive eating, until one considers the motivation which is often behind that excess: self-centered loneliness with indiscriminate sieges of oral gratification. One Ciacco ("Fats"), a fellow Florentine, addresses Dante from the slime. He vents his own alienation and misery, then gives an acid survey of the rottenness which will continue to seep from their native city.

The metaphoric effect is equally powerful in canto 12, when Dante and Vergil enter the pathless wood of the suicides, where the souls have been turned to dead trees which bleed at the touch and are fed on by Harpies, who represent the guilt of self-destruction. Through this same wood run the souls of persons who in life madly spent all they owned. They are being chased and torn to pieces by hunting dogs. Dante's decision to put suicides here among souls who have been violent against themselves seems reasonable. That he should sense a comparable wish for death among those who are impatient to destroy their wealth shows a marvelous awareness of the darker corners of the human situation. Like the cold rain upon the Gluttonous, it is a superb reach of intelligence and intuition.

The last four cantos describe the ninth and lowest circle of Hell, which contains the perpetrators of the subtlest, most complicated frauds imaginable. First described are the giants of classical legend who tried to scale Heaven and challenge Jove, and the biblical Nimrod, who directed the attempt to build the Tower of Babel. At the bottom of Hell's pit is the frozen lake Cocytus. There, the traitors, who through intellect and will achieved the most drastic perversion of love, are frozen in unrepentant attitudes of hatred. These are the souls of those who betrayed kin, fatherland, guests, and, lowest of all, those who betrayed their lords. Fed ultimately by all the rivers of Hell, the ice itself may be blood-colored. Tears, a symbol of compassion, freeze instantly there. The famous agony of Count Ugolino of Pisa, who, with his children, starved to death in prison, mirrors perfectly these pitiless surroundings. Ugolino and the others are at Hell's bottom because they violated the promise-keeping which is the root of every social and spiritual relationship, for man becomes ethical on the basis of his fidelity to promises of loyalty, hospitality, and the like. The cannibalism which the traitor Ugolino enacts as he devours the skull of the person who betrayed him suggests the ultimate negation of social behavior, where humanity and bestiality are no longer distinguishable.

Satan, the angel once nearest to God, now occupies the lowest extremity of Hell, held in ice up to his chest. This is the summary image of the first third of *The Divine Comedy*. At the center of the heart of darkness is this living death, presided over by the first of God's creatures to defy Him. Satan has three faces here, red, yellow, and black, which probably refer to the races of humanity through which his first evil is continued. A parody of the Triune God, his face is the inversion of the spiritual number three. Two batlike wings flap under each face, making a freezing wind which keeps the lake frozen. There is no other movement observable here, unless one includes the tears from those three pairs of eyes, which drip in a bloody mixture from Satan's chins. The draft from his wings evidently freezes all tears but his own. If these tears and blood, which are appalling reminders of the sacramental water and blood which flowed from the side of the Redeemer on the first Good Friday, represent the misery which sin causes, they reveal no contrition whatsoever, for the wings are operated by a will which is still rebellious and an icy egotism which will never cease to oppose God. Even the blindly passionate wind which heaved Paolo and Francesca about would be a welcome alternative to those hopeless gusts.

Each of Satan's mouths chews on a famous traitor. Situated highest, the mouth of the red face tortures the most notorious traitor of all: Judas Iscariot. In the lower mouths are the two others who make up this Satanic Eucharist,

Brutus and Cassius, who subverted God's plan for world empire under Rome by assassinating Julius Caesar. In Dante's conception, sacred and imperial history, although they are separate, are both founded on God's will, and therefore must stand responsible before His justice. In this sense, the things of God and the things of Caesar must ultimately converge. In the midst of these ironies is the supreme irony of Satan's powerlessness, which makes him, for all of his gigantic size, ridiculous. He and the giants are mastodons in a museum. Dante and Vergil climb down this hulk out of Hell and see the stars for the first time since early Friday morning.

When Vergil and Dante have climbed down past Satan's navel, they have reached the point farthest from God. What was below is now above them, and Satan appears upside down, a fitting final aspect of the Arch-Rebel. The pair are now in the Earth's southern hemisphere, facing an island with a mountain called Purgatory, formed of the land which retreated to avoid Satan when he fell. The Earthly Paradise is on the top of that mountain. It was closed at the expulsion of Adam and Eve, but since Christ's death it has been open to souls purified in Purgatory. Actually, Scripture gives few specific details about Hell, and none at all about Purgatory.

In Purgatory, medieval Christians believed, the residual effects of sins admitted, confessed, and forgiven were removed before the soul entered Paradise. The soul permitted to enter Purgatory was saved and would surely see God someday. Furthermore, these souls could be helped by the prayers of people still on Earth and could enjoy communication with the suffering souls around them. This is quite different from the isolation and hopeless sense of loss in Hell.

If the topic of the *Inferno* is the just punishment of sin, the topic of *Purgatory* is the discipline of perfection. It is a more serenely organized piece of writing, with a pace which is generally more constant. After the terraces of the ante-Purgatory, the mountain has seven cornices, each devoted to purging the stain of one of the deadly sins. Every cornice contains a penance, a meditation, a prayer, a guardian angel, and a benediction. The ascent from one area to another is often accompanied by a brief essay on some topic in natural or moral philosophy. The idea of an ante-Purgatory was probably Dante's own. In its two terraces are the souls of those who delayed repenting until the moment of their death. Having waited too long in life to do what was necessary to be saved, they must wait for some time before they can begin the ascent. In the first terrace, are the souls who, although excommunicated by the Church, delayed repentance until the last moments of life. In terrace two, are those who delayed similarly, although they always lived within the Church; included here are the souls of the indolent, the unshriven, and the preoccupied.

Saint Peter's Gate is the entrance to Purgatory proper. Three steps of Penance lead up to it: confession, contrition, and satisfaction. At the gate, an angelic custodian inscribes seven *P*'s, signifying the Seven Deadly Sins (*peccatum* is the Latin for sin), on the forehead of each soul. The letters will be erased one at a time as the soul passes from cornice to cornice. The Seven Deadly Sins were the most widely used description of human evil in the Middle Ages. Somehow or other, every transgression was thought to have come from one of those seven: Lust, Gluttony, Avarice, Sloth, Wrath, Envy, and Pride. Each cornice has a penance appropriate to the stain left by one of those sins. The soul may be made to perform a penitential exercise which symbolically describes the effects of the sin committed, or as counterbalance it may have to perform actions which suggest the virtue directly opposed to the sin. Sometimes souls are assigned to do both.

The meditation in each cornice consists of a whip, or example of the opposing virtue, and a bridle, which is made up of horrid instances of the sin in question. These are followed by a prayer taken from the Psalms or hymns of the Church, then by a benediction (one of the Beatitudes), which is spoken by the angel of the cornice, who then erases a *P* from the soul's forehead. The soul then moves up the Pass of Pardon to the next cornice.

The boundary line for a Hell or Purgatory can be difficult for even a severely legalistic planner to draw. Those souls closest to the entrance of Hell had lost all hope of salvation, though by a narrow margin. In *Purgatory*, those closest to the boundary have avoided that loss by a similarly narrow margin. Dante's Hell begins with the neutrals, those who chose not to choose. They are a faceless mob condemned to chase a whirling standard forever. Next is the Limbo of the unbaptized and virtuous pagans. Dante could not imagine salvation for them, even though their poetry and ideas had nurtured him, but neither could he condemn them for light denied. Thus, the virtuous pagans appear in a dim but pastoral setting, and the poets among them admit Dante to their number. The first terrace of Purgatory also involves fine distinctions, but ones in which the poet is less personally involved. To be excommunicated was not a sin in itself, but a person who was separated from the Church by a sin which called for excommunication, and who put off repentance until the last minutes of life, was grasping salvation by its coattails. Appropriately, these excommunicates and the other late repentants in the second terrace are the only souls in Purgatory who have to undergo a punishment—that is, a wait. All of the others are cheerfully engaged in a healing process which will continue until they are ready for Paradise.

Ascending through the cornices of Purgatory is in one way like backing up the spiral road out of Hell. The lowest part of Hell, where the proudest act ever committed is being punished, corresponds to the first cornice, where the stains of pride are being removed. The cornice of Lust, the least of the Seven Deadly Sins, is nearest the top of the mountain, as Lust was farthest from the frozen lake at the bottom of Hell. The descent became increasingly difficult for Dante and Vergil as each circle delivered something more bleak or dangerous. The trek upward in Purgatory is a happy jettisoning of old heaviness, done in the midst of general enthusiasm and encouragement. Instead of Charon, who grudgingly ferried the two across Acheron, an angel of the Lord lightly takes a hundred singing souls across to the island where Mount Purgatory stands. Indeed, the change of mood exhilarates Dante so thoroughly that he all but loses his sense of mission as he listens to the singing of Casella, an old friend and musician.

There are subtle changes in Vergil's presence at this point. He is temporarily eclipsed in the early cantos by the appearance of the astringent Cato, who represents the discipline that will be needed for the lively chores ahead. Moreover, Vergil has not been here before, so although he is still a fount of good sense, he is seeing everything for the first time. He can only partly answer certain questions Dante asks, such as the one about the efficacy of human prayer. Dante will have to wait for Beatrice to explain such matters fully, and interpreters will come forth intermittently to talk about what Vergil cannot be expected to recognize.

Dante and Vergil emerge from Hell on Easter morning at dawn and reach the island shortly after that. They are in the second terrace of ante-Purgatory when the sun begins to set. Night-climbing is not permitted, so the two are led to a beautiful valley, where the souls of preoccupied rulers dwell. The cycle of day and night and the natural beauty of the valley indicate their presence still on Earth, in the middle state. The significance of not attempting a penitential climb in the dark is fairly clear, but as night falls, two angels descend to keep watch over the valley. They immediately chase off a serpent who has marauded there. Dante is brilliantly suggestive here. The sentry angels are dressed in green, which is a sign of both hope and penance, but that they should be there at all is puzzling. The point seems to be that, at least in ante-Purgatory, temptation is still a possibility. The fiery swords that the angels bear and the presence of the enemy serpent recall the Fall in Eden, and indeed the theme at the core of this journey is the return to that garden and man's state before he sinned.

The morning dream which Dante has in that valley is also charged with details which add significance to all that will happen. Having his own share of Old Adam's nature, he says, he nods off, and in the first light, the time of holy and prophetic dreams, he sees a golden eagle in midair, about to swoop toward its prey. He thinks of Zeus snatching the boy Ganymede up to Heaven, but then he conjectures that this eagle must always hunt here, so it need not have anything to do with him. Then the eagle comes for him like lightning, and takes him up to the circle of fire which surrounds the Earth, where they burn together with a heat which wakens him and ends the dream. He finds that Saint Lucy has carried him to Saint Peter's Gate—the beginning of Purgatory proper.

This dream illuminates the rest of the story until the final line, although it is possible to interpret its simpler elements at once. Lucy is one of the three ladies (the other two are Beatrice and the Blessed Virgin) who decided to help Dante out of the dark wood earlier. Lucy personifies the beckoning power of Divine Light by literally transporting Dante to the start of this second phase of his journey. The golden eagle, a bird sacred to Jove and also an emblem of the empire, is doing a comparable thing. Here are two faces of the Godhead, one maternally encouraging, the other ravenously assertive, together making up a richly complicated insight which comes not from a Vergilian lecture or the remark of a dead soul, but from a dream, where the discourse is intuitive and mystical. The progress up the mountain will for the most part involve intellectual and ethical knowledge, but as it is happening the totality of Dante's being will be moving toward a Divine Love which is beyond language and rational understanding, and for which a burning heaven is the most appropriate metaphor. The movement up the cornices will be clear and steady, so uniform as to be tedious at times. It will require the light of day, but the total movement of the self with the Deity is perhaps best reflected in dreamlight, because Dante is giving his readers not only an encyclopedia of morality but also an imitation of a psychological process.

The removal of the vestiges of sin will render the soul fitter and more able to see the Beatific Vision in its full glory. In Purgatory, all souls are headed homeward, and each step is easier and more satisfying. Innocence, man's state before sin, is the first destination, and from there a more glorious vision will begin, one which the most artful words can only partially describe.

Signs that Eden is near begin in the sixth cornice, with the Gluttonous. By this time, Publius Papinius Statius, a pagan Latin poet who became a Christian, has joined the party; Dante believes that Vergil's reason and literary art need the supplement of revelation so that everything that is about to happen can be fully appreciated. Vergil had pagan glimmerings of Eden and the prelapsarian state when he wrote of a virtuous Golden Age once enjoyed by humankind, but glimmerings are not enough. Before them in the path, they see a tall tree, watered from above by a cascade. The tree bears ambrosial fruit, but a voice forbids anyone to eat it. Examples of Temperance are then described, which are the goad or whip to counter the vice. The souls of the Gluttonous, all emaciated, suffer from being denied the sweet-smelling fruit, but, as one of them tells Dante, they come to the tree with the same desire that Christ brought to the Cross, for both sufferings bring redemption. They see another tree which also keeps its fruit from a gathering of gluttonous souls. A voice tells them to ignore the tree, which is the sort that fed Eve's greed. The connection between the sin of Gluttony and the eating of the forbidden fruit was a point commonly made from medieval pulpits. Particularly noteworthy here is the easy flow of allusions to the Fall of Man and to the suffering on the Cross which compensated for it. The classical story of Tantalus' punishment in the Underworld may have inspired Dante's description of the Gluttonous, but the tree of Eden and the tree of the Cross are clearly the central points of reference here.

When the three travelers finally reach the Earthly Paradise, they see not a garden but a forest, a sacred wood wherein dwells the primal innocence which seemed so far away in the dark wood of the *Inferno*, in canto 1. The sacred wood has a single inhabitant, Matilda, who is there to explain these environs and make straight the way of Beatrice, who appears in a spectacular allegorical event called the Procession of the Sacrament. Only eyes which have regained the first innocence are ready for such a vision. Looking eastward, which is by tradition the holiest direction, Dante sees a brilliant light spread through the forest, and a procession led by seven candlesticks to a chanting of "Hosanna." Next come twenty-four elders, heads crowned with lilies, and after them four beasts surrounding the triumphal cart drawn by a griffin, whose birdlike features are gold, and elsewhere red and white. Three ladies, colored respectively, red, green, and white, dance in a circle by the right wheel; four in purple dance by the left wheel, led by one who has a third eye. Two old men come next, one dressed as a physician, the other carrying a sword. They are followed by four humbly dressed processants, and then by a very old man, going in a visionary trance. These last seven all wear red flowers.

Medieval religious processions were usually staged to affirm a crucial matter of doctrine or devotion. The key notion in this masquelike procession is the unity of sacred revelation since the Fall of Man. The twenty-four elders refer to the books of the Old Testament, their lily crowns suggesting pure righteousness. The Benedictus they sing is a reminder that the Old Testament symbolically anticipates events in the New Testament. The four beasts are the beasts of the Apocalypse and the signs of the four Evangelists. The griffin, which is part eagle and part lion, traditionally refers to the two natures of Christ, its gold suggesting divinity, its red and white, humanity. White and red are also the colors respectively of the Old and New Testaments, and of the bread and wine in the Eucharist. The ladies by the right wheel are Faith (white), Hope (green), and Charity (red); by the left wheel are the four cardinal virtues: Prudence (with the third eye), Temperance, Fortitude, and Justice. Behind the cart are Luke, Paul, and the Epistles of Peter, James, John, and Jude. The old man is the Revelation of Saint John. The red flowers they all wear signify the New Testament.

Then Beatrice appears on the cart in a red dress and green cloak, her head crowned with olive leaves. At this moment, Dante realizes that Vergil, the man of natural wisdom, is no longer with him. Beatrice, who might as well be called Revelation here, tells Dante to look at the entire procession. All of it is she, Beatrice says. Beatrice's words are the fullest manifestation so far of the significance of one passionate event which occurred when the poet was nine years old. What the God-Man brought into history, she is. The Incarnation which the Old Testament faintly surmised, and which the New

Testament celebrates, she is, with every holy virtue in attendance. The same can be said of the transsubstantiated Host on the altar.

After a rebuke from Beatrice for the wandering ways of his own life, which is perhaps his own rightful dose of the purgatorial suffering he has been content to watch, Dante faints with shame. When he revives, Matilda is drawing him across the stream of forgetfulness. With the memory of evil now gone, he can watch with original innocence as the procession heads toward the Tree of Knowledge, where human sin began. Many medieval writings connected the Tree of Knowledge with the tree on which Christ was crucified. Lore had it that the seeds of the fruit from the first tree were buried on the tongue of Adam and then grew to become the tree of the Cross. Christ was often referred to as the Second Adam, come to reverse the catastrophe caused by the first. Here, the Griffin (Christ) moves the cart with Beatrice (the Word and its Incarnation) past the site on which the temptation and Fall occurred and joins the shaft of the cart to a barren tree, which immediately blossoms. The Griffin then ascends, leaving Beatrice at the roots of the tree. She now represents the Church which Christ at his ascension left behind to care for the mankind He had redeemed.

The role of the Empire in God's plan is stressed here, too. An eagle slashes at the tree, just as Roman persecution maimed the Church. Then a gaunt fox appears, probably to represent the heresies of the Church's early history. After the fox has prowled about the cart, the eagle descends again, this time to feather the cart from its own breast. This no doubt represents the symbiotic relationship between Church and State in the Holy Roman Empire. That liaison is followed by a dragon which damages the cart, causing it to change into the many-headed beast of the Apocalypse, on top of which is enthroned a whore consorting with giants. The imagery suggests the later corruption of the Church caused by its consorting with earthly powers. Thus, Dante sketches a symbolic history of the decay of the Church which Christ and Peter founded. The point is one he makes directly in many places: that in Christian history, Church and Empire need to maintain separate identities as they pursue God's plan. The atmosphere of these last cantos has been gradually shifting toward Apocalypse, which Beatrice continues by prophesying revenge for what has been allowed to happen to Christendom, but the final canto returns to the theme of a purgatorial journey. Dante now drinks from Eunoe, the water of Good Remembrance, which renders him finally free from the tarnish of an earthly life and ready for a direct vision of the Godhead.

Readers who think of Dante as the poet of Hell often have read only the first third of his masterpiece. The joy which quickens every step of the *Purgatory* makes it an exhilarating sequel to the *Inferno*, but that joy is only a hint of what awaits Dante in the vision of Paradise. The *Inferno* and *Purgatory* are preparatory visions, the first stressing the reality of evil and its effects, the second showing that it is possible to remove every one of those effects.

Purgatory and *Paradise* form the main part of the comedic structure, which leaves the unhappiness of the *Inferno* far behind.

Dante's *Paradise* is a description of Godhead, as much of it as his eyes could register, and as much as his memory could retain. Medieval literary audiences loved well-executed descriptions, and the *Inferno* and *Purgatory* contain some extraordinarily effective ones. Once the poet has left the substantive world, images on which to base descriptions are no longer obvious. Hell and Purgatory are constructed and described according to sinful human actions, which had been traditionally identified and discussed in concrete images. Social history abounds with vivid examples of depravity, but there has never been a great store of fictions or metaphors to describe the state of the soul enjoying Heavenly rewards. Moreover, the step-by-step journey into Hell and up the purgatorial mountain involves a sense of time and space which is inappropriate to the simultaneity of eternity. Thus, the metaphor of the journey does not quite fit a vision of Heaven, although to accommodate human communication and understanding, the vision had to be subdivided and presented in some sequence. Dante reminds his audience, however, that this is only a strategy to help them see.

Until one reaches the presence of God, the Being than Whom none is higher, one has to understand every phenomenon, even heavenly bliss, hierarchically. Every soul in Heaven is completely happy, but even heavenly bliss has its degrees. To describe Paradise, Dante looks outward from Earth to the concentric spheres of the planets and beyond them to the Empyrean, where the Divine Presence begins. Because, moving outward, each successive planet is closer to God, each one can be a gathering point for increasingly elevated forms of blessedness. With the rather technical exception of the souls on the Moon, the imagery Dante uses to describe the souls he meets is nonrepresentational, even approaching abstraction with voices, lights, and patterns. Dante was familiar with the tradition of the cosmic voyage, a literary form which went back to the Stoic philosophers, in which a guide takes a troubled individual to the outer spheres, to provide consolation by demonstrating the littleness of troubled Earth when compared to the grand harmony of all Creation. A powerful counterpoint develops in *Paradise* between accounts of the sordidness of contemporary Italian society and the charity and communion above. Part of the image of Paradise is thus accomplished through negative description, using earthly examples to emphasize what Heaven is not.

The *Inferno* does not start with a poetic invocation. Dante rushes directly into the troubled middle of things. *Purgatory* has an invocation to Calliope, the Muse of epic poetry. It is crucial but perfunctory, and it suits the hopeful premises of that work. The invocation to *Paradise* is a fitting start to a sublime task. It tells what a poet requires to describe his Creator. He starts with the notion that what he has seen is not possible to relate, because when the mind nears that which it has always wanted, memory weakens. Even so, he will sing about that part of it which has remained with him. He calls upon Apollo, a god traditionally associated with light, wisdom, and prophecy, to breathe into him and use him like a bellows to utter song worthy of what memory of Paradise he still has left. Dante's audience would have been comfortable with an invocation to a pagan deity, because they believed that many pagan myths were glimpses of Christian light which could be used to make poetry more articulate. As an inspiration to soul and art, Apollo resembles the Holy Spirit, but he also carries all the rich associations of the classical literary tradition.

If Apollo will be generous, Dante continues, he will approach the laurel tree to take those famous leaves, now so neglected by an unheroic and unpoetic age, to create poetry which will ignite better imaginations than his own. From that tree, then, may come light for all future ages. The highly prophetic *Paradise* deserves to be under the keeping of Apollo. The poet approaches the laurel tree sacred to Apollo as he gathers strength to take his pilgrim self from Eden and the last visible traces of earthly things. The tree of tantalizing punishment for the Gluttonous and the tree of the first sin are replaced here by a tree reflecting the highest moral calling of art. As the images of Eden and sin recede, the laurel tree and the tree of Redemption converge. Dante looks at Beatrice looking at the sun, which is both Apollo's planet and a traditional symbol for God. It is the same sun he saw that morning in the dark wood, but then he was looking through sinful eyes. The eagle, Dante's symbol for the Empire, was thought to be able to look directly into the sun; the suggestion here is that Beatrice, who stands for all revelation, and the eagle are one. It might seem curious that an image of imperial order should be presented at a moment of intimacy between self and Godhead, but Dante will make a similar point throughout *Paradise*: that religious mysticism and social history are different but not antithetical routes to God. The eagle which seized Dante in a dream and took him on high to burn was as much the call of empire as it was a private religious impulse.

Dante is not able to look directly at the sun for long. As he looks at Beatrice looking at eternity, he begins to hear the music coming from the harmonious motion of the heavenly spheres, a sound no mortal has heard since Adam sinned. Instantly, Dante realizes that he has left Earth with Beatrice. The vision which follows, the organization of which is only a metaphor for the ineffable, involves ten Heavens, each of the first seven associated with a planet—Moon, Mercury, Venus, Sun, Mars, Jupiter, Saturn—the eighth Heaven with the zodiac and fixed stars, the ninth the Crystalline Heaven of the *Primum Mobile*, or First Mover, through which motion was imparted to all the other spheres, and beyond that the Empyrean, or realm of God. In the first seven Heavens, the souls are located in the planet with which their earthly activities could be associated, although in actuality each of them is in the Empyrean with God. According to Dante, the first three Heavens are touched by the shadow of Earth. On the Moon, the planet nearest Earth, are those souls who through no fault of their own proved inconstant in vows they had made to God. They were not sinners, only less perfect in salvation. Next is the Heaven of Mercury, filled with souls who lived virtuous lives serving the social order, but who were motivated at least in part by worldly ambition. The sphere of Venus is for those who followed Eros in life but now are delighted to wheel with celestial movement.

In the Heaven of the Sun are spirits whose wisdom furthered the understanding of God on Earth. Mars houses those who gave their lives for the Christian faith, while Jupiter houses the souls of the Just. The second three Heavens (Sun, Mars, and Jupiter) celebrate the virtuous achievements of the active life, but the contemplatives abide above them, in the circle of Saturn. The theme of the eighth Heaven is the Church triumphant, with Christ and the saints in full radiance. The ninth and tenth Heavens, respectively the *Primum Mobile* and the Empyrean, are given to the various direct manifestations of God. They take up the last six cantos, which trail off as even Dante's imagination begins to fade before its task.

The mood of *Paradise* is perfect joy which has no end and which leaves not even a trace of unfulfilled desire. The spirits describe that joy by what they do and say. There is a hierarchy of blessedness here, but it exists without anyone feeling envy or deprivation. Just as the courtesy and charity of Purgatory take one above the hatred and cupidity of Hell, so the perfect happiness here lifts one even higher, particularly through the praises for its perfect Source. The points of Christian doctrine and philosophy which are explained to Dante as he moves from Heaven to Heaven with Beatrice are rarefied, some barely fixable in mind or language. To follow these thoughts, the reader must move with Dante past the recognizable specifics of time and place. This commentary can only sample that exquisite brightness. One might begin with the notion that the rewards of Heaven justify everything that man can know about God's plan. *Paradise* is a celebration and vindication of the Church and all of its traditions, and of the plan for justice on earth through empire. It is also an opportunity for a citizen poet and visionary to justify himself to the audience of the world.

The Heaven of the Sun provides a satisfying example of Dante's love for the true Faith and the ideal Church. When he and Beatrice ascend to this Heaven, twelve lights carol around them, and one, Saint Thomas Aquinas, speaks. Aquinas belongs with the wisdom and illumination of the Sun. Mastering Aristotelian thought, he put its processes at the service of Christian theology. Among medieval Scholastic philosophers, he was supreme, and as a member of the Dominican Order (whose standard is a blazing sun), he studied and wrote to combat the heresies of unbelievers. Aquinas speaks not to praise a great university scholastic, however, but to praise Saint Francis of Assisi. Saint Francis was a street preacher, a disciple of the poor, whose spontaneous, instinctive love of God did not move through learned syllogisms. Aquinas tells a lively allegory about Saint Francis and the woman in his life, Lady Poverty. Poverty had been a neglected widow since her first spouse died on the Cross twelve centuries before. Indeed Poverty and Christ were so inseparable that during the Crucifixion she leapt on the Cross, like a wanton lover. Aquinas compares Francis' taking the vow of poverty to a wedding, an orgiastic celebration at which the guests (Saint Francis' followers) all hasten to follow this couple; as an Order, they will spread preaching and conversion throughout the world. This earthy description of Saint Francis' love for an ideal is no blasphemy: it is a charming reminder of how far the saint actually was from sensuality.

Then a Franciscan, Saint Bonaventura, praises the life work of Saint Dominic, founder of the order to which Aquinas belonged. Dominic, says Bonaventura, was the skillful gardener, sent to cull, trim, and order the plot of Faith and bring it new vitality. It is, like Aquinas' remarks about Francis, a graceful compliment, from lights which glow more brightly as they praise others. The ecstatic preacher and the systematizer of doctrine both work God's will and complement each other. At the same time, the reader cannot forget the diatribes of Aquinas and Bonaventura against the state of those orders.

Dante continually arranges his descriptions of Heaven to portray the idea of perfect happiness, although he relentlessly turns to bitter reminders of what human choice has rendered impossible on Earth. He never puts down the lash of satire for long. If *Paradise* is the happy conclusion of a comedy, it is also filled with astringent reminders that human history is a process of social and moral decay, much like the image of the Old Man of Crete in *Inferno* 14, which starts with a golden head and ends with rotting feet. At points Dante is apocalyptic about this decay, and he foretells destruction for his sinful age. He also implies that one day a strong figure will punish those selfish wrongdoers and usher in an age of justice.

Despite his outcries as an embittered satirist and doomsayer, Dante knows that both sacred and secular history are processes of God's justice, even when they seem to be operating at cross-purposes. In the Heaven of Mercury, Dante interviews Justinian, the Roman Emperor and codifier of law, who outlines the historic progress of the Empire. For Justinian, history is the flight of God's sacred eagle. He describes the earliest tribes in Italy, the Punic Wars, and the emperors. Justinian's most startling point is that the highest privilege of Roman justice was the punishment of Christ. The Crucifixion was a legal act, conducted by duly constituted Roman authority, with Pontius Pilate as the agent. It made the Redemption possible. At the same time, as Beatrice will later explain, the legality of the act under Roman law did not remove the need to avenge what had been done to Christ's person, so, somewhat paradoxically, the destruction of Jerusalem was also justified. The path of Divine Justice moved from ancient Rome to the Holy Roman Empire, thanks to

Charlemagne, but that magnificent progress has fallen to puny, contemptible heirs, as the Guelphs and Ghibellines of Dante's time continually ruin that justice with their feuding.

Dante's view of the workings of Divine Justice comes with surprises, as when he puts in the Heaven of Jove one Rhipeus, whom Vergil in the *Aeneid* called the most just among the Trojans. Presumably, Rhipeus was a pagan. That he should be in Heaven and the author who wrote about him in Hell is an irony, but Dante means to emphasize the presence of an appetite for justice in the Trojan line even before it settled in Italy.

If the ways of Justice can seem mysterious, Dante had no doubt that they would someday set in balance all the wrongs he had suffered. In Hell, Dante's anger at old enemies sometimes made him spiteful and almost pruriently interested in their pain. He paid particular attention to the part of Hell where barratry, the crime of making personal profit out of public trust, is punished by immersion in a pit of boiling tar. The episode is personal, for Dante was convicted and sentenced to exile on charges of barratry. For all the thrashing about among devils and damned souls in the pit of barrators, not so much as a drop of tar touches the poet. That is his answer to the capricious charges against him.

By placing his fictional journey in 1300, several years before the beginning of the political turmoil in Florence which resulted in his exile, Dante was able to present himself as a pilgrim ignorant of what is to come. This allows the heavenly hosts to refer to his coming suffering as an unjust but transient ordeal. It is a powerful response to his oppressors, because it allows him to assert the righteousness of his own cause and the maliciousness of his enemies through voices which are not to be contradicted, because their foreknowledge comes from the Divine Presence. The highest and most justified reaction to his future sufferings will come when Dante sees how little they amount to in the eye of eternity.

Dante's self-justification in *Paradise* shows a legitimate holy pride in ancestry and a certainty about his own destiny, despite the disgrace which is brewing for him. In the Heaven of Mars, the souls of those who died for the Faith form a cross. One of them, Dante's great-great-grandfather Cacciaguida, reminds him of the simple and virtuous old stock from which he is descended, in a line extending back to ancient Roman times. Cacciaguida hails Dante as a solitary continuation of this earlier nobility, then names clearly what had been hinted about in Hell and Purgatory: exile, poverty, a life at tables and under roofs not his own. Cacciaguida instructs Dante not to temper so much as a word, but to be a gadfly to degenerate Florence as Justice works its way.

Paradise is always ascending toward the vision of God, at which paradoxically it will evaporate, because it is only a human artifact. Actually, Dante is given three manifestations of God's presence. In the *Primum Mobile*, he sees God symbolically as a point of light surrounded by nine rings, each ring representing an order of angels. These nine rings of angels are in pointed contrast to the geocentric world, where the most slowly moving sphere, that of the Moon, is closest to the corruptible center. Here, as Beatrice explains, the fastest and brightest angelic circle, that of the Seraphim, is closest to the point of light. The definition of God as an indivisible point of light may seem unusual, given the traditions of a transcendent, all-encompassing Divinity. Dante was familiar with a definition of God as a sphere whose center is everywhere and whose circumference is nowhere, a concept which neatly implies the traditional idea of God's absolute and indivisible simplicity and His absolute interminability and simultaneity. The image of the point of light and the concentric circles of angels is perhaps as close as the human intelligence can come through symbols to understanding God's essence.

The image of God which Dante is given when he enters the Empyrean is a product of faith and revelation; it is the closest Dante can come directly to God, and this is the image with which *The Divine Comedy* must end. The Empyrean contains the souls of the Blessed on ascending tiers of thrones arranged to form petals of a white rose, as they will appear on Judgment Day. With the rose, a symbol of Divine Love, Dante moves finally beyond time and space in a blinding brightness as a river of Divine Grace pours from an incalculable height. In the center of the rose is a circle of light, the glory of God. It is time now for the final vision, but Dante discovers that Beatrice has left him to take her place among the Blessed. She has sent the great mystic and contemplative Saint Bernard to be his final guide. Doctrine and revelation, which Beatrice represented, have advanced as far as they can. Only ecstasy can go beyond that.

Under Bernard's direction, Dante's journey ends where it was first conceived, for there are the Virgin, and Lucia, whom the Virgin had sent to Beatrice, who in turn summoned Vergil to aid Dante in the descent to Hell. Now Saint Bernard prays for Mary's intercession, so that they can look at God without the instruments of metaphor or symbol. It is, as Dante says, the end of all yearning, satisfying and rendering obsolete the last vestiges of desire in the soul. In one mystical moment, Dante sees all creation held together by love. Then he sees three circles, each one a different color, occupying one space. It is the Trinity. The first two circles (the Father and the Son) reflect on each other, and the third (the Holy Ghost) seems a flame coming equally from the first two. It is a vision beyond logic and intellect. In trying to encompass it, Dante falls, like Icarus, back to his everyday human self. Dante ends with the remark that, whatever the limitations of his own understanding, Love was at the heart of what he saw, that same Love which moves the sun and the stars.

Major publications other than poetry

NONFICTION: *Epistolae*, c. 1300-1321 (*The Epistles*); *De vulgari eloquentia*, c. 1306 (English translation, 1890); *Il convivio*, c. 1307 (*The Banquet*, 1909); *De monarchia*, c. 1313 (*On World Government*); *Eclogae*, 1319 (*The Eclogues*); *Quaestio de aqua et terra*, 1320; *Translation of the Latin Works of Dante Alighieri*, 1904.

Bibliography

Auerbach, Erich. *Dante: Poet of the Secular World*, 1961.

Bergin, Thomas G. *Dante*, 1965.

Grandgent, C. H. *Companion to the Divine Comedy*, 1975. Edited by Charles S. Singleton.

Sayers, Dorothy L. *Introductory Papers on Dante*, 1954.

_____ . *Further Papers on Dante*, 1957.

Singleton, Charles S. *Dante Studies I*, 1954.

_____ . *Dante Studies II*, 1958.

_____ . *An Essay on the Vita Nuova*, 1949.

Williams, Charles. *The Figure of Beatrice*, 1961.

Thomas A. Van

RUBÉN DARÍO

Born: Metapa, Nicaragua; January 18, 1867
Died: León, Nicaragua; February 6, 1916

Principal poem and collections

Azul, 1888; *Prosas profanas*, 1896 (*Profane Hymns and Other Poems*, 1922); *Cantos de vida y esperanza*, 1905; *Canto a la Argentina*, 1914; *Selected Poems of Rubén Darío*, 1965 (Lysander Kemp, translator).

Other literary forms

Rubén Darío's fame rests primarily on his poetry, but he wrote serious prose as well. *Azul* (azure) his first major publication, contained poems and short stories alike. Both the poetry and the prose portions were widely acclaimed, but Darío's mature work includes almost no fiction. He published several volumes of essays based on his experience as a foreign correspondent, a traveler, and a diplomat, and two such collections have gained international attention: *La caravana pasa* (1903; the caravan passes) was among the earliest chronicles of the experience of American artists in Paris, while *Tierras solares* (1904; the sunny lands) is a collection of affectionate and melancholy essays celebrating the countryside of southern Spain, which Darío considered the common ground of Spanish and Latin American history. Darío also published literary criticism, political commentary, an autobiography and exegeses of his own works.

The most famous of Darío's critical works is *Historias de mis libros* (1914; stories of my books), a compilation of three explanatory pieces he wrote about his greatest works of poetry, *Azul*, *Profane Hymns*, and *Cantos de vida y esperanza*. In *Historias de mis libros* he responded to the most frequent criticism of his work, that he had abandoned the traditional themes of Latin America in pursuit of a European art. He branded the criticism "myopic" and answered that the literature of the New World needed no more stylized odes to nature or patriotic battle hymns.

Achievements

Darío was a giant of Spanish-language literature and a pioneer of the literature of the American continents. One of the founders of the indigenous Latin American literary movement known as *Modernismo*, Darío introduced European influences—particularly from France—to the poetry of Latin America, but perhaps more important, he introduced the *Modernismo* of Latin America to Europe. His dramatic innovations in theme, language, meter, and rhyme influenced the poetry of both the New World and the Old.

The publication of *Azul* in 1888 was acclaimed by European as well as South American critics, and the book's title was adopted by the *Azure Review*, a Mexican journal that became a principal forum for South America's experimental *Modernista* poetry. When Darío was only twenty-one years old, the influential Madrid critic Juan Valera praised the Nicaraguan's "singular artistic and poetic talent" and the "pure Spanish form" of his writing. With the publication of later works, Darío's renown grew, and he was widely acknowledged as a spokesman for Latin American culture.

Darío was a colorful public figure, equally at home in Paris, Madrid, and Latin America. He traveled constantly and was acquainted with literary figures throughout Europe and Latin America. He exerted a profound cultural influence through his poetry, his literary criticism, and his journalism. At the height of his fame, he was Nicaragua's minister to Spain; an internationally celebrated lecturer, poet, and journalist; and an éminence grise among artists of Europe and the Americas. In a 1934 tribute, Chile's Pablo Neruda and Spain's Federico García Lorca pronounced Darío "the poet of America and Spain."

Biography

Rubén Darío's life was adventurous and Bohemian. He traveled constantly in Europe and the Americas, renowned for his literary achievements but dogged by debt, sickness, and alcoholism throughout his life.

Darío was born in 1867 to a poor, part-Indian family in rural Nicaragua. He published his first poem at the age of thirteen, and his early promise as a poet won for him scholarships which enabled him to gain an education.

In 1886, Darío left Nicaragua for Santiago, Chile. There, he suffered a life of severe poverty and wrote in obscurity until the publication of *Azul*. Through Darío's friend Pedro Balmaceda, the son of Chile's president, *Azul* came to the attention of Juan Valera, a Spanish critic attentive to South American literature. Valera published an encouraging review in Spain and Latin America in 1889, but although this brought Darío literary recognition, it did little to ease his poverty. In the same year, the poet returned to Central America, where his writing in literary journals and other periodicals won regional fame for him.

In 1892, Darío traveled to Europe as an assistant to a relative who was an official of the Nicaraguan government. He made his first visits to Madrid and to Paris, developing a lifelong love for the artistic communities of Europe. Upon his return to Central America, Darío called on Dr. Rafael Nuñez, a former president of Colombia, who was like Darío, a writer. Nuñez arranged for a consular appointment for Darío in Buenos Aires, Argentina. Darío remained in Buenos Aires from 1893 to 1898, writing for many Latin American newspapers and other periodicals, including *La nación*, Argentina's most influential newspaper. In the course of his Argentine stay, Darío's literary reputation continued to grow. *Profane Hymns*, his second major volume, was published in 1896 and attracted critical attention in Spain and South America alike. Both the work's literary maturity and treatment of erotic themes ensured Darío's notoriety in the Spanish-speaking literary world.

In 1898, Darío returned to Europe as a foreign correspondent for *La nación*. In the course of the following ten years, he became a fixture of the literary life in Spain and France. He collaborated in establishing a number of fledgling literary journals, contributed to periodicals in Europe and Latin America, and produced important works of nonfiction as well as collections of poetry. Despite his commission from *La nación* and appointments to consular positions for Nicaragua in both Paris and Madrid, however, Darío's financial difficulties continued.

In 1907, Darío returned to Nicaragua to an enthusiastic public reception but stayed in his native country only briefly; he remained restless until his death, spending the last ten years of his life traveling throughout Central America and Europe, holding a variety of diplomatic and ceremonial posts, lecturing, and publishing poetry and essays in periodicals of both continents. In 1914, he published his last major work, *Canto a la Argentina*, commissioned by *La nación* on the occasion of Argentina's centenary of independence.

In 1915, Darío took his last trip home from Europe. His health was poor, and he died the following year in León, Nicaragua, at the age of forty-nine.

Analysis

Rubén Darío is remembered as one of the first poetic voices of postcolonial Latin America, enormously influential as a founder of *Modernismo*. His work, however, underwent constant change, and no single school can claim him. He was acclaimed a Prometheus who brought modern trends of European art to newly independent Latin America; at the same time, he was an innovator in poetic form who exercised a major influence on the poetry of twentieth century Spain. In his later years, Darío retreated from the exotic imagery of *Modernismo* and returned to more traditional Latin American themes, including patriotism and religion.

The birth of *Modernismo* in Latin America coincided with South America's transition from colonialism to independence. The declining influence of Spanish culture made way for new literary sources. Latin American intellectuals had long recognized French culture as the navigational star for their society, which was throwing off the control of monarchies. Thus, in the late nineteenth century, with much of Latin America freed from the cultural sway of Spain, the influence of France was everywhere ascendant, particularly in the universities and in the world of the arts. Darío's work in particular and *Modernismo* in general derived primarily from the interplay between French and Spanish culture, with a rich diversity of other foreign influences.

At its heart, *Modernismo* was an assertion of artistic freedom—the manifesto of those whom Darío described as a "new generation of American writers [with] an immense thirst for progress and a lively enthusiasm." The *Modern-*

istas idealized art, seeking to range freely for symbolic images in the worlds of the fantastic, the mysterious, and the spiritual. Emphasizing the eclectic internationalism that characterized the movement, Darío spoke of a "close material and spiritual commerce with the different nations of the world. . . ."

Darío's work spanned thirty-five years. It consists of thousands of poems, most of them short and many of them in sonnet form. Darío's best-known works also include longer pieces, and his shorter works are sometimes grouped as suites of poems with common themes.

The most common subjects of Darío's poetry are the members of his international family of friends, his romantic loves, and the world of nature. In the tradition of French Parnassianism, he portrayed his subjects through dramatic ideals, using lavish symbolic imagery. Whatever the subject, Darío's portraits are rich in exotic imagery and symbolism. The world of his images is European as much as it is American. In places real and imagined, the reader finds unusual animals and woodland flora, and characters plucked from myth and history. Darío's poetry abounds in allusion, and he often arrays his poetic portraits of the most commonplace themes with the exotic trim of myth and history.

Early evidence of Darío's debt to French art and literature appears in the 1884 poem "A Víctor Hugo" (to Victor Hugo), a paean directed not only to the French master but also to an enumerated multitude of figures who inspired the seventeen-year-old Darío: authors, scientists, and philosophers from Europe and the United States as well as figures from mythology and the Bible. The poem describes the explosion that Hugo touched off in the heart of the self-proclaimed "sad troubadour from the New World." Throughout the work, Darío blends his pious attention to the noise and movement of nature with the voices of myth and history. The influential Spanish critic Juan Valera acknowledged the obvious: the poetry of the young Darío was marked by an immersion in the images and ideas of centuries of Western civilization. Throughout his literary life, Darío wore his new religion proudly.

"A Víctor Hugo" explodes with pithy tributes to Darío's Olympus of heroes. Venus smiles. Apollo discourses with Erato, the Muse of love poetry, and with her sister Muses. Christ preaches and dies. Galileo utters his apocryphal words of defiance ("And still, I say, it moves"). Benjamin Franklin, Robert Fulton, and Ferdinand de Lesseps move the Earth with their inspired plans.

International recognition did not immediately follow the publication of "A Víctor Hugo," but the work heralded Darío's fame. In it, he affirmed his proud association with the artist. His profusion of references to the geniuses of Western civilization, too, reflected his captivation by European art and writing. Finally, his portrait of the world was of an extraordinary setting, a site of spectacular animation, anticipating explicitly *Modernista* works. While emotional and sincere, his descriptions were not so much true to life as true to an ideal.

At the close of "A Víctor Hugo," the New World's sad but well-read troubadour echoes a famous theme of Spain's first poet of the modern era, Gustavo Adolfo Bécquer: the yearning to give voice to the transcendent and the frustration at the limits of language. Darío unconvincingly gasps: "Oh, but I am left breathless at my lyre/ And unable to continue my song." The breathless recollection of Hugo, France's "immortal genius" and "prophet," however, provides a reviving breeze: "Thoughts of your just fame/ Echo in my mind/ And ardor inflames my heart. . . ."

The publication of *Azul* in 1888 marked the beginning of Darío's international recognition. An unusual combination of short stories and poetry, the collection revealed not only Darío's ebullience but also his sympathy with the Parnassian school, with its exotic symbolism, lavish portrayal of ideals through striking imagery, and departure from metric formalities.

The centerpiece of *Azul* is the suite of four poems that constitute "El año lírico" (the lyrical year), corresponding to the seasons and beginning with spring. The poems describe settings rich in exotic scenery and stirring with activity. "Primaveral" (spring) is by far the most dramatic. It portrays a vast forest alive with the awakening activity of nature. Darío's treatment of the arrival of spring, with suggestions of pagan and mythic ritual, reveals his fascination with a favorite theme of nineteenth and twentieth century European art and literature: the vision of untamed nature as the face of the savage world. The theme received its most celebrated treatment in Igor Stravinsky's ballet, *Le Sacre du printemps* (*The Rite of Spring*), which premiered in Paris in 1913. Darío's "Primaveral" begins with an invitation to the same celebration. The poem is composed of six stanzas of nearly uniform length, five of which end with the antiphonal cry: "Oh, my beloved, It is the sweet springtime!" The grand forest hosts the bathing nymphs, a stalking Pan, and the stirring Muses. Throughout the poem, colors flicker in the light. The locusts chirp to the sun, and all of nature highlights the beauty of a woman's face. "Primaveral" is not simply a seasonal celebration of love; the forest is the beautiful face of the world.

Azul also introduced influential formal innovations. The traditional Spanish sonnet of the nineteenth century consisted of rhymed lines with an even distribution of metric feet within the lines. Darío's sonnets generally abide by those conventions, but he experimented with longer lines and innovative patterns of rhyme. His sonnet "Caupolicán" (added to editions of *Azul* after 1890) is an early example. Each of its lines far exceeds the conventional eleven metric feet; in addition, Darío's rhyme scheme is unorthodox, and instead of the usual rhyming device of assonance, he employs sharp, syllabic rhymes. The first quatrain of the sonnet is representative:

> Es algo formidable que vio la vieja raza;
> robusto tronco de árbol al hombro de un campeón

salvaje y aguerrido, cuya fornida maza
blandiera el brazo de Hércules, o el brazo de Sansón.

(They saw Something formidable, the now-gone ancient race:
A robust tree trunk on the shoulder of the champion
Savage and war-wise with the mighty mace
Fit for the arm of Hercules or the arm of a Samson.)

Azul, if not the first *Modernista* work in Latin America, is a literary landmark and supremely representative of the movement. Its departure from formality and its thematic audacity reveal the literary freedom of what was then a new, and largely young, generation of artists in Latin America, apace of Europe's artistic evolution.

With his next major collection, *Profane Hymns*, Darío established his reputation as a mature poet and aroused controversy as well. Published in 1896, while Darío was living in Argentina, the work received considerable attention in Spain. Although it developed themes familiar to readers of *Azul*, it also included many poems exalting erotic love. The Spanish poet Pedro Salinas, a Darío partisan, describes the work as the "daydream of a cultured and erotic man."

In exploring sexual themes, Darío was both playful and frank, enhancing his reputation as a libertine and a rascal, and he provoked predictable outrage from some conservative critics. Others saw uncommon beauty and innovation in the work, and *Profane Hymns* won acclaim, particularly among young readers in Europe.

One of the best-known poems in the collection *Profane Hymns*, "Blasón" ("Blazon") is a panegyric to the swan (*Modernista* doctrine and French Parnassians). The work contributed to one of literary history's most colorful exchanges, a contest between Darío and his contemporary, the Mexican poet Enrique González Martínez, fought by symbolic proxies.

In "Blazon," Darío proudly adopts the swan as his blazon—his emblem. He sings of the swan's haunting unreality and decorative beauty in numerous poems, extolling its mythic and regal qualities—"Olympic is the swan, . . . Wings, short and pure . . . as the sun they seek." In time, the swan became closely associated both with Darío and with *Modernismo*, symbolizing the depiction of the exquisite, for which the *Modernistas* strived.

Some Latin American artists believed that Darío was guilty of excessive fidelity to the symbols, themes, and forms of European art. The growing "New World" movement did not entirely reject *Modernismo* but rather scolded what it perceived as its symbolic excesses and favored development of truly Latin American themes. In his later works, Darío himself showed just such an inclination, but at the height of his swan worship, he was a target of the New World movement.

González Martínez chose to attack the symbol of the swan in his famous repudiation of the elegant excesses of *Modernismo*, "Tuércele el cuello al cisne" ("Wring the Swan's Neck"), something of a New World credo. The 1911 work began, "Wring the neck of the deceitfully-plumed swan/ Who sings his white note to the blue of the fountain." Ironically, by the time "Wring the Swan's Neck" was published, Darío had turned to themes more conspicuously South American, including traditional Christian subjects and songs to the awakening continent.

This growing South Americanism is obvious in the last of Darío's three great collections, *Cantos de vida y esperanza*. Published when Darío was thirty-eight and in the depths of ill health and despondency, the work was widely acclaimed in Europe and South America and recognized as a new departure for the poet. Although it carries on themes associated with Darío's early works, it also includes a number of poems featuring traditional Christian imagery as well as several political poems—both uncommon in his previous collections.

"A Roosevelt" ("To Roosevelt"), the best known of the *Cantos de vida y esperanza*, is sharply political. It voices a stern warning to the United States to forswear colonial designs on Latin America. The poem is a confident address to President Theodore Roosevelt, a celebrated big-game hunter, whose personification of the United States is clear.

"To Roosevelt" followed close on the heels of Spanish defeat in the Spanish-American War. Voicing as it did a solemn warning to the United States and a disarming affinity with Spain, the poem did much to enhance the reputation of Darío, then living in Europe, as a spokesman of Latin America. The poem boasts of the proud Spanish spirit and the strong literary traditions of Latin America—both ironic choices for Darío—as the sources of South America's potential resistance to the United States.

Darío enjoys a lasting place in Hispanic literature. His art reunited Spain and its former empire after the wars of independence. He infused Latin American literature with the cosmopolitanism of the European avant-garde, while his own achievement drew European critical attention to the literary activity of Latin America. He was, to many, the quintessential American artist: an earnest student of tradition and an eager captive of the future.

Major publications other than poetry

SHORT FICTION: *Cuentos completos de Rubén Darío*, 1950 (Ernesto Mejía Sánchez, editor).

NONFICTION: *La caravana pasa*, 1903; *Tierras solares*, 1904; *Historias de mis libros*, 1914.

ANTHOLOGIES: *Obras desconocidas de Rubén Darío*, 1934 (Raúl Silva Castro, editor); *Escritos inéditos de Rubén Darío*, 1938 (Erwin K. Mapes, editor); *Rubén Darío, Obras completas*, 1950-1953 (5 volumes).

Bibliography

Andrian, Gustave. *Modern Spanish Prose*, 1969.
Salinas, Pedro. *La poesía de Rubén Darío*, 1957.
Sánchez-Reulet, Anibal, ed. *Homenaje a Rubén Darío (1867-1967)*, 1967.
Torres-Rioseco, Arturo. *The Epic of Latin American Literature*, 1964.
Watland, Charles. *Poet Errant: A Biography of Rubén Darío*, 1965.

David Nerkle

JOVAN DUČIĆ

Born: Trebinje, Yugoslavia; February 17, 1874(?)
Died: Gary, Indiana; April 7, 1943

Principal collections

Pjesme, 1901; *Jadranski sonetti*, 1906; *Pesme*, 1908; *Plave legende*, 1908; *Sabrana dela*, 1929-1932 (5 volumes), 1969 (6 volumes); *Lirika*, 1943; *Izabrana dela*, 1982.

Other literary forms

Although Jovan Dučić was preoccupied with poetry, he wrote in several other genres. His travelogues, *Gradovi i himere* (1932; cities and chimeras), contain his impressions gathered during journeys to Switzerland, France, Italy, Greece, Egypt, and other countries. More testimonies to his erudition than reports of his actual experiences, they deal with the history and cultural background of those places rather than with the present. *Gradovi i himere* is the best book of its kind in Serbian literature. A number of historical-cultural essays are collected in the book *Blago Cara Radovana* (1932; the treasure of czar Radovan). They offer Dučić's views on happiness, love, women, friendship, youth, old age, poets, heroes, and prophets. Dučić also wrote numerous articles on Yugoslav writers, his predecessors as well as his contemporaries, in which he presented not only opinions on these writers but also glimpses of his own literary views and accomplishments. Toward the end of his life he wrote a book about a Serb who went to Russia and became an influential figure at the court of Peter the Great, *Grof Sava Vladislavić* (1942; Count Sava Vladislavić). It is an ambitious pseudohistorical study that reads more like a novel than history. Dučić also wrote numerous essays and articles about cultural, national, social, and political issues of the day.

Achievements

Dučić appeared at a crucial point in the history of Serbian literature, at the turn of the century, when the epoch of Romantic and realist poetry was coming to a close and another, usually referred to as *Moderna*, was just beginning. By introducing new themes and sources of inspiration, Dučić was very instrumental in setting Serbian poetry on a new course. He was an aesthete, with a refined taste and an aristocratic spirit. In his poetry, he strove for formal excellence expressed through clarity, precision, elegance, musical quality, and picturesque images. His subject matter and unique style, reflecting the manner of French verse—Parnassian, Symbolist, *décadent*—brought a new spirit to Serbian verse. Unlike previous Serbian poets, who were either Romantically or realistically oriented, Dučić was attracted to esoteric, sophisticated, thought-provoking, and soul-searching themes, creating his own lonely world of imagination and reacting to it in a highly subjective manner. His poetry reveals a sensitive artist with a basically pessimistic outlook. He has sometimes been criticized for this, as well as for his inclination toward art for art's sake. His supreme craftsmanship, however, no one denies. Dučić represents one of the highest achievements in Serbian and in all south Slavic literatures, a fame that increases as time goes on.

Biography

There still exists some confusion about the date of Jovan Dučić's birth. He was born into a prominent Serbian family in Trebinje, a picturesque little town in Herzegovina, at that time under Turkish occupation, in the 1870's— that much is known. As a boy he moved to Mostar, a Herzegovinian cultural center, and later to Sarajevo. After he was graduated, he taught at schools in Bosnia and in Mostar, where he was frequently harassed by Austrian authorities for his nationalist activities. In Mostar, he participated in cultural activities, joined a literary circle, edited literary journals, and began to write poetry. Supported by the Serbian government, he studied liberal arts at the University of Geneva. During his study there and on frequent visits to Paris, he fell under the influence of French culture, particularly that represented by the *décadent* and Symbolist poets, which would have a decisive impact on his literary development. Upon his return to Serbia in 1907, he entered diplomatic service and served in that capacity for the rest of his life in various capitals of the world. At the same time, he published poetry and prose works and came to be recognized as one of the leading Serbian writers. He was in Lisbon during World War II and moved to the United States in 1941. Until his death less than two years later, Dučić actively supported the nationalist side of the guerrilla struggle against the Germans in his native country. His book *Lirika* (lyric poems) appeared the day he died. He is buried at the Serbian shrine in Libertyville, Illinois. At his request, his papers and library were sent to his native Trebinje.

Analysis

Jovan Dučić wrote poetry during his entire mature life. His first poems followed in the footsteps of the leading Serbian poet, Vojislav Ilić, at the end of the nineteenth century. Ilić employed a mixture of Romanticism, realism, and neoclassicism, all of which appealed to the young Dučić, especially in view of his patriotic fervor. During his study in Switzerland and prolonged stays in France, Dučić moved away from national regionalism as a result of his falling under the influence of the Parnassians and, later, the Symbolists. Despite some striking similarities to French poets, however, he developed his own style, thus successfully transplanting foreign influences onto a soil uniquely his own. In the latter part of his poetic career, he was free from any foreign influence. Ironically, his own influence on Serbian poets was minimal despite attempts by many to emulate him.

There are three more or less distinct periods in his poetic development. The first (1886-1908) was the period of naïve beginnings, fervent patriotism, love of nature, pronounced musicality, and Romantic sentimentalism. The strong French influence later in this period manifested itself through accentuated pessimism, melancholy, affectation, and a strict attention to form. This development, as Milan Kašanin sees it, had not only aesthetic but also historical significance, for the French predilection for intellectualism and rationalism replaced in Dučić's poetry the emotion and folkloristic regionalism dominant in Serbian poetry up to that time. Changes in Dučić, in turn, paved the way for historical changes in Serbian poetry in the first decade of the twentieth century. Dučić carried these and other signs of French influence, notably that of Albert Samain, Henri de Régnier, Sully-Prudhomme, Charles Baudelaire, Théophile Gautier, and José Maria de Hérédia, into his second period (1908-1932), but during this period he was able to transform such influence into a synthesis of his earlier Romantic preoccupations and the French "linear" spirit and discipline. In this period, he turned inward, searching for lasting themes and grappling with such perennial problems as man's isolation, love, search for faith, and reconciliation with death. It was not until his third and last period (1932-1943) that he was able to give full expression to this synthesis. Refining it further, he wrote his most mature works, although they consisted more of prose than of poetry. His last poems, some of them undoubtedly his best, return to the simplicity of his earlier period, as if closing the circle.

Dučić wrote a great deal of poetry, but, always placing high demands on his craft, he later renounced much of it; in fact, he explicitly forbade the republication of his earliest poetry. As a consequence, his entire authorized poetic output consists of only one medium-sized volume. He was also versatile in his choice of subject matter and in his stylistic approaches. His poems can be grouped according to their overriding themes into patriotic-historical poems; poems focusing on nature; love poems; and predominantly meditative poems. Sometimes a poem is limited to one of these themes; more often, however, it combines two or more of them.

Dučić wrote poems on patriotic and historical themes, undoubtedly under the influence of folk poetry, the Serbian poets still writing in a Romantic vein, and the general patriotic enthusiasm of his countrymen. These early poems are rather bombastic, full of rhetoric, declamatory, though quite sincere. Later, he moved away from purely patriotic themes and turned to history. Only during the two world wars, especially during World War I, did he return to patriotic poetry, for obvious reasons. Inspired by the enormous suffering, valiant efforts, and glorious exploits of his people, he wrote several excellent poems, of which "Ave Serbia!" and "The Hymn of the Victors" are especially notable. In somewhat intellectual fashion Dučić sings not of battles but of the suffering necessary for victory. Love for one's country he calls "a drop of poisonous milk," hinting at its opiumlike intoxication. Only that country is blessed "where children unearth a rusted sword" and "paths of greatness lead over fallen heroes." "Glory, that is the terrible sun of the martyrs," he exclaims in praise of the World War I victors. He would raise his voice once again during the second world cataclysm, this time more in anger and despair over the tragic fate of his people, whose end he did not live to see. His historical poems are in a much lighter vein, devoid of the tragic aura of his patriotic poetry. In the cycle "Carski soneti" (the imperial sonnets) he returns to the glory of Serbian medieval empire, and in the cycle "Dubrovačke poeme" (the Dubrovnik poems) he extolls the virtues and the sunny ambience of the Ragusan Republic, which alone escaped several centuries of Turkish occupation. While the former cycle is unrestrained in its glorification of the pomp and strength of the old Serbian empire, the latter is amusing, humorous, at times irreverent, but above all lighthearted and warm. These poems are read today only out of curiosity and for amusement, although some of them show Dučić's craftsmanship at its best.

Dučić's poems about nature are both varied and limited in scope. While it is true that he touches upon many phenomena and objects in nature, his approach tends to be somewhat one-sided. This one-sidedness can be seen in his choice of motifs, which are repeated time and again, although in endless variations. Among such often-repeated motifs are the sea, the sun, morning, evening, night, and natural objects that are usually isolated in their surroundings—no doubt reflecting the poet's own isolation and loneliness despite his appearance as a very happy and self-satisfied person. Even the titles of the cycles reveal the concentration on certain motifs: "Jutarnje pesme" (morning poems), "Večernje pesme" (evening poems), and "Sunčane pesme" (sun poems). Dučić's nature poems are not descriptive per se; rather, description is used primarily to evoke an atmosphere or to underscore the poet's melancholy mood. In the poem "Sat" ("The Clock"), for example, the very first verse sets the desired tone: "A sick, murky day, the sky impenetrable." The tolling of the tower clock contributes to general hopelessness: "Last roses are slowly dying . . . poplars are shedding their last leaves." The entire scene is permeated with "a horrible foreboding and the panic of things." In his treatment of nature Dučić emulates the Parnassians and the Symbolists; but he also endeavors to "spiritualize" nature, as Pero Slijepčević remarks, to present it as something outside and above the poet's perception of it. When a strong musicality is added to his regular versification, the impact of his poem, whether it is read or listened to, is powerful and lasting.

Other poems, such as those in "Sunčane pesme," are almost exactly the opposite: sunny, joyful, invigorating. Thus the poem "April" evokes a fairy-tale setting: the sky resembles a field covered with roses, the green hill is full of snails, and the sun's gold glitters in mud puddles. The titles of other poems in the Sun cycle—which translate as dawn, a forest, the sun, rain, a pine-tree, the wind, and so on—suggest a symphonic picture of nature, as Miodrag Pavlović observes, a picture that nourishes one's imagination and captivates with its seemingly effortless simplicity.

Dučić is a poet of the Mediterranean *joie de vivre* and closeness to nature, his pessimistic posturing notwithstanding. This fact explains the abundance of sounds and acoustic impressions, with form and color following closely. As a native of a region close to the Adriatic Sea and having spent most of his life in cosmopolitan centers, he shows little interest in the inland territories of the Balkans and Europe, concentrating on landscapes at or near the sea, both in his poetry and in his travelogues, most of which depict places in the Mediterranean area.

Dučić goes to nature not so much to enjoy it as to meditate in it. Many of his poems depict silence as the most salutary state for the poet's musing about life and the meaning of existence. There he finds "loneliness, in eternal silence, pale, by the river" and "evening waters streaming in quiet sadness, and weeping willows rustling forgetfulness." It is hard to say whether such attitudes stem from affectation or from the need to give his mood adequate expression. Critics have often accused him of affectation and artificiality, but in doing so, they overlook his remarkable ability to create with a few masterful strokes a picture of a landscape capable of moving the reader. Despite certain mannerisms, clichés, and repetitiousness, Dučić's poems about nature are highly ingenious in approach and execution. They belong to the best of their kind in Serbian poetry.

Dučić has been accused of even greater affectation and artificiality in his love poetry, probably because the woman in his poems is seldom a being made of flesh and blood but rather only a vision of an unknown woman, an eternal creature without specific abode or age. She does not exist nor did she ever exist, Dučić admits. Instead of endowing his emotions with a concrete substance, he creates a woman cult, placing her at the altar of an unrealizable dream. She is "the principle that builds and destroys, the God's spirit in every string and line . . . an inexhaustible well of pride and shame . . . an endless desert where the suns of despair rise and set" ("Poem to a Woman"). She is also a constant source of pain and unhappiness, mainly because she does not exist in her own right but only as the poet's chimera: "You have shone in the sun of my heart: for, everything we love, we have created ourselves." Seeing in woman a goddess, a cosmic principle, and destiny, it is not surprising that Dučić cannot find happiness and satisfaction in love. Even though he yearns for satisfaction, he is convinced beforehand of his failure. It is interesting that, as Slijepčević remarks, Dučić never sings about the beginning or the duration of love but only about its end.

It is easy to see only affectation in attitudes such as these, but such an approach does not exhaust the complexity of Dučić's love poetry. The fact is that he did not always advocate such an ethereal relationship. In his earliest poems (later repudiated), as well as in his poems in prose, he does speak of lust, sensual excesses, and even devouring passion. In private life, he was known as an insatiable, often ruthless lover. As he matured as a poet, however, the ideal of a woman beyond reach—but also beyond corruption and decay— slowly took shape: "Remain unreachable, speechless, and distant—for, the dream of happiness means more than happiness" ("Poem to a Woman"). Yet, despite the withdrawal and lack of confidence, he refuses to dwell on the transience of love, counterposing love to death as one of the few forces that could overcome it. One cycle of his poems is entitled "Poems of Love and Death." By elevating woman to the level of deity, he establishes love as one of the three basic themes of high poetry: God, death, and love. Thus, Dučić's love poetry transcends the Romantic, realist, and Symbolist approach to love, all of which had, at one point or another, taken their turn in shaping his poetic profile. As in his nature poetry, he approaches love in a nontraditional, primarily intellectual way. Love is no longer a manifestation of only feelings but also of thought. In the process, Dučić has created some of the best love poems in Serbian literature, despite some admitted flaws.

Many of Dučić's poems about nature and love show a distinct propensity for meditation, just as many of his purely meditative poems are related to nature and love. Dučić's meditative bent derives not only from his nature but also from his firm belief that only the meditative element and intellectualism could pull Serbian literature out of the confines of narrow regionalism. His time in France and Switzerland, as well as in other parts of the world, only confirmed that belief. In order to achieve that goal, he sometimes strained too hard. On the other hand, some of his meditative poems are genuine artistic achievements.

Dučić never developed his own philosophy, nor was he systematic in expressing his thoughts in his poems. There is no doubt, however, that he was fond of philosophizing and couching his thoughts on many subjects in poetic fashion. Even in his prose works, where his meditativeness is more pronounced, he often expresses his thoughts poetically. From the many poems which are either completely or partially suffused with meditation, several topics clearly emerge. In these works, Dučić frequently addresses God. Even though he sees Him in all things, offering His hand "whenever my ship tilts," the poet cannot always suppress doubts about His whereabouts at the time "when a criminal sharpens his knife somewhere" ("Poems to God"). Most of Dučić's references to God are the result of the constant interplay of faith and doubt. Death, "the only thing we did not invent . . . more real than reality . . . the only truth and the only fairy tale, the sum of all symbols" ("Poems of Death"), is also often depicted by Dučić. In accord with his basically pessimistic attitude, he speaks of death as of an inevitable outcome that can be halted temporarily only by love. The experience of love, too, often gives Dučić an opportunity to reflect. Poetry itself is the subject of meditation, as in his famous "My Poetry," in which he pleads with his muse to be beautiful and proud only for him and to ignore the rest of the world as if it were hidden in a mysterious fog. This aptly illustrates his belief in *l'art pour l'art*, of which he was the leading proponent in Serbian literature.

Some critics maintain that the reflective poems are the weakest in Dučić's oeuvre. Others believe that this particular characteristic lends his poetry an aura of cosmopolitanism and sophistication that helped Serbian poetry overcome its century-long limitations, as Dučić believed it would. Moreover, far from being trite or superfluous, his meditativeness inspires the reader to do his own thinking.

Dučić's poems in prose in *Plave legende* (blue legends) stand out as a curiosity in Serbian poetry, because no other Serbian poet had written prose poems in such a sustained and dedicated fashion. They are also a further testimony to Dučić's versatility and poetic prowess. The thirty-seven poems in this collection cover the ground of his lyric poetry: one finds poems about nature, love, faith, gods, and human behavior in general. The most striking difference lies in the frequent depiction of the ancient world, of pagan and classical antiquity as well as of early Christianity. Dučić, who seldom concerned himself with the present, found in these escapes into the past a convenient idiom to give poetic expression to his thoughts and sentiments. His treatment of love here is much bolder and earthier and that of faith much less reverent than in his lyric poetry, and his conclusions about human nature seem to be more realistic. "The Sun" and "The Little Princess" are generally considered to be the best of these prose poems.

Dučić's style has often been singled out as the most significant and accomplished aspect of his poetry, often at the expense of other qualities. He demanded of himself, as well as of other writers, rigorous attention to matters of style, considering himself to be a craftsman in a poetic workshop. He constantly revised his works, not hesitating to disown those he did not deem worthy. He remained a student of poetry even when others thought of him as a complete artist, and he had no patience with those who neglected style.

In matters of versification, Dučić shows a remarkable versatility. His most common form is a variation of the Alexandrine, which he used almost exclusively in his later periods (except in the last book published during his lifetime, *Lirika*). He started with hexameter, octameter, and decameter, and settled on the Alexandrine, although he used many variations of these and other meters. All of his verses rhyme, but even here there is great variety from poem to poem, even within a single poem. Enjambment is not infrequent. Most of his poems consist of four to six quatrains. He wrote many sonnets; some of the cycles are composed entirely of them.

The texture of Dučić's verse is characterized above all by strong musicality, achieved through a skillful use of vowels, cadence, and resonance, and by avoiding harsh elements such as dissonant consonants, corrupted speech, and provincialisms. The inner rhythm is achieved by strict adherence to the rules of versification, especially those of meter, stress, and caesura, although he sometimes deviates if his highly sensitive ear tells him to do so. This is possible in Serbo-Croatian, where morphological and syntactic rules allow such variations.

The wealth of images and metaphors in Dučić's poetry has often been pointed out. The originality of such figures is undeniable: the armies of night are sailing and the flags of darkness are waving; a horny moon has entangled itself in the branches of old chestnut trees; his poetry is quiet as marble, cold as a shadow; a sea willow resembles a nymph condemned to become a tree-rustling sadness. Dučić frequently employs personification: a row of black poplars marches through the wheatfield; water fountains are crying; the dawn looks into the window with the childlike eyes of a doe; a snake is taking off its shirt in the blackberry bush. Even with such a wealth of imagery and metaphor, Dučić's verse is always clear and fully expressed, never overloaded with meaning, yet never devoid of it. The purity of his language, his striking and bold innovations, and his musical fluidity all contribute to a powerful total effect.

While it is true that many of these characteristics can be traced to the influence of the Parnassians and the Symbolists, it is also true that without his own immense talent Dučić could not have become what he was—a leading poet of his generation, a pathfinder and epoch-maker in Serbian literature, and one of the important writers in world literature of the twentieth century. Only the fact that his skillfully composed poetry is extremely difficult to translate has limited his appeal and reputation in the rest of the world.

Major publications other than poetry
NOVEL: *Grof Sava Vladislavić*, 1942.
NONFICTION: *Blago Cara Radovana*, 1932; *Gradovi i himere*, 1932.

Bibliography
Begić, Midhat. "Modernistička gama Dučićeva," in *Raskršća I*, 1957, pp. 171-198.
Goy, E. D. "The Poetry of Jovan Dučić," in *Gorski vijenac*, 1970.
Kašanin, Milan. "Usamljenik," in *Letopis matice srpske*. CCCCI (1968), pp. 351-372.
Mihailovich, V. D. "Yugoslav Literature," in *World Literature Since 1945*, 1973.
Pavlović, Kosta St. *Jovan Dučić*, 1967.
Pavlović, Miodrag. "Jovan Dučić, danas," in *Delo*. X (1964), pp. 1191-1228.
Popović, Bogdan. "Teme i misli u Dučićevom pesništvu," in *Sabrana dela*. I (1929), pp. 11-22.

Skerlić, Jovan, "Jovan Dučić: *Pjesme*," in *Letopis matice srpske*. CCX (1901),
    pp. 77-86.
Slijepčević, Pero. "Jovan Dučić," in *Sabrani ogledi*. I (1956), pp. 93-148.

Vasa D. Mihailovich